S0-ALH-292

THE BURMA SPRING

THE BURMA SPRING

AUNG SAN SUU KYI AND THE NEW STRUGGLE FOR THE SOUL OF A NATION

RENA PEDERSON

FOREWORD BY LAURA BUSH

PEGASUS BOOKS
NEW YORK LONDON

THE BURMA SPRING

Pegasus Books LLC
80 Broad Street, 5th Floor
New York, NY 10004

First Pegasus Books cloth edition January 2015

Interior design by Maria Fernandez

Library of Congress Cataloging-in-Publication Data is available.

ISBN: 978-1-60598-667-8

10 9 8 7 6 5 4 3 2 1

Printed in the United States of America
Distributed by W. W. Norton & Company

To the brave people of Burma
and the hope for a better tomorrow

"We are dependent on persons who set examples, persons who can symbolize what we are seeking and mobilize the best in us. Aung San Suu Kyi is just such a person. . . . Knowing she is there gives us confidence and faith in the power of good."

—Nobel Peace Prize Chairman
Francis Sejersted 1991

CONTENTS

FOREWORD

BY LAURA BUSH

Rena Pederson's story of Nobel Peace Prize winner Aung San Suu Kyi and the people of Burma's struggle for freedom is an important one. I have followed closely, and with optimism, the changes taking place in Myanmar. My inspiration for this concern has always been Daw Aung San Suu Kyi. Her brave leadership gives hope to the men and women of Myanmar, and to freedom lovers worldwide.

In 2006, I convened a roundtable at the United Nations to address the issues of Burma's ethnic conflicts, drug trafficking, and the many thousands of displaced persons. We listened as Burmese activist Hseng Noung described the rape victims in conflict areas. The youngest victim was 8. The oldest was 80. Her words silenced the room.

In 2008, with my daughter Barbara, I visited the remote and crowded refugee camps on the mountainous border between Myanmar and Thailand. There, I saw the tireless efforts of Dr. Cynthia Maung to provide lifesaving medical aid for hundreds of refugees in need. I sat with victims of land mine explosions who had lost legs or feet and were waiting quietly for basic care.

Finally, in 2012, after her long isolation under house arrest had ended, I was able to meet Daw Suu in person as she was honored with the Congressional Gold Medal. Daw Suu is not only a symbol of courage, but she is a woman of tremendous humor, honesty, and grace.

Former Secretary of State Hillary Clinton and I serve as co-chairs of the Suu Foundation. With Daw Suu's vision and guidance, the foundation supports education and improved healthcare in Myanmar. The hope that now grows in Myanmar is a tribute to Daw Suu.

Today, through the George W. Bush Institute's Liberty and Leadership Forum, President Bush and I are working with democracy advocates. We hosted a class of young leaders from all faiths and all regions of Myanmar. These young people read the foundational thoughts of John Locke and James Madison, as well as the inspiring speeches of American presidents from Lyndon Johnson to Ronald Reagan to Barack Obama. They visited George Washington's historic home, Mount Vernon, and watched Fourth of July fireworks light up the sky over our nation's capitol.

Now, these young leaders are back home in Myanmar with the challenging new tasks of reform and reconciliation. They will need the help of the world to make sure that Myanmar has more than a veneer of democracy. And our shared hope is that they will find the kind of lasting peace that the Burmese have sought for so long.

EDITOR'S NOTE

In 1989, Burma's military rulers changed the official English name of the country from "the Union of Burma" to "the Union of Myanmar." And in 2010, they changed it once more to "The Republic of the Union of Myanmar."

Some countries—including the United States and the United Kingdom—continued to use the country name Burma because the military government that changed the name to Myanmar had not been elected democratically. Since there is now a quasi-civilian government in place, the growing trend has been to use the Myanmar nomenclature around the world.

Because it was still U.S. State Department policy to continue using the country name Burma at the time of this book's writing, that is the term used predominantly here. Myanmar is also used where appropriate.

PROLOGUE

"This is Burma, and it will be quite unlike any land you know about."

—Rudyard Kipling, 1898

Knowing Burma is elusive. The names are tricky for Westerners to pronounce. There are dozens of ethnic groups and generals to sort out.

But the human drama begs you: Don't look away. There are saints as well as soldiers at every turn. The sights and sounds are intoxicating—with an undercurrent of danger.

Under military rule since the 1960s, Burma became a poisoned Shangri-La, a garden of good and evil. For decades, everyone was watched. People disappeared in the night. After the military takeover, Burma became known as "a tropical East Berlin"—the citizens were walled in and democracy walled out. Most of the country missed the modernity of the 20th century as a succession of generals kept a "bamboo curtain" around the country. Only recently have they begun to loosen their grip.

Despite its hardships, Burma has retained the otherworldly appeal that Kipling so admired. Away from the bustle of Rangoon and Mandalay, you discover lakes of dream-like blue and quiet villages untouched by time. Giant golden temples—Eiffel Towers of faith—dot the landscape and remind you that Burma is the heartland of Theravāda Buddhism, the oldest surviving branch of the "teaching of the elders."

Most Burmese—both men and women—still wear the traditional wrap-around sarong called a *longyi*, so they walk with an easy, languid grace. It is said that the Burmese are "the most charming oppressed people in the world," and it is true. Their earnest efforts to please ("Tea for you?") make it easy to fall under Burma's spell.

Geographically, it's a country the size of Texas, but with about twice the population, more than 50 million.

The overall shape of the country is often described as that of a kite with a drooping tail. Or, depending on your sense of poetry, a jagged diamond with a falling teardrop.

Burma is bounded to the west by India, once the Proud Raj of the British Empire. To the north looms the colossus of China. And to the east, there's the free-wheeling marketplace of Thailand. It's a strategically important neighborhood for world powers and the criminal underworld—including a "Golden Triangle," where a major share of the world's heroin and meth-amphetamines are produced.

The jagged Himalayas make a forbidding barrier around the upper half of the country. The bottom half opens up to the Bay of Bengal. There are miles of honeymoon-perfect beach that most hotel chains have never seen.

Four mighty rivers run through Burma from north to south: the Irrawaddy, the Salween, the Chindwin, and the Sittang. The great Irrawaddy River arises in Tibet and powers down through Burma for more than a thousand miles to the Andaman Sea, creating harbors for commerce legal and illegal.

Today, China is trying to build a series of dams on Burma's waterways to generate hydropower for its thriving provinces. A giant pipeline has already been constructed to bring oil and gas from Burma to energy-hungry China. Meanwhile, more than 70 percent of the Burmese lack electricity, cell phones, cars, indoor plumbing, or healthcare.

Under British rule, Burma became the leading rice producer in the world and was known as "Asia's Rice Bowl." Its universities were among the best in the region. The vast riches of the country include rubies, gold, copper, tungsten, uranium, and teak. Yet those resources have been squandered by powerful generals and their cronies. Today Burma must import rice and its schools are in disrepair.

Uniting the country is difficult because there are more than 135 ethnic groups in Burma. They include the Padaungs, whose "giraffe women" are known for wearing brass neck rings up to their chins. Then there are the Nagas, renowned for many years as headhunters in leather thongs, and the Taron, a rare group of pygmies, barely four feet tall, now threatened with extinction. The Karen, Kachin, and Chin peoples—who were Christianized by American and British missionaries in the 18th century—have been under siege by the military for more than 60 years, the longest civil war in the world. Those groups still struggle for autonomy today.

By far the largest ethnic group is the Bamar or "Burman" people, who are predominantly Buddhist. With 68 percent of the population, the Burmans dominate the country and control the military, known as the "Tatmadaw." The British named the country "Burma" after the Burmans; military rulers have changed the name to the older form of "Myanmar."

This is an ancient and proud nation. People have thrived in these abundant lands for 15,000 years. Control has passed from kings in silk turbans with fleets of elephants to British governors, to the hard-fisted generals, to the beginnings of democracy today.

The same scent of sandalwood and profits that drew Portuguese traders in the 1600s now draws merchants from Ford and Coca-Cola. Starbucks is on the way.

With an appeal all its own, Burma beckons and beguiles. After only one day in Mandalay in the 1800s, Rudyard Kipling wrote, "Personally I love the Burman with the blind favoritism born of first impressions. When I die, I will be a Burman, with 20 yards of real King's silk that has been made in Mandalay about my body and a succession of cigarettes between my lips."

Over time, one begins to understand why warriors like Genghis Khan and statesmen like Randolph Churchill would want to get their hands on Burma. And why others would fight to free it.

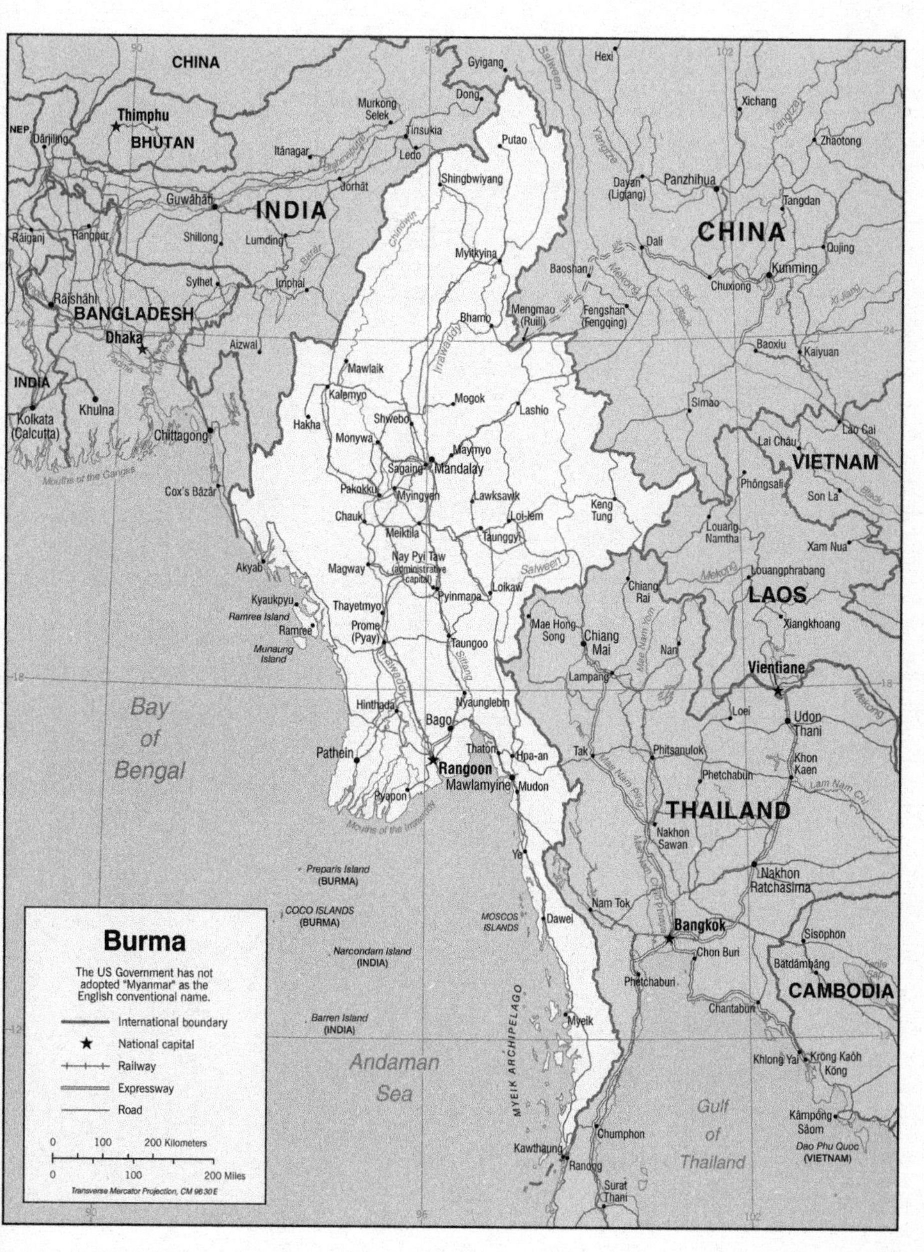

Burma
The US Government has not adopted "Myanmar" as the English conventional name.
International boundary
National capital
Railway
Expressway
Road
0 100 200 Kilometers
0 100 200 Miles
Transverse Mercator Projection, CM 96 30 E
CHINA
Thimphu
BHUTAN
NEP.
Darjiling
INDIA
Guwāhāti
Shillong
Lumding
Imphal
Sylhet
Itānagar
Jorhāt
Tinsukia
Ledo
Murkong Selek
Dong
Gyigang
Putao
Shingbwiyang
Myitkyina
Bhamo
Mengmao (Ruili)
Baoshan
Fengshan (Fengqing)
Rāiganj
Rangpur
Rājshāhi
BANGLADESH
Dhaka
Khulna
Kolkata (Calcutta)
Chittagong
Cox's Bāzār
Aizwal
Mouths of the Ganges
Mawlaik
Kalemyo
Hakha
Mogok
Lashio
Shwebo
Monywa
Maymyo
Sagaing
Mandalay
Pakokku
Myingyan
Lawksawk
Chauk
Meiktila
Loi-lem
Taunggyi
Keng Tung
Nay Pyi Taw (administrative capital)
Magway
Akyab
Kyaukpyu
Ramree Island
Ramree
Munaung Island
Thayetmyo
Prome (Pyay)
Pyinmana
Loikaw
Taungoo
Hinthada
Nyaunglebin
Bago
Pathein
Thaton
Hpa-an
Rangoon
Mawlamyine
Mudon
Pyapon
Mouths of the Irrawaddy
Ye
Dawei
Myeik
Kawthaung
MYEIK ARCHIPELAGO
MOSCOS ISLANDS
Preparis Island (BURMA)
COCO ISLANDS (BURMA)
Narcondam Island (INDIA)
Barren Island (INDIA)
Bay of Bengal
Andaman Sea
Gulf of Thailand
Chindwin
Irrawaddy
Sittang
Salween
Mekong
Yangtze
Red
Black
Hexi
Xichang
Zhaotong
Dayan (Lijiang)
Panzhihua
Tangdan
CHINA
Dali
Qujing
Kunming
Chuxiong
Baoxiu
Kaiyuan
Simao
Lao Cai
Lai Châu
VIETNAM
Phôngsali
Son La
Louang Namtha
Xam Nua
Louangphrabang
LAOS
Xiangkhoang
Chiang Rai
Mae Hong Song
Chiang Mai
Nan
Lampang
Vientiane
Loei
Udon Thani
Tak
Phitsanulok
Phetchabun
Khon Kaen
THAILAND
Nakhon Sawan
Nakhon Ratchasima
Nam Tok
Bangkok
Chon Buri
Sisophon
Batdâmbâng
CAMBODIA
Phetchaburi
Chantaburi
Khlong Yai
Krŏng Kaôh Kŏng
Kâmpóng Saôm
Dao Phu Quoc (VIETNAM)
Chumphon
Ranong
Surat Thani

BURMA (MYANMAR)

INTRODUCTION

"If you allow yourself to be intimidated, then you will go on being intimidated."

—Aung San Suu Kyi

It was the story about her piano that first caught my attention.

I was skimming through the morning paper in 1991, coffee in hand. A front page story in the *New York Times* made me pause. It was about a woman with the unusual name of Aung San Suu Kyi. She had been awarded the Nobel Peace Prize for her efforts to bring democracy to Burma. The article said she was being held under house arrest in Rangoon, cut off from the world, her husband, and their two young sons. To keep her mind occupied, she often played the piano for hour after hour, alone.

I sensed in that moment that the woman confined to her house was someone extraordinary. The image of a lone prisoner playing Bach and Chopin a world away from her family stuck with me. I started looking for more articles about Aung San Suu Kyi. The ruling generals in Burma had ignored her party's overwhelming victory in the 1990 elections. Instead of conceding, they surrounded her home with guards and threw hundreds of her political colleagues into prison. Soldiers cut her phone line in the most literal sense—they stormed in one day with scissors, snipped the cord, and took the offending instrument away. At the time, Suu Kyi had been in the middle of an interview with the BBC.

As the days and years went by, Aung San Suu Kyi had to sell her personal possessions and furniture, piece by piece, chair by chair, to get by. To pass the hours, she cleaned her house, exercised on a NordicTrack cross-trainer, and tended to the wilting remains of her mother's garden. She began meditating every day to stay spiritually centered. Settling down her restless mind was difficult at first, but she kept trying. She listened to the BBC on a short-wave radio to keep up with world news. She studied to improve her French and Japanese. And she played Mozart and Chopin on the old family upright. It gave her mental strength to keep up the discipline of playing the piano. The music filled the empty house. And when she got angry or frustrated, which her circumstances often warranted, she banged out her frustrations on the Yamaha piano. But over time, parts of the piano broke. It fell terribly out of tune. The Burmese generals refused to allow anyone to repair the piano. It was a tiny bit of malice, compared to the horrors the military was committing throughout the country, but it stuck in my mind. The generals were denying their prize prisoner even the company of Chopin.

After that, I wondered, what did Aung Sang Suu Kyi do to keep her wits? She had to give up her gardening when people started taking photos of her in her courtyard, like tourists gawking at Greta Garbo. She went for months on end without hearing from her family. How does she go on, I wondered, when the rest of the world forgets she is there?

Years passed. Aung San Suu Kyi kept up her fight for democracy despite impossible odds. Although there were multiple attempts on her life, she did not go wobbly, as Margaret Thatcher would say. Glimpses in the news of the waif-thin woman were rare, but enough to see her head held high, a defiant flower tucked into her hair. Over time, I could see how her example was beginning to inspire people around the world, even if they couldn't find Burma on a map. Crowds of people began protesting her captivity, from Kuala Lumpur to Dallas to Prague. Something about the defiant struggle by this sparrow of a woman had touched a moral chord around the world.

When her Nobel Peace Prize was announced in 1991, committee chairman Francis Sejersted said, *"We are dependent on persons who set examples, persons who can symbolize what we are seeking and mobilize the best in us. Aung San Suu Kyi is just such a person. . . . Knowing she is there gives us confidence and faith in the power of good."*

Though the committee's choices for the Peace Prize often are controversial, this time the consensus was they got it right. The world community cheered. Why did the story of a solitary woman in far-off Rangoon resonate in so many corners? Some will say it was because she was pretty and photogenic and articulate, but more likely, as Sejersted observed, it was that she provided an example the world sorely needed. Every age needs its heroic archetypes, "moral celebrities" like Helen Keller, Mother Teresa, Martin Luther King Jr., Nelson Mandela, Cesar Chavez, Billy Graham, and now Aung San Suu Kyi. They give us a reminder of ethical character in a world without strong moorings. For sure, it would be a mistake to turn Suu Kyi into some kind of saint, although some of her most devoted fans already have. No human being can live up to such elevated expectations. But it would be a greater mistake to ignore someone who has raised the bar higher for so many. The time would come when people would see Aung San Suu Kyi as a human being in full, flawed and fallible like everyone else, but dedicated to serving her people.

Aung San Suu Kyi gets her unusual name from her family: "Aung San" from her father, "Suu" from her grandmother on her father's side, and "Kyi" from her mother Khin Kyi.

The easiest way to pronounce her name is to start with unsung as in unsung hero—then add Suu like the English girl's name Sue and Kyi, which is pronounced "Chee" like the Cheeto snacks. Phonetically, you might sound it out as "awn-sawn-soo-chee."

She is frequently called Daw Aung San Suu Kyi. "Daw" is not part of her name, but is an honorific, similar to madam, for older, revered women, literally meaning "aunt," a term of respect. She is also often referred to as Daw Suu by the Burmese or "Amay Suu," meaning "Mother Suu" by some of her followers.

—~—

As I followed Aung San Suu Kyi's struggle over the next decade, I often wondered, *"What makes this stubborn woman tick?"* From time to time, I wrote newspaper editorials calling for her release, hoping they helped keep her cause in public view. As more years passed, penning those editorials from the safety of a newspaper office seemed like watching the life-and-death struggle in Burma through a telescope. I felt compelled to get closer to reality and see what was happening for myself. It was time to see Aung San Suu Kyi in person. I began looking for a way to get past the military security to meet her. What was she *really* like, I wondered? Had all those editorials been merited? It took more than a year of persistent requests through back channels, but at long last a meeting was arranged. There were no guarantees of safety or success. But "The Lady" did not disappoint.

CHAPTER ONE

RANGOON, 2003

> "Foreign writers and journalists are denied entry to Burma. Occasionally some are able to slip into the country posing as tourists, but if they are discovered their notebooks and photographic film are confiscated and they are swiftly deported. For the Burmese people they interview, the repercussions are infinitely greater . . . providing foreigners with information that the regime considers inimical is punished with a seven-year prison sentence."
>
> —Emma Larkin,
> *Finding George Orwell in Burma*

So there I was in Rangoon, listening to the tired hum of the vintage ceiling fan in my hotel room, as it went slowly around . . . and . . . around . . . again. The hotel was a stately former British governor's mansion with vaulted teak ceilings and high-backed rattan furniture in the lobby. It was the kind of once-grand place where you'd expect to encounter a foreign diplomat at the next dinner table. Or a divorcee from the U.S., taking the geographic cure to get as far away as she could to forget. Or perhaps a man with a burn scar covering one side of his face, making a whispered deal. People tend come to places like Burma to escape something or find something. As a jaded newspaper editor, that included me on both counts, I suppose. Burma was anything but humdrum.

Peering out from my room window, I could hear the chirpy chatter of French tourists having breakfast in the tropical courtyard below. I was hungering to go down and join them for a buttery croissant and thick black coffee, but I couldn't leave my room because I was waiting for the call that would confirm my interview with Aung San Suu Kyi. I tried to fill the time by reading a newspaper, but all the papers in the hotel were several days old and full of government propaganda. The lead headline in the *New Light of Myanmar* blared: "WIPE OUT THOSE INCITING UNREST AND VIOLENCE!" I was forced to return to a dog-eared paperback of George Orwell's *Burmese Days* that a previous visitor had left behind. Ten o'clock. No phone call. The French tourists left for a day of sightseeing. There was no sound but the slamming of doors as maids went from room to room to clean. Eleven o'clock. No phone call. I drank cup after cup of tea and read the same paragraph again in the Orwell book. It was noon. I was running out of time to meet with Suu Kyi before my flight home. Staring at the phone didn't help.

I had requested an interview for the last day of my trip because I could be thrown out of Burma for having an unapproved meeting with Suu Kyi. At the time, no press visas were granted and you could be arrested for interviewing "activists." My plan was to soak in as much information about the country as I could before being shown the door. I had used the first weeks of my trip to bicycle along back roads and byways, often sharing the right-of-way with farmers stoically hauling crops in ancient wooden carts. The ox carts plodded ahead so slowly they didn't even stir up dust. As I pedaled along, I could only marvel at the raw natural beauty of Burma all around. The teak trees overhead had leaves as big as green kites. You've never seen leaves on a tree so big, like something in a Maurice Sendak children's book. There is a fairy-quality to the scenery in Burma, a world apart. Jagged mountains framed the far horizon like a granite fence. Sometimes the only sound was my own tires bumping through ruts in the road. This was a land that time forgot, and soon my time didn't matter. The afternoon felt four years long. My bike itinerary allowed me to cycle through remote villages rarely seen by tourists. Most people lived in simple bamboo huts with a hand-pumped well in the yard. They slept on straw mats or low wooden beds that looked hand-hewn. There was little other furniture. Most villages didn't have electricity. Even fewer had phones. Or newspapers or TV, for that matter. But they all knew who Aung San Suu Kyi was.

One man with a ramshackle store—where he sold odds and ends like broken wristwatches and wooden carvings of elephants—looked carefully around before taking me back to a small, dark room off the rear of the shop. There was no light to switch on, so I had to squint to see what he was pointing to: a photo of Suu Kyi's father, General Aung San, reverently displayed on the back wall and carefully hidden from street view. "He is Daw Suu's father," he whispered, using the "Daw" title of respect for women. I nodded silently that I understood, with just a frisson of pride that I had been trusted to see the treasured photo, making me a co-conspirator. Still, I didn't dare tell the man that I was hoping to see Suu Kyi herself. I couldn't risk having someone tip off officials to stop me, even someone who seemed simpatico. The list of offenses that could land you in prison in Burma in 2003 included:

- Telling jokes about the military junta
- Writing poems about democracy
- Blogging about injustices
- Reporting about oppression
- Holding a gathering of more than five people
- Marching peacefully to protest high gas prices
- Being a member of the 1988 student protests
- Making a documentary about orphans from the cyclone
- Providing medical care for AIDS victims without approval
- Taking photos of military installations or troops
- Carrying a sign protesting the house arrest of Aung San Suu Kyi
- Posting a cartoon of General Than Shwe on a blog

- Speaking to journalists
- Speaking to international human-rights groups
- Taking photos of human-rights abuses
- Complaining to the International Labor Organization about slave labor
- Praying in public for Aung San Suu Kyi's release
- Singing a song critical of the military regime
- Driving up to Aung San Suu Kyi's house

References in the press to the widespread poverty were censored, as well as references to corruption, bribery, disease—and Aung San Suu Kyi. The Press Scrutiny Board made sure that Aung San Suu Kyi was not seen in print—unless it was something to make her look bad. Among the magazine covers that had been censored was one featuring a penguin on an ice floe and another showing a woman seated among fallen flowers. Both were interpreted as veiled references to Suu Kyi and banned.

Despite such surreal circumstances, most Burmese people went out of their way to be hospitable. My first impression of the Burmese was how gracious they were, with their eager smiles and polite ways. Tilting their heads downward and placing their hands together in front of them as if in prayer, they nodded their respects. As I explored deeper, away from the city-center streets where armed soldiers stood watch on every corner, it became apparent that underneath the politeness and hospitality, there was an edge of fear. It brought to mind the dramas where people nervously go through the motions of trying to appear at ease to visitors because they know there's a killer in the back room holding a gun to a loved one's head. Probe beyond the pleasantries and you find everyday working people are too scared and too beaten down to speak out. Rather than mention Aung San Suu Kyi's name out loud, they referred to her as "The Lady." When I tried to ask people about Suu Kyi in public, they would nervously look around and avoid answering. Later, when we were out of earshot from others, they would lean close and whisper, "We love her. We love The Lady." Their discretion was well warranted. As many as one in four people in Burma were said to be informers for the government. Even the snitchers had to be careful, because others might be listening to them. One of my flights was canceled because military officers had cavalierly commandeered the commercial airplane for their own personal use. The passengers were left stranded in the dingy airport for the rest of the day. Everyone sat in silence and waited. No one dared complain. Those who speak out risk arrest or worse. The result is a collective paranoia. You never know who might be the Judas in a conversation.

—∾—

Speaking your mind in Burma was dangerous because, in addition to the military and the police, there were multiple "civilian" groups on the government payroll to keep citizens in check.

By far the most powerful group was the Union Solidarity and Development Association (USDA), which claimed 24 million members. The USDA was officially described as a "civilian welfare" group to provide social services. But most of those so-called services (perks and money) went to the USDA members themselves, payment for serving as the junta's eyes and ears and enforcers. The USDA tattled on any anti-government activity and sometimes administered harsh retribution.

Other groups used as spies and surrogates at the time included:

- A civil militia called the Swan Arr Shin ("Masters of Force") acted as a civilian Gestapo, cracking down on those who didn't toe the line or those the government simply wanted out of the way. They have often been compared to the deadly "Ton Ton Macoute" of the Duvalier regime in Haiti, who murdered opposition members at the dictator's behest.
- The Township Peace and Development Councils (TDPC) conducted surveillance of residents' movements and checked to see if citizens had unapproved guests in their homes. It was against the law to have overnight visitors without permission.
- The Village Peace and Development Councils (VPDC), or Ya Ya Ka, collected taxes and often were ordered by the military to provide forced labor to build roads or to seize food for the army.

In effect, most people in Burma were under constant surveillance by layer on layer of oppression.

—∾—

Once he was sure that no one else was close enough to hear, a wrinkled old man who operated a bicycle taxi in the historic ruins of the ancient city of Bagan told me how the government had ordered everyone in his neighborhood to move their homes in a week. The junta didn't want their bamboo huts to clutter the view for tourists and planned to use prime plots for resorts built by government cronies. The soldiers cleared out thousands of families who had lived in Bagan for generations. Many were caretakers of the ancient temples, whose roots went back to the "temple slaves" of the 11th century. The old man wrote a letter in protest, arguing that the government had no right to take his house. Later that day, soldiers came to his home. They threw him in prison for four months. The old man became seriously ill in the filthy prison and lost a great deal of weight. He said he was still recovering. His thin arms and legs looked like bamboo sticks. He explained that after the government confiscated his home, the substitute site they finally gave him was in a floodplain. When the monsoon rains came, the new house he had hurriedly built was swept away. His family lost everything. "Trouble never comes alone," he sighed as he bicycled by his old neighborhood. He was surviving by pedaling the occasional tourist by the temples—and what used to be his neighborhood—on a battered bicycle that had been made in China.

In another candid moment, a young man in Rangoon told me that several of his friends were killed during the student revolt of 1988. He had a university degree, but he was forced to drive a cab to earn a living. He pointed to one of the many blood-red billboards with ominous messages that dominated traffic circles in Rangoon. The signs warned citizens to beware of "external elements" and "foreign stooges," a not-so-subtle swipe at Aung San Suu Kyi and her Western connections. They proclaimed that the Tatmadaw, as the Burmese Army is known, would "Crush all those harming the union" and would protect "The People's Desire." The former student scoffed, "The people's desire! The *people's* desire is for the government to leave them alone! The *government's* desire is that the people suffer!"

He was infuriated that most people around the world didn't know that the massacre of students in Burma in 1988 was much worse than the Chinese crackdown in Tiananmen Square the following year. The death toll at Tiananmen Square was estimated at 200 to 1,000 and ignited global outrage. But many thousands more died in Burma. An estimated 3,000 to 10,000 people perished in Burma in 1988—and the world did little. No one in the outside world saw the Burmese slaughter on their TVs because the country was so isolated, the former student said bitterly, "So it was as if it did not even happen."

He had a point. The tragedies in Burma rarely made the news. Getting the word *out* to the world about the horrors in Burma was incredibly difficult because foreign journalists were generally not granted visas. Getting the news *into* Burma was just as difficult. I could watch the watered-down international version of CNN on cable TV at my hotel, but most Burmese could not. The government controlled the newspapers and the TV stations in the country as well as the only Internet servers. Guests in better hotels could use a computer in the hotel business office, but with the understanding that every word was being monitored. The domestic press was licensed, watched, and generally stifled. Leading journalists, such as newspaper editor U Win Tin, had spent much of their adult life in prison. Many did not survive their incarceration—including a correspondent for a Japanese newspaper and the former chair of the All Burma Journalist's Association. One photographer died at a military intelligence detention center after his newspaper published a photograph of the dreaded military intelligence chief at the time, Gen. Khin Nyunt, alongside a highly negative report.

In 2003, freedom of expression, association, and assembly all were strictly limited in Burma—and had been for decades. Owning a fax machine without a permit was illegal. Gatherings of more than five people were banned.

The all-powerful Press Scrutiny and Registration Division, which was riddled with members of Military Intelligence, censored all the media.

The official *New Light of Myanmar* newspaper was dominated by photos of the generals at official ceremonies and routinely referred to Suu Kyi as an "evil tool of foreign interests." The *Myanmar Times*, a new English-language weekly that was created mainly to appeal to foreign readers, published more international news, but did not dare print articles critical of the military regime and was said to have close links with Burmese military intelligence at the time.

More than 1,400 political prisoners were believed to be in prison or under detention when I visited in 2003, including approximately 135 members of Suu Kyi's National League for Democracy party (NLD) and more than a dozen journalists, including the editor of the *First Eleven* sports magazine. The sports editor's offense? He had dared to publish an article questioning how international grant money to develop soccer in the country had been spent.

As I traveled around the country, I saw children under the age of 12 working long days in conditions that OSHA would condemn, breathing harsh chemicals in lacquer factories and standing on stools to stir steaming-hot vats in silk factories. According to human-rights groups, more than a third of Burmese children have jobs to help support their families. Because their parents couldn't afford to pay for schooling, children in tattered clothes often trailed after foreign visitors at tourist attractions, begging for money or food or pencils.

Working conditions at the notorious Ivanhoe copper mines reportedly had been "improved," according to the government press, but when I went to look at the area there were hundreds of workers sleeping on the ground in fields between their shifts. Their only shelter was some flimsy sheets of plastic strung over them, with no apparent facilities.

As we bumped along the punishing rural roads that left no bone unjarred, we found work crews of villagers who had been coerced by authorities to rebuild the roads ruined by monsoon rains. Even grandmotherly-looking women were down on their bony knees, digging out rocks with their bare hands. One of the defining features of the Burma military regimes has been the use of forced labor. Amnesty International reported in the 1990s:

"Conditions in the labor camps are so harsh that hundreds of prisoners have died as a result. Military Intelligence personnel regularly interrogate prisoners to the point of unconsciousness. Even the possession of almost any reading material is punishable. Elderly, sick, and even handicapped people are placed in leg irons and forced to work." The practice of using forced labor is euphemistically described by the military as "people's contributions."

The military junta claimed to have eliminated leprosy, but the disfigured victims who sat by the side of the road with their palms outstretched and their heads down in shame were proof of the lie. One Baptist hospital in Moulmein alone was serving several hundred leprosy inpatients. The doctor, a handsome young man in a crisp white shirt, had studied to become a heart surgeon, but because he was a Christian, the pro-Buddhist government sent him to the leprosy hospital instead.

According to World Bank figures at the time, more than a third of the population was trying to get by on little more than $1 a day. Spending on health and education combined was barely two percent of the official budget and perhaps a stretch at that. Meanwhile, the military generals lived behind high walls in villas with multi-car garages.

The more I witnessed how deeply oppressed and poor the people of Burma were, the more I realized how extraordinary Suu Kyi was for standing up to the regime on their behalf. She was the only hope they had. The United Nations voiced support for change in resolutions now and then, but did little more. Why? China and Russia, which did not want their own human-rights issues on the table, routinely blocked attempts to get the U.N. Security Council to take action in Burma. Neighboring countries like Thailand and Malaysia tsk-tsked publicly—and then made back-door deals with junta business surrogates. Corruption had become systemic under military rule. Meanwhile, Suu Kyi continued calling for an end to fighting. She called for wider access to education, rule of law, and jobs for the poor as opposed to what was slavery in all but name. The Lady refused to let go. She was not giving up.

But would I get to meet her? I had only one afternoon left. I couldn't leave Burma without talking to Suu Kyi, because she was making Burma legible to the world. Without her mystique, the Burma struggle was just another miserable situation in a faraway place. After their takeover in

1962, the generals had kept Burma so closed off that the county had faded from the world's view. As novelist Amitav Ghosh put it, General Ne Win "slammed the shutters and switched off the lights. Burma became the dark house of the neighborhood, huddled behind an impenetrable, overgrown fence. It was to remain shuttered for almost three decades." As a result, most people around the world didn't know that villages were being looted and burned by the army every week. They didn't know that army soldiers had raped thousands of ethnic women from the Kachin, Shan, and Karen areas of the country. It was rarely reported that ethnic Christians had suffered targeted abuse, their churches burned, their ministers tortured, their women brutalized. The "religious cleansing" was invisible because the ethnic areas were under siege and access was heavily restricted. No press and no human-rights observers were allowed. International Red Cross observers were barred from inspecting the prison conditions. It was no wonder that most people around the world didn't know that AIDS, sex trafficking, and drug abuse were at epidemic levels in Burma. Or that some 40 percent of the children in Burma were malnourished, starving while the Tatmadaw generals and their wives went on shopping sprees in Singapore.

The World Health Organization has listed the health system in Burma as the second worst in the world (just ahead of Sierra Leone). The annual health budget: less than $1 a person.

While Burma used to be one of the most literate nations in Southeast Asia, the successive military regimes had closed most of the schools since the 1960s, preserving the best education for military elites. The United Nations reported that Burma spent only 28 cents per student a year on its public schools.

According to UNICEF, the under-five child mortality in Burma averaged 104 deaths per 1,000 children, the second-highest rate (after Afghanistan) outside of Africa. Four out of 10 children were reported malnourished, and the average life expectancy is less than 50 years.

Doctors Without Borders has estimated that Burma also has the worst HIV crisis in Southeast Asia and appears to be a breeding ground for more dangerous forms of the virus. Malaria, a treatable and preventable disease, is still the leading cause of mortality, and new drug-resistant forms of malaria have been reported along the Burma borders crowded with refugees.

—~—

I had been asking questions about the harsh conditions in the country wherever I could, so I began to worry that someone could have snitched about my inquiries while I waited for the call about my appointment. Perhaps her call wouldn't come, but the police might? My suitcases had been rifled through several times when I wasn't in my hotel room. Once I returned from breakfast to find a different combination lock on my suitcase than the black one I had fastened on it. Who was looking through my suitcase? Did they think I wouldn't notice that the new lock on it was red instead of black? Or did they want me know they had been there?

Several times at night, I had awakened at the sound of someone trying to turn the doorknob on my hotel door. It didn't take long to realize things can go wrong in a heartbeat in Burma. So when the phone finally jangled that afternoon like an alarm clock, I was startled. I had a feeling it was not good news. "So sorry, but the interview has been canceled," a man's voice said. Urgent problems had come up. "The Lady" would need to reschedule. Perhaps some other day.

"I *can't*," I rushed to say before the man could hang up. "My flight home is tomorrow. Can't you do something? *Please*? I may not be able to come back. I used my savings to come."

There was a long pause. "I'll try," the man said. Click.

It took several more phone calls, but a meeting was arranged late in the afternoon. The next hurdle was getting past the guards into Suu Kyi's compound. To get past the security check, I would have to pretend I was not a journalist. As I got into the car with my escort, I felt both exhilarated and numb. My escort, a diplomat who had helped arrange the meeting, was jumpy. She pointed out the extra soldiers along the roadway as we drove down Army Boulevard. Every quarter mile, there was a soldier standing guard. More could be seen standing behind the trees. The Armed Services Day parade was coming soon, she explained. The route was being secured weeks in advance, just in case anyone had any foolish thoughts of making trouble. With a sidewise glance at my camera, she cautioned me that taking photos of soldiers was punishable by 20 years in prison. I nodded. I had heard that. She went on: Do you understand that interviewing Aung San Suu Kyi could get you thrown out of the country? Yes. My bag was packed. I had a new red lock on it.

As we turned into the street where Suu Kyi lives at 54 University Avenue, about a dozen soldiers blocked the way. Resting on lounge chairs by barricades, they looked like extras from a "Rambo" movie. All of them carried assault weapons and wore dark green fatigues. Wraparound sunglasses masked their eyes. They did not smile. They peered through the window into our car and ordered us to show our IDs. My escort handed over her diplomatic ID, but grabbed my wrist to stop me as I reached for my passport. Speaking in Burmese, she explained to the guards that I had "no rank." She assured them emphatically, "She is *nobody*." I nodded in agreement. A soldier leaned through the window to look me over. All I could see in his sunglasses was my own reflection. I had worn a feminine, pastel-colored pantsuit very deliberately, hoping I would not look like a typical American reporter, who tended to be men in well-traveled jeans and quick-dry hiking shirts from REI or Whole Earth Provisions. While I held my breath, the guards looked me over, and then huddled for several excruciating minutes. The leader came back to the car window and handed us a sheet on a clipboard to sign. Perhaps to cut the tension, my escort suggested, under her breath, "Why don't you sign 'Laura Bush'?" I could only hope the guards didn't see the startled look on my face. "I don't think so," I whispered back, imagining the trouble that forging the First Lady's name could get me into. Many years later, I would learn why Laura Bush's name had come up in such an unexpected circumstance.

After several more tense minutes, we were waved ahead to Aung San Suu Kyi's home. Guards had removed the street number "54" from the front gate in an effort to deny Suu Kyi's presence. Everyone in the country knew where her house was anyway. When our driver pulled up to the tall iron gate, an elderly man with a warm, gap-toothed smile rushed over to swing it open for us to drive through. As he shut the gate behind us with a loud clank, I suddenly realized: *I'm here*. This was the place I had read about so many times. Suu Kyi's weathered house was in an area near Rangoon University that was dotted with stately old homes. The courtyard to her house had a quiet, timeless feel. In years past, Suu Kyi had appeared at the big iron gates many times, standing on a box or table to speak over the fence from the courtyard to her followers, trading smiles and waves for cheers. Tattered flags of red and white, the colors of her National League for Democracy party, still drooped on the rusting gate, evidence of a freer time. Now, even the bamboo stalks in the yard looked bedraggled. Suu Kyi's two-story home, with its colonial-era architecture and arched *porte cochere*, might have once been imposing, but now it was sadly in need of paint and repair. We stepped inside to a reception room that was immaculately clean but sparsely furnished. A single wooden table and a few chairs were placed in the center. Family photos on the wall were the only decorations. There was a large photograph of Suu Kyi's mother as an earnest young woman, unaware of tragedies to come. Another photo showed Suu Kyi's father when he was a political leader on the way up. He was posed like a young prince in an oversized chair, looking straight at the camera with a determined look in his eyes.

I was studying the photos so intently that I did not hear Aung San Suu Kyi enter the room. She announced herself with a crisp "Good afternoon!" in a precise, Oxford-polished accent. Despite a day of considerable difficulties, she seemed completely at ease. She offered graciously to pour tea. At the time, Suu Kyi was 57 years old. She had a distinctive, delicate look, sometimes described as an Asian version of Audrey Hepburn, thin and elegant. Her friends say she weighs 105 pounds at most. She had visibly aged since the glamour-girl photos on democracy posters were taken. Her high cheekbones had lost some of their photogenic roundness and her face seemed drawn, yet she was still an exceptionally striking woman. She wore her onyx-black hair tied at the back at her neck with a small spray of flowers, her trademark.

Well aware that she had urgent matters to attend to (and that we could be interrupted by the guards at any minute), I told her that I had honed my questions down to twenty.

"Twenty questions?" she said with a bemused smile. "It sounds like a quiz show!" But she answered every one. And stayed for more.

I asked first, how was her health after thirteen years of confinement? I had read that at one point during a hunger strike she had lost twelve pounds in twelve days and ended up on intravenous support. Another time when she had little money to buy food, she had suffered from malnutrition to the extent that her hair fell out.

Suu Kyi reassured me that her health was fine except for spondylitis, an inflammation of the vertebrae. She treats it with neck exercises, she said. "Perhaps everyone in Burma needs to stiffen their spine," she said, with a self-mocking smile.

The playfulness in her manner was a pleasant surprise. "The Lady" was a tease. Though she is sometimes criticized for having the prim and proper manner of a governess, her voice took on a sharp, reproving edge only when she began describing the injustice around her. She pointed out that the government led by Senior General Than Shwe claimed publicly to have released her from house arrest the year before, yet the road to her house was still guarded around the clock. Once she had gone out to meet with friends at a restaurant—the government closed the restaurant the next day. It never re-opened, and the owners went into hiding. Suu Kyi did not visit a restaurant again. Likewise, if she went to the food market herself to get fresh supplies, the vendors' stalls were often shut down afterwards. As a result, she had to leave the grocery shopping to two women, loyal members of her political party, who stayed in her home to assist her and were, in effect, voluntary prisoners with her.

"When I was supposedly released a year ago, the government made a series of promises," Suu Kyi said, getting right to the point. "It has not yet kept them." She spoke with such deliberate emphasis that she seemed to put a period after every word: "It. Has. Not. Yet. Kept. Them."

"The government promised that it would begin discussions about the transition to democracy. They have *not*. They promised they would release all the political prisoners. They have *not*," she said. There were some 1,400 political prisoners in the prisons at the time.

"They also promised that independent newspapers would be able to publish," she said, adding with an arched eyebrow, "You haven't seen one, *have you*?" She had applied for a newspaper license for her party immediately after her so-called "release" the year before, she said, "And it has not been approved *yet*."

Her candor was striking. I could see the color drain from my escort's face every time Suu Kyi said something that could get us all arrested. I had been warned that the house might be wiretapped, yet Suu Kyi unabashedly was criticizing the military government to a member of the Western media. She was not lowering her voice or tempering her views. No wonder she makes the generals nervous, I thought.

The generals had tried for years to diminish Suu Kyi's stature by claiming she was not a true Burmese because she had married a foreigner. They liked to refer to her as "Mrs. Aris" to underscore the point that she had a British husband. Look, they sneered, she's sleeping with the enemy, she's in bed with the country that colonized and humiliated Burma for so long. Or they dismissed her condescendingly, saying "She is just a *housewife*." At times, they taunted that she was a "Western fashion girl" or "political stunt princess." They tried to brand her as the tool of the CIA and Western powers, saying she was a "neo-Imperialist" or "the ax handle of the neo-colonialists." But still the people were drawn to her by the thousands.

A few weeks before her first arrest in 1989, Suu Kyi had been asked by a reporter from *AsiaWeek* if she thought the authorities would move against her and she replied, "I suppose they'll try. They've been trying that all the time with false propaganda about me—all sorts of nonsense. Things like I have four husbands, three husbands, two husbands. That I am a Communist—although in some circles they say I am CIA. They even have been trying to get prominent monks to say I have been insulting the Buddha!"

The generals later would float false rumors that she had abused an employee and was a negligent mother, all in transparent attempts to ruin her reputation. The generals tried to thwart her every move, even during the brief periods in the mid-1990s when they claimed she was "freed" from house arrest. Whenever the generals wanted to curry international favor or increase tourism, they would announce her "release," but not relax their grip. One summer she attempted to leave Rangoon to visit the families of political prisoners, but was halted abruptly on the road by the military. The soldiers forcibly lifted her car with a forklift truck—and pointed the vehicle back in the direction that she had come from.

On another occasion when she traveled to a province outside of Rangoon for a speech, she discovered that the town square was deserted. The government had threatened to arrest people if they attended her rally. None of the townspeople dared show up. Suu Kyi responded by announcing that she was going to a town in a different province—and then secretly switched directions and returned to the first site. This time, thousands of supporters were able to turn out and greet her, cheering and boldly wearing the red and white of her party.

Not long before our talk, Suu Kyi had tried to speak in the western part of Burma, in Rakhine State. Though the gathering was peaceful, local authorities dispatched police and a fire engine to the town center. The firemen began to turn the fire hose on the crowd. As people around her panicked, Suu Kyi stepped up on the side of the fire truck and exhorted the people to stay calm. She chided the local security forces, telling them their job was not to bully the people, but to serve them. Suu Kyi then asked the fire captain to move the truck because it was scaring people. He refused. Undaunted, she climbed to the top of the fire truck and began giving her speech from there. Not wanting to furnish her with a platform, the authorities agreed to move the truck away. Suu Kyi continued her rally.

The incident greatly bothered her, she said, because the government was subverting respected civic organizations such as the Burmese Red Cross and the Fire Brigade by compelling them to threaten people.

She was even more troubled, she said, by recent reports compiled by ethnic women in the Shan State that documented the rapes of thousands of women and girls by Burmese soldiers. The military apparently was using rape to subjugate the ethnic areas that were still resisting their control.

"These allegations must be taken very seriously as a violation of human rights," she said. "The soldiers *must* be held accountable. We *must* protect the most vulnerable among us, women and children. It is the *government* that must be held responsible for this violence."

What was especially remarkable about Suu Kyi's comments was that she was not making the charges from the safety of a think-tank in Washington, D.C., or the op-ed pages of the *New York Times*. She was quite alone in 2003, and her every move watched.

I asked Suu Kyi: Would it help to call for a United Nations force to come in and supervise new elections, as was done in Cambodia in 1992?

She shook her head no. She was concerned that an armed international intervention would provoke a violent confrontation with the military. "More violence is not the answer," she said. She said her conscience as a Buddhist required her to keep calling for a *negotiated* transition to democracy and *peaceful* reconciliation. She returned repeatedly to the point that the world community needed to press the regime to "sit down and talk *peaceably*." Once they do that, she said crisply, "We will be able to work out our problems quite speedily."

She paused to serve more tea like a solicitous hostess, lifting the china teapot to pour without skipping a beat in her analysis of the situation. She reminded me that Burma was once one of the richest countries in Asia, with vast teak forests, rubies, sapphires, and oil. Today it had become one of the poorest. Once it was the leading producer of rice in the world. Today it has to import rice. Just a few weeks before my visit, the government had seized most of the private bank accounts in the country. Many families lost their life savings.

"We are in *serious* economic trouble," Suu Kyi acknowledged, but all the trouble stemmed from bad governance. "We can't do anything about the *appalling* social and economic problems until we do something about the *government*."

I could see my escort visibly flinch through the corner of my eye. These were seditious statements. On the other hand, Suu Kyi seemed to have no qualms about speaking out. Nor did she seem discouraged at the seemingly impossible task before her, piloting the country and the military toward democracy. To the contrary, she seemed coolly intent on seeing her mission through. There was no fear in her. She had already faced danger many times.

In 1996, when Suu Kyi was attempting to speak at a high school, her car was attacked by a gang of men identified as government-paid members of the Union Solidarity and Development Association (USDA). Stones were thrown at her car and the vehicle was battered with iron rods. Suu Kyi's senior adviser, U Tin Oo, suffered a cut to his face when the windshield was shattered. A hole was torn in the car by blows from the iron rods. Riot police and soldiers stood by without intervening except to arrest several NLD supporters who witnessed the attack.

In 2000, riot police surrounded Aung San Suu Kyi's motorcade as she tried to travel to Dala, a poor slum area across the river from Rangoon. She was stranded in her car for nine days. For day after day, Suu Kyi had only minimal food and water before the police authorities finally allowed her to return to Rangoon, carried on a stretcher. As soon as she recovered, she ventured out again. She tried to travel by train to the Mandalay area with U Tin Oo, the former general who had helped found the National League for Democracy. When the two arrived at the train station, they were surrounded by armed guards and jostled roughly. After a tense standoff, they were forcibly barred from boarding the train. Suu Kyi went back out to speak as soon as she could.

As we talked, I asked Suu Kyi if it scared her that she was under constant threat of "accidental" death. She smiled at the question. One eyebrow arched up slightly. "*Scared*? If that's their goal, they have not succeeded," she said.

The closest she has come to acknowledging the stress from her tribulations came in a 1995 interview for *Vanity Fair*, when she revealed that she worried at times that her health would give out. "Sometimes I didn't even have enough money to eat. I became so weak from malnourishment that my hair fell out, and I couldn't get out of bed. I was afraid that I had damaged my heart. Every time I moved, my heart went thump-thump-thump, and it was hard to breathe. I fell to nearly 90 pounds from my normal 106. I thought to myself that I would die of heart failure, not starvation at all. Then my eyes started to go bad. I developed spondylitis, which is a degeneration of the spinal column," she told the magazine. She paused for a moment, then pointed a finger to her head and added, "But they never got me up here.'" She would not allow herself to falter, because that would be a victory for her captors. She disciplined her diet to stay as healthy as possible and disciplined her mind to stay focused.

She was not frightened at being alone, she reassured me. The only real prison is fear itself, she insisted, if it keeps people from doing what they know is right. While she was under house arrest in the 1990s, she sent out word to the remnants of her party not to be frightened: "You must go and give them a message that I said, 'Don't be scared.'"

She fights fear herself, she told me, by meditating and developing positive feelings toward all, including her jailers. She explained, "If you have a positive feeling towards other people, they can't do anything to you—they can't frighten you. You cannot really be frightened of people you do not hate. Hate and fear go hand and hand."

That forgive-your-enemy approach is precisely what set Aung San Suu Kyi apart from activists in many parts of the world. She has never called for revenge, a pound of flesh, a chance to turn the tables on her jailers in spite. She has never called for the masses to storm the barricades and risk wholesale bloodshed. She has called for forgiveness. Which astounded even her jailers.

As she explained, if she began to hate or harm her oppressors, then her life's work will have been in vain, because she will have forfeited her core Buddhist beliefs: Loving kindness. Compassion. And right intention. She would not return hate with hate.

Though morality is a topic that seems to bring out bombast in American politicians, Suu Kyi managed to weave moral concerns into our conversation repeatedly without sounding sanctimonious. She had been isolated by her house arrest, but not so isolated that word didn't reach her about the corruption around her. She was concerned that everyday people could not transact business without paying a bribe, known as "tea money." She knew that to get a car license, some *kyat* must be slipped to the clerk. She was aware that parents were expected to pay teachers to get good grades for their children—and that a payoff was even expected for hospital services. She knew that Burma had become a narco-state, one of the leading producers of heroin and methamphetamines in the world. Nearly half of the hand pickers working in jade mines used heroin to get through the day, and 40 percent of them were infected by HIV. She knew that sex traffickers were transporting countless women across the border to servitude in China and brothels in Thailand.

That corrosion of national character could not be ignored, she said. "It will require more than a change in laws, it will require renewed respect for *values*," she said, locking eye contact to bring home her point.

Suu Kyi sees her campaign for democracy as a struggle for the very soul of Burma, not just a contest for seats in the Parliament. She often has called it Burma's "revolution of the spirit." As a result, her politics are not so much "left" or "right," but her own hybrid—a sort of Parliamentary Buddhism. Her goal is to combine the peaceful tenets of Buddhism with democracy, rule of law, and open markets.

In her early speeches, Suu Kyi would encourage crowds, "Aspire to be noble. Aspire to be as noble as can be." Often she would close her talks with the Buddhist blessing, "May you be free from danger, and may you be happy in body and mind."

Once she was asked if such beliefs made her old-fashioned. She replied drily, "Well, talking about morality, right and wrong, love and kindness, is considered rather old-fashioned these days, isn't it? But after all, the world is spherical. Perhaps the whole thing will come around again, and maybe I'm ahead of the times."

Her critics over the years have found that approach dangerously naïve. In the face of the junta's daily brutality, it seemed like walking up to a tank with a flower. Some in her party wanted more direct action. After all, they reminded, her father had taken up arms to fight for independence. Gandhi had called for national strikes in India. Yet Suu Kyi had her own endgame in mind. She stuck to her message of peaceful transition. Without a revolution of the spirit, she continued to say, the result of a violent regime change would probably be yet another heavy-handed government that would take on the bloody stain of the old order.

Aung San Suu Kyi's insistence that resorting to violence only begets more violence echoed a popular Burmese folk story. The legend was often circulated during the student riots of 1988. According to writer Emma Larkin, the story told of a dragon that terrorized a village and demanded the sacrifice of a virgin each year. Every year a brave young warrior would scale the mountains to fight the dragon and prevent the sacrifice. But each time, the warrior would perish. Then one year, a young man was able to get a glimpse of the dragon's lair, which was stocked with piles of gems and gold. Inspired and inflamed, the warrior marshaled the wherewithal to slay the dragon with his sword and claim the treasure. But as he sat on the corpse, admiring his spoils of victory, the young warrior noticed he was beginning to grow scales and then horns and a tail. He had turned into a dragon himself.

—~—

The need to break the cycle of violence in Burma had become Aung San Suu Kyi's mantra. "There are those," she explained to me, "who believe the only way we can remove the authoritarian regime and replace it with a democratic one is through violent means. But then, in the future, those who do not approve of a democratic government would be encouraged to try violent means of toppling it, because we would have set a precedent that you bring about political change through violence. I would like to set strongly the precedent that you can bring about political change through political *settlement* and not through violence."

Her position was not just taking the moral high road, it was also the most pragmatic option: Defeating the massive Burmese army by force was simply not feasible. With more than 400,000 soldiers, the Burmese army is one of the largest armies in Southeast Asia. Known as the "Tatmadaw," the army's goal of total national domination is reflected in their motto: "One blood, one voice, one command." The military's influence also permeates the economy through a honeycomb of insider business deals that have made the generals and their families hugely rich. Many of them live in mansions in the "Golden Valley" section of Rangoon with garages full of cars. They have vacation homes in the hills and beaches, as well as fortunes banked in Singapore and Dubai. The military had become interwoven into nearly every sector of the economy: construction, mining, transportation, banking.

The only pragmatic way of getting the military to relax its powerful grip would be negotiating a transition. Suu Kyi often pointed to precedents in other countries—the rapprochement in Chile after the Pinochet military regime, the re-unification of East and West Germany, the transition in South Africa after the end of apartheid, and the peace between the Hutu and Tutsi factions in Rwanda after brutal genocide there. Reconciliation has worked in other places, she emphasized to me, and it could be done in Burma.

"Our people deserve a government that will make sure they are not waked up in the middle of the night and pulled off to goodness knows where," she said, her voice breaking with an angry flash of emotion.

The only other time her composure cracked was when I asked about her two sons. Because it had been many years since the generals had granted visas for them to visit, I asked if she was in contact with them. Her eyes flickered with moisture as she answered briskly, "Yes, of course." She did not elaborate, and it was clear she would not. The separation from her sons was not something she dwelled on publicly. It was years later before she would admit to the BBC, "Of course I regret not having been able to spend time with my family. One wants to be together with one's family. That's what families are about. Of course, I have regrets about that. Personal regrets. I would like to have been together with my family. I would like to have seen my sons growing up. But I don't have doubts about the fact that I had to choose to stay with my people here," she said, with a firmness that indicated: case closed.

She does not encourage melodrama and told her friend Alan Clements she doesn't like it. "One has to live life on an even keel. You get down to work and don't just stand there despairing. That's what I would say to people who feel helpless and despairing. 'Don't just sit there. Do something.'" She used the analogy of a pot on the stove that had boiled over. Instead of "getting into a tiz," she suggested, it's much more effective to get to work cleaning up the mess on the stove.

She adamantly has refused over the years to describe the personal price she has paid for leading the democracy movement as a sacrifice. "If you *choose* to do something, then you shouldn't say it's a sacrifice, because nobody forced you to do it. It's a choice." That legalistic response may be her way of deflecting too much sympathy about the personal cost of her house arrest. She is acutely mindful that many others have been tortured in prison or have died in the struggle for democracy. In 1996, she wrote poignantly, *"This is the eighth winter that I have not been able to get into bed at night without thinking of prisoners of conscience and other inmates of jails all over Burma. As I lie on a good mattress under a mosquito net, warm in my cocoon of blankets, I cannot help but remember that many of my political colleagues are lying in bleak cells on thin mats through which seeps the peculiarly unpleasant chill of a concrete floor. Both their clothing and their blankets would be quite inadequate and they would be unprotected by mosquito nets."*

Though she did have more comfort in her home than her colleagues in prison, Suu Kyi's accommodations appeared as spare as a Shaker cabin. Much of her parents' furniture had been sold off, repurchased, and then sold off again. Her upstairs bedroom was furnished with only basic necessities, including the mosquito net on her bed that she considered a "luxury." There are only three seasons in Burma, she has said: hot, rainy, and cold. All three seasons can be punishing. When the roof of the dilapidated house leaked, Suu Kyi had to dash around her house, placing pots and pans under the streaming water. When it became cold, she covered her bed with a blanket given to her father in 1947 by ethnic Chin friends, or a Japanese blanket from her parents' wedding bed. Her bedroom reportedly was filled with photographs of her mother and brothers, her husband and sons. Her kitchen was meagerly stocked with what her companions could afford at the market. She had once loved experimenting in the kitchen and taught herself how to make chicken fricassee with dumplings after reading about it in a Nero Wolfe detective novel. During her house arrest, she had to make do with simpler fare. The dining table was more likely to be covered with work papers than cuisine.

Part of her self-discipline has been mending her own clothes and cleaning her house, in keeping with her mother's strict teaching to always be presentable. On the day of our talk, she was dressed in a cotton blouse and *longyi*, the traditional Burmese sarong. They were made out of simple cloth, and yet looked elegant. I wanted to find out more details about her girlhood growing up in Rangoon, so we talked about the Methodist school she had attended, where she had learned to make good grades and sing hymns. "The Methodists have the *best* hymns," she said, laughing at the memory. When I asked her how tall she was, she insisted that we both take off our shoes and stand side-by-side to measure who was taller. She was not quite 5 feet, 3 inches tall, but her proper posture made her seem taller.

My escort interrupted. She was worried that I was overstaying our time. We should leave before the guards became suspicious, she said. As we walked toward the door, I couldn't resist asking one more question. What had happened to the piano that had first piqued my interest in Suu Kyi and brought me there? Had Suu Kyi been able to play the piano, now that the military had supposedly "relaxed" her house arrest?

"Oh, no, I'm afraid not," she said, making light of it, "I'm afraid my fingers have quite forgotten how to play. I wouldn't want to torture others with my playing—or torture myself. "

I later learned that the old Yamaha piano had been repaired at some point, but Suu Kyi had less time to play as her political activities increased. But she would never complain. She knew all too well that her colleagues had given up far more in their prison cells than sonatas.

As we departed, Suu Kyi walked with us to the door and invited us to please come again. We all knew that would be highly difficult and unlikely. I asked if there was anything I could do to help her. She looked me in the eye and said, "Here's what you can do. Keep a light shining on this place. Without the light, we would go back into the shadows, so please keep a light." I said that I would.

As we drove away through the tall gates, I looked back through the rear window of the car. Aung San Suu Kyi was standing on the steps of her house, watching us leave. She seemed to gaze for a moment at what was left of her neglected garden. Then she turned and went back into her house.

Our car sped down University Avenue and away from the guards at the barricade. My escort was exhilarated. We had gotten away. Her job was done. But not mine. I was determined to learn more about this struggle for the soul of Burma.

What I didn't know was that Aung San Suu Kyi was about to face a desperate fight for her life. I was one of the last journalists to interview her for the next seven years.

CHAPTER TWO

THE LADY VANISHES

"It was just like the hell boiling over."

—Survivor of 2003 attack on
Aung San Suu Kyi

Just a few months after our conversation, on May 30, 2003, Daw Aung San Suu Kyi's motorcade was attacked in a bloody ambush. For days, it was not known exactly what had happened, and people around the world were held in suspense. Was "The Lady" still alive? Was she being held by the junta somewhere? Not known. Was she seriously injured by a blow to the head as reported? Or a broken arm? Also not known. All the Burmese military government would say was that Aung San Suu Kyi had been taken into "protective custody." She disappeared from view.

Many weeks passed before pieces of the story could be put together. In contrast to earlier attempts on Suu Kyi's life, this time international legal organizations were attuned to the Burma democracy struggle and they stepped in to document the mayhem. According to their reports, this is what happened:

Aung San Suu Kyi had been given permission by authorities to travel that spring to northern Burma, where she planned to open a series of her National League for Democracy offices and launch new youth groups. She left Rangoon on May 6 with a makeshift convoy of several hundred supporters. Yet while she was wending her way from village to village, drawing greater and greater crowds as she went along, the military regime began preparing an ambush of major proportions.

Members of the military-affiliated USDA (Union Solidarity and Development Association) and the Swan Arr Shin, the Gestapo-like group made up of thugs and former convicts, were mobilized from eight townships near Suu Kyi's planned route. More than 5,000 men were provided attack training at a high school in Depayin, a town to the north of Mandalay. An armada of 56 large trucks and 10 smaller vehicles such as jeeps was brought to the campus for their use. Carpenters were brought in to make crude weapons—sharp and thick bamboo sticks, pointed iron rods, and wooden bats. Clerks from the local township offices were ordered to help distribute the weapons to the trainees. And just days before Aung San Suu Kyi was scheduled to arrive in Depayin, residents who lived along the route were forbidden by authorities to welcome her motorcade. They were ordered to stay in their houses.

The plan of attack looked like a military operation, only this assault was directed at unarmed citizens. More than a thousand of the trained assailants were assigned to follow Aung San Suu Kyi as her convoy moved toward Depayin on May 30. Three thousand others were to hide in the woods and thick bushes at a designated location along the road. Another thousand were to be deployed at a barricade further down the road, a second designated "killing field." Lights were brought in to illuminate the two locations. Attackers were given whistles and walkie-talkies to communicate with each other. Supervisors for the operation used code words of the kind normally used in military maneuvers. A deadly trap was being set.

Suu Kyi had a security team, but it was largely composed of young volunteers from the NLD Youth group, who left their studies or farmwork to provide an improvised cordon of protection along her way. Concerns about her safety were ever-present, even though the junta had claimed her current release at that time was "unconditional." The ruling generals had trumpeted that a new chapter had been opened in the history of Burma and every citizen could take part in political activities. But that was not the reality. As I had seen, access to Aung San Suu Kyi was still restricted. Her home was guarded and her movements monitored and hampered. When she ventured out to speak, her followers were harassed, jostled, and threatened. But none of that rose to the level of the violence that was about to occur.

A traveling party with approximately ten cars and dozens of motorcycles had been assembled by the NLD for the spring trip. Several hundred democracy supporters were on board, including a contingent of monks. It wasn't long before the trouble began. On May 16, when Suu Kyi's motorcade was entering the city of Myitkyina, her supporters were confronted by more than 300 protesters brandishing clubs, stone catapults, and sharpened farm chopping tools. The protesters held up signs and shouted, "We don't want people who don't support USDA!" Suu Kyi's NLD supporters countered by chanting, "Long live Daw Aung San Suu Kyi." When they did, police and military intelligence members brazenly took their photos with video and still cameras.

The harassment was bothersome and unpleasant, but not unusual or totally unexpected. The NLD had picked up rumors before the trip that troops with bamboo clubs were being trained by the USDA. They had heard that villagers had been ordered to furnish meal packets for the assailants.

Suu Kyi cautioned her supporters to avoid any words or behavior that might lead to a confrontation. As one volunteer recalled, "Daw Suu had told us that if we were wearing the NLD uniform of white shirt and Kachin sarong, we had to bear with a bowed head whatever was done to us, and must not retaliate."

Aung San Suu Kyi went ahead with her scheduled speeches, but events soon took on an ominous tone. A scout car of her security volunteers was traveling ahead of her motorcade in order to report back on any threatening conditions. The scouts suddenly encountered a group of USDA protesters on the road who were massing to deter Suu Kyi on her way to the next stop at a town called Monywa. When the scout team tried to turn around and go back to warn Suu Kyi, the protesters forcibly blocked their way. The security scouts drove hurriedly on ahead to Monywa and alerted supporters, who raced back to the confrontation area by the hundreds on motorcycles. Because the NLD supporters outnumbered the USDA protesters and because a large contingent of monks was accompanying her, Suu Kyi was able to pass through the hostile mob. When she arrived at Monywa at dusk, she was greeted by the astonishing sight of thousands of people holding up candles. The government had cut off all the electric power to the town. People showed up anyway and brought candles as it began to grow dark. The crowd was so big that Suu Kyi had great difficulty reaching the clock tower in the center of town to speak. Her team sensed that more trouble was looming, but the next morning Suu Kyi rose early as usual. She inaugurated another NLD office and youth group despite angry interruptions from some protesters, who later admitted they had been given free meals and money to disturb the event.

Suu Kyi had planned to pay her respects to the abbot at the local Zawtika monastery, but arrived to discover he had been "invited" elsewhere by the military. In another portentous sign, area army commanders ordered the monks with Suu Kyi's group to leave immediately, apparently removing them from the line of fire. Some stayed anyway. Suu Kyi was undaunted. She made a point of stopping at another monastery briefly and kept to her afternoon schedule of speeches. She made time to go check on an NLD colleague who had been in prison.

It was nearing twilight when her convoy finally drew near a farming community known as Kyi Ywa. The village was not far from their goal of the town of Depayin, where they had planned to spend the night. Suu Kyi's group was running late because the roads were bad and so many people were turning out to see "The Lady" that it had slowed movement. Suu Kyi's security team was on high alert because some of the NLD supporters had been beaten and arrested by police in Monywa earlier in the day. As usual, the scout car traveled on ahead, but this time the car did not return. Several convoy members were sent out on motorcycles to find out why. They did not return, either. Concerns were heightened when Suu Kyi's group realized that no traffic was coming from the opposite direction. Something was clearly amiss. Their convoy had been tailed by military intelligence vehicles and motorcycles all day, but now volunteers in the rear spotted a long line of buses and vans following them at a moderate distance. Suu

Kyi decided to press on. It was dangerous in the dark and supporters were waiting for them in Depayin.

Fifty-one-year-old Nyunt Nyunt, an NLD volunteer from Mandalay, would later remember how moving it was to look out the car window as they headed toward Depayin and see how many people had trekked from distant villages to wait by the roadside in hopes of getting a glimpse of Aung San Suu Kyi. They called out to her, "Aunty!" or "Kyi Ahma!" (Big Sister). "They were poor starving people," she remembered. "I saw amongst them old grandmothers quivering and waving neem tree sprigs to welcome us."

When they arrived at Kyi Ywa village about 7:30 or 8 P.M., Nyunt Nyunt recalled, they were greeted by a large, cheering crowd. Many of the villagers attempted to join Suu Kyi's convoy in cars and motorcycles, but were forcibly held back by police. Hundreds of the villagers still managed to follow the NLD group to the edge of town. Suu Kyi's entourage had gone less than 200 yards down the road, when events suddenly unraveled.

Two men dressed like monks stood in the middle of the road, blocking their way. Because Suu Kyi's car was in the lead of the caravan, her chief of security, Ko Tun Zaw Zaw, stepped off the running board of her Toyota to find out what the monks wanted. The monks said they had been waiting a long time and that people nearby wanted Suu Kyi to give them a speech. Ko Tun Zaw Zaw told them, "Revered monk, it is very late and there is no time. Please excuse your disciples." The monks insisted, still barring the way. When Ko Tun Zaw Zaw relayed the problem to Suu Kyi, she said would talk to the people who had been waiting. But before she could, hundreds of the armed men who had been shadowing her convoy swarmed out of their trucks as if on cue. They attacked the villagers who were accompanying the NLD group and then the rear of the motorcade itself, including the monks who had refused orders from the authorities to leave. A surreal, bloody melee ensued.

The frenzied attackers chanted what seemed to be a scripted message, mocking the NLD members as "ax handles" (a term for tools of foreign interests) and taunting the women as wives of "Kalah," a particularly offensive term for Indians and Westerners. With no mercy, the attackers relentlessly bludgeoned the NLD supporters with iron rods and bricks. Some were run over with trucks.

Then, at the sound of a loud whistle, the 3,000 attackers who had been hiding in the roadside bushes came rushing out. Some were dressed like monks, but wore red armbands so they would not be mistaken for the real monks who were still in Suu Kyi's convoy.

Nyunt Nyunt, the volunteer from Mandalay, saw other women she knew jerked from cars, stripped, and assaulted in the road. She could hear one assailant yelling "We have built bridges and roads on which you all can walk, race-destroying women! You want to be wives of Kalah! Before you make yourselves wives of Kalah, become our wives!" She could see the attackers wrapping the NLD women's hair around their hands and pounding their faces against the road. They continued pounding their heads on the ground until the women died. After she was beaten on the head and back with bricks, Nyunt Nyunt collapsed.

When she regained consciousness briefly, Nyunt Nyunt saw her pinni jacket had been torn off, her sarong ripped. Her shoes and the sling bag with her money were gone. She was covered with blood. Somehow she found her mangled glasses on the ground and as she looked around, she could see the driver of her car was dead, his eye protruding. Her friend U Chit Tin had blood spilling out of three big cuts on his head and was vomiting blood. As he died, he told her, "My duties have been fulfilled. Tell them at my office. I have fulfilled my obligations." She lost consciousness again.

The air was filled with screams and the sound of heads and arm bones being smashed with iron rods. Many of the eyewitnesses later testified they would never forget the popping sound of human heads being cracked open. The horrible sound would haunt them forever.

A shrieking horde of attackers surrounded Suu Kyi's car. Her young security guards linked hands to protect her in a double circle around her car. They were attacked with particular vengeance, with repeated blows to their heads. The assailants taunted those who tried to protect Suu Kyi as they struck, "Are you death-defying force for Kalah woman? If so, die!" NLD photographer Tin Maung Oo was killed on the spot.

Suu Kyi was injured when either a rock or a brick smashed through the back window. The attackers attempted to pull her out through the broken window, grabbing and pulling at her. According to witnesses, her horrified young bodyguards yelled "Aunty, run! Run!" as the assailants jabbed sharpened bamboo sticks through the shattered window at her face. Suu Kyi refused to be intimidated. She called out to her followers not to fight back, and she called out to the attackers not to harm anyone. Further back in the convoy, her 76-year-old deputy, U Tin Oo, had stepped out of the micro-van he was riding in to calm the crowd, only to be battered and dragged away.

Numerous witnesses later testified that the attackers appeared drunk or drugged and that their eyes were red and wild. Some evidence was found later that a half-drum full of liquor had been provided for assailants, who were told they could drink as much as they wished. It also appeared that the attackers had been trained to strike systematically at the head. Survivors said the killing sites looked like a movie set because spotlights had been installed in the trees by the road. Toyota Dyna trucks had been positioned with their headlights turned on to illuminate the carnage.

One of the survivors, Toe Lwin, said he was standing by Suu Kyi's car and saw even elderly people being beaten to the ground. "I told them to stop beating people and asked them to go back. Suddenly, they started to hit Daw Suu's car. First I tried to cover it. Then they started to beat me. They hit my head three times and I collapsed."

Suu Kyi's driver that night was a handsome young law student named Kyaw Soe Lin, who had been given the prized assignment of driving her as a reward for helping organize legal aid for the NLD. When they came under heavy attack, Kyaw Soe Lin pleaded with the mob, protesting that "The Lady" was in the car, but the attacks only intensified. To his horror, he could see her young bodyguards being beaten senseless all around the car. Her colleagues yelled "Drive on!" but Suu Kyi refused. She said she could not abandon those who loved her. She wanted to stay to help them. Her young driver wouldn't let her get out of the car. He decided to do what needed to be done and stomped on the gas pedal.

To the driver's surprise, the Toyota pitched and swerved erratically out of his control. Something was wrong. He could not go forward. The attackers had apparently jammed a wooden stick in the wheel mechanism so the vehicle would lurch when driven forward, perhaps to make their deaths look like an accident or at least impede their escape. Thinking quickly,

Kyaw Soe Lin reversed the car and the wooden stick broke. While he was struggling with the Toyota, attackers broke the car windows on both sides. The battered car was covered with blood and filled with broken glass inside. The headlights and mirrors were smashed to pieces.

At last, Kyaw Soe Lin was able to floor the accelerator and get the car moving forward. He worried he might run over some of the youth members who had been knocked to the ground, but there was little choice. He tried his best to avoid them. As soon as he got far enough away from the thick of the fighting, he got out of the car to see what the matter with the car was. His hands trembling, he did his best to fix the damage from the stick. As they limped along the road, he saw several hundred members of the USDA in uniforms standing by with posters. They seemed shocked to see the car as some of the NLD bodyguards were still clinging for life to the top and sides of the vehicle. Kyaw Soe Lin worried that the protesters might pull them off, so he pretended he was going to drive the car into the USDA crowd and they scattered. As he drove on, the rest of the car windows were shattered by attackers who ran after them. He and Aung San Suu Kyi were struck through the windows by stones and bricks and sticks. But he kept on driving.

"Aunty asked me if I was okay, and I said I was fine and kept on going," Kyaw Soe Lin told Democratic Voice of Burma years later. He then saw a large wooden blockade in the road ahead. He was afraid they would be beaten to death if he stopped, so he drove through it. The one-lane country road had become a deadly obstacle course. Barbed wire had been stretched across the road to prevent the ambush victims from escaping. A row of trucks blocked the way ahead. Kyaw Soe Lin spotted a small gap between the vehicles, grabbed the steering wheel tight, and drove thorough. But their way was not clear yet. Next they encountered a line of policemen with their guns pointed at the car. Kyaw Soe Lin drove straight toward them and they jumped aside.

Suu Kyi told him not to stop until they reached Depayin. If only they could reach Depayin, he thought, they might be safe with the NLD supporters there. But in the confusion, he had somehow taken a wrong turn in the dark. He wasn't sure exactly where they were. He thought they were drawing close to their destination. But as they neared a small town called

Yea-U, security personnel stopped the vehicle and asked who was in the car. Suu Kyi's group was told to wait. About 30 minutes later, a large number of military personnel arrived. "They came out carrying guns and surrounded us. Then an army official, apparently a battalion commander, arrived. He put a gun to my temple and asked us to go with them," Kyaw Soe Lin said. "Aunty nodded us to go, so we did."

The small group of survivors from the car were taken to the Yea-U jail, where they saw people wearing the same armbands as their attackers. Suu Kyi calmly told the police and intelligence officials that she would cooperate with them if they promised to abide by legal procedures. They promised to abide with the law and took her away.

Suu Kyi was taken to a military hospital for stitches for her injuries and then sequestered at a military camp some 30 miles from Rangoon. As the days passed and international outcry about her whereabouts grew louder, the government released a statement that they had placed Suu Kyi in custody to "protect her." She was then secretly transferred to Insein Prison, a penal complex notorious for its unsanitary conditions, meager food rations, disease, and torture. As the daughter of war hero Aung San, she was given the privilege of a separate space with a wooden bed and toilet, but she had no access to news or visitors—and no assurance that the foul food she was being given was not poisoned. She ate little if any. Her health began to deteriorate.

—w—

Insein Prison, whose name appropriately is pronounced like "insane," is located on the outskirts of Rangoon in the town of Insein. Built by the British in the 1800s, Insein was considered the largest prison ever built in the British Empire. At the time of Suu Kyi's arrest, it had grown to a population of more than 10,000 and housed many of the 2,100 political prisoners in the country.

The prison has been described as the "darkest hell-hole in Burma." Inmates report some wards are so crowded that prisoners sleep on concrete floors in rows on their sides or have to take turns sleeping. Some are confined to "dark cells" in former dog kennels where they have no access to light or a toilet and cannot stand up.

Water for bathing often is allotted by the cupful—in the same cup that prisoners must use for meals. Food is usually contaminated and most prisoners suffer from dysentery. Abuse includes beatings, keeping inmates shackled in chains, attacks by dogs, sexual abuse, and injections with contaminated needles. As recently as late 2010, prisoners reported being burned with cigarettes and tortured with electroshocks.

With only three prison doctors to treat 10,000 inmates, diseases such as tuberculosis, scabies, and malaria are rife. Mental illness is widespread.

When a United Nations envoy finally was allowed to see Suu Kyi more than a week after she was taken to Insein Prison, he was surprised to find her in "good spirits," even though she was still in the same clothing she had been captured in. She apologized for not being able to receive him more properly.

Months later, Suu Kyi's physician was allowed to visit her at the prison after continued international clamor. Her health was deteriorating rapidly. He convinced authorities that she needed immediate medical care. In September 2003, she underwent a hysterectomy at a nearby hospital with guards at the door. Undergoing major surgery while still under military guard was a risk that she must have understood well, but endured.

Bombarded by rising international concern about her whereabouts and well-being, the military government quietly placed her under strict security in her home. Junta Foreign Minister Win Aung downplayed her heavily restrictive detainment, telling the diplomatic community "We don't call this house arrest. . . . We are helping her to overcome the health problems."

Meanwhile, an ad hoc commission on the Depayin massacre was convened by the Burma Lawyers' Council and the National Council of the Union of Burma. The commission reported that the attack was clearly premeditated and well organized. They cited as evidence:

- Several thousand persons were brought to a remote rural location for the specific purpose of attacking the convoy.
- The attackers were all well armed and located strategically at two killing sites.

- Before Aung San Suu Kyi's motorcade arrived, local authorities ordered people living in nearby villages to stay indoors.
- The authorities systematically searched for and arrested survivors of the attack.

The consensus of the reports was that the massacre was carried out by pro-junta forces consisting of members of the USDA and the Swan Arr Shin ("Masters of Force") militia, the cadre of thugs and convicts often used by the junta to disrupt protests. A report by the U.N. Special Rapporteur on Human Rights, Professor Paulo Sergio Pinheiro, summed it up bluntly: *"There is prima facie evidence that the Depayin incident could not have happened without the connivance of State agents."*

Subsequent reports on the Depayin attack brought to light official involvement at many levels. Later on the night of the attack, an estimated 80 riot policemen, with shields and sticks, arrived at the scene around 11 P.M. in four Dyna trucks and two cars that looked like Pajero jeeps. The bodies of the dead and dying were loaded into trucks to be disposed of like garbage. Witnesses saw the police change the location of abandoned NLD cars to make it look as if they had been traveling the other direction. Two trucks were set up to look as if they had had a head-on collision. Photos were taken of what was now made to look like an accident scene. The next morning, municipal policemen came to wash the blood from the roads with water and brooms.

The Depayin massacre rang alarm bells in human-rights circles. The bloodshed was troubling in a singular way. It was different from the government crackdown on demonstrators in 1988. Depayin was a well-organized, systematic assault, committed by thousands of perpetrators under the direct control of national and local authorities against unarmed civilians, including a Nobel Peace Laureate, her supporters, and other innocent people. The respected Asian Legal Resource Center, which has consultative status with the United Nations, concluded that the slaughter was a clear violation of Article 7.1 of the Rome Statute of the International Criminal Court and therefore a crime against humanity.

And yet, a decade later there would still be no serious action taken on the massacre and no one held accountable. Most of the beaten were later arrested and imprisoned. None of the beaters were.

The government claimed only four people were killed in the incident. Conservative estimates at the time were that 70 to 100 democracy supporters were killed during the "Black Friday" attack. Other estimates by human-rights groups placed the total at three times that, closer to 282 people. The dead included a doctor, members of the women's wing, and Suu Kyi's head of security, Ko Tun Zaw Zaw. In addition, some 256 of Suu Kyi's followers were taken into custody at the scene or hunted down later. They included her trusted adviser, U Tin Oo, the deputy leader of the NLD, who had tried to stop the violence. He was taken into custody without trial, placed in solitary confinement for eight months, and then held under house arrest for seven years for reasons that were never specified. The junta kept him under arrest until he was well into his eighties.

Those who were not taken into custody at Depayin fled for their lives. Nyunt Nyunt, the NLD volunteer from Mandalay who had been bludgeoned unconscious with bricks, continued blacking out as she staggered away from the killing scene. Several of the younger NLD members helped her get to a monastery, where she was hidden in the bushes and later given treatment. Though her head was still caked with blood and flies and she was too weak to walk, her NLD colleagues managed to boost her up and onto a train headed to Monywa and safety. Min Thein, then a 33-year-old youth organizer, remembered hiding in a car under the bodies of several dead and injured league members before escaping. "Blood from their wounds flowed over me," he told investigators with the Ad Hoc Commission. Another youth organizer, 23-year-old Phoe Zaw, said he helped carry the limp bodies of the injured to the Depayin Hospital. Phoe Zaw said the government forbade hospital staff from helping NLD members, but they did anyway. After receiving treatment, the injured league members were arrested.

Aung San Suu Kyi's young driver, Kyaw Soe Lin, was held for days without food, then transferred to Shwebo Prison, where he was given worse food than the rapists and thieves he was celled with. Hooded and shackled, he was taken to another prison where he was only given a handful of unhusked rice with rotting fish paste that made some people vomit. Then the interrogations began. He was told to say that the people in the villages who had welcomed them were the ones who attacked the convoy.

He refused. As a result he was tortured, stripped naked, and hot candle wax dripped on his body until he was covered with burns. He was forced to sit on his haunches and kicked like a football, even in his face. He was singled out, he was told, because he was the driver for "The Lady."

As he told a reporter seven years later, "They stank of alcohol as they tortured us. Then they threatened us—they said they will electrify us; keep us in the pouring rain. Not me alone, but all of those with me were beaten up. The sounds of 'I'm scared' and smashing—I heard these. It wasn't that painful when I was beaten up, it was more painful in my heart when [other people] were beaten."

His punishment included being placed in the worst detention cells. His cell was only slightly higher than standing height. Because it was rainy season, water often was several inches deep. He could not sleep. He could not sit. When he had arrived, he was handcuffed with his hands behind his back; his arms were pinned back for a month. His drunken jailers came to interrogate him at midnight and in the morning; the abuse continued throughout the day. When he was released, he considered it fortunate that his detention was "only" six months. He had made it out of a nightmare alive.

Outrage to the attack was expressed by much of the international community, human-rights groups, and even the Association of Southeast Asian Nations (ASEAN), which had more often than not turned a blind eye to the Burmese abuses. The massacre was proof that ASEAN's tepid policy of "constructive engagement" with the generals had failed to bring the junta closer to norms of international behavior.

The billionaire prime minister of Thailand, Thaksin Shinawatra, who had personal business interests in Burma, downplayed Suu Kyi's incarceration, saying "She is in no danger whatsoever." He claimed the Burmese government was becoming "more open" and warned that if Suu Kyi remained "stubborn," it would be "helpless for her."

In contrast, Foreign Secretary Blas Ople from the Philippines, the ASEAN country with the *least* business interests in Burma, took the toughest stand. He declared, "The goal is not merely the release of Madame Suu Kyi, but the release of the entire people of Burma from a regime of oppression and repression."

For a time it had appeared that ASEAN—finally—might take action against its most reprehensible member. Yet after Suu Kyi was transferred from Insein Prison to house arrest, ASEAN leaders went back to a complacent posture.

To stave off pressure from the rest of the world, the Burmese regime suddenly offered to put together a plan for democratization. They called it their "Seven-Point Roadmap to Democracy." The first step was the resumption of a previous National Convention that had been adjourned after criticism that it was rigged and had little true democratic participation. After the Depayin outrage, the generals decided to resume the stage-managed process to draft a new Constitution. This time, the generals were determined to lock military control into the Constitution—and lock out Aung San Suu Kyi, by prohibiting people married to foreigners from holding office.

The sham constitutional process gave the international community the cover to turn its attention to other matters. And that meant the Burmese generals had gotten away with murder.

Who should have been held accountable? At the time, the military regime was ruling under the name of the State Peace and Development Council (SPDC), which had replaced the State Law and Order Restoration Council (SLORC), which had replaced the role of the Burma Socialist Program Party (BSPP) created by the first military dictatorship in the 1960s. The senior general who was the ultimate authority in 2003 was a dour, colorless career officer named Than Shwe, Chairman of the SPDC and Commander-in-Chief of the Defense Services. Than Shwe had a jowly bulldog countenance, no charisma, and little education. He had worked his way up the military chain of command by currying favor with commanders and eliminating rivals. People spoke fearfully of Than Shwe in code as "Number 1," just as they had with the previous dictator, General Ne Win. Than Shwe was known to loathe Aung San Suu Kyi and had gone so far as to forbid anyone from saying her name in his presence; doing so sent him into rages. The contrast between the two was stark: She was doggedly clinging to noble ideals; he was ruthless in clinging to power. She was beloved by the people; he was feared. She had international respect; his name was little known outside of Burma. She had won multiple awards for her courage; he had been placed on *Parade* magazine's list of the worst dictators in the world.

Many months after the Depayin attack, Than Shwe acknowledged in a letter to regional diplomats that the attack had indeed been premeditated, but he claimed it was to protect the country from disorder, the military's usual excuse. He asserted that the regime was "compelled to take firm measures to prevent the country from sliding down the road to anarchy and disintegration." He charged that the NLD was "conspiring to create an anarchic situation . . . with a view of attaining power" by Aung San Suu Kyi's birthday on June 19. She spent her 58th birthday in prison instead.

Word eventually leaked out that a lieutenant general named Soe Win, who ranked as Secretary-2 in the regime, had been responsible for orchestrating the Depayin attack. Rather than being brought to justice, he was rewarded by Than Shwe with successive promotions and accompanied the senior general on state visits to Vietnam and China.

The feared Chief of Intelligence, General Khin Nyunt, who ranked as Secretary-1, later claimed that the order to attack was given without his knowledge and that he had intervened to save Aung San Suu Kyi after the attack. He was quoted by a Thai newspaper as saying, "I sent my men to snatch her from the mob that night and they brought her to safety to a nearby army cantonment."

Though he was responsible for enforcing the climate of terror and torture, Westerners considered Khin Nyunt the most modern and liberal of the generals, the most likely to embrace reforms. He may have overplayed his hand, however. After serving only a year as prime minister, Khin Nyunt resigned for "health reasons" and was placed under house arrest for seven years for corruption. He was replaced as prime minister by none other than Soe Win, who had become widely known in the country as "the Butcher of Depayin."

The United Nations Security Council should have conducted an investigation of the Depayin massacre similar to its investigation two years later of the assassination of Lebanese Prime Minister Rafik Hariri. But they did not.

Aung San Suu Kyi had been on the verge of uniting the country for change when the regime cracked down at Depayin. She was drawing as many as 40,000 people at a time to her rallies, despite intense harassment from the USDA and the Swan Arr Shin militia. Photos of her on the campaign trail just before the Depayin attack show Suu Kyi relaxing between speeches by perching barefooted on the limb of a tree. She looks tired, but happy to be out on her own. For a brief time, she had been free.

—~—

Before setting out on the fateful campaign foray in May, Suu Kyi had secretly videotaped a message in April to be played at a Freedom Forum event in Washington, D.C. honoring young people who had shown "Free Spirits." In the video, she implored the students in the United States to keep in mind what it must be like for young people in her country to grow up without being able to speak freely or vote. "They are not allowed to take wing," she said. "So I would like to count on you, you young people who are able to stretch your wings and fly and to soar, to help *our* young people do the same thing."

A friend had urged her to tell the story in the Freedom Forum video about the incident in which she had climbed atop a fire truck to stop the crew from spraying her supporters with their fire hoses. Her friend thought it would illustrate the difficulties she faced.

"No, I don't want to complain," Suu Kyi said.

"You have to complain," the friend replied.

"It's not about me," Suu Kyi insisted.

But for the junta, it *was* all about her. A few weeks after the Freedom Forum video was taped, her convoy was attacked at Depayin. The main offices of her NLD party were padlocked and put under guard in Rangoon. Other party offices around the country were shuttered. The Depayin Massacre was a watershed event. It marked the beginning of a prolonged crackdown on Aung San Suu Kyi personally and a near total shutdown of her party operations. Access to her physician, her attorney, and international authorities was cut off. She could not leave her house or talk to the media. Mail was often suspended. The junta had failed to kill Suu Kyi at Depayin, but they succeeded in isolating her even more than before.

But if the military thought that they could silence Aung San Suu Kyi by cutting her off from all outside contact, they miscalculated.

CHAPTER THREE

THE RETURN OF THE NATIVE

"The world views her as one of the great heroes of our time."
—His Holiness the Dalai Lama

After the Depayin massacre, Aung San Suu Kyi's advocates around the world struggled to keep her story in public view, as she could no longer be seen or heard. Birthday parties were organized with an empty chair for the guest of honor. In a rare display of unity, 112 former presidents and prime ministers called for her release.

Her stature grew in absentia. Aung San Suu Kyi became even more famous. While she was invisible, her fight for freedom became more visible. The drama of the woman held prisoner in a house by a lake assumed almost mythical, cultish proportions, like a fable about a princess held hostage in her castle by dark forces.

Journalists started describing Suu Kyi as the "Titanium Orchid" and "Steel Butterfly." But none of those labels adequately captured the complexity of the woman who was being held in her home—or explained what made her take up such a dangerous, lonely mission.

To understand what brought Aung San Suu Kyi to her destiny at 54 University Avenue, you must start with the beginning, her family tree. A brief introduction says that her father, General Aung San, was the "father" of the independence movement in Burma. Brilliant and daring, he persuaded the British to give Burma its independence after World War II. He was known throughout the country as the "Bogyoke" (bo-joke), which is Burmese for "The General." He was organizing a democratic government when he was assassinated by political rivals in 1947. Suu Kyi was only two years old. After her father's death, her mother, Khin Kyi, became a national figure in her own right, elected to Parliament and named Ambassador to India.

As a teen-ager, young Suu Kyi attended a girl's school in Delhi while her mother was ambassador. One of the lessons that she absorbed in Delhi was how Mahatma Gandhi stubbornly and shrewdly used nonviolence to free India from British control. She then went to England to attend Oxford University, where she met and later married a British college student named Michael Vaillancourt Aris. He was tall with sandy-colored hair, bookish, deeply interested in Asia, and determined at first sight to win Suu Kyi. Michael Aris went on to become a well-known Himalayan scholar on Tibet and Bhutan. Suu Kyi settled into university life at Oxford as a mother of two sons, Alexander and Kim. She was known to her neighbors as a dutiful housewife, but she dreamed of becoming a scholar and writer herself. She was working on her doctoral thesis when her domestic scenario was abruptly interrupted in 1988.

The boys had gone upstairs to bed and Suu and Michael were reading when the phone rang around 11 P.M. Suu Kyi rose from her chair to answer the phone. An aunt told her: "Your mother has had a stroke. It was quite a bad one. I think you should come." Suu Kyi put down the phone, went to their bedroom, and began to pack. Her husband did not realize something was wrong until he noticed that Suu Kyi had gotten out a suitcase. It was the kind of distress call about an aging parent that many families know all too well. But as Michael later wrote, he had a premonition then that their lives would never be the same.

The next morning, Suu Kyi walked briskly down the street from her home to the station and took a bus to Heathrow Airport for the long flight overseas.

When asked about her return to Burma that spring, Suu Kyi has said she had no political aspirations when she first arrived in Rangoon. "When I arrived in Rangoon to take care of my mother, my only intention regarding politics was to start several libraries in my father's memory." She had reassured the ruling generals as much when they called her in for questioning during an earlier visit to Burma in 1974. They were blunt: *Was she going to engage in anti-government activities?* No, she said, she had no intention of getting involved in Burmese politics so long as she lived outside the country. She had remained true to her word. As she boarded the plane at Heathrow in 1988, she was expecting to do her duty for her mother and then return to her husband, children, and thesis.

Yet when Aung San Suu Kyi landed in Rangoon, the air was charged with danger. Spring 1988 was a time of massive demonstrations in Burma, led by students who were demanding a democratic system. After 20 years of General Ne Win's disastrous military dictatorship, people were suffering deeply across the country. As one observer put it, Ne Win had turned into Burma's Stalin. He had done away with elections, muzzled the press, jailed critics, and forced people into labor camps. His "Burmese Way to Socialism" had become the way to ruin. Burma, once one of the most prosperous and literate nations in Southeast Asia, was now classified as a Least Developed Country by the United Nations, a "basket case" dependent on foreign help to get by. As a university student in the 1930s, General Ne Win had campaigned for independence from the British—now students were campaigning for independence from him.

Protests had started in the universities over the lack of freedom in the country, but gained momentum when Win abruptly and bizarrely canceled most denominations of currency. A highly superstitious man, Ne Win decreed the government would only recognize 45 and 90 kyat notes in the future. Why? Because those denominations were divisible by nine, which a soothsayer had suggested would be a lucky number for the general. But by canceling the majority of the currency, the savings of many Burmese disappeared overnight. Most people hid their cash away because they did not trust the government-controlled banks; now their money was worthless. Students had lost all their money for tuition and the chance for a better life.

Students from the Rangoon Institute of Technology took their anger to the streets, smashing windows and traffic lights in Rangoon. The universities were closed and students sent home. At the same time, villagers in rural areas started protesting the inept government policies that required farmers to sell below market rates. Burma was boiling with anger everywhere.

Riot police had shot to death 200 demonstrators, most of them students protesting government policies and demanding free, multiparty elections. Even larger demonstrations were then ignited by a small, seemingly random incident, much like the "Arab Spring" would be sparked by the death of a street vendor who set himself on fire in Tunisia decades later. In Burma's case, three students were taking a break at a tea shop near the Rangoon Institute of Technology on Insein Road. When they tried to listen to contemporary music on one of their cassettes, a brawl broke out with some older men who objected to the music and may have been drunk. All the brawlers were jailed; the older men were soon released, but not the students. Hundreds of other students returned to the tea shop to protest. When a riot erupted, the Lon Htein, the hardened police units similar to Hitler's "brownshirts," were brought in. More students were wounded. Matters got rapidly worse from there.

On March 16, students marching on Prome Road were confronted near Inya Lake by the Lon Htein riot police. Many were beaten to death or drowned, as soldiers held their heads underwater in the lake until they quit struggling. Some of the women were gang-raped.

On March 17, soldiers and riot police entered Rangoon University and arrested hundreds of students. Forty-one of the students suffocated to death after they were locked in a police van in the sweltering heat.

The commander of the security forces was Gen. Sein Lwin, known as "The Butcher." He had suppressed dissent at Rangoon University in 1962 by force and dynamited the student union to eliminate debate at its source. Once again, Sein Lwin was put in charge of beating back the protests in

1988, and he showed no quarter. Ne Win claimed that "hoodlums" had brought on the confrontations and the police had to keep order.

Evidence of the March mayhem was still evident at Rangoon General Hospital when Suu Kyi arrived to see her mother in April. Many of the doctors, nurses, and relatives of the wounded told Suu Kyi about the perilous state of the country. People were starving and living in fear. Corruption was mounting. Suu Kyi took this all in, but kept her own counsel. She said later, "I don't think I would have come back just to take part in the demonstrations. The first part of it started when my mother was in the hospital and I was in the hospital with her. People were in and out all the time talking about it. There were all sorts of pamphlets floating around. Everything was happening around me."

Despite the ongoing violence, Michael and the boys came to Rangoon to be with Suu Kyi that summer. With little hope for her mother's recovery, Suu Kyi had moved Khin Kyi from the hospital to their weathered villa on Inya Lake. She converted the downstairs area into a hospital room for her mother and made sure that Khin Kyi could see her garden through the window. Suu Kyi became her mother's chief nurse, although she had help from a cook and housekeepers as well as Khin Kyi's sister, who had come to live in one of the small houses in the family compound after her husband died.

But everything around them portended something ominous. The weather that summer of '88 was oppressively hot and humid. It added to the sense that something unpleasant was about to happen. During the hot season in Burma—March to May—temperatures often reach over 100 degrees. During the rainy season—May to October—temperatures are even steamier as monsoon rains beat down, drenching everything in sheets of rain. Rangoon typically receives nearly 100 inches of rain a year, more than eight inches a month. July and August, when the student protests were at their height in 1988, are the two rainiest months.

Rangoon students sent Ne Win an ultimatum: Make a full accounting of those responsible for the violent crackdowns, or face "trouble." Ne Win did not respond. Three days later, thousands of students gathered for rallies at the shuttered Rangoon University campus. This time, thousands of other citizens joined in. Buddhist monks stepped forward, violating a ban on their involvement in political matters. The Lon Htein security force charged into the crowd with lethal ferocity. Instead of fleeing for safety down side streets to hide out, the protesters ran to the sacred Shwedagon Pagoda and mounted more protests from there.

By July, curfews were in place. People were on edge. An important announcement was said to be coming. Suu Kyi and Michael Aris sat transfixed before the radio in her mother's house on July 23. General Ne Win shocked the country by announcing that he was resigning as Chairman of the ruling Socialist Program Party to spend more time with his children and grandchildren. Even more stunning, Ne Win said that a referendum on the country's political future would be scheduled. The raging public discontent could no longer be ignored.

Suu Kyi, like the rest of the country, was "electrified," Michael wrote later. "I think it was at this moment more than any other that Suu made up her mind to step forward."

Here, at last, was the people's chance to take control of their destiny. Or was it? Although Ne Win had expressed concern for the welfare of the people in his resignation speech, within days he announced that one of his henchman, "The Butcher" Sein Lwin, would serve as president. Two other Ne Win acolytes got top positions: the hard-line General Saw Maung become commander in chief of the Tatmadaw, and Khin Nyunt, the crafty head of Military Intelligence, gained the additional rank of brigadier general. It was not an encouraging sign.

Public unrest continued to grow. The All Burma Federation of Student Unions (ABFSU) called for a general strike precisely at 8:08 A.M. on August 8, 1988. Known as the "Four Eights," the date was chosen by the activists for its numerological significance. They hoped 8-8-88 would be auspicious. And it was.

Hundreds of thousands of students, teachers, dockworkers, civil servants, and monks poured into the streets, exhilarated at the prospect of an end to one-party rule. They held up bright yellow banners emblazoned with a peacock, the symbol of the democracy movement, or photos of Aung San. Similar protests were staged in Mandalay, the second largest city, and Moulmein.

Then around midnight, President Sein Lwin ordered the troops to fire. Unarmed people on the streets and sidewalks were shot indiscriminately.

Witnesses said soldiers grabbed some young women by the hair and smashed their heads into the sidewalk.

A medical volunteer at Rangoon General Hospital told Human Rights Watch: "Army trucks dumped both dead and wounded from all over Rangoon outside the hospital. Some kids had a bullet wound in their arms or legs—and then a bayonet gash in their throats or chests. Some were also totally disfigured by bayonet cuts."

As the hospitals filled to overflowing with the wounded, doctors and nurses put up signs begging the soldiers to quit firing. Nurses in their white uniforms smeared with blood left the hospital to join the marchers. They, too, were shot.

Tom Meuer, a visiting American businessman, was staying at the Inya Lake Hotel that week. The hotel had been built in 1962 by the Soviets, a gift from Nikita Khrushchev. It was considered the most modern hotel in the city, a favorite of Westerners. Reports began filtering into the hotel about students fighting for their lives in other parts of the city. Meuer vividly remembers hearing that some students defended themselves by ripping spokes out of their bicycle wheels to make "jinglees," that could be hurled like arrows with slingshots. Other students packed mud into hardened balls to aim for the soldier's eyes. But they were no match for the soldiers' automatic weapons.

Ne Win had warned in his retirement speech that if there were more demonstrations, "We will shoot to hit . . . there will be no firing into the air. So, in the future, I am warning the demonstrators they won't be treated lightly." For once, he kept his word. When the protests continued, the military and security forces shot to kill. The shootings and arrests continued until there was so much turmoil that "The Butcher" Sein Lwin resigned as president on August 12. He was replaced by Dr. Maung Maung, a historian known as "The Puppet," who was a friend of Ne Win's. The country was reeling.

Many of the pro-democracy demonstrators who were shot carried signs with pictures of Suu Kyi's father. Protests were staged in front of the U.S. embassy, because the U.S. was seen as a symbol of democracy, and those demonstrators were shot as well. Between August 8 and 13, the Burmese police and military forces had killed at least 3,000 people, possibly as many as 10,000.

Democracy activists began urging Suu Kyi to take up her father's banner. She decided to seek the counsel of a half-dozen former military leaders who had turned against Ne Win as a matter of conscience. She trusted the judgment of these older men who had served in the Burma Independence Army during her father's era. Back then, the army was a respected institution. One of those she sought out was former General U Kyi Maung, who had been put in prison by Ne Win after he let it be known that he didn't think it was proper for the military to be involved in politics.

At first, U Kyi Maung was unsure that Suu Kyi was ready to lead. His initial impression was that she was shy and looked very young. "She must have been about 42 at the time, but she could have passed for a girl of 17," he told writer Alan Clements. After repeated requests from others in the movement, he agreed to take on a leadership role in the democracy movement with her. He figured she needed all the help possible.

Another veteran Suu Kyi consulted was General U Tin Oo, who had become so popular as a major general that Ne Win feared he was becoming a rival and put him in prison on trumped-up charges of treason. When U Tin Oo first met Suu Kyi, he was struck by how much her features and gestures were like her father's. "She resembled him in almost every way. I thought she was a female replica," he told Clements. Suu Kyi asked if Tin Oo had personally known her father and the last time he had seen him. Yes, he knew him well, Tin Oo said. He had last seen the Bogyoke when he went to Maymo to meet with the Shan leaders in northern Burma. Suu Kyi wanted to know, did he notice a small girl being carried by someone on the sidelines? "That was me," she said, "that was me!" They talked at length and Tin Oo became convinced that Suu Kyi was the one to carry on her father's work. She had a clear mind and a "strong head."

Despite the bloodshed and chaos, the fledgling democracy movement was gaining structure and momentum. Even U Nu, the ineffectual prime minister who had been deposed by Ne Win, joined the movement for a time although he was more than 80 years old. Suu Kyi remained a coach on the sidelines, deferring to others who had more experience. Her top priority was still caring for her dying mother. But privately, she discussed playing a greater political role with her husband.

Michael would later write how impressed he was that his wife was able to juggle the pressure to lead the democracy movement with the need to care for her mother during her last months. Despite all the frenetic activity in the house, he said, it never lost the sense of being a haven of love and care. "Suu is an astonishing person by any standards, and I think I can say I know her after 20 years of marriage, but I shall never quite understand how she managed to divide her efforts so equally between the devoted care of her incapacitated, dying mother and all the activity which brought her the leadership of the struggle for human rights and democracy in her country," he wrote. "It has something to do with her inflexible sense of duty and her sure grasp of what is right and wrong—qualities that can sit as a dead weight on some shoulders, but which she carries with such grace."

Protests were becoming a daily event in Rangoon. Suu Kyi counseled the activists who had begun gathering regularly in her home that they needed to be "for" something, not just against Ne Win. At the same time, she wrote an open letter to the military government, proposing that a committee be formed to take the country toward multiparty elections. She played Ne Win's own words back to him: "If we should have to choose between the good of the party and the good of the nation, we should choose the good of the nation."

Then she began making the speeches that would propel her to the very center of the storm.

On August 24, she was asked to say a few words to the crowd gathered outside Rangoon General Hospital. "It was Daw Suu's first appearance in public and we thought she wouldn't be able to speak Burmese fluently because she had spent years in England," said Moe Thu, a prominent writer. Suu Kyi surprised them all with her fluency in the Burmese language. Her remarks at the hospital were brief and served mainly to announce that she would deliver a full speech a few days later at the Shwedagon Pagoda.

The military leaders had spies in the hospital audience and moved quickly to try to sabotage her next appearance. People were told that Suu Kyi would speak in a different part of town, not at the Shwedagon Pagoda. As head of Military Intelligence, Burma's version of the KGB known as "M-Eye," Khin Myint launched a virulent propaganda campaign against Suu Kyi. Pamphlets accused her of being the puppet of Western powers and a "genocidal prostitute." Some caricatures of her were later described by one journalist as "startlingly obscene." One even depicted Michael as a Communist Jew working in Moscow.

Plans went ahead for a major speech on August 26. A sea of people flooded the slope beneath the revered Shwedagon Pagoda to hear the Bogyoke's daughter speak. By midday, the crowd was estimated to be larger than 500,000. Some climbed trees in hopes of getting a glimpse of Suu Kyi.

It was fitting that Aung San Suu Kyi made her political debut at Shwedagon Pagoda, the holiest site in Burma. The gilded dome dominates the Rangoon skyline from an elevated position on a hill in the city center. Shaped somewhat like a Hershey's chocolate kiss, the structure has a wide base and a dome that slopes gently up. Hence the name Shwedagon, which translates to "Golden Victory Mound."

Shwedagon is believed to be the largest gilded *zedi*, or Buddhist mounded shrine, in the world. The pagoda also is sometimes called a *stupa* because it houses Buddhist relics, notably eight hairs of Gautama, the historical Buddha.

Pairs of giant stone *chinthe*—mythical lions—guard the entrances to the pagoda. According to records kept by monks, the pagoda was built before Gautama died in 486 B.C., which would make it some 2,500 years old. Archeologists disagree and contend it was constructed in the sixth century A.D. Either way, it is an ancient treasure.

Wars and earthquakes have caused serious damage over the centuries, so the pagoda had to be rebuilt several times until it reached its current height of 320 feet, the equivalent of a 32-story building. By the sixteenth century, the pagoda had become the most famous place of pilgrimage in all of Burma. The first Westerner to write home in awe about it was a gentleman merchant from London named Ralph Fitch, who noted in 1586 that Shwedagon was "the fairest place in the world."

The crown, called a *hti*, is decorated with 5,448 diamonds and 2,317 rubies. The top is tipped with a 76-carat diamond, far outweighing even the 45-carat Hope Diamond.

The glittering dome is made of genuine gold plates attached by rivets. People all over the country, as well as rulers, have donated gold over the years to maintain the pagoda, a tradition started in the fifteenth century by a queen who gave her weight in gold.

In modern times, leaders in the democracy movement have gathered at the shrine to reinforce their cause. In 1920, Rangoon University students met at one of the pavilions to plot a protest against colonial practices; and in 1936, students camped out again on the terraces as part of another protest. In 1938, oilfield workers on strike also established their protest camp at the golden pagoda.

Foreigners have not always shown the same regard for the shrine as locals, which resulted in what is called the "Shoe Problem." Protests were triggered when foreign visitors and British officials in the 1800s balked at honoring the tradition of removing their shoes before entering the holy site. British authorities finally issued a regulation in 1919 prohibiting footwear in the pagoda. However, they put in an exception that government employees on official business were allowed footwear. That exception clause continued to create resentment as a religious affront and contributed to the growing nationalist movement. Today, all visitors must remove their shoes to enter the pagoda.

The shrine has special significance for Aung San Suu Kyi's family and the democracy movement: In January 1946, General Aung demanded "Independence now!" from the British at the stupa, with a thinly veiled threat of a general strike. Forty-two years later, his daughter addressed an even larger group of people at the golden pavilion, calling for a new day of peaceful change.

—w—

Despite rumors of an assassination attempt, perhaps planted by military intelligence, Suu Kyi refused to wear a bulletproof vest to the speech at the golden pagoda. She did concede to having her family travel in separate cars as a protective measure. Nyo Ohn Myint, a history teacher at the University of Rangoon, drove Michael to the pagoda and noticed he was nervous. It was the first time his wife had given such an important speech in public. And she might well be killed.

As the family caravan drew near the pagoda, their cars could not go ahead because the streets were filled with a wall of people. They would have to walk the rest of the way. To protect Suu Kyi, a team of bodyguards picked her up and carried her the final distance. Seeing who it was, people stepped back to open a path through the crowd for Suu Kyi. She made her way to the stage. Shortly after 11 A.M., Suu Kyi stepped up to the microphones, looking like a schoolgirl in a simple white cotton blouse, with a white flower in her hair. Because of the death threats, the other young women around her were all dressed the same, to make it difficult to single her out. But it was soon apparent which one was the Bogyoke's daughter as she stepped forward to the microphone.

The crowd was chanting "Doh A Yay! Doh A Yay!" (Our rights! Our rights!). The noise was deafening.

Suu Kyi captured the crowd's attention by calling out, "Revered monks and people! It is the students who have paved the way for this rally . . . I therefore request you all to observe a moment's silence for those students who have lost their lives." The crowd was quiet. Suu Kyi called on the people to honor the fallen students so as to "share the merit of their deeds among all of us." It not only was a dramatic opening, but a strategic use of the Buddhist concept of "sharing merit," good deeds, because it implied that the democracy struggle by the students was for the good of the *sasana*, the Buddhist community. That subtly placed the government on the wrong side of the community and Buddhism. The general's daughter was already showing signs of being a shrewd chess player.

Any uncertainty that people might have felt about her loyalty to Burma was allayed when she called the Shwedagon Pagoda, where her father has championed democracy decades before, "the soul of the nation." She told the crowd that the rally was aimed at informing the whole world that the will of the Burmese people was for a multiparty, democratic system of government. She implored the crowd to work together with the many ethnic minorities in the country for democracy. To achieve *true* national unity, she told them, they would need to show discipline and put their differences aside. She asked them "to demonstrate clearly and distinctly their capacity to forgive."

For its part, she said, the Army would need to become a national force that the people could trust. "May the armed forces become one which will uphold the honor and dignity of our country," she said, with the implicit message that at present, it did not.

The crowd was so large—more than five times the size of a Super Bowl crowd—that it was impossible for her words to be heard down all the streets where people were straining to hear and see anything at all. Snatches of paraphrased quotes were passed from person to person, like a prized package being relayed hand to hand. "She said we must unite. . . ." "She said the army must earn our respect. . . ."

People in the audience nodded appreciatively as she read her speech. She alluded to her father's assassination by saying "People have been saying I know nothing of Burmese politics. The trouble is, I know *too much*." They cheered. The girl had moxie.

Suu Kyi spoke frankly about the junta's personal criticisms against her: "It is true that I have lived abroad. It is also true that I am married to a foreigner. These facts will never interfere with or lessen my love and devotion for my country by any measure or degree."

She then concluded with one of the most oft-quoted lines from the speech: "I could not, as my father's daughter, remain indifferent to all that is going on. The national crisis could, in fact, be called the *second* struggle for independence."

The crowd roared its approval. There was hope. The Bogyoke's daughter was back to help them.

Years later, one of those in the audience that day, U Win Khet, a prominent Burmese novelist, would recall the power of the moment with tears in his eyes. "What surprised me, what surprised us all, was how *mature* she was. She spoke elegantly, but simply, so that everyone could understand exactly what she meant. It may be an old man's delusion, but for me, she became Aung San in August 1988. Her actions, her commitment, most of all her manner, were exactly *his*."

Nita Yin Yin May, who would later work for the Burmese section of the BBC, remembered that she had never seen such a big crowd in her life. "I thought she was going to be just another general's daughter, but then she started talking to the people. I was overwhelmed. This is the one; this is the one we were looking for. She was a true leader. I was very much impressed."

Many of those in the crowd had brought treasured photos of Suu Kyi's father to hold up. Others waved the Burmese one-*kyat* bill, which featured the Bogyoke's portrait. It was obvious to all around that the image of the independence hero greatly resembled his daughter on the stage. Some waved the French tricolor flag, signaling that a new people's revolution was at hand.

In the midst of the excitement, history teacher Nyo Ohn Myint looked over and noticed Michael, standing to the side of the throng around his wife. He was clearly proud, the activist recalled, but he also wore a sadly prescient look on his face, "kind of like, I'm going to lose my wife and my privacy and my family." On the drive back to the house on University Drive, people in the car were "amazed, excited," Nyo Ohn Myint said, while Michael was silent, lost in thought. His Suu was becoming their Suu.

After her sensational debut, Suu Kyi was besieged with interview requests from journalists who wanted to know: What was she going to do next? Would she stay and lead, or go? She told *The Times* of London, "I am one of a large majority of people in Burma struggling for democracy. It is my aim to help the people attain democracy without further violence or loss of life." Asked what specific role she might play, she said she did not yet see a particular role: "I shall wait on events to see how I can be of most use." She was careful to underscore, "A life in politics holds no attraction for me. At the moment I serve as a kind of unifying force because of my father's name." It was an appropriately modest stance. Suu Kyi knew it would be presumptuous of her to assume a greater role, having just arrived on the scene. And she was still clinging to the notion that she could help her people in some way and return to her family in due time.

Ne Win and his spymaster Khin Nyunt continued doing everything they could to undercut Suu Kyi's appeal. They wanted to stir up enough unrest to justify military action. On the day Suu Kyi spoke at Shwedagon Pagoda, more than 5,000 prisoners were let out of Insein Prison to fill the streets and alleys with mischief and mayhem. Hundreds of mental-asylum inmates were also set free. Looting, vandalism, and arson spread. A known prostitute who was caught committing arson confessed that she had been given money and drugs by the authorities to create damage that could be blamed on the democracy movement. In an even more heinous scheme, five men tried to poison the water supply near a children's hospital. They were apprehended by witnesses and confessed to being Military Intelligence agents, part of Khin Nyunt's terror squad.

Later Suu Kyi would observe in her essay, *In the Eye of the Revolution*, "It is a strange and horrifying situation where the people are trying to preserve order and unity, while a faction of the government does its utmost to promote anarchy."

On September 18, less than a month after the landmark Shwedagon speech, martial law was declared again. There was a surprising twist: General Saw Maung, who was the head of the army and had served with Ne Win in the Fourth Burma Rifles during the war, announced that the military was officially taking over from Ne Win's socialist/authoritarian/military government. He promised the new military regime would not "cling to power for long." People were not convinced, especially when Saw Maung proceeded to crack down hard after crowds gathered to protest the alleged coup. An estimated thousand demonstrators were killed. Additional troops were trucked in from the countryside and crowds were dispersed with barrages of bullets. Doctors and nurses at Rangoon General Hospital reported that the casualties included children. Some of the dead had been shot in the back. Some were shot between the eyes at close range.

On the morning of the so-called military "coup" on September 18, a hundred soldiers surrounded Suu Kyi's home. Trucks with mounted guns were put in place to block the gates. Suu Kyi, Michael, and a good number of the democracy activists who were meeting at the house were trapped. They were kept awake all through the night by the sound of machine-gun fire ricocheting across the city and wondered, would they be attacked next? They did not know if they would be lined up in the courtyard and shot or taken to prison. Some of the activists wanted to respond with any kind of weapons they could fashion and were ready to rip out their bicycle spokes to make the sharp-pointed jinglees, but Suu Kyi insisted they stick to their principles of nonviolence. One of the activists, the history teacher Nyo Ohn Myint, was so worried about Suu Kyi's safety that he was prepared to hoist her over the compound wall if troops moved in to take her.

After two intense days, the soldiers left the lakeside compound. Their mission had been accomplished: A new military regime was in control of the country.

Suu Kyi sent an urgent appeal to the United Nations: "I would like every country in the world to recognize that the people are Burma are being shot down for no reason at all."

Nothing happened.

General Saw Maung announced that the ruling government would henceforth be called the State Law and Order Restoration Council (SLORC), but the name change fooled no one; this was a continuation of the previous military regime. Ominously, Khin Nyunt, the head of Military Intelligence, became SLORC's "Secretary One." And a lieutenant general named Than Shwe, who had been Ne Win's obedient deputy chief of staff, emerged as SLORC's vice chairman. Like the tiger waiting quietly for dinner to come his way, Than Shwe began waiting for his chance to move up even higher.

The new SLORC team decreed that the country's name be changed from Burma to "Myanmar," claiming that the name "Burma" was a vestige of colonialism. The name Yangon (meaning "end of strife") was likewise resurrected for the city of Rangoon, returning to the name given by King Alaungpaya back in 1755. Yet if the name changes were meant to stimulate a sense of nationalism, it didn't work as intended. People continued to pour into the streets to protest military control. Hundreds more were killed. To defuse the resurgent unrest, Gen. Saw Maung made a peace offering: He promised that democratic elections would be held in May 1990.

It was the opening the democracy activists had been waiting for. Former general-turned-democracy leader U Tin Oo, who had been present at Suu Kyi's Shwedagon speech, told Suu Kyi she *must* assume a leadership position. He insisted: "We cannot make it alone." She listened carefully and simply said, "All right, fine. Let's go forward and work together."

And with that, Aung San Suu Kyi took up her father's banner. Her fate was now interwoven with that of the Burmese people.

CHAPTER FOUR

THE CANDIDATE

> "Politics is seen as a duty and as a destiny. You just have to follow that. If that is your fate and that is your role, it is a responsibility given to you. And you cannot just avoid it."
>
> —Aung San Suu Kyi

Meeting primarily at Suu Kyi's family home, the democracy advocates formed a new political party by pulling together a host of smaller political groups. On September 27, 1988, a month after the brutal repression of the democracy protests, they announced the formation of the National League for Democracy (NLD). The key leaders were Suu Kyi, former army commander U Tin Oo, and another former general named Aung Gyi. Aung Gyi was considered savvy about business and a supporter of free markets. He had broken ranks with Ne Win in protest of economic policies that were bankrupting the nation. His business expertise would be an asset for the NLD.

Suu Kyi was given the special honor of being named the general secretary of the party although the older men were considered senior to her. She was a newcomer and a political novice, but she was the daughter of Aung San.

Almost overnight, Aung San Suu Kyi went from being a housewife-graduate student to the leader of the democracy movement in Burma. Later, her husband, Michael, would say that it came as no surprise that Suu Kyi would be drawn into the forefront of the struggle. "She predicted what would happen to us as a couple 20 years ago on the eve of our marriage. It wasn't a flash of intuition or insight. It was a knowledge that she would have to render service to her people at some time," he said. However, he had imagined it would happen much later in life, when their children were grown. "But fate and history never work in an orderly way," he mused. "Timings are unpredictable and do not wait upon convenience."

Because the Aris children had returned to school in England that fall, journalists and party members began asking Suu Kyi how long she would stay. She answered, "I am going to stand by the democracy movement all the way. Which is braver or more necessary? To stay or to leave?" She clearly had her father's scrappy genes.

Michael tried to remain in Rangoon with her as long as he could, but the junta refused to extend his visa. He was forced to return to England and university life in Oxford, which now seemed awfully staid. And lonely.

Suu Kyi threw herself into campaigning across Burma, a nation the size of Texas. She traveled the country, speaking to as many as a dozen villages in one day. She wrote to Michael, "Traveling by bullock cart and small boats in the blazing sun—alas, your Suu is getting weather-beaten; none of that pampered elegance left as she tramps the countryside spattered with mud, straggly-haired, breathing in dust and pouring with sweat!"

Large crowds turned out to hear her despite constant harassment by soldiers. She wrote to Michael that often "people had been told not to go out of their houses, not to wave, etc., and gunshots had been fired to frighten them." But the people kept coming. And she kept traveling to speak to them.

Suu Kyi began a letter-writing campaign to the United Nations and Amnesty International. She reported that the military junta was killing even monks in the streets. She wrote that students were being rounded up, stripped naked, and used as slave labor—some were being used as human minesweepers for the military. Suu Kyi implored human-rights groups to press the U.N. to intervene. She implored other countries to stop selling the weapons to the junta that were being used against the Burmese people. But nothing happened.

She also protested formally to the SLORC leaders about the violence and repeatedly requested a dialogue with the generals, but there was no reply.

She turned to the people to speak up for themselves. Many of her countrymen were so worn down by decades of oppression that they thought democracy was out of their reach. Suu Kyi insisted it was possible if they rose above their fears and got involved. If they wanted democracy, they would have to work for it, she instructed. "You've got to join in. The more people are involved, the quicker we'll reach our goal," she urged. By the hundreds and the thousands, they began joining the NLD. Suu Kyi was learning that being a leader meant persuading people to step out of hiding.

As her voice was getting stronger that fall, her mother's was fading. Daw Khin Kyi's condition had deteriorated considerably after the new military regime took over that summer. She did not last many months more. On December 27, 1988, Daw Khin Kyi died at the age of 76. The military allowed a full public funeral in recognition of her long service to the country. Although Michael had been forced out of the country that fall, he was allowed to return with their sons to be with his wife for the funeral services. Suu's older brother Aung San Oo, was even permitted to attend the memorial service, although he had relocated in the U.S. after getting a degree in engineering and was now an American citizen. Customarily, Burmese who had renounced their citizenship would be denied a visa, but the generals made an exception for the funeral of the Bogyoke's widow.

A crowd estimated at more than 200,000 gathered in a solemn show of respect for the woman who was considered First Lady of Burma. Almost unbelievably, the army, students, and politicians came peacefully together for a few hours to pay tribute to Daw Khin Kyi. The leading generals, who had supervised the slaughter of demonstrators, even paid a courtesy call at the family compound. Aung San Suu Kyi applauded the peaceful concord, saying it showed that the people and the military could cooperate.

But the goodwill from the generals did not continue.

Shortly after the funeral, the Tatmadaw stepped up their crackdown on anyone who expressed anti-government or pro-democracy sentiments. When Suu Kyi went to speak at events in Rangoon, she was constantly followed by soldiers in army trucks telling people not to listen to her. The trucks carried loudspeakers that blared music to drown out her words. When Suu Kyi traveled to the countryside, the army raised barbed-wire fences to keep people away and arrested her followers.

The harassment became more menacing as her popularity grew in 1989. One of the incidents would assume legendary status, but according to British biographer Justin Wintle, Suu Kyi actually had been accosted three other times the same day. The incidents occurred as Suu Kyi and her traveling group were visiting the rice-growing Delta region April 4–6. The harassments began early in the morning, just as the mists were lifting from the marshy rice growing area. Suu Kyi's contingent had just arrived at a muddy boat landing when they were surrounded by a company of soldiers that ordered them to leave. Suu Kyi held her ground. She told the company captain her group had every right to be there to speak to the people. The captain was no match for her cool, firm authority. He relented for the moment. But when the NLD group returned from a day of traveling from village to village, they were met at the boat landing by the troops, who insisted that their boat could not land. "Ignore him," Suu Kyi directed her colleagues, "I'll land first." As they went ashore, they were surrounded by soldiers, who pinched and shoved them, trying to provoke an all-out fight. Suu Kyi cautioned her followers not to be drawn into a conflict; the group ignored the assaults and walked away. They still had quite a distance to travel .

As it turned out, they were not out of danger yet. Suu Kyi's party continued on their way, but their path was blocked yet again by a group of soldiers with automatic weapons. It had been a long, trying day, but Suu Kyi teased the soldiers gently, "You really shouldn't bully me so much. You must let us pass." Her goodwill was disarming. The soldiers let her by.

The final, most dramatic confrontation occurred as they were walking down the road to the town of Danubyu. British director John Boorman would dramatize the incident in his 1995 movie about the democracy movement, *Beyond Rangoon*. But even that riveting cinematic version did not capture the heart-stopping confrontation.

It was late in the day, after the tiring visits and repeated tussles with soldiers. As Suu Kyi and her supporters rounded a corner in the road, they encountered a detachment of soldiers kneeling in firing position, their gun barrels pointed straight at the NLD group. The air crackled with tension. The soldiers ordered Suu Kyi's group to walk on the side of the road. They complied. However, as they moved forward, it became apparent that the soldiers were aiming to shoot them whether they were on the side of the road or the middle.

Win Thein, a broad-shouldered Rangoon University student, stepped in front of Suu Kyi to protect her. As he walked ahead, he nervously turned around to check on Suu Kyi. She motioned to him to keep moving ahead. As he proceeded toward the raised rifles, she kept pace with him, step by step, her head up and her small shoulders held square.

A captain ordered the soldiers to prepare to fire. His heart racing, Win Thein turned around to check on Suu Kyi again. She had waved to the rest of their colleagues to stand back, yet she continued to walk forward. Win Thein heard the countdown to fire begin, "One. . . ." He froze and closed his eyes, preparing for the shots that would take their lives.

Suu Kyi walked past him toward the troops, looking the soldiers squarely in the eye, while motioning her team to stand back, out of the line of fire. The countdown continued, "Two. . . ." The members of the little group were holding their breath, paralyzed. "Three. . . ." But the order to fire was interrupted abruptly. A major who had been watching Suu Kyi suddenly stepped forward and ordered the soldiers to lower their weapons. He couldn't let them shoot someone so brave. As a result, the major was sent to prison. Suu Kyi continued going out to speak.

Later she explained that she had motioned her colleagues away because "It seemed much simpler to provide them with a *single* target rather than to bring everyone in."

The incident catapulted Suu Kyi into something more than just General Aung San's daughter. After that, she was treated with a respect that had less to do with who her father was and more to do with the courage that she was displaying. Suu Kyi was showing she had her own steel.

The generals continued trying to undermine her, claiming her marriage to a foreigner disqualified her as a candidate because she might leak state secrets to foreign governments. Foreigners are sometimes derided with the epithet "kalah" or "kalar" in Burma, reflecting the lingering resentment against their old British landlords, their Indian collaborators, and non-Burmans in general. Attacks about Suu Kyi's marriage to a "kalar" grew so intense that at one point, Suu Kyi and Michael discussed the possibility of divorce, but only as a way to get around SLORC's roadblocks to her election. They eventually decided against separating, because they figured SLORC would only have thought up other excuses to criticize Suu Kyi.

Suu Kyi often used her wry humor to deflect the slanders. At a speech at Meiktila in central Burma, an elderly man in the crowd asked her why she had married a foreigner. She replied, "I married a foreigner because I grew up in foreign places. If I had grown up in Meiktila, then perhaps I would have married—*you*." The crowd roared with delight as the old man blushed.

Although danger was around every corner during the campaign, there were moments of exhilaration and camaraderie as the NLD supporters carried their message out into the country. History teacher Nyo Ohn Myint had been persuaded by Suu Kyi to stay with the democracy movement rather than return to his position at Rangoon University. He helped organize the NLD youth movement and often served with the students as one of Suu Kyi's bodyguards. He told of a rare day when the NLD entourage took a break from campaigning. The group was near Maungmagan Beach in southern Burma. The young people decided to take an impromptu swim. They ran into the water, splashing each other and playing like children. Suu Kyi walked along the beach by herself, lifting the hem of her longyi as she moved across the sand and the tide lapped at her bare feet. "Aunty, come join us!" the students shouted. She smiled and continued walking. But she let the ocean spray soak the bottom of her longyi. "She was laughing," Nyo Ohn Myint recalled. "She looked so free." Many of the students on that trip would soon be imprisoned. He was forced to flee the country and did not see her again.

After her mother passed away, Suu Kyi took on an even more demanding campaign schedule. During one 13-day stretch, she campaigned in more than 50 villages. The NLD had adopted the straw peasant's hat, the *kamauk*, as one of its symbols, to show their support for the long-suffering farmers and manual laborers who were the poorest of the poor. Crowds everywhere began showing up at her rallies wearing the cone-shaped straw hats, and so did Suu Kyi. Sometimes she appeared in the traditional dress of the area she was visiting, donning red-and-black Kachin attire on a visit to the north. She did not consider the ethnic tribes adversaries, as some of the majority Burmans did. To the contrary, she was eager to build bridges with them, like her father. Only when the Burmese people were united across tribal and ethnic lines could they stabilize the country.

Knowing that veneration for her father's name was still strong throughout the country, Suu Kyi often worked his democracy campaign into her speeches. She began emphasizing that each individual was entitled to human rights, every person deserved a voice in their governance. This was a new concept for people who had been oppressed for centuries—by their own military, the British before them, and powerful kings before that. Bertil Lintner, the veteran South East Asian Journalist, covered Suu Kyi's campaign and observed, "Thousands of people were waiting in the scorching sun for hours. Suddenly, you could see a white car somewhere in the distance trailing a cloud of dust. The cheers were incredible. She got out, very relaxed, surrounded by her students, her bodyguards, smiled and everybody and was garlanded. She went up on stage and started talking. She talked for two or three hours, and nobody left. Not even the children. She was using very simple, down-to-earth words."

Suu Kyi drew on the lessons she had learned about Gandhi as a schoolgirl and preached that nonviolence was not just the best way, but the only way to win their freedom. With democracy, she promised, their problems could be resolved with votes, not bullets. She reassured audiences that democracy was fully compatible with the Buddhist values they had grown up with and was not some foreign notion being imposed on their culture. A constitution that respected everyone's human rights was a natural fit with their core Buddhist tenets of tolerance and compassion, she would explain.

The more speeches she gave, the more Suu Kyi's message evolved into a new formula: spiritual renewal + political renewal = freedom. She began emphasizing that Burma not only needed *democracy*, it needed a revival of its ancient values such as honor, trust, and faith. She could see that military rule had corrupted much more than the economy. She realized that getting and keeping freedom would require reviving the traditional concepts of *personal virtue*. She coached audiences to understand that without the iron grip of military rule to impose order on the country, the people would have to *self-govern*—and governing themselves would require a return to moral values. It was their duty, she reminded crowds.

She pointed out that even the ancient kings had had responsibilities to their subjects: The 10 rules that Buddhist kings were supposed to be bound by were liberality, morality, self-sacrifice, integrity, kindness, austerity, non-anger, nonviolence, forbearance, and non-opposition to the will of the people. Those precepts were still valid, she contended, and perfectly compatible with democracy. She didn't have to say that the current rulers had not met those duties.

The junta responded by decreeing that the NLD could no longer distribute its pamphlets. Her party members parried by recording Suu's speeches on videotape and circulating them clandestinely. People who were starved for change often paid a week's wages for a Suu Kyi video. They had never seen anything like her before. Suu Kyi had glamour as well as intelligence. Like her mother, she often wore flowers in her hair, sometimes as many as three. The more she traveled and spoke and smiled and waved, the more the popular response swelled into something akin to hero worship. People began copying the style of her jacket and longyi. Followers who had been praying *for* her safety, began offering prayers *to* her. Rumors spread that she could be a *bodhisattva*, an enlightened person, who out of compassion forgoes nirvana in order to save others. Some said she was an incarnation of the ancient Goddess of Mercy. Stories even began circulating that some of the Buddha statues in the pagodas were growing breasts. What actually happened was that people were visiting the pagodas to pray for Suu Kyi and were observing the custom of buying small swatches of gold leaf to pat on the likeness of Buddha as an offering. So many placed the gold leaf over the hearts of the statues that their chests appeared to bulge. Rumors reverberated around the country that the phenomenon was an endorsement by Buddha of Suu Kyi's leadership. The military regime became so worried that they cordoned off some of the temples.

Suu Kyi tried to deflect the intensifying personal adulation by reminding crowds repeatedly that she was not the only one working for Burmese democracy and that she could not work miracles. "I keep telling the people that I cannot do it alone. Nor can the National League for Democracy.

Everybody who really wants democracy has to do his or her own bit—you can always find a way."

Yet the glorification continued. Some gave her nicknames like "The Madonna of University Avenue." The more people exalted Suu Kyi as a political savior, the more the military seemed to fear her. They stepped up efforts to besmirch her reputation by alleging she had been married multiple times and performed "wifely duties" for foreigners. They tried to turn people away from her party by planting rumors that the NLD was part of a "Communist conspiracy." In truth, there were members of NLD who were disillusioned former members of the Burmese Communist Party. The NLD had an "open door" policy: Anyone who promised to work peacefully for democracy, whether they were former soldiers or former Communists, could join. A sharp disagreement soon developed among the NLD leadership about whether the Communist elements should be included in the party. Former general Aung Gyi, who was chairman of the party and part of the founding NLD leadership, was adamantly opposed to allowing the former Communists a role. They were having far too much influence in the country already, he argued.

—~—

As Army Vice Chief of Staff, Minister of Trade and Industry, and Chairman of the Burma Oil Co., Aung Gyi had once been General Ne Win's No. 2 man. The son of a well-to-do Chinese textile merchant and a Burmese woman, Aung Gyi rose to the rank of brigadier general and proved himself a shrewd bargainer as Ne Win's right-hand man. He led 1960 negotiations that fixed Burma's borders with Red China and talks with Japan that produced $170 million in World War II reparations and loans.

Despite his insistence "I have no training in economics," Aung Gyi built a modest army PX-type operation into the giant Burma Economic Development Corp., running 34 firms ranging from banking to fisheries. Some years the profits from the operations ran as high as $2,500,000. Though Aung Gyi often insisted that he was a socialist, in reality he proved a tough-minded pragmatist who openly advocated cooperation with private industry, much in contrast to Ne Win's preference for nationalizing industry.

—∞—

Just two months after the NLD was formed, Aung Gyi left the party. It appeared the party was falling apart at the top. How could a group in such disarray possibly hope to win an election? Some blamed Suu Kyi for the schism. She was difficult to work with and stubborn, they said, a complaint that would resurface in the future. Others suspected that Aung Gyi had remained uncomfortably close to high friends in the military and might even have been working to help them behind the NLD and Suu Kyi's back. After leaving the NLD, Aung Gyi set up his own political party. However, he was able to elect only one candidate in the 1988 elections, compared to 392 for the NLD. Suspicions circulated that the tough and handsome former general might have been playing a double game. At one point, he had been considered General Ne Win's heir apparent. He had defended "The Old Man" from time to time after he left the military, causing people to speculate, over the years, which side was he really on?

The dispute proved a painful learning experience for Suu Kyi. She had taken quiet note when Aung Gyi urged people not to "feel bad" about the military following the student massacre in 1988. She kept her concerns that he might be too loyal to the military rulers to herself. Even after their split, she said little. Yet Aung Gyi continued criticizing Aung San Suu Kyi. He alleged in foreign interviews 10 years later that she had allowed Communists too much sway in the early party decisions. He suggested that General Ne Win should be asked back to fix the country. Tellingly, when Ne Win died in 2002, Aung Gyi had been among the few who attended the old general's funeral. His loyalty to the dictator had endured. Trusting Aung Gyi had been a mistake, Suu Kyi would later admit, a political ingénue's misjudgment. She would learn to trust her instincts.

—∞—

There would be other frictions within the party ranks—the "growing pains" of any political movement, especially for a party that was a conglomeration of interests ruled by a committee. And there were regrettable examples of violence by some in the democracy movement. In Moulmein, several government officials had to be rescued by the Burmese Navy to prevent their being lynched by angry democracy activists. Some democracy supporters took out their vengeance on known Military Intelligence operatives with their own version of vigilante justice. Pity the hapless MI agent or soldier who found himself surrounded in an alley by people who had seen their loved ones murdered by the military regime. Some of those associated with the regime were torn or hacked to death. Had it not been for the intervention of monks, more would have died in the revenge killings. The bloody reprisals seemed to confirm Suu Kyi's warnings: Violence would only trigger more violence. Additionally, it gave SLORC more impetus for violent retaliation, and the generals did not need much provocation.

SLORC continued to tighten its grip on the country and ratcheted up controls on the domestic media. As a result, the NLD had to turn to the foreign media to get their message out. Stories and speeches were leaked to international sources like the BBC and Voice of America, which also could be heard by citizens in Burma. Those early connections to Western media would prove provident. They paved the way for an international campaign over the years to help Suu Kyi and the democracy movement.

The NLD set up an office for Suu Kyi down the street from her home at 54 University Avenue so she could meet with the growing numbers of people who wanted to see her. The office was tiny, with only enough room for a desk and a few chairs. The joke was that if Suu Kyi had not been so petite, there would not have been space for a visitor. But the little office enabled her to talk privately with people outside of her home. Suu Kyi would listen carefully. Usually the visitors wanted to help the NLD or to complain about the military. After an appropriate period of time, Suu Kyi would gracefully say that she had many more people to see and moved on to the next visitor.

One day, one of her party members alerted her that a captain of the Tatmadaw, disguised as a monk, was waiting to see her and quite possibly was a spy. Rather than find an excuse to turn him away, Suu Kyi insisted gleefully "Then certainly, I want to see him!" As it turned out, the captain had not come to snoop, but to show his respect.

Support for the NLD was growing by the day. This emboldened Suu Kyi. She stepped up her criticism of the real power behind SLORC: General Ne Win. Although he had allegedly relinquished control, it was becoming evident that Ne Win actually was still orchestrating events from behind the scenes. Although others feared to criticize Ne Win by name and used the code words "Number One" or "The Old Man," Suu Kyi began to lay the blame for Burma's problems directly on Ne Win. She blamed him for running the country into the ground. She accused him of perverting the army her father had founded, from the professional institution into an occupying force. "My father didn't build up the Burmese Army in order to suppress the people," she accused. She began punching back hard against the SLORC rulers. She even dared to brand the ruling generals as "liars" who had no intention of transferring power to civilians.

And her daring was contagious. Some of SLORC's own troops had begun cheering Suu Kyi at events. By June 1989, Ne Win was increasingly alarmed by the trends. He had presumed that SLORC's puppet party, the National Union Party, would easily beat Suu Kyi's NLD. He had calculated that the NLD's loosely bound coalition of small groups would fall apart. It was not part of Ne Win's plan that Aung San's daughter would become as popular as a rock star.

A year had passed since Suu Kyi's debut speech at Shwedagon, and the democracy forces were gaining steady support. The summer rainy season was steaming up again as Martyr's Day, the July 19 anniversary of Aung San's assassination, was nearing. Suu Kyi had planned a rally at her father's grave in Rangoon. The SLORC generals decided something needed to be done to keep the observance from being turned into major anti-government demonstration. They cancelled Martyr's Day. Soldiers poured into Rangoon and Mandalay. Mass arrests of NLD members began. Foreign journalists were deported to Thailand with the chilling explanation that they were not supposed to see what might happen next. Telephone lines into Burma were cut. Not wanting to subject her party members to a "killing field," Suu Kyi cancelled her rally. She issued a statement: "Let the world know that under this military administration, we are prisoners in our own country."

She awoke the next morning to discover that University Avenue was barricaded with barbed wire and a wall of trucks. Her first thoughts were safety for her sons, Alexander and Kim. They were then 16 and 12 and were with her in Rangoon for the summer. Michael had left them there to go to Scotland for his father's funeral. Suu calmly arranged for a friend to take care of the boys if she were taken away. "They had gotten quite used to seeing people being taken away and put into prison," she said later, "so I packed a small bag." She reasoned that if the generals were going to put her in prison, "then at least I should have a bag packed with essentials, such as a toothbrush and change of clothes."

As tension mounted, Ma Thanegi, her secretary, offered to distract the boys. They played cards and Monopoly while they waited for their mother to be arrested. As the day wore on, Suu Kyi gathered the forty NLD volunteers who had gathered at the compound and advised them to go home while they could. All forty, including Ma Thanegi, were seized as they tried to walk out down the road in front of Suu Kyi's home. They were trucked off to Insein Prison.

At 4 P.M., the chairman of the Township Law and Order Restoration Council, an army major, appeared at the door with a squad of soldiers. He read a detention order to Suu Kyi. She was confined to her home and could not leave the compound to campaign. However, she could leave the country on the condition that she never return.

Perplexed, young Kim asked his mother, was she being taken away? No, she explained matter-of-factly, she was merely going to be locked up in the family compound. Her calm confidence made it seem as if the soldiers were just borrowing her house keys for a while.

Kim then asked the chairman if his mother would be kept as an "A" class prisoner or a "B" class prisoner. Someone apparently had told him about colonial times when political prisoners were given "B" status, better treatment and more privileges than the criminal "C" class. "A" class was reserved for Very Important Prisoners, such as retired prime ministers. "The chairman was somewhat disconcerted by Kim's question and replied that I would not be taken to prison," Suu Kyi recounted in a speech years later, "This was how I learnt that I would be placed under house arrest under a section of the law that had previously never been invoked."

Suu Kyi would later recall that when she was first placed under house arrest, her mother's garden was quite beautiful: "There were lots of white Madonna lilies, fields and fields of them, and frangipani and fragrant yellow jasmine and gardenias, all highly scented flowers. There was also a flower called 'Yesterday, Today and Tomorrow.' " The garden was never again as lovely. Her house became her jail for nearly two decades.

The soldiers cut the telephone wire and began ransacking the house, looking for damning documents. Drawers were dumped out, closets searched, files combed. The soldiers carted off boxes of party documents until 4 A.M.

Kim would later say that when the soldiers stormed into the house to search for incriminating evidence, "there was a huge amount of activity and lots of guns and shouting." As a young boy, he was not fully aware of what it was all about, but found it "incredibly exciting." He told a British publication called *The Weekly*, "Mother tried to be reassuring, at least when I was around, and I can't remember ever being frightened."

Suu Kyi was never charged and never put on trial, but was sentenced indefinitely to her home. Spokesmen for SLORC claimed the generals were being merciful for not putting Suu Kyi on trial, because if they had, she would have been tried for treason, and the penalty for treason is death. Suu Kyi, they insisted, was a prisoner in her own home by choice. She was trying to call attention to her herself, SLORC stated, "because she had grown bored with her life in England."

When Suu Kyi learned that most of her colleagues had been placed in prison, she became deeply distressed that they were enduring harsh conditions while she was jailed in her home. Not wanting special favors for herself, Suu Kyi went on a hunger strike the day after her detention to protest. She demanded that she be taken to prison to be with her NLD colleagues. SLORC did not reply.

Michael was still in Scotland, dealing with the loss of his father, when he heard on the radio that his wife had been placed under guard. He immediately asked for permission to re-enter the country and take care of his family. SLORC officials, thinking that he might persuade his meddlesome wife to come home with him, granted the visa. Suu Kyi, however, had made it clear the only way she would leave the country was if she were bound in chains.

Fearing they might have made a mistake in allowing her husband to come back, the junta surrounded his plane with soldiers when it landed. Armed guards took Aris to what passed for a VIP lounge in the dismal Rangoon airport, a box-like World War II structure with cement floors and bad lighting. They informed him that he could visit his wife for two weeks, but with conditions: He could not leave the home without an escort, and he could not meet with British diplomatic officials or NLD members. He agreed. When he finally was taken to his wife's family home, the exhausted professor discovered that his wife was on Day 3 of her hunger strike and losing strength. She was willing to starve herself to death on principle, and there was nothing he could do to dissuade her.

While he was dealing with the drama inside the lakeside home, an international drama about his disappearance was taking place. The last time the Oxford professor had been seen publicly was when he was driven away from the airport under armed guard. He had not been sighted since. The British Embassy, fearing the worst, made repeated requests for information about his whereabouts. SLORC would not divulge where he was.

For 22 days, the professor effectively disappeared from sight. "I had vanished," he said later. The situation was catnip for the British press, which pounced on the story. Fleet Street raised the alarm: Oxford professor missing! Beautiful wife under arrest! Children's safety in question! Then, word of Suu Kyi's hunger strike got out and she replaced her husband on the front pages again as a real-life damsel in distress.

There was little that Michael could do as his wife refused to take food. Suu Kyi continued requesting that she be jailed with her colleagues, thinking her presence might keep jailers from treating them as harshly. More than anyone, her husband understood that her mind was set on protesting with the only means she possessed—her own life. For days, Suu Kyi accepted only water, losing 12 pounds and falling well below a weight of 100 pounds. She initially spent her time talking with her family, reading, resting. Michael tried to appear as calm as she was. When her condition grew grave, she finally was persuaded by her physician to accept an intravenous lifeline. She suspended her hunger strike after 12 days when a military officer assured her that her party colleagues would not be tortured and would receive fair trials. That promise, like many others, would not be kept. Yet it was enough to persuade her to resume leading the democracy struggle as best as she could from inside the confines of her home.

After Suu Kyi had recovered from the hunger strike, Michael and the boys returned to England. "Dad took Alex and me home," Kim recalled later, "and Mum stayed on." As it turned out, it would be the last time they were all together as a family. The junta cancelled the boys' passports, making it difficult for them to come back. They were not allowed to return until 1992, when they were given permission to come, without their father, for a short visit. Suu Kyi later would acknowledge that she missed them constantly. She kept their image and memory alive by thinking of them as if they were not really apart.

Her hunger strike had earned her the front cover of *Time* magazine; but afterwards, her detention was scarcely noted. The world was preoccupied in 1989 with other matters: The Soviet Union was breaking apart and the Cold War was ending. The *Exxon Valdez* was spewing oil in Alaska. Islamic extremists had issued a fatwa against Salman Rushdie. U.S. forces invaded Panama to capture Manuel Noriega. Unarmed students were massacred at Tiananmen Square. Some years are thick with historic importance and others are thin; 1989 was packed with events of import. As a result, the Burma crisis in 1989 was eclipsed. It was largely thanks to Suu Kyi's incarceration in her house that Burma at least found a small niche in the news agenda. Amnesty International declared Daw Aung San Suu Kyi a "prisoner of conscience."

SLORC was not deterred by the growing censure from international human-rights groups. The generals said they would go ahead with their announced plans for an election the next year, partly to satisfy potential foreign investors. The catch was that Aung San Suu Kyi would be formally disqualified as a candidate because she had allegedly committed a crime against national security. The SLORC generals claimed that she had been influenced by unsavory anti-government elements who wanted to seize power for their own ends, so she needed to be restrained "for her own good and the good of the country."

In order to prevent the junta using Suu Kyi's incarceration as an excuse to ban her party from the election, the NLD announced that Aung San Suu Kyi was no longer officially the general secretary of the party. They continued their campaign through the fall of 1989 without her. The decision came as a shock to Suu Kyi. Although she understood the necessity of that decision, it meant that she was now separated from the party she had founded, in addition to her family.

Much later, she revealed in a speech in India, "When I heard on the radio, suddenly and unexpectedly one day, that the Central Executive Committee had expelled me from the party for the simple reason that I happened to be under detention, I felt myself to be in a curious no man's land, far away from everything except my own volition. I realized that pressure must have been exerted on the party and that it must be going through a very difficult period. Finally I decided that it was for me to keep faith with my party as long as it kept faith with our cause, regardless of their official position with regard to me. I thought of Nehru's ability to keep true to Gandhi in spite of serious differences between them and it strengthened my conviction that we had to cleave to comrades and colleagues despite dissension and disagreement."

SLORC, sensing a PR opportunity, claimed Suu Kyi had been formally disqualified as a candidate because she had committed a crime against national security. They claimed that she "had been influenced by anti-government opportunistic politicians and insurgent groups in their attempt to seize political power for their own end. . . . For her own good and for the good of the country she had to be restrained in order to prevent her from promoting the cause of these unsavory political elements who found their way and got themselves into positions of influence around her to create disunity among the only unified establishment left in the country [the military], which was endeavoring to stabilize the situation created by the political vacuum." Few believed them. The generals were not only verbose, they were not credible.

In the beginning, separation from her family depressed Suu Kyi, but she has said that any pain or longing "simply became part of my daily life." She maintained a strict regimen: Up by 4:30 A.M. for an hour of meditation. She had not had much time to devote to meditation as a young mother, but on the advice of NLD members who had been imprisoned, she began a serious meditation regimen that shaped her days and her outlook from then on. Usually she would also spend an hour and a half listening to the world news on radio. She had a laptop computer on which she could write. She exercised on a NordicTrack treadmill Michael had given her and played Bach on the battered family piano. "It takes me to a different place," she said of her playing. "It's a challenge because I am so bad at it—and also a joy, because sometimes you find your fingers going the way they should and not the way they think they should and then you enjoy it."

She read extensively, savoring volumes by Rabindranath Tagore, the first Asian writer to win the Nobel Prize in Literature. She read Nehru's autobiography and his *Discovery of India*, along with the novels of Jane Austen and John le Carré. Then there was cleaning and sewing to keep up with. She generally was in bed by nine.

Suu Kyi taught her guards to speak a little English and discussed her views on democracy with them. She posted sayings of her father and Nehru on large pieces of paper in her house so her guards would see them as they came and went. She hand-copied a long paragraph from Nehru's autobiography and hung it near the entrance to her home. It questioned whether the so-called "law and order" that states and governments impose on people is actually an *absence* of law and order because it is coercive. Nehru maintained it was the duty of the state to preserve righteousness and the absence of fear. This was much more desirable, he wrote, than "enforcing 'order' on a frightened populace!" The soldiers outside Suu Kyi's door may not have been well educated, but they got the message.

Suu Kyi sensed that all her doings were being relayed to the authorities, so she made a point of dressing nicely every morning, putting jasmine in her hair even though there was no one to admire the touch of beauty. That was very dispiriting for the generals, recalled a friend. "They were expecting her to be bedraggled and unnerved. She never gave them the opportunity."

Privately she anguished over the fate of her supporters and, more than once, cried for them, trying to figure out a way to deal with her feeling of powerlessness to help those who had been loyal to her and to a democratic Burma. She tried to remain positive and sent her imprisoned party members blessings through her meditations. She was learning to concentrate on her breathing and see herself "from the outside," by practicing insight meditation. To calm her mind and her temper, she meditated. To put aside her longing for her family, she meditated.

Michael was allowed to visit for a fortnight during Christmas in 1989. Yet when he arrived at the compound, he discovered that his wife was none too happy to see him. The junta had not informed her that her husband was on his way. Caught by surprise, she surmised that the military had allowed Aris back into the country in order to somehow appear sympathetic to the world or to use him to convince her to leave. She was furious that the generals were trying to use her family to manipulate her. She asked Michael to stay in the small villa on the property until she could make the point to SLORC that they should have communicated with her first. Michael, who had just traveled more than 5,000 miles around the world to see his wife, agreed. He, too, had concluded the generals had let him back in the country in hopes he would persuade his wife to come home. He stayed in the guest house. To resolve the impasse, which was becoming an embarrassment to the junta, an army officer finally consented to inform Suu Kyi officially of the authorities' decision to let her husband return.

The junta then tried to capitalize on the confusion with her husband's arrival by leaking stories that Suu Kyi had turned away her husband at the door. They claimed it was proof that their marriage was in trouble. In truth, whatever stresses there had been on the marriage over the years, the extraordinary crisis they now found themselves in made their relationship stronger. Michael would later observe that those weeks together, not knowing what the future would bring, brought the couple closer together than ever before. "Those days I spent alone with her that last time, completely isolated from the world, are among my happiest memories of our many years of marriage," he has said. They had long talks that encompassed their life together, their options for the future. She was memorizing a number of Buddhist sutras and playing her favorite pieces on the piano, giving the home a peaceful feel. He had brought Christmas presents for her and spread the presentations out over several days to make the moments last longer.

Back in England, Michael told the press, "She is in good health, in good spirits. She is completely isolated from the world by the presence of armed guards. It is very difficult to tell what will happen from now on because of the lack of contact."

Throughout the months leading up to the May 1990 elections, the junta continued trying to smear Aung San Suu Kyi and her family. Articles were published in junta-controlled newspapers protesting the "tainted race" of her children, who were at boarding schools in Britain but had retained Burmese citizenship. The regime alleged that Suu Kyi was corrupting the youth who were flocking to her cause. They claimed she had profaned the Buddha because she had described him as "an ordinary person like us" during one of her speeches. She was called unpatriotic for criticizing the change of the country's name from Burma to Myanmar. Junta spokesmen even luridly alleged that Suu Kyi had told a student that a better shift from "B" to "M" in a name would be changing the name of Buddha to *Moatta*, the Burmese word for testicle.

Despite their calumnies and the fact that almost all the top NLD leadership was under arrest, the NLD won the May 1990 election by a landslide, securing 60 percent of the popular vote and approximately 80 percent of the seats. The puppet party of the military, the National Union Party (NUP), won only 10 seats out of 485 contested.

The victory should have meant that Aung San Suu Kyi would be chosen by her party to lead the nation. But the military government refused to let the NLD take power and kept Suu Kyi locked in her house. They rejected the election results and continued to rule with gun in hand. SLORC would later claim the election was never intended to select new national leadership, but merely to select delegates for a constitutional convention. Their lame attempt to retroactively recast the vote did not fool anyone. SLORC had hijacked the 1990 election.

Historian Josef Silverstein has speculated that the generals, in their hubris, had intended for the election to be a "Burmese version of Indonesian *wayang kulit* (shadow puppets) with the soldiers-in-power acting as the *dalang* (puppeteer) moving the puppets (the parties and leaders) behind the lighted cloth and controlling their speech." But instead, their staged event turned into a revolt against the military and for the party of Aung San Suu Kyi.

Not taking any chances that Suu Kyi could regroup her followers and try again, the military leaders extended her detention after the election. And to preempt more unrest on the anniversary of the "Four Eights," the generals cracked down hard on any protesters. Foreign diplomats reported seeing monks and students killed from the windows of their embassies. Asia Watch reported that political prisoners were being subjected to torture, including electric shocks, beatings, and cigarette burns. More than 100 political protesters were sentenced to death that summer. By fall, reports were coming out of the country that the soldiers were storming into foreign embassies and monasteries searching for dissidents who had sought refuge.

—~—

As the government suppressed dissent inside the country, efforts to support the democracy movement sprang up outside the country. Suu Kyi's cousin, Dr. Sein Win, fled to Washington, D.C. and set up the National Coalition Government of the Union of Burma (NCGUB). He declared that the coalition was the legitimate government of Burma and included many of the elected NLD representatives.

At the same time, new advocacy groups emerged, including the Burma Action Group (later renamed the Campaign for Burma U.K.) in Great Britain and the Free Burma Coalition in the U.S.A.

For their part, the regime had hired several American firms to try to improve their image. But it was impossible to put a Madison Avenue gloss on shooting down students and locking up the winner of an election. The government may have won the day after the election, but they were losing the PR war.

CHAPTER FIVE

THE PRIZE WINNER

"We are dependent on persons who set examples, persons who can symbolize what we are seeking and mobilize the best in us. Aung San Suu Kyi is just such a person."

—Nobel Committee Chairman Francis Sejersted

In England, Michael Aris had to grapple with being the primary caregiver in his family as well as being the spokesperson for his wife. He did the best he could, although by nature he was a bookish, reserved man unaccustomed to the public spotlight.

Privately, he began lobbying for his wife's release in 1990. He had to be careful about talking on the record publicly, for fear the Burmese government would accuse him of being a foreigner interfering in their affairs and subject his wife to even worse conditions. Very quietly, he initiated or assisted efforts to recognize her courage. His college graciously agreed to give him a leave to work on behalf of his wife's release. One of his colleagues, John Finnis, a Professor of Law and Political Philosophy, agreed to propose Suu Kyi for the Nobel Peace Prize. Winning such an award was a long shot for a little-known person in a little-known country. But Michael was determined to make more people aware of her lonely and dangerous cause.

His efforts soon began to bear fruit. Near the end of 1990, Norway awarded Aung San Suu Kyi the Rafto Prize for Human Rights. In July 1991, the European Parliament awarded her the Sakharov Prize for Freedom of Thought. Because she was still isolated in her home, she was not able to accept or acknowledge the awards.

Among those who took notice of Suu Kyi's struggle was Václav Havel, the courageous writer-playwright who had been imprisoned himself for agitating against Soviet rule in Czechoslovakia. Though he had developed serious respiratory problems as a result of his incarcerations in dank conditions, he was putting together a new democratic government in Prague. Even in the midst of his own transformative work, Havel took note of Suu Kyi's principled sacrifices in Burma. At the time, Havel was considered the favorite to win the 1991 Nobel Peace Prize for inspiring the "Velvet Revolution" against Soviet rule in Czechoslovakia. Yet Havel was convinced Suu Kyi was far more deserving. He was among the 90 who nominated Aung San Suu Kyi for the prize, in effect forgoing his own chance for the award.

Although they never met, Václav Havel and Suu Kyi developed a long-distance mutual-admiration society. She borrowed a TV to follow the democracy movement in Eastern Europe in 1989 and asked for Havel's books and essays on human rights during her extended detention.

While Suu Kyi was speaking out for democracy in Burma in 1988 and 1989, Havel led his country to multi-party democracy. He became the last president of Czechoslovakia in 1989 and the first president of the new Czech Republic in 1993.

Having served four years at a stretch in prison, he understood what it was like to be cut off from the world. He also knew what it was like to live under constant government surveillance and harassment.

One of his most famous essays, "The Power of the Powerless," Havel described how people in authoritarian states all "live within a lie." He knew what it was like to be in "hopeless places and be a witness." A passionate supporter of nonviolent resistance, Havel's motto was "Truth and love must prevail over lies and hate."

Like Suu Kyi, he came to realize that his purpose was to motivate people to reach higher. "I feel that the dormant goodwill in people needs to be stirred," he wrote. "People need to hear that it makes sense to behave decently or to help others, to place common interests above their own, to respect the elementary rules of human coexistence." That's a sentence Suu Kyi could have written as well.

Philosophically, Havel and Aung San Suu Kyi were soul mates. His writing strengthened her, and her example strengthened him.

—ʌʌʌ—

On October 14, 1991, the Norwegian Nobel Committee announced that it had selected Aung San Suu Kyi as the winner of the 1991 Nobel Peace Prize. It was a development that the dictators in Burma hadn't anticipated. The eyes of the world suddenly became focused on the slight, Buddhist woman who was jailed in her home and forbidden from picking up her award. As Havel and others had hoped, the prize put the glare of international attention on her captors as well, which meant that killing or torturing Suu Kyi would be too reckless a move even for a junta that made murder, rape, and human bondage cornerstones of its policy. The Peace Prize, at least for a time, became Suu Kyi's life-insurance policy.

Aung San Suu Kyi knew she had been nominated for the award, because she had heard on the BBC that she was among the finalists. Yet when the Nobel Committee announced the honor, Suu Kyi was surprised to hear her name. She had actually won! At the time, she could not receive phone calls or visitors, so there was little she could do to celebrate or share the news. She could not attend the ceremony in Oslo, but she managed to send out word that she would donate the $1.3 million in prize money to establish a health and education foundation for the benefit of the Burmese people, which she did. Her thoughts on receiving the award were not known until four years later, when the first foreign visitors were allowed to see her. She told U.S. Congressman Bill Richardson and *New York Times* reporter Philip

Shenon that she had felt humbled when she heard the announcement. "I was very grateful," she said. "The prize meant that the whole movement for democracy will receive a lot more recognition."

Many years later, she revealed that it "did not seem quite real because in a sense I did not feel myself to be quite real at that time." She said that often during those early days of house arrest, it felt as though she was no longer part of the real world. "There was the house which was my world . . . there was the world of others who also were not free but who were together in prison as a community . . . and there was the world of the free; each was a different planet pursuing its own separate course in an indifferent universe. What the Nobel Peace Prize did was to draw me once again into the world of other human beings outside the isolated area in which I lived, to restore a sense of reality to me. This did not happen instantly, of course, but as the days and months went by and news of reactions to the award came over the airwaves, I began to understand the significance of the Nobel Prize. It had made me *real* once again; it had drawn me back into the wider human community. And what was more important, the Nobel Prize had drawn the attention of the world to the struggle for democracy and human rights in Burma. We were not going to be *forgotten*."

People in Rangoon had greeted the news on the BBC's Burmese service with jubilation. They saw the award as a resounding reproof to the military regime.

When he heard the announcement that Suu Kyi had won, Václav Havel, who was then President of the Czech Republic, memorably called Suu Kyi "an outstanding example of the power of the powerless." He said, "Aung San Suu Kyi cannot be silenced because she speaks the truth and because her words reflect basic Burmese and universal concepts. . . . She speaks for all of us who search for justice."

Michael Aris, who was working as a visiting professor that fall semester at Harvard University, described his reaction as one of "great joy and pride." He said it was his "hope and prayer" that the award would lead to the lasting peace his wife was seeking and to the reunification of their family. "We miss her very much," he said.

A week before traveling to Oslo for the award ceremony, Michael gave a surprisingly candid interview in his cluttered Harvard office to a *Los Angeles*

Times reporter, Josh Getlin. Taking frequent drags from a cigarette, he said their world had been "turned upside down" by the separation and events in Burma. "No family should have to live this way," he said. "But she's a political animal and I'm not. I'm not a diplomat. I am simply a human being who misses his wife, trying to make some sense of cataclysmic events."

Michael admitted to Getlin that he was struggling with the role reversal of being the supportive spouse waiting for the brave hero to come home. "People do point that out," he said. "And they say, 'What is that wimp of the husband doing to get her out, hmmm? What about it?'

"I'd be so happy to change places with Suu," he said. "I'd be *delighted*. Solitary confinement isn't a problem for me as long as I have books. I'd love to be locked up for three to four years . . . but of course, it's no joke, it's no picnic. When you are talking about a place as dark and distant as Burma, you remember that so many people are suffering. Suu has made her commitment to her people, and she's locked up with them. I support her decision.

"Today the finger of fear touches everyone in Burma," he added. "But it's not for me to say what should be done, or interfere. I'm not Burmese. I'm just a husband, trying to support my wife in the best way I can."

Rather than accept the award himself the next week for his wife, Michael decided it was more appropriate that their sons, Alexander and Kim, accept the award on behalf of their mother. Their presence would remind the world that the junta was holding their mother in captivity. Dressed in suit and tie, Alexander Aris, who was now a tall and slender young man of 18, stepped forward to speak for his mother:

"Firstly, I know that she would begin by saying that she accepts the Nobel Prize for Peace not in her own name but in the name of all the people of Burma. She would say that this prize belongs not to her but to all those men, women, and children who, even as I speak, continue to sacrifice their well-being, their freedom, and their lives in pursuit of a democratic Burma. Theirs is the prize and theirs will be the eventual victory in Burma's long struggle for peace, freedom, and democracy."

Reading the words that had been carefully crafted by his father, Alexander spoke of his mother's Buddhist faith as well as her belief in democracy. "I know that if she were free today my mother would, in thanking you, also ask you to pray that the oppressors and the oppressed should throw down their weapons and join together to build a nation founded on humanity in the spirit of peace."

Although his mother was often described as a political dissident, he said, her quest is basically *spiritual.* He pointed out that she often has said "The quintessential revolution is that of the spirit." She truly believes, he said, that to live the full life, "one must have the courage to bear the responsibility of the needs of others . . . one must want to bear this responsibility."

He closed by reminding that she had said, "The quest for democracy in Burma is the struggle of a people to live whole, meaningful lives as free and equal members of the world community. It is part of the unceasing human endeavor to prove that the spirit of man can transcend the flaws of his nature."

Suu Kyi's presence was deeply felt throughout the event, even though she was thousands of miles away under heavy guard. Her young sons stood as straight on stage in their new suits as their mother would have hoped. They were placed in front of a vivid, enlarged photograph of a smiling Suu Kyi that had been taken when she was still free. In the musical selections before the award, a Burmese musician played some of her favorite music on a Burmese harp.

Outside the hall, Suu Kyi's photograph seemed to be everywhere. Marchers held up photos of her in a torchlight procession. Her face was on the front page of every newspaper. Posters of her were displayed in bookstore windows featuring both the English and Norwegian editions of her new book. Michael, in a touching gesture of support, had gathered a collection of his wife's writings and edited them for publication as *Freedom from Fear.* The quiet professor, who had never sought the spotlight, was now escorting his sons to royal galas and suffering through countless interviews with the press.

In his presentation speech, Nobel Committee Chairman Francis Sejersted captured the meaning of the moment: "We are dependent on persons who set examples, persons who can symbolize what we are seeking and mobilize the best in us. Aung San Suu Kyi is just such a person. . . . Knowing she is there gives us confidence and faith in the power of good."

He then went beyond his prepared remarks to add: "Suu Kyi's struggle is one of the most extraordinary examples of civil courage in Asia in recent decades." Sejersted said he hoped the Peace Prize would put pressure on the Burmese junta to speed Aung San Suu Kyi's release.

What was little known was the generals did offer to release Suu Kyi after the award was announced. The catch was that she would have to leave the country forever. She refused to do so unless the military authorities 1) freed all political prisoners, 2) turned power over to civilians, 3) let her address the country over television and radio for 50 minutes, and 4) allowed her to walk in a public procession to the Rangoon airport.

The generals did not respond to her counter-offer. She remained jailed in her house.

Thus began six more years of house arrest—the first of several long stretches of detention. Michael Aris became a single father in what his Oxford friend Peter Carey described as "bachelor digs" in Oxford. In time, Alexander would go to school in London and then to attend college in the U.S. Kim moved into a boarding school. "It was jolly difficult," Carey said of those years. "The warm heart of the Aris household" was no longer there.

Carey credited Aris with carrying on "a very brave, very lonely, very courageous struggle to bring up his children in an air of normality and do what he could for Suu."

Young Kim Aris would later say of his father that "He had to be flexible—allowing her to get on with what she needed to do, supporting her, looking after us, keeping his own work going. He had a lot of his plate, really."

As the months went by, Michael reported to the press, "We, her family, are denied all contact with her whatsoever. We know nothing of her condition except that she is quite alone."

CHAPTER SIX

A DAUGHTER OF DESTINY

"My father was a child of his times who grew into a man for all time."

—Aung San Suu Kyi

After her house arrest in 1989 and the sham election that followed in 1990, Aung San Suu Kyi was catapulted into the headlines as a prisoner of conscience. And yet, most people outside of Burma knew very little about her. They knew from the headlines that she had won the Nobel Prize in 1991 and she was locked in her home, but little else. Who was this woman? Where did she get the nerve to stand up to an army? Was she born with that courage, or did she develop it? The answer is both.

As a child, the spindly-legged and sad-eyed Suu Kyi was afraid of the dark. Her older brothers were not. She purposefully conquered her fear by standing alone in their home late at night. While everyone else was comfortably asleep, she would slip downstairs to get a glass of milk by herself. When the night sounds and dark shadows made her heart race with anxiety, she would force herself to stand still in the pitch-black room until she overcame her fear. Then she would go back up the shadowy stairs to her bed. Her friend from her days at Oxford University, Ann Pasternak Slater, describes that stubborn self-discipline as "her rooted reluctance to accept defeat."

The story of how that timid little girl became a symbol of strength for millions of others begins with her parents. Although her father is more famous as a national hero than her mother, Aung San Suu Kyi is the sum of *two* very remarkable people.

In her book of essays, *Freedom from Fear*, Suu Kyi wrote, "Since my father died when I was only two years old, it cannot really be said that I knew him. I was taught to think of him as a loving and indulgent father, and as an upright and honorable man who put the welfare of his country above his own interests. It was only when I grew older and started collecting material on his life and achievements that I began to learn what he had really been like and how much he had managed to achieve in his 32 years."

Aung San was born in Natmauk, a small township in the dusty and dry central region of Burma. His father, U Pha, was from fairly well-to-do farming stock by rural standards of the time and became a lawyer. His mother, Daw Suu, was a woman from old landed gentry. She was a spirited woman and doted on her youngest son. The last of six, he was a favored child.

As a boy, Aung San had been sickly. He was late to learn to speak and reluctant to go to school unless his mother went too. For a time, he wanted to become a novice monk. He was drawn to the noble ideals of self-sacrifice and, perhaps, the prospect of getting to ride a prancing white pony through the village square like the other novice monks in the township. His mother insisted he must learn to read and write first. Aung San drove himself to become a top student with the passion that would become characteristic of his life. In high school, he made the highest score in the country on nationwide exams and won a scholarship to attend college.

The more Aung San learned, the more politically aware he became about the British colonial world around him. The path of a monk no longer appealed to him; he wanted to be a man of action. He later wrote that even as a boy, he dreamed of ways, even magic tricks, to run the British out of

Burma. He no doubt had heard such rebellious sentiments around his home. One of his mother's uncles, U Min Yaung, had led resistance groups against the British after they took over the country in 1885. When he was captured, he was beheaded. It was a point of family pride that the uncle was a patriot and martyr because he had refused to be a subject of the "kalahs," the foreigners from the West. Aung San was intent on carrying on that spirit. When he arrived at the University of Rangoon in 1933, he lost no time in becoming a leader in the student movement protesting British rule.

According to his own accounts, Aung San earned an arts degree in English literature, modern history, and politics in 1937. He won scholarships and prizes and seemed destined for a bright academic career. For a time he read law, but he eventually dropped his legal studies—politics drew him away.

As a voracious reader, Aung San knew the power of words. He sought out a position as editor of the student magazine so he could get involved in the debate on political issues. The magazine was named *Oway* after the distinctive call of the peacock, the proud symbol of the independence movement. Before long, Aung San was in trouble with school authorities for printing an article called "Hell hound turned loose," which alleged a senior university official had visited prostitutes. Aung San didn't write the article, but he and another student who would become famous, U Nu, were expelled for refusing to reveal the article's author. Their expulsion from the university became the match that inflamed student discontent and led to the momentous student strike of 1936.

Rangoon University, where Aung San was studying, was the incubator for the democracy movement in Burma, a center of political ferment as well as learning, so he was in the thick of political action in the country.

The university had been formed in 1920 with the merger of two colleges founded in the 1800s: Rangoon College and Judson College. Rangoon College, which had been established by the British, was attended primarily by elite Indians and ethnic Burmans. Judson College, which had been founded by Baptist missionaries, was attended mostly by ethnic Karens and Christians.

The combined University of Rangoon was patterned on the University of Cambridge and University of Oxford and grew into one of the leading educational institutions in Asia. It also became a hotbed of unrest. All three nationwide strikes against the British (1920, 1936, and 1938) began at Rangoon University, where students were free to learn about ideas and talk about them, or at least for a while.

—~—

On campus, Aung San did not look destined for "Most Likely to Succeed." He was so intent on challenging the status quo that he cared little about his appearance. He rarely bathed. His clothes were generally unkempt or threadbare. His dormitory room was an uninviting jumble of books and papers. At one point his bed was infested with bedbugs, but Aung San was too preoccupied with politics to care. Even when he became a political organizer after graduation, he slept on the floor of the political office. His clothing was so raggedy that visitors mistook him for a servant boy.

Friends noted that Aung San kept part of himself detached and distant. He could be chilly or quite curt to others, especially those he considered elitist or less dedicated to the cause of the people than he was.

Bo Let Ya, who was one of Aung San's closest friends in his student days and in politics, described him as an odd character in many ways. "He had the look of a man of mixed Chinese blood, an undernourished one at that. His manners were crude, and he was not a sociable person. He would often sit for hours, deep in his own thoughts. Talk to him and he might not respond. He did not wear his clothes well, and add to this his stern appearance, and who would find it easy to get on with him?" But if they did earn his trust, Bo Let Ya said, "One would find many lovable traits in his character. All in all, he was an unforgettable person."

U Nu, his colleague on the staff at *Oway*, described Aung San as "precise and realistic . . . he wrote pure and pithy prose in English and Burmese; he was precise and hardworking; he was a thinker." During their days as impoverished student organizers, others would express a longing for a good meal or soft music, U Nu recalled, but Aung San would never complain or yearn for creature comforts: "He was not soft, he was made of steel, and with his strength, he made a revolution."

Others described him in their recollections as "brutally frank," "arrogant," and "high-handed." Yet they praised him as "thoroughly practical" and expected the same rationality from his friends. He could "analyze calmly and formulate clear and effective plans." Depending on the mood, he could talk all night—or sit in unapproachable silence. When he was in a good mood, his laughter was hearty, loud, and uninhibited. He smoked but did not drink. He was shy around women. His code of rectitude was one of prim self-control that he saw as befitting a patriot. He did not have time for frivolous activities and had no patience with the pretentious parlor manners practiced by the British and their acolytes. Often he would pass colleagues in the street without a word of greeting or nod, so at times he didn't seem "normal." And yet there was *something* about Aung San that drew people to him. More often than not, they selected him as their leader.

His daughter, who became fascinated as an adult with finding out more about the father she never knew, wrote in a sketch about him that "He was a moody young man, taciturn and garrulous by turns, indifferent to social niceties. His close friends, however, spoke of his warmth; only his shyness made him appear stern and aloof to those with whom he was not at ease." She could have been speaking about herself as well.

At Rangoon University, her father's mind was absorbed in the radical new ideas about social justice that were rippling around the world in the first decades of the 20th century. Intellectuals were talking about the liberation of the oppressed working class from Russia to Mexico. Aung San also had been influenced by a Buddhist monk from the 1880s named Thakin Kodaw Hmaing, who dreamed of a world where people lived in freedom and harmony. Aung San and the other angry young men around him joined a group called the *Dohbama Asi-ayone* ("We Burmese Organization"). They studied Marxism and called each other *Thakin*, which meant "master." The term was usually used to address European elites, similar to the Indian term "sahib." Applying the term to themselves was a way for the college students to thumb their noses at their British rulers and imply that *they* were the true masters of their country. Like others who had been subjugated by foreign armies, their resentment was deep.

The Burmese had been doubly humiliated: After completing the conquest of their country in 1885, the British did not designate Burma as a separate part of its empire, but declared it a province in its India holdings, an annex. Not only was their king deposed and sent packing to exile in India, the Burmese were further shamed by being made subordinates to their larger neighbor. Ethnic Indians were brought in to rule over the Burmese. Indian soldiers were brought in to reinforce the British troops. Indians were given prime posts in the civil service in Burma and dominated the economy as merchants and moneylenders. For the Burmese, it was like being conquered by India as well as by the British. The Indians, themselves chafing under British rule, often relished being the ones subjugating other people instead of being the ones subjugated. They could be as harsh or haughty as the British and were deeply resented.

For decades, the local Burmese were afforded few rights and had no political autonomy. By 1923, as unrest simmered, the British permitted Burmese nationals to hold some select government offices, but under firm British auspices. In 1935, the British separated Burma from India, giving the country its own constitution, an elected assembly of Burmese nationals, and some measure of self-governance—but still under strict British oversight. The Burmese knew they were not really masters of their own affairs. They still felt like second-class citizens in their own country.

—w—

The Burmese grievances against the British were considerable. The British had introduced a civil service and built schools, roads, and hospitals, but had failed to hear the voice of the Burmese.

Although Burma had produced significant wealth under British colonial rule, the Burmese people had profited very little themselves. Almost all of the benefit went to British officials and their imported Indian minions. As one observer put it, the Burmese had gone from being poor in a poor country to being poor in a richer one.

When World War II erupted, more than half the population in Rangoon was Indian. Resentment grew against those who were brought in by the British and given preference.

The economic inequality led to banditry as more people from impoverished villages became "dacoits." Tax levies only added to the perception of servitude to the British and began triggering violent protests.

The cultural inequality also fueled resentment. The foreigners looked down on the Burmese because they were less educated and poor. The British took Burmese for their mistresses or "temporary wives" and often left behind Anglo-Burmese children when they returned to their own families in England. The British were served by Burmese servants in their homes and clubs, but did not socialize with locals. Burmese were barred from membership in the elite clubs—the Pegu, the Boat Club, and the Gymkhana.

The British effort to separate church and state by imposing a strictly secular government was particularly resented by the majority Burmans and the hundreds of thousands of Buddhist monks in the country. The kings traditionally had supported the monks financially. That was in part a royal way of buying support, but it also reinforced the tradition that Burma was a Buddhist nation. The British did not support the monks financially. Worse, they had shown their disrespect by not taking off their shoes when entering Buddhist temples.

—∞—

As discontent festered, the British responded with heavy-handed repression. A local tax protest in 1930 led by a charismatic monk named Saya San grew into a national insurrection that took two years and 10,000 troops to put down. Saya San was executed by hanging. Then in 1938, a wave of protests erupted in the oilfields that grew into a larger general strike. As workers and students picketed the massive red-brick Secretariat, the seat of colonial government in Rangoon, British mounted police galloped into the streets and beat a university student to death with their batons. In Mandalay, soldiers even fired on a protest led by unarmed monks, killing 17 people.

The crackdowns only heightened dissatisfaction. Though many Burmese went to British schools and spoke English fluently, the new generation of university-educated Burmese, such as Aung San, bitterly resented their British overseers. They were drawn toward Communism as a way to uplift the long-suffering common man in Burma. In 1939, Aung San and other disaffected young rebels founded the Communist Party of Burma. They began calling for a national uprising.

Aung San's first efforts to give a political speech in English were a disaster. He knew the vocabulary from his book learning, but his pronunciation was so mangled that his sentences could not be understood. People in the audience jeered. He doggedly finished the speech anyway—and then practiced for hour after hour to bring his English to a respectable level, shouting out speeches to the bushes on campus. He would not accept less than the best from himself. That intense drive and daredevil courage drew others to him. Once when he was scheduled to speak at a rally, he was cautioned by authorities *not* to speak about problems in the ethnic Chin territory, or else he would be arrested. When his time came to speak, Aung San began by saying exactly what he had been warned not to speak about: the problems in the Chin territory. A warrant was issued immediately for his arrest. Aung San sought refuge with friends and hunkered down. He continued his work, wearing a pulled-down hat to hide his face when darting from meeting to meeting.

Worried about the mounting agitation, the British colonial government hunted down several members of Aung San's Thakin group in 1940 and arrested them. That crackdown played into the hands of the Japanese, who already were preparing for an armed sweep across Asia. The Japanese secretly were courting young Burmese who might help them against the British. Aung San inadvertently fell into their hands.

Aung San had managed to escape the British manhunt for University of Rangoon student leaders by disguising himself as a Chinese crewman on a Norwegian boat heading to China. His goal was to contact Chinese Communist leaders in the port of Amoy. With idealistic naïveté, he had hoped to find some Communists who would help Burma's drive for independence. Instead, he was stranded in an island settlement with a friend who had accompanied him. The two did not speak the language and had difficulty making connections. They ran out of what little money they had and were getting desperate for food when Japanese intelligence agents spotted them and took them into custody. They were flown to Tokyo to meet with Colonel Keiji Suzuki. Suzuki was head of the *Minami Kihan*, an ultra-secret organization whose assignment was to speed the takeover of Burma. The cunning Suzuki offered to help Aung San and his friends get rid of British rule by assisting the Japanese invasion. Aung San was not predisposed to partner with the bellicose Japanese, but he secured his way home by agreeing to collaborate with them. The impressionable young leader may have had his head turned somewhat by the flattering Japanese treatment he received during his stay, as he took to wearing a kimono, learned Japanese, and took a Japanese name. But he balked when Suzuki offered him a woman for his pleasure. The straitlaced Aung San refused, thinking the older man was trying to corrupt or compromise him.

In March 1941, Aung San secretly returned to Rangoon on board a Japanese freighter. He selected 29 key members of the Thakin group to help him, and together they became known as the "30 Comrades." Together, they would form the beginning of the Burmese national army and become the stuff of legend. With youthful bravado, they gave themselves bold new wartime names: Aung San's *nom de guerre* was Bo Teza (Powerful General). With the help of Suzuki and his secret agents, the young men were spirited outside the country to be trained in guerrilla warfare. On their return, the "30 Comrades" provided insider information and assistance to the Japanese. Their secret collaboration enabled the Japanese to seize Burma from the British with brutal dispatch in 1942.

Once in control, the Japanese helped the "30 Comrades" put together a new Burmese army called the Burma Independence Army (BIA). The crafty Colonel Suzuki was named the general in charge. Aung San was made a major general and chief of staff, the highest-ranking Burmese officer. Only 27 years old, he would thereafter be known as the *Bogyoke*—"The General."

Aung San had his own quiet reservations about the Japanese power-sharing arrangement but sold the deal to his comrades as a necessary step toward independence. The Japanese wooed them with clever propaganda, proclaiming they were creating "Asia for the Asiatics" and exhorting "Down with the white men." That chauvinistic approach played very effectively on the emotions of young Burmese who chafed at British control. Many of the best and the brightest of the time joined the BIA.

Aung San's BIA troops were earnest but inexperienced. They made mistakes during the war that would have repercussions later. The most serious blunder was an overzealous campaign against the ethnic Karen population. The green BIA troops feared a possible rebellion by the Karen. Many of the Karen had served in British military units before the war and were sympathetic to the British. The BIA soldiers started executing Karens suspected of disloyalty. Dozens were murdered. A Catholic mission headquarters as well as an orphanage were burned down. The Karen retaliated. Soon, violence rippled across the Delta region where the Karen population was concentrated. Only the intervention of the Japanese stopped the runaway killings. The episodes tarnished the BIA and Aung San. And the violence set the stage for an ongoing civil war between the Burmese government, which was predominantly Buddhist, and the Karen ethnic group, which was considerably Christian. The conflict would last more than 60 years and become the longest-running civil war in the world.

It wasn't long after the Japanese took over Burma in 1942 that Aung San and his young colleagues began souring on the relationship. The Japanese did not turn out to be equitable "partners." In fact, they were even more brutal overlords than the British. They helped themselves to whatever they wanted, commandeering Burmese property, furniture, and livestock. They transformed the Anglican cathedral into a brewery to make sake and sauces. They converted the genteel Pegu Club into a brothel. A system of "comfort girls," which had been used in Korea and China to force local women to provide sex for the military, was put in place in Burma. Burmese men seethed with hatred for the Japanese as they saw their women placed in degrading servitude. Burmese soldiers felt further humiliated by the Japanese practice of slapping them in the face publicly to show who was boss. As one of Aung San's colleagues put it, "If the British sucked our blood, the Japanese ground our bones!"

After nearly two years of Japanese rule, Aung San was deeply disillusioned by the empty promises of independence from the Japanese. He was invited to Japan again and was presented with a flattering award by the emperor, but he was not so easily swayed as before. He had risen to become a minister of defense under the Japanese, but without real authority, and he knew it. He also knew that his countrymen were being used for forced labor on roads and bridges by the Japanese. His single-minded goal was still the same: true self-rule for the Burmese.

As early as 1943, Aung San was considering changing sides to partner with the British and the Americans. He calculated that he would have more leverage if he switched his allegiance while he could still be of some assistance to the Allies in winning the war. He began looking for a way to make a switch. It was a dangerous move. Winston Churchill had branded him a "traitor rebel leader." The British troops might shoot him on sight. Aung San reached out to undercover intelligence units in the area—Detachment 101 of the Office of Strategic Services (OSS), the predecessor of the Central Intelligence Agency, and the British counterpart, Force 136. Covert communication was established.

Aung San began speaking out against the Japanese in 1944 and on March 27, 1945 led Burmese troops in large-scale resistance to the Japanese. That campaign would later be celebrated as "Resistance Day," a national holiday, and today is called "Armed Forces Day."

Arrangements were made in May 1945 to quietly take Aung San to the headquarters of the Allied Commander in Burma, Lt. General William Slim.

Some of the British officers thought Aung San should be strung up immediately when he arrived for betraying the British to the Japanese. General Slim, however, had anticipated Aung San's 11th-hour chess move to the Allied side. The British general gave his personal guarantee that Aung San would have safe passage to his camp.

The visit by Aung San was a bold gamble. He was venturing into the enemy camp alone, placing himself in jeopardy of being killed or imprisoned. Yet he knew the chances of arranging independence for Burma would be dimmer than ever if his forces went down to defeat with the Japanese. He needed to make a deal with the Allies.

According to wartime reports, when Aung San was escorted into Slim's temporary headquarters, the two generals saluted and then began to take the measure of each other. It was a well-matched duel. On one side stood the slight, youthful-looking Aung San, dressed in the Japanese uniform of a major general, shoulders back and head up proud to show he was a man of backbone. On the other side stood Slim, the thick-chested, square-jawed veteran of horrific battles such as Gallipoli. He was a man on the verge of victory in Burma and in no mood to be tricked.

Slim listened to Aung San's offer of his sword and his assistance. He replied that Aung San's cooperation, while helpful, thank you very much, would only be of marginal help in routing the Japanese at that point.

Unfazed, Aung San contended that his Burmese troops were already demonstrating their worth to the Allies with their resistance; they were shooting hundreds of Japanese who were trying to flee across the border to Thailand.

Slim told Aung San that he had been urged to put him on trial. He noted that Aung San was in considerable jeopardy at that very moment. He tested him: "What makes you think you can trust me?"

Without hesitation, Aung San replied, "Because you are an English gentleman."

Slim couldn't resist a laugh. He asked Aung San if he had felt that way about the British, why had he been trying so hard to kick them out? Aung San countered that it was not that he disliked the British per se, but that he did not want any foreigners to run his country.

Enjoying the verbal jousting, Slim teased Aung San that the only reason he had come was because the Allies were winning.

Aung San shot back, "It wouldn't be much good coming to you if you weren't, would it?"

Slim was impressed. He concluded that Aung San was an authentic fellow who was committed to serving his people. The general later wrote, "I liked his honesty. In fact, I was beginning to like Aung San. [He] was not the ambitious, unscrupulous guerrilla leader I had expected. He was certainly ambitious and meant to secure for himself a dominant position in post-war Burma, but I judged him to be a genuine patriot and a well-balanced realist . . . I could do business with Aung San."

General Slim accepted General Aung San's sword and his offer to provide 10,000 Burmese soldiers for the Allied war effort. Renamed the "Patriotic Burmese Forces," Aung San's troops helped recapture Rangoon, although they were not given a major combat role. They were used primarily to guard bridges and ammunition dumps, either because the Burmese soldiers were not fully trusted yet or were needed to provide stability after the war.

Nearly 50 years later, when his daughter Aung San Suu Kyi was asked whether her dad had reneged on both the British and the Japanese by switching sides twice during the war, she bristled: "He didn't renege on any deal with the British. He didn't renege on any deal with the Japanese, either. I think you could say it was the other way around. The Japanese reneged on the deal with the Burmese. They promised to give independence to Burma, and they did not."

It took courage, she maintained, to join ranks with uncomfortable bedfellows in pursuit of true independence. As Winston Churchill would say of his own switch from one party to another, "Any one can rat—it takes real courage to re-rat." Aung San had shown he had the guts to walk into the enemy camp—and walk out with a deal. His daughter would have to go face-to-face with her adversaries as well.

The young general had learned from his wartime mistakes and setbacks; he was maturing into a national leader. British historian Maurice Collis observed, "He had the faculty, which belongs to superior talent, of continuing to learn; his mind expanded as he rose. Though with little knowledge of the outside world and only moderately well educated, he yet made the transition from commander of guerrilla bands to headship of a state without incongruity or much apparent effort. His natural gifts of mind and character sufficed."

After the war, Aung San moved quickly to pull together a political party that could lead the nation to independence. He gave it the tongue-twisting name of the Anti-Fascist People's Freedom League (AFPFL). The AFPFL was an alliance of the Communist Party, the Burma National Army, and the Socialist Party—all of which Aung San had a hand in founding. It was a precarious alliance of discontent. Aung San constantly had to cajole and coach the country's factions to quit sparring against each other and work together for independence. In 1946, he gave a speech in which he stressed the responsibility of all Burmese to help. "I am a person who is very popular with the public. But I am neither a god, wizard, or magician."

Aung San became the de facto prime minister of Burma in September 1946 when he accepted the British governor's invitation to become deputy chairman of the Executive Council charting the way forward. He was given the portfolios of defense and external affairs, which meant dealing with the British on the independence issue.

Despite Aung San's relentless entreaties for independence, the British were not initially keen on giving up control after the war. It took a series of strikes—by police, government workers, and rail unions—to get them to the table. On his way to resume talks in London, Aung San made it clear at a press conference in Delhi that the Burmese wanted *full* independence, not just participation as a dominion in the British commonwealth like India and Australia. He warned that the Burmese were prepared to wage "violent or nonviolent struggle or both" to achieve that independence. He still hoped for the best, he said as headed to London, but was prepared for the worst.

He got the best. In January 1947, Aung San and British Prime Minister Clement Atlee signed an agreement, the Aung San-Atlee Agreement, granting Burma's independence within a year, including the ethnic areas.

The agreement was the breakthrough that Aung San had long sought. He posed for newspaper photos in the bitter London cold in an impressive military greatcoat that made his small frame look more substantial. The wool coat was a present from his friend Jawaharlal Nehru, who had become the first prime minister of India. When Aung San had stopped in Delhi on his way to the London talks, Nehru was appalled by Aung San's soiled and worn military uniform. Nehru ordered that new clothing be tailored in a rush for his friend that was more fitting for a national leader. The resulting flannel suit and a British-issued greatcoat were the most handsome clothes Aung San ever possessed.

After the agreement with Atlee was signed, Aung San put aside his customary reserve to celebrate with a reception at the Dorchester Hotel. He proved to be a gracious host to the polished guests. The young general seemed to have realized for the first time that he was now a player on the world stage.

He was receiving credit for bringing Burma the prize of independence, but he had picked up critics as well. When his former colleagues in the Communist movement accused him of "selling out" to the British, he turned away from them. He booted his brother-in-law Than Tun and the Communist Party of Burma from his AFPFL organization and moved on. His allies praised him for being relentless; his enemies criticized him for being ruthless.

He risked alienating his former army colleagues by not inviting any of them to join him in governing the country. Like America's George Washington, Aung San was a believer in civilian control, and he gave up command of the army to assemble the democratic government. He then transferred command of the troops to a capable, Sandhurst-trained Karen officer. This sent a signal of respect for ethnic professionals, but not selecting a Burman officer as commander in chief did not sit well with some of his fellow Burmans. With every decision he made, friction was created with those who disagreed, but Aung San stuck to his principles.

"My father made it abundantly clear that the army was meant to serve the people, that it should abide by principles of justice and honor, and that unless it could win and keep the trust and respect of the people, its purpose would be vitiated. He never intended the army to meddle in government. A liberal and a democrat, he saw from the fascist Japanese army the dangers of military absolutism," his daughter would write.

Edward Law-Yone, who had served briefly with the American OSS intelligence unit during the war, went by to meet Aung San while he was assembling the government at the recommendation of friends. Their memorable meeting was described by his daughter Wendy Law-Yone in a memoir based on her father's papers, *The Golden Parasol.* According to her account, her father still had on his OSS uniform when he went to meet Aung San because he could not afford new clothes. The former general questioned him sharply: Why was he still in uniform? Why was he there?

Her father found Aung San brusque, shy, and shockingly young. "But for his gaunt face and the brooding, slightly petulant eyes, he might have passed for a junior cadet. His uniform looked lived in and hung loosely on his angular frame," Wendy Law-Yone recounted.

When Aung San found out how much the Americans were paying Law-Yone to wind down their OSS affairs in Burma, he blurted, "Too much!" The general huffed that when Law-Yone came to work for the government, he would have to take less money. Law-Yone took that as a left-handed job offer and countered that he deserved more money because he was "a terrific guy." The general broke into a laugh and softened. With that, a cordial relationship began, although Law-Yone still found Aung San an "impenetrably private and taciturn person."

Law-Yone noted that from time to time, the general would drift off into a kind of deep thought during their occasional conversations, but when arguing a point, he did not hesitate to interrupt, contradict, or change the subject.

They discussed Aung San's concerns about the ethnic Kachin territory in northern Burma, which was Law-Yone's homeland, and agreed bridges of goodwill needed to be built to the Kachin people in the northern territories as well as the ethnic Karen in other regions. They differed on the merits of Communism—Law-Yone was skeptical of the Communist movement, while Aung San still found merit in the new ideology. Aung San challenged, "Why are you always running down Communism? There are many things I find appealing about Communism." Yet when Law-Yone gave a copy of the *Communist Manifesto* to Aung San's brother Aung Than, Aung San rebuked him sharply, "Leave him alone."

According to his daughter, Law-Yone found Aung San a man of many contradictions, but one thing was clear: the Bogyoke doted on his children and often had one of them in his arms while he was working in his office. He also could be gracious, inviting Law-Yone to his house on Tower Street to meet his wife Khin Kyi. Law-Yone warned his own wife that the general had a lot on his mind and might be rude. To his surprise, when they arrived for tea, the general came out to open the door of their car. In contrast to his ill-fitting uniform, he was dressed formally and neatly in the traditional Burmese attire for males, a long silk longyi called a *pasoe*, a crisp white jacket, and a head scarf called a *gaung baung* of pale silk on his head. With a show of gentility that apparently had been cultivated by his wife, the war hero poured tea like a perfect host and showed off photos of their children. As the visitors prepared to leave, Aung San asked his wife to gather some vegetables from their garden, which he presented as a gift to the Law-Yones with a bow from the waist.

Aung San was not so gracious a few weeks later when Law-Yone called again. The general kept Law-Yone waiting for 20 minutes, then greeted him gruffly with "Oh, it's you. What do you want?"

According to Wendy Law-Yone, her father got along with Aung San by returning his gruffness with cheeky good humor. In contrast to the brash general, Law-Yone was known for his charm—during the war, he had talked his way past a military checkpoint by using a yellow card that he got out of a toothpaste box as a pass. He was also a gifted writer and went on to become the influential editor of *The Nation* newspaper. According to the recollections gathered by his daughter, Law-Yone occasionally got close enough to see the earthy side of the intellectual leader. When Aung San gave a major speech at the Shwedagon pagoda in 1946, the sound system broke down. Law-Yone overheard Aung San fuming, "(expletive) useless!"

By that time, Law-Yone had indeed gone to work for the government as a supervisor in the railway system. After a particularly uncomfortable meeting with the testy general about a transportation strike that had brought all the fledgling government services to a halt, Law-Yone dared to follow Aung San out to his car. He invited the general to lunch as he was getting into his sleek new Wolseley sedan, a British-built car with a shiny black paint job and bright chrome grill. It was one of the few indulgences of power that Aung San allowed himself, perhaps to reflect the authority of his position as he traveled the country. Aung San shook his head regretfully there was no time for lunch; problems were stacking up faster than he could address them. As the car started rolling, the general asked how Law-Yone liked his new job at the railways. Terrific, Law-Yone told him, adding mischievously that Aung San's government had ended up paying him more than the Americans had for his OSS work. Aung San stuck his arm out the window as the elegant Wolseley pulled away and flashed an upraised, bony finger back at Law-Yone, the universal soldier's sign language.

—w—

The picture that emerges from Aung San's contemporaries is of a complex man, a tightly wound bundle of contradictions, a visionary driven to move his country forward. A visit to his former home on Tower Street, which has been preserved as a museum, revealed other facets to his personality. I had tried to visit the museum several times during my trips, but it was closed most of the time during the most repressive periods of military rule. The gates were padlocked with heavy chains. Unmarked security cars were parked nearby to keep a watch on visitors who tried to get through the fence. The only day visitors supposedly were allowed to visit was on July 19, the anniversary of Aung San's death, but maybe not even then. After the regime loosened some of their restrictions in 2011, the museum was reopened.

The house stands out on the high part of a hill in a residential area that used to be a suburb of Rangoon. It is a unique fusion of Tudor and tropical architecture, topped by a prominent turret and skirted by a shaded veranda to escape the heat. The turret is the most defining characteristic, giving it the appearance of a small white castle. A spiral staircase led up from the master bedroom to a room inside the turret. The room had one window that looked out toward the gleaming Shwedagon pagoda. The room was Aung San's meditation room, where he escaped from the worries of governing.

The house has a tranquil appeal. Surrounded by several acres of garden, it is quieter and cooler than the streets outside; a breeze brings the scent of bougainvilleas into the open windows of the house. A scrawled handwritten note left by Aung San on the wooden dining table requests his favorite dish—boiled garden peas and Indian-style *nan* bread. It's easy to imagine what family life in the house had been like. The big teak armchairs in the living areas seem to invite long conversations. Wooden single beds in the children's rooms are draped with mosquito netting. But the most telling room is the library. The 240 books crowded onto shelves show far-ranging interests. They include *A History of the World, The King's English, Oliver Cromwell's Letters and Speeches, Modern Japan,* and *Great Soldiers,* along with histories of France and Britain and China. There are technical books on mechanics, air defense, and political economy. And on the literary side, works by D. H. Lawrence and Upton Sinclair. The collection reveals a man hungry for knowledge. He was drawn to a life of the mind and often said that someday he would like to retire from politics and write. When his schedule allowed, Aung San preferred to walk the two kilometers to his office rather than take his Wolseley out of the garage; it gave him time to think.

The vast majority of the Burmese people considered Aung San as "the just man" of the hour after the war, a leader who put the interests of the nation above his own. However, one murky incident from the war continued to shadow him. Aung San had participated in the execution of a village headman. The headman, a civilian who may have been an Indian and a Muslim, was accused of communicating with the British and organizing opposition to the Japanese. Some accounts say Aung San personally killed the unarmed headman with a bayonet, others say he tried to administer the death penalty by sword, but the blow failed to kill the man and a soldier finished the task. When the incident became an issue after the war, Aung San did not deny the killing. He maintained it was justifiable in wartime. His enemies disagreed and came very close having him tried for murder. The British governor-general of Burma at the time, Reginald Dorman-Smith, harbored deep mistrust of Aung San and wanted him shot on sight as a traitor after the war. Dorman-Smith was overruled by Lord Mountbatten, who sensed Aung San's arrest or death would trigger a revolt. Mountbatten risked his own credibility to support Aung San when Dorman-Smith tried to have Aung San put on trial for the death of the headman. Aung San was given clemency for the wartime incident, but it remained a blemish on his legacy, along with the bloody persecution of Karen villagers by Aung San's army when they were fighting for the Japanese. Although many of the Karen had indeed been sympathetic to the British, Aung San's soldiers had used undue force against them. Large numbers of unarmed villagers were killed, perhaps the consequence of the army's inexperience, misguided zeal, or prejudice against ethnic peoples.

Those anti-minority incidents did not reflect the personal philosophy that Aung San had expressed over the years. As a student leader, he had pursued a progressive course, urging cultural autonomy for the minorities, full equality for women, and freedom of religious worship:

- He called for unity and reconciliation with ethnic groups, saying he had learned from a Karen soldier that the only difference between a Burmese and a Karen was that the Burmese like to play cards and the Karen enjoyed fishing in the woods.
- He called for better public healthcare and education.
- He said there must be no discrimination on grounds of race, religion, class, or sex.

In an eloquent speech to the AFPFL, he challenged people to join him in building a new state and not be afraid of getting involved in politics. "Politics, in its true sense, permeates life. But some of us still say that 'politics' is dirty. Is that correct? Of course not! It is not politics that is dirty, but only those who choose to dirty it. And what is politics? Is it something high above the reach of the common man? The truth is, politics is neither high nor low, neither magic nor astrology nor alchemy. Nor is it dangerous ground to tread on. Nor is it narrow nationalism either. It *lives*. It is *us*. . . . The worker wants to earn higher wages and better conditions of life. The peasant wants to improve his land and his lot. The clerk and the official want more than the drudgery of office, they seek freedom from want and worry. The trader and the broker want fair opportunities for trading and business. For all these people, their striving for a better life, their pursuit of happiness, is politics."

It was time for the people to get involved, he said, and and "build themselves a nobler, happier life."

You can hear his voice and his idealism in his speeches. He was breaking new ground by urging people to put aside their long-standing religious and ethnic prejudices to work together for the good of a united and independent Burma. By the time of the Aung San-Atlee Agreement in 1947, Aung San had become even more acutely aware that the ethnic minorities in Burma must feel welcome in a new government, or else the union would fall apart. He began intensifying his efforts to bring the ethnic groups together in a federal system of power-sharing. Not a minute could be wasted. Aung San sensed that he might not have long to live.

He wept in a meeting with Dorman-Smith and prophesied his impending death, saying "How long do national heroes last? Not long, in this country; they have too many enemies. Three years is the most they can hope to survive. I do not give myself more than another 18 months of life." His astrologer had warned him he would be killed.

He also knew that his number of enemies was growing. His flashing temper and frankness had been assets as a rebel, but as a civilian leader his temperament began isolating him from some of his former associates. He had criticized Lt. Col. Ne Win, one of his former colleagues in the original "30 Comrades," in front of his men for womanizing, drunkenness, and gambling—and suggested replacing him with a more disciplined Karen soldier. Aung San scathingly criticized newspapers and those who were critical of the independence process as "goat testicles." He was an impulsive truth-teller, which was hard on the people around him. He needed smoother social skills to build coalitions that would support the difficult decisions he was making, but he was impatient to move the country forward and felt his time was limited. During the last months of his life, he began to speak of the loneliness of leadership. He spoke wistfully of the time he might be able to leave his grinding duties and live quietly with his family.

His economic plans also made Western allies nervous. In a three-hour speech at Shwedagon Pagoda, Aung San described his vision for Burma as an independent version of socialism with state ownership of key industries. While he needed international investment in his country, he remained wary of the capitalist policies of the colonial powers that had taken advantage of his people. He envisioned a more socially responsible kind of capital investment. The British and the Americans were concerned that such ideas might lead him closer to the Soviet style of state control. What if Burma drifted closer to the Communist camp than the West? Had they fought for Burma only to lose it again?

Aung San stirred other concerns among his own ethnic Burman population. The dominant Burmans wanted Buddhism to be designated the state religion. A devout Buddhist himself, Aung San praised the virtues of Buddhism, but warned that no faith should be named the state religion, because all faiths should be respected. That angered some in the Buddhist majority. What if he gave equal power to the religious and ethnic minorities, the Muslims and the Christians? Would they lose influence? Would their Buddhist heritage be diminished?

Racing the clock and his growing list of enemies, Aung San traveled upcountry to the village of Panglong in the Shan States to persuade the minority ethnic groups—the Shan, Chin, Karen, and Kachin—to join a new union. His promise to them was that their rights would be respected and "if Burma receives one kyat, you will also get one kyat." He offered what would become known as the Panglong Agreement, a one-page document.

It stated that the central government would not "operate in respect to the Frontier Areas in any matter which would deprive any portion of those areas of the autonomy which it now enjoys in internal administration." It was a landmark concession.

Still, some of the ethnic groups remained aloof. Knitting together the 135 different ethnic groups in the country was not going to be easy:

- The Karenni believed they *already* had an independent state.
- The Muslim Rohingyas, the Wa, and the Pa-O were suspicious of anyone in power, especially a Burman.
- The Karen, the third-largest ethnic group, had good reason to mistrust Aung San after his troops' abuse during the war. They wanted their own state of "Karenistan."
- The Shan, the second-largest ethnic group, had operated as a largely autonomous region under both the British and the Japanese, and wanted to make sure they would retain that autonomy in a new federal union.

Aung San offered a brilliant compromise: If the minority groups such as the Shan would stay in the federal union for 10 years to give the country time to rebuild from the war, they could apply for secession at the end of that 10-year-period if they were displeased by the federal arrangement. That persuaded the powerful and proud Shan sawbwas (princes) to come on board. It was the breakthrough Aung San needed. Enough of the other minority populations accepted the Panglong promise to move the concept forward. In February 1947, Aung San signed the Panglong accord with the majority of the leaders of ethnic nationalities, who agreed to work with him and the Burman majority for independence.

British prime minister Clement Atlee later said that by dealing with the minority communities on generous lines, Aung San had proved he was becoming "a statesman of considerable capacity and wisdom." Voters in Burma agreed. A few months after the Panglong breakthrough, in April 1947, Aung San's AFPFL party won a landslide victory in the election to choose a constitutional assembly, taking 196 out of 202 seats. The assembly would write Burma's first truly independent constitution.

The nation felt a gentle euphoria: they had an inspiring leader and were on the way to self-rule. That progress was held together by the charisma and promises of Aung San, but it was progress. The young hero seemed to be on the verge of uniting his country. The British were going to officially withdraw after the first of the year, and Aung San would be prime minister.

Then tragedy struck.

The first flowering of Burmese democracy was wiped out in one morning on July 19, 1947. A green army jeep with what turned out to be fake license plates pulled up outside the imposing red-brick Secretariat building in downtown Rangoon where Aung San and his new Executive Council were meeting. Without warning, a team of gunmen with semi-automatic weapons rushed into the building and overcame the lone security guard. They burst into the Executive Council meeting a few minutes after 10:30 A.M. It has become a part of Burmese lore that when one of the assassins pointed his Sten submachine gun toward the assembled group, Aung San stood up from the head of the conference table and stretched his open hand outward, appealing for peace. But he was shot 13 times at point-blank range in a rapid burst of fire. His body crumpled to the floor under the table. The deafening sound of repeated rounds of automatic gunfire filled the room, shot after shot after shot. Six of Aung San's cabinet ministers, including his older brother Ba Win, were killed, along with the cabinet secretary. Aung San's entire leadership team was wiped out, just as they were preparing for the transfer of power from the British.

Blame for the assassination was assigned to a political rival named U Saw. He was an ambitious lawyer who had made his name by helping defend the celebrated rebel Saya San in 1931. U Saw then served as a prime minister during British rule, earning a reputation for being malleable and not particularly principled. The British described U Saw as being "rascally," but with a certain oily charm. Before the war, he was believed to be secretly in the pay of the Japanese. However, he also helped make covert arrangements for the Americans to outfit their "Flying Tiger" planes in Burma, perhaps benefiting financially from both sides at the same time. As a former prime minister, U Saw had the rank to accompany Aung San to the negotiations for the Atlee Agreement, but he was overshadowed by the young defense minister. On his return, the chagrined older leader began stirring up dissent against Aung San. U Saw believed that *he* deserved to be the first leader of independent Burma, rather than the upstart Aung San. When Aung San added insult to his injured pride by not including him on the first Executive Council, U Saw was incensed. U Saw schemed that if Aung San were unseated by force—as adversaries customarily had been dispatched in Burma—the leaderless country would have to turn to him because of his experience. Instead, U Saw and eight accomplices were tried, convicted, and sentenced to death.

After their hangings, conspiracy rumors continued to swirl for many years. The most persistent suspicion was that British leaders who did not like and did not trust Aung San had been involved. Some circumstantial evidence pointed to the Brits: the weapons used in the attack had been stolen from a British arms depot and provided to U Saw by two British officers. Had the British finally gotten their revenge on the Bogyoke? The question was never resolved, and the records of the case were sealed. There was no shortage of people with a motive to remove Aung San, including the rebuffed Communist factions and ethnic groups who wanted the country run their way. But the case against U Saw prevailed.

Some British remained sharply critical after Aung San's death. The British historian Hugh Tinker wrote in a 1961 history of Burma that except for his last six months, Aung San's whole life "was devoted to bitter and often unscrupulous opposition to Britain; his methods were often violent and sometimes cruel; he acted treacherously, first to the British and then to the Japanese; his concept of independence was narrowly nationalistic; and he failed to grasp the potentialities of the new multi-racial Commonwealth."

Others like F. S. V. Donnison, the British administrator in the Far East, credited Aung San with developing statesmanlike qualities which showed that his character could grow with events. For the last 10 months of his life, he was virtually prime minister, realizing for the first time the size of his country, the plurality of its races, and the complexity of its problems; the volume of work took its toll on his health, and at times he was out of his depth, but he was man enough to acknowledge it, winning the respect of the British administrators with whom he was now in daily contact. His assassination deprived his country of the one man who might have been able to enforce discipline on his followers in the lawless years that lay ahead.

The people of Burma would only remember that Aung San had refused bravely to be subjugated by either the British or the Japanese, and had died trying to establish self-rule for his people. They named streets after him, erected statues of him, and put his likeness on their currency.

As the stunned country grieved, the democracy process was suspended. The bodies of the martyrs lay in state in glass coffins at Jubilee Hall for month after month as thousands passed by to pay their respects. The remains were not interred until nine months after the assassination, when a fitting Martyrs Monument could be completed. Those who came by to honor the fallen general included poor farmers in their straw hats as well as the diplomats in formal attire; missionaries as well as monks. One young boy recalled years later that everyone was in shock; all he could remember was that General Aung San seemed much smaller as he lay in state than expected. He had seemed larger than life to everyone.

Year's later, Aung San's daughter would write a fitting epitaph in an essay: "My father's greatest strengths were the largeness of his spirit and an immense capacity to learn from his experiences. He recognized his faults and worked to remedy them. His life is a lesson in revolutionary politics, the hardness and the heartbreak of it. At the same time, it is an inspiration which proves the simple truth that a good leader who serves honestly will be loved and cherished throughout the history of his nation."

—∞—

Burmese leaders regrouped as best they could after the assassinations. Six months after Aung San's death, independence came at last for Burma. The time and date were selected by astrologers—4 P.M. on January 4, 1948. Burma was finally free. *Time* magazine reported: "Thousands of Burmans caroused amiably along Rangoon's steamy, tropical waterfront. Some still recalled the day in 1885 when Burma's last king, the brash Thibaw, sailed into exile and the British took over. Now, British rule was at an end. Atop the gloomy Government House, where the Union Jack had flown for 62 years under British rule, the new red-white-and-blue Burmese flag now fluttered. State musicians in classical court dress played the sonorous 'drum song' and happy throngs chanted the plaintive national anthem: 'Until the end of time, this is our land. . . .'"

Yet the new nation would have a difficult time enjoying the blessings of sovereignty, even with large infusions of British and American aid. The country had been ravaged twice as a battleground during World War II, first by the Japanese as they fought their way in and then by the Allies as they fought their way back in. Burma was left in shambles. According to British historian Sir Reginald Coupland, "Burma suffered more from the war than any other Asiatic country save possibly Japan herself." Many of the Burmese towns were reduced to ashes by air raids. Oilfield equipment, mine equipment, and much of the river transport had been destroyed by the British as they retreated. The Japanese had compounded those losses by confiscating usable equipment and furniture. When they left, rice and teak exports were at a standstill. Burma, once the rice bowl of Asia, needed much more than replanting and rebuilding. It needed to be resuscitated.

In the turbulent months that followed Aung San's untimely death, his former college friend U Nu took over the leadership of the AFPFL and won the vote to become the first prime minister of independent Burma. U Nu had been president of the student movement at Rangoon University when Aung San was secretary, but he had been eclipsed by the more charismatic agitator. Now it was his turn. U Nu was an intelligent, public-spirited man, but he lacked the personal force and political skill to bring the country's indigenous groups and political factions together. And as the former British ambassador Sir Nicholas Fenn later observed, the assassination of Aung San and half his cabinet meant Burma became independent with "a second-eleven cabinet."

Unrest boiled over. The Communists broke with U Nu, and a battalion from the Burma army joined them. The Socialists resigned en masse. The country was not even a year old, and it had already splintered into the Red Flag and White Flag Communists, the Yellow Band (formerly Aung San's army), and a half-dozen ethnic groups.

U Nu, a devout Theravāda Buddhist, further inflamed relations with the minority Christian populations by prodding Parliament to declare Buddhism as the state religion, something Aung San had promised would never happen. The bright hope of tolerance that Aung San had generated at Panglong was snuffed out.

In spite of those problems, the country's infrastructure was gradually being rebuilt, work that had started under Aung San. Burma's per capita GDP grew at a rate of 3 percent in the 1950s, thanks to its natural riches and an eager-to-work population. Rangoon University became competitive with the University of Malaya and Hong Kong University. Prominent Burmese families finally became members of the posh Pegu Club and the Boat Club. It was their turn to play tennis and go sailing on Inya Lake, built by the British for their private recreation.

Yet the country continued to reel with political discontent and ethnic rebellions. The escalating ethnic agitation undermined U Nu's ability to govern and opened the door to military control. U Nu feared he could no longer hold a majority in parliament. He asked General Ne Win, the minister of defense, to form a "caretaker" government in 1958 and restore order to the country. Ne Win gladly took over and began using the army, originally created by Aung San to defend against external enemies, to crack down on internal dissent.

In 1960, when U Nu won back enough electoral support to return to power, Ne Win initially relinquished control. Then two years later, the general took power back. Ne Win claimed he was protecting the country from falling apart. In truth, his taste of power had fed his own ambitions. The general had deliberately derailed positive talks that Prime Minister U Nu had been having with the sawbwas, the powerful Shan princes, who controlled almost a third of Burma. Contrary to Ne Win's claims that the ethnic leaders were plotting trouble, they had come to Rangoon seeking a compromise. The opening for peace was slammed shut. Ne Win's soldiers rounded up U Nu and the sawbwas at gunpoint and locked them up. The first of Burma's harsh military dictatorships had begun.

—ℳ—

Ne Win, whose given name was Shu Maung, was born into an educated middle-class family in the small town of Paungdale about 200 miles north of Rangoon. He spent two years at Rangoon University and took biology as his main subject, with hopes of becoming a doctor. However, he failed a key biology exam in 1931 and was expelled from the university. He went to work as a postal clerk to earn a living, but he kept up contact with former university colleagues who were protesting British rule. As a result, he became one of the young "Thakins" who joined Aung San in the *Dobama Asiayone* "We Burmans Association." He then became one of the "Thirty Comrades" who secretly went with Aung San to undergo military training on Hainan Island to help the Japanese push the British out of Burma. Like the other "Thirty Comrades," he adopted a *nom de guerre*, Ne Win, which meant "Sun of Glory."

Ne Win's flagrant womanizing and drinking hurt his advancement in the army while Aung San was in charge. Aung San did not tolerate licentious behavior. But after the war, Ne Win landed leadership positions in the new army. He was placed in charge of efforts to roust the Communists from their strongholds as commander of the 4th Burma Rifles. During the 14 years when Burma had a struggling parliamentary government, Ne Win rose in Army ranks. He emerged as second in command of the army after a daring confrontation with his rivals.

When the country continued to be riven with political divisions, Ne Win created special attack battalions under his personal command to crack down on insurgents. The attack units proved brutally effective. The Tatmadaw, as the army was affectionately called during Aung San's liberation days, was being converted into a tool of oppression under Ne Win.

In 1949, Ne Win was appointed chief of staff of the armed forces and given total control of the army. He began a policy of "Four Cuts" to crack down on insurgents—cutting off food, funds, intelligence, and recruits. Ne Win's soldiers took what they wanted from the fields and destroyed villages sympathetic to the insurgents. Subsequent military governments would adopt his cutthroat strategies against ethnic groups with even greater ferocity.

One of Ne Win's up-and-coming deputies was a dour officer named Than Shwe. He also was from a small town and had begun his career as a postal clerk. In time, Than Shwe would eclipse Ne Win in notoriety—and hold Aung San's daughter prisoner.

—∾—

Ne Win served as the head of state in Burma for nearly two decades of eccentric autocracy. Obsessively xenophobic, Ne Win nationalized oil fields and industries, kicked out all foreign missionaries, created a state school system to reduce the influence of Western schools, and arrested dissidents. Although Ne Win had been an early colleague of Suu Kyi's father during the independence movement, he proved the antithesis of Aung San and his ideal of selfless service. Ne Win made so many enemies with his corrupt administration that he had to employ a food taster. In contrast with Aung San's probity, Ne Win enjoyed the lavish lifestyle of a Caesar and was prone to drinking and gambling. While he appeared puritanical at times by banning such pleasures as ballroom dancing and horse racing, his personal life was torrid. He had between six and eight wives and even more mistresses. When he wasn't playing golf, he was consulting with astrologers on what to do next, or visiting a psychiatrist in Switzerland for a mysterious, undisclosed personality disorder. One report in the *Far Eastern Economic Review* in 1984 said that his privately chartered jet was delayed on one of his visits to Switzerland "because chests of jade and precious stones carried on board had been stacked incorrectly and had to be reloaded."

When an astrologer warned that his politics had moved too far to the left, Ne Win followed the astroger's advice and ordered that street traffic be moved from the left lane to the right lane, although steering wheels remained on the right side of the vehicles, which made it difficult to drive safely. Deeply superstitious, one of the spells he used to ward off misfortune called for shooting his reflection in the mirror to confuse evil spirits. He was said to bathe in dolphin's blood to restore his youth.

Ne Win's erratic behavior included fits of temper fueled by alcohol, megalomania, and paranoia. In one of the most infamous incidents, he was furious that his favorite daughter Sanda Win was keeping company with a British dental technician, a "kalah." When he discovered she was not at home and heard loud party music wafting across the water from the Inya Lake Hotel, he assumed she was out dancing with the foreigner. He stormed into the ballroom with armed soldiers. People melted away from the dance floor, and the band music faded to a halt as the furious Ne Win climbed onto the bandstand. His daughter and her *kalah* boyfriend did not appear to be present, but by that time Ne Win was so enraged that he grabbed the drummer's drumsticks and plunged them through the drum skin. Amplified by the microphones, the rip made a terrible sound. As he was leaving, a European woman stood up to protest the behavior. According to some accounts, Ne Win pushed her down so forcefully that he half-ripped the top of her dress off. His bodyguards pummeled her outraged husband to the floor.

Some international observers initially had hopes that Ne Win could move the country forward. Former *New York Times* editor Joseph Lelyveld, who was a Fulbright scholar and correspondent for *The Times* in Burma in the 1960s, remembers seeing Ne Win proudly riding in his full dress uniform in an open car when Chinese leader Zhou En-lai visited Rangoon. "He had a kind of nutty candor and some idea of the rest of the world, however limited," Lelyveld recalls. "He was highly regarded in those [early] days. No one suspected he'd prove to be as erratic as he later showed himself to be. Most Western diplomats in those days regarded him as a modernizing figure. . . . They were, of course, spectacularly wrong."

Ne Win's government blindly pursued a policy of autarky, which consisted of national self-sufficiency and non-reliance on foreign imports or economic aid. They began isolating Burma from the world. The needs of everyday people had to be supplied by the black market and smuggling, while the central government slowly slid into bankruptcy. Average incomes fell from $670 a year in 1960 to $200 in 1989. Ne Win's "Burmese Way to Socialism" turned out to be the way to deeper poverty. After 20 years of his rule, Burma would have to apply for status as a Least Developed Nation to get relief from debts. It was during this period of decline and deprivation that Burma became a major producer and exporter of opium—while the military government looked the other way.

When students from Rangoon University staged peaceful protests in 1962, Ne Win sent crack troops to break up the uprising. Dozens of students were shot, and the student union building was dynamited. Reports said that some of the wounded students were still alive when the army took their bodies away and crushed them at the sewage treatment plant in Rangoon. The government claimed that 16 students died; families said more than 100 had been killed.

The ruthless oppression caused many in the educated workforce to emigrate, the beginning of a sustained "brain drain." Newspapers, radio, and TV were taken over. Persecution of minority groups increased. Torture in prisons became standard practice. To erode the family and tribal bonds of ethnic groups, rape was employed on a widespread basis as a weapon of war. To build up the army, boy soldiers as young as 12 or 13 were recruited. A pattern was set for the reign of fear that would continue for more than half a century.

Even after he "resigned" as head of state in 1978, Ne Win maintained the de facto power behind the scenes as the head of his ruling Burma Socialist Program Party—until events spiraled out of control in 1988 and civilian protests began erupting against his regime. As his soldiers cracked down, the Rangoon hospitals were overflowing with victims and the sidewalks were blotted with blood. It was at that turbulent moment that Aung San Suu Kyi returned to Rangoon to care for her ailing mother. The day was coming soon when she would pick up her father's banner for freedom.

> "Because he died so young, it's difficult for me to think of him as an old person. I tend to look upon him as a friend as well as a father. I feel as if he is somebody who would have stood by me when I was in trouble. I always think, 'I may be alone, but I know I have your backing.'"
>
> —Aung San Suu Kyi

CHAPTER SEVEN

KHIN KYI

> "Aung San had married a woman who had not only the courage and warmth he needed in his life's companion, but also the steadfastness and dignity to uphold his ideals after he was gone."
>
> —Aung San Suu Kyi

Aung San Suu Kyi's mother is not as well known as her father, but her influence on Suu Kyi's life should not be overlooked. While Suu Kyi inherited much of her looks, her intellect, and temperament from her father, it was her dutiful and upright mother, Daw Khin Kyi, who raised her.

Suu Kyi often credits her mother with teaching her to respect the values her father stood for, especially to be brave. "She emphasized that fear was not something you should encourage. In fact, she would get very angry with me if I was frightened. She did not like cowardice at all. And she would get very angry about the fact that I used to be afraid of the dark. She would not encourage such namby-pamby feelings. She thought very highly of courage, responsibility, spiritual service, and caring. My mother was an extremely upright woman."

That helps explain why Suu Kyi forced herself to go downstairs at night as a child to conquer her fear of the dark. Her mother expected her to be a brave little soldier, like her father.

Suu Kyi's descriptions of her mother over the years are telling:

- "My mother was one of those parents who always said you had to share. In her opinion, selfishness was one of the worst sins that anybody would be capable of. She always used to say, 'so-and-so is so selfish!' I heard this as a tremendous condemnation. So I would say I learned a lot from my mother. She believed in serving others and in gaining satisfaction and happiness from giving rather than taking."
- "My mother instilled in me the principle that wrongdoing never pays, and my own experience has proved that to be true."
- ". . . my mother always taught me to think of them [the ethnic peoples] as very close to us, emphasizing how loyal they were. She always spoke of them with great respect and warmth."

Because her children had been too young to get to know their father well, Khin Kyi made sure they were aware of his remarkable life from their earliest years. Her often-told memories of her husband were reinforced by Aung San's former colleagues in the army and politics, who kept up their ties with the fallen leader's family. Suu Kyi would later say that she was literally cradled in the arms of her father's soldiers, who felt it their duty to tell his children what a great man the Bogyoke had been. "Even though I never really knew him, I was always told how much the Burmese people loved and revered him," she said.

Suu Kyi said she seemed to recall her father coming in after work and sweeping her into her arms, but was not sure whether she actually remembered it, or was told about it so many times by her mother that it seemed real.

When I first interviewed Suu Kyi, I deliberately asked her about her mother several times, because so much had already been written about her father but very little about her mother. What attributes did she share with her *mother*? "A sense of *duty*," she said instantly. After some thought, she added, "Discipline . . . courage . . . determination . . . I think I get those qualities from *both* my parents."

In 1995, she told *New York Times* writer Claudia Dreifus that her father also had been very influenced by her mother. "One of the reasons I think my father must have been a wonderful person is because my mother was very strong. She was, by choice, a career woman, and was not the domesticated type. Until she married my father. And I think she was completely won over by his principles and by the fact that he was a very lovable person, of which most people are not very aware. People think of him as a tough soldier and an astute politician, but he was very warm-hearted and loving."

Her mother was a remarkable woman, she said—very strong, very strict. "She brought me up as she thought my father would have. Her strength was above normal. Sometimes I think by nature she was braver than my father. I think my father, like me, had to learn to be brave. My mother was afraid of nothing."

Her mother's story begins in the Myaungmya area, a rice-farming and fishing area in the southern Delta. Khin Kyi was the eighth of ten children and affectionately known in her family as "Baby." She started out in local schools, but was considered bright enough to be sent by her family to get a better education at the Kemmendine Girls' School. The school had been started by Baptist missionaries in the 1800s and was open to all ethnic groups. Khin Kyi did well academically, but was not able to gain admission to Rangoon University. She had her heart set on getting a college education, so she persisted and was able to gain entrance to Morton Lane Teacher Training College, another Baptist school, in Moulmein.

Khin Kyi returned to her hometown to teach at a government school, but soon became restless in the sleepy provincial town. Two of her older sisters had become nurses, so she went to Rangoon to be trained as a nurse at the General Hospital, an impressive three-story facility built in the Victorian style by the British, with red brick walls and distinctive yellow trim. It was the premier hospital in the country, a teaching hospital for medical students and nurses. Khin Kyi learned fast and gained a reputation as a can-do nurse. She was the kind of woman who did not blanch at the sight of a soldier with an arm cleaved to the bone by a machete. She stayed calm and on task even while a pregnant woman was shrieking with pain in delivery and hemorrhaging. She was redoubtable.

Even in those early days, Khin Kyi showed an interest in advancing the roles of women that would continue the rest of her life. She joined the Women's Freedom League, which promoted women's rights. She also transferred to a maternity hospital for a while, to gain an extra credential in midwifery. She was so valued for her skilled support in operating rooms that she was persuaded to return to the General Hospital just as war broke out in December 1941.

A large number of her patients were Indian residents, who had thrived under British control as privileged civil servants and merchants. When the Japanese marched into Burma and the British fled, the Indians had to flee for their lives as well. Many were too sick to travel, so a medical ship was arranged to transfer the Indian patients to Calcutta. Khin Kyi was one of the few nurses who volunteered for the hazardous duty. Helping the ailing Indians to escape was not a popular decision, as many Burmese resented their preferential status. Khin Kyi considered it her duty to care for the sick, no matter what their background. After escorting the Indian patients to safety, she made it back to Burma on one of the last vessels allowed back into the Rangoon port before the Japanese closed the shipping lanes. Khin Kyi went immediately back to General Hospital to care for the wounded being rushed in from the war.

One busy day, a cranky patient named Aung San was admitted to the hospital. The general was exhausted and had contracted malaria while helping the Japanese take over Burma. He was only 27, but he had already gained the reputation as a hero and was serving as minister of defense. The senior staff at the hospital decided that it would not be proper to assign one of the trainees to someone of his stature, so they assigned Khin Kyi, one of the most respected members of the staff, to tend to him. She made a point of wearing a cheerful flower in her hair every day and insisted the headstrong general follow the doctor's orders to the letter if he wanted to get well enough to return to his post. It was just the kind of tough love that Aung San needed. He not only recovered, he fell in love. It was a rare personal detour for him. He had only recently declared to his military colleagues that it would be better for true patriots to be castrated "like oxen," rather than risk romantic affairs that would distract them from their mission. Then he got distracted himself.

Writing of her parents' hospital romance in her biography of her father, Suu Kyi said her mother had "handled Aung San with firmness, tenderness, and good humor. The formidable commander-in-chief was thoroughly captivated."

Aung San was indeed besotted. But it was an unlikely pairing: He was 27. Khin Kyi was 30, a bit beyond the traditional marrying age. He was an intellectual elite from the top university. She had gone to missionary schools and was a nurse, not one of the more prestigious careers. He was a devoted Buddhist. She was from a mixed-faith family. Khin Kyi's father, a fairly prosperous farmer and huntsman, had been persuaded to convert to Christianity by his hunting friends. Her mother stayed staunchly Buddhist. Young Khin Kyi grew up with the freedom to worship in both traditions.

On paper, they did not appear suited for each other. But they were young and tender-hearted and there was a war changing the world around them. Khin Kyi was not as pretty or photogenic as her famous daughter would be; but when she smiled, she was radiant. And when she was with Aung San, he smiled too, a marked contrast to his usual intensity.

He wanted to get married right away. She held back, worrying that his affection might only be the passing attachment that wounded soldiers form with their caregivers. Aung San would not give up. He refused to eat unless she fed him by hand. Once he was well enough to be released, he wooed her with boat trips on Inya Lake. Four months after they met, Khin Kyi agreed to marry him.

The wedding was almost called off at the last minute. Aung San's Japanese officers feted him with an all-night bachelor party of carousing to make up for his years of abstinence. The morning before his wedding day, he staggered home half-drunk with a couple of young beauties in hand. Khin Kyi, who was a teetotaling Baptist, got word and was not amused. She told him she was calling the wedding off. Aung San swore he would never get drunk again. She accepted him at his word and forgave him. They were married on September 6, 1942, and he kept his promise.

—~—

It was during this same period that Khin Kyi's sister met and married one of Aung San's close Thakin colleagues, Than Tun, who became a key leader of the Communist movement in Burma.

Than Tun was considered by some as one of the brightest of the young Burmese radicals, but Aung San was the one who made things happen.

In later years, when Than Tun strongly disagreed with his decisions, Aung San had to make the difficult decision to part ways with his brother-in-law. The family relationship was a casualty of the independence movement.

Aung San was under enormous pressure during their first years of married life. Publicly, he was serving his Japanese bosses as minister of defense. Privately, he was looking for a way to escape Japanese domination. He was determined to keep Burmese independence hopes alive. Aung San began secret meetings with the British. Had his efforts been discovered, he would have been shot by the Japanese for treason. His wife became his trusted confidante and refuge.

By the spring of 1945, the Allies were taking back Burma, road by road, town by town. It was no longer safe for Khin Kyi to stay in Japanese-held Rangoon. She had to flee to the Delta region for safety. Khin Kyi was six months pregnant with her third child and had her two toddler boys with her. She hunkered down with the children amidst friends and relatives who would not betray her. Being invisible was not easy in her condition, but Khin Kyi managed to stay out of sight. She did not emerge from hiding until two months later in May, when Rangoon had been retaken by the British with the help of her husband's forces. A daughter who looked much like her father was born a month later, June 19, as the war was winding down.

By the time the war ended, the family had settled into a two-bedroom house at 25 Tower Lane. The picturesque wooden structure had a reception room downstairs, where Aung San could meet with important officials. His home was always open to visitors, who could come by to talk with him at any time. The house also had a large yard with an ornamental pond in back, where the children could play and Khin Kyi could garden. Aung San and Khin Kyi shared the master bedroom with his considerable library, while their children shared the other bedroom.

Khin Kyi had gotten pregnant every year of their marriage, so they now had three children, born in rapid succession during the war years: Aung San Oo, the oldest boy, was born in 1943; Aung San Lin, a second son, was born in 1944; and Aung San Suu Kyi was born in 1945. A second girl, Aung San Chit (Chit meaning "love"), was born in 1946 but died not long after her birth.

The children all carried Aung San's name in addition to their given names to reflect their father's prominence. Their daughter Aung San Suu Kyi was also given the name of two strong women in the family: Suu from her father's esteemed mother, and Kyi from her own mother Khin Kyi. All together, the combined names translated to "Strange Collection of Bright Victories." While that designation may have seemed an unlikely name when Aung San Suu Kyi was a child, her life did indeed turn out to be an unusual series of triumphs. Since she was born on a Tuesday, Burmese astrology predicted the child would have an honest character.

The home at 25 Tower Lane was not palatial, but it came with nursemaids to help with the children and a cook, which was essential since cooking was not one of Khin Kyi's strengths. Aung San liked to come home for lunch to see her and the children. He was often away tending to government matters, but when he was home, the couple enjoyed typical domestic life in the evening. She mended and embroidered. He read. He was quite content with his wife; she humanized him.

In a 1947 article in the *Myanmar Review*, an official named U Thein told about being invited to their home for a reception and being impressed by the general's relationship with his wife. Aung San had arrived late. The governor, a host of officials, and his wife were waiting for him. "I shall never forget the look on Mrs. Aung San's face when he did eventually turn up. It was not only relief. There was love and tenderness, and a good-natured protest in the look. I was convinced that the Bogyoke's happiest moments must be when he was at home with his wife and children. It was, therefore, a huge sacrifice that he left home so long and so often to serve the state."

As the guests thinned out and U Thein and his wife prepared to leave, Khin Kyi introduced them to her husband. He startled them by abruptly asking who they thought was the more handsome of the two, him or his wife? They were taken aback and struggled for the right response, as his wife was not a classic beauty. Suddenly, U Thein realized that Aung San was trying to compliment his wife in his socially awkward way. U Thein dodged politely, saying that he could ask the same question about himself and his own wife. Aung San smiled appreciatively and put his arms around Khin Kyi, teasing, "I never had to woo my wife, you know, for she did all the wooing." U Thein feigned surprise and said that was not what he had heard. He added that their marriage was further proof that "none but the brave deserved the fair." The host was pleased.

When he traveled, Aung San took his wife with him as often as he could. He liked to introduce her at events and josh that she was not interested in him when he was a politician, but when he was a general, she took interest. The line wasn't particularly funny, but crowds laughed respectfully and Khin Kyi smiled patiently. She knew her presence allowed her husband to cope with the pressure he was under.

Rebuilding the country's railroads and oilfields and schools after the war presented a daily deskload of problems for Aung San. On top of the reconstruction problems, there were urgent challenges from the Communists who wanted to take over and the ethnic groups who wanted more say-so in their own governance. Aung San continued meeting with the discontented ethnic leaders. He must somehow get their support for a unified Burma, or the country would splinter apart. Divisions were deep and compromises over power-sharing came hard. The minority populations occupied roughly two thirds of the country's total area. He could not ignore them. He must win them over.

Because of its central geographic location in Asia, Burma has been a crossroads for millennia. The people who flowed in are remarkably diverse.

The government has identified 135 different ethnic groups. These groups comprise eight major national ethnic races: Kachin, Kayah, Kayin, Chin, Mon, Bamar, Rakhine, and Shan.

Some of the ethnic groups are of Sino-Tibetan origin; some are closely related to the Thai people. Some groups speak Mandarin Chinese. Others speak the ancient Pali languages from the Indian subcontinent. Under British rule, some of the largest ethnic areas—the Shan States ruled by princely sawbwas, the Chill Hills, and mountainous Kachin tracts—were known as the "Frontier areas" and were administered separately.

To complicate matters, there are other populations that are not officially recognized—such as the Rohingya, who have historically been ostracized and denied citizenship.

Each ethnic group regards the protection of their individual languages, customs, culture, and natural resources as important to their national identity. In many instances, revenues from gold, gems, petroleum, and timber that provide the bulk of Burma's wealth have been at stake.

—ɯ—

Building bridges with the diverse ethnic groups was essential for Aung San to fulfill the independence dream, but earning their trust had been complicated by the war and his own troops. Clashes had occurred between some of Aung San's troops and ethnic groups that were suspected of siding with the British.

One of the most tragic incidents took place in the Myaungmya district, where Khin Kyi's parents lived. The incident was triggered when a friend of Japanese Colonel Suzuki was killed during a raid by pro-British Karen insurgents on the Japanese forces. Aung San's troops were ordered by the Japanese to seek reprisals. Two Karen villages in the Myaungmya district, close to Khin Kyi's former home, were targeted for demolition. In what came to be known as "the Myaungmya massacre," the villages were destroyed and all their occupants killed. In Myaungmya itself, a former member of parliament and a cabinet minister were hacked to death along with 150 other Karens.

Aung San was in a different part of the country at the time and played no role in the slaughter, but the incident caused him grievous concern. It hit painfully close to home. After the Myaungmya massacre, he raised his quiet meetings with Karen leaders and other ethnic groups into something more open and forthright, promising respect for minority rights and their religions once Burma became truly independent after the war.

Marriage had given Aung San an even deeper appreciation for the need for tolerance and inclusion in the country. His wife deferred to her husband and honored his Buddhist faith after their marriage, although she had grown up in a mixed-faith home. There was a Buddhist altar in their house, at which they prayed, meditated, and made offerings. Yet her father, a Christian, was a welcome and beloved visitor. Aung San could see that prejudice against other faiths was unjust and tried to live out the model of coexistence that he hoped his country would follow. He took care to include a Muslim leader, U Abdul Razak, in his interim cabinet, as well as a Karen tribal leader, Mahn Ba Khaing, and a Shan leader, Sao San Tun, who was the sawbwa (prince) of Mong Pawng.

With typical frankness, Aung San tackled the issue of ethnic and religious prejudice head-on in his speeches. "In the past, we shouted slogans: 'Our race, our religions, our language.' Those slogans have gone obsolete now," he said. He pointed out to audiences that in America, people sprang from many stocks but speak a common language. As for religion, it should be a matter of individual *conscience*, not politics, he said.

"If we want the nation to prosper, we must pool our resources, manpower, wealth, skills, and work together. If we are divided—the Karens, the Shans, the Kachins, the Chins, the Burmese, the Mons, and the Arakanese—each pulling in a different direction, the Union will be torn, and we will come to grief. Let us unite and work together and see what we can accomplish," he said as he campaigned across the country for unity.

The Panglong agreement that he worked out was not perfect, but it patched together enough goodwill with the contentious "frontier areas" for the nation-building to move forward. That progress was abruptly ended on July 19, 1947, when assassins rushed into the Secretariat building and took Aung San's life.

—∞—

On the day he was assassinated, Aung had hugged his children good-bye and headed off to work, sticking to his schedule despite warnings of danger. He had received word three days earlier that a plot against him was afoot, but he left home that day with a smile for his children. His much-wounded body was taken to Rangoon General Hospital only hours later.

When his wife received word about the attack, she rushed to the hospital, the same red-brick building where she had helped save so many lives. But it was too late to help her husband. According to reports, blood was still oozing from his wounds as she gently cradled his head in her lap. She sat silent for a long time, too deeply stunned to weep. Then, drawing on her skills as a nurse, she gently wiped away the blood and cleaned her husband's wounds so his body could be prepared for display for mourners. Photos taken while his body lay in state show the widow Khin Kyi sitting by the side of the coffin in a plain wooden chair, her shoulders slumped in fatigue and grief. Thousands filed by his open coffin for weeks on end.

—∞—

Those who had been on the other side of Aung San's temper or politics may not have mourned him as a national hero, but to the vast majority of the Burmese public he had represented the hope of a better life. For them and for future generations, he would remain a brave hero, a martyr for his country.

However, Khin Kyi could not spend the rest of her life looking back. There was the pressing problem of how to support three children. A small honorarium had been awarded by the new government to each of the murdered cabinet ministers' wives, but it was not enough to provide for ongoing expenses and the children's education. Khin Kyi quietly made contact with the Rangoon General Hospital to see if she might resume her nursing career. The administrators were more than happy to welcome her back. But by then, Aung San's old college classmate U Nu was serving as prime minister. He thought a more dignified position should be found for the widow of the country's fallen leader. Khin Kyi was named the director of the National Women and Children's Welfare

Board. As a former midwife, she was well acquainted with the difficulties that women faced in Burma and was drawn to the idea of helping them. She was subsequently elected a member of the first post-independence Parliament, helping fulfill the dream her husband had fought for. And in 1953, she was appointed Burma's first minister of social welfare. Khin Kyi became known an adept administrator and was often commended for her highly disciplined management skills. Her kitchen table had once again become a sounding board for political talk, only now she was presiding.

Khin Kyi was not the first woman to be active in Burmese politics. Many of the kings had been closely advised by the queens. Indeed, the independent Mon Kingdom in Pegu had once had a "female king" named Shin Saw Bu.

In modern times, a woman was elected for the first time to the Legislature in 1929. Daw Mya Sein, a respected headmistress, participated in the 1932 Burma Round Table conference about independence in London and was an emissary to China in 1939–40.

Women traditionally had enjoyed more privileges in Burma than in many societies of the time. The inheritance of specific oil wells, for instance, belonged exclusively to women; in some cases the inheritance to the headmanship of a village was through the female line. To this day, there are no family surnames in Burma and a woman keeps her own name after marriage.

The "arranged marriage," customary in a large part of Asia, can still be found in a few segments of Burma; but even there, the parents cannot choose a partner for their daughter without offering her the right of refusal. Most Burmese young people marry for love—or at least choose their own partners.

Other practices found in parts of Asia—such as immolation of widows, female infanticide, foot-binding, and child brides—have never been prevalent in Burma. Some speculate the reason is that most Burmans practiced a purer form of Buddhism that emphasized that all human beings should be treated with loving kindness, including women.

There are tenets of Buddhism, however, that cast women in an unfavorable light—those who misbehave may be punished by being reborn as women. Women cannot reach the highest ranks in Buddhism. Men traditionally are considered the "head of house" and have the privilege of being able to eat first, but women often manage the home finances.

Female literacy was near that of men after World War II, and women held positions of respect as academics and professions such as medicine. After the imposition of military rule in 1962, women were increasingly marginalized. Military men dominated all facets of the country's life.

—~—

After her husband's death, Khin Kyi tried to establish a sense of normality for her children. She made sure they honored their father's memory and understood they had a civic obligation as his children. Each month, she held a memorial for their father in the house, led by Buddhist monks from the monastery near the house on Tower Lane. Khin Kyi discouraged her children from feeling ill will toward their father's assassins, according to biographer Whitney Stewart. She often would remind them that if you hurt people for revenge or wish them harm, you will suffer in your next life. She taught them the law of karma: Each one must control his or her own ignorance, hatred, and desire—or suffer the consequences in this life or the next.

Yet Khin Kyi's efforts to stabilize her children's lives were interrupted by another tragedy in the spring of 1953. Her second son, Aung San Lin, who was Suu Kyi's closest playmate, was drowned in an accident at their home on Tower Lane.

The 8-year-old boy had been playing with his sister by the pond on the grounds of their home. He dropped his toy gun and went back to get it. His sandal came off in the mud. Running to catch up with his sister, he handed her the toy gun before racing back to get his sandal. He never returned. It was believed he somehow got stuck in the gluey mud, fell into the pond, and drowned.

When word reached Khin Kyi, she was shocked and stricken once again. She stoically decided it was her duty to stay at her desk and finish her work before leaving to tend to yet another unfathomable family tragedy. Some people found that unusual, but they didn't understand Khin Kyi's deeply rooted sense of responsibility. And the pain of coming home to a dead child.

Her young daughter was devastated. Her spunky brother had been her best friend. Suu Kyi would write later, "In some ways, I believe my brother's death affected me more than my father's. I was seven-and-a-half when he died and we were very close. We shared the same room and played together."

After Aung San Lin's death, Prime Minister U Nu made it possible for Khin Kyi to move the family away from the house on Tower Lane and its mixed memories. Another house was found at an address that would later become famous: 54 University Avenue. The change of scene helped heal the loss for the two surviving children, who found it difficult to play in their garden with the pond in view. Psychologists say that a child who has lost both a parent and a sibling at a very young age will likely experience anxiety about abandonment or become fearful. That Aung San Suu Kyi did not retreat from life is a tribute to her own resolve, her mother's example, and the comforting embrace of the extended family of friends and relatives who gathered in the home.

Relatives from both her father's side of the family and her mother's side had come frequently to visit after her father died, so there was usually a family member at the house even though her mother often was away at work. Suu Kyi has said the strongest male role model in her life was her mother's father, U Pho Hynin. He doted on his granddaughter and was much loved in return. When she was old enough, Suu Kyi often was asked by her grandfather, who was a Christian and had become blind, to read the Bible to him. She read to him for hours and learned his favorite passages by heart.

During the same period, a great-aunt would tell her stories from the *Jakata*, the tales about the Buddha's life. "She knew the whole story of the Buddha's life. Her knowledge of Buddhism was really, very, very broad, and she taught us a lot, especially me because I was a girl. I learned about Buddhism the easy way," Suu Kyi would recall much later. Like most Buddhists, they had a small altar at home, where they could make offerings of flowers, fruit, or incense every morning. But there also would be a Bible on the table downstairs. As result, young Suu grew up conversant with both faiths, learning scriptures such as "Perfect love casts out fear" as well as the core Buddhist teachings on suffering, impermanence, and loving kindness.

That ecumenical upbringing helped shape her tolerant view of people of other faiths. "I'm all for a broadminded attitude," she told an Indian interviewer in 1996. "People of all different religions should be given the opportunity to pursue good in their own way. I assume that is what religion is all about. Religion is about increasing peace and harmony in the world. Everyone should be given a chance to create peace and harmony in their own way."

A steady stream of distinguished figures made their way to Khin Kyi's home and had strong influence on the widow's children as they grew older. U Myint Thein, a distinguished chief justice, was a loyal family friend. U Ohn, a journalist who had known Aung San and had served as ambassador to the Court of St. James and Moscow, brought Suu Kyi books and gave her long lists of books to read in English and Burmese.

Even though she was not an avid reader herself, Khin Kyi had made it a point to promote reading to her children because of her husband's love of literature. She took her children to the library every two weeks. Reading became Suu's passion. When she was 10, she had wanted to become a soldier like her father. By the time she was 14, when she was enthralled by reading, she decided she would become a writer instead. Suu Kyi was a good student and reinforced her schoolwork with constant reading, even taking a book along while going shopping with her mother so she could read in the car. She began with fairy tales and graduated to Sherlock Holmes. When a cousin gave her a copy of "The Blue Carbuncle," she became hooked on the Baker Street sleuth because he could use his observation and scientific knowledge to figure out the villain well ahead of the police. She became a fan of detective fiction and was discerning enough to read between the lines. It is said she deduced at a young age that Georges Simenon's brainy Inspector Maigret preferred small Provençal restaurants, while John le Carré's lonely George Smiley, in contrast, never seemed to eat at all. "The first autobiography I ever read was providently, or prophetically, or perhaps both, *Seven Years Solitary*, by a Hungarian woman who had been in the wrong faction during the Communist Party purges of the early 1960s. At thirteen years old, I was fascinated by the determination and ingenuity with which one woman alone was able to keep her mind shapr and her spirit unbroken through the years when her only human contact was with men whose everyday preoccupation was to try to break her," she revealed in *Aung San Suu Kyi: A Portrait in Words and Pictures*.

Her inquisitive tastes led her on to the classics of literature and a wide range of contemporary writers. In interviews over the years, she demonstrated a well-stocked mind, quoting with ease from Soviet dissident Natan Sharansky, British author Rebecca West, Czech president Václav Havel, Martin Luther King Jr., philosopher Karl Popper, and Thich Nhat Hanh, the Vietnamese monk, poet, and peacemaker.

People from the various ethnic groups often stayed in their home. When Khin Kyi was working on health issues, nurses would come from all over the country to Rangoon for classes on child care. Khin Kyi would invite them to stay at her home, and her quiet, earnest young daughter took it all in. Visitors would recall the polite young girl with the long braided plaits of dark hair coming downstairs to be presented to guests and staying to listen.

The story is told that young Suu Kyi had such an inquisitive nature that she would pester her mother with questions when she came home from work. Even when her mother lay down on the bed to rest, Suu Kyi would quiz her for answers about things she had read about that day, like "Why is water called water?" She would circle her mother's bed, asking a question every time she came to the foot of the bed. Her mother, no doubt sensing her daughter wanted attention, made sure to answer every question. "Never once did she say, 'I'm too tired. Don't go on asking me these questions,'" Suu Kyi would recall later.

Though she was a caring woman and a convivial companion with her friends, Khin Kyi was a no-nonsense taskmaster with her children. They not only were taught to sit up straight at the table, their backs were not allowed to touch the back of their chairs. The Asian tradition called for a respectful formality between generations and especially between children and their elders. Then, too, Khin Kyi was more concerned about giving her children the skills to survive than being their friend. At times when she would talk about her upbringing, Suu Kyi would say that she had a very Burmese relationship with her mother, which meant her mother did not discuss personal problems with her. "Parents don't do that in a Burmese context. There is a certain reserve between the generations. Mothers of my mother's generation just don't have heart to heart talks with their daughters." Her mother had been "very strict," she acknowledged, perhaps too much so, but that discipline had often stood her in good stead in many of life's unpleasant and unpredictable twists.

Khin Kyi also instilled in her young daughter a sense of self-management, including keeping her appearance neat and clean. Her mother did not allow her to leave the house for school or come down to meet guests unless she had combed her hair and looked presentable. Khin Kyi's rationale was that people generally judge your inside by looking at your outside, so appearance was important. Just as her mother put flowers in her hair as a feminine touch that her father admired, Suu Kyi would later tuck flowers into her thick dark hair.

—∾—

Khin Kyi knew well that education was the best insurance policy for life's challenges, so she made sure her children got the best education available. Suu Kyi and her brothers had started school at St. Francis Convent, a co-ed private school near their home. They began learning English at an early age, because Khin Kyi had observed from the British that it was essential for upward mobility. Young Suu showed so much academic promise that she transferred at the age of 12 to the more highly regarded Methodist English High School (MEHS).

At the time, most Burmese elites sent their children to schools operated by churches, such as the Anglican St. John's Boy's School or the Roman Catholic St. Paul's High School, or the Methodist English High School. MEHS was considered the best school in Burma—even dictator Ne Win sent his six children there. Parents sometimes moved from other parts of the country to Rangoon so their children could study at MEHS.

—∾—

As I interviewed people over the years, I was struck by how many of the democracy leaders and top professionals seemed to have attended the same school, MEHS. Why, I wondered, had a *Christian* school become so prominent in a *Buddhist* country? Why had so many of the democracy advocates come from the same school? Tracing back the story of how Aung San Suu Kyi ended up at MEHS turned out to be the Burmese equivalent of C. S. Lewis's wardrobe with a magic back door. It led to the story of how Christianity got a foothold in feudal Burma in the 1800s and altered the status quo for the next two centuries. The missionaries were an injection of Western thought into the isolated kingdom. The resulting cultural tension was the prologue to the struggle for the soul of Burma today.

The beginning can be traced back to Adoniram Judson, who was born in 1788 in Malden, Massachusetts with a Biblical name that sounded as if it would someday be chiseled into granite. And it would be, in Burma. Judson is often cited as the first American to become a Protestant missionary to Asia and one of the first to set forth from the U.S. for a foreign mission.

While Judson was studying at the new Andover Theological Seminary in 1810, he read about a British missionary who was trying to convert the people of "Burmah," a land of golden temples. At the time, Lewis and Clark had just trekked to the other side of the American continent. Adoniram Judson sailed to the other side of the world to become a Bible-toting version of Indiana Jones.

When he and his wife Ann arrived in Rangoon by schooner in 1813, they discovered what another visitor of the time described as "A miserable, dirty town, containing eight thousand or ten thousand inhabitants, the houses being built with bamboo and teak planks, with thatched roofs—almost without drainage, and intersected by muddy creeks, through which the tide flowed at high water. It had altogether a mean, uninviting appearance."

The Judsons settled in a bamboo hut and learned the hard way that the Buddhists in Burma did not want to convert to Christianity. The reason was simple: the king forbid it. Buddhism was the state religion. The penalty for conversion was death.

It was six years before Judson made his first convert, a timber worker from the northern hill tribes who floated logs down to Rangoon. After ten years, he had only ten followers. Judson sometimes walked for months through the jungle to meet with villagers. He survived multiple imprisonments by the king. He endured being hung upside down in his prison cell and being marched barefoot in shackles for miles over rugged territory. But he wouldn't give up his work. When Judson asked the king for permission to at least let him do missionary work among the illiterate hill tribes, the monarch laughed and told him he would have a better chance teaching the royal dog.

Both of the Judsons would struggle for years with illness—cholera, dysentery, malaria, smallpox, and tuberculosis were widespread and unchallenged, as they are in many areas today. All their children died from disease that would be preventable today. Judson would have three wives who died from illness in the tropics, along with many of the missionaries who followed him to the land of golden temples.

But Burma, as now, was a paradise of frangipani and jasmine, exotic fruits and kind neighbors. Judson's letters home were read from pulpits across New England and inspired many more missionaries—not just Baptist, but Methodist, Anglican, and Catholic—to come to Burma. By the time of Judson's death, there were 210,000 Christians, one out of every 58 Burmese.

After his death in 1850, Judson's influence lived on—a college in Rangoon was given his name and formed the beginning of what is now Rangoon University. His name was preserved in marble in churches in Rangoon and Moulmein. He also would be remembered for his remarkable translation of the Bible in Burmese, his dictionaries of the Burmese languages, and the printing press he brought to Burma, which printed the grammars used to teach children to read.

His first wife Ann started a Rangoon elementary school that became the model for missionary schools that sprang up across the country, Baptist, Anglican, Catholic, and Methodist. That network of church schools, along with the British government schools and the indigenous monastery schools, helped make Burma one of the most literate countries in Asia. The missionaries were not only teachers who brought new ways of thinking, but also doctors who brought new ways of healing, and agriculture experts who brought modern methods of growing crops and sturdier breeds of pigs and chickens.

Although Western church leaders were expelled in the 1960s, Baptist, Assemblies of God, Catholic, Methodist, and Anglican churches still maintain devoted followings today. Christians in Burma make up seven percent of the population, many of them Baptists and from ethnic areas.

Burma is home to the third-largest population of Baptists in the world, after the U.S. and India.

To the xenophobic leaders in the military, however, the Christian intrusion was another vestige of Western colonialism—*religious imperialism.* The missionaries had brought with them the Western concepts of human rights and self-rule. That was a threatening combination for Burmese rulers in Adoniram Judson's day. And now.

In order to preserve their control, Burmese generals since the 1960s have continually tried to suppress Christian populations as well as Muslims. The Jewish population has been largely driven out. Unlike the more broad-minded General Aung San, the succession of military rulers has resented and resisted Western concepts of freedom of religion, freedom to speak, and freedom of the press.

That was the paradox of the Christian influx into Burma: The missionaries sowed the seeds of conflicts with the military by introducing the Western concepts of democracy and human rights—and at the same time inspired the leaders of the democracy movement with the schools they created. In other words, they helped create the problem and the solution.

After the military repression of the 1988 protests, many of the MEHS graduates became members of Aung San Suu Kyi's party, the National League for Democracy. Like Suu Kyi, they had been educated to lead at MEHS. They took to heart the school motto, "Not for school, but for life do we learn." While the school had Christian roots, the curriculum was based on a classic British model and Buddhist students were not under any pressure to convert. Most did not. But they did excel.

The founders of MEHS, Frank and Karis Manton, would become close friends with Suu Kyi's mother in Rangoon. Their story was a bookend to hers, with a war in between.

According to family memoirs, the Mantons first came to Burma in the midst of the Depression in 1937. The Methodist Church sent the Mantons to lead the Methodist English Church in Rangoon. They settled into a large wooden house behind the church school. Those were happy years, but war clouds were gathering. On December 23, 1941, just weeks after Pearl Harbor, the Japanese conducted their first bombing raid on Rangoon. Frank Manton volunteered as an ambulance driver to pick up the dead and wounded. The second raid took place on Christmas Day. American and British authorities ordered women and children out of the country just days after Christmas. A ship was leaving the next morning. Karis Manton and the children would have to be on it. The entire city was blacked out in anticipation of continuing air raids, so Karis used very small candles to pack one suitcase in the dim light for herself and each of her three children. When they said good-bye to Frank at 6 A.M. the next morning, they did not know if they would ever see each other again. Karis and the three children—ages four, two, and three months—sailed across the Bay of Bengal and then traveled by train hundreds of miles to a hill station in the far north of India called Almora. Karis Manton would look out at the snow-capped Himalayas and wait for her husband Frank.

Frank Manton stayed on through the continued bombing of Rangoon by the Japanese, hoping each wave of roaring destruction would be the last. He helped as an ambulance driver, carrying those who survived from the rubble of their homes to General Hospital where Khin Kyi was working day and night, improvising care with dwindling supplies. He continued volunteering until the British declared Rangoon an "open city"—they would no longer try to defend the inhabitants against the Japanese onslaught. Frank packed a small suitcase with his Bible and hymnbook, grabbed his walking stick, and fit as many people as he could into his 12-horsepower Opel. They headed north from Rangoon on the road to Mandalay, along with a somber parade of people walking and riding whatever they could, bicycles, oxcarts, civil service cars. From Mandalay, he drove on to Monywa, where he abandoned his car in exchange for riverboat passage up the Chindwin River. It was the quickest way north. The Japanese army was taking over the country, mile by mile. As soon as he arrived in Kalawa to the north, Frank started—along with hundreds of thousands of fellow refugees—on the long trek to India. It was on that road that at some 50,000 people died from what they called "black water fever" or malignant malaria. The mountain jungle was as dense as any in the world, rough on feet, hands, tempers. With the Japanese army continuing to advance, there was no time to rest, but Frank paused when he could to take black-and-white movies of the desperate diaspora. Frank survived the walk of hundreds of miles to northern India and cabled home that he was alive. He found a way to go by train to where his family was staying in Almora. It was a grateful reunion.

After recuperating, Frank was reassigned to be minister of a church in Bombay. The young family moved into the parsonage, which was an apartment above the church. Though they had little, they welcomed many refugees who were fleeing from the Japanese war in both Burma and China. Some of those refugees included members of Karis's family who had been serving as missionaries in China. Her young brother and her family narrowly escaped the conflict in China and flew out over the famous "hump" of the Himalayas from Kunming to Assam. For a time, there were quite a few missionary cousins who had survived ordeals crowded into the apartment over the church.

During the hot season, Karis Manton took the children to the hill station of Mussoorie in the foothills of the Himalayas to get out of the heat of the plains and to attend the Woodstock School there. The school had been founded back in 1854—and had become a very international school. The youngest Manton—William Arthur—arrived a month after Karis's 41st birthday, and was prominently given the nickname "Sufficient" to round out those of the other children, Sissy, Sunny, and Sandy.

The half-dozen Mantons sailed from Bombay back to the U.S. on a troop ship on August 12, 1944. All the mothers and 25 children were gathered in one cabin, while all the fathers and other men bunked below in the hold. The ship was shadowed by Japanese subs as it left Bombay, but arrived safely in Long Beach, California after a zigzag journey across the Pacific. The Mantons settled in New Jersey until the war was over, but felt called to return to Rangoon. They made a small profit by selling their home and used it to return to their work in Burma.

There was no housing in Rangoon for them because more than 12,000 permanent buildings had been destroyed during the war. Frank Manton bunked where he could in Rangoon, while the rest of the family returned to the Woodstock School in India. That proved provident, as the family was up in the hills when the violent schism of India and Pakistan occurred in the summer of 1947. The world around them was again in turmoil. Millions were killed while Muslims fled to the newly created Pakistan and Hindus rushed from Pakistan back to the newly independent India. By the end of the year, the rest of the family was able to join Frank in Rangoon, traveling by train and by ship with as much war-surplus food as they could buy and carry from Calcutta. The big item was #10 tins of peanut butter by the case.

Having seen firsthand the turbulence of the independence of India and Pakistan, the Mantons were about to be "present at the creation" of the other large British colony that was being given its independence, Burma.

The Manton family returned to Rangoon six months after the assassination of Aung San and half his cabinet. The country was still in shock. The Mantons went to pay their respects to the fallen leader, who was still in a glass-enclosed coffin in Jubilee Hall until a memorial site could be constructed.

Though the country remained in mourning, the Mantons were relieved to be together at last. They lived with another missionary family in a three-story building, where at first all six of the family shared one large room partitioned off by cupboards and curtains. When the other couple moved to another residence, they had the luxury of two rooms for the six of them.

As 1947 was drawing to a close, they were told that independence would arrive at 4:20 A.M. on January 4, 1948—a time pronounced as auspicious by the leading astrologers. Accordingly, the Mantons got up at 4 A.M. and lit candles to place in the windows. At 4:20 A.M., they heard the booms of a 21-gun salute from the HMS *Birmingham* as the last British governor went up the light cruiser's gangway. The Union of Burma was born.

The British were gone. Burma was independent. But not united. The various ethnic groups tried to assert their own independence. Revolt was all around as the ethnic nations wrestled for autonomy and political forces like the Communists wrestled for power.

It was during those anxious days that Karis became good friends with many of the Burmese women leaders, starting with Daw Khin Kyi, the widow of the martyred founder of modern Burma. Khin Kyi was well aware of the many problems that women and children faced in Burma and became the country's first minister of social welfare, providing services to people suffering from poverty and other social ills. She was instrumental in founding volunteer societies like the National Council of Women of

Burma to mobilize women in the country. Karis Manton was the only non-Burmese woman asked by Khin Kyi to join that premiere group of women leaders. The NCWB undertook many social welfare projects throughout the country. Karis later served as president, an honor given to no other foreigner. She was accepted as a Burmese woman leader until she left in 1966.

In the meantime, Frank Manton had thrown himself into rebuilding the Methodist institutions that were destroyed or damaged during the war. The Methodist English Church in the heart of Rangoon was not destroyed by Japanese bombing, because it had been the Burma headquarters of Subhas Chandra Bose, the charismatic Indian nationalist who tried to rid India of British rule during the war. The church with its massive teak arches in the sanctuary had survived, but the Methodist School some 75 yards away was destroyed by British bombing as they retook Burma because it was closer to the Japanese War Office, a prime target. The school had to be completely rebuilt and staffed. It was a tall challenge in the lean post-war years.

Frank Manton gained a partner in what looked like an impossible task when Mrs. Doreen Logie came to call. Mrs. Logie was a Eurasian born in Burma of Indian and British parents. She had been teaching school in Burma before the war and had recently returned from India with her Scots husband George, who was the Burma representative of the Valvoline Oil Company. Mrs. Logie could not find a place for her five-year-old daughter Gillian to go to school since the Methodist English Girls School had been reduced to rubble by the bombing. She called on Rev. Manton and told him many other parents faced the same problem. He suggested that she use the vestry of his church to start a primary school and see what happened. She placed an ad in the local paper saying she would register children who spoke English and wished to learn in English. They soon had 30 students, enough to start a class, but not all the new students spoke English at a proficient level. Rather, their parents were determined that their children would learn the language of the powerful British and American people.

Thanks to a $10,000 donation from American Methodists—a donation that would have a long-lasting impact—a sturdy red-brick school was built. Frank Manton was the superintendent of the school as well as minister of the church and choir director. Doreen Logie was the principal of the school, lead teacher, and church organist. They were an odd team—he was an intense American, slender with sandy-red hair and stomach problems. She was quite British and proper, shorter, and a bit plump, with dark hair and eyes. Together the made the school a showcase for excellence.

By the end of the first term, there were 90 students. Attendance continued to climb, reinforcing the need for a new building. The only problem was that there was no money for construction. The Crusade Fund, which had been formed by American Methodists, chipped in more than $1 million over the next few years to complete the construction. Little did the American Methodists far away know that their donations would provide the foundation for the democracy movement in Burma.

Frank oversaw the construction work, while Doreen Logie ran the school. Karis minded the Manton children and church details. By the time the school had grown to more than 100 students, Frank was able to move some classes from the sanctuary to the school next door. By 1949, the major reconstruction was completed and a U-shaped parsonage was added in back of the church, with bedrooms on one side, living spaces on the other, and an open garden area in the middle suitable for church socials.

By 1960, the school at 26 Signal Pagoda Road had grown to 4,500 students and 500 staff. There were so many students, the school had to be divided into morning and afternoon schools.

In 1998, a minister of Burma's military cabinet acknowledged that MEHS was "the best school in Burma." Many would agree. The school has educated several generations of leaders who came from all walks of life. In one classroom alone, twenty out of forty students became medical doctors or obtained PhDs. Many of the leaders of the student rebellion in 1988 were MEHS graduates, as were a large number of the early members of the National League of Democracy. Hundreds more who left for the United States have played valuable roles in the democracy movement:

- Maureen Aung Thwin is director of the Soros Foundation's Burma Project and would prove instrumental in providing leadership training for democracy supporters, including monks.

- Kwan Kwan Wang was Hillary Clinton's roommate at Yale Law School and lobbied for Madeleine Albright's visit to meet Aung San Suu Kyi when Albright was U.S. Ambassador to the U.N.
- Louisa Benson filed the slave-labor lawsuit against Unocal and obtained a confidential $30 million settlement for those harmed by the construction of the Unocal natural gas pipeline from Burma to Thailand.
- Richard Yukhin would become a successful financier in the United States and become a widely read critic of the military regime in the media, as well as a champion for Burmese refuges.
- Harn Yanghwe, a Shan, was the son of Burma's first president and heads the European office of the democratic resistance overseas.
- Tin Maung Thaw became one of the founders of the U.S. Campaign for Burma.
- Soe Thinn became head of the Burmese section of Radio Free Asia.

It is estimated that only a minority of the original MEHS alumni remain in Burma—while alumni overseas have been at the forefront of keeping the democracy movement alive by long distance. Almost all of them give the credit for the school's impact to the indomitable Doreen Logie.

MEHS graduate Richard Yukhin remembers Mrs. Logie as a strict disciplinarian. "I shared office space with her," he says, meaning considerable hours of detention. She tried to tame his hijinks by double-promoting him so he would have to work extra-hard on his schoolwork to keep up and have less time for rebelling. Her plan succeeded. He went on to Yale.

Others agree that Mrs. Logie ran the school very correctly and did not "take any nonsense." Despite the impact of her "caning ceremonies," they describe her as "lovely" and say "Everyone loved her." Her name became synonymous with the school.

What happened to the indomitable Mrs. Logie and Rev. and Mrs. Manton?

Rev. Frank Manton later took on a greater share of Methodist Church work in all of Burma, performing all the functions of bishop, but without the title. He was long-time chairman of the Rangoon Charitable Society and for a time was president of the American Association of Burma. Karis Manton became extremely active in grassroots work on behalf of the church, serving as national president of the YWCA. The Mantons retired in the U.S., and both passed away in the late 1980s. Their long years of service to Burma—and the contributions of Adoniram Judson before them—are testament that Americans have been deeply involved with the people of Burma for two centuries.

Doreen Logie was forced to flee Burma when Ne Win ordered non-Burmese out of the country in October 1964 and the school was seized. When she was 86 and living in Worcestershire, England, more than 100 of her former pupils and staff traveled to England from as far away as Australia, Hong Kong, and the U.S. to say thank you.

MEHS was renamed State High School No. 1 Dagon when Gen. Ne Win nationalized the schools in 1964. While it is still considered one of the best of the state-run schools, the achievements of the Manton-Logie era in Burma remain unmatched.

One of Suu Kyi's best friends at the Methodist school was a very bright Chinese girl named Jenny Lim. Jenny sat next to Suu Kyi in the eighth grade. They were both members of the Girl Guides, which had been introduced in Burma by Suu Kyi's mother as a way of improving the lives of women and girls in Burma. Jenny Lim describes the young Suu Kyi as a shy child who dressed so plainly, she looked like an orphan. "She was not dressed in any fancy way as the daughter of the Bogyoke. She had long braids and dressed in the simple school uniforms. She used to tell me that the other kids, our contemporaries, had money and she didn't."

The Bogyoke's family was prominent, but not well-to-do. Khin Kyi had to sell what little jewelry she had during the war to help her husband's new Burmese Independence Army. Though Prime Minister U Nu had gifted the Bogyoke's widow with the home at 54 University Avenue, it was furnished with simple wooden chairs and beds.

Because her mother worked, Suu Kyi often was looked after by family members or a governess. Jenny Lim remembers, "When I would go to the movies, I would look up to the balcony and she would be there with her governess. Her mother never went with her, as she had responsibilities."

After her brother Aung San Lin drowned, Suu Kyi became more isolated. She no longer had her favorite playmate. "Suu had an older brother that she respected as an older brother, but he already was in competition with her," Lim said. The differences between the siblings, which would lead to a painful schism in later years, were already noticeable when they were young. Aung San Oo was moody and insecure; his sister was inquisitive and playful. After his father's death, Aung San Oo became more introverted and remained so. Those who met him later in life most often described him as "boring."

Jenny Lim became Suu Kyi's friend and confidante at the Methodist school. They sat next to each other at the back of the classroom and discovered they both felt different from the other students. "It was a lonely existence. I happened to be a Chinese girl and a Christian, so I didn't go with the typical Burmese crowd. She was the Bogyoke's daughter, so I didn't think I would be able to associate with her, but I became her best friend. She is very gentle, but she appears tough to some people."

At MEHS, Suu showed a special talent for learning languages, but her favorite class was Burmese literature. As a self-confessed "bookworm," Suu Kyi preferred reading and writing to math and science, but by applying herself with gritty determination, she was able to place first in her class in every subject by the time she was 15.

Richard Yukhin, one of her classmates, says the days they attended MEHS during the 1950s were a happy interlude before the military leaders turned against their own people. As the son of respected academics, Yukhin had access to the Rangoon Sailing Club and remembers Rangoon as an enjoyable place to grow up despite any political tensions. The students at MEHS listened to American records and watched American movies. Their prom photos, with the boys in crisp white shirts and suits and the girls in skirts with petticoats, could have come from a TV episode of *Happy Days*.

Most MEHS students went on to study at the University of Rangoon, which was enjoying its heyday. The engineering college had professorial exchange programs with MIT. Johns Hopkins University also had a campus in Rangoon that offered a master's degree. Burma's medical schools were considered among the best in the region.

A 1957 broadcast of Edward R. Murrow's *See It Now* TV series spotlighted Burma's neutral status during the Cold War of the 1950s. It included excerpts from a lecture at Rangoon University by Dr. Kyaw Thet, who had taught history at Yale University.

The packed audience for the TV lecture was filled with clean-cut Burmese students, all dressed as neatly as if they were going to church. Professor Thet explained that Burma had benefited greatly from some of the democratic ideas and values that the British believed in, although "the British probably didn't think they applied to us."

Much was expected of the daughter of the Bogyoke, so Suu Kyi had worked hard to become No. 1 in her class at MEHS. Richard Yukhin nominated her to be "head prefect," or president, of their class. But Suu Kyi did not get to serve. When her mother was named ambassador to India and Nepal in 1960, Suu Kyi suddenly had to change schools. Her older brother Aung San Oo was sent off to boarding school in England, while Khin Kyi took her teenaged daughter with her to India.

Khin Kyi had proved so capable as minister of Social Welfare that in 1960 she was appointed ambassador to India with special responsibility for Nepal, becoming Burma's first woman ambassador. The young Delta village girl who could not gain admission to Rangoon University was now handling a diplomatic portfolio in one of the most important posts in Asia. By all accounts, she handled the assignment with dignity and skill.

Suu Kyi would later tell the *New York Times*, "My mother was head of the household, and a capable one, and so without going out of her way to do that, she showed me that a woman can be as capable and as efficient as any man. But she did not spell it out for me. She was not of the generation that talked of women's rights. My mother, for instance, was ambassador to India, but she did not think of it as something she had achieved as a woman."

Though the ambassadorial appointment was a high honor for her mother, it meant that Suu Kyi had to leave her MEHS school friends just as she was being accepted as a leader. She would miss all the proms and social events that other students got to enjoy.

Transplanted to New Delhi, Suu Kyi studied at what was considered the best girls' school, the Convent of Jesus and Mary, which was tucked behind the Sacred Heart Cathedral in central Delhi. When she arrived, Suu Kyi was just a girl of 15, still wearing long, thick braids of hair with bangs. She found herself a person apart—a Buddhist in a predominantly Hindu culture attending a Catholic day school where all the students recited the school motto, *Semper Jesu et Maria Laudentur* ("Praised be forever Jesus and Mary"). She did not join many school clubs, but made close friends. One of them, Malavika Karlelar, would later recall those convent school years when they were ingénues, sheltered from the real world.

Karlelar wrote: "Suu's mother, the gracious Daw Khin Kyi, Burma's ambassador to India at the time, would brook no indiscipline. Sloppiness or slouching was out. For habitual loungers to whom divans with bolsters signified ultimate bliss, Suu's upright posture was a constant reminder of how young ladies should conduct themselves."

The convent had a strict regimen that included well-starched divided skirts—all the better to protect their modesty—that could be no more than one inch above the knee. Learning was mostly by rote, so they were exhilarated when they graduated to Lady Shri Ram College and discovered—ideas. They were swept away by the intellectual challenge of Rousseau's concepts of childhood and Hobbes's *Leviathan*. "Notions of liberty and freedom via Locke and Hume made their way to our receptive minds—still reveling in having escaped from the shackles of a convent. It mattered little to us that an Indian women's college in the 1960s meant incarceration of another kind, though I do recall many arguments with the authorities over why the college gates had to be so securely locked!" Karlelar remembered.

Because there were no boys in sight, the young women had to play all the male roles in college plays. When Suu Kyi wrote a witty spoof of *Antony and Cleopatra*, she had to play Mark Antony in the school production, wearing someone's mother's sari.

Suu Kyi became president of the Debate Club and dove into the political-science discussions. Karlelar speculated that their "Nocturnal coffee sessions on the implications of Machiavelli's *Il Principe*, lodged safely in her sprightly mind," may have come in handy in the years ahead when Suu Kyi was forced to understand the ways of despots.

In India, Suu Kyi was often on her own while her mother worked at the embassy, although she was surrounded by retainers at their elegant new home. Prime Minister Nehru had made sure that the widow of his friend Aung San had proper accommodations. The residence provided for Khin Kyi at 24 Akbar Road was a large house with extensive grounds and a magnificent garden. Such elegant surroundings normally would have been reserved for only the most senior Indian officials, but the home was assigned to Daw Khin Kyi as a special mark of esteem. It was by far the most luxurious home that Suu Kyi would ever live in.

Young Suu adapted to her new surroundings by pouring herself into her studies. She wrote papers for school with the title "What is Democracy?" and began delving into the life and works of Mohandas Gandhi. She was fascinated by how the Indian leader used passive resistance strategies of satyagraha to achieve his goals. She already was prejudiced against violence by her father's murder, and Gandhi's nonviolent approach reinforced her feelings. Explaining her nonviolent position to the *New York Times* in 1989, she said, "My father died because there were people who preferred guns to solve political problems."

She sent many letters to her friend Jenny Lim back in Rangoon, filled with typical teenaged insecurity and longing. What were their friends doing? What was she missing at their school? Being a stranger in a new land, Suu did what many foreigners do when displaced: she clung more fiercely to her national identity. She continued to wear simple Burmese clothes and sometimes came to class with her cheeks covered with the beige *thanaka* cream that young women in Burma traditionally wear on their faces as sunscreen and decoration. Surrounded by foreign faiths, she began learning more about her own Buddhist faith. A monk that the family had known in Rangoon, U Rewata Dhamma, became one of Suu Kyi's Buddhist mentors.

Just as she constantly was made aware of her father's courage, Suu Kyi often heard stories about her mother's courage as a nurse during the war, when her quick wits and persuasive skills were called into play. It was said that when Rangoon was subjected to frequent air raids in the middle of the night, her mother was unruffled. "My mother impressed and annoyed her fellow nurses with her insouciance in the face of danger," Suu Kyi wrote. "She would insist on dressing neatly before going down to the bomb shelter and when friends in a tearing hurry to get to safety scolded her for what they deemed to be mad behavior, she would retort lightly: 'If I am going to die, I might as well die looking beautiful.'"

She told the BBC in a 2012 documentary that because she grew up with such a self-reliant mother, she took it for granted that women could do anything. "Although I always knew about my father and I was very proud of him and looked up to him, not just as my father but the great hero of our country, actually it was my mother who was the head of the household and she, as far as I could see, she could do anything that men could do. I don't think she ever expected me to go into politics. I think she just wanted me to be a well-educated person who was worthy of my father."

Suu Kyi often attended the diplomatic parties that went with her mother's job and was described by visitors as alert, polite, serious, and proper. Suu's mother arranged for her daughter to learn the refinements that a young lady needed in important circles. This was the era when young women were taught how to enter a room, how to sit properly at the dinner table, how to pour tea. Suu was tutored in the fine art of Japanese flower arranging and took riding lessons at the exercise grounds of the presidential bodyguard.

At the riding school, she met Prime Minister Nehru's grandsons, Rajiv and Sanjay. Like her, they were children of privilege, learning how to lead. And like her, they would encounter tragedy early. The boy's mother, Indira Nehru Gandhi, would become Prime Minister of India and was assassinated by her own bodyguards in 1984. The younger son, Sanjay, was considered the more politically ambitious, but was killed in an airplane crash in 1980. The more free-spirited son, Rajiv, became an airline pilot. Yet he answered the call to serve in 1984 and proved a progressive, far-sighted prime minister, only to be assassinated by Tamil rebels in 1991. Like Suu Kyi, Rajiv Gandhi had married a foreigner, a striking Italian woman named Sonia. After his death, Sonia Gandhi became president of the ruling party, the Indian National Congress, and a powerful political broker in the world's second-largest state by population.

Suu Kyi had heard stories about the head of the political dynasty, Jawaharlal Nehru, since she was a toddler. He was known in her family as a loyal friend named "Panditji." But she met him in person for the first time as a girl of 16 at the railway station in New Delhi. She was impressed with the confident, aristocratic way the prime minister exercised his power. He seemed not to care what others thought about him and ignored them. In the years ahead, she would come to admire Nehru's writing from prison about perseverance and self-reliance as much as Gandhi's concept of nonviolence. Both men shaped her world view.

Every day in India turned out to be a political tutorial in one way or another, as Suu Kyi was a watchful participant in many diplomatic functions. But what Suu Kyi enjoyed most was her piano lessons. She took up playing the piano with great enthusiasm and practiced for hours to improve. Reading about Suu's private lessons in piano and ballet, her young friend Jenny Lim back in Rangoon could only marvel that her shy young friend had moved into a far different realm.

—~—

When British writer Harriet O'Brien came to visit her old friend Khin Kyi in New Delhi, she found that young Aung San Suu Kyi was developing a presence all her own. She was more confident and more willing to plunge into the conversation about politics. "She was 17 or 18 and she was already a commanding person . . . her mother was a bit more relaxed than Suu. You could have a good chuckle with her. Suu was more correct."

When Suu Kyi graduated from Lady Shri Ram College with a degree in politics in 1964, the question for the family became: What should she do next? Return to Rangoon for a career or a husband? Or perhaps pursue another degree at her father's alma mater, the University of Rangoon? Returning to school in Burma was problematic. Ne Win had dynamited the Student Union building at the University of Rangoon a few years before in an attempt to stifle student unrest; the university had been closed for several months. The campus remained in Ne Win's crosshairs.

Suu Kyi's older brother Aung San Oo, who had been studying electrical engineering at Imperial College at the University of London, strongly encouraged Suu Kyi to broaden her education by studying at one of the vaunted universities in England. His suggestion would change the trajectory of her life.

Two of her mother's closest friends cinched the decision. While she was serving as ambassador in Delhi, her mother had become friends with Sir Paul Gore-Booth, Britain's high commissioner in India, and his wife, Patricia Gore-Booth. When Suu Kyi was accepted for study at St. Hugh's College, one of the five women's colleges in Oxford, the Gore-Booths offered their house in Chelsea as a home away from home. Their generous gesture gave Khin Kyi the reassurance she needed to let her daughter go.

—∿—

The decision to send her children overseas to school later came back to haunt Khin Kyi. Unlike Prime Minister U Nu, General Ne Win did not have protective feelings toward Aung San's family. His administration spread the story that Khin Kyi had abused funds while ambassador. Anyone who knew Khin Kyi's rectitude knew it was not in her character, but it was damaging nonetheless. Ne Win alleged that Khin Kyi had improperly used some of her government funds to pay for her children's education. Government stipends were allowed for diplomatic personnel to send their children to college, but only to colleges in Burma or the country where they were posted, Ne Win contended. He tried to use the dispute to diminish the standing of the Bogyoke's widow. It was the last straw for Khin Kyi, who stepped down as ambassador rather than continue representing the repressive, erratic Ne Win government and seeing her reputation slandered.

Despite that discord, Khin Kyi's achievements were rewarded with honors from the United States, Yugoslavia, and Thailand. Even the Rangoon military government awarded her the country's prestigious Maha Thiri Thudhamma prize, given for service to Burmese social and religious life.

Khin Kyi did not return to public life and was content to live away from the spotlight for the first time in many years. The poet Tin Moe, who often visited her lakeside home in Rangoon, said Khin Kyi would chat about what was going on in Burma while gardening or sitting in the kitchen. She was very well informed and knew a lot about politics, he observed, although she did not tend to parade her knowledge in public. Late in life, she turned down a biography proposal by one of Burma's most popular writers. She preferred to stay in the background and let her martyred husband receive the accolades.

Harriet O'Brien, who was the daughter of a British diplomat posted to Burma, remembers going with her father to visit Khin Kyi. She listened in as they shared the latest gossip about local political intrigues, which Khin Kyi recounted with great wit. The visits followed a pattern: They would be taken on a trip around her garden to admire the orchids and roses. Touring the small garden also provided a means of talking more openly. Indoors, there was always the danger of being overheard by the wrong people. "More delicate conversations would also take place outside as a matter of course," O'Brien said.

After the garden visit, they would gather in the sitting room or dining room, where they would be offered something to eat, perhaps sticky rice with coconut milk and jaggary (palm sugar). When it was time to go, a fond Burmese "kiss" would be exchanged, not a peck on the check but a gentle cheek-to-cheek rub on each side of the face.

On one occasion, Khin Kyi told the O'Briens that she had been diagnosed with diabetes. As nurse, she faced the diagnosis pragmatically: "God is good. In this country it is difficult to get sugar, and now the doctors tell me I should not take it anyway."

Khin Kyi had insisted her children be brought up with her husband's Buddhist traditions and followed Buddhist tenets faithfully herself all her life, but when she was ailing, she also found comfort in Christian traditions that she had learned as a girl along with Buddhism. When her diabetes weakened her to the point she could no longer go out, local ministers who were friends came to her home at 54 University Avenue. Baptist minister Arthur Ko Lay, the long-time pastor of the historic Judson Baptist Church in downtown Rangoon, was a frequent visitor, along with the Methodist bishop, Zothan Mawia. Bishop Mawia told me, "She was very fond of singing hymns, so we used to sing hymns together."

Arthur Ko Lay remembered that one of Khin Kyi's favorite hymns was "I Would Be True." The minister told me that the lyrics to the 1906 hymn in particular struck a chord with both Khin Kyi and her daughter because of the emphasis on duty and service:

> I would be true, for there are those who trust me;
> I would be pure, for there are those who care;
> I would be strong, for there is much to suffer;
> I would be brave, for there is much to dare;
> I would be brave, for there is much to dare.
>
> I would be friend of all—the foe, the friendless;
> I would be giving, and forget the gift;
> I would be humble, for I know my weakness;
> I would look up, and laugh, and love and lift.
> I would look up, and laugh, and love and lift.

"Khin Kyi was very intelligent," Ko Lay recalled. "Even though she was isolated, she got all her information somehow. When we had discussions, she would give us information." As her health grew worse, she would call Ko Lay or Bishop Mawia to come pray with her. Ko Lay rode on his bicycle to her house, always stopping to pick up a coconut or chocolate. Khin Kyi liked to have candy on hand to give to the children of friends who sometimes came to visit her. If there were five children, he remembered, she would give out five pieces of chocolate, one piece for each. "She was very disciplined," Ko Lay remembered, "a woman of discipline and integrity."

After Khin Kyi had a series of strokes, she was bedridden and had difficulty speaking. Special friends—poets, diplomats, monks, ministers—continued to come sit with her. Their presence comforted her. Her daughter was far away in England but would be coming home when she was most needed.

CHAPTER EIGHT

"SUU"

> "All my memories of her at Oxford have certain recurring elements: cleanliness, determination, curiosity, a fierce purity. . . . Many, like me, must first have been drawn to Suu by her beauty. Our perdurable love and admiration are for her pilgrim soul—for her courage, determination and abiding moral strength. . . ."
>
> —Ann Pasternak Slater

When Aung San Suu Kyi arrived in England, it was the first time in her life that she had not been under her mother's wing. Had she stayed in Burma, she would have gotten a much different education. The military regime shunted students to remote campuses where they couldn't make trouble; many of the leading intellectuals were arrested or left the country for freer shores; the university's curriculum was severely censored and limited. She also would have met a different husband.

As it was, Aung San Suu Kyi entered St. Hugh's College in Oxford in 1964. The college was young by Oxford standards. It was founded in 1886 by Elizabeth Wordsworth, the great-niece of the poet, to provide a quality education for women, especially women of limited means. The campus was a square of stately brick buildings with a spacious green quad at the center, the very picture of idyllic college life. Suu Kyi would later say that while she was a student there, she was "carefree, happy, nice."

Suu Kyi was accepted into a degree program of Philosophy, Politics, and Economics, known as PPE on campus. PPE was what her advisers thought she should take; she would have preferred literature because of her great love of reading, or even forestry, a side interest of hers, perhaps inspired by her country's bountiful forests.

While Suu Kyi often spent weekends and holidays at the Gore-Booths' home in England, she spent most summers with her mother in India or Burma, so she was well aware that political conditions in her home country were deteriorating.

Just as a new world was opening for Suu overseas, Ne Win was forcing Burma into a closed isolation. Opposition parties and independent newspapers were banned. In contrast to the students struggling with repression in Burma, college students in England were stretching their freedoms. They were protesting the American war in Vietnam, listening to the beat of the Beatles and Rolling Stones on pirate radio stations, growing their hair long, experimenting with drugs and sex. Suu Kyi kept her distance from the counterculture trends. She shuttled back and forth between two worlds in transition, Burma and England, and was a person apart in both of them.

She definitely stood out on the St. Hugh's campus. She was slender and pretty and cut a distinctive figure in her wraparound longyi sarong. In contrast, British young girls were sporting the "mod" style of miniskirts. "By the popular morality of the time, Suu was a pure Oriental traditionalist. Even the way she held herself was straitlaced," her friend Ann Slater has said. Suu Kyi made some concessions to campus culture—she eventually swapped her long braids for a ponytail and her longyi for a pair of white jeans. In lighter moments many years later, she admitted to being quite the catch during her student days. "I turned a few heads," she said.

"With her jet-black hair pulled back into some sort of ponytail with a flower behind her ear, she was like something out of a fairy tale, an Oriental princess. She moved like a princess, she was very conscience of her graces," recalled Suzanne Hoelgaard, an Aris family friend and Suu Kyi colleague.

Even then, there were signs of the indomitable will beneath the feminine exterior. "She has a very sweet and very loving and very sensitive and kind of all-embacing side," Hoelgaard recalled in a BBC documentary, "but she also has a very, very iron, hard, determined—you might almost call it a ruthless side—to her character that she will pursue her goal, whatever it is, to the end."

Suu Kyi made several close British friends during those college years, but many of her friends were from Ghana, India, Thailand, Sri Lanka, from all over the world. She was well aware that she was a foreigner in Britain and as an "outsider" she had an affinity with other foreigners.

Although she joined the Oxford debating society, Suu Kyi did not get involved in campus politics and repeatedly resisted attempts to get her involved in Burmese issues. She did not want to stir up headlines back home—either by giving the impression of supporting Ne Win's government or opposing it from the safety of Oxford. When General Ne Win came to England on a state visit, he invited her to meet him for lunch. She declined. She did not want to socialize with the man who was sabotaging her father's work for a democratic, pluralistic Burma. He would remember the snub.

Suu Kyi was known among her classmates for her naïve rectitude. She had lived a cloistered existence at church schools and was an innocent abroad. Though many students spent as much time in the pubs at Oxford as they did in the hallowed libraries, the only time Suu Kyi tried drinking at St. Hugh's was as an experiment to see what alcohol tasted like. Her senior year, she purchased a miniature bottle of wine and took it back to her dormitory to drink surreptitiously in the bathroom. She didn't care for it, and that was that. Many of her classmates often sneaked back to the dorm over the garden wall after a night of partying in a practice called "climbing in," but Suu never had done so. Toward the end of her undergraduate experience, she persuaded a friend to boost her up and over the wall after a dinner date even though the night was still young and there was no need to sneak in over the wall. She was determined to experience "climbing in." She did not take the same experimental approach to "sleeping around."

Though sex was all the talk among the other coeds, she demurred. Her college friend Ann Pasternak tells the anecdote that one of their amazed dorm mates once pressed Suu, "Don't you want to sleep with someone?" No, Suu Kyi replied, standing her ground, she would just "go to bed hugging my pillow" until she was married. While she had college crushes and close friendships, they did not turn into enduring romantic relationships.

She would soon meet the man she would marry, although she didn't realize it at first. Anthony Aris, a young friend of Suu Kyi's surrogate parents, the Gore-Booths, happened to meet Suu at their Chelsea home. He promptly told his twin brother Michael, who was studying Tibetan at the University of Durham, "Oh, you must come see this remarkable Burmese woman at St. Hugh's!"

Michael Aris came to see the girl from Burma for himself. "He came to see me at Oxford on the pretext that he had come to see some Tibetan Lamas, perhaps killing two birds with one stone. Perhaps he had come to see the Lamas, but came to see me as well," she said later. He was smitten at once.

However, Suu Kyi had no intention of getting serious about a British suitor. She made it clear that she intended to marry a Burmese man some day. Marriage to a foreigner would have been a betrayal of her Burmese heritage. For the daughter of the Bogyoke, leader of the revolt against the British, in particular it was unthinkable to marry a British citizen. The Burmese harbored deep resentments that British soldiers who had taken Burmese women as "temporary" wives often deserted them and their offspring when their tours of duty ended. Even when legal marriages did take place, the Anglo husbands often would ship out and leave behind a small sum of money for the upkeep of the children. Sometimes the Anglo-Burmese children were removed from their Burmese mothers and placed in convent schools run by Europeans, where their Burmese heritage was often undermined. The issue of mixed marriage was so sensitive that it had helped propel the independence movement against the British. Aware of the taboo, Suu Kyi kept up a correspondence with Michael, but also kept her distance.

She received her Bachelor of Arts degree in Philosophy, Politics, and Economics from St. Hugh's in 1967, but without distinction. Suu Kyi received only a third-class rating on her final exams. Her poor academic performance surprised many of her friends and colleagues. They had seen her intellectual agility for themselves. They surmised her mind was elsewhere, probably on the literature she loved. They were partly right. She had enjoyed reading the novels of Jane Austen much more than her economics textbooks. She also had not been happy in her PPE classes, which struck her as too theoretical and impractical to help Burma with its problems. She tried twice to change her major, first to forestry and then to English Literature, but was turned down because of Oxford's strict rules against such changes. Suu Kyi stayed the course, but her heart and her head were not in PPE. She would later recall those carefree college days as the summer of her life, "When I went on the Cherwell with friends in a punt, or sat reading on the lawn at St. Hugh's, or in the library—not looking at a book, but out of the windows."

After receiving her degree, she tried teaching for a year at an English preparatory school, where she taught high school students, but it wasn't a fit. And she worked as a research assistant for Asian historian Hugh Tinker, but that wasn't quite a fit either. She sensed her true vocation was elsewhere.

—∾—

Thanks to another family connection, an invitation came to pursue a career in America. In 1969, Suu Kyi moved to New York City. She shared a small apartment at 49th Street and First Avenue that overlooked the East River with Daw Than E, a long-time family friend. Suu Kyi liked to call the older woman her "emergency aunt" and "Auntie Dora," which was the Christian name Than E had been given at Baptist missionary school in Burma. Considered quite a beauty in her youth, Daw Than E had gained fame as a popular singer and recording artist before the war. When the Japanese invaded Burma, she fled to India and went to work for All Radio India in New Delhi and then the radio service for the U.S. Office of War Information in San Francisco. She spoke English fluently because she had studied in England as well as the University of Rangoon. In fact, Than E had been living in England in 1947 when General Aung San traveled to London to meet with Clement Atlee. He remembered listening to her records while he and Khin Kyi were dating and invited her to dine with the Burmese delegation several times at their suite at the Dorchester Hotel. The group spent the evenings recalling simple pleasures of Burmese life and sharing the hope of better days to come.

When Suu Kyi arrived in New York, Daw Than E had just returned from four years in Algeria, where she had volunteered to help an organization that constructed housing for people displaced by the struggle against French rule. Suu Kyi had joined her in Algiers during her first summer vacation from Oxford in 1965. She lived and worked with volunteers on a reconstruction project because she wanted to be with ordinary Algerians rather than government officials or elites. She saw firsthand the hardships that poor people had suffered during the years of French occupation and the harsh regimes that followed independence. In many ways, the situation in Algeria echoed the festering problems in her home country. The authoritarian ruler Ben Bella was supplanted by his defense minister, Hoari Boumedienne, while Suu Kyi was in Algeria. Boumedienne promised a more moderate regime. While he did move the country away from Ben Bella's tilt toward Communism, Boumedienne used the military to keep the country firmly in his grip. As in Burma, the Algerian media was tightly restricted. The one legal party was relegated to a toothless role. Suu Kyi's natural sympathies went to the long-suffering people of Algeria. They had little access to schooling and the literacy rate was less than 10 percent. She saw up close how difficult it was to bring power to the powerless without education. She saw how difficult it was to dislodge a military regime.

Once she had reconnected with Daw Than E in New York, Suu Kyi planned to do postgraduate studies at New York University. But after several weeks of difficulty navigating across Manhattan, her advising professor suggested it might be too difficult to continue commuting by bus every day. At Daw Than E's suggestion, Suu Kyi applied for a job at the U.N. where her "emergency aunt" worked. The timing was propitious—it just so happened that U Thant of Burma was serving as the Secretary General at the time. He, too, had known and admired Suu Kyi's father. Suu Kyi was given a job as assistant secretary, Advisory Committee on Administrative and Budgetary Questions. The staff job, though largely clerical, gave her the opportunity to observe the inner workings of key U.N. agencies such as the U.N. Development Program and the World Health Organization. To stay in touch with the needs of everyday people outside of the rarefied workings of the U.N., Suu Kyi volunteered at Bellevue Hospital, which was within walking distance of the U.N. and Than E's apartment. Just as she once had read scripture to her grandfather, Suu Kyi patiently spent hours during her weekends off reading to destitute patients with mental or alcohol problems and comforting them.

Though there was a significant age difference between them, Suu Kyi and Daw Than E got along well. Together, they were able to stay close to their Burmese culture, speaking their native tongue and cooking their Burmese food. Their friends called their flat "a Burmese home in Manhattan." U Thant, who had become an unofficial "uncle" to Suu Kyi, often invited her to Sunday-afternoon socials at his home in the upscale Riverdale area of the Bronx. She and Daw Than E also were invited to many of the diplomatic events that were part of the U.N. cocktails-and-canapés circuit. At such soirées, they would occasionally find themselves in the company of representatives from General Ne Win's military government. They had to be careful to avoid awkward encounters. Since Suu Kyi's mother had resigned her ambassadorship, the general's emissaries considered her daughter's loyalty suspect. They took note when Suu Kyi refused to meet with Ne Win in England. And when Suu Kyi went to work at the U.N., they worried that she might be maneuvering to challenge them. Their mistrust was deepened by the fact she was living with Daw Than E, who had once refused a request from Ne Win to sing at a dinner he hosted. When the general had suggested she "sing for her supper," she shot back, "I'll sing for my supper after I've had it." She finished her dinner and, pointedly, did not sing.

When Daw Than E and Suu Kyi were invited to the home of Ne Win's diplomatic envoy, U Soe Tin, they were understandably surprised and wary. Their suspicions increased when they arrived to find several military visitors from Rangoon in attendance. Something was going on. A large number of Burmese ambassadors from around the world, who were in town for the U.N. General Assembly, were also gathered there. Suu Kyi was steered toward an empty chair at one end of the room, and Daw Than E was seated pointedly in a chair some distance from her. After brief pleasantries, a colonel named Lwin took over the conversation and began interrogating Suu Kyi. *Why* had she not surrendered her diplomatic passport when her mother resigned? Did she know it was *unlawful* to keep the diplomatic passport? *Why* was she working as a staff member at the U.N. rather than with the *Burmese* delegation? The subtext was clear: Ne Win had orchestrated the interrogation session to find out if the Bogyoke's daughter was plotting against him.

Suu Kyi remained unflappable. She had applied for a new, regular passport in London and had never heard back from the embassy, she explained. She could not very well surrender her old passport until she received a new one, could she? And as for her job, she had a right to earn a living. How could Colonel Lwin object to that? As it happened, the Burmese ambassador to Great Britain was in the room; when asked if Suu Kyi had indeed applied for a new passport, he had to admit that she had applied, but he had delayed giving the passport to her because he was still awaiting instructions from Rangoon about whether to grant approval. The embarrassed Colonel Lwin found himself caught in the trap he had intended for Suu Kyi. His accusations were not discussed further. The encounter was uncomfortable, but Suu Kyi proved she could hold her own under pressure.

Ne Win need not have worried. Just as she had eschewed Burmese politics while she was a student in England, Suu Kyi generally avoided Burmese issues while she was at the United Nations. She spent most of her time simply absorbing the heady experience of living in Manhattan in the late 1960s, which turned out to be a tumultuous period in American history. Social turmoil was exploding all around her. Bobby Kennedy and Martin Luther King Jr. had been assassinated and their assailants, Sirhan Sirhan and James Earl Ray, were brought to trial the year Suu Kyi arrived in the U.S. Race riots had rocked major cities, and racial tension was simmering on the streets of New York while she lived there. Students were in open rebellion on the campus of Columbia University. Protesters against the Vietnam War were shot at Kent State. John Lennon was singing "Give Peace a Chance" and Country Joe and the Fish were asking "One, two, three, what are we fighting for?" Woodstock was staged in upstate New York, with more rock stars and marijuana joints than had ever been assembled in one place before.

As she often was in her life, the very proper Suu Kyi was a person apart from the anti-establishment turmoil around her, but she was a keen student and absorbed important lessons. "The young people were for love and not for war," Suu Kyi said of that period. "There was a feeling of tremendous vigor. I had been moved by Martin Luther King's 'I Have a Dream' speech and how he tried to better the lot of the black people without fostering feelings of hate. It's hate that is the problem, not violence. Violence is simply the symptom of hate." Suu Kyi may have led a sheltered life under Khin Kyi's wing, but now she was seeing on the streets how social issues can erupt into violence.

It was a heady time. New York seemed the center of the world. Suu Kyi was young and single and thrilled to be in the big city. She especially enjoyed going to concerts at Lincoln Center. A friend from Oxford, Robin Christopher, had been posted to the U.N. with the British Foreign Service. They enjoyed entertaining at small dinner parties with junior foreign service officers. Once the young diplomats even serenaded "Uncle" U Thant during a rollicking night of Christmas caroling around the city. The image of Suu Kyi singing "Good King Wenceslas" on a cross-town bus while dressed in her best Burmese attire is a glimpse of her carefree side. Eager to learn all she could about America, she explored the East Coast by bus and train, traveling up to Boston and down to Washington, D.C. She even used her vacation time to board a Greyhound bus and see America for herself. She rode by bus all the way from New York to California.

Suu Kyi had stayed in touch with her old MEHS friend Jenny Lim over the years and discovered she was living nearby in New Jersey. On a day off, she took the train to New Jersey to visit Jenny, who was working as a medical technician and would later become a dentist. Jenny Lim proudly showed off the equipment in the laboratory where she worked and remembers that Suu Kyi wistfully remarked how much she enjoyed biology and wished she had been able to study forestry and the environment as she had once intended. They had lunch and talked about their experiences in America and friends back home. According to Jenny Lim, there was no hint at the time that Suu Kyi was seriously considering marriage to her suitor Michael Aris. Than E also would say later that Michael Aris was enamored while Suu Kyi was in New York and the two were keeping up a correspondence, but Suu Kyi had "no ideas about being taken by anybody at that time."

However, her relationship with Michael continued long-distance. His courtship had become more serious by mail. He had not been able to study in Tibet, as he had hoped, because of the Chinese occupation of the Himalayan country, so he was in neighboring Bhutan, "little Tibet." He had taken a job as tutor to the royal family in Bhutan and was conducting research for his Ph.D. in Tibetan literature. Michael was determined to marry Suu Kyi and have her join him in Bhutan. He wrote, he called. The two grew closer, but she still had ambitions of an academic career herself and wasn't quite ready to leave the U.S. She was making inquiries about graduate school at Northern Illinois University and the Fletcher School of Diplomacy at Tufts when Michael stopped by New York in 1970 on his way home to England for a vacation. He wanted to make his case in person. She agreed to visit him in Bhutan. In 1971, she arranged a trip to visit her mother in Burma, traveled on to India to see friends, and then to Bhutan to be with Michael. The visit to the tiny Himalayan kingdom, with its emphasis on loving kindness, drew her closer to her Buddhist faith and Michael, who had become devoted to the tenets of Buddhism through his studies. She had been away from her country for a long time and had not actively engaged in her Buddhist faith in England or New York, other than to perform acts of compassion. Bhutan called her back to the charity, forbearance, and calm of Buddhism. She and Michael studied together at the feet of a Buddhist master who had been one of the Fourteenth Dalai Lama's teachers. Though it was cold and snowy, Michael suggested that they visit Taktsang, "the lair of the pregnant tigress," an ancient complex of temples high in the mountains. Taktsang is to Bhutan what the Taj Mahal is to India, one of the country's oldest and most beautiful sites. Built in 1692, the monastery perches on a sheer mountain cliff like a bird nest high on a skyscraper ledge. Legend has it that in the 8th century, the Guru Padmasambhava, who introduced Buddhism to most of Bhutan, flew on the back of a tigress to subdue a powerful deity at the site, giving it the name Taktsang, meaning "Tiger's Nest." On many days, clouds shroud the monastery, enhancing its mythic aura of remoteness. Pilgrims have to climb an almost vertical stairway to reach the main buildings, 3,000 feet above the Paro Valley. But the 90-minute hike straight up has its rewards: a view like no other. There, at the top of the world, Michael Aris proposed to Aung San Suu Kyi. She said yes. They decided to marry later that year in England during the Christmas holidays, when he could travel home from his job.

"He didn't catch me that easily, it took quite some time," she acknowledged later. The decision was difficult for Suu Kyi, although she cared deeply for Michael. She was well aware of the prejudice against marrying foreigners. She worried that the marriage would make it seem she was turning her back on her country. During the eight months that followed their engagement, she wrote him 187 letters, pouring out her heart and her concerns. She worried, *"Sometimes I am beset by fears that circumstances and national considerations might tear us apart just when we are so happy in each other that separation would be torment. And yet such fears are so futile and inconsequential if we love and cherish each other as much as we can while we can. I am sure love and compassion will triumph in the end."* She warned him even more explicitly in another letter that if they married, she might have to return to Burma. *"I only ask one thing,"* she wrote him, *"That should my people need me, you would help me to do my duty by them."* In yet another letter, she asked *"Would you mind very much should such a situation arise? How probable it is, I do not know, but the possibility is there."* He promised to support her if that day arrived—and when it did two decades later, he kept his word.

They were married in a Buddhist ceremony at the Chelsea home of the Gore-Booths on New Year's Day 1972. Their college friend Robin Christopher was there to help wind a symbolic thread around the couple in keeping with the Buddhist tradition. But there were notable absences. The Burmese ambassador to Britain, Chit Myaing, did not attend. He later explained, "The Burmese people would not like the daughter of Aung San marrying a foreigner. I knew that if I attended the wedding, I would be fired that day." Suu Kyi's brother Aung San Oo also did not attend. More painful was the fact that her mother Daw Khin Kyi did not come to see her daughter married. Her mother was said to be deeply disappointed that Suu Kyi had not married a Burmese. The fact that Michael was an Englishman was an added affront to the woman whose husband had led the fight against British rule and who had seen many Burmese women abandoned by their British husbands. Over time, Khin Kyi would come to appreciate her new son-in-law and welcome him warmly to her home in Rangoon and understand that their relationship was as deep and loving as hers was with Bogyoke. But on the day of her wedding, Suu Kyi was without family support. Photos of that day show her looking more like a wide-eyed teenager with her thick bangs than a 26-year-old woman of the world. Swathed in frothy white lace, she looks directly into the camera and smiles with composure. She had just married the man she had grown to love—and jeopardized her relationship with her mother and her country in the process.

"She had a feeling of mission even then," said Martin Moorland, a former ambassador to Burma. "But in spite of that mission, she decided to marry someone she loved."

Michael Vaillancourt Aris had a unique pedigree that made him a perfect bridge between Suu Kyi's Asian heritage and her adopted British home.

He had inherited an attraction for faraway places: His great grandfather had been an explorer in the Pacific Islands. His father John, a British Council administrator, was posted in Havana when Michael and his twin brother Anthony were born. His mother, Josette Vaillancourt, was the daughter of a French-Canadian diplomat and had studied painting in Montreal.

And he understood the importance of a spiritual life. Michael had attended a Benedictine school as a boy that emphasized the metaphysical. He became fascinated with Asia after his father brought him a prayer wheel from India. With characteristic intensity, he learned the translations of the Tibetan letters on the prayer wheel, then began a quest to learn more about Tibet and its next-door neighbor, Bhutan. Having devoted himself to Asian studies, Michael understood Buddhism and Burma. It was a big plus on his side, as he courted Suu Kyi, that he respected her heritage and traditions.

Shortly after their wedding, the newlyweds returned to live in Thimphu in Bhutan. In addition to serving as the royal tutor, Michael was the head of the kingdom's translation department and its official history researcher.

Because of her prior experience at the United Nations, Suu Kyi was hired by the foreign minister of Bhutan to advise him on matters related to the U.N. Michael's boyhood dreams of living in a foreign kingdom with a beautiful princess had come true.

In reality, living conditions for the honeymooners were primitive. Relating to the politics of the royal court as outsiders was not always easy. Some of the archaic protocols rankled Suu Kyi. She was not only expected to kowtow to the king, kneeling and bowing so low that her head touched the ground, she was expected to prostrate herself before all the princesses. And there were quite a few princesses. For entertainment, there was little for the young couple to do but hike in the rugged mountains. Their favorite companion was a shaggy Himalayan terrier they affectionately called "Puppy."

After a little less than a year in Bhutan, Suu Kyi discovered she was pregnant. The young couple began transitioning back to England so they could start their family there and Michael could finish his book with the research he had done during his six years in Bhutan. Their first son, Alexander Aris, was born in 1973 in London and given the additional Burmese name of Myint San Aung. When Michael was given a special assignment shortly thereafter to lead a project in Nepal, Suu brought along young Alexander. They stopped in Burma on the way to introduce her mother to Suu's new husband and son. Whatever reservations Daw Khin Kyi had harbored about the marriage melted. Photos from the visit show her beaming with pride as she cradled her first grandson.

After less than a year in Nepal, Suu Kyi and Michael returned to England, where he became a research fellow at St. John's College at Oxford. Another son, Kim Aris, named after the hero of the Kipling tale, was born in 1977 in Oxford and was given the Burmese name of Htein Lin, which had also been her father's birth name.

Suu Kyi became a busy stay-at-home mom. They were living in a faculty flat provided by St. John's College that had high ceilings and tall windows, but little space for a growing family. The kitchen was dark and cramped. There was only one bedroom, which presented a challenge when friends from Burma or Bhutan showed up to visit. The Arises accommodated them as best they could. Their small space and budget were often taxed. To help make ends meet, Suu Kyi worked in what was then called the "Oriental Department" of the Bodleian Library, the university's ancient and grand research library with its stately, soaring ceilings and centuries of books.

Suu's college friend Ann Pasternak Slater lived around the corner. She remembers seeing Suu Kyi pedaling on her bicycle from the library, loaded down with bags of the least expensive vegetables and fruit she could carry. When Slater would come to call, she often would find Suu Kyi preparing Japanese fish dishes or busy at her sewing machine, making curtains or clothing for the family. After young Kim was born, Suu's homemaking duties left little time to resume her own studies. The constant work of caring for a young family kept her lean and she lost some of the roundness in her face that had made her look younger than her years in the past. Her face began taking on the spare elegance that would one day become famous on posters and book covers.

According to her friends, Suu Kyi poured herself into becoming a devoted wife for her scholar husband. She not only ironed his shirts, she ironed his socks and shorts. She cooked all their meals and cleaned their house herself. Although Michael came from a somewhat genteel family, his own resources as a junior academic were limited. Suu Kyi went to classes to learn how to sew her own clothes.

While their Oxford life had its challenges, Suu developed a fond relationship with Michael's mother and step-mother, along with several older female mentors. Perhaps because her own mother was so far away, she became close to an older neighbor named Nessa McKenzie and a surrogate "aunt" named Mathane Fend, who had been a famous pre-war singer in Britain.

Family photos show the Arises on weekend family picnics sharing a picnic basket on the grass in the English countryside. Often it was Suu, dressed in cut-off jeans, who did the grilling over the portable barbecue grill.

The first thing that people who knew him say about Michael is that he was highly intelligent, reserved, and "professorial," usually wearing a tweed jacket, corduroy pants, and Hush Puppie-style shoes to his book-lined office. After working for four years on his Ph.D. thesis about Bhutan, he had gained recognition as a rising star in Himalayan studies. He received a series of research fellowships at Oxford. His path-breaking work in Bhutan had earned a place as an Oxford "don," a distinguished professor and scholar. Though Michael may not have been as charismatic as his wife, he was by all accounts an upright and likable man, what his friends described as "an Edwardian gentleman." He would prove a loving and dutiful husband under the formidable circumstances to come.

For her part, Suu reportedly was the consummate mother, supervising her sons' homework and organizing their birthday parties. She gained a reputation as a strict mother, making sure there was no cheating when the boys and neighborhood children engaged in games. This was her "governessy" side, which could turn some people away. But most who knew her during that period describe her unfailing cheerfulness and "serenity" as her most distinctive feature. What stands out in Pasternak's memory about Suu Kyi's Oxford days was her kindness to the oddball campus characters that others shunned. While others kept their distance from a crotchety old artist who lived in the Oxford community, Suu would invite her for meals. She visited the old woman regularly to make sure she was all right after the woman had become senile, knowing well that widows are often dependent on the kindness of others.

Eventually the Aris family moved from their cramped quarters to larger, more attractive accommodations in the Park Town area of North Oxford. The historic area was not as fashionable as it once had been, but it was a step up. The streets were wide and the 19th-century houses were adorned with wisteria. Finances remained tight as the boys began school. With the boys away at classes during the day, Suu began entertaining thoughts of resuming her own education. She was determined to show she could do better than her lackluster undergraduate performance. She re-applied to take a second undergraduate degree at St. Hugh's in English literature. School officials rejected her application. She was crestfallen. Her friends saw her frustration and intellectual restlessness. At times she would be witty and engaging, at other times she was distant, aloof.

"She was petite . . . formidable . . . fixed you with her eye and obviously had a strong set of principles by which she led her life. There is a quality about her like steel, but not grandstanding. She did not ever say, 'I am the daughter of Aung San, the founder of modern Burma,'" recalled Peter

Carey, a close friend and Southeast Asia historian at Oxford. Yet he could see that she was looking for a distinctive role. As he observed, "She hadn't yet found her true calling."

"In the 1980's, my image of Suu is very much of someone casting around for a role for herself, a position for herself," Peter Carey remembered. "She would ask, 'Is this my destiny, to be a housewife? To be the partner of an Oxford don?"

Her friend Ann Pasternak Slater also sensed that Suu Kyi wanted a higher level of achievement, both for herself and her husband. "I think that created a certain amount of anxiety in her," Pasternak Slater has written. "There was a restlessness in her life." She had been brought up to believe she had a special obligation in life, but so far her life was fairly ordinary.

Suu Kyi talked about someday establishing a new library in Rangoon, or setting up a scholarship program for young Burmese students to study overseas. Her country was never far from her mind, and she was well aware of her father's revered place in Burmese history. When a visiting professor joked at Oxford that her father was like Elvis Presley because it had been a "good career move" for him to die young, she heard about it and was incensed. She had inherited her father's temper. Over the years, many people had told her that her gestures, blunt speech, and bright eyes made her a "female replica" of the general. She became increasingly drawn to learning more about the father she had lost. She acquired a considerable library of books and papers in Burmese and English about him. Occasionally, she would meet former British colonials who had served in Burma at the end of the war. She would quiz them, did they know Gen. Aung San? What was he like? What did he look like? "One of them said, 'He did look a little like Yul Brynner,' with his Japanese military haircut, which she liked quite a lot," recalled Carey. "I think she always had this incredible sort of daughter's hero worship for her father, considering the father he was." She became determined to write a biography of her father and began learning Japanese so she could research his wartime experience in Japan.

However, Suu Kyi still needed to prove her academic bona fides. She decided to write a doctoral thesis on Burmese political history for London University and applied as a postgraduate student at the School of Oriental and African Studies (SOAS). She wanted to expand a sketch she had published in 1984 into a full-fledged biography of her father. But again, her application was rejected. One of the faculty reviewers who was instrumental in blocking her application was Professor Robert Taylor, a Burma specialist. He happened to be the same professor who had made the wisecrack comparing her father to Elvis Presley. According to British biographer Justin Wintle, Taylor did not think Suu Kyi had a sufficient understanding of political theory to become a college teacher, the usual goal for obtaining a Ph.D. Taylor later defended himself by saying that Suu Kyi simply did not meet the criteria for the Ph.D. program, which required obtaining a Master's degree first, something she did not want to do. However, he acknowledged that there was some animus between the two. When she published a paper in India about the incomplete nature of Burma's nationalism experience, he was highly critical as a discussant to her paper. Not long after that criticism, she found herself seated at a table with Taylor at a dinner party. She left the table and sat steaming in the corner, unwilling to make small talk with someone who had demeaned her abilities. Years later, she was asked to review a book written by Taylor that was considered friendly to the military regime. She could have delivered a withering critique by pointing out the atrocities being committed by the government, but she chose the stiletto rather than the ax. She wrote that while the book contained useful statistical data, Taylor did not understand Burmese politics or culture. To prove it, she pointed out that he had mangled many Burmese words and the errors could be found throughout the book. She had learned the game of academic condescension well.

With her husband's continued encouragement, Suu Kyi reapplied to SOAS, this time to research a Ph.D. on Burmese *literature* instead of political history. The change played to her strengths: she was well read in her country's classics and had spent many hours talking about Burmese literature with one of her mother's friends, U Tin Moe, who was a Professor of Burmese Literature at Rangoon University. This time, she was accepted—and received high reviews for her written and oral examinations. Even better, she discovered that SOAS had an exchange program with the Center for Southeast Asian Studies at Kyoto University in Japan, which meant she could now go research her father's experiences in Japan. She had just turned 40 and was on her way to scoring the academic achievement that had eluded her before.

Suu Kyi wangled a research grant to go to Kyoto and decided to take her 8-year-old son Kim with her. Alexander was old enough for boarding school, but young Kim was not, so she took him rather than be separated for the eight months. It was not an easy adjustment for either one. Suu Kyi struggled to learn Japanese by taping words to the mirror each day. Kim suffered in school because he did not understand what was being said in his classes. She chafed at the restrictive Japanese society. Still, she made some friends and she and Kim bicycled on the campus together. In order to learn more about her father's leadership, she interviewed old war comrades in Japan who had met him and sifted through historical records that were not available outside Japan.

Professor David Steinberg, Director of Asian Studies at Georgetown University, recalls meeting Suu Kyi for the first time by accident while she was studying in Kyoto in 1986. "We had quite a respectable exchange, walked up the river afterwards, and had a long talk," he remembers. He came away thinking that she was bright and gracious, like many of the foreign graduate students he worked with, but nothing more. Then they met again in 1989, after she had begun her campaign for democracy in Burma. "It was just before her arrest. I immediately sensed she was different. She had an aura, a presence about her. She really did. I am not usually impressed, but she had changed from a quasi-academic person to a person with a real presence. You can meet members of royal families who have been trained since birth to have that kind of presence, but she had acquired it on her own. She was *very* impressive. While I don't agree with her on a lot of things, I think she is a very brave, remarkable woman."

Suu Kyi had begun a transformative shift in Japan. While still a homemaker, she was becoming a researcher with a world view, someone to be taken seriously. After her study in Kyoto, Suu Kyi and Kim were reunited with Michael and Alexander at the Indian Institute of Advanced Studies (IIAS) in Simla, India. Michael had a fellowship position at IIAS and had obtained a guest fellowship for her. Simla turned out to be an academic idyll for them. Simla had been the summer capital when the British ruled India, a hill town where the Raj officials could escape the 100-degree heat of the plains. The Aris family was housed in the Viceregal Lodge, a sprawling colonial retreat with big balconies and huge turret rooms, along with other scholars from around the world. An American academic couple, Michael and Kenton Clymer, had children the same age and often would share dinners with the Aris family. They noticed how close the family seemed. Michael and Suu Kyi often called each other "Darling" or "Sweetheart" and actually seemed to mean it.

Each morning in Simla, the Arises sat down to breakfast together and then worked together on their projects. Michael credited Suu Kyi with helping him edit some of his writings, and he later returned the favor by editing a collection of her essays. She wrote about Burmese literature and the influence that literature has on nationalism, as well as about intellectual life in Burma under colonialism.

For Suu Kyi, the year researching her father's life in Japan plus her time writing about Burmese culture in Simla was a reawakening of her Asian heritage after many years in Britain.

When they traveled from India to Rangoon to visit her mother in 1987, Suu Kyi had her sons go through the Buddhist initiation ceremony for young monks, *shinbyu*. They spent the customary two weeks as novices. Their heads were shaved, they donned saffron robes. With bare feet and alms bowls, the Bogyoke's grandsons went out to seek the day's meal, learning the lessons of charity that had held Burmese society together for centuries.

By 1988, the family had returned to Oxford to resume their former schedule. Suu Kyi was finishing work on her doctoral thesis. Then fate intervened and she received the call that she was needed to return to Rangoon to care for her ailing mother. A chapter of her thesis was on her husband's computer when she left.

As Suu tended to her mother that spring, life went on as usual back in Park Town in England. Alexander, now a tall teen-ager, rode his bike to school, and young Kim scooted to prep school on a skateboard. The family assumed Suu Kyi's absence was only temporary, like her study in Japan.

CHAPTER NINE

THE LADY OF THE LAKE

> "Whatever they do to me, that's between them and me; I can take it. What's more important is what they are doing to the country."
>
> —Aung San Suu Kyi

Aung San Suu Kyi's family had not expected easy circumstances when she returned to Burma to care for her mother, but they certainly could not have imagined that she would end up imprisoned in her family home. As her confinement wore on, Suu Kyi's health deteriorated. At times she did not have enough to eat. An egg once a week was a luxury. Her weight fell to 90 pounds. Her eyesight suffered, and her spine began to degenerate. The few times that Michael was allowed back in the country to see her, he brought suitcases full of food as well as books.

Those aid packages were rare, however, and she had to sell some of the furnishings in the house for food. She did not find out until later that her military guards had purchased back her furniture with their own money. They kept it in a warehouse to return to her. During a brief period when she was granted enough freedom to have access to her personal funds, she insisted on repaying the guards for the furniture. It was not uncommon for the soldiers guarding her to become attached to the woman who bore her isolation with such dignity and grace. She was unfailingly kind to them and spoke to them as equals. As soon as the generals found out that the soldiers were developing loyalties to "The Lady," they began rotating her guards on a regular basis.

In an attempt to break her spirit, the junta did not allow Suu Kyi to see her children for more than two and a half years. "I felt very guilty about not looking after them," she said. "There are things you do together as a family that you don't do with other people. It's very special, so when a family splits up, it is never good." The only antidote to such feelings, she said, was knowing that others had it much worse. "I knew that my children were safe with my husband in England, whereas a lot of my colleagues were in the terrible position of being in prison themselves and not knowing how safe their children were going to be."

When she finally got to see her younger son Kim for the first time in years, she was stunned to discover how much he had grown. "I would not have recognized him if I had seen him on the street!" He brought his favorite music with him and taught her to appreciate Jamaican singer Bob Marley. "I began to like Bob Marley," she said, quoting from one of his most popular songs, "'Stand up, get up, stand up for your rights.' Perfect for us."

She would not allow her spirit to be broken by the junta. To make her independence clear, she refused any help from the authorities. When she believed the government thought it was doing her a favor by letting her write to her family, she stopped writing altogether. Her stubborn pride would not let her accept token favors from her jailers, even if it cost her what little contact she had with her family.

The junta not only denied access to her family for long periods, they rebuffed repeated requests from U.N. emissaries to visit her. They snubbed a Nobel Peace Prize delegation, which was led by the Dalai Lama in 1993 and included a half-dozen other winners. The laureates had to convene in Bangkok instead. The unprecedented assemblage of laureates held a press conference lamenting the treatment of Aung San Suu Kyi. The junta did not respond.

—∾—

In 1994, the military regime did allow a visit to Rangoon by U.S. Congressman Bill Richardson, a Democrat from New Mexico with foreign-policy interests.

Richardson had visited the country before as part of a congressional delegation and met with Secretary No. 1 Khin Nyunt. The powerful general seemed to enjoy the 6-foot-2 Congressman's spunk and sense of humor, but turned down his request to meet with Aung San Suu Kyi. Testing the depth of the Congressman's interest or perhaps stringing the Congressman along, the master of manipulation said that if Richardson came back, he would be allowed to meet with her. Richardson accepted his dare and returned a year later. During the interim, he went to see Michael in England, who deferred all of his questions about Burma's politics to his wife. "Ask Suu," Michael would say, "ask Suu."

When a meeting was finally arranged for February 14, 1994, Suu Kyi was not sure she could trust anyone that the junta allowed to see her, assuming the generals might be trying to manipulate her. She insisted that *New York Times* reporter Philip Shenon be included in the meeting to report what transpired. A local U.N. Development Program representative, Jehan Raheem, was also included. Suu Kyi's suspicions that the generals were exploiting the meeting in some way were partly right—the regime was hoping to look more tolerant to the Clinton administration because they wanted foreign funds to beef up their military arsenal and add infrastructure for tourists. For his part, Richardson was hoping to negotiate Aung San Suu Kyi's release.

The Richardson group became the first visitors to see the Nobel laureate, other than her doctor and family, since her house arrest in 1989. The Congressman found Aung San Suu Kyi "enormously bright and engaging." He later told me, "We had a wonderful meeting, a very interesting two hours. The meeting was tense at first. She was testing me to make sure she was not being used for Khin Nyunt's purposes."

He was struck by what a "bright, charismatic" person she was, but found her "distant." When he pressed Suu Kyi about what she would do if she were in power, she corrected him, "It's not *my* vision. We must not emphasize this personality business. I'm quite happy to be a figurehead . . . [but] I'm not Burma." There were plenty of other able people who could lead the country, she insisted, if only they were allowed.

Richardson said it was his view that Secretary No. 1 Khin Nyunt should talk with Suu Kyi. She retorted, "I have always said he should talk to me." When Richardson and Raheem asked what she thought about using development money as a carrot, she countered, "Where is the stick?"

The meeting was being taped by the junta, which she knew, so she made a point of emphasizing that whatever their differences, the SLORC generals had no reason to fear her and could benefit much by talking with her and the NLD. When Richardson noted her Spartan household and offered to obtain some modern conveniences for her, she said she wanted only an open honest dialogue with SLORC, nothing else.

"The main thrust of her message to the world and to me," Richardson said afterward, "was that despite the physical and mental discomforts to her, and the loss of seeing her children grow up, the most important facet of her life was standing up for democracy for the people of Burma, and not surrendering her principles by agreeing to have luxuries and other advantages that the SLORC had offered her."

The Congressman also noted afterward that she appeared thin and tense; she had mentioned that the lack of nutrition had caused a back problem. "She seemed to be under a lot of pressure because she was having difficulty getting access to her children and her husband. She said she particularly missed her children," he said. When he asked what he could do for her, she replied, "Nothing, nothing." He persisted, "Isn't there something I could do?" She eventually said yes, she would like to get out of house arrest.

Though Suu Kyi emphasized to the visiting Americans that she was ready and willing to talk with the generals, there was no response from the regime after they left. Months went by with no further contact. Suu Kyi was the lonely lady of the lake once again. She studied the lives of other leaders who had been imprisoned: Václav Havel of Czechoslovakia, imprisoned four years; Gandhi of India, nearly seven years; Nehru of India for nine years; and Nelson Mandela of South Africa for 27 years. She said one reason their movements had succeeded was that while confined, the leaders had an opportunity to grow spiritually and strengthen their determination. She redoubled her efforts to master the vipassana meditation techniques, whose name means to see things as they really are.

Half a year after Richardson's visit, Suu Kyi suddenly was summoned to a state guest house. She was taken to meet with her SLORC captors twice in the fall of 1994. That meant she was able to see the men who were calling the shots in person for the first time: Senior General Than Shwe, and Secretary No. 1 Khin Nyunt, the head of military intelligence. The details of their conversations have never been released or discussed by either side. Photos from one of the meetings show Suu Kyi dressed in an elegant pink sarong, looking demure and feminine. She clearly had dressed her best for the meeting. The two generals are in uniform, striding forward with cocky smiles on their faces. Photos of the other meeting show Suu Kyi dressed in a more traditional lilac blouse and longyi, warily reaching out to shake heads with an equally wary Than Shwe. There does not appear to be any rapport between them.

The SLORC generals later claimed that a "dialogue" had been conducted with the opposition, but nothing constructive came from the conversations. A former military intelligence officer, Major Aung Lin Htun, later revealed that the two top generals realized after the meetings that they were comparatively inexperienced and "not capable of negotiating with Aung San Suu Kyi." The intelligence officer recalled, "After the meeting, they said, 'Suu Kyi is not easy.'" United Nations envoy Razali Ismail also later told biographer Benedict Rogers that Suu Kyi's principled intelligence "frightened the hell out of the military."

Than Shwe, in particular, was frustrated that Suu Kyi would not bend to his will. How dare she? He never met with her again and never allowed her name to be spoken in his presence. In meetings, she was referred to indirectly as "That troublemaker" or "That woman."

Nine more months passed before the SLORC generals allowed Suu Kyi some freedom of movement. In July 1995, a white limousine showed up at her house unannounced. The Rangoon chief of police had been dispatched to inform Suu Kyi that her house arrest was over. The SLORC generals did not explain their reasons. The diplomatic community speculated that either 1) the junta was trying to eliminate her as a negative issue because they had declared 1995–1996 as "Visit Myanmar Year" to boost tourism and fill the swank hotels that their cronies had constructed, 2) the Japanese government was holding back on further development assistance until Suu Kyi was freed, 3) the SLORC generals believed they had sufficiently weakened the NLD and Suu Kyi so that they were no longer a viable threat, or 4) all of the above.

Only hours after the arrest order was lifted, Suu Kyi met with the key "uncles" of the democracy movement: U Tin Oo and U Kyi Maung, who had been released from their own imprisonment. Joining them was U Aung Shwe, who had led the NLD while the two leaders were detained. The group quickly decided, as she put it, "to pick up where we had left off six years ago."

As quickly as it could be arranged, she went to the home of the British ambassador to use the phone to call her husband. They both calmly said "Hello" and then matter-of-factly discussed their next plans. Both had been schooled in the British tradition of "Keep Calm and Carry On." And both were well versed in the Buddhist precepts of detachment, or non-attachment. What they didn't know was that events were ahead that would put those coping mechanisms to even greater tests.

For the time being, Suu Kyi's new window of freedom meant that she could communicate again with the international community. Being able to "see and be seen" led to two new relationships that would prove critical to her democracy efforts in the future: First Lady Hillary Clinton and U.N. Representative Madeline Albright. Both would go on to serve as secretary of state, and both would champion Suu Kyi's efforts in Burma.

The women first made a connection through the historic Fourth World Conference on Women in Beijing. The Beijing Conference—the largest ever convened by the U.N.—brought together 17,000 participants from 189 countries in 1995 to talk about the need for women's empowerment.

Aung San Suu Kyi was invited to be the kickoff speaker. She couldn't come in person because of the ever-present risk of not being allowed back into her country again. Even taping a video and getting it smuggled out through diplomatic channels had been difficult. Suu Kyi opened the talk by explaining she had only been released from six years of house arrest the month before. "The regaining of my freedom has in turn imposed a duty on me to work for the freedom of other women and men in my country who have suffered far more—and who continue to suffer far more—than I have. It is this duty which prevents me from joining you today," she said.

Her calm, composed manner captivated the participants from around the world, most of whom had never seen or heard of her before. The most often quoted sound bite from her speech was "For millennia, women have dedicated themselves almost exclusively to the task of nurturing, protecting, and caring for the young and the old, striving for the conditions of peace that favor life as a whole. To this can be added the fact that—to the best of my knowledge—no war was ever started by women. But it is women and children who have always suffered most in situations of conflict."

Suu Kyi pointed out that in her own country, no women participate in the highest levels of government or the judiciary. In the 1990 election, only 14 of the 485 members of Parliament who were elected were women—and all of those were from her own party. They, along with their male colleagues, had not been allowed to take office.

She observed that there was an age-old prejudice the world over to the effect that women talk too much and asked teasingly, "Is this really a *weakness*? Could it not in fact be a *strength*? Recent scientific research on the human brain has revealed that women are better at verbal skills while men tend toward physical action. . . . Surely these discoveries indicate that women have a most valuable contribution to make in situations of conflict, by leading the way to solutions based on dialogue rather than on viciousness or violence?"

The crowd cheered like delegates at a political convention. In one short speech, Suu Kyi had gained thousands of new allies around the world.

One of the other "stars" at the event was American First Lady Hillary Rodham Clinton. She had championed equal rights for women since her college days at Wellesley. She went on to support programs to help women and children while her husband was governor of Arkansas for five terms. But at the time of the 1995 women's conference, Mrs. Clinton was still plagued by criticism for her prominent role in her husband's ill-fated attempt at healthcare reform in 1993. Her standing also had been tarnished by their involvement in the failed Whitewater land deal in Arkansas, which was still in the news. The timing of her scheduled speech at the global event in Beijing raised questions because tensions were high at the time between the government of China and the U.S. The First Lady was under pressure from Congress and the media to pull out of the event. Yet Mrs. Clinton was determined to deliver a message to China about its human-rights violations, and she wanted to speak out about the discrimination against women worldwide. She felt withdrawing might send the wrong signal on both fronts. The publicity about her appearance only intensified the spotlight on what might have otherwise been another U.N. talking session. As it turned out, her speech was a defining moment for the convention and for her.

In the most-often-quoted segment, the First Lady dramatically opened a series of sentences with the same phrase like a rhythmic drum beat:

> "It is a violation of human rights when babies are denied food, or drowned or suffocated or their spines broken, simply because they are born girls.
>
> "It is a violation of human rights when women and girls are sold into the slavery of prostitution.
>
> "It is a violation of human rights when women are doused with gasoline, set on fire and burned to death because their marriage dowries are deemed too small. . . .
>
> "It is a violation of human rights when young girls are brutalized by the painful and degrading practice of genital mutilation. . . ."

She listed more abuses before concluding, "If there is one message that echoes from this conference, let it be that human rights are women's rights and women's rights are human rights, once and for all." Mrs. Clinton had found her voice. And a new friend. The video presentation by Aung San Suu Kyi was the first time Hillary Clinton had seen the Nobel laureate speak. But she was well aware of her fight for democracy. The First Lady had been encouraged to help the democracy movement by her former roommate at Yale Law School, Kwan Kwan Tan. Kwan Kwan was an ethnic Chinese who was a graduate of the Methodist English High School in Rangoon, the same school Aung San Suu Kyi had attended. Kwan Kwan had come from Burma to Yale to pursue graduate legal studies. Hillary Clinton later noted in her autobiography, *Living History*, that Kwan Kwan was "a delightful living companion and a graceful performer of Burmese dance." Kwan Kwan later married another Yale Law School student, Bill Wang, and became a successful attorney in San Francisco.

That random roommate assignment in 1970 would prove vitally helpful for the democracy movement in Burma decades later, although Kwan Kwan Wang's role remained behind the scenes. She had not tried to publicize or capitalize on her connection to Hillary as her former roommate became more high-profile along with her husband. According to friends, Kwan Kwan Wang's brother did not even know the two had been roommates. But after Bill Clinton was elected president in 1992, Kwan Kwan Wang quietly went to visit her former roommate at the White House. She asked her school friend to please do what she could to help the people of Burma. Hillary said she would. And kept her word. She and Kwan Kwan Wang would continue their conversations about the democracy movement in Burma from then on. And the time would come when Mrs. Clinton could use her influence to make a breakthrough in relations with Burma.

After hearing Aung San Suu Kyi's speech to the Beijing Conference, Hillary Clinton and Madeleine Albright, who was the U.S. Ambassador to the United Nations at the time, signed a conference poster to send as a gift to her. Both Clinton and Albright were alumnae of Wellesley, which encouraged its female students to be change agents. And both were now champions of Aung San Suu Kyi.

Immediately after the conference, Albright took the autographed poster with her to Rangoon to present to Suu Kyi in person. That made Albright the most senior official to visit Burma since Ne Win's coup d'etat in 1962. Ambassador Albright had known Michael during the time she was a professor at Georgetown University. When he needed to contact Czech revolutionary leader Václav Havel in 1991 to write a forward for Suu Kyi's book of essays, *Freedom from Fear*, Albright had been the intermediary. She knew Aung San Suu Kyi's story well.

Suu Kyi prepared for the ambassador's visit in a touching way—she scrubbed the walls and floor of her house by hand and washed and ironed the curtains by herself.

Years later, Albright told me that Aung San Suu Kyi was the most compelling figure she had ever met, and by then she had met more than her share of impressive leaders as secretary of state. "She is a combination of very beautiful and fragile," Albright said. "I'll never forget how she looked, with a lavender skirt and flowers in her hair. But she was tough. When we had a conversation about what needed to be done, she was tough, a combination of fragile and very strong."

Albright also met with the SLORC generals on the same trip, with the aim of exploring the possibility of improving U.S.-Burmese relations. They reminded her of the manipulative "Big Brother" party leaders in George Orwell's dystopian novel *1984*. "They were patronizing," she remembered. "They referred to Aung San Suu Kyi as 'our little sister,' and said they had to protect her. They claimed everyone in Burma walked around with happy faces." Albright left thinking, who do they think they are fooling?

Albright issued a press statement September 11, 1995 that said "Khin Nyunt expressed the belief that the SLORC had broad public support, and observed that the Burmese people smile a lot. I said that it has been my experience, in a lifetime of studying repressive societies, that dictators often delude themselves into believing they have popular support, but that people often smile not because they are happy, but because they are afraid." Her visit was the most high-level attempt to engage the junta, but nothing came of it. The generals were in control, and they had no intention of letting go.

Debate over "what to do about Burma" see-sawed through five American administrations—from the Reagan administration to the Obama administration. After the generals slaughtered democracy supporters in 1988 and refused to honor the 1990 elections, the Reagan administration took a series of steps. The U.S. refused to recognize the change of the country's name to Myanmar by what it considered an illicit government. The American ambassador was withdrawn from Rangoon. For the next two decades, limited diplomatic operations would be carried out by a *chargé d'affaires*. And in its last months in office, the Reagan administration suspended all arms sales and foreign assistance to Burma, with the exception of humanitarian aid.

Congress joined in by passing the Customs and Trade Act in 1990, enabling the president to impose new sanctions against Burma. But rather than impose new sanctions when he took office, President George H. W. Bush opted to try other measures first. He decertified Burma from the list of states cooperating in anti-narcotics efforts instead. That move meant that aid and loans were blocked from the Export-Import Bank, the Overseas Private Investment Corporation, and other international financial institutions receiving U.S. funds. The decertification also enabled the Bush administration to revoke Burma's trade benefits under the Generalized System of Preferences.

But such attempts produced little change because Burma's trade partners in Asia continued business as usual. Frustrated by the lack of political improvement in Burma, a bipartisan movement began in Congress to get the generals' attention. A flurry of resolutions condemned the repression. Funding was approved for pro-democracy programs. In 1993, the Senate passed a resolution calling on President Clinton to work for the immediate release of the Burmese opposition leader Aung San Suu Kyi and for adoption of a United Nations embargo against Rangoon. President Clinton expressed support for the resolution, but did not take steps to implement it.

As the repression in Burma mounted, a bipartisan group of Senators and Representatives ramped up a campaign for stiff economic and trade sanctions on Burma. The juggernaut was led by influential leaders in the Senate such as Sens. Mitch McConnell, R-Kentucky; John McCain, R-Arizona; and Dianne Feinstein, D-Calif.

In the House, the charge was led by Dana Rohrabacher, R-Calif., and Tom Lantos, D-Calif. They would later be joined in the sanctions effort by Rep. Joe Crowley, D-N.Y., and all would remain faithful supporters of human rights in Burma throughout their careers.

In 1996, an amendment was added to the 1997 Foreign Appropriations Act to allow the president to determine if and when to impose sanctions on Burma. That measure gave the Clinton administration the diplomatic flexibility to decide whether the regime, operating under the name SLORC at the time, had improved its human rights policy and whether sanctions were needed.

A tug-of-war went on internally in the Clinton administration—would sanctions or engagement get better results? Those who had visited Burma and met Aung San Suu Kyi personally tended to favor sanctions. Madeleine Albright, the new secretary of state, and Congressman Bill Richardson, who had become the U.S. Ambassador to the United Nations, argued for a get-tough approach. They had seen the repressive conditions in the country. But some of the administration's economic advisors and the National Security Advisor, Sandy Berger, were not enthusiastic about economic sanctions. They were worried about the effect on U.S. companies operating in Burma, such as the oil giant Unocal. They also were concerned that the move might derail Washington's relationship with the Association of Southeast Asian Nations (ASEAN).

Complicating matters, a strong campaign was being conducted by the business lobby in Washington to block sanctions. The American companies argued that the Clinton administration would be hurting domestic businesses for political purposes.

At the same time, the administration was also under growing pressure from human-rights groups and Congress. Some local jurisdictions had already moved on their own to sanction the SLORC regime. The state of Massachusetts and the city of San Francisco had enacted laws penalizing multinational companies that were doing business in Burma by making them ineligible for government contracts. As a result, Apple Computer Inc. had pulled out of Burma. PepsiCo Inc. had likewise announced it would leave, partly due to pressure from shareholders.

In the end, Secretary Albright and Ambassador Richardson, with support from Hillary Clinton, carried the day in the debate. The administration decided to impose sanctions. Mrs. Clinton had kept her pledge to Kwan Kwan Wang to support the democracy movement; Secretary Albright and Ambassador Richardson had kept their assurances to Aung San Suu Kyi that they would not forget the people of Burma.

On May 20, 1997, President Clinton issued Executive Order 13047, banning most new U.S. investment in "economic development of resources in Burma." To justify the ban, the president cited a "constant and continuing pattern of severe repression" of the democratic opposition by Burma's ruling junta. Clinton said the SLORC had "arrested and detained large numbers of students and opposition supporters, sentenced dozens to long-term imprisonment, and prevented the expression of political views by the democratic opposition."

Clinton stressed that under Rangoon's "brutal military regime, Burma remains the world's leading producer of opium and heroin and tolerates drug trafficking and traffickers in defiance of the views of the international community."

He added that relations between the Burmese government and the U.S. would improve only if there was "a program on democratization and respect for human rights."

During this same period, Suu Kyi was trying to resume her campaigns around the country. She told the Reuters news agency, "The future, of course, is democracy for Burma. It is going to happen, and I'm going to be here when it happens." But she was rarely allowed to travel outside Rangoon, although the regime claimed she had been "released." When she did leave her house, military intelligence would tail her. And often when she attempted to travel outside the city of Rangoon, she was forced back after standoffs with the military.

In March 1996, Suu Kyi was thwarted when she tried to attend the trial of comedian Par Par Lay and his Moustache Brothers troupe in Mandalay. She had gotten to know the trio of comedians the summer before when they performed their vaudeville-style act in her Rangoon home. As far as biting satire goes, it was paper tiger fare. They sang a corny song about the generals, and Par Par Lay joked, "You used to call a thief a thief; now you call him a government servant."

The audience guffawed, but there were junta snitches in the audience. When the comedians returned home to Mandalay, they were arrested. Suu

Kyi wanted to go to Mandalay to support their freedom of speech. She boarded the train bound for Mandalay, but her train car was decoupled and left behind at the station. Authorities blamed a "last-minute problem."

Behind closed doors at the Mandalay prison, Par Par Lay was sentenced to seven years' imprisonment for telling jokes—which the junta described in their Orwellian indictment as intending "to spread false news, knowing beforehand that it is untrue." For part of his sentence, the comedian was held in a labor camp, where he was forced to work with iron bars binding his legs. When he was ordered to break rocks, other prisoners offered to help with his share in return for the comic relief of some of his famous jokes. Even that was a risk, Par Pay Lay said afterward; if guards did not like a prisoner, they shot him in front of the others.

The comedian was released in 2001, but was kept under constant surveillance by military intelligence. With incredible bravery, he resumed his show of music, folk dancing, and sly political jabs in the garage of his home in Mandalay.

He not only dared to put posters of Aung San Suu Kyi on the walls of his garage/theater, he and his brothers Lu Maw and Lu Zaw used the proceeds from their performances to assist political prisoners and their families.

One of his jokes was about a tsunami that had did not hit Burma as expected. The joke was about why Burma was spared. The answer was that three corrupt Burmese generals had died and for their crimes were reborn as lowly fish. When they saw the deadly wave coming, they told it to turn back from Burma, saying, "We already ruined it."

Par Par Lay was arrested again in 2007, yet after his release continued his satirical shows until his death in 2013.

Though the world was told that Suu Kyi had been "released" and was free to continue her work, even more threatening incidents followed. In November 1996, a vehicle carrying Suu Kyi and other senior NLD members was attacked by some 200 government-sponsored thugs from the Union Solidarity and Development Association (USDA), the regime's brutish surveillance and enforcement corps. Armed with knives and clubs, the

USDA assailants attacked Suu Kyi's car on the Kabaraye Pagoda Road. They rocked her car violently back and forth. They beat it with iron bars and smashed the rear window. Government troops stood nearby and looked on without moving a step to help.

Suu Kyi later told reporters from *The Progressive*, "It was quite interesting. [She laughs.] I was fairly detached. I saw it all as an observer. There were all these faces crowding in toward the car, and there was one man in front with an iron bar in his hand who I assume was the one who made the big gash in my windscreen. I just said, 'Keep moving.' I made the decision that we were simply going to continue on to meet the crowds that had come to support us. One of the boys who was in the car with us was a bit angry about the whole thing, so I spent some time calming him down and telling him not to be angry. But it was clear to us that the attack was a deliberate attempt to harm us badly or even kill us. It is, of course, very serious. But we do not consider our own personal safety as any more serious than the safety and security of the people in general."

The government continued trying to undermine Suu Kyi with posters suggesting crude sexual behavior or insinuating that she was anti-Buddhist. They printed photos on the front pages of state media of chocolates and fashion magazines that her husband had sent her. One journalist observed that their accusations followed a pattern: "Suu Kyi is married to a foreigner. She has Western ideas. She is not really one of us."

Suu Kyi endured the harassment with as much grace as possible, but from time to time she did become frustrated by the indignities and dangers the military was subjecting her to. At one point she said to a friend, "Look at me, I'm over 50. At this age, I should be leading a quiet life. But then I think of Mandela. The poor man's 80 and he's still working."

She had to be careful when she chatted with people in public, because the military would interrogate anyone she talked with. She would occasionally go to diplomatic receptions, but had to stop going to restaurants or the local markets because the authorities often would close down the places she visited. She shifted her social life toward private gatherings with people that she could trust, and often she would invite friends to her home.

"She likes a good party," recalls a Western diplomat who was stationed in Rangoon during that time. "She would have parties at her house. People could bring cakes and we would bring food and drink. It was not very often, but every once in a while she would have something and invite friends. We had a few laughs. She has kept a healthy sense of humor, which I think has been very important to her survival, to be able to laugh at things."

—∿—

Those who met Suu Kyi during this time often expressed surprise that she had such a playful sense of humor. As the attacks on her grew, she noted tongue-in-cheek to a journalist, "It's very different from living in academia in Oxford. We called someone vicious for a review in *The Times* literary supplement. We didn't know what vicious was."

She can be staid in formal settings, but she often likes to leaven proceedings with wry observations. In a Q-and-A with students, she was asked what childhood experiences changed her life. "I became who I am because I was lucky in choosing my parents," she said as the audience responded with laughter. "I made sure I had the best parents possible for the situation."

"Suu is funny. She has an abundant sense of humor," her early NLD colleague U Kyi Maung said. "When we are together in a group, say in meetings, she is always telling jokes. Always. We all do. This is the atmosphere we work in."

It is a Burmese trait to understate hardships; making light about their situation is natural. Many of Suu Kyi's friends tell stories about her ability to find things to delight in, even when situations look dire. Her NLD colleague U Kyi Maung was one of the last to see her before her house detention in 1989 and the first person she requested to see when she was freed in 1995. As he drove up to her house, Suu was standing on her doorstep and quipped, "Uncle, what took you so long, six years to drive a mile?" Visitors who were allowed to see her when she was confined in her house or in prison all emerged with the same comment: Daw Aung San Suu Kyi was in amazingly good spirits.

During one phone interview with a reporter, the buzzing on her telephone line from military wiretaps became so loud that she could barely be heard. She laughed audibly when the tape recorders clicked on and off, telling the reporter, "We couldn't survive without our sense of humor."

Having a healthy appreciation of the ridiculous not only cut the tension, it also helped the activists stay emotionally detached from the constant threat of death or arrest. When Suu Kyi was released in 1995, she wryly told audiences, "I have been free for more than a month. Some people may think that that is long enough. Others may think that is not quite long enough."

During our first interview, I mentioned that I was surprised to be taller that she was. Suu Kyi took the challenge with a playful laugh. "Oh, you think so?" she said. "Stand up, and we'll see. Take off your shoes." Side by side, she was about an inch taller. She was visibly pleased.

When the generals continued to refuse her offers to have a dialogue with them, she told Hannah Beech of *Time* magazine, "I wish I could have tea with them every Saturday, a friendly tea." Beech asked, what if they turn down a nice cup of tea? Suu Kyi teased back, "We could always have coffee."

She admits to interviewers that playing Mozart made her happy, but she preferred Bach, who made her calm, explaining, "I need calm in my life." But she also needed humor to see her though. She told David Pilling of *The Financial Times* the story of an Englishman who was due to travel to Burma some years before. "He went to his local pub as usual and said he was going to visit Burma on holiday. And one of his mates said, 'Should you be going? That lady with the unpronounceable name said you must not go.' I was very touched. He couldn't pronounce my name, but he'd obviously taken my message to heart!" Then, she added, "I thought, next time I am able to go to England, I must go to that pub."

That human side of Suu Kyi is often missed by people who only see the dignified, reserved woman in the news giving speeches. Debbie Stothard, the coordinator of the advocacy group Altsean Burma, remembers meeting Aung San Suu Kyi for the first time during Suu Kyi's brief hiatus from full house arrest in 1995–96. A meeting was being held at the NLD headquarters in Rangoon. "Suddenly there was electricity in the air, a lot of movement outside the house, cars and people arriving, and then this little old white car, a decades-old car, pulls up and drives up to the house, and there is ASSK. We were standing inside the house and she called out to us as she walked up, 'Don't come out to greet us, don't give MI an easy opportunity to photograph you, stay inside in the shade.'"

Suu Kyi climbed up the stairs to discover Stothard and a group of visitors from Stockholm, Malaysia, the Philippines, and Indonesia, who had been waiting a while to meet her. Her first concern was for the visitors. "Have you eaten?" she asked, since it was past midday. No, they had not. Suu Kyi began organizing food for the group, sandwiches, whatever could be found. Since the visitors spoke a variety of languages and she was fluent in four, she offered to assist as a translator.

Introduced to Stothard, Suu Kyi expressed surprise that the democracy advocate, who was 33 at the time, was so young. She had often heard Stothard being interviewed on the radio about the democracy movement and had imagined a much older woman. Suu Kyi was curious how the younger woman had gotten involved with the Burma cause, where she lived, how she was doing. "Everyone was talking about politics and the work, but she wanted to get to know all the people who were there and talk about *them*," Stothard remembers. Stothard knew more than most about how much deprivation Suu Kyi had endured and the risks she still faced. She was so overwhelmed by Suu Kyi's warmth in the face of such difficulties that she broke into tears. "She gave me a tissue and comforted *me*," Stothard remembered.

The meeting was the first of many that Stothard had with Suu Kyi during that period. Since the regime had a stranglehold on the Burmese media, outreach to the foreign media was essential to get news out about the democracy movement. Stothard had a television background, so she gave Aung San Suu Kyi coaching on her media skills. She advised Suu Kyi to repeat her messages to establish her democracy "brand," much like a commercial media campaign. Stothard also showed her how to improve her presentation skills on TV by looking directly into the camera lens and keeping her comments short. Suu Kyi's speaking style—simple, frank, and clear—made her a natural.

As they spent time together, Stothard noticed that Suu Kyi particularly enjoyed visiting monasteries. "She shows a great deal of respect to the monks and nuns. She sees the importance of the religious community in Burma and is respectful of all religions. She is quite a spiritual person herself and believes in prayer. She would often tell people, 'Pray for us, prayers help.' She really believes in that."

—∾—

David Eubank, another visitor during that period of brief access, also came away impressed that Suu Kyi asked him to pray for her. Eubank, a former Green Beret, came from a missionary family that was working in Thailand with Burmese refugees. He admired Aung San Suu Kyi's courageous efforts and went to meet with her during her period of access in 1996 to tell her about his work. Afterward, he wrote that although he knew she was not a Christian, when he met with her he felt God's presence. "She exudes faith and told me her favorite scripture was John 8:32, 'You shall know the truth and the truth shall set you free.'" When he asked what he could do to help her, she asked him simply to pray for Burma.

Eubank took the request seriously. He went on to found a "Global Day of Prayer for Burma" that would be observed every year on March 9 by thousands of churches around the world. He also was inspired to create a unique guerrilla/humanitarian organization based in Thailand called the Burma Free Rangers. Despite the extreme risk, his backpack missionary teams regularly slip over the border from Thailand into conflict areas of Burma. The teams provide desperately needed medical care and humanitarian services for villagers caught in the crossfire between the Burmese military and ethnic groups. And by daring to go where others cannot, the Burma Free Rangers have in many instances provided eyewitness accounts and documentation of the military's human-rights abuses hidden from international view in the remote jungles of Burma.

The Eubank encounter was another demonstration of Aung San Suu Kyi's gift for establishing a rapport with people on brief acquaintance. As biographer Justin Wintle pointed out, when she met with a reporter from the *Irish Times*, Suu Kyi took care to point out to her that her father and other independence leaders had admired Michael Collins, one of the leaders in the Irish independence movement. As one reporter admitted in *The Economist*, "We all fell a little bit in love with her."

But her charm did not work on everyone who journeyed to see her. In 1997, Richard Armitage, who had served as an assistant secretary of defense and spearheaded American security policy in the Pacific, visited Rangoon with two other former high-ranking American diplomats—Michel Armacost, former U.S. Ambassador to the Philippines and Japan, and Morton Abramowitz, former U.S. Ambassador to Thailand. The purpose of the officials' trip ostensibly was to initiate a dialogue that would lead to a solution to the political stalemate in Burma. The Americans talked with the SLORC generals about economic issues and met with Aung San Suu Kyi for three hours.

When I interviewed Armitage several years later, he remembered Suu Kyi's unique presence and determination, but said he thought she was "coquette-ish" in their meeting, using her looks as well as her intellect to persuade the visitors to align with her views. He thought she "played to the audience of three guys, nothing over the top in any way, shape or form, but she knew she was an attractive woman."

His cool response might have been due to the fact that their views on economic sanctions were diametrically opposed. She supported them; he did not. Armitage was put off that Suu Kyi did not seem concerned about the possible suffering that might be caused by the sanctions that had recently been imposed by the Clinton administration. And she did not seem inclined to compromise.

Armitage strongly believed that sanctions hurt working people more than leaders. What's more, he thought sanctions tended to assume a "life of their own" and were difficult to remove. He believed that restrictions on visas for government leaders and their supporters offered more flexibility with less harm to the poor.

Observers at the time pointed out that such views may have reflected the fact that the trip was sponsored by the Washington-based Burma/Myanmar Forum, which received funding from oil companies such as Unocal. The American oil industry remained opposed to the sanctions President Bill Clinton had imposed on Burma—and worried that the Burma Sanctions Act might lead to similar actions against Nigeria, Indonesia, and perhaps even China. Considerable lobbying money was being spent to oppose the use of sanctions.

The debate on the usefulness of sanctions would continue for years to come, with strong feelings on both sides of the issue. Suu Kyi's personal assistant, Ma Thanegi, who had kept Suu Kyi's sons busy playing board games when her house was first surrounded by soldiers in 1989, became a vocal critic of the sanctions. Their friendship did not survive Thanegi's public criticism.

Although Armitage may have had philosophical differences with Suu Kyi on sanctions, it did not lessen his support for democracy in Southeast Asia. He had served in Vietnam during the American conflict there. As U.S. forces pulled out, he helped rescue 30,000 Vietnamese by guiding a flotilla of refugees across the Pacific to the Philippines.

His career would intersect with Aung San Suu Kyi again in 2003 when he was serving as deputy secretary of state and her campaign convoy was brutally attacked by military henchmen in Depayin. Armitage applied great pressure to get Suu Kyi transferred from the prison to the relative safety of her home.

And he implemented visa sanctions against the regime generals and their families and associates, which significantly impacted their ability to travel.

During Suu Kyi's brief periods of relative freedom in the 1990s, visitors would bring her the creature comforts she had long done without—cosmetics and her favorite chocolate—as well as books and CDs. "People felt they had to send me books about people who were in prison," she told Edward Klein in a *Vanity Fair* interview in 1995. "I read a lot of biographies. They taught me how other people faced problems in life. Mandela, Sakharov, Mother Teresa."

Along with her books, her radio was a constant lifeline to the world. It was from the radio that she heard about NLD activities in the vicinity of her own house. And it was from the radio that she learned of the breaching of the Berlin wall, the collapse of the Soviet bloc, the moves toward constitutional change in Chile, the progress of democratization in South Korea, and the dismantling of apartheid in South Africa.

As she later said in the prestigious Reith Lectures on BBC, "The books I received intermittently from my family included the works of Václav Havel, the memoirs of Sakharov, biographies of Nelson and Winnie Mandela, the writings of Timothy Garton Ash. Europe, South Africa, South America, Asia—wherever there were peoples calling for justice and freedom, there were our friends and allies."

She was particularly drawn to the thoughts of her Nobel champion, Czech leader Václav Havel, as he worked for freedom from Soviet rule. Like her, he was convinced that there was a huge potential of goodwill slumbering within the people who were trapped in totalitarian regimes. He believed that the dormant goodwill in people needed to be *stirred*. People need to hear repeatedly that it makes sense to behave decently or to help others. They need to be encouraged over and over to place common interest above their own, to respect the elementary rules of human coexistence.

Like him, she believed in the power of a truthful word. She was convinced that every human heart has a conscience, that there is a moral origin to all politics, that moral standards have a place in all spheres of social life, including economics. She understood that if people do not try to discover, or rediscover, what is noble and good within themselves, rather than settle for the base compromises of fearful survival, then more will be lost than good governance.

Neither had any illusions that they would rid their countries of wrongdoing. This was a war that has been waged for centuries, Havel pointed out, and will continue to be waged, on principle, because it is the right thing to do. It was their job as leaders to draw out the best in beaten-down people, even if others considered it a hopeless task. In her enforced solitude, Suu Kyi understood what Havel meant when he wrote "Hope is not the conviction that something will turn out well, but the certainty that something makes sense, regardless of how it turns out."

Over time, she acquired a collection of textbooks on how a society deals with a past period of repression after it becomes democratic, like the truth and reconciliation commissions in Guatemala and in South Africa. "She has a whole bookshelf of political science books," a former diplomat said. "She really believes that Burma will need a period not of *retribution*, but of growth, institution building, and economic revitalization. They will need to train people how to run a country, how to serve in public office, how to deal with the international community. The returnees will have to come back. There will be no time for retribution, she believes. They will have to skip that phase. People in Burma have become bitter and their bitterness has become understandably petty. Her role is to provide a vision of democracy, of sound management and good government that people can aspire to. She understands all that—she's had a lot of time to think it through."

—∞—

Suu Kyi also realized during her release that she needed to rebuild her party. The NLD was moribund. Most of the key leaders had been imprisoned after the 1990 elections. Revitalizing the party was no easy task, since many NLD offices were still closed. The party was barred from using fax machines or distributing pamphlets and flyers. People inside and outside the party complained that the sclerotic NLD leadership was incapable of mounting a viable campaign against the military regime. Most of the elderly "uncles" in charge were in their 80s and 90s. They were clinging to their positions on the NLD executive committee like an entitlement.

Wikileaks cables later showed that American diplomats were scathing in their criticism of the ineffectual old guard: "The way the Uncles run the NLD indicates the party is not the last great hope for democracy and Burma," a cable reported. "The Party is strictly hierarchical, new ideas are not solicited or encouraged from younger members, and the Uncles regularly expel members they believe are 'too active.' NLD youth repeatedly complain to us they are frustrated with the party leaders . . . lack of unity among the pro-democracy opposition remains one of the biggest obstacles to democratic change in Burma."

Out of respect and custom, Suu Kyi had deferred to the older men since the time of the formation of the NLD. When some of them were sent to prison, she was genuinely concerned for them. She still relied on the advice of senior advisers such as U Tin Oo and U Win Tin. That said, she was well aware that the Executive Committee was now too geriatric to function. Once she got the chance, Suu Kyi began efforts to enlarge the committee and recruit new, young members to key roles. Often those efforts were thwarted by the old guard on the Executive Committee.

Dealing with those internal challenges and the repeated attempts by the regime to restrict her movements did crack her composure from time to time. Reporters often were warned by friends that she could be "spikey" and sharp. Those who witnessed her temper flareups said they were a surprising contrast to her cool, controlled demeanor in public. British Ambassador Robert Gordon, a close friend, admitted to the BBC, "When she's angry she can be really quite ferocious. You can see her eyes flashing. No wonder she was held in such awe and dread by the generals! She was thought by the dictators endowed by some supernatural power that enabled her to cast power over the country as a whole."

Others argued that most of the time, Suu Kyi tolerated a great deal without losing her cool. A former American public-affairs officer in Rangoon said, "She is a precise person who knows the way things should be and wants them to be, but I would not describe her as temperamental or hot-headed, not at all. She has a powerful, insightful mind. She does not get angry at things that might annoy someone else—once when she came to our house to dinner, there was a photographer there who came up and stuck a camera in her face and took several shots with a flash. She just sort of flinched and went on with the conversation. She didn't get angry at all. I think I would have. I've seen her in crowds—she does not get angry when people press all around her. She *does* get angry when someone is intellectually lazy, she has very high standards in that sense. The regime tries to characterize her as someone who is very inflexible. Actually that's not true. She has tried to be very flexible in dealing with the regime, has offered repeatedly to meet with them, dialogue with them. That's anything but inflexible."

She did consistently offer to dialogue with the generals, but was not afraid to differ with them publicly. When the junta introduced their "Visit Myanmar" campaign in 1996 to boost tourism, she opposed it, saying, "We are totally against the 'Visit Myanmar' campaign. This is tantamount to supporting authoritarianism in Burma. Tourists should wait until Burma is a freer and happier country."

She was adamant: Countries should not provide official aid to Burma, and corporations should not to invest in the country, until progress toward democracy was made. As she insisted, "they will get better returns for their money if they invest in a country that is stable and has a strong framework of just laws."

She was not going to budge until there was evidence of positive change. That did not endear her to the generals. Or to those with differing views. What seemed like constancy to her could sometimes seem like obstinacy to those who preferred different tactics over the years. But her constancy enabled her to stay on task—at great cost—which endeared her to the masses of people who knew only she was taking difficult stands for them.

—∾—

Because Suu Kyi couldn't go to the public as much as she wanted, the public came to her. By the thousands.

So many people had started gathering outside the gate of her home by 1996 that that it was decided she should go out and speak to them. Fearful that the petite Suu Kyi would be crushed if she went into the crowd, her party colleagues pushed a wooden table up to the tall fence so that she could stand on it and speak over the top of the fence to the crowds. At first the fence-top chats were held daily, but they began to consume too much of her time. "Wouldn't it be better to turn up every other day?" she suggested to the crowd. She needed time to meet with her party leaders, so the chats at the gate were reduced to every Saturday and Sunday afternoon. A couple of large speakers were attached to trees so she could be heard over the crowd.

At 4 P.M. sharp, Aung San Suu Kyi would mount the wooden table, always with fresh flowers in her hair, and usually holding a notepad to write down questions from the crowd.

Large crowds of people flocked to the gate, sitting on old newspapers and plastic bags on the sidewalk to cheer "The Lady," laugh at her little jokes, and listen to her political encouragement. Claudia Dreifus reported in the *New York Times*: "Thousands of Burmese come in from all over the countryside to participate in her 'free speech' meetings. They bring their children. They take tape recorders and video cameras. Though Suu Kyi explains such concepts as freedom of the press and the right to assembly in the most elegant Burmese, certain English phrases slip through: 'social contract,' 'Martin Luther King' and 'It's not fair.'"

Though the regime had banned opposition rallies, Suu Kyi kept up the sessions to make the point that people should be able to speak and gather freely. The people continued coming to the sessions at the gate even though government spies took note of all in attendance and often videotaped them. Some of those who attended would "disappear" for questioning later. Why did they risk it? A worker in the crowd expressed what many in the crowd felt: "Whatever happens, she gives us hope." A retired government official who came nearly every Saturday and Sunday explained, "I come, because I think what she says is the truth, and nobody else is saying it."

Though they often had to wait hours to save their place in the audience, people were orderly. Vendors started coming to provide refreshments, hawking skewers of blackened children and betel-nut chews for a buzz of energy. Traffic on the road outside her home often clogged up as buses and taxis slowed down so people could hang out of the windows to catch a glimpse of the "The Lady."

Nodding and smiling in response to the cheers from the crowd, Suu Kyi usually would speak for exactly one hour, discussing education, democracy, or human rights.

Every week she had a teachable point. "If you want democracy, you'll have to work for it," she exhorted. "You've got to join in. The more people are involved, the quicker we'll reach our goal." Once she told of how a woman, inspired by her talks, went to cash a check, and when the bank clerk started to deduct a fee for a calendar issued by the military, she protested. "But I did not request a calendar." The clerk kept trying to charge for the calendar. The woman stood her ground. Taken aback, the clerk cashed the check in full. Suu Kyi pointed to that small personal victory as a step toward democracy. If everyone could resist in some small way, she said, they would begin to feel empowered as human beings.

Often Aung San Suu Kyi answered questions submitted by the audience. Most were serious queries, but some were sly jabs at the military dictatorship, such as, "Why do the wives of government leaders wear diamond jewelry?" A pointed question indeed, when most of the Burmese citizenry were barely living above the poverty line.

At the end of the hour-long session, Suu Kyi would instruct the crowd of supporters to go home. Sometimes she would remain at the gate, watching to ensure that people got away without arrest or harassment.

News accounts said the average turnout for the over-the-fence talks was 3,000 per speech. The junta responded to the talks by printing commentaries in state-run papers with complaints such as "If we are going to discuss matters of mutual benefit, it will be necessary to close the soap opera on University Street." Another pro-junta opinion piece said "The puppet princess and her director who manipulates from behind the curtain should be withdrawn from the Myanmar stage."

The SLORC generals let it be known that they would not discuss matters of mutual interest with the NLD unless Suu Kyi left Burma. She responded that she would be willing to discuss anything—except leaving the country.

Suu Kyi spoke frankly about the military misrule at the fence-top sessions, even though she knew the generals might shut down the public access as a result. In particular, she criticized the new constitution that SLORC was trying to ram through. Even though the NLD had won the vast majority of the seats in the 1990 election, the party was only given 86 seats in the 677-member National Convention to draft the constitution. The regime had already moved the goal post once, by falsely claiming after the 1990 election that balloting was not intended to elect members of Parliament, as everyone in the country had believed, but to elect members of a constitution-drafting convention. By that standard, Suu Kyi's NLD party should have had the *majority* of seats at the constitutional convention, not a small minority. In effect, the regime had kept the NLD team on the bench even though they were the winners.

At one point, Suu Kyi ordered her delegates to walk out in protest against the way the convention was being manipulated. The NLD delegates were not allowed to speak. Without debate, the generals packed provisions into the constitution that would stack the future Parliament with military representatives. All of the executive branch would be dominated by the military. And, demonstrating why no one would ever accuse them of subtlety, the generals had inserted provisions aimed at Suu Kyi that specified no one with children who had a foreign passport and citizenship could serve as president, and this was after the government had canceled her sons' Burmese passports and citizenship, leaving them no other option than their British passports. The constitutional convention had been hijacked. Suu Kyi announced that the NLD would draw up its own draft of a constitution instead.

The SLORC generals then checkmated that move. They proclaimed a new law that prohibited separate constitutional drafts, with penalties ranging from five to 20 years in prison. After the law was issued, Suu Kyi and her followers toned down their public criticisms of the sham convention but continued to document its failings. The NLD leaders were in a double bind: they couldn't participate freely in the constitution drafting process, and they could not offer an alternative.

Though the challenges facing the democracy movement seemed to grow more daunting by the day, Suu Kyi used her weekend talks to offer words of hope. She talked about the Buddhist law of impermanence. "All things change eventually," she said, "even the government of Burma"

Critics at the time said that if she had been a shrewder and more flexible politician, she would have found an accommodation within the constitutional drafting process that would have made it possible to share power with the military. But the problem was that it takes two to have a dialogue. The generals would not even let the NLD speak.

Despite the momentary uplift of the pep rallies at the gate, the 1990s were mostly times of loss for Suu Kyi. She was able to see her husband only five times in eight years, and her children even less than that.

The separation was difficult for everyone in the family. Michael reportedly was tormented by his inability to help his wife. He continued to press for her freedom and to accept awards on her behalf, but he could offer little more than moral support. When her detention stretched into years, Michael was asked if he was considering a legal separation of some sort. He brushed such suggestions aside, saying firmly, "I am a one-woman man." Without regular correspondence or visits, he could only worry from afar about her well-being. In 1992, there had been a report in *The Times* that his wife was on another hunger strike. Michael had no way of knowing why or what her condition was, but stated that he stood by her and was confident she was doing "what she believes is right." As it turned out, the rumor was false.

On another occasion, he had been preparing for a Christmas visit, only to receive a cryptic note from his wife advising him not to come because she did not have the money to receive him properly. It was a coded way of saying that conditions were not right for him to come, but what did that mean? It was hardly a reassuring holiday message. Day to day, Michael could not be sure of Suu Kyi's safety; and night to night, he could only wonder if he would ever see his wife again. Yet despite all the difficulties, not once did he urge her to back down and return to her family. "She wouldn't have done it anyway," their youngest son Kim said. "I think Dad must have known that."

From 1995 on, the regime refused all of Michael's requests for a visa to visit his wife. Michael coped as best he could at home, but for all practical purposes he had become a single father. Friends observed that the house in Oxford was not the same without the disciplined, feminine presence of Suu Kyi. Michael lacked her domestic organizing skills. Kim would remember that his mother was a "fantastic cook," which his father was not. When his mother was home, he said, "We ate well and there were always friends coming and things happening, and we had some fantastic travels together. Without her, I suppose we lived a simpler life."

As a grown man, Kim noted in a BBC documentary that his father tried his best and had a droll sense of humor, "But fathers aren't motherly." A distance developed between them, he said, because it was a "father-son relationship, rather than mother and son." As a family friend put it, Michael was a scholar; "it wasn't a natural default mode to play football with the children."

In the documentary, *Aung San Suu Kyi: Lady of No Fear*, historian Peter Carey, one of Michael's colleagues and a family friend, says that the boys grew up somewhat "baffled" by their mother's decision to stay in Burma. They endured a unique emotional roller-coaster during their teen years. "It was very tough for them. If your mother dies, you can come to terms with that. But if your mother is alive and you can hear her being talked about, but you cannot reach her, it's like Persephone in the Underworld.'"

During the 1990s, the boys were able to speak to their "Mum" on the telephone from time to time, but always with the knowledge that their words were overheard and noted. Max Horsley, who was friends with Kim while they were students at The Dragon School in Oxford, told *The London Daily Mail*, "The pain Kim suffered at growing up without his mother was heartbreaking to see. I remember he would try to telephone her every night after school, although sometimes he couldn't get through or would be cut off, probably deliberately by the regime. He was just a little boy who didn't understand why his mother couldn't be with him or why he couldn't be with her. It was very difficult for him to take in. He would beg her, 'Please come home, Mum. We miss you terribly. Why aren't you here?' The separation reduced him to tears."

The boys visited their mother whenever the junta would allow it, but the flights were long and costly. Often the junta would give permission for a visit and then, cruelly, withdraw it. A school friend of Kim's who came with him on one of his visits to Rangoon remembered that there was hardly any furniture in Suu Kyi's house in Rangoon, which was in poor condition. "I can remember a piano with half of the keys broken," he told *The Daily Mail*. "Once, when we were there, she clutched his arm as they sat together. She just wouldn't let it go. It was as if she feared that if she let go of his arm he would walk out and she would never see him again. There was really anguish there."

As he grew older, Kim would say later, he became more comfortable with the situation, "but we all missed her badly."

By the time the Aris boys reached adulthood, they had come to realize why their mother made the decisions that she did and admired her for it. "It must have been incredibly difficult for her," Kim said. "It wasn't easy for us, but I am proud she took that decision."

Asked once to describe his mother, Kim said, "She is a very calm person. She doesn't get angry and she has a strong will."

As reports of her travails filtered out of Burma, Michael would anxiously seek back-channel information from diplomatic sources to find out if his wife was all right. Often they did not know. At one press conference, all he could say was that he had not seen his wife in 18 months and had not received a letter in a year. "All contact has ceased," he said. "I am sorry I cannot give you more encouraging news."

In January 1998, Michael rang his friend Peter Carey and said, "I've got two pieces of news, one good, one bad. I've got cancer. But I'm going to beat it." However, the prostate cancer was advanced. It had spread to his spine and his lungs. Michael did not have long to live. When it became apparent that the cancer was terminal, Michael intensified his efforts to see "my Suu." Yet the Burmese government kept refusing his repeated requests for a visa. He made more than thirty applications so he could see his wife one last time. They were all denied.

A multi-national effort began to help the rapidly weakening Oxford professor see his wife before he died. Appeals to the Burmese junta to allow Michael an entrance visa were made by the United States, Great Britain, and several other countries. The Dalai Lama, U.N. Secretary General Kofi Annan, and Pope John Paul II entreated the junta to show mercy and grant the visa. They refused. The generals claimed that they did not have the facilities to care for Michael, and suggested that Suu Kyi leave the country instead if she wanted to see her husband.

Instead of granting the visa for Michael, the junta piled more psychological pressure on Aung San Suu Kyi. They printed commentaries alleging what a bad wife Suu Kyi was and asking, why didn't she do what decent wives would do and go to the side of her dying husband? They were pouring salt in the wound, said British ambassador Robert Gordon, as everyone knew full well that once she crossed Burma's borders, she would never be allowed to return.

It was a dreadful "Sophie's choice," between her dying husband and her struggling country. Suu Kyi and Michael both knew that if she left to be with Michael during his final months, the regime would have finally gotten their chance to kick her out for good. She would lose both her husband and her country. What would happen then to the many people in Burma who were counting on her? They both understood that without her prominent presence, international attention might fade and there could be a large-scale persecution of the democracy activists she would be leaving behind. How could she justify leaving to be with her family when so many of her colleagues were in prison without their loved ones? It was an intensely difficult time. Coming to terms with the harsh options before her, her friends say, took prayer and the deep faith of a lifelong Buddhist. She told *Dateline NBC* in 2000 that her decision in the end was what she had warned her husband many years before: "My country first."

That did not mean that she didn't try to help her husband when he was ailing. She rang up her family friend, Lady Gore-Booth in England, and beseeched her, "Please do something." But his cancer was already too advanced for her to help. Because the phone line in her home had been disconnected, she arranged to await his call at the home of the British ambassador. After the calls, Ambassador Gordon remembered, "Sometimes my wife would need to comfort her a bit." Military intelligence soon figured out that Suu Kyi was circumventing their telephone block by going to the British ambassador's house to call her husband. One evening, Michael and Suu had just said hello when the line went dead at the ambassador's home. In a rare moment of utter despair, Suu Kyi burst into tears and sobbed.

Michael's friends worried that the swift path of the cancer was linked to the stress he had been under as the standard-bearer and white knight for his wife. He continued to say he was going to overcome the cancer, he was going to beat it, he had to.

As late as March 19, 1999, Michael was still trying to get a visa to visit his wife. He passed away a week later in a London hospice. In a final bit of cruel irony, a visa was approved by the Burmese regime the day he died, March 27, 1999. It was his 53rd birthday. On his last day, he told his friend Robin Christopher, "Tell Suu we have done our best."

A farewell film that Suu Kyi recorded for her husband at the British embassy, which was smuggled out of the country, arrived two days after he died. She asked her sons to gather flowers from the meadows on her behalf to put on his memorial.

In his obituary, a friend spoke of his enduring love for his wife, a "love that tyranny could not crush." At his memorial, his friends recalled fondly "his deep throaty laugh, his benign and avuncular presence and great scholarly knowledge." They remembered how he lovingly gave them packets for his wife if they were traveling to Rangoon, tucking in rolls of toilet paper along with the complete works of Shakespeare. The memorial service was a pastiche of his life: His sons read the Lord's Prayer, honoring his upbringing as a Catholic; a chamber quartet played Bach and Pachelbel; and Buddhist monks prayed and chanted. One of his Tibetan students spoke of the wisdom that Suu Kyi and Michael had learned from a Tibeto-Bhutanese Lama, who taught that the happiness of the individual is insignificant compared to that of the many; therefore the one should serve the other. A Buddhist memorial service also was held in Rangoon at Suu Kyi's home. When asked to comment, Suu Kyi said simply, "I feel so fortunate to have had such a wonderful husband who has always given me the understanding I needed; nothing can take that away from me."

Suu Kyi's faithful housekeeper Khin Khin Win later told the BBC, "He was the man for her. She treasured him. She said he was the thing she valued most in her life. She's always able to control her feelings; I couldn't tell what she was thinking, but from what I saw, she suffered terribly. Since she was a child, she has kept herself under control, no matter how deeply she feels. She never shows it, but she did say she had lost the most valuable person in her life."

Robin Christopher, who was serving at the time as British Ambassador to Indonesia, flew to Burma to console the new widow. "There was the sense of 'that chapter of my life is over. It is closed. I will now focus totally on the future and my country.'"

Some Southeast Asian leaders, normally reluctant to criticize their incorrigible neighbor, expressed shock and dismay at the Burmese government's callousness in refusing a visa to Michael. Shamed by the outpouring of international criticism, the junta generals allowed Alexander and Kim Aris to come to Burma shortly after their father's death to see their mother.

After Michael's death, his family helped look after his sons. Both young men grew up to become tall, dark-haired blends of their parents. Their family circumstances took a toll on both boys—Alexander dropped out of college for a year, and Kim dropped out entirely.

Alexander traveled to the U.S. to attend college, but went back to England for a year to mull his future. He then returned to the U.S. and enrolled in Northern Illinois University in DeKalb, where he studied mathematical sciences and philosophy. He later joined a Buddhist commune in the Portland, Oregon area and became a practitioner of the ancient Chinese meditation therapy Qigong. He has written that the meditation brought him comfort with the "great and unnecessary burden" he had been carrying in his life. According to a *Daily Mail* report, he lives simply, is a vegan, rides a bicycle, has no refrigerator, and cooks on a wood stove with twigs and scrap wood he has collected. Though it appears he has retreated from the world, his friends say he speaks proudly of his mother and speaks with her often on the phone.

Kim remained in London. Always the more free-wheeling of the two, he became a carpenter and decorator. He married and has two young children, Jasmine and Jamie, but is divorced. At one point, he was reportedly living in a narrowboat, a small covered boat, in Oxford.

While their mother was under house arrest, both sons avoided speaking out publicly lest they worsen her predicament. Neither has any involvement in Burmese politics. "It's probably best that we don't," Kim has said. "It wouldn't help her, and she wouldn't want it. It's something she wants to do herself." Still, he thinks of his mother, he said, "all the time."

Over time, Suu Kyi would say less and less about how much she missed her sons. She often rebuffed interviewers by saying crisply, "I don't answer personal questions." But there were instances when she let down her reserve with friends. Film director Moe Thu, a longtime family friend, told the BBC that when he was in prison, the government came to tell him that his wife had passed away. He was allowed to go to her funeral and was impressed that Aung San Suu Kyi came to pay her respects and comfort him. It broke his heart, he said, when she told him in a rueful, pensive moment, "We are not a good wife, good husband," because his wife had passed away when he was gone and her husband passed away while she was gone. He said she told him, "'You know I think I'm not even a good mother also because my son started smoking.' She never got to take care of her sons."

—∾—

By 1998, the regime began racheting up the pressure on Aung San Suu Kyi and her followers. Blockades were placed around her house from time to time to discourage people from gawking or gathering at her gate. Crowds that gathered anyway were warned they could face twenty years in prison to attending her gate-side talks. That inspired even more people to attend. When the Tatmadaw sealed off University Avenue, Aung San Suu Kyi blithely moved the pep talks to a different street. That feint was foiled when a mob of the junta's USDA supporters attacked Suu Kyi's car with sticks and stones while she was en route to the new site, wounding her adviser U Tin Oo.

Her colleagues were increasingly worried about her safety, but as she told the *New York Times* that year, "If the army really wants to kill me they can do it without any problems at all, so there is no point in making elaborate security arrangements. It is not bravado or anything like that. I suppose I am just rather down to earth and I just don't see the point to this worry."

In July and August 1998, the pressure on her was intensified. Suu Kyi tried to meet with NLD members outside Rangoon, but police stopped her car. In July, she was trapped in her car for five days before soldiers forcibly removed her driver from the car and drove her home under guard. In August, she held out for 11 days before the extra food and water she had brought ran out. She stopped drinking liquids to avoid having to urinate in public. Her car finally was turned around and she was escorted home. The experience left Suu Kyi deeply bruised from the manhandling, dehydrated, and exhausted. She had intended to tell her NLD party members in Bassein not to obey a recent military order to report to the authorities twice a day under the "Habitual Offenders Act," a law generally reserved for heinous criminals. She was not able to do so because her car was surrounded by soldiers, sandbags, and barbed wire barricades. The military government later claimed in a statement, "In fact, there existed none of these around the car. It is their own rigid and confrontational policy which has made them spend the night in the car."

Aung San Suu Kyi was incensed by the incident, and the harassment became continual:

- When students tried to ramp up protests again, Aung San Suu Kyi was put under stricter guard in her home, "for her own protection."
- When the NLD attempted to hold a national conference, the junta put 800 to 1,200 NLD members under "temporary" detention.
- When Aung San Suu Kyi was contacted about sending a video message to the U.N. Human Rights Commission, the junta accused her of having contact with "dissidents" and "armed terrorists." They warned that she and her party members could be given the death penalty or life in prison for treason.

Aung San Suu Kyi kept going out to speak anyway, only to be trapped in her car again on the way to the poverty-filled Dala area. The junta said in state newspapers that she was on "holiday" and was put in protective custody for her protection—on a stretch of road that happened to be infested with malarial mosquitoes. This time, Suu Kyi was trapped in her car for nine days and had to be returned to her home in an ambulance. She had trained herself to get by without food and water for long stretches, but she was only human and collapsed.

Still, Suu Kyi would not give in to the pressure. She went with U Tin Oo to the rail station in Rangoon to attend an NLD meeting in Mandalay. When they arrived, the station had been cordoned off. Dozens of NLD supporters were arrested. U Tin Oo and several other uncles on the Executive Committee were taken to Insein Prison. Suu Kyi was forced roughly into a car and driven to her home unceremoniously.

Once again, Suu Kyi was placed under house arrest in September 2000. The junta claimed it was to protect her from being used by "criminal and terrorist elements."

—~—

Her perseverance did not go unnoticed by the international community. President Bill Clinton, in the closing weeks of his presidential term, awarded Aung San Suu Kyi the Presidential Medal of Freedom on December 7, 2000. Accepting the award on his mother's behalf in 2000, Alexander Aris stood nearly as tall as the 6-foot-2 president.

"She sits confined, as we speak here, in her home in Rangoon, unable to speak to her people or the world." Mr. Clinton said as he presented the award. "But her struggle continues and her spirit still inspires us."

Paying tribute to the democracy leader, he added: "She has seen her supporters beaten, tortured, and killed, yet she has never responded to hatred and violence in kind. All she has ever asked for is peaceful dialogue.

"The only weapons the Burmese people have are the words of reason and the example of this astonishingly brave woman," he added. "America will also be a friend to freedom in Burma—a friend for as long as it takes to reach the goal for which she has sacrificed so very much."

—~—

When the rest of the world celebrated the beginning of a new millennium in 2001 with champagne and fireworks, Aung San Suu Kyi was under guard at 54 University Avenue again. Whenever U.N. envoys were allowed to see her, they invariably reported afterward that she seemed in "good spirits."

CHAPTER TEN

THE LIVES OF OTHERS

"We will surely get to our destination if we join hands."
—Aung San Suu Kyi

One by one, most of Aung San Suu Kyi's closest associates were taken away, imprisoned, and abused throughout the course of the 1990s. Although the circumstances that she was enduring were difficult and often dangerous, she was acutely aware that others were sacrificing far more. She told a reporter after her release in 2002, "Many have suffered more than I have, much more. I don't have the right to complain."

It's true she never complained about her own hardships, but she did grow angry at the unspeakable treatment her friends and colleagues suffered. Considering what the people closest to her endured, it is easy to understand why she banged her piano keys so hard in frustration that some of the strings and keys broke.

Suu Kyi's closest cousin, **Aye Win**, a bookish, bespectacled accountant, served as her secretary. He was awakened in the middle of the night—1 A.M. is the junta's favorite calling time—and taken to prison on unspecified charges in 1996. He was held in Insein Prison five years, the maximum allowable without charges. Aye Win had offered to assist Suu Kyi out of a sense of family duty. His father was Aung San's brother and was assassinated in 1947 along with the other members of the country's first cabinet. Before he was taken away to prison in 1996, Aye Win reassured a visiting journalist who was nervous about the risk of interviewing him, that the reporter did not have anything to worry about because he had the power of the U.S. government behind him. "It is we Burmese who have to worry," Aye Win told him. "All we have is Aung San's daughter."

—∞—

Another of her volunteer secretaries, **Win Htein**, was arrested in 1989 at Aung San Suu Kyi's home for his role in the 1988 uprisings. He was kept in Insein Prison for five years. The torture he endured included three days without water, five days kneeling on the cement floor, lying handcuffed with a hood on his head, and more than two years in solitary confinement. He was then rearrested in 1996 along with 262 other NLD supporters and members of Parliament as the junta thwarted their attempt to form a Congress. Win Htein was sentenced to another 14 years in prison, supposedly for providing information to the media about Burma's agricultural decline under military rule. He was released in 2008 as part of a ballyhooed general amnesty, only to be rearrested 17 hours later.

—∞—

Suu Kyi's 27-year old Muslim bodyguard, **Maung San Hlaing**, vanished on the way to a local video shop in 1996. He was later seen in Insein Prison. Military authorities accused him of providing information to foreign journalists about the use of torture in prisons. Myanmar citizens who reported the use of torture risked imprisonment and torture themselves. Maung San Hlaing, also known as "Evak" and "Tin Hlaing," was sentenced to seven years' imprisonment. His mistake was being interviewed on camera in Suu Kyi's home compound. The government-controlled media reported that

Suu Kyi's assistant had given foreign journalists "concocted news" about torture and other "false and fabricated events."

—w—

Win Thein, the young man who bravely stepped ahead of Suu Kyi during the dramatic "High Noon" showdown on the road to Danubyu during the 1989 election campaign, was picked up by Military Intelligence not long after the incident and taken before a military tribunal. He spent the next 14 years in prison. His original sentence was three years, but the punishment was extended when he was caught circulating a human-rights report critical of the government to the other prisoners. When he was finally released in 2003, he fled to Thailand. Like many other political refuges, he struggled to get by in the refugee-packed border town of Mae Sot. He remained a loyal advocate of Aung San Suu Kyi.

—w—

U Tin Moe, a professor of Burmese Literature at Rangoon University who was the Poet Laureate of Burma, was a close friend of Suu Kyi's mother Khin Kyi. At her mother's recommendation, Suu Kyi sought out the rumpled professor for his advice when she was working part-time at the Bodleian Library at Oxford, helping to build up the Burmese collection. Tin Moe not only helped her locate copies of Burmese classics, he gave her tutorials on Burmese literature, which later helped Suu Kyi when she applied for the doctoral program in literature at London University. Tin Moe, who was highly critical of Ne Win's dictatorship, recognized Suu Kyi's leadership potential and often urged her, "You must help our country." When she returned to Burma in 1988, he became active in the new pro-democracy movement and headed one of her NLD committees. As a result, he was imprisoned in Insein Prison in 1991 for four years. All of his published works were banned. In jail, Tin Moe was prohibited from possessing any reading or writing materials. He was pleased when he discovered that one of his short poems had been scratched on the dirty cell walls by a previous prisoner, a poem for which he was famous: "The cigarette's burnt down, the sun is brown, will someone please take me home now." In defiance of the authorities, U Tin Moe wrote a poem celebrating the life of Michael Aris after his death.

A teddy bear of a man with a thick thatch of gray hair that stood straight up in places, Tin Moe loved nothing better than presiding over literary conversation at Rangoon restaurants over dishes heaped with noodles and tea salad and young eels, serving food to his companions along with insights about Tolstoy. When the authorities started threatening him with re-arrest if he continued supporting the NLD, Tin Moe decided in 1999 that it was time to flee. He knew he was too old to survive another incarceration. Obtaining a passport required considerable cunning, because he had been barred from leaving the country without permission. Fortunately for him, the immigration officials did not have enough literary savvy to recognize his real name on the passport: U Ba Gyan. No one even knew he had fled the country. His escape was discovered when authorities heard him being interviewed on the Burmese Service of the BBC. U Tin Moe died in exile in California in 2007.

Largely unknown to the public outside of the country, Burma's most prominent political prisoner after Daw Suu is **Min Ko Naing**. That is the *nom de guerre* meaning "Conqueror of Kings," of a young man named Paw U Tun, the fiery student leader of the nationwide uprising in the summer of 1988.

Throughout the 1980s, as a student at the Rangoon Arts and Sciences University, Min Ko Naing had somehow managed to build a nationwide political-dissident network in the shadow of one of the world's most watchful police states. He called it the All Burma Federation of Student Unions (ABFSU).

A talented orator, his passion at rallies brought out millions of Burmese into the streets in 1988. More than any other student leader at the time, he had the ability to inspire crowds and then calm them down at tense times. He matched that with a gift for organizing people for large-scale events.

Constantly in danger, he told crowds, "I'll never die. Physically I might be dead, but many more Min Ko Naings will appear to take my place. As you know, Min Ko Naing can only conquer a bad king. If the ruler is good, we will carry him on our shoulders."

Min Ko Naing was arrested early in 1989 and sentenced to 20 years, later reduced to 10 years. Though suffering from ill health in solitary confinement for most of these years, Min Ko Naing was defiant. On the rare occasions he was able to send a message outside, he simply said, "Don't give up."

When I met Min Ko Naing in 2013, he had been recently been released from a second long stint in prison. He was soon turning 50 and had spent 25 of those years in prison. As he walked into the hotel restaurant where we were meeting, all heads turned. The room buzzed as people watched him with admiration like a movie star. It was apparent that the two prison cohorts who came with him held him in high esteem as well—one cut his food for him when he was busy talking, one checked his cell phone messages. I found him immensely likable: soft-spoken, thoughtful, extremely bright—not the brash type I had imagined as the Conquerer of Kings. With his boyishly tousled hair, he still looked like a student. He had an odd twist to his mouth, the result of slightly prominent front teeth, which gave him a unique, vulnerable appearance. As we talked, he made no mention of the fact that he had been tortured repeatedly; once forced to stand in water for two weeks before collapsing. He spoke only of the need to help the lost generation of patriotic students who had spent most of the best years of their lives in prison. He pointed out that the key successes of the movement were because of the efforts of ordinary people. "We should always remember the goodness of unsung heroes who gave their lives," he said. "We faced brutal responses, but people marched on. I want this to remain in history as unforgettable."

His personal plans? In addition to launching a new civic society organization to promote democracy, Min Ko Naing said he was finally starting a long-deferred career—as a painter. He had drawn caricatures of the generals as a student and started painting in prison with materials his family brought him. Now he was painting the beautiful landscapes and scenes of children playing that he had dreamed about in prison.

Though people often spoke of him as a potential rival to Aung San Suu Kyi, he said he was not interested in running for office himself and would do all he could to help Aung San Suu Kyi and the NLD.

Like the poet and novelist that he is, he later described the need to keep up reforms by saying "The people are like the sky, which is always there for us, and the government or the men in power are like the clouds, which visit the sky temporarily."

—w—

Daw Yin Yin May, a matronly-looking woman with a warm smile, worked in the information office at the British Embassy when the democracy movement sprang up in 1988. Known to her friends as "Nita," she first encountered Aung San Suu Kyi in 1988 when she heard her speech at the Shwedagon Pagoda. Nita May recalls, "She had a certain aura about her that was instantly captivating. The whole speech moved me profoundly. I remember coming away thinking—a leader is born."

Nita May met with Suu Kyi several times that year and followed her during her campaign trips around Rangoon. She visited Suu Kyi's house almost every day and was able to attend press conferences as part of her job at the embassy. Her position also enabled her to surreptitiously slip letters to Suu Kyi from her husband and friends abroad. She relayed information back to the British officials and the BBC's Burma Service about the democracy movement. It was a risky role. In time, Nita May was accused by the Burmese authorities of being a British spy and taken to interrogation camps multiple times.

A few months after Aung San Suu Kyi was placed under house arrest in 1989, Daw Nita May was incarcerated in Insein Prison. Security forces coerced a false confession out of her. She was sentenced to three years of hard labor. While incarcerated, she gave birth to a son with little medical support. She handed the boy over to her family for care because the prison was not a suitable place for an infant. "I felt it was my sentence, not the baby's," she explained. A year later, when she was released, she returned to her family and her post at the Embassy and then left the country to work as a producer for the BBC Burmese Service in London. She was honored with the Order of the British Empire for her work to support the democracy movement.

When Aung San Suu Kyi was released from her house arrest in 1995, Daw Nita May interviewed her for the BBC. "Her first question was about my youngest boy," Nita May said.

Burma's leading journalist, **U Win Tin**, also paid a dear price for supporting Aung San Suu Kyi and the NLD democracy movement. He served more than 19 years in jail—almost all of them in solitary confinement. His first arrest in 1989 was for offering hospitality in his home to an NLD member and his companion. He was interrogated, deprived of sleep, food, and medicine when he was arrested. According to Aung San Suu Kyi, "His interrogators wished to force him to admit that he was my adviser on political tactics, in other words, that he was my puppet master." U Win Tin refused to give any information about the NLD inner workings or to make a false confession. He was sentenced to three years of hard labor at the age of 59. That sentence was extended to 12 years. Then it was extended again. Win Tin was kept most of the time in "the center of hell, the dog cells. He was routinely beaten and on one occasion interrogated for five days straight. He lost most of his teeth from the beatings. The guards refused to let him get dentures for eight years, forcing him to gum his food. He also suffered two heart attacks and a slipped disc and lost one testicle in a botched hernia operation in a hospital cell. While he was locked in prison, he lost his home and his daughter was forced into exile.

Yet when asked by his interrogators to resign from the National League for Democracy, he refused.

When asked to sign a statement promising he would not engage in politics again, he refused.

"I could not bow down to them," he said. "No, I could not do it. I wrote poems to keep myself from going crazy. I did mathematics with chalk on the floor."

Altogether, he was kept in prison more than 7,000 days. After his release, Win Tin said it was the isolation from other people that had caused him the greatest distress. "The hardest thing was the separation from other people. Even when I was in the hospital, I was put in a different room. You long to have a discussion with your friends. You feel as if you are losing your mind," he said.

When Win Tin was released in 2008 at the age of 78, he was the country's longest-serving political prisoner, locked up because of his views and words. He was released as part of a wider release of prisoners that the government called "a gesture of loving kindness and goodwill."

After his release, Win Tin made efforts to re-organize the NLD. He re-established weekly meetings of the party's Central Executive Committee, which had been held irregularly since the Depayin massacre in 2003. He also resumed a regular roundtable called "Youth and Future" that Aung San Suu Kyi had attended in the past. And to keep faith with the thousands of "forgotten prisoners" languishing behind bars, the old journalist visited family members of political prisoners to offer moral support.

When I met with him in 2013, he had only recently gotten out of the hospital again, the consequence of prison ailments, but he was smiling and welcoming, his eyes twinkling behind big black glasses. He lived in a small two-room hut in the garden of a relative's house, with the only decorations being a shelf of books and a large photo of Aung San Suu Kyi. He had just turned 83 and continued to wear blue shirts the same color as his prison shirts to remind people that the country is not totally free so long as the military controls Parliament.

Win Tin remained convinced that Suu Kyi had the best chance of getting the ruling generals to relax their grip: "I can confront the junta personally, but I cannot organize other people to do the same. Only she can do that." Despite the long years he spent in prison, Win Tin's memories of "The Lady" campaigning in 1989 were still vivid to him. "She drew crowds that were a mile deep. People could not see her, but they came anyway. There was hope and expectation and I pray I will see this again," he said. "She is great. She is wise and committed, hard-working and far-sighted. We believe she can lead our country."

—w—

Being a journalist is a life-threatening choice in Burma. The vague and draconian Electronic Act is often used to arrest many reporters—like the arrest of a young female video journalist with the Democratic Voice of Burma in late 2009. Hla Hla Win was sentenced to 20 years in prison under the Electronic Act. Her crime? She had interviewed monks in Pakokku about the uprising that had begun in local monasteries two years before.

In October 2010, Nyi Nyi Tun, editor of the *Kandarawaddy* news publication, was sentenced to 13 years in prison on vague charges of crimes against the state. He was originally detained in 2009 on suspicion of abetting bomb blasts in Rangoon. Although those allegations were later discarded, Nyi Nyi Tun was interrogated and tortured. He was charged with associating with exile-run news groups and unauthorized use of electronic media. His newspaper was shut down.

Research by the Committee to Protect Journalists in 2010 showed that Burma had at least 12 journalists behind bars as elections were being held, the second-highest tally in Asia. (Only China exceeded the number, with more than 24 journalists jailed.) The Democratic Voice of Burma, which works from exile in Thailand, told CPJ that a dozen of its undercover reporters are also being held by Burmese authorities on various charges, but that they must remain anonymous because their sentences could be extended if they were revealed to be DVB journalists.

The most powerful portrait of the repression in Burma was produced by Democratic Voice of Burma video crews, who secretly documented the bloody crackdown on protests in *Burma VJ*, which was nominated for an Academy Award in 2009. As the narrator-in-hiding of the film, "Joshua," watches the military brutalize the protesters, he says, with fear and sadness, "I feel the world is forgetting about us."

Even in 2013, when press laws were supposedly relaxed, police arrested five journalists from the *Unity Journal* for reporting on an alleged chemical weapons factory. They were given sentences of 10 years in prison for a single news story. Another journalist from Democratic Voice of Burma was imprisoned for "disturbing a civil servant" and trespassing after attempting to interview an education official about corruption allegations. And a *Mizzima* journalist was arrested for leading a demonstration to protest the intimidation of the media.

—~—

As the years and the struggle went on in the 1990s, not all of the early NLD supporters stayed on board. The greatest loss was **U Kyi Maung,** who quietly bowed out of the top leadership in 1997. U Kyi Maung had been one of the first of the influential former generals to welcome Aung San Suu Kyi to party leadership. He was the man most responsible for leading the party to victory in 1990 while Aung San Su Kyi and U Tin Oo were under arrest. Gaining freedom for Burma had been his life's work. As a young student at Rangoon University, he had marched at the head of demonstrations against colonial rule in 1938, holding high the flag of the Students' Union. He was one of the first students to be struck down by the mounted police. During the war, he served in Aung San's Burma Independence Army and remained with the armed forces as a top regional commander until 1963. A staunch believer in the importance of an apolitical, professional army, he was strongly opposed to the military takeover led by General Ne Win in 1962. That wasn't a popular view with Ne Win. U Kyi Maung was asked to retire. He then was imprisoned twice, for a total of seven years, on suspicion of opposing the military.

When the democracy movement broke out in 1988, U Kyi Maung was arrested for the third time, but only for a month. He went on to become one of the 12 members of the NLD Executive Committee and vice chairman of the party. When Aung San Suu Kyi and U Tin Oo were put under house arrest in July 1989, U Kyi Maung held the NLD together. He deftly masterminded the victorious election campaign while avoiding arrest himself. He also won election to the Parliament and probably would have played a prominent role in a new government had the military handed over power. Instead, he was arrested a fourth time after the 1990 election and imprisoned until 1996. Once freed, he often stood side by side by Aung San Suu Kyi at the gate of her house and gave speeches to the crowds.

One of the photos from that period shows U Kyi Maung and Aung San Suu Kyi in a relaxed moment, laughing genially while they work. What happened to end the laughter? A mild-manned man, U Kyi Maung was known to his friends as "Colonel" and was popular for his sense of humor and straightforward manner.

U Kyi Maung's decision to leave the party in 1997 caused considerable concern that the democracy movement might implode without him. His reason for leaving was never publicly revealed. All that was known was that there were three strong personalities in charge, then suddenly there were two. The military regime, always eager to cast Aung San Suu Kyi in the worst possible light, claimed U Kyi Maung had sharp differences with Suu Kyi. When I asked Suu Kyi about it in a 2011 interview, she said there had never been a split. "I don't know why people call it a split. We disagreed on some things, but there was not a split," she said crisply. I felt the temperature in the room drop slightly. One of the fascinating things about Aung San Suu Kyi's charisma is that when she pulls back into herself, you feel it. As someone once observed, it is like window blinds opening and closing. It was clear she would say no more.

Whatever the cause of the fracture with U Kyi Maung, he remained widely admired for keeping his differences private to minimize harm to the democracy movement. He did not switch his allegiance to any other party and was never active in politics again. Nor did he ever issue a statement for why he left the party. The NLD carried on. But Suu Kyi had lost a close friend and ally, for reasons still unknown.

Other prominent party defectors did speak out. The most notable was **Ma Thanegi**, the assistant who had kept the Aris boys busy playing Monopoly while their mother was being arrested in 1989. Ma Thanegi, who had attended the Methodist English High School along with many of the democracy activists, worked as an artist and writer before she volunteered to help Suu Kyi as a personal assistant in her home office. In the early days of the democracy movement, she answered the phone, took notes at meetings, and traveled with Suu Kyi. A decade later, Ma Thanegi told an interviewer that those early days "were filled with high hopes, fun, and optimism. Even when I recall the times of danger, I have no regrets." She was taken into custody the same day soldiers placed Suu Kyi under house arrest and was kept in Insein Prison for three years.

When Suu Kyi was released from house arrest in 1995, Ma Thanegi returned to help her with errands. But she soon parted ways with Suu Kyi. They had argued so much, Ma Thanegi said, that she left. An articulate woman with a trendy haircut and intellectual-looking glasses, Ma Thanegi began criticizing the democracy movement's tactics. She faulted the NLD for opposing the constitutional process, essentially saying it was better to be inside the tent than outside. She challenged Suu Kyi's call for foreign investors to isolate Burma. She opposed sanctions. She wrote articles for *The New Yorker, International Herald Tribune,* and *Far Eastern Economic Review* as well as local, government-controlled media criticizing Suu Kyi's policies. She complained Suu Kyi's approach "came at a real price for the rest of us."

Democracy advocates accused Ma Thanegi of being a paid shill for the government, a traitor to the democracy movement. When she traveled to the U.S. for a speaking tour, activists disrupted her speaking events, peppering her with questions until she had to leave. Ma Thanegi insisted she still respected Aung San Suu Kyi, but felt compelled to speak her conscience and convictions. She contined to have a successful career as an author and cultural critic. Suu Kyi does not discuss her former assistant or her criticism.

—∿—

Many of those who survived their prison experience in the 1990s told of being beaten, burned, shackled, stabbed. Some had salt and chemicals rubbed into open wounds. Women often suffered particular indignities. Some were raped, used as porters, or tortured for the amusement of the guards. Some had body parts amputated. One woman who met with a visiting U.N. Special Rapporteur could not describe her horrors—her tongue had been cut out by soldiers.

The prison network in Burma reportedly numbers 43 prisons and some 100 labor camps scattered across the country. They range from the infamous Insein Prison, built by the British in 1871, to remote camps in the chilly mountains along the Burma-China border. More than 200,000 prisoners were being held before the elections in fall 2010. Some 2,170 of those were monks, activists, lawyers, politicians, relief workers, and journalists. It was estimated that there is one doctor for every 8,000 inmates in the prison system.

—∿—

One of those who did not get out of prison alive was Suu Kyi's godfather and one of her closest friends. His name was **James Leander Nichols**, but

Suu Kyi called him "Uncle Leo." Nichols died in 1996 after being taken to Insein Prison. The official reason for his arrest was that he was operating unregistered phone lines and fax machines in his home. His real sin was being a close friend of Aung San Suu Kyi.

Military authorities had been racheting up the pressure on people helping Suu Kyi after she began drawing crowds to the front of her house during 1995 and 1996. They discovered that Nichols had been using his fax to send Suu Kyi's newspaper column, "Letter from Burma," to Japan's *Mainichi Shimbun*, which in turn shared her column with Western newspapers. To shut down her access, the military hauled in Nichols and confiscated his assets.

When he was arrested, Nichols was 65 and in poor health. He suffered from diabetes, hypertension, and heart problems. After his death, Amnesty International protested that Nichols had been forced to undergo sleep deprivation for night after night in prison and was denied medical treatment. Government officials claimed Nichols was found unconscious in his cell after "suffering a stroke" and was transferred to a hospital, where he died one hour later. Most others believe he died in the prison after weeks of torture. Authorities refused to release his body for an independent autopsy. They hurriedly buried Nichols within 27 hours of his death. No family members were allowed at the burial service. Yet as the details of the days before his death emerged, the middle-aged businessman became a symbol of the struggle against the barbarity in Burma. Nichols had the kind of life story that novelists dream of. He was a slightly mysterious figure, of mixed Greek-Burmese parentage. He had turned his hybrid heritage into a business advantage, becoming so successful at bridging the Burmese and European worlds that he represented the business interests of Norway, Denmark, Finland, and Switzerland as honorary consul in Rangoon for many years.

Nichols's father was part of a Greek family that owned the Stevedoring Shipping Company in Rangoon. His family was well off and sent young Nichols to school in India, which probably saved his life during the Japanese occupation of Burma in 1942. His father died in the war. Nichols returned to work with his uncle and brother and became general manager of the United Liner Agencies. He married and had several children, who left during Ne Win's dictatorship for safer locations in Australia and the United States. Nichols stayed on.

His shipping company was nationalized after Ne Win came to power in 1962. Shortly afterwards, Nichols was appointed honorary consul-general for the three Scandinavian countries and Switzerland, who needed someone with his savoir faire to help them navigate the treacheries of the time. Nichols was briefly arrested in 1980 and forced to give up his official representations, but he quietly resumed his consular work behind the scenes.

Nichols was not a political man, but he knew injustice when he saw it. He did what he could to help by devoting himself to making money and distributing it to worthy causes such as orphanages. His donations never appeared on the government lists as he discreetly found ways to donate to Buddhist, Muslim, and Christian charities. He himself was a Catholic.

Though he was half Burmese, Nichols had more European features, with a high forehead and thinning gray hair. He was a bit taller than most Burmese and wore glasses. Over the years, he had acquired the mannerly demeanor of an international broker. Thanks to his business success, he was able to help Aung San Suu Kyi by performing small favors such as finding her a gardener and handymen for her house. He lent her his car on occasion. Rumors persisted that he was the NLD's secret banker, which both he and the NLD denied.

After Aung San Suu Kyi's release from house arrest in July 1995, Nichols would stop by her house for breakfast every Friday. He was one of the first arrested when the military cracked down in April 1996. Soldiers swept across Rangoon, arresting Nichols and more than 250 NLD members just as they were preparing to attend a party conference at Aung San Suu Kyi's house. Nichols was sentenced to three years in prison. The Burmese official media accused him of "providing general expenses for the democratic stunt actress." It is more likely that military intelligence tapped his phones lines and wanted to remove his connections to the international media.

As a close friend of Suu Kyi's, he was subjected to especially harsh treatment in prison. Although prisoners normally can wear their own clothing to prison, police stripped Nichols of his tailored clothes and forced him to wear a loud yellow sports shirt and a standard white prison longyi that was too small for him. The guards placed Nichols in solitary confinement, forced him to sit or stand in painful positions, and interrogated him for hours on end about his dealings with Aung San Suu Kyi. In particular, the guards liked to show their hatred of him by forcing him to endure the degrading positions of subservience called "Poun-san." The Poun-san practices included requiring him to sit cross-legged with his hands on his knees, with his back straight and head bowed to them in subjugation, or squatting and standing in painful and humiliating positions for hours, until he collapsed to the floor.

Like many of the prisoners, Nichols contracted acute dysentery from the foul, unsanitary conditions. He had nothing to clean himself or a change of clothes, which caused him considerable embarrassment. Though they had very little by way of food or clothes themselves, the other prisoners shared the meager bits of biscuit they had stashed away as well as their own clothing. They helped him wash his soiled garments with shards of soap they had saved, knowing they could be subjected to severe punishment in the dreaded "dog cells" for doing so. They were deeply touched by the humble man who said he was honored to be among them when he found out that he was in the section for political prisoners. When they walked by his cell, he would call to them through the opening in his cell door, "Thank you, thank you."

Nichols was particularly dismayed when he heard about the long sentences given to four others arrested at the same time as he was for their political work. He repeatedly cried out, "Oh, my God, oh my God!" Nichols could not believe his ears and tried to find out more about their well-being. He vowed to the other prisoners in his section that he would tell the world about their suffering when he got out. He did not get that chance.

According to other prisoners, the guards interrogated Nichols for six nights in a row about Western involvement in Burma as well as Suu Kyi's personal life. By then he was vomiting and suffering from dizziness. He was disoriented and had great difficulty walking. According to a fellow political prisoner named Moe Aye, before Nichols was taken away the last time, he said to his cell neighbors, "I'll lie down on the floor if they force me to stand to ask questions this time. I can't take this anymore. . . . I'll be lucky if I make it back. If I can't make it back, please tell everyone here for me that I owe them for their kind help."

Moe Aye, who was later released, wrote that he saw Nichols taken away by the Military Intelligence service in the back of a truck carrying empty rice pots. "As usual, there was a hood over his head. . . . That was the last time we saw him." About a week later, Moe Aye heard that Nichols had died. "All that we were told was that he was forced to choose the path in which there was no way back," he said. At the time, a commentary in a government-controlled newspaper in Burma said that Leo Nichols was an "unimportant crook who met his due fate." The commentary claimed that Nichols deserved his fate because he had been "reckless with food and lazy and sought luxury." It also claimed that Nichols was not mistreated and that he had masseurs and people fanning him in prison. Such was the handiwork of Military Intelligence, under the direction of General Khin Nyunt.

It was a measure of Leo Nichols's courage that he had continued providing support to Aung San Suu Kyi even though he knew the risks. He had been arrested twice before. In addition to his 1980 arrest for his work for foreign countries, he was picked up in 1989 at the same time as Aung San Suu Kyi's first house arrest, but was released soon after. A prominent Muslim businessman who was arrested during the same period died for lack of medical treatment. Leo Nichols continued to support the democracy movement for more than six years. He was not willing to sit by while the military regime tried to destroy his goddaughter and the country.

After Nichols's death, Aung San Suu Kyi had hoped to attend a proper memorial for her loyal friend. But a scheduled Catholic memorial service for Nichols was called off out of concern that undercover military intelligence agents, who were sure to watch over the burial service, would arrest those who attended.

Nichols's death turned out to be a signal moment for the international community. The regime's persecution of ethnic groups had long been considered unconscionable and the jailing of critics on the slightest pretext was indefensible, but torturing a respected businessman to death for having a fax machine was a new barbarity. As one shocked diplomat put it, the Burmese generals were descending rung by rung into the darker realms of power, where other human lives had no value.

Though Burma rarely sentenced political prisoners to death *officially* and formal executions inside prisons were rare, the ruling generals had found sinister ways to make sure that many democracy leaders never left the prisons alive. Stories of political prisoners who died in Burma's prisons regularly surfaced in the 1990s: Student leaders in their early 20s were found with broken ribs and smashed faces and proclaimed dead of "natural causes" . . . members of Parliament were reported dead of leukemia or "heart attacks" . . . an ex-Navy commander and a respected member of the High Court died with no explanation before their sentences were completed . . . 40 monks who had protested the harsh conditions in the country were never seen again. Many others perished who were transferred to remote prisons and contracted malaria, tuberculosis, and AIDS in prison. Some went blind. Others committed suicide.

> "Those of us who decided to work for democracy in Burma made our choice in the conviction that the danger of standing up for basic human rights in a repressive society was preferable to the safety of a quiescent life in servitude. Ours is a nonviolent movement that depends on faith in the human predilection for fair play and compassion.
>
> "Some would insist that man is primarily an economic animal interested only in his material well-being. This is too narrow a view of a species which has produced numberless brave men and women who are prepared to undergo relentless persecution to uphold deeply held beliefs and principles. It is my pride and inspiration that such men and women exist in my country today."
>
> —Aung San Suu Kyi,
> *International Herald Tribune*,
> February 1997

—∾—

The loss of many of her closest friends as well as her husband was not the only heartache Suu Kyi would endure. Her sole remaining sibling, her older brother, Aung San Oo, began siding with the military against her. Though their relationship had become increasingly distant as they became adults, it was a sharp wound when her brother become an ally of the military dictatorship—especially when he joined the generals in trying to take her house away from her.

Aung San Oo had harbored resentments against his sister for many years. While she was allowed to stay with their mother when she went to India, he was sent by himself to a boarding school called Dover College in Kent, England. He was not a top student, but managed to go on to study at Imperial College in London, which had a respected program in engineering, which was Aung San Oo's strong suit. With his quiet and moody ways, Aung San did not make many close friendships during his years in England and often felt slighted by the Burmese community there. He did not stay in England after he obtained his engineering degree and instead went to the United States, where he worked for a time at the Mostek memory chip company in Dallas and then as a computer engineer for the U.S. Navy in San Diego. He did not indicate any interest in the democracy struggle in his home country. While his sister's political party was campaigning in the 1990 election, Aung San Oo did not take part.

He married Lei Lei Nwe Thein, a university employee who was his junior by about 10 years. His mother disapproved of his choice so strongly that when she died, Suu Kyi advised her brother that it was best that he not bring his wife to his mother's funeral in deference to her wishes. It did not help their frayed relationship that Suu Kyi's spouse, a foreigner, was allowed to attend. Aung San Oo remained alienated from his sister for most of the next decade, living quietly with his wife in a modest 1,200-square-foot house. His neighbors were not even aware Aung San Oo was related to the Nobel Peace Prize winner until Burmese activists picketed his home in 2000 to protest because he had filed a legal claim to his mother's house.

Daw Khin Kyi had left the house to both her children in her will, with the provision that if they sold, the proceeds must go to a charity. For 12 years after her death, Aung San Oo showed no interest in the property, until he filed a claim. Observers blamed his wife, who had made frequent trips to Burma, for his sudden desire to take possession of the house. "We believe his wife is influencing him," Khin Maung Win, a member of the Burma Lawyer's Council, told a reporter. "She has been doing business and is seeking business opportunities from the junta."

Lei Lei Nwe Thein rejected the notion that she was manipulating her husband in an interview with Radio Free Burma, insisting "My husband is not a weak man." She said he had brought the lawsuit because the statute of limitations for filing a claim was running out and he wanted to "legalize his share of the property." She also claimed he was merely trying to follow his mother's wishes and turn the house into a memorial. "We have never thought about living in the house," she said. "The only thing she (Aung San Suu Kyi) has to do is accept this. Her refusal causes all kinds of trouble."

Others had a different view of the reasons behind the dispute. Aung Lin Htut, the former deputy chief of mission for the Burmese Embassy in Washington, later said in an interview that the lawsuit was generated by the Burmese government to hurt Suu Kyi. He claimed that the Burmese ambassador at the time received an order from Rangoon to get Aung San Oo's signature on the lawsuit in exchange for promises of business opportunities for his wife and her family.

If the brother won in court, legal analysts said, it would pave the way for him to sell his share to a government-run charity, giving the military access to the property. The military regime could then take half of the 54 University Avenue property away from Aung San Suu Kyi. The brother, they concluded, was being used as a pawn by the junta to corner the queen.

The junta's chess maneuver was thwarted by a surprise move. Although judges in Burma usually delivered verdicts in line with the government's wishes, the High Court ruled in 2001 against Aung San Oo in favor of Suu Kyi, much to the surprise of legal observers. The reason was simple: As a U.S. citizen, Aung San Oo could not legally hold property in Burma and therefore could not claim a half-share of the house.

That was not the end of the sibling feud, however. With the assistance of the military government, Aung San Oo and his wife began establishing themselves as public figures in Burma. In 2005, Aung San Oo constructed a large mansion on a prime location within the exclusive Archaeological Zone in Bagan, which could not have been done without government approval. Since Aung San Oo cannot hold property, his wife's family is believed to have acted as proxy on his behalf. Those who had spoken with the couple said Lei Lei Nwe Thein wanted her husband to have the prominence she believed he deserved as the oldest son of the Bogyoke. The military government was happy to encourage those ambitions. The regime gave permission for Aung San Oo and Lei Lei Nwe Thein to lay a wreath at the tomb of his father on Martyr's Day in 2007, the 60th anniversary of his father's death. Permission was denied to his sister. She was still under arrest in the family home. By this time, Aung San Suu Kyi had endured four years of near total isolation since the generals had tried to kill her at Depayin in 2003. As she would continue to insist, others had endured far worse. She was painfully aware that many of them had suffered simply because of their closeness to her. She had many hours to think about who to trust—and what had happened to those she did.

CHAPTER 11

THE GENERAL IN HIS LABYRINTH

> "Than Shwe will stay in power as much as he can because he's worried about his own future. He has created a lot of enemies over the past five or ten years."
>
> —Aung Zaw, editor of *Irrawaddy* news magazine

In photos, General Than Shwe often looks ill at ease, as if he might need some Maalox. He is unsmiling, his limpid eyes looking warily to the side. His flat, square face and drooping expression earned him the nickname "Bulldog" as a young officer. The chest of his uniform is covered with a colorful quilt of medals in rows of five across, although his victories have been behind closed doors, not on the battlefield.

To many Burmese, Than Shwe [tawn-schway], like Ne Win, was known as "No. 1," or "The Old Man." For more than two decades, they did not dare not say his name aloud, for fear a snitch might report some alleged disloyalty. Some simply refer to him as "the invisible hand."

Unlike many dictators, you don't see Than Shwe's face in public squares in Burma like Chairman Mao's giant portrait in Tiananmen Square. You don't see his portrait on the national currency, like Fidel Castro's bearded image on the Cuban peso. Than Shwe's face and name are little known to people outside of Burma, unless they happened to see him listed in *Parade* magazine's annual ranking of "The Worst Dictators in the World." As recently as 2013, Than Shwe was in fourth place, behind Robert Mugabe of Zimbabwe, Omar al Bashir of Sudan, and Kim Jong-Il of North Korea. Although he doesn't have as high a profile as those despots, Than Shwe has earned his place on the international murderer's row. His record shows he has authorized military attacks on ethnic villages that have left nearly a million people displaced and homeless. He is the one who gave the order to attack Aung San Suu Kyi at Depayin. He authorized the imprisonment and torture of thousands of democracy supporters. He is the one who gave the order to attack monks who protested conditions in the country. He is responsible for the use of land mines in civilian areas, the rapes of tens of thousands of ethnic women, and the abduction of child soldiers as young as 11—all documented by human-rights groups who have been powerless to bring Than Shwe to justice, largely because of China's protective votes on the United Nations Security Council.

To understand the cold-blooded general who has held Burma—and Aung San Suu Kyi—in his grip for more than two decades, the best place to start is the country's new national capital, Naypyidaw. The surreal capital city is Than Shwe's fortress and monument to himself. If you want a fitting symbol for the struggle for the soul of Burma, the costly capital may be it.

In 2006, Than Shwe had the seat of government abruptly moved from Rangoon to a capital built in secret 100 miles to the north. He named his ostentatious new capital "Naypyidaw," which translates to "The Abode of Kings." The multi-billion-dollar city is ten times the size of Singapore. The labyrinth of Parliament buildings and palatial private homes is a sterile, lifeless combination of Kublai Khan's Xanadu and Hitler's Eagle's Nest at Berchtesgaden—a place for the powerful to rule and retreat.

Because Aung San Suu Kyi was still being held prisoner in her home when I visited in 2009, I went to Naypyidaw to get a better understanding of her jailers. Options to travel to the remote capital were limited at the time. Visitors could apply for permission to fly in (risky for journalists trying to stay below the radar on a tourist visa). Or drive on the new superhighway built primarily for government officials (risking roadway security checks). Another possibility was traveling on the rickety train system, but Burma's trains are not known for reliability, safety, or comfort. Or, as a last resort, visitors could travel for nine uncomfortable hours from Rangoon over a back road that has seen more oxen than axles (the more punishing but inconspicuous choice of smugglers and journalists).

I took the punishing back-road route. The only way to describe the day-long drive in the stifling heat with no shock absorbers was "The Shake and Bake Tour." Our vintage Toyota sedan overheated every hour or so, which meant pulling to the side of the road, opening the hood to the hope of a breeze, and splashing the engine with bottled water that we had stashed in the trunk of the car. By mid-afternoon, we had limped into the only gasoline station on the route. While the driver sprayed water on the steaming engine with a hose, I went in search of a cold drink, running smack into a Burmese military officer in uniform who had apparently dropped into the roadhouse for a cool beer. We nodded in silent complicity. I won't tell on you, I thought, if you don't tell on me.

As it grew dark, we continued bumping along the rutted road, sharing the lane with people bicycling home in the twilight from a long day at manual work. Soon the only light was the occasional flicker of a candle in nearby farmhouses. Like most of rural Burma, the area around Naypyidaw had little or no electricity; families got by with candles and lanterns. Occasionally, one of the larger tea shops by the side of the road had a TV mounted on the wall for customers to watch. Most nights, such tea shops are packed with people of all ages watching soccer matches, the national obsession. When the matches are over, a long line of villagers could be seen walking for miles single-file down the side of the road to their homes, with only the stars for street lights.

The surprise was that as we drew closer to Naypyidaw, the night skies came ablaze like a Hollywood set. Thanks to a huge new hydropower station—built by Chinese engineers—electricity is available for the generals 24 hours a day. Our potholed farm road miraculously turned into an eight-lane freeway lit up with arched street lights. The halogen lights gave the scene an amber *Twilight Zone* glow that was eery; the wide freeway was so empty, it looked like an airport runway. There were no cars on the road but ours for long stretches at a time—only an occasional SUV with tinted black windows speeding by us into the distance.

The landscape was fairly bleak as we approached the city, except for an enormous construction project where work was going on round the clock underneath bright spotlights attached to construction cranes. The lighting made it look like a scene from Dante's *Inferno*, a giant erector set with a swarm of people working in the night heat. What was that gigantic project? My guide explained that a reproduction of the Shwedagon Pagoda was being constructed as a showcase for General Than Shwe's piety. The pagoda would enshrine a rare tooth relic of the Buddha, purchased by Than Shwe's family at considerable cost for the pagoda. The monumental pagoda is sometimes called "The Peace Pagoda," but the official name is Uppatasanti, which translates to "protection against calamity." Names are important in Burma; it is telling that Uppatasanti also is the name of a *sutra* (a collection of aphorisms to teach some aspect of life), prepared by a monk in the early 16th century. The sutra is supposed to be recited in time of crisis, especially in the face of foreign invasion, one of Than Shwe's greatest fears. The new golden pagoda—and Naypyidaw itself—are testament to Than Shwe's paranoia. Having grasped power by deposing others, he lives with the fear of being deposed himself—or being brought to an international court. Building the pagoda is one of his many efforts to balance the scales of justice with civic deeds.

And just in case the golden pagoda does not earn the senior general enough merit to defray fate, a special home has been constructed near the pagoda for a pair of white elephants, which are believed to be harbingers of good fortune for kings and anxious generals.

—~—

In Burma, albino elephants are revered as "the Lord White Elephant." Their discovery is a sign that rulers will prosper.

The rare creatures are not actually white—mouse-colored would be more accurate. Their skin is pinkish-beige rather than the grayish hue of most elephants. With their red-rimmed eyes, the white elephants are distinctive.

According to legend, a white elephant appeared to the Buddha's mother before he was born and presented her with a sacred lotus flower. Some say that in another existence, Gautama Buddha himself had been a white elephant.

Over time, Burmese kings came to believe that the pachyderms were blessed—so they were pampered in extravagant surroundings, draped with diamonds, and fed in gold troughs. A treasured white elephant calf was often nursed by women of the court, who lined up for the honor of having the pale trunk seize on one of their proffered breasts, while they swooned at the sensual experience.

Arriving in the ancient capital of Pegu in 1587, a traveler reported that there were four white elephants that lived in a gold house. The elephants were bathed under a white silk canopy in the river, their feet scrubbed by attendants with silver basins.

While the acquisition of a white elephant was considered a good omen, the demise of one could foretell doom. Not long after King Thibaw's favorite white elephants died, the monarch was ousted by the British in 1885.

Senior General Than Shwe desperately wanted one of the power symbols to signify his own kingly rule. When one of the pale elephants was spotted on Burma's western coast in early 2010, army troops and veterinarians were sent out armed with tranquilizer darts to capture it. Villagers were forced to leave their crops and help with the search, without pay.

After months of searching, not one, but two of the rare white creatures were captured. They were shackled in splendid isolation at Naypyidaw, Than Shwe's latest prisoners.

—∾—

The total cost of building Naypyidaw remains a mystery, but economist Sean Turnell, an expert on the Burmese economy at Macquarie University in Sydney, has estimated the cost at $4 billion to $5 billion. Opposition groups were quick to point out that the money could have been better spent in a country where the per capita annual income was $280 at the time—less than 80 cents a day

Time magazine's correspondent Hannah Beech told about meeting a 15-year-old girl working on the highway to Naypyidaw in the 110-degree heat. She had been working on the road since she was 11, carrying heavy rocks in her hands and on her head. And what was her daily pay? $1.50. All she had to look forward to was one day reaching the end of the road. "I have heard that Naypyidaw has so much electricity that nighttime looks like day," she told the American reporter. "Can you imagine such a beautiful place?"

The capital may be architecturally beautiful, but it is conspicuously empty and uncomfortably quiet. A 20-lane boulevard was built to prevent traffic jams, but there were barely any cars. The Parliament Buildings, the Pyithu Hluttaw, are accessible by bridges over moats, like medieval castles. Distances between buildings are vast—designed, so it is said, in case of an aerial attack, to limit adjacent damage.

We visited a new shopping mall that sported cheap Chinese-made goods, but not much else. Salespeople sat on white plastic chairs, looking bored. One area of Naypyidaw was designated for hotels and another for restaurants, which gives the capital a sense of order, but not community. The only entertainment for families at the time was the Naypyidaw Zoological Gardens, the largest in Burma. The new zoo boasts a respectable contingent of elephants, crocodiles, deer, leopards, monkeys, and zebras, all trucked in from the old zoo in Rangoon. (When the zoo and government officials were relocated, a local comedian announced, "All our animals are going to Naypyidaw." He was jailed.) Although most of the wild animals were housed in attractive, landscaped cages on the day I visited, a baby bear was chained to a tree out in the open, where children poked at the bawling cub with twigs, an unsettling sight. There were other dissonant aspects: The star attraction is a penguin house that is air-conditioned 24 hours a day—in a country of chronic power shortages. Special food had to be shipped in for the penguins—at a time when there were news reports of people in drought-stricken areas reduced to eating rats.

The zoo's grand entrance itself is in stark contrast with the dusty ruin of the rest of the country. Visitors are greeted by a huge fountain spraying water over a half-dozen giant white elephants triumphantly raising their trunks to the air. Burmese pop music—which sounds like a bouncy blend of Abba and Alvin and the Chipmunks—blared with non-stop good cheer from loudspeakers, much like other theme parks around the world. But to remind zoo visitors who their host was, a tall guard tower loomed nearby and a security guard stood near the ticket office.

In an effort to provide another tourist attraction to draw visitors to Naypyidaw, the junta opened a Gems Museum. The star attraction is one of the world's largest sapphires—standing 6.7 inches high (17.018 cm) and weighing 26 pounds (11.8 kg), which the museum estimates is a whopping 63,000 carats.

The three-story museum also features the largest jade stone, weighing in at 152 pounds (69 kg), largest ruby with 21,450 carats, and largest natural pearl (845 carats).

The displays are a shining example of how the military regime has exploited the vast treasure in Burma's hills. Since the museum is government-owned, all proceeds go to the junta.

—⁂—

Burma has often been described as the jewelry box for the world. It is stocked with deposits of ruby, diamond, cat's eye, emerald, topaz, pearl, sapphire, coral, garnet, and rare jade.

Gem sales are held throughout the year for traders, who come primarily from China, Hong Kong, and Thailand. Annual sales are in the billions; gems are Burma's third-largest export after natural gas and agricultural products—and under-the-table drugs

The most highly-sought gems are the rare "pigeon's blood" rubies and sapphires mined in the Mogok region north of Mandalay, dubbed the "Valley of Rubies." Some estimate that Burma accounts for 90 percent of the world's ruby production.

Just as "blood diamonds" are used to finance violence in Africa, the gems of Burma help finance the military regime. The junta has contrived to hold a majority share in the mines. The regime issues the licenses for each mining project. It runs the gem auctions in Rangoon. To become a partner in a mine requires being either a senior government official, or a close ally of the regime.

According to the U.S. State Department, a large number of the partners in the mining operations have direct ties to the opium and heroin trade. Impoverished mineworkers often are paid with heroin, and the needle-sharing on payday has led to tragic rates of HIV infection in the mining areas.

The gemstones that do not find their way to the government-run auctions usually are smuggled out of the country, in black-market operations that also may have ties to government officials, or those involved in the drug trade. The illicit traffic feeds a murky underworld of violence.

Burma produces at least $4.3 billion in high-quality jade a year, and it is estimated that at least half of that is spirited over the border into China with little or no taxation.

Residents in the mining area—who are often members of ethnic minorities and Christians—have largely been shut out of the gem profits from their own lands. Their lands are often confiscated by the government and complicit companies. That is why the region has often been at the forefront of demonstrations against military control.

—w—

In Naypyidaw, it is said that an elite Special Forces battalion watches over the generals in their lair. Three light infantry divisions, which are believed to be loyal to Than Shwe, are stationed not far from the center of the city. Roads to the generals' quarter are blocked, creating a fortress within a fortress.

The secret quarter for the generals is a network of bunkers and luxury houses with resort-like perks. According to various reports, the generals rarely venture out, emerging only to play golf at one of two golf courses or gamble in the five-star hotels. Their private tennis courts are screened from public view. A gate in the middle of some trees is said to lead to a nightclub for the Tatmadaw elite. A closed exit from a roundabout is the entrance to what a cabbie called the "top man restaurant." Another gate with red warning lights reportedly leads to a park and playground for the generals' families. And what's behind the razor wire at a wide intersection that was guarded by police? "Than Shwe house," it is whispered. Aerial photos of Than Shwe's retreat show a sprawling mansion with a U-shaped ceremonial driveway in front and a large swimming pool in back. According to Bangkok-based Burma analyst Larry Jagan, the palatial residence includes pillars coated in jade and Italian slate costing millions of dollars. When Than Shwe became dissatisfied with the Italian slate, he had it pulled out and replaced with even more expensive Chinese marble. As he grew older and struggled with health problems—possibly diabetes and a cancer scare—he ceased going to an office and only rarely left his residence. Those he wanted to see came to him.

In a different quarter, government employees are housed in rows of four-story apartment buildings. The roofs are color-coded in bright shades of pink, blue, and green—blue for Health, green for Agriculture and Irrigation, pink for Ministry of Home Affairs. The only non-conformity I could see was a small Christmas tree in one of the apartment windows. It was a brave touch; the regime had been closing down house churches in Rangoon that winter as part of its efforts to limit the growth of Christian groups.

It was hard to escape the feeling of being watched in Naypyidaw; there were security forces on the corners, at the intersections, in the zoo, at the shopping mall. And people standing along the road who seemed to be looking at everyone else going by. Intently.

Reports have surfaced that the junta built a series of tunnels—with the help of North Korean engineers—underneath the capital. Rumors have swirled—are the tunnels part of a nuclear project? Escape routes?

My hotel in Naypyidaw, the Aureum Palace, looked like many other tropical resorts around the world—palm trees, pool, patio—except for a few details. A guard post on stilts was a short walk from my door. At night, there were thumping noises against the walls that woke me up in the middle of the night. I later found out it was the sound of security patrols sweeping the grounds with metal detectors, looking for bombs.

I stacked my suitcases against the door every night—this was getting to be a habit—because the lock on the door to my room did not work. I had reported the broken lock to the front desk. When I returned to my room there was a "repair crew" of three people inside my room. After several hours huddled around the door, they indicated they were finished; I tipped them, they smiled, they left. The lock still didn't work and could easily be opened from the outside without a key.

For more than a week, I had been subjected to hang-up calls in the middle of the night. Someone was apparently checking to see if I was in my room. Or just wanted to let me know they were checking.

At such times, I asked myself what on earth was I doing in Burma again? Cell phones were not readily available then, so I couldn't call out. My guide disappeared every evening to stay at a cheaper hotel. The repeated hangup calls did not add up to a good night's sleep. Then I would remember Suu Kyi standing alone in her house as a child to will away her fears, and I would feel foolish for being anxious. "Shine the light on what is happening here," Suu Kyi had said, don't let people forget us. I would later find out she had said similar things to others, including Congressman Bill Richardson, who would go on to champion the democracy movement as ambassadorto the U.N., and Derek Mitchell, who videotaped Suu Kyi in 1995 as a young staffer at the National Democratic Institute and went on to become U.S. Ambassador to Burma. Like me, they found it hard to look away from the plight of so many people.

After half a dozen trips to Burma, I had seen that fear is contagious; I could see how it spreads like a virus from person to person in the furtive glances of people in the market, in the street. But I could also see how courage was contagious, too, in the stories of people who were put in prison and went right back out and protested again. Oprah Winfrey and Suu Kyi were right, I thought. Risk-taking is like a muscle: the more you use it, the stronger you get.

I had noticed that those who proudly displayed Aung San Suu Kyi's photo in their homes understood the galvanizing power of example—like the remarkable journalist U Win Tin, who could not be muzzled despite long years of punishing treatment in prison. He kept a photo of Suu Kyi on his bookshelf. Or like Dr. Cynthia Maung, who ran a clinic on the Thai border for Burmese refugees, many of whom had lost limbs to landmines and had crawled in for help. She had photos of Suu Kyi in her hospital. Or like the comedians the Moustache Brothers, who dared to mock power and posted Suu Kyi's photo in their garage theater. They all had demonstrated human integrity under difficult circumstances. They had stayed the course.

Many of the younger members of the National League for Democracy that I had interviewed had been inspired by Aung San Suu Kyi's bravery—like Zin Mar Aung, who had been in prison for 10 years for distributing political poetry at the university. She had started political science classes to train young leaders. Then there was Charm Tong, who co-founded the

Shan Women's Action Network (SWAN) when she was only 17. SWAN proved instrumental in documenting the army violence against women and children in Burma. Their role model was "The Lady." Aung San Suu Kyi was still locked up in her house six long years after Depayin, but her example was all around.

—∾—

Naypyidaw was one place I did not find any photos of Suu Kyi in 2009. In fact, no mention of her name was allowed in the state newspapers at the time. I was usually the only guest in the hotel restaurant for breakfast or dinner, and I had gotten accustomed to not having anyone to talk to. One of the eager-to-please waiters proudly confided to me one evening, "We have five people staying with us!" Sure enough, the next morning, two Thai diplomats showed up for breakfast and three businessmen—one Scottish, one British, and one French—showed up for dinner. Like the real estate salesmen in David Mamet's play *Glengarry Glen Ross*, they spent the evening in loud, macho, sometimes profane talk. The Scot proclaimed Hendricks Gin is the best (bleeping) gin in the world. The Brit proclaimed the Liverpool Football Club was (bleeping) superior to Manchester United. The Frenchman seemed unimpressed by everything they said. I could see them turning their heads occasionally to watch me, so as I prepared to leave, I stopped by their table and introduced myself.

"I must say we've never seen an American woman here before—especially by herself," the Scot ventured. "What are you doing here?"

"I'm an educator doing research on Burma," I said, fibbing just slightly. "What do you guys do?"

They looked at each other knowingly and didn't answer. There was an awkward silence. I tried again, "Is this your first time here?" "Oh no, we've been here 49 times," the Scot answered. "It's not a bad place, although the (bleeping) menu does get old." They all laughed heartily. I understood—the only entrée for the second night in a row had been chicken with cashews. We chatted for a few more minutes, but I could not get them to reveal what business they were conducting on the sly; an intriguing omission since their countries had sanctions against dealing with the junta.

Burma is that kind of place, where people who hope to make a killing of one kind or another keep their cards close.

The attitude toward foreign influence in Naypyidaw was not benign. The following instructions were displayed in newspapers daily and pasted on roadside billboards throughout the city.

THE PEOPLE'S DESIRE

- Oppose those relying on External Elements, acting as stooges, holding negative views.
- Oppose those trying to jeopardize the stability of the state and national progress.
- Oppose foreign nations interfering in the internal affairs of the state.
- Crush all internal and external destructive elements as the common enemy.

When U.S. diplomats were first given a tour of Naypyidaw, they reported back to Washington in cables that were later revealed by Wikileaks that the city was "green and empty." Civil servants forced to relocate there virtually overnight encountered problems with water quality and bugs. The embassy cables reported, "They claim they want to resign, but are not allowed to. The scattered nature of the buildings in the midst of nothing reinforces the sense of isolation. Nothing gives the impression of a workable city. No wonder the civil servants are unhappy. If you are planning to visit, make sure you bring a good book, because there is nothing much else to do."

And there was little to look at as well, minus three giant visages. At General Than Shwe's instruction, statues of Burma's three mighty kings were erected in his new capital city:

Anawrahta, the warrior king who unified the country during his reign from 1044 to 1077 A.D. and imposed Theravāda Buddhism as the state religion;

Bayinnaug, who reunified the kingdom and conquered the Shan States, Siam (Thailand), and Laos during his rule from 1550 to 1581 A.D.;

And *Alaungpya*, who later reunified the country again from 1752 to 1760 A.D. He founded Yangon (Rangoon) and the Konbaung Dynasty, which lasted until the British annexation of upper and lower Burma in 1886.

The larger-than-life statues are often used a backdrop for the viewing stand where General Than Shwe and other top leaders sit to review parades of the country's military might.

As an amateur historian, Than Shwe must have intended the giant royal statues as a way to make Burmese proud of their historical past. Most interpreted it as an advertisement of his power. He also may have hoped that Naypyidaw would be Burma's gleaming answer to the modernity in Singapore and Hong Kong. But it was widely interpreted as self-indulgence and disregard for the poor throughout the country. The capital not only became Than Shwe's monument to himself, it also became his indictment. Its excesses are his excesses. Its coldness is his coldness.

Than Shwe was apparently aware that the moving of the capital was considered a wasteful move by some in the international community. According to biographer Benedict Rogers, a former American military attaché in Rangoon approached Than Shwe at a diplomatic reception to introduce himself. But before he could finish his sentence, Than Shwe began reciting, "Canberra-Sydney, Washington, D.C.-New York, The Hague-Amsterdam, Ottawa-Toronto. Many countries have an administrative capital separate from the major economic and population centers." Then he walked away.

When it first became apparent that the regime was moving the seat of government from Rangoon to central Burma, the obvious question was not only "Why?" but "Why *there*?" The new site was in the middle of nowhere, adjacent to a sleepy farming town called Pyinmana.

The U.S. Embassy staff speculated that from a larger historical perspective, the move was not as arbitrary as it might seem. "It was customary for Burmese kings to shift their capital periodically for political, economic, or supernatural reasons," an embassy cable pointed out. "Though Rangoon has been Burma's capital city since colonial days, it has been administered by Burmese only since 1948. It is clear that Senior General Than Shwe increasingly views himself as the inheritor of the mantle passed down through the centuries by Burma's great builder kings. Thus, through a monarchial lens, a move to Pyinmana after nearly 60 years in Rangoon is a logical and consistent step to take."

Pyinmana, the small town adjacent to Naypyidaw, also has played a role in the country's military history before. The Allies were forced out of the country in 1942 by the Japanese. Pynimana then was used as a headquarters by General Aung San while he assembled his young army. He figured the comparatively remote location, flanked by dense forest and a mountain range, would make it easy to launch guerrilla warfare against invaders. The Japanese army later headquartered there for the same reasons. And for quite a few years after the war, it was the stronghold of Communist activity.

Than Shwe's regime was well aware of those precedents, but there was one thing they failed to note: They built the new capital on a major earthquake fault line. Several worrisome tremors have been registered since Naypyidaw was constructed.

~

Diplomats in Burma say there are likely several reasons why the regime wanted to replant the government offices, other than Than Shwe's vanity:

STRATEGIC

The top generals are in constant fear of being invaded. From their perspective, a heavily guarded command center in a central plain was more defensible than the sprawling port city of Rangoon. The regime leaders reportedly worry that an attack might come from the country's western shore, which is open to the Bay of Bengal; or perhaps from Thailand into the Karen State in the east, where there is long-standing opposition to the regime. The generals also feared the port of Rangoon could be easily cut off and was vulnerable to invasion or bombing. They are said to have pored over the American invasion plans for Iraq and Afghanistan to prepare for possible U.S. invasion strategies into Burma. They built tunnels, bought MiG fighters from Russia, and began work on nuclear weapons with the assistance of North Korea. Than Shwe reportedly vowed that if the U.S. invaded, the diplomats at the U.S. embassy would be killed first.

The senior general also feared that masses of his own people might take to the streets again in Rangoon or elsewhere. By hunkering down in Naypyidaw, the junta could safely run the country's administrative affairs from there, while sending troops to quell protests or a national uprising.

SUPERSTITION

An equally prevalent view is that Than Shwe built the new city on the advice of his astrologer, who reportedly warned him of an impending catastrophe that could only be avoided by moving the seat of government. As an extra precaution, Than Shwe had ordered that the Parliament complex have 31 buildings, an allusion to the Buddhist concept of 31 planes of existence. Moving day for government workers was set for November, the 11th month, because the number 11 is considered auspicious. According to Buddhist tradition, there are "eleven fires" that are fueled by human attachment: greed, hatred, delusion, birth, aging, death, grief, lamentation, pain, sorrow, and despair. Accordingly, a convoy of 11 battalions and 11 ministries left Rangoon for Naypyidaw in 1,100 trucks at the 11th minute of the 11th hour of the 11th day of the 11th month.

—∾—

While it may seem strange to Western readers to move an entire capital city based on superstition, occult practices are as much a part of life in Burma as fish paste and rice. Since they have had the most to lose, kings and generals have long sought supernatural guidance. After seizing power in 1962, General Ne Win is said to have relied heavily on astrologers and numerologists for policy advice. His decision in 1970 to change from driving on the left-hand side of the road to the right-hand side came after an astrologer warned that Burma had moved too far to the left, putting Ne Win at risk. A great number of accidents resulted.

The strongman also practiced "yadaya," an occult practice to warn off adversity. After a soothsayer warned Ne Win that there might be a bloodbath, he was advised to stand in front of a mirror and trample on meat to simulate the blood. He also was advised to shoot his image in the mirror to ward off an assassination attempt. He once asked his pilot to circle his birthplace while he was seated in the plane on a wooden horse—all to preserve his rule.

Than Shwe is reputed to be even more superstitious than his predecessor. In his authoritative biography of the dictator, Benedict Rogers reported that Than Shwe has seven personal astrologers, including several who focused solely on Aung San Suu Kyi. Many of his most bizarre acts actually have been attempts to thwart the democracy leader's influence, based on advice from soothsayers:

For example, when the democracy movement was becoming a threat to the regime in the 1990s, seven peacocks—the symbol of Suu Kyi's National League for Democracy—were brought to a pagoda and sacrificed. The throats of the shrieking birds were slit, their bodies offered to the shrine.

In 2007, even though Aung San Suu Kyi was confined to her house, the regime ordered everyone in the country to grow the Jatropha plant, sometimes called "physic nut." Even those who lived in cities were ordered to grow the shrub in their back yards and balconies. People were puzzled. What was going on? The nut could be used to produce candles, soap, and biodiesel fuel, but the real reason for the change seemed to be that the Burmese name for the nut, *kyet suu*, has the astrological meaning of Monday-Tuesday, whereas Suu Kyi's name means Tuesday-Monday. According to *Irrawaddy* magazine, an astrologer suggested that Suu Kyi's power could be neutralized by planting *kyet suu* everywhere. The crops were generally a failure.

That same year, farmers in one division were ordered to grow sunflowers instead of their staple crop of rice. Why? Sunflowers are called *nay kyar*, meaning "long stay." Than Shwe apparently had been advised that the new crop would ensure his "long stay" in power, even if it meant hard-pressed farmers had to survive on sunflower seeds.

In one of the most outlandish incidents, Than Shwe and other top generals appeared in a nationally televised ceremony wearing the Burmese equivalent of women's dresses. In Burma, both men and women wear sarong-style wraps, but the patterns are different for each. The generals' sarongs in the public display looked decidedly feminine.

Many interpreted the fashion show as *yadaya* to counteract an astrologer's prediction that a woman would rule Burma. It was speculated that the generals were trying to fulfill the prophecy for themselves with a deception or to somehow neutralize Suu Kyi's power. Either way, they became objects of ridicule for milling around on TV in women's apparel.

—∾—

Such thinking may not appear rational in the 21st century, but it is perfectly in keeping with deep-seated cultural beliefs in Burma. Superstitious customs are not considered in conflict with the Theravāda Buddhist philosophy that is practiced by the majority of the populace. That's why Burmese tradition embraces the continued worship of ancient "Nat" spirits that preceded the introduction of Buddhism more than 2,000 years ago, as well as astrology and numerology. It is not unusual to find animist Nat shrines around Buddhist shrines.

What are Nats? The word is often translated as "spirit," but Nats are more than that, a uniquely Burmese blend of fairies and ghosts. The Nats are a collection of guardian spirits of people, real or legendary, who died a violent or wrongful death. Just as Westerners might turn to a rabbit's foot for good luck or step over a crack in the sidewalk to avoid bad luck, the Burmese turn to the Nats for favors and placate them with gifts to avoid their ire, better safe than sorry. Little boxes that look like bird houses can be spotted throughout the country, often as the base of banyan trees, with young bamboo shoots and incense as offerings, and sometimes a small empty bed inside.

When the great King Anawrahta of Bagan unified the country in the eleventh century and made Buddhism the national religion, he banned Nat worship, but he could not get his people to give up the tradition. Realizing he couldn't overcome the popular superstitions, Anawrahta employed the shrewd strategy of designating 37 "official" Nats and making Nat worship compatible, but *secondary* to Buddhism. He had Nats placed in the Shwedagon Pagoda in various positions of worshipping the Buddha to illustrate his point and eventually succeeded in making Buddhism dominant. Today many Buddhists bring offerings to both, a belt-and-suspenders approach. As the Burmese say, "Love the Buddha, fear the Nats."

The Burmese also place great stock in astrology and include astrological signs inside Buddhist shrines. Most Burmese have an astrological chart drawn up at birth and consult fortune-tellers to guide their daily lives.

Natural phenomena such as earthquakes and cyclones, or the collapse of a pagoda, are interpreted as serious omens of celestial disfavor. Birth times and dates are considered destiny. As a Burmese friend once explained to me, "You can explain someone's behavior by saying, 'She was born at 10 on a Tuesday. What else do you expect?'"

For everyday people in Burma, whose lives turn on the whims of dictators and nature, this mixed bag of beliefs helps them cope with the uncertainty and fear of everyday life. Life is too precarious not to cover all the possibilities.

For dictators like Than Shwe, who are constantly fearful of being deposed, consulting an astrologer makes more sense than consulting polling data like Western leaders. For him, what the fortune-teller says is more important than what the people say.

According to Andrew Seith at the Asia Griffith Institute, Burma is not alone in having leaders who observe such practices. Indira Gandhi secretly consulted astrologers. Indonesian presidents Sukarno and Suharto both allowed superstitions to influence policy decisions. Sri Lankan president Rajapaksa declared that he consulted astrologers. Even in cosmopolitan commercial centers such as Singapore and Hong Kong, lucky numbers are highly prized.

It is believed that General Than Shwe developed his reliance on the supernatural from his influential wife Kyaing Kyaing. Kyaing Kyaing is reported to use *yadaya* black magic rituals to ward off bad luck and ensure her husband's power.

When the country was preparing to vote on the regime-rigged Constitution in 2008, Kyaing Kyaing was seen climbing on the base of the Shwedagon Pagoda in an area banned to women. According to *Irrawaddy* magazine, she walked around the structure three times followed by attendants who sheltered her with gold-and-white umbrellas and shouted, *"Aung Pyi,"* which means "victory" in Burmese.

An embassy cable in 2008 revealed by Wikileaks reported rumors that Kyaing Kyaing had suffered a stroke when she fell down the steps of a Rangoon pagoda. She was said to have been praying and meditating for several hours on top of a map of Burma in an effort to prolong her life and power. The Embassy noted, "A month ago, we received reports that she had circled Burma's most sacred pagoda, the Shwedagon, with a dog and a pig on instructions from astrologers."

One of Than Shwe's acts of voodoo nearly turned into an international incident. When United Nations chief Ban Ki-moon and envoy Ibrahim Gambari made obligatory visits to Shwedagon Pagoda in 2006 on separate occasions, they were guided to what appeared to be a new jade statue of Buddha. It had never been seen in public before. Each of the U.N. dignitaries was ostentatiously photographed making an offering and praying in front of the sculpture. Neither one realized until it was pointed out later that the statue was not the enlightened Buddha. It was an effigy of Than Shwe in a Buddha-like pose. The embarrassed local officials who arranged the bizarre ceremonies said they had been ordered to carry out the charade by Than Shwe. The incident confirmed: the general was either more narcissistic or superstitious than anyone had realized.

Than Shwe's superstitious quirks turn out to be one of the more interesting things about him. Highly reclusive with a wooden personality, he is living proof that not all dictators are charismatic. A stocky man with large glasses on a flat, wide nose, he looks uncomfortable at state occasions, as if his uniforms were over-starched and he would be more comfortable at home. He is not known to drink or smoke—unlike the hedonistic Ne Win. His military colleagues recall that as a young officer, instead of going out to have drinks with the guys, Than Shwe went home to his family. His interests did not appear far-ranging; he talked some about Buddhism, little else that was noteworthy. For many years, he chewed betel leaf, a mild stimulant popular with working people that can stain teeth red.

Asked to describe the dictator, Mark Canning, the former British ambassador to Myanmar who has met the junta chief several times, said he was "small, plump, slow moving, and physically unimposing."

The puzzle is, how did a man who is most often described as "dull" come to control the lives of more than 50 million people?

Canning says, "He projects no obvious sense of menace or intimidation. He's far from the image of a fire-breathing demagogue. . . . He gives every impression of being what he in fact is—someone who has maneuvered himself from lowly beginnings to the top of the military pile, with guile, intrigue and, where necessary, *force*."

—∾—

Than Shwe got his start in life in 1933 when Burma was under British rule. He was born in Minzu village, near Kyaukse, in central Burma. The hardscrabble farming area was known only for its turmeric, mango, and onions. Than Shwe is believed to have gotten only a minimum education at state schools and did not finish high school. He found work as a postal clerk, but realized after a few years that there were better opportunities in the military. He enrolled at the age of 20 in Officer Training School in Meiktila. Other trainees remembered mostly that he chewed betel nut, a rather messy habit that requires spitting, like chewing tobacco, and that he was rather dull and quiet—"not outstanding."

As a second lieutenant in the 1950s, he was with units that fought against the Shan and Karen ethnic populations, who were resisting control by the Burman ethnic majority. Than Shwe was described by his colleagues as being "battle shy" and is not believed to have earned any distinction for bravery. In fact, one former soldier claimed Than Shwe switched off his radio before a battle and disappeared for two days.

By keeping his head down, Than Shwe advanced to the rank of captain in five years. Just like executives on Wall Street, he moved up the ladder by befriending mentors who could help him land better assignments. His climb in the ranks included: lieutenant colonel (1972), colonel (1978), Commander of the Military District of South West (1983), Vice Chief of Staff of the Army, brigadier-general and Vice-Minister of Defense (1985), and then major-general (1986).

How Than Shwe maneuvered ahead is instructive: In February 1958, he moved from the infantry to the Psychological Warfare Department in Rangoon. He got along well with his bosses, and it wasn't long before he was sent to Mandalay to serve as head of the Psychological Warfare Department. The former postal clerk taught the sinister arts of manipulating others and learned the lessons well himself. His approach echoed the maxim posted at the military intelligence school: "Reveal little, listen, look and gather all you can."

After General Ne Win took over the government in 1962, Than Shwe was assigned to the Central School of Political Sciences to teach Ne Win's new ideology, the "Burmese Way to Socialism." One former diplomat described the hybrid dogma as "an amalgam of Karl Marx and Groucho

Marx." Than Shwe was careful not to voice his own opinions. He stuck close to the official doctrine of nationalizing industries and expelling foreign interests.

Though he had no academic credentials of his own, he soon became head of the Political History Department. He seemed to relish the country's history of kings and conquerors; in later years, he would surprise visitors with rambling discourses on ancient leaders. Students found him awkward to talk to.

After six years of teaching, Than Shwe realized there was little chance of advancing rank in the school. He asked to return to the infantry. He was promoted to major in early 1969 and assigned to the 77th Infantry Division. While stationed in Mon State, he married a woman named Kyaing Kyaing. She was not from purely Burman ethnic stock—her father was Chinese and her mother was ethnic Pa-O. According to various accounts, she had been married before to an army officer and her husband was killed in battle. The commanding officer reportedly asked the bachelor officers in the division, who would volunteer to marry their fallen comrade's wife to honor his sacrifice? Lots supposedly were drawn and Than Shwe drew the wedding lot. Whatever the origin of their relationship, Kyaing Kyaing would soon become the driving force in Than Shwe's career.

By the end of the year, Than Shwe was promoted again and sent to the War Office in Rangoon, where he helped lead hard-nosed operations against the Karen insurgents in the Delta. That meant he was directing attacks on ethnic villages while young Aung San Suu Kyi was working at the United Nations in New York.

Than Shwe continued to work his way up the military chain of command, becoming lieutenant colonel of the 88th Light Infantry in Shan State, where the Tatmadaw was aggressively combating insurgents. Than Shwe returned to the War Office in 1975 at a higher rank, but according to *Irrawaddy*, still brought his betel nut to work and still did not seem particularly noteworthy.

His wife Kyaing Kyaing, anxious to advance her husband's career, often consulted palm readers, astrologers, and monks. In 1980, she reportedly went with some of the other officer's wives to consult a famous astrologer named U Nyan Zaw. The astrologer told her that one day her husband would be king of Burma. Incredulous, Kyaing Kyaing revisited the astrologer to double-check the prediction. The fortune teller insisted: Than Shwe was destined to be the leader of the country. It was in the stars. When Than Shwe was promoted to commander of the 88th Light Infantry Division at the age of 47, Kyaing Kyaing was convinced that the stars were right.

Than Shwe soon got two lucky breaks that vaulted him closer to the top. The first came when Ne Win deposed a general who was getting too flamboyantly powerful. The shakeup created an opening for Than Shwe to become head of the Southwestern Command in the Irrawaddy Delta region. Those who worked with him said Than Shwe gave long, dull speeches and seemed mostly interested in constructing roads and bridges, but was otherwise a fairly normal, okay guy. He claimed to have improved education in the region and boosted the literacy rate, but those claims appear to have been for propaganda purposes.

His second felicitous opportunity came when the Ne Win decided he could no longer trust his upper echelon of officers. Looking for some fresh faces that would be non-threatening, he asked military leaders who was the youngest officer in their ranks? "Bulldog," they said. With that, Than Shwe became deputy commander of Burma's armed forces in 1986. A former electrician named Saw Maung, who was an unassuming guy and considered a loyal officer, became the commander-in-chief. Neither had a university degree or had ever traveled outside the country. According to *Irrawaddy* editor Aung Zaw, the two were so socially inexperienced that Ne Win reportedly ordered that they be taught how to use a knife and fork and be sent to some diplomatic functions to learn how to behave.

When Than Shwe moved into the inner power circle, he was still living a low-key domestic life. His wife prepared meals in the kitchen. They raised five daughters and three sons. His oldest daughter drove herself to college; few of the other students knew her father was a general. Than Shwe liked to watch international soccer matches and Chinese martial arts movies. He was said to regularly read *Time* magazine, which was his primary window to the outside world, and later was known to surf the Internet. He played golf, but unlike North Korean leader Kim Jong-Il, never claimed to hit 11 holes-in-one on his first round of golf.

U.N. officials and diplomats who met him said he was generally "cold and humorless," but could be charming and friendly when he wanted to. Though he presided without remorse over attacks against ethnic groups and implemented forced labor practices, there was little sign of the cruelty, corruption, and pretensions of grandeur that would come to dominate his family and regime a few years later.

For many years, U.S. diplomats assumed Than Shwe did not speak English. He did—and well enough to correct his translator. Colleagues said he didn't say much in meetings, but was always willing to say things to please the commander, a "yes man." No one took much notice of his views, but that was the secret of his success. Than Shwe knew that if you showed off too much, the people above you and the people below you didn't like it and might find ways to get rid of you. His contemporaries may not have thought Than Shwe was smart, but he was smart enough to slip by them.

Ne Win made the fatal mistake of thinking that his deputy Than Shwe was non-threatening. The Bulldog bided his time. He did not question authority. He helped put down the student rebellion of 1988 without blinking at the bloodshed.

The size and sustainability of the continued demonstrations against the regime in 1988 convinced Ne Win that some cosmetic changes were needed to make people think their concerns had been heard. He invited his new army leaders, Generals Saw Maung and Than Shwe, to carry out a faux *coup d'etat*. In the resulting government, Saw Maung became chairman of the new State Law and Order Restoration Council (SLORC), which served as a 21-member cabinet. Than Shwe became vice chairman. Than Shwe also was promoted to the rank of full general and later became commander in chief of the Army. Khin Nyunt—the powerful intelligence chief who had spearheaded the persecution of the 1988 student leaders—was rewarded by being named Secretary-1.

It soon became apparent that Ne Win was still running the country from behind the scenes. Saw Maung, Than Shwe, and Khin Nyunt were all seen making regular visits to his residence. When asked about the visits, Saw Maung said it was like going to see a parent.

The new junta took quick steps to put their own brand of nationalism on the country by force. They disbanded the Parliament, as well as the Council of Justice and the Attorney General's office. They began expanding the Tatmadaw to 321,000, double the pre-1988 size. They stepped up their purchases of arms and began beefing up intelligence capabilities to sniff out external and internal threats. In 1989, they changed the capital's name from Rangoon to Yangon and the country's name from Burma to the Union of Myanmar, ostensibly to remove the colonial designations in favor of more ancient nomenclature. And they began moving away from Ne Win's disastrous version of socialism to allow more private investment, which just so happened to benefit their own families and friends.

But the generals made a major miscalculation: they failed to hear the voice of the people. When the NLD swept to victory in the polls in 1990, the new SLORC leaders were surprised to see that Aung San Suu Kyi's party received strong support even from within their own military ranks. They had promised to hand over power to the winner, but they had presumed that would be their own party, the National Union Party. They concocted the story that the ballot was actually to elect representatives to write a new constitution, not to serve in Parliament. It was a transparent lie, but it bought them time and kept them in power.

After SLORC refused to honor the NLD's victory, Saw Maung and Than Shwe not only kept Aung San Suu Kyi locked in her house, they tried to make sure she would never, ever win another referendum. The generals claimed that two previous constitutions—one written in 1947 under the leadership of Suu Kyi's father, Aung San, and the other in 1974 during Ne Win's rule—contained a clause precluding anyone married to a foreigner, or having spent more than 20 years out of the country, from ever becoming president. Both applied to Suu Kyi.

Gen. Khin Nyunt, the powerful interior minister and chief of military intelligence, even claimed that the alleged clause in Section 10-E had been written into the 1947 constitution by the revered General Aung San himself! Yet, according to the NLD, it was not Aung San, but the SLORC generals themselves who had added that exclusionary clause—immediately before the elections in 1990.

Suu Kyi commented that it seemed ridiculous that the government would rewrite a clause in the constitution to apply to one specific individual. But they did. And would keep looking for ways to bar her from leadership.

Some said Than Shwe's ascension to power during SLORC's rule was due to "his ability to bore everyone else into submission." In reality, he used his position as the second most powerful general in SLORC to hire and fire strategically within the War Office. He shored up his power base by appointing loyal officers to senior positions. They included Gen. Soe Win, who would later carry out the Depayin attack on Aung San Suu Kyi; Gen. Maung Aye, a hard-liner who would become Than Shwe's partner in throttling dissent; Gen. Shwe Mann, who would later become speaker in Parliament; and Gen. Thein Sein, who would later be anointed president.

It worked to Than Shwe's advantage that the continuing protests for democracy in the early 1990s put SLORC chairman Saw Maung under intense pressure. He was said to have begun drinking at home and began acting erratically in public. He referred to himself in incoherent ramblings as the reincarnation of the ancient Burmese king Kyansittha. In one outburst, he waved his pistol on a military golf course and screamed, "I am Kyansittha," which also means "the remaining soldier."

In April 1992, it was announced on the radio that Saw Maung was resigning for health reasons—before Saw Maung was told. He was leaving for work when he discovered his house was surrounded by soldiers. Saw Maung was placed under house arrest by his deputy, Than Shwe. He died of a heart attack five years later. There was lingering suspicion that Than Shwe and/or Khin Nyunt might have caused his precipitous mental decline by drugging him somehow.

With Saw Maung removed, Than Shwe immediately pronounced himself the new Senior General. He became the head of SLORC and the commander in chief of the Armed Forces. Kyaing Kyaing's astrologer had been right. Than Shwe, the former postman and high school dropout, was the new King of Burma.

Than Shwe had been fortunate to begin his military rise while General Ne Win was enlarging the armed forces, which created more opportunities for Than Shwe to move up.

After World War II, only a few thousand soldiers remained in the Burmese Army. Ne Win enlarged the Tatmadaw to more than 150,000 soldiers to combat the Communist movement and rebellious ethnic groups. When his turn at the top came, Than Shwe enlarged the national forces to more than 400,000, to keep control of the county.

During the late 1950s and early 1960s, only 50 officer cadets graduated annually from the Defense Services Academy. Toward the end of Ne Win's dictatorship, some 120 officer cadets graduated per year. Under Than Shwe, the graduating class at the military academy multiplied to more than 2,000.

By 2011, 24 percent of the country's national budget was reportedly earmarked for the military, compared with 4 percent for education and 1.3 percent for health services.

—w—

Than Shwe was ruling over a country the size of France and yet he was still so reclusive that most Burmese had never heard his voice. Initially, he was seen by the West as a more moderate dictator than his predecessors. He took several positive steps to further that impression: He relaxed the socialist stranglehold on the economy. He championed Burma's admission to the Association of Southeast Asian Nations (ASEAN). He cracked down on some of the corruption in the government.

Than Shwe then moved with the cunning of a serpent. He expanded his power base, eliminated his rivals, controlled information, and built a military elite to carry out his wishes.

As he gained more and more power, Than Shwe became less and less accountable to anyone else. In 1993, when he reached the age of 60, the mandatory retirement age, he simply made a new law to extend it.

He launched the Union Solidarity and Development Association (USDA) as a social organization purportedly to foster "political leadership" among civilians. In truth, it was a civilian militia to protect the state from internal threats. Civil servants, teachers, and students were coerced into joining the USDA. They became his eyes and ears and enforcers—USDA thugs repeatedly attacked Aung San Suu Kyi and her supporters. Machiavelli would have been impressed. Than Shwe had deputized a huge segment of the country as his personal henchmen and made it sound like the Rotary Club. As a Burmese saying goes, "the ruler has a thousand ears." Than Shwe now had millions.

In 1997, Than Shwe abolished the unfortunately named SLORC and reconstituted control under the more dignified sounding State Peace and Development Council (SPDC). The new SPDC consisted of 11 senior military officers plus Than Shwe as chairman and commander in chief of the armed forces. The Tatmadaw was stacked with officers that Than Shwe had groomed. Than Shwe knew that so long as the army was in his grip, the country was too.

In 2004, Than Shwe moved to eliminate the main competition to his power. He purged the powerful prime minister and intelligence chief, Khin Nyunt. Khin Nyunt had served Than Shwe with skill as his ruthless enforcer. He had masterminded efforts to smear Aung San Suu Kyi and hound democracy activists into prison. He had earned the nickname "The Prince of Darkness" by presiding over a reign of surveillance and torture. However, Khin Nyunt's core loyalty to Than Shwe was suspect because he had originally had been a protégé of Ne Win's. University-educated, Khin Nyunt was more sophisticated and articulate than his betel-chewing boss. He wore Western-style suits with grace; his hair was carefully parted, Ivy League style. Worse, his wife was a physician, well-educated and well-spoken—which earned her the extreme dislike of Than Shwe's wife Kyaing Kyaing, who was not.

Khin Nyunt also made the mistake of courting praise in the foreign media for being more moderate and more progressive. Congressman Bill Richardson had praised Khin Nyunt's leadership in a press conference and suggested he was more willing to negotiate with Aung San Suu Kyi, which was another strike against him.

Than Shwe had the intelligence chief arrested on charges of corruption and taken to Insein Prison—where he was locked in a bungalow that he had originally ordered built to keep Aung San Suu Kyi. He was given a suspended sentence of 44 years and placed under house arrest indefinitely. Like General Ne Win and General Saw Maung before him, the powerful spy chief had been outmaneuvered by Than Shwe. Hundreds of his supporters in the Directorate of the Defense Services Intelligence were purged at the same time. The country's intelligence capability was weakened for years, but the message was sent: those who got in Than Shwe's way disappeared.

Ironically, one of Khin Nyunt's last acts would provide a way for Than Shwe to deflect criticism and perpetuate his rule.

The savvy spymaster came up with the idea of a seven-point "Roadmap to Democracy." The idea was to gradually move the country and the economy toward more openness, what Than Shwe called a "discipline-flourishing democracy."

The first step would be to revive the sidetracked constitutional convention that the military had pretended was a substitute for honoring the winners of the 1990 election. The constitution-writing process had dragged on for more than seven years and then was largely abandoned until Khin Nyunt suggested dusting it off.

The "Roadmap" provided a smokescreen of reform for the junta. The revived constitution-writing process was rigged to perpetuate their control. Twenty-five percent of the seats in Parliament were reserved for the military. All top leadership had to have served in the military. And a Supreme Council of former generals was placed over the president and Parliament.

Two special provisions were inserted at Than Shwe's request: Section 59(f) decreed that no one whose spouse or children were foreign nationals could serve in top leadership positions. That ruled out one candidate in particular: Aung San Suu Kyi.

Another provision, Chapter 14, Section 445, specified that no member of SLORC or the SPDC could be held legally accountable for their actions while performing their duties. "The Bulldog" had granted himself amnesty in the constitution for a long list of crimes against humanity.

It's difficult to say the exact moment when the socially awkward postman was transformed into a cold-blooded dictator, but it most likely happened over time. As his hold on power grew, the casualties did too, like bones around a dragon. The new emperor had state-run media to clothe him in honor daily. The *New Light of Myanmar* praised his initiatives and windy speeches by printing fawning articles.

When journalist Joshua Kurlantzick visited in 2006, he noticed increased efforts to build up Than Shwe's image like North Korea's "Dear Leader."

Photos were regularly printed of the unsmiling senior general greeting foreign dignitaries, donating to temples, opening new bridges. The nightly news opened with scenes of Than Shwe inspecting crops or troops. According to veteran Burma-watcher Larry Jagan, the government even produced a propaganda film in which the face of one of the famous Burmese kings morphed into the face of—Than Shwe.

Than Shwe continued to rule with the armor of his rank and ego, unmoved by the suffering of the poor in the country. His power was absolute after the removal of Khin Nyunt. Top officers owed their high standing to him; some even idealized him for building up the military's might. But a sizable body of evidence was being compiled by international organizations that could leave the dictator liable to prosecution in an international tribunal, or at the least mark him as a monster in history. In particular, the International Human Rights Clinic at Harvard University has documented the egregious human-rights abuses in Burma—forced labor, forced displacement, sexual violence, extrajudicial killings, and torture. In 2009, the Clinic released a major report, *Crimes in Burma*, which showed that there was a *prima facie* case of international criminal law violations occurring in the country. The Clinic recommended strongly that the U.N. Security Council act to establish a Commission of Inquiry to investigate these grave breaches further. By 2010, the U.N. Special Rapporteur and more than a dozen other countries supported calls for such a Commission if the government did not take action to investigate and prosecute abuses in the country. A Myanmar Human Rights Commission was formed in 2011, but could not investigate former leaders because of the indemnity placed in the constitution by Than Shwe. The U.N. Security Council has not approved an official inquiry, and no effective international action has been taken to convene a Commission of Inquiry.

Than Shwe's offenses over two decades are far too many to list, but even a brief accounting demonstrates there is much in Than Shwe's record that should cause him problems in this life and the next:

GENOCIDE

Those who have never seen a murder victim, and most people have not, may find it hard to imagine the deaths of hundreds of people at a time; but under Than Shwe's rule, wholesale killings became the order of the day. Ethnic minority groups—especially those that were Christians or Muslims—were singled out for persecution. Under Than Shwe's direction, the Tatmadaw was sent out to "Burmanize" the country by force.

As early as 1991, Than Shwe and Khin Nyunt oversaw a campaign in the Irrawaddy Delta that was code-named "Operation Storm." The generals brought in Chinese-made helicopters, jet fighters, and naval vessels to hunt down suspected ethnic Karen "rebels" who, for the most part, were just ordinary villagers. According to the regime's figures, 275 "enemy combatants" were killed in the campaign, 13 were arrested, and three surrendered, but the numbers are widely believed to be much higher. Than Shwe had given a "shoot to kill" order, and many villagers were simply executed or killed in the air bombing raids. According to Aung Zaw of *Irrawaddy*, "The survivors were not necessarily the lucky ones. Hundreds of Karen villagers—some as young as 15—were thrown into prison and subjected to torture and inhumane interrogation techniques. Some Karen villagers are reportedly still being detained in prison, but they are not listed by political prisoner campaign groups because nobody knows who they are."

In April 1993, Than Shwe ordered the Western Regional Command to kill over 400 ethnic Rohingyas, who were predominantly Muslim, in Arakan State's Buthidaung Maungdaw Township. The attacks were punishment for attacks by some Rohingya rebels on the Burmese army. The army rounded up more than 400 people, including civilians, and as soon as they received their orders from headquarters, killed them all.

In 1996, Than Shwe ordered his commanders in Shan State, Karenni State, Pegu Division, Karen State, Mon State, and Tenasserim Division to relocate villages and kill entire families, including infants, of anyone who defied the orders. The U.N. Special Rapporteur estimated that more than 3,000 villages were vacated by force over the next decade of scorched-earth attacks. By 2006, more than 540,000 people were displaced in eastern Burma alone, without homes, without a way of earning a living, without medical care.

RELIGIOUS CLEANSING

The vendetta against Christians began heating up in 1966 after General Ne Win seized control and expelled foreign missionaries in a xenophobic crackdown. Believers who had born in Burma carried on church work but found their path increasingly blocked by authorities. Permission was required for the most mundane of church activities, from baptisms to nativity plays. Christians were barred from positions of responsibility even though they traditionally have been well-educated in missionary schools. During Than Shwe's rule, that suppression turned into deadly, predatory oppression.

Under Than Shwe, Burma shared a place on the U.S. State Department's list of worst religious offenders with China, Iran, North Korea, and Sudan. In addition to anti-Christian abuses, Muslim and Jewish cemeteries routinely have been desecrated and razed to provide land for projects benefiting military cronies. Muslim groups like the Rohingya have been denied right of citizenship and have to get permission even to get married.

Not all the villages where Christian homes were destroyed were targeted primarily because they were Christian—often they were caught in the crossfire because of their proximity to resistance armed groups. Homes in the predominantly Buddhist Shan area were also burned. The problem of religious prejudice is often intertwined with armed conflict and political persecution.

That said, there have been specific instances where religious prejudice was an animating factor. A 2007 regime memo to army troops in the largely Christian Karen area of eastern Burma gave directions on how to eliminate Christians from the state. Seizure of livestock, destruction of crops, as well as abduction of children for use as porters, human minesweepers, and soldiers were approved tactics. Rape was frequently used as a weapon. In many parts of the country, churches not only were destroyed, but Buddhist temples also were constructed on the sites. Crosses were defaced or taken down.

In a series of events documented in fall 2011, the pastor of Banggaw Kachin Baptist Church was arrested by soldiers while speaking on the telephone in a shop. His whereabouts are unknown. During that same period, soldiers looted donation boxes in the Assemblies of God church in Muk Chyuk village and tortured the assistant to the pastor to death. Some 50 members of the church were seized as porters. Soldiers also fired multiple rounds of bullets into a Roman Catholic church in Namsan Yang village, where 23 worshippers, mostly women and elderly people, had gathered in the sanctuary for an early Sunday morning service. After destroying the Catholic church, the soldiers took over a Baptist church and burned it.

In many regions, harassment is an ongoing problem. Church elders in a 150-year-old Baptist church confided to me that their members are increasingly afraid to attend services. The loss of financial support has meant fewer resources to support causes like the nearby Christian Leprosy Hospital. As a result, the hospital has little medicine for the hundreds of sufferers who come for help, many without hands or feet. The government claims leprosy is no longer a threat, although there are an estimated 3,000 new cases a year.

Christians in Kachin State in the mountainous north told me they were ordered to submit written requests 15 days in advance to conduct Bible studies or Sunday school classes. House churches in Rangoon were closed and historic cathedrals subjected to bureaucratic harassment to stymie their operations. In the Karen area in eastern Burma near Thailand, churches were being burned even while Burma was courting approval to become chair of the Association of Southeast Asian Nations (ASEAN) in 2014.

According to Human Rights Watch, the junta regularly arrested and imprisoned the predominantly Christian ethnic Chin during Than Shwe's rule to intimidate villagers and stifle dissent. The HRW study from 2005 to 2008 documented army abuses that included confiscating and extorting money, food, and property; exacting forced labor; and coercing people to plant crops for the military. One Chin man told Human Rights Watch, "We are like slaves, we have to do everything [the army] tells us to do."

In 2010–2011, Physicians for Human Rights documented the conscription or murder of children under 15 and the rape of Christian women, men, and children in Chin State. Religious symbols such as crosses were removed by the military. In one instance, female genitalia were drawn on the cross, and in another the cross was used to prop up guns turned on villagers. Almost 92 percent of all surveyed households reported a family member subjected to forced labor. More than 62 percent reported working under the threat of physical harm, and 15 percent had been tortured. Although some see the religious persecution as a side issue in the Burmese struggle for democracy, it is part and parcel of the story, a symptom of the regime's drive to "Burmanize" the country by suppressing minority languages, religion, and culture by force.

PORTERS AS SLAVE LABOR

Farmers and their families regularly are forced to leave their fields to porter goods for the Burmese army, build roads, or construct army posts, which means they cannot tend to their crops, their main means of support for their families. One Chin woman told Human Rights Watch, "The army has called me many times to porter, more than 10 times. When I cannot carry their bags, they beat me. [The soldiers] get angry and slap us and kick us. . . . They said: 'You are living under our authority. You have no choice. You must do what we say.'"

Using forced labor has been a Tatmadaw practice under Than Shwe since as far back as 1995. At that time, Than Shwe and Khin Nyunt directed the final assault on Manerplaw, a city on the Thai border. The ethnic Karen people had hoped Manerplaw would be the capital of their long-dreamed-of Kawthoolei State ("The Green Land"). Students and members of the NLD sought sanctuary there after the 1990 elections were annulled. In violation of international law, Burmese troops forced thousands of villagers in the region to serve as porters to carry the heavy artillery that would be used to shell Manerplaw. Some were kidnapped from tea shops, some were taken from hospitals. Writer Alan Clements witnessed the infantry and artillery attacks against Manerplaw. While trying to document the battles, he encountered a bloated and mutilated body floating in the nearby river, face up. The man was naked except for his underwear. Both arms had been pulled from their sockets and twisted behind his back. There were large chunks of flesh missing from his inner thighs where he had been tortured. His face was blackened as if he had been bludgeoned with a rifle butt or heavy stick. Clements wrote, "This was the usual fate of a military porter. . . . These porters, usually young men, were forcibly seized and taken into the war zone to serve as pack animals for military supplies and as human mine sweepers. Numerous shallow mass graves were being discovered throughout the region, filled with the mutilated bodies of these conscripted laborers."

MURDER

In 1998, Than Shwe ordered the murder of scores of unarmed villagers and Thai fishermen. According to Aung Lin Htut, formerly the deputy chief of mission at the Burmese mission in Washington, D.C., 81 people, including women and children, were shot and buried on Christie Island after straying into a remote military zone. After one general hesitated to kill the unarmed civilians, fearing the commander who had given the order was drunk, he was told the instruction came directly from "Aba Gyi" or "Great Father," a term used to refer to General Than Shwe.

Aung Lin Htut, who had served as a General Staff officer with the military intelligence in the War Office during the 1990s, later wrote that when there were domestic disturbances, Senior General Than Shwe told his top officers, "Don't even spare the residual quarter!" His officers interpreted that to mean that all civilians who did not obey the orders of the military should be killed. They took his emphatic order as a green light to put to death civilians and to use forced labor and rape without compunction. Aung Lin Htut said Than Shwe's angry orders often exploded as outbursts: "Eliminate them! Don't even leave an infant alive! They are just kala [a degrading term for people of Indian descent and other foreigners], not humans! Sentence them to the maximum imprisonment!"

RAPE

The Shan Women's Action Network (SWAN) and other ethnic women's groups have documented that rape is routinely used as a weapon by the Tatmadaw against ethnic populations. Troops from 52 army battalions were involved in the incidents of rape documented by SWAN, compelling evidence that the practice of rape is accepted throughout the ranks of the Burmese military. More than 60 percent of the incidents documented involved gang rape. In many of the gang-rape cases, the victims were also killed by the troops. Rape allegations against soldiers rarely, if ever, result in prosecution or punishment.

In one documented incident, three women aged 18, 35, and 37 were at their farm in the Kho Lam area when they were arrested by 80 SPDC troops. They were kept for four days and three nights, during which time they were repeatedly gang-raped before being released.

In another case, a school meeting was held at a middle school in Lai Kha town, two teenage girls questioned why Burmese people were forcing village people off their land. Two security guards at the school ordered the girls to go to the commander of the nearby military base. The commander locked up the girls. At night he took turns taking one of the girls into his bedroom and raping her at gunpoint. After raping the girls in turn for four days and four nights, the commander demanded that the parents pay 15,000 kyat for the release of each of them.

In dozens of other documented cases, women were kept by the regime's troops for periods of up to four months for the purposes of rape. In one example, four female and six male villagers were seized while they were working at a farm and forced to carry military equipment and go with the troops while they patrolled deserted villages. The women were raped almost every night. They not only were forced to serve as unpaid military porters for almost four months, they also were also forced to serve as sex slaves.

CHILD SOLDIERS

When Than Shwe was presiding at graduation ceremonies at the Defense Services Academy in 1996, senior military leaders accompanying him said he told them that if the army needed more soldiers, they should recruit children if necessary. Human Rights Watch issued a report in October 2002 confirming that child soldiers made up more than more than a fifth of the Burma Army. More than 70,000 youngsters under the age of 18 were forced to serve in the national army, the largest number in the world. Although Burma had ratified the U.N. Convention on the Rights of the Child in 1991, the military regime continued to ignore its provisions, including the prohibition on the use of child soldiers. And although ethnic armies also resorted to using child recruits, international observers reported the abuse by the Burmese Tatmadaw was more widespread. The guns that the young boys had to carry often were taller than they were.

One 12-year-old forced into army service told Human Rights Watch, *"They asked me, 'Do you want to join the army?' I refused and they punched me. Then they asked again, 'Do you want to join the army?' I refused again and they punched me again. They did this seven times and I still refused. They punched my face, my chest, my forehead, and they cut open my eyebrow and it bled. I was bleeding from the eyebrow and the mouth."*

The child soldiers are subject to beatings and systematic humiliation during training. One 14-year-old boy told of being held in a detention room with 60 other forced recruits. One was a playmate from his village who was only 11 years old. *"He often cried because he didn't get enough food, and then he was beaten by the guards. I also cried often because I didn't want to join the army. I was beaten twice a day for crying. . . . We couldn't sleep. There were also rats and ants in the room. . . . For a toilet they'd dug a hole in the ground and it had a wooden cover over it. . . . There was a terrible smell. . . . Some of my friends were crying. . . . Two or three boys got sick and died."*

Often the child soldiers are refused contact with their families and face severe reprisals if they try to escape. A 16-year-old boy recruited in 2001 remembered what happened to a trainee who was caught trying to go home. He was beaten on the head and back with sticks for about an hour and a half. When he fell, he was propped back up and beaten until he was unconscious. He was left in leg stocks for a week, the other recruit remembered. *"Then he couldn't eat anything and they sent him to hospital. He died in the hospital."*

Once deployed, the boys are forced to engage in combat and participate in human-rights abuses against civilians. Two boys, ages 13 and 15 at the time, told Human Rights Watch they had served in units that massacred a group of 15 women and children in Shan State in early 2001. The 13-year-old testified, *"They took the babies away from their mothers. We gathered them in one place and sent a report to headquarters by radio. . . . The order that came over the radio was to kill them all. . . . Then six of the corporals loaded their guns and shot them. They fired on auto. The women had no time to shout. I saw it. I felt very bad because there were all these people in front of me, and they killed them all. Their bodies were left there. The soldiers were holding the babies and the babies were crying. After the mothers were killed, they killed the babies. Three of the privates killed them. They swung them by their legs and smashed them against a rock. I saw it."*

The Burmese government has denied any recruitment of children and reported to the U.N. that "There are no children in armed conflict."

TORTURE OF POLITICAL PRISONERS

The Council on Foreign Relations produced a report in 2003, chaired by Mathea Falco, a former assistant secretary of state, that claimed more than 1,300 democracy supporters were being held behind bars in Burma in a penal system that included 35 prisons and 100 labor camps at the time. Amnesty International described human-rights violations in Burma as "widespread and systematic." As many as a million Burmese were sent to jungle gulags or shipped to rural work camps and forced to perform manual labor—all during Than Shwe's tenure.

Also in contravention of international law, political prisoners have been savagely beaten and tortured as a state policy. As former prisoner Bo Kyi wrote, *"Many people don't know people were tortured. Many people don't know about the darkness in Burma. . . . If the regime cannot find the person they are hunting, they take a hostage instead: a father, a mother, a husband, a wife."*

Aung Hlaing Win, a 30-year-old member of the National League for Democracy, was sitting in a local restaurant eating his dinner in May 2005. He was suddenly accosted by several men and taken to an unknown location. Seven days later, he was dead. Aung Hlaing Win was tortured to death in one of Burma's interrogation centers. Though an autopsy revealed his body had marks consistent with torture, Aung Hlaing Win's death was ruled a result of natural causes. He was cremated without his family's knowledge, and the authorities attempted to bribe his family to keep quiet. The authorities who tortured him are known, and though his family has filed his case in court, no action was taken against his torturers.

According to the Assistance Association for Political Prisoners (AAPP), shackles are used not only while prisoners are being transported, but as a means of punishment. One man said he had to wear shackles for three months, rubbing his flesh away. The shackles usually have an iron bar between the feet, which keeps the legs permanently astride. The usual iron bar is between a foot and a half and two feet long, but some are as short as six inches long, making it impossible for prisoners to walk.

The political prisoners are also sometimes tied down to chairs, tables, and to the prison bars, according to human rights reports. Often they are stripped naked even in winter months and placed in pitch-black cells with no light, no sleeping mat, no chamber pot for days on end. They were punched, kicked, slapped, kneed, their skin rubbed off their shins with metal rods. They were beaten with a variety of implements, including wood batons, truncheons, rifle butts, electric cords, chair legs, broomsticks, and plastic pipes.

Some of the torture was painfully novel—one man had his legs placed in stocks, and the hair on his shins plucked out. Yet another man was made to lick up his own spit during his beatings. A few men have had their hands tied behind their back with rope, and then were suspended from this rope until only their big toes could touch the ground for support. They were kept in this position for as many as three days, forced to defecate on themselves.

Political prisoners have also been made to walk across, kneel on, or crawl on their stomachs across sharpened stones, glass, metal, and gravel, slicing their skin to pieces. This is referred to often as "walking on the beach." Some political prisoners have experienced "tick-tock" torture wherein a single spot on a person's body is beaten rhythmically every second for hours on end. This torture causes severe physiological damage. As one political prisoner reported to the AAPP, "I was beaten on the head with a wooden ruler. . . . It was non-stop, like the ticking of a clock. One hit for every second. It was a regular beat. For three days, non-stop my head was hit every second with the ruler. There was only one target that they kept hitting; it felt like a hammer hitting my head every time. . . . I still get terrible headaches. . . ."

Cigarettes, hot wax, lighters, and electric rods have all been used to burn political prisoners on the most sensitive parts of the body, including the genitals. One man explains: "Prisoners were always threatened. They said that they had the right to kill us, stop our visits with our family, and keep us in the jail for a long time. It was not jail, it was hell. All prisoners were always frightened about what would be done to us by the officers."

To make matters worse, the dank cells in prison teem with a variety of animals and insects, which the authorities made no real effort to remove. Some of the animals and insects spread disease, posing an additional threat to the political prisoners' health. Rats, mice, snakes, scorpions, spiders, worms, lizards, leeches, cats, lice, flies, maggots, and bird droppings have all been reported in the cells. One woman reported there were 35 rats in her cell. They ran across her body in the dark.

When U.N. Special Rapporteur on Human Rights Paulo Sergio Pinheiro went to interview those political prisoners about their conditions in prison in March 2003, he discovered that the regime had hidden a microphone under the table. The regime apparently was trying to gain information that could be used to incriminate and jail other political activists. Pinheiro left the country in protest.

Despite the great risk, women often led the way in exposing the repression under Than Shwe. In addition to the Shan Women's Action Network

ABOVE: Aung San Suu Kyi as a child in 1951.
BELOW: The 2008 Congressional Medal of Honor featuring Aung San Suu Kyi.

TOP LEFT: Aung San Suu Kyi and Michael Aris on their wedding day. TOP RIGHT: The newlywed couple on their honeymoon. CENTER: General Aung San and his young family. His daughter is at the bottom in the white dress. LEFT: Khin Kyi with her children.

ABOVE: Aung San Suu Kyi and Senator Jim Webb. *Courtesy of the U.S. State Department.* BELOW: Senator Hillary Clinton and Aung San Suu Kyi meet for the first time. *Courtesy of the U.S. State Department.*

President Obama meeting with Aung San Suu Kyi.

ABOVE LEFT: General Aung San in traditional Burmese attire. ABOVE RIGHT: A popular image of General Aung San. BELOW: A political cartoon in *The Irrawaddy* satirizing Hillary Clinton's meeting with the Burmese leadership.

THE
IRRAWADDY

"NICE TO MEET YOU! LET ME HELP YOU THROUGH..."

By HARN LAY / THE IRRAWADDY — Wednesday, November 30, 2011

ABOVE LEFT: Clinton and Suu Kyi. ABOVE RIGHT: Aung San Suu Kyi meeting with U.S. Chargé d'Affaires Larry Dinger (left) and Assistant Secretary of State Kurt Campbell (right). BELOW: Author Rena Pederson with Aung San Suu Kyi and the dog Tai Chi Toe, who was a gift from Suu Kyi's son.

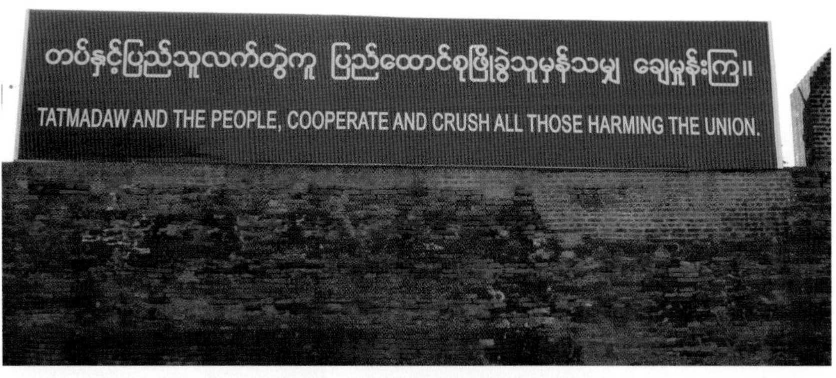

Military regime signs around the country, 2003–2010.

General Than Shwe making merit at a Buddist temple.

Monks marching through the streets of Rangoon during the Saffron Revolution.

Aung San Suu Kyi on the cover of *Time* in 2011. *Courtesy of Time Inc.*

Kim, Michael Aris, and Alexander attend the Nobel Peace Prize ceremony in place of Aung San Suu Kyi. *Image courtesy of Reuters.*

ichael Aris with sons Kim and Alexander, September 12, 1991. *Image Courtesy Corbis nages.*

David Ben-Gurion with General Ne Win.

TOP: General Than Shwe.
CENTER LEFT: President Thein Sein. CENTER RIGHT: Hillary Clinton, now Secretary of State, with President Thein Sein. *Courtesy of the U.S. State Department.* BOTTOM LEFT: First Lady Laura Bush speaks on a panel at the United Nations about bringing democracy to Burma.

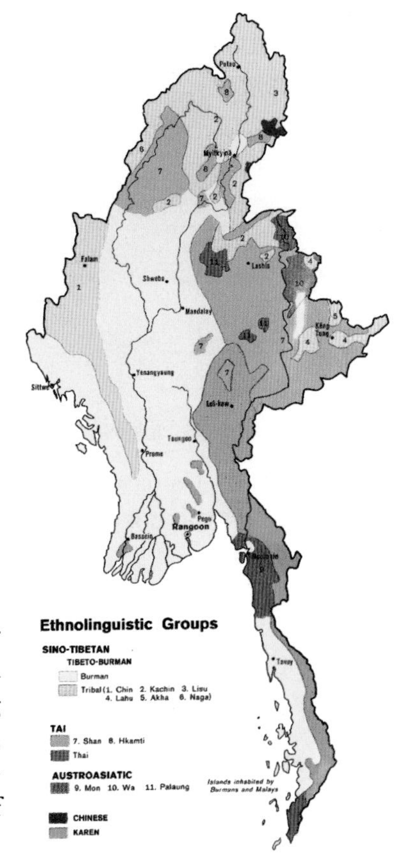

TOP: Former general Shwe Mann, Speaker of the House and potential presidential candidate. CENTER: General Min Aung Laing, Commander of the Armed Forces, and another potential presidential candidate. RIGHT: An ethnographic map of Myanmar.

The house at 54 University Avenue next to Inya Lake, where Suu Kyi spent decades under house arrest. *Courtesy of the Associated Press.*

Aung San Suu Kyi's house from another angle. *Photo by John Bishop.*

ABOVE: Aung San Suu Kyi greeting her followers from the fence of her home. *Courtesy of Campaign for Burma in the United Kingdom.* BELOW: Greeting the crowds after her release from house arrest. *Courtesy of Agence France-Presse.*

exposure of the use of rape as a weapon, the Palaung Women's Organization documented the growth of the drug trade in 2009 in their report "Poisoned Hills." The Karen Women's Organization documented the abuses experienced or witnessed by women who have taken leadership roles in their villages in a report called "Walking Among Sharp Knives" in 2010. The abuse that has been documented includes:

- People burned alive
- Crucifixions
- Rape, including gang rape
- Many forms of torture, including beatings and water torture
- People buried up to their heads in earth and beaten to death
- Arbitrary executions
- Beheadings
- Slave labor

One woman reported that she was forced to carry heavy loads as a porter for soldiers and was tied up at night with ropes that were jerked as she tried to sleep. When she protested the torture, she was raped. Other women were used as minesweepers, forced to walk ahead of soldiers in areas peppered with land mines.

Another woman, who served as village chief for five years because no one else wanted the job, said the military came to her village searching for insurgents. They forced several people into a hole, covered them with earth up to their necks, and stomped on them. Another female village chief, who had endured beatings herself, said villagers were arrested while working on their farms, tied up, and crucified before their throats were finally cut.

The government denied the allegations, saying its soldiers were only engaged in anti-terrorist operations.

Than Shwe and his generals continued for year after year to get away with their crimes against their own people, despite the growing body of documentation by human-rights groups and international organizations. The sanctions imposed by the Clinton administration in 1997 were hurtful, but not enough to topple or deter Than Shwe's regime. However, there was evidence that Than Shwe knew he had much to atone for. He stepped up his efforts to "make merit" by donating to pagodas and building pagodas. And his guards began wearing their guns even when escorting him inside pagodas to make donations—the monks weren't going to hurt him, but the possibility was increasing that his own people or his own soldiers might.

And as early as 2001, Than Shwe began expressing concern that he might be indicted by an international criminal tribunal. A personal representative was dispatched to the Burmese embassy in Washington, D.C. with a top-secret request: Could the embassy find out if the U.S. government had any intention of bringing the Burmese generals before an international criminal tribunal? At the time, Slobodan Milošević of Yugoslavia, Charles Taylor of Liberia, Pol Pot of Cambodia, and Omar al-Bashir of Sudan were all facing charges in different internationally sponsored tribunals. But not Than Shwe. The Burmese embassy responded to Than Shwe that the U.S. had no time think about Burma at the moment. It was September 2001 and attacks had just been made on the World Trade Center and the Pentagon.

The lull in international attention allowed the Burmese regime to expand their tentacles of power. They extended their reach into every sector of the economy in Burma. The generals became vastly wealthy themselves by creating an ever-larger fraternity of guilt. Than Shwe had corrupted the military; now he corrupted the country.

CHAPTER TWELVE

THE LORDS OF THE SUNSET

> "The irony is that corruption and bribery has since spread like cancer to the top levels of Than Shwe's regime, and people in Burma now joke that it is not only a butcher, but also thieves and dacoits, who run the country."
>
> —Aung Zaw, "The Dictators"

As Than Shwe's power became more absolute, his personal wealth soared and his family started taking on royal airs. He began requiring others to address him and his family members with regal courtesy titles, the kind of pomp only used in Burmese theatre. At times, other obsequious gestures were required of subordinates, such as getting down on their knees to honor the ruling family and speaking only when spoken to in their presence. Than Shwe was said to place visitors to his home in chairs lower than his, just as the dictator Ne Win had, and kings before him.

But the most ostentatious display of royal pretension was the infamous 2006 wedding of Than Shwe's daughter Thandar Shwe. Bootleg video footage showed the general's plump daughter draped in what looked like seven diamond necklaces. The video became such an underground hit on YouTube that possession was made a crime punishable by imprisonment.

Some observers estimated that the cascade of gifts showered on the newlyweds—cars, apartments, jewels, envelopes stuffed with cash—totaled as much as $50 million.

And how much did the dour Father of the Bride pay for the elegant buffet, champagne, and a five-tier wedding cake?

The senior general apparently got off light. He didn't have to pay for his daughter's wedding. The junta's business cronies picked up the tab, estimated at $300,000.

The main wedding planner reportedly was Tun Myint Naing, the son of one of Burma's most infamous drug lords, who has re-invented himself as Steven Law, a billionaire businessman. Law has been placed on the U.S. Treasury Department sanctions list for illicit dealings. He is the chair of the Asia World conglomerate, the largest in Burma, with interests in five-star hotels, airport construction, toll roads, and giant hydropower projects—most of which involve high-level government contracts. According to British journalists Peter Beaumont and Alex Duval Smith, the catering for the gala wedding was arranged by Law through his hotel connections. They reported in *The Guardian* that the most of the other expenses were footed by another crony, Tay Za, who is head of the Htoo Trading Company, a major conglomerate, and founder of Bagan Airlines. Tay Za also is on the U.S. sanctions list for illicit business dealings.

Than Shwe could have come up with the cash himself. He is believed to have several billion dollars stashed in banks in Singapore, Dubai, Macau, and China. Following in the tradition of Burmese monarchs, Than Shwe's family controls the ownership of lucrative oil wells and gold mines. His share of deals brokered on his watch—giant port projects, dams, real estate projects—is estimated in the millions. The name Than Shwe translates to "million golden" for good reason. In 2011, the military government transferred ownership of over 1,000 acres of rubber plantations, jade mines, and gold mines to the junta chief and his family, according to business sources in Rangoon.

Than Shwe reportedly has a multi-story colonial villa in Rangoon, plus a holiday villa on Burma's west coast with an infinity pool overlooking five miles of the stunningly beautiful Ngwe Saung (Silver Beach). He also has a hilltop vacation home in Pyin Oo Lwin, the cool and quiet hilltown once known as Maymyo, where British officers escaped the tropic heat. And then there is his home in the new capital, Naypyidaw, where it has been reported that the general keeps a huge stash of cash in a bunker below the mansion, just in case.

Not bad for a guy whose monthly pay is officially $1,000.

His wife Kyaing Kyaing and members of her family are said to have shares in Air Bagan, the airline founded by Tay Za. Than Shwe's daughters also have shares in Tay Za's hotels in popular beach resort towns. And they are shareholders in a hospital near Inya Lake, which was sold off to Tay Za as part of the government's privatization process. Two of Than Shwe's sons own hotels in Naypyidaw as well as gas stations that have been doled out to insiders. When a large number of properties were transferred by the government to Than Shwe and his family in 2011, jade and gold mines that had been under the care of the regime's Ministry of Mines were transferred to his daughters. A source from the regime's Ministry of Finance and Revenue (MFR) also told *Irrawaddy* magazine that the ownership of premises in Rangoon, Naypyidaw, and Maymyo, as well as over 30 vehicles, were put in the names of Than Shwe's children and grandchildren.

In addition, Than Shwe's favorite grandson, Nay Shwe Thway Aung (nicknamed Pho La Pyae "Full Moon"), was given a directorship of Yadanabon Cyber City, a 10,000-acre IT park while he was still in high school. The grandson later was given a prime position as president of the Universities Champions Football League. A Ministry of Finance and Revenue source has reported that Nay Shwe Thway Aung has been given key parcels of land in Rangoon to develop that previously belonged to the government, including properties from the Ministry of Industry 1, the Ministry of Science and Technology, the Department of Atomic Energy, and the Ministry of Industry 2. He also reportedly has taken over the land of the duty-free market in Yankin township. According to the *Asia Sentinel*, one of the grandson's money-making activities as a commercial broker is helping companies to clear customs at the country's ports, enabling them to illegally import goods upon receipt of a "tax" payable to him.

Although only in his early 20s, Than Shwe's favorite grandson Nay Shwe Thway Aung has power and influence beyond his years. He also has been a magnet for controversy. As a teenager, he and some friends allegedly kidnapped a famous model and actress and kept her against her will for several days.

According to the *Irrawaddy* news magazine, Than Shwe's grandson sent associates to shut down a coffee shop that had been opened by sons of other officials. He also may have sent toughs to rough up a rival in a business deal. In addition, Nay Shwe Thway Aung was implicated in a drug scandal in 2009. Two of his friends, the Burmese tycoon Maung Weik and a son of a lieutenant general, were arrested after a member of the Than Shwe family found some pills thought to be the drug Ecstasy on the grandson's person. He also was accused of attacking a police officer, apparently for not clearing traffic for him in Rangoon.

Despite the controversies, Than Shwe proudly took Nay Shwe Thway Aung with him on state visits, creating the impression that he considered the young man the rising star in the family dynasty.

—∿∿—

The sticky web of insider deals also has enveloped the top generals around Than Shwe:

According to Reuters, Than Shwe's longtime second-in-command, General Maung Aye, known for his heavy drinking and love of golf, profited handsomely from his close connections to the chairman of KBZ Group. The KBZ Group controls two airlines, the country's largest private bank, Kanbawza Bank, and lucrative jade and gem mining concessions. The Democratic Voice of Burma reported that the Kanbawza Bank "was started in Shan State by the then-unknown and apparently 'asset-less' teacher, Aung Ko Win, who happened to meet and befriend General Maung Aye." At the time, Aung Ko Win was in charge of purchasing goods at Shan Yoma Shopping Center in Tachilek, where Gen. Maung Aye served as commander of the Eastern Command. According to *Irrawaddy*, Maung Aye asked Aung Ko Win to run the ruby and sapphire mines in Mong Hsu. Aung Ko Win was then seen as the "adopted son" of the powerful general and granted concessions in cement and cigarettes, along with other enterprises. The Kanbawza bank has grown to become one of the biggest and most important financial institutions in Burma.

General Khin Nyunt, the once-powerful intelligence chief, had ties to U Eike Htun, the head of the Olympic Construction Company and a key figure of Asia Wealth Bank, according to multiple reports. The *Irrawaddy* news magazine has alleged that U Eike Htun had connections to the drug trade. His Asia Wealth Bank has received substantial support from Chinese business interests. Spychief Khin Nyunt also has been closely connected to U Htay Myint, who is head of the sprawling Yuzana Company, which has interests in housing, supermarkets, fisheries, hotels, and shopping plazas.

The Yuzana founder, U Htay Myint, would later become a member of Parliament. He was also was given licenses by Senior General Than Shwe to operate giant plantations for tapioca, sugar cane, and cassava in the Hukawng Valley, which had been declared the largest tiger preserve in the world in 2004. The preserve, the size of Vermont, was intended to save the shrinking population of tigers, along with gibbons and elephants. It was endorsed by the Wildlife Conservation Society and supported with $400,000 from the U.S. Fish and Wildlife Service. Then from 2006 to 2010, the Yuzana Company moved in with an armada of backhoes and bulldozers that ripped up native forests and bamboo groves. The lands of small farmers who had lived in the valley for generations were confiscated to make room for the plantations—and the most recent reports have indicated that almost all the tigers have been driven out of their habitat. The regime also opened the tiger reserve to oil-drilling and gold-mining operations.

Wikileaks of embassy cables in 2007 noted that while the third-ranking general at the time, General Shwe Mann, "may not be as notoriously corrupt as some of his colleagues, Shwe Mann has solid connections to regime business cronies. He is reported to be a director in Tay Za's Htoo Construction Company, and is also allegedly involved in fertilizer, brokerage, and fish export businesses."

Lucrative petrol-station permits were given to the two sons of General Thura Shwe Mann as well as to Tay Za's Htoo Trading Company and Steven Law's Asia World in 2010 according to *Mizzima News*. Petrol concessions also went to the junta-controlled organization, the Union Solidarity and Development Association (15 stations) and to Myanmar Economic Holdings—a company that funnels income to the junta (14 stations). The Democratic Voice of Burma has estimated that 70 percent of the property that was auctioned off to private enterprise when the government began liberalizing the economy in 2010 ended up in the hands of cronies of the military rulers.

The sons of General Shwe Mann also show up in a clutch of cozy relationships—one son was hired to work for Tay Za and another is married to the daughter of another crony. One has interests in jade mines in Kachin lands in the North. Both benefited from their ownership of Redlink, a telecommunications firm given preference by the government.

General Thein Sein, the dutiful Than Shwe loyalist who would become prime minister and then president, is often described as the "least corrupt" of the generals. When one of his daughters was married in Naypyidaw in 2009, great care was taken to show more restraint than the notorious wedding of his boss's daughter several years before.

I happened to be in Naypyidaw the day that Thein Sein's daughter was married and attempted to go by the wedding site to get a glimpse of the guests. All the roads around the ceremonial government site were blocked and heavily armed. I asked my driver to pull into an adjacent area where limousine drivers were parked. Then I paid him extra to go chat up the drivers and see what he could find out about the people attending the wedding. I scrunched down in the back seat and waited. About 20 minutes later, he came back wide-eyed with amazement. He had gotten close enough to see the stream of guests in their finest silks, carrying in gifts. The other drivers told him their customers brought keys to cars and apartments as gifts. The parade of wealth was like something out of a dream for a man who wore the same neatly cleaned shirt day after day. I could see the wonder on his face and sensed that he wished he could have just a little of that luxury, too. No diamond necklaces were being captured in cell-phone videos that day; Thein Sein was too smart for that. He is said to return gifts he believes are inappropriate. But that would be the exception for the military elite, not the norm.

The chain of sweetheart deals between the military and business allies has created a cadre of superwealthy in Burma while most of the people remained impoverished. In 2013, *The Wall Street Journal* and *Reuters* cited a World Ultra Wealth Report by Wealth-X, which said that Burma has 40 billionaires who have accrued more than $3 billion in wealth.

Because of the lack of transparency, it is difficult to track the byzantine array of connections, but by piecing together news accounts and reports by watchdog groups you can compile a picture of the extent of the corrupt practices. Some of the most detailed information about the crony capitalists has surfaced through classified American embassy cables from 2005 to 2009 that have been posted by Wikileaks. One of those cables described how Win Aung, owner of Dagon International Construction Company and Dagon Timber, was using his close connections to the regime to amass great wealth. Although Dagon International specializes in building luxury housing projects, it won contracts to build roads and government dormitories in Naypyidaw. The embassy reported that Dagon Timber illegally exports millions in teak logs to China annually, substantially more than the reported exports of $161,000. Win Aung also has interests in the tourist industry, and his Palm Beach Resort is one of General Than Shwe's favorites.

Another cable described Zaw Zaw, managing director of the construction company Max Myanmar and chairman of the Myanmar Football Federation, as an up-and-coming crony. The cable said Zaw Zaw actively seeks favor with the senior generals and competes with top crony Tay Za for key construction projects by volunteering to do them at a lower cost. The cable said, "The GOB (Government of Burma) gave Max Myanmar the concession for all the roads in Naypyidaw and paid the company with import licenses, properties, and housing development permits. In addition to his construction company, Zaw Zaw controls most used car and motorcycle imports, has a concession for timber exports, and owns two luxury hotels. He is considered close to General Maung Aye and Than Shwe's grandson, Nay Shwe Thway Aung."

The cable went on to explain, "Max Myanmar was one of eight companies that built Naypyidaw. . . . He also built the Royal Kumudra Hotel, one of Naypyidaw's first five-star hotels. Instead of being paid for the construction work, Zaw Zaw reportedly received 10 permits, valued at $180,000 each, to import new cars. (Tay Za and Steven Law each received 15 permits for work done in Naypyidaw.) He also received several properties in Rangoon, where he plans to construct housing developments."

—⁓—

For centuries, "The Lords of the Sunset" were the powerful hereditary princes of the Shan States of Burma, called *Sawbwas* or *Saophas*. In many ways, the sawbwas were as grand as the famous maharajahs of India, with as many elephants and even more rubies. Some of their estates were as large as Massachusetts and Connecticut combined and included prize teak forests that made generations rich. Their hills later proved a sublime place to grow opium poppies.

The name *saopha* translated to "Master of the Sky," and a saopha wife was called the *mahadevi*, "Goddess of Heaven." When General Ne Win was given control of Burma under Prime Minister U Nu, he stripped the princely sawbwas of their feudal powers in exchange for comfortable pensions for life in 1959.

Under Ne Win, the military began profiting from the riches in the Shan States and neighboring Kachin lands. Under Than Shwe's rule, the military became the new "Lords of the Sunset."

—⁓—

While Aung San Suu Kyi and most of the opposition leaders were locked up during the 1990s and early 2000s, Than Shwe had created what democracy advocate Maung Zarni, a research fellow at the London School of Economics, has called a "pocket army" to protect his interests—"a national mafia."

In contrast to General Aung San's hope for civilian control of the army, General Than Shwe transformed the military into a privileged ruling class presiding *over* civilians. In a prime example, the training ground for Tatmadaw officers—the Defense Services Academy (DSA)—was expanded dramatically under Than Shwe's rule. Signs at the DSA campus now proclaim that the academy is preparing the "Triumphant Elite of the Future." Under Than Shwe, members of the military were provided access to the best educational facilities in the country, while other campuses were shut down or moved to remote locations, making it extremely difficult for the rest of the population to get an education. Those who rose in the army ranks then had access to a cozy network of business connections through graft or by marriage.

The incestuous intermarriage of military power and money vastly complicates the challenge of opening the country to the kind of responsible international investments that could reinforce democracy. Transparency International has cited Burma as one of the world's most corrupt countries, ranking 172nd out of 176. When asked if corruption is a big obstacle to establishing democracy in Burma, democracy leader Aung San Suu Kyi replied, with typical frankness, "Corruption is certainly a big obstacle. I'm just wondering whether we couldn't find a stronger word than 'obstacle.'"

Suu Kyi explained in a 1995 interview with *New York Times* writer Claudia Dreifus that one of the ways that the government has tried to stop people from being involved in the democracy movement is to encourage them to take an interest in business, not politics. "That is, if you are concentrated on just making *money* in this country, you have to indulge in a lot of things that are . . . not quite strict. There is a lot of bribery and corruption going on. You do lose the morality if you are told to concentrate only on making money and if you are made to feel as long as you are making money you won't get into trouble. So people think that it is much more dangerous to support the democracy movement than to bribe somebody."

Bertil Lintner, who has covered politics and corruption in Southeast Asia for decades, agrees that the systemic corruption has become a way for the generals in Burma to control the population because everyone has a vested interest in the system. As he told me, "Everyone who comes to the wedding brings car keys for gifts . . . students have to pay for exam papers . . . doctors sell medicine on the black market. Basically, it is a criminal system—*where everyone becomes guilty of something.*"

This presents the democracy supporters in Burma with a major dilemma: how can they cut through the Gordian knot of military rule that is interwoven with a corrupt economic system?

Aung San Suu Kyi suggests with her "Revolution of the Spirit" that the generals will have to help unravel the knot themselves, for their own good. For those who are Buddhists, that will mean embracing reform in order to avoid a punishing fate in their next life.

For the less devout, that will mean gambling that they will get an even larger share of the pie if they help grow the pie bigger—and growing the pie will require a legal climate that can draw greater international investment.

The high degree of difficulty of decoupling the rich ties between the military and their partners in profits is exemplified in two individuals: Tay Za and Steven Law.

TAY ZA—THE ROCK STAR

Tay Za has been described as Burma's first billionaire, although there are several others who could claim that title if accurate figures were available. The U.S. Treasury calls Tay Za "an arms dealer and financial henchman of Burma's repressive junta." For many years, he has been considered Than Shwe's top crony. Diplomats told Reuters that Tay Za strategically curried favor with Than Shwe and other generals, giving their children roles in his businesses in exchange for coveted contracts and import licenses in highly profitable sectors: trading, logistics, property, agro-industries, tourism, oil, and retail.

In years past, when Than Shwe and his family went on vacation, they often went the beach where Tay Za owned resorts. When Than Shwe wanted five armored Toyota Land Cruisers, Tay Za provided them. When Than Shwe needed surgery, Tay Za rushed him to medical facilities in Singapore because the hospitals in Burma were far from adequate.

How did Tay Za get so close to power? He was born in 1964 to an army officer who was a protégé of General Aung San. He named his son after the independence hero, whose wartime alias was "Teza," a Sanskrit word that means radiant or bright; Tay Za is an alternative spelling.

Tay Za followed in his father's footsteps by attending army cadet school, but he dropped out to marry a girlfriend. He was eking out a start in business when protests against military rule erupted in 1988. Tay Za joined the street marches in Rangoon. He has said that his family was still close to Suu Kyi's at the time. Before she was arrested in 1989, Suu Kyi stayed at his family compound outside Rangoon and was driven around in his car.

Tay Za did not stay an anti-government protester long. In 1990, he launched Htoo Trading, using the name of his wife's family, who were respected merchants. His first enterprise was leasing a rice mill from his mother-in-law. Then he moved into timber and showed an early talent for wheeling and dealing. By obtaining logging permits in remote areas, he was able to harvest logs at $10 each and then sell then for $500 or more. With what would become typical braggadocio, he soon claimed he was the biggest timber extractor in Burma. He leveraged those logging profits into real estate, including his first hotel.

According to American diplomatic cables, Tay Za began his relationship with the military in early 1990, when he befriended the head of procurement for the Ministry of Defense. He then parlayed his good relations with the Russian ambassador into sales rep positions with Russian companies, including the Military Industrial Group (MAPO), Aviaexport, and the helicopter company Rostvertol. He formed Myanmar Avia Export and earned hefty commissions from sales to the military junta of arms, ammunition, supplies, Mi-17 helicopters, and MiG-29s. His take for arranging the regime's purchase of 10 MiG-29 jet fighters from Russia alone was reportedly $130 million.

Timber continued to roll in a reliable revenue stream. By 2005, Tay Za controlled an estimated 80 percent of the country's logging business. He became one of the few with permission to harvest logs in "brown," or militarily contested, areas. According to American embassy cables, the government gave Htoo logging concessions in Kachin State, where locals had been resisting Burmese control for nearly 60 years. The locals then complained that they lost a significant source of revenue when Tay Za was allowed to move in, to no avail. "Travelers to the region tell of a steady stream of Htoo trucks plying the road from Kachin State, loaded with teak logs for export," the cables reported.

Over the next decade, valuable concessions in timber, cement, and liquor sectors enlarged Tay Za's empire. Htoo Group grew into a major conglomerate. Tay Za created Air Bagan, the first private airline in Burma. He acquired 17 luxury hotels in prime locations in key tourist destinations.

Rumors began circulating that his rapid rise was fueled with money and privileges from Than Shwe and his family, which Tay Za denied. Others say Than Shwe was impressed by Tay Za's glitzy style during a visit to his beach resort. Tay Za also cultivated a friendship with rising stars such as third-ranking General Shwe Mann when he was still a colonel.

While many other cronies tended to avoid the limelight, Tay Za danced in it—sometimes taking the stage himself at gala dinners to grab the microphone and sing. Taxi drivers proudly point out his home in Rangoon, which is close to the American embassy and Aung San Suu Kyi's home. His neo-classical mansion at the corner of Inya Road and University Drive is easy to spot because of the trophy cars in the driveway, including a canary-yellow Lamborghini, a Ferrari, and a Rolls-Royce.

Tay Za is the kind of hip CEO who wears black jeans and an expensive sweater with loafers to interviews. He has a reputation as a fun-loving and generous boss. He shows up at company picnics. He sends employees overseas to study, hired the country's first female pilot, and shares profits with top managers. He is said to pay for expensive holidays in the posh Maldives for his office staff.

When Than Shwe, a football fan along with his grandson, ordered Burmese business moguls to create a national football league, Tay Za suited up. He threw his energies and money into establishing the Yangon United Football Club and likes to play in club matches. (His rival crony, Steven Law, launched the Magway Football Club.)

Yet while Tay Za gained fame as a bold entrepreneur, he is not known as an astute manager. There were reports over the years that his seat-of-the-pants management style could not keep up with his far-flung holdings. At times, his flashy investments in aviation and hotels had to be subsidized by his profits from junta-granted concessions for timber and gems as well as lucrative import licenses. Embassy cables reported that the roller-coaster of cash-flow problems was bringing him close to bankruptcy.

Tay Za frequently blamed his financial difficulties on Western sanctions, which hampered his profits and kept his children from attending prestigious colleges abroad—one of his sons was so frustrated that he could not get a visa to elite schools in London and Sydney that he appealed to the European Union high court, saying he should not be punished because of his father—and the court agreed.

Yet when Tay Za's projects were riding high and the profits were rolling in, he bragged that he had done very, very well *despite* sanctions. According to American embassy cables, Tay Za made frequent trips to Singapore, where he owns a home and does his banking. "The Singaporean Ambassador confided in the embassy that Tay Za had purchased two $7 million homes on a gambling resort island off the coast of Singapore," the cables reported. "We have also heard that he used his connections in Singapore to secretly arrange Than Shwe's emergency medical treatment there last January. Tay Za has personally designed and built homes for Than Shwe and his family." He was said to be the favorite of Than Shwe's wife, Kyaing Kyaing, who often was seen riding in his Mercedes-Benz in downtown Rangoon. Tay Za regularly took generals on golfing trips or invited them on trips where they are wined and dined and entertained by models and actresses. In turn, he took the general's wives on lavish shopping sprees in Singapore.

The inside story on his operations was laid out in a 2009 cable from the American embassy. The diplomatic cable noted that regime officials often turn to Tay Za for hotel and airline freebies or capital for the regime's projects. "He also became the regime's key broker, negotiating with investors from China and Russia on a number of different public and private projects. In return, Tay Za obtained lucrative construction contracts, valuable import permits, and access to the regime."

Not all the generals admired Tay Za's flamboyant talents. One embassy source quoted General Shwe Mann, the third-ranking general in the regime, as saying Tay Za had become a liability because his conspicuous consumption was drawing international scrutiny that reflected "poorly" on the regime. The source quoted in the cable said Generals Maung Aye and Shwe Mann were shifting their preference to other cronies for new projects and licenses in return for their "allegiance." Those in favor included Zaw Zaw, who was close to Than Shwe's favorite grandson. Zaw Zaw gave Than Shwe's favored grandson a position during the time he owned the Delta football team. In return, Zaw Zaw's company, Max Myanmar, was said to have received several new construction contracts, including completing work on the Rangoon-to-Naypyidaw

Highway. Max Myanmar also was working with Steven Law's Asia World to finish construction on the new Parliament building and Presidential Palace in Naypyidaw after Tay Za reportedly lost those contracts.

The high-flying Tay Za seemed undaunted by any business setbacks. At the request of the regime, he teamed up with the Myanmar Gem Traders Association to promote Burmese jade and gems in Kunming. He flew 40 merchants to Kunming on his Air Bagan free of charge. His companies expanded their share of the mobile telecommunications sector through his partnership with a Chinese cell-phone company and sales of mobile-phone SIM cards. He constructed a vacation home close to General Than Shwe in the hills overlooking Pyin Oo Lwin, the colonial retreat.

Though Tay Za's day-to-day management skills may be in doubt, his Donald Trump-ish flair never is. Tay Za is given credit for doing a masterful job of turning the historic Governor's House in Pyin Oo Lwin into a luxury hotel with Wi-Fi, jacuzzis, and satellite TV. He also has restored the majestic, teak-columned Kandawgyi Hotel in downtown Rangoon and helped beautify the adjacent lake. As a fan of French food, he added a posh French restaurant, "Agnes," to the Kandawgyi Hotel that has become a see-and-be-seen venue. If it sometimes seems as if Tay Za is around every corner in Burma, he is.

According to diplomatic cables, benefits to Tay Za from regime leaders have included highly lucrative permits to import and export agriculture products. He imports large quantities of the palm oil used in everything from baked goods to soap; his permits to export beans and pulses alone brought in more than $60 million. Tay Za also had one of the country's few permits to import cement, a valuable asset while the government built its new capital in Naypyidaw.

His Htoo Construction has built a rail terminal as well as luxury housing. Reportedly at Than Shwe's request, Tay Za spent $2 million to build a luxury mall near Sule Pagoda that features designer goods that the majority of the country cannot afford.

Other businesses in the Tay Za empire include heavy land and marine transport, plantations, telecommunications, oil exploration, rice mills, and vehicle imports.

According to the *Irrawaddy*, his wife, Thida Zaw, who is also on the sanctions list, bought the London Cigarette Company and is believed to control Burma's tobacco industry.

In a 2007 diplomatic cable, Tay Za was described as a "rock star." Never one to hide his wealth, Tay Za and his family reportedly own more than 20 houses in Rangoon and Singapore, and are often seen driving around town in their fleet of expensive imported cars. Tay Za also acts as a purchasing agent for the military government, buying luxury items for regime members and flying them back to Rangoon on Air Bagan planes. "He earns his money by charging a 20 percent surcharge," an embassy cable revealed.

"Tay Za has a reputation for being charming, charismatic, and generous," embassy cables noted. He once threw an elaborate party to celebrate an anniversary for Air Bagan that cost $25,000—at a time when he had reported the airline only made a profit of $51,000 that year.

Other embassy cables noted the dark underside to Tay Za's extravagant ways: A police contact had reported that the millionaire owes an "indicted narcotics trafficker $10 million for wagers on soccer matches and may have to pay the debt with assets from his holding companies."

After Tay Za bought two helicopters as gifts for the government, he was allowed to build a hotel in the ancient capital city of Bagan. He also got a contract to build a controversial 13-story observation tower in the Bagan Architectural Zone, which includes more than 2,200 historic temples. The modern tower was heavily criticized as aesthetically out of place in a historic site that rivals Macchu Pichu and Angkor Wat.

But according to Aung Zaw at *Irrawaddy* magazine, more serious damage may have been done in Bagan by the construction of Tay Za's five-star Aureum Palace hotel in the area, which is said to have plowed through ancient artifacts. The final approval of Bagan as a UNESCO World Heritage Site reportedly has been delayed because of the clumsy modern renovations. Tay Za's supporters counter that he also helped restore the Bagan palace of King Anawrahta in Bagan at considerable personal expense and believes he is helping the country.

In 2002, a report on deforestation by the U.K.-based advocacy group Global Witness claimed the Htoo Company's logging and resource extraction activities (jade, gold) are responsible for much of the environmental degradation in Burma.

The damage from gold-mining in Kachin state by junta cronies and military proxy companies also was documented by Images Asia Environment Desk (E-Desk) in collaboration with the Pan Kachin Development Society in 2004. Their photos show rivers ruined by the mercury and cyanide used to extract gold. Gold is being extracted in large amounts and at breakneck pace from throughout Kachin State with hydraulic equipment and barges without regard to the environment or living needs of nearby villagers. What used to be clean water in the Mali Hka River—which flows into the Irrawaddy River, the lifeline of the country—is now tainted by the toxic chemicals from gold mining. That is jeopardizing the ecosystem of the entire river basin, potentially impacting 20 million people who live and work on the river.

Environmental critics also contend that Tay Za's resort hotels often are built without regard to the natural environment. This has raised concern that he has received permission to develop property in the Myeik Archipelago, a lacework of 800 islands in southern Burma with shimmering beaches and some of the world's most important marine biodiversity.

The sinister side to Tay Za's enterprises was apparent in a 2009 cable describing Tay Za's top assistant, Lu Lu, also known as Kwan Lu Chan, Chan Kwan Lu, and Zaw Min. At the time, Lu Lu was vice chairman at Air Bagan and Tay Za's main adviser. The American diplomatic cables reported that Lu Lu is known in business circles to be "cunning and ruthless" and boasts to businessmen that he taught Tay Za "all he knows." Because he is of Chinese origin, Lu Lu is Tay Za's liaison to Chinese investors. He allegedly set up different firms in China on Tay Za's behalf and owns several companies on his own. Although he is married to an American citizen, the embassy recommended that Lu Lu be added to the sanctions list and went on to explain that he owns several jade and gem mines, often selling high-quality gems to the senior generals' wives.

The embassy reported that "Rumors abound that Tay Za has long smuggled Chinese weapons into Burma via his aviation and trading businesses." An embassy source alleged that Lu Lu has close ties to the senior management of the Chinese firm Norinco, formally known as the China North Industries Corporation. Norinco manufactures trucks, cars, motorcycles, oilfield equipment, chemicals, explosives, and a wide range of armaments, including amphibious assault weapons, anti-aircraft and anti-missile systems, "high-effect destruction systems," anti-riot equipment, and small arms.

The cables contend that Lu Lu was the mastermind behind Tay Za's involvement in the arms trade, including helicopters and explosives that could be used in ethnic areas. Lu Lu also was believed to have secured agreements between Htoo Trading and Norinco for a gold-mine partnership in the Mandalay area and the purchase of a controversial copper-mine project near Monywa in central Burma that is known as Myanmar Ivanhoe Copper Co., Ltd. (MICCL). That toxic mining project would later explode into an environmental scandal that Aung San Suu Kyi would try to resolve in 2013; she ended up losing face instead.

In the beginning, the giant Ivanhoe copper mine was a 50/50 deal between a Canadian company and a Burmese state-owned enterprise called Mining Enterprise-1. Operations of Myanmar Ivanhoe Copper Co., Ltd. (MICCL) began in 1994. For many years, the copper project was Burma's largest mine and a top source of revenue for the junta.

The mine also was chronically controversial because of labor conditions and environmental pollution. The Canadians eventually tried to get out of the deal, according to the American embassy cables, because of *"the GOB (government of Burma)'s continued interference in operations, refusal to pay Ivanhoe its share of profits, and unreasonable demands for increased taxes."*

According to leaked American cables, the Canadians wanted to sell the mining operation directly to the Chinese, but were afraid that the Burmese military government would block the sale. In 2008, they sold the troublesome project for $100 million to the Burmese state mining company, which turned around and sold it to Norinco for $250 million. Tay Za pocketed $50 million in consulting fees for his role as a broker. The mine has remained controversial because of land confiscations and environmental dangers.

Questions later were raised about the transaction—wasn't the sale by Canadian investors to a Burmese entity a violation of Canadian economic sanctions against Burma? At the time, Tay Za was subject to Canadian sanctions as well as American and EU sanctions. Despite the sanctions, the Than Shwe regime and Tay Za reaped a steep profit.

Even more troubling than Tay Za's ties to controversial Chinese investments were reports that he has helped broker Russian and North Korean assistance for the junta's nuclear ambitions. According to the *Asia Times*, Tay Za was part of the delegation led by General Maung Aye, the junta's second-ranking official, to Russia in 2006 to discuss weapons purchases as well as the construction of a nuclear reactor. A former Htoo Trading bookkeeper subsequently claimed that Tay Za was involved in brokering sites for two nuclear reactors and shipping equipment to the sites, often under cover of darkness.

The Democratic Voice of Burma news organization in Thailand reported in 2010 that while Burma was not yet capable of building nuclear facilities or a nuclear bomb in a professional way, the military regime had expended large sums seeking expertise and equipment. Defectors told of working on nuclear projects; a veteran IAEA inspector also found suspicious equipment. Though no smoking gun was uncovered, the intent was evident. Reports have persisted that the government is mining uranium in restricted areas and has continued contacts with North Korea, despite objections from the United States. Moscow has agreed to supply Burma with a small nuclear reactor for civilian use.

In 2010, Tay Za narrowly survived a helicopter crash in the northern hills while scouting out investment properties. With only a handful of candy bars and two bottles of water for provisions, the group of six trudged through waist-deep snow to a sheltering rock, where they huddled against the high winds, calling out to one another every five minutes to stay awake. The 47-year-old mogul told reporters later, "I didn't expect to make it."

Military search crews fanned out across the northern hills looking for the missing tycoon. After three days, the small group was found and rescued. Tay Za suffered frostbite and kidney damage. He came away from the incident claiming to be a changed man. He pledged to devote more time to his foundation and made contributions to Suu Kyi's National League for Democracy. His Htoo Foundation—which has made showy donations for water wells, eye care, schools—won an award for "National Best Social Welfare Team Award," which Tay Za gladly accepted at the Presidential Residence in Naypyidaw in 2014. He has also pledged $1 million for a journalism foundation to support better reporting.

As part of his efforts to rehabilitate his image, Tay Za is said to have hired PR firms in Washington, D.C. to lobby to have his name expunged from the U.S. Treasury Department's list of sanctioned "Specially Designated Nationals" (SDN), but with no immediate results.

Tay Za's name continued to come up in questionable deals involving Russia and North Korea. In late 2013, state-run newspapers reported that Burma and Russia were strengthening cooperation on military technology. The announcement was made after a high-level trip to Russia by Senior General Min Aung Hlaing, the powerful new commander-in-chief of Burma's armed forces. Notably, the trip coincided with one by Tay Za.

People in high places in the U.S. also paid attention when Tay Za continued brokering deals between the Burmese government and North Korea. In 2013, the U.S. was influential in shutting down bank accounts of Tay Za's investment firm in Singapore on suspicion that it had made transactions involving North Korean-linked companies. It was believed that at least one of the companies supported through Tay Za's Singaporean bank accounts—Fortune Sun–was a front company set up by North Korea's Tanchon Commercial Bank. The United Nations sanctioned Tanchon in 2009, calling it the main "financial entity responsible for sales of conventional arms, ballistic missiles and goods related to the manufacture of such items."

In an interview with *Forbes Asia* in 2014, Tay Za defended the fact that he made the Korean payments on behalf of Burma's government. He explained that he heads the business association in charge of importing fuel, and made $300 million in transfers for the government, which is blocked from buying on much of the global market. Transaction records show that most of the payments were made to Fortune Sun under the previous military regime, but one was made eight months after a semi-civilian, semi-reform government assumed office in March 2011.

In May 2012, President Thein Sein claimed Burma has never had nuclear cooperation with North Korea but has made deals for conventional weapons. He said Burma would honor United Nations Security Council resolutions and would no longer buy weapons from North Korea.

Yet a year later, in July 2013, the United States placed sanctions on a Burmese general, saying he had violated the U.N. Security Council embargo on arms deals with North Korea.

As is often is the case with murky transactions in Burma, what the government and business cronies say does not always bear up to scrutiny. Who can you believe? Until there is more transparency and accountability in the financial system, it's impossible to say.

STEVEN LAW: FLYING UNDER THE RADAR

In 2007, the U.S. embassy staff cabled a side-by-side comparison of Tay Za and Steven Law. "Despite being the senior generals' two favorite cronies, Steven Law and Tay Za could not be more different. Steven Law, the son of a known drug smuggler, keeps a low profile and conducts his business with little fanfare. Known as a consummate businessman, Law is lauded for his ability to get the job done professionally and quickly. Tay Za is the polar opposite: a spotlight loving man with little business experience. He used his connections with the regime to get rich, flaunting his money and status, as well as his connections with the regime."

The embassy added, "Despite coming from a wealthy family (his father is the notorious drug trafficker, Lo Hsing Han), Law does not flaunt his money but instead does his best to avoid the limelight. Steven Law, who is known to be discreet and soft spoken, lives modestly and rarely makes public appearances. Even his offices are sparsely furnished."

Steven Law may operate below the radar, but if you travel to Burma, it's almost impossible to avoid his reach.

> If you fly in to Rangoon, he built the international terminal.
>
> If you ship in goods, he owns the busiest wharf.
>
> If you drive from Rangoon to Mandalay, he controls the toll road.
>
> If you stay in a top hotel like the Traders or the Sedona in Rangoon, he's one of the owners.
>
> If you visit the new capital in Naypyidaw, he built a good part of it.

And if you want to escape the tropical heat with a cool beer, Steven Law probably brewed it. Law owns Myanmar Brewery in partnership with a conglomerate run by the military called Myanmar Economic Holdings (UMEHL). Together, they sell two-thirds of the beer consumed in Burma under the labels of Myanmar Beer, Double Strong, and Andaman Gold. You can buy them in his grocery stores.

It's easy to see why Steven Law is known in Burma's business circles as the regime's most accomplished crony. American diplomats were told by a member of the Tuesday Breakfast Club, a group of prominent businessmen who meet regularly, that when the regime wants to build something, the senior generals choose Steven Law's construction company, Asia World. The consensus in the Breakfast Group was that Law is a highly competent and accomplished businessman; he finishes projects quickly and efficiently. The only problem was that most of the other businessmen still didn't trust him.

Despite his commercial prowess, Law is not popular with his business peers. As a U.S. embassy cable reported, "Several businessmen, pointing to his family's drug smuggling connections, argued that Steven Law cannot be trusted. He has a close relationship with the Chinese, [the business source said] and some people believe that the Chinese are using Law to gain greater access to Burma's natural resources."

—w—

The fact that Chinese businessmen have become the richest group in the country has created resentment in Burma.

In an interview with an Italian journalist in 2011, Burmese tycoon Tay Za complained that "Too many Chinese have taken out citizenship and are now boasting they are the richest. But they're not pure Burmese."

Burmese businessmen complained to U.S. embassy officials that Steven Law, whose family is Chinese with roots in the Kokang region close to China, had become wealthy thanks to his involvement in mega-projects run by Chinese state-owned corporations.

Some of Steven Law's major investments include:

- A Sino-Burmese pipeline project that takes oil and gas from the Burma coast 1,950 km (1,220 miles) to the energy-hungry Yunnan province in China.
- The Kyaukpyu deep-sea port on the island of Ramree to service China's shipping needs.
- The controversial Myitsone and Tasang hydro-power dams. Chinese companies own 80 percent of the $3.6 billion Myitsone project, and almost all of the power generated will go to China, not Burma, where 75 percent of the people lack electricity.
- Asia World also appears to have secured lucrative contracts to extract timber and mine gold from the Myitsone Dam site.

In particular, the troubled Myitsone Dam in Northern Burma has drawn criticism since its beginnings for several reasons:

In the first place, the dam is located in a sacred area for the local Kachin population, and the Irrawaddy River is known as the "mother river" for all Burmese. Dredging up the area is considered a sacrilege.

Second, the enormous project—with a reservoir the size of Singapore—would send 90 percent of the electric power it produced to China. If fully implemented, the hydro project would consist of seven dams that would generate more electricity than the massive Three Gorges Dam in China, with little benefit to Burma.

Third, the dam is in a known fault-line area and would have tremendous environmental and social impact for the region. It would require the relocation of local villages and affect fisheries, sediment flows, and the livelihoods of people hundreds of kilometers downstream.

The controversy has been exacerbated by the widespread belief that the negotiation of the contract between the military government, Asia World, and the Chinese state-owned China Power Investment Corporation (CPI) was tainted by corruption. *Irrawaddy* magazine reported allegations that Senior General Than Shwe would receive a 25 percent cut of Asia World's broker fees. The hydro-power project was temporarily suspended in 2011 after major demonstrations against it, which Aung San Suu Kyi supported. In 2014, Chinese officials expressed optimism that the project could be restarted with changes made to provide more benefits to Burmese.

Because of the Myitsone controversy, it was assumed the Burmese government might try to avoid the appearance of inside dealing when bids were opened in 2013 to upgrade and operate the main airport in Rangoon—a contract said to be worth $1 billion over 30 years. But did the Burmese government choose a U.S. consortium that included aerospace giant Boeing? Or one of the other internationally respected bidders? No. The rich airport contract went to Steven Law.

—

Steven Law's story demonstrates the double whammy of drugs and corruption that confronts democracy reformers. Some of Burma's biggest businesses—banks, construction, timber, and more—are believed to have been founded with drug profits and may still benefit from illegal trafficking or money laundering. Will those enterprises welcome a more open democracy and fair judicial system? Or thwart changes behind the scenes? Will the former generals feasting on the buffet of Burma's riches agree to play by the rules?

Steven Law's rise is a case in point. He was born as Tun Myint Naing on May 16, 1958. He is the son of Chang Feng Hsuan Lo (a.k.a. Kyat Phone Shin) and Lo Hsing Han, a known drug lord and founder and chairman of Asia World Company. In addition to owning Asia World, one of Burma's most successful construction and trading companies, Steven Law and his wife Cecilia Ng own businesses in Singapore and have interests in Thailand. Cecilia Ng (a.k.a. Ng Sor Hong) is often described as operating an "underground banking system" in Singapore to conduct her husband's business transactions, otherwise known as money-laundering.

The family business started with Steven Law's father, Lo Hsing Han, who was described by the U.S. Treasury as the "Godfather of Heroin" and "one of the world's key heroin traffickers dating back to the early 1970s." Law, the Treasury document adds, "joined his father's drug empire in the 1990s and has since become one of the wealthiest individuals in Burma." Law has denied involvement in drug trafficking, but the U.S. has placed him on sanctions lists along with his wife.

Based on information from the Drug Enforcement Administration (DEA) office in Rangoon as well as business contacts, the American embassy listed 24 of Steven Law's known aliases and name variations:

Steven Law
Stephen Law
Stephen Lo
Stephen Ping Chung Lo
Steven Ping Chung Lo
Stephen
Steven Naing
Win Naing
Htun Myint Naing
Myint Naing Htun
Myint Naing Tun
U Tun Myint Naing
Tun Myint Naing
A Chiu
Lo Ping Chung
Lo Ping Zhong
Lo Ping Hau
Lo Ping Haw
Ping Chung Lo
Ping Shao Lo
Pin Shao Lo
Ping Han Lo
Abdul Halim

According to embassy contacts, the Asia World Group controls investments in Burma totaling more than $500 million. Established in 1992 as an agricultural and animal feed products company, Asia World then constructed the now-defunct Equatorial Hotel in Rangoon, as well as several high-rise office buildings. By 1996, Steven Law was partnering with Malaysian billionaire Robert Kuok, to build luxury hotels in Rangoon. These included the Traders Hotel in the heart of Rangoon (owned and operated by Shangri-la Hotels and subsequently renamed the Sule Shangri-La), and the Sedona Hotels in Rangoon and Mandalay. While the Chamber of Commerce lists the Traders and Sedona Hotels as 100 percent foreign-owned, embassy sources confirmed that Steven Law owns a percentage of the hotels in partnership with the Malaysian and Singaporean owners.

—~—

Steven Law has partnered with Malaysian-born billionaire Robert Kuok, who also is ethnic Chinese, on a number of real estate ventures in Burma.

Kuok has been ranked by the Bloomberg Billionaire Index as the world's 38th-richest person, with a fortune estimated at more than $19 billion in 2013. Kuok, who founded the luxury Shangri-La Hotel chain, maintains his office in Hong Kong. He is said to enjoy close ties with China's top leaders in Beijing.

Kuok built his fortune by becoming the leading sugar producer in Malaysia and was known as "The Sugar King." He then added large stakes in palm oil, shipping, and property. He also owns Hong Kong's *South China Morning Post*, once considered the world's most profitable daily newspaper.

Like Kuok, Law has diversified from hotels into other interests, such as palm-oil processing plants, paper mills, and garment factories. More problematic for those who worry that Steven Law may still have ties to his father's drug domain are his transportation investments. Law has assembled a transportation network that would provide a ideal system for shipping contraband of all sorts: the deep-sea port where major cargo comes and goes; the toll road from the two urban centers of Rangoon to Mandalay; the Leo Express bus line in northern Burma, the epicenter of drug trafficking; and a shipping line that transports goods from Singapore to Rangoon.

Law also won the rights to build the highway to Muse, on the China-Burma border—a golden corridor for opium crops, heroin processing, and methamphetamine labs. Clandestine factories in the nearby foothills crank out the drugs that are shipped throughout Asia.

In addition, Law owns a plastic-bag company. To make plastic bags, the company imports large quantities of acetic anhydride. Another use of acetic anhydride is the manufacture of heroin. While certainly not conclusive evidence of guilt, the links in Steven Law's empire continue to arouse DEA suspicions because of his family pedigree. The Bush administration named Law "a regime crony also suspected of drug trafficking activities."

The difficulty of following the money was illustrated by a January 2009 drug seizure. The high-profile seizure was made on a Singaporean ship named *Kota Tegap* that was docked at the Asia World Port Terminal in Rangoon, which is owned by Steven Law. Blocks of heroin worth as much as $100 million were found in a container headed to Singapore and Italy. The container was reportedly owned by the Myanmar Timber Enterprise, a government-owned business that is on the U.S. sanctions list. The raid on the suspect ship was galvanized by foreign anti-drug agents. According to Washington-based Radio Free Asia, Interpol in Singapore asked the Burmese police to seize the ship. Without that intervention, it's unlikely the Burmese authorities would have acted.

—

Burma has become a mecca for the drug trade, but it was not always so. Arab traders had introduced opium to the subcontinent as early as 400 B.C., but it did not take root in Burma as it had in India and China because Burmese kings strongly discouraged its use, a sentiment that Buddhist monks shared. In the 1800s, King Thibaw placed an outright prohibition on opium and alcohol use by the dominant Burman ethnic group. Minority groups—such as the hill tribes and the Chinese—could obtain and use opium, but not the majority Burman community.

When the British conquered Upper Burma in 1885, deposing Thibaw and sending him to exile in India, they initially kept the opium ban in place, a move applauded by the many American and British missionaries in the country who saw the drug as damaging to Burmese society and their conversion efforts.

In the rest of the subcontinent, opium use for medicinal and mood-altering purposes was a widespread practice. Opium was an important household remedy for diarrhea, dysentery, chills, malarial attacks, asthma, coughs, and rheumatic pains. Mothers routinely gave small doses of opium daily to infants to keep them quiet.

Whereas earlier users had mixed the opium with savory spices or water, Dutch sailors, who brought tobacco shipments with them, taught the Chinese to smoke opium by mixing a pinch of it with chopped tobacco or betel leaves. The result was more potent than eating or drinking the drug and led to more widespread recreational use—and more addiction.

The British then figured out a way to commercialize opium cultivation on a larger scale in India. Lord Cornwallis had become governor general of the East India Company after his unhappy experience in the American colonies. He set up an agency in India in 1797 to license selected farmers to grow poppy. The British then were able to control the market by making all *unlicensed* cultivation a criminal offense. The opium that was grown on the licensed farms was largely shipped to China, where it was exchanged for silks and other fine goods.

With the influx of supply from India, the practice of smoking opium took hold in China with ferocity. By the early 1800s, the habit had spread throughout the country, to the great alarm of the Qing emperors.

When the Qing leaders tried to seize foreign opium to stem the influx, the British fought back with the Opium Wars. They overwhelmed the weaker Chinese defenses and forced the Qing Emperor to legalize the import of opium.

Throughout the 19th century, opium was one of British India's most lucrative exports. At its peak, the trade was 16 percent of India's revenues. Thousands of tons were exported from Bombay and Calcutta to some 13 to 14 million consumers in China and Southeast Asia.

It was only after a Parliamentary crusade against the Indo-Chinese opium trade as morally indefensible that an agreement was signed with the Qing leaders to reduce shipments.

The next great venue for opium production on an international scale would be Burma, courtesy of the Chinese soldiers who migrated into northern Burma after World War II.

—~—

To understand the poppies-to-riches saga of Steven Law's family, you have to start with the turbulent period after World War II. Remnants of the Kuomintang (KMT) army of Nationalist leader Chiang Kai-shek—who had sided with the Allies during the war—escaped into northern Burma after the war. They had to flee when Mao Tse-tung's Communists gained control of China. The exiled KMT leaders were hoping to return to power in China with the assistance of the new American Central Intelligence Agency (CIA). To fund their operations, they used drug profits. Many of the KMT soldiers from the Yunnan Province in China had brought their penchant for growing opium with them. It wasn't long before trespassing KMT soldiers were either exacting "taxes" from local farmers to pay for their military operations against China, or growing opium poppies themselves in the Shan hills. Over time, those operations grew into full-blown drug production in the foothills of Burma, which would become part of the notorious "Golden Triangle" of Burma, Laos, and Thailand.

Those poppy fields produced a series of drug lords who would develop profitable links to the military leaders. One of the most notorious drug lords was a larger-than-life character named Khun Sa. As a young man, Khun Sa was called Chang Shi-fu. His father was a KMT soldier who had come from China, and his mother a Shan villager. Growing up, the boy learned the cutthroat business of opium dealing as well as military basics from the KMT troops that had fled into Burma. He gave himself the *nom de guerre* "Khun Sa," meaning "Prince Prosperous." As is so often the case in Burma, names are destiny. Khun Sa went on to form his own army and funded it with his drug profits.

Khun Sa originally sided with the Burmese military government. He received drug money and weapons in return for fighting against Shan rebels who were resisting dominance from Rangoon.

When his army had expanded to more than 800 men, Khun Sa stopped cooperating with the Burmese government. He took control of a large area in the Shan and Wa states in northern Burma and went into opium production. He renamed his group the Shan United Army and began fighting for Shan independence and fighting *against* the Burmese government. His army grew to 10,000 men and then 20,000, the largest private army in the region. More than 20 heroin factories were under his control. Khun Sa became known as the most powerful drug trafficker in the Golden Triangle.

According to scholar Alfred McCoy, under Khun Sa's cunning leadership Burma's opium production soared 500 percent. Burma's share of the New York City market jumped from 5 to 80 percent between 1984 and 1990. By the end of the decade, Khun Sa controlled more than half of the world's heroin supply—making him history's most powerful drug lord. American drug agents dubbed him the "Prince of Death." One DEA agent said, "He has delivered as much evil to this world as any mafia don has done in our history."

Khun Sa's kingly hideout in the Golden Triangle was equipped with satellite televisions, schools, and surface-to-air missiles. "They say I have horns and fangs. Actually, I am a king without a crown," he once boasted to a reporter. The chain-smoking warlord entertained visitors to his jungle kingdom with Taiwanese pop songs and grew orchids and strawberries like a gentleman farmer. He sent letters to several U.S. presidents. Peter Bourne, an adviser to former U.S. president Jimmy Carter, once called him "one of the most impressive national leaders I have met."

Khun Sa claimed that he was only involved in the drug business to further the cause of the Shan people struggling for autonomy. On one occasion he offered to sell his entire opium haul to the U.S. government in exchange for money to start economic development in the impoverished Shan areas. "My people grow opium," he said. "And they are not doing it for fun. They do it because they need to buy rice to eat and clothes to wear."

Yet in the mid-1990s Khun Sa fell out with Shan leaders and had to switch his allegiance yet again, swinging his support back to the Burmese military junta, which was now under the control of Than Shwe and the intelligence chief Khin Nyunt. Though the U.S. had offered a $2 million reward for his capture, the drug warlord was able to make a deal with the Burmese regime to hide in plain sight. In 1996, the junta announced that Khun Sa had "surrendered." In truth, a mutually beneficial accommodation had been made with the assistance of General Maung Aye, who had served as commander in the northeast region. The drug don was allowed to live in a posh new house in the "millionaire quarter" of Rangoon. He got valuable concessions to run bus lines and toll roads, as well as prime plots of land for his children to develop. Though Khun Sa died of natural causes in 2007 at the age of 73, his reputation as the man who out-foxed the U.S. and the Burmese military junta remains—so much so that in a final irony, his name was still included on American economic sanctions lists in 2013.

While Khun Sa's influence was in flux, other drug lords and their families came to power. One of those was the Lo family of junta business crony Steven Law.

Steven Law's father, drug lord Lo Hsing Han, would have an on-and-off relationship with the military government, much like Khun Sa. Born poor into a Chinese family in the Kokang region in the northern region of the Shan States, Lo initially tried to make money with video parlors and liquor stores. He then became a troop commander for a local prince, one of the Shan sawbwas, who was rebelling against the Burmese military. After the Burmese government cashed out the princes, it didn't take Lo Hsing Han long to realize he should probably switch sides.

Lo Hsing Han finagled an appointment as head of some "home guards" in the Kokang region of Shan State. The home guards benefited richly from drug franchises. As a top commander, Lo emerged as a leading trafficker in Southeast Asia in the 1970s. He set up some 17 heroin refineries in the Kokang region and earned sobriquets such as "King of the Golden Triangle" and "King of Heroin."

When Rangoon authorities disbanded the Kokang home guard that had been his base, Lo switched sides and teamed up with rebels in the area who were fighting *against* the Rangoon government. He was arrested in Thailand, perhaps betrayed by corrupt Thai police, and deported back to Burma. The military regime charged Lo with treason rather than drug trafficking, apparently because he had their permission to sell drugs, and sentenced him to death. Enough of the Burmese top brass were on his payroll that the charges were eventually eased; he only endured house arrest and was released in 1980 to rebuild his drug empire. By 1991, two dozen new Lo refineries dotted the northern hills. Lo Hsing Han had developed a preference for exchanging sacks of heroin for gold bars, hence the famous name "The Golden Triangle."

Lo won his way back into favor with the junta by helping General Khin Nyunt negotiate an accommodation with the Communist Party of Burma, which had been fighting against the Burmese government since the 1950s. In effect, the pact bought peace with drugs. The Communists were allowed to profit freely from the drug business in the northern "no-man's-land" of Burma. Some of them became Lo Hsing Han's business partners. According to DEA Rangoon, Khin Nyunt also give Lo Hsing Han a "concession" for heroin production in return for his help brokering the cease-fire.

DEA sources say Lo Hsing Han's success came from making a superior product. In his case, that was No. 4 grade China White. It was marketed in plastic bags with the brand name "Double UO Globe" and the words "100% pure" in Chinese characters.

Unlike the dirty brown variety of heroin from Afghanistan, the leading producer, the Burma China White could be injected, not merely smoked, which increased the public health risk of HIV and hepatitis. The effects were longer-lasting. And addictive.

Like any attentive manager, Lo Hsing Han reportedly oversaw every stage in the heroin-making product chain, from paying farmers who grew the poppies on their hilly plots in northern Burma . . . to the transport of raw poppy gum in huge sacks on the backs of hundreds of mules that navigated the narrow jungle paths . . . to the refineries near the border with Thailand, where the gum was processed . . . and shipped to markets overseas.

DEA sources say it was Lo Hsing Han who shipped to Vietnam the heroin that ravaged 10 percent of America's forces in the 1960s and 1970s.

By 1998, it was said that Lo Hsing Han's exports equaled all of Burma's legitimate exports put together. He plowed his profits into a new conglomerate he named Asia World. In time, that conglomerate would be taken over by his American-educated son Steven Law, whom we "met" earlier.

Lo earned the gratitude of the ruling generals by paying a "whitening tax" on his profits into Burma's bare treasury. He had a home on the 16th hole of the municipal golf course, and when he traveled he often had escorts of soldiers in army vehicles. When his son got married in 1995, there were at least three generals and four cabinet members in attendance. Lo Hsing Han himself remained close to former prime minister Khin Nyunt in the 1990s and used this friendship to advance Asia World's legitimate and illegitimate operations.

Although Khin Nyunt was ousted in 2004, Lo Hsing Han's son Steven Law continued to have excellent relations with senior generals such as Vice Senior General Maung Aye. Steven Law reportedly also traveled with Senior General Than Shwe on trips to China and built Than Shwe's home in Naypyidaw.

When the Bush administration imposed tougher sanctions on businesses supporting Burma's military government in February 2008, the companies owned by Steven Law were prominently included.

—~—

In 2011, I made the drive from Rangoon to Mandalay and on up to the northern hills to Muse, the gateway to China and all manner of goods, legal and illegal. On the Rangoon-to-Mandalay stretch, there were toll booths at regular intervals with signs saying they were operated by Steven Law's Asia World. The experience was unsettling. Every time we stopped to pay more kyat at the toll, we were benefiting Steven Law.

The only good thing about the toll road was that it was in better condition than the rest of the roads on the trip. Our car wheezed its way up the corkscrew turns around the mountains on what used to be part of the famous Burma Road. We stopped in the Lashio area—where Lo Hsing Han used to have his palatial headquarters, serviced by burlesque dancers from the Ukraine as well as chemists. We had arranged to meet with farmers who wanted to avoid the pitfalls of producing poppy. They were trying to switch to growing corn.

The project had been started by American soldiers who fought in Burma during World War II. They had been members of the first detachment of the OSS (Office of Strategic Services), the predecessor of the CIA. The OSS had waged an undercover war against the Japanese behind the lines in Burma. After the war, the Americans wanted to do something to help the brave Kachin people who had assisted them during the war, often saving their lives. The Americans started the "Old Soldiers Project" in the 1990s to provide seeds and assistance so the farmers could grow legal crops to support their families. The program had grown to include hundreds of farms and villages. But by 2011, most of the old soldiers were dying off, which made it more difficult to keep up support. Funding had been obtained years before by U.S. Rep. Bill Richardson, when he was representing New Mexico in Congress, but now the appropriation was drying up. The wars in Afghanistan and Iraq were draining resources.

Dozens of farmers in faded cotton longyis and flip-flops gathered to show off corn cribs that were filled to the brim with giant golden ears of corn, a variety that had been recommended by Texas A&M University. Many of the farmers said the corn program had done so well that they no longer grew poppy for profit, but since funding from the U.S. was dwindling, they did not know where they would get the money for seeds the next year. Growing poppy was dangerous, but *not* growing poppy was dangerous too. There was pressure from elements of the Burmese military and the ethnic militias to grow poppy and "pay tax." But the farmers said they had seen the toll that heroin abuse was starting to take in their own villages. Too many families had been affected. They didn't want to be part of the drug poison.

They said their way of life in the villages was deteriorating because of the drugs and the crime and human trafficking that came with it. Almost every home had also been touched by sex trafficking, they said. At first, they said, the Chinese from across the northern border came to their villages offering good jobs for women as maids and in factories to the north. When the women did not return, the villagers realized something was wrong. The few women who escaped told of being forced to serve as sex slaves or to work in subhuman conditions. After that, village women refused to go with the recruiters. The recruiters then started stealing the women and girls by force from the streets, sometimes from their homes. Most were never seen again. "It cracked our hearts," one of the farmers said.

I told them I would relay their concerns about funding for the crop program to the embassy, which I later did, but to no avail: there was no more funding for the crop program.

It was late in the afternoon when we headed on toward Muse, when I noticed that an increasing stream of young men on motorcycles had begun racing past us from the Muse direction. Many of them wore dark scarves, so they looked like Ninja warriors speeding into the dark. Swoosh, swoosh, swoosh. The motorcycles sped by so fast, I had trouble snapping a photo. I had counted several dozen in the space of a few minutes before I asked my guide, who are all these guys on motorcycles?

"Drug runners. Young boys who are hired by the drug lords," I was told. "They come out late in the day from the hills, where the drug labs are hidden. They'll ride all night to deliver the drugs to their contacts."

For hours, the dark motorcycles continued racing by, swoosh, swoosh.

At one point, we were startled when we rounded a corner to discover a large group of the motorcycle drivers waiting. Several dozen of the motorcyclists were pulled over together by the side of the road. My heart skipped a few beats as I thought at first they were waiting to ambush us. Had we stumbled into some transaction that they wouldn't want anyone to witness? Oh man, this is it, I thought.

But it turned out that the drug runners had merely pulled over to wait for the policeman they would have to bribe to continue their way down the road. With their scarves down and helmets off, they looked like really young teenagers. They stared expressionlessly at us as our car inched around them. They did not smile and wave.

We drove on to Muse, but the sound of the motorcycles roaring down the road, one after another and another, stayed with me. Swoosh. I couldn't stop thinking of how many lives would be harmed by the cargo they carried. And of the farmers who were asking for help to grow something else.

—~—

When Burma became independent in 1948, the annual production of opium was 30 tons. Under military rule, the production increased some 8,000 percent to about 2,757 tons in 1992–93.

Burma was the world's biggest producer of opium poppy gum, the main ingredient in heroin, until 2003, when Afghanistan took the lead. As their share of the heroin market declined, many of the major drug lords diversified into the manufacture of methamphetamines.

In recent years, the production of poppy has been on the increase again. The U.N. Office on Drugs and Crime estimated that Burma produced 870 tons of opium in 2013, a 26 percent increase over 2012 and the highest figure recorded in a decade. During the same period, drug eradication efforts plunged.

UNODC spokesmen cited the deep poverty in the country as one of the main causes of the increased poppy production. Ethnic minorities in the highland areas say they grow poppy because they have no viable alternative. More than 300,000 households were believed to be involved in poppy cultivation.

Most Burma opium currently is processed into heroin and trafficked in China and Southeast Asia. Demand for heroin remains strong, according to the UNODC, because there are so many young people in the region of drug-using age.

Myitkyina, the capital of Kachin State in northern Burma, is believed to have one of the highest addiction rates in the world because of the easy availability of heroin. The Kachin Baptist Convention, a regional network of half a million parishioners, has estimated that nearly 80 percent of the local Kachin youth are drug users. It also has been reported that half of the students at the local university in Myitkyina—the region's bridge to the future—are addicted. The problem is even more pervasive in mining areas, where work conditions are punishing and pay is often in opium. According to the U.N. Office on Drugs and Crime, there are about 300,000 addicts in Burma, most of them in Kachin and Shan states in the northeast.

Residents in the ethnic areas where poppy is grown, such as Kachin State and Shan State, allege that the Burmese military government looked the other way while the northern areas became soaked in drugs as part of a long-term plan to destroy the ethnic minorities and take over their lands.

While sometimes exaggerated, the conspiracy theories may have some basis in fact. Aung Lynn Htut, a former General Staff officer with military intelligence during the 1990s, wrote that when it came to drugs, General Than Shwe's mantra had been, "Narcotics harm no Burmese. Drugs only harm the U.S. and Thailand. So let the Americans and Thai die!" A study for the South-East Asian Information Network by researchers Dr. Chris Breyer and Faith Doherty in the 1990s concluded that the SLORC generals allowed heroin to circulate freely and cheaply in Burma in the hope that it "pacifies" the rebellious young.

When the SLORC regime was put together after the 1988 popular revolt, cash was desperately needed to make up for the ruined economy they had inherited from Ne Win. The SLORC generals reportedly set a goal of doubling the country's drug exports. They succeeded beyond their expectations. Within a few years, Burma was producing more than 60 percent of the world's heroin supply, valued at more than $40 billion a year.

According to the International Monetary Fund, SLORC used its new drug revenues to buy $1.2 billion in military hardware. The U.S. embassy in Rangoon acknowledged that exports of opium were on a par with legal exports, if not greater. Banks in Rangoon began offering openly to launder money for a 40 percent commission.

By 1997, Secretary of State Madeleine Albright called the Burmese junta a collection of "drug traffickers and thugs." She said, "Drug traffickers who once spent their days leading mule trains down jungle tracks are now leading lights in Burma's new market economy. We are increasingly concerned that Burma's drug traffickers, with official encouragement, are laundering their profits through Burmese banks and companies—some of which are joint ventures with foreign businesses," she said.

The Clinton administration estimated that nearly two thirds of the heroin that entered the U.S. in 1997 came from Burma. At that time, the value of a kilogram (2.2 pounds) of raw opium gum was around $150. The value on the street of the heroin cut from that same opium gum was nearly 10 times as much.

Publicly, the junta supported drug reduction. Privately, the generals benefited enormously from the drug trade. Drug lords could be seen playing golf with military officials. The U.S. tried throughout the years to cooperate with the military on drug eradication, providing training and helicopters; then it was discovered the generals were using the helicopters to attack ethnic groups instead.

In the 1990s, Burma was No. 1 in the world, producing 2,560 tons of opium gum, compared to 1,239 in Afghanistan. The Taliban rulers at the time considered the drug business un-Islamic and punishable by death, so production had slowed there. But when the Taliban government was pushed aside in 2002, drug growers rushed back into business in Afghanistan with a vengeance. The balance shifted. The Afghan hills became the leading producer of opium in the world with a whopping 6,250 tons, and Burma's share officially went down to 800 tons.

The shift prompted international agencies to predict that Burma would become an "opium-free nation" in the near future. It didn't happen. By late 2009, U.N. reports confirmed that opium cultivation in Burma was on the increase again. Drug-control measures were unraveling, with opium farming expanding year after year. What happened? The price of the heroin went up, making opium poppies a more lucrative crop for drug kings. At the same time, the ethnic armies rebelling against the Burmese government were increasingly trading drugs in order to buy more weapons.

Even more troubling, the Burmese drug lords had perfected a new drug product: methamphetamines. Bertil Lintner, a journalist who has covered the Golden Triangle drug trade for decades, says many of the drug kingpins shifted their focus to methamphetamines. They shifted not only because Afghanistan took over the market for heroin once the religious injunction against growing poppy was lifted, but also because the synthetic drugs do not depend on unreliable weather or soil. Since the methamphetamines are easier to manufacture, they can be sold at a 300-percent profit. As a new century dawned in 2001, dozens of new processing plants were cranking out methamphetamines in northeast Burma. The tablets were then shipped into Thailand, where the drug is known as *yaba*, "crazy medicine." Another synthetic drug, Ecstasy, which became dangerously chic in the U.S., was first produced in Burma.

The Burmese *yaba* is cheap—about the price of a couple of bottles of beer—accessible and ruinous. Apart from making people stay awake, the *yaba* can cause hallucinations and severe dehydration. The heart rate is increased, making some users dangerously paranoid. After the effects wear off, depression sets in. Suicides are not uncommon.

Although most Burmese heroin now goes into Asian markets, the surge of Burmese heroin into the U.S. in the 1980s and 1990s dramatically altered the drug scene in American cities.

The surge meant that the retail price of heroin in New York dropped from $1.81 a milligram in 1988 to just 37 cents in 1994, providing an inexpensive temptation.

In the 1980s, the average purity of refined heroin was estimated at 7 percent. By 1991, the figure had risen to 26.6 percent. By 1995, it had increased to 39.7 percent. That meant that the "China White" supplied from Burma was popular because it was so pure that it could be injected, making the effects more immediate and intense. That took away much of the stigma for young people who wanted to experiment but weren't keen on injections, although extended use usually led to injections. Heroin crossed over from back alleys into the suburbs of America.

By the late 1990s, it was estimated that there were 600,000 heroin users in the U.S. The number of emergency-room visits for overdoses spiked. It was during this period that entertainment figures like Kurt Cobain and River Phoenix died of overdoses.

Americans may not have known how to find Burma on the map, but Burma had found America.

The 2014 UNODC report showed that seizures of methamphetamine in Asia have tripled over the past five years, largely originating in Burma.

What was ominous about the resurgence of drug production in Burma is the growth in partnerships with narcotics organizations around the world. Though the drug-trafficking in Burma still is dominated by ethnic Chinese gangs, networking with transnational crime syndicates from around the world is increasing, according to the U.N. Office on Drugs and Crime.

—∿—

The spreading tentacles of the drug trade in Burma underscore the urgent need for what Aung San Suu Kyi calls a "revolution of the spirit," as well as rule of law. But the violent forces that are co-dependent on drug revenue will be hard to convert or prosecute. The U.S. Department of State has offered for many years a reward of $2 million for information leading to the arrest or conviction of Wei Hsueh-kang, the commander of the United Wa State Army's (UWSA) Southern Military Command in the Wa region in northern Burma. He also has also been indicted for federal drug violations in the Eastern District of New York. The UWSA is currently the dominant heroin-trafficking group in Southeast Asia and Wei Hsueh-kang is believed to be in hiding in the Wa hills. The Wa army is estimated at 30,000 troops, making it the largest ethnic army in Burma. The Wa organization is reported to be a major player in the opium, heroin, and amphetamine drug trade.

Wei Hseuh-kang got his start in the drug business in the wild Wa hills with his two of his seven brothers. He is believed to have been born in 1946 in southern Yunnan near the Burma border. His father was an opium farmer and soldier in the KMT, his mother a local villager. When the nationalist forces retreated into Burma, Wei's family settled in the Wa region, which previously had been known for its fierce headhunters. Like Khun Sa, Wei grew up watching how the KMT profited from the opium harvests. He became a master of the trade. He and his brothers, Wei Hsueh Lung and Wei Hsueh Ying, were associated with the KMT-CIA spy network along the Yunnan frontier in the early 1950s.

Later Wei joined Khun Sa's forces on the Thai border and for a time served as his treasurer, a position of great trust. As the drug lord's financial officer, he traveled to West Germany, Taiwan, and many other countries around the world, according to investigator reporter Bertil Lintner. Wei later fell out with Khun Sa, who suspected that his wily money manager had his hand in the till. Wei was imprisoned, but managed to escape. He returned to the Wa hills to set up his own heroin empire. Making use of old Wa connections and his considerable financial acumen, he helped mastermind the building of the United Wa State Army.

Wei's clout increased after the Burmese junta signed a cease-fire with the UWSA in 1989, allowing their syndicates to expand heroin production—a peace-for-drugs tradeoff. Within a year, 17 new refineries opened on the China border, and by 1996 opium production had tripled. When the Khin Nyunt made a similar deal with the Communist Party of Burma to cease their opposition, the Communists then sold their poppy harvests to Wei, whose refineries turned the opium into heroin.

In the late 1990s, the United Wa State Army did a market study, much like any other international business, and determined that the opium business was freighted with negatives, such as the loss of market share to Afghanistan and rising overhead costs including payments to the junta. Amphetamines, on the other hand, had the benefit of easier production because there is no growing season. No large workforce was required. The chemical ingredients were easily acquired. The labs could be located near consumer markets. There was a high return on investment and a diversified product line. The products included amphetamine-type stimulants (ATS) known as "speed" for laborers; the designer drug MDMA known as "Ecstasy" for middle-class youth; "Ketamine," an anesthetic generally used for animals that is abused by young people at "rave" parties; and "crystal" methamphetamine known as "Ice" in Burma and as "Yaba" in Thailand. The UWSA added up the potential profits and shifted its business plan to an emphasis on amphetamines.

According to the BBC, some 50 amphetamine/methamphetamine labs soon sprang up in the southern Shan area, where there was easy access to the border and chemicals. Each of the labs could produce 100,000 *yaba* pills a day. Publicly the Wa leaders claimed to have eliminated their opium/heroin line. In truth, their opiate production was demoted under their new business plan, but not discarded.

Wei reportedly took the helm of the Wa amphetamine operations and has been the driving force behind the man-made drug production in the Golden Triangle since then. It has made him a very rich man. Thanks to the vast amounts that Wei has made trafficking drugs, his Hong Pang Company includes lumber interests, farms, retail outlets, liquor distilleries, gas stations, a cement factory, gas stations, a drinking-water business, electronics, pirated CDs and DVDs, and department stores as well as gems and fine jewelry. The company also owns thousands of acres of fruit orchards and coal and jade mines.

Little is known about Wei, because unlike Khun Sa, he does not give interviews, and unlike Steven Law, he does not appear publicly. He is known to be brutal—associates who dare to undercut his price, or skim some profit for themselves, are likely to be found dead.

Wei has a handful of homes, including a luxurious mansion carved into the hillside in the Wa hills that looks like a small college. He reportedly does not drink, smoke, or womanize, and prefers to spend his time watching movies on DVDs. On the rare occasions that he ventures out in the daylight, he usually is covered up by a jacket up to his neck, perhaps to camouflage a bullet-proof vest, the uniform of a billionaire in splendid, paranoid isolation.

Like the bounty offered for Khun Sa, a $2 million reward was offered by the U.S. in 1993 in return for information leading to Wei's capture. Eighteen years later, in 2011, the U.S. was distributing "Wanted" information about Wei in Thai nightspots on plastic beer-bottle holders, coasters, and matchbooks, still trying to capture him.

Wei was one of the first heroin dealers indicted in the U.S. in 2005 under "drug kingpin" legislation. The indictment charged Wei and his brothers with importing more than a ton of heroin, with a street value of $1 billion, into the U.S. since 1985. The U.S. Department of State labeled the Wa army as the "largest drug-trafficking army in the world." It was estimated that in 2006 alone, the UWSA had refined three tons of heroin. His amphetamine operations have flooded the market since then.

In recent years, the drug lord and his Hong Pang Company sought approval from the military government for gold-mining concessions and several major highway projects—and received it. He has been running full-scale jade-mining operations in the Phakant area of northern Burma through a Hong Pang subsidiary called Myanmar Daguang Co. According to the *Kachinland News*, Wei was allowed to use heavy-duty mining equipment—hydraulic lifts and 12-wheel trucks—in the prime jade area along with another familiar name: Tay Za, whose Htoo Trading Company also was granted jade concessions in the resource-rich Kachin region.

—

In an interview with *The Progressive* in 1997 while she was relatively free from house arrest, Aung San Suu Kyi expressed her concern about the growing drug proliferation in Burma. The surge in drugs, she said, was not only harmful for the people of Burma, but for people around the world. The government should be helping people who grew poppy to find other ways of earning a living, she said. But in reality, the government was reaping almost as much benefit from the drug trade as the drug lords.

She was especially troubled about the increasing availability and use of heroin on college campuses in Burma. The government appeared more interested in stamping out political activity on campuses than drug addiction, she noted.

She was asked why she thought the heroin used by students at the time was sometimes nicknamed "freedom from fear"—the same name as her famous essay.

"Perhaps it means that the only way the students can escape from the fear of the repression of the government is by taking drugs," she said. "That would be very sad, wouldn't it?"

The cost to Burma and the world of the outpouring of drugs from Burma is impossible to calculate—along with contamination of the environment by destructive mining practices and the loss of teak forests, tigers, and the dolphins native to the Irrawaddy River. Corruption in Burma is exacting a toll on wildlife as well as human beings.

Kachin State has been dubbed one of eight "hotspots of biodiversity" in the world, meaning that it contains a large number of species that are experiencing exceptional loss of habitat. The area being exploited by reckless business projects is home to the red panda, leopards, elephants, the Malayan sun bear, and 580 species of birds, the largest in Southeast Asia. The exotic beauty that has made Burma famous for centuries hangs in the balance while democracy advocates struggle for a more responsible governance.

Even if Suu Kyi and her NLD party are able to bring a more legitimate democracy to Burma, so much of the economy and money is tied up in the drug trade and other corrupt activities that it may take a long and deliberate process to change things. Václav Havel had observed that the former Soviet regime in Eastern Europe had "systematically mobilized the worst human qualities, like selfishness, envy, and hatred." Corruption thrives in the darkness of authoritarian regimes.

Suu Kyi has been criticized for calling for "Rule of Law" over and over like a mantra, but she has a point: equitable laws and an honest judiciary are fundamental for a stable nation. Rule of law in keeping with international norms would lead to more transparency and accountability—and ultimately prosperity for more people, not just the generals and their cronies.

Suu Kyi has warned in blunt fashion that the country does not need "the kind of reforms that may benefit any particular group or individual or organization." Instead, she has told world leaders that what Burma needs in order to improve the lives of its people is to address corruption and the legal system, and to build up its capacity with education, jobs, and training. Burma needs to "build up a strong basic foundation for reform success," she told the World Economic Forum, saying that unemployment among young people in Burma is a "time bomb" and that there is "a grave lack of people" with skills to carry the country forward. "We do not want more investment to mean more possibilities for corruption . . . or greater inequality . . . or greater privileges for the already-privileged. We want investment to mean jobs, as many jobs as possible."

But it would take a series of devastating events before the military would begin making changes that eventually could shore up the rule of law and open the door to new investment. In the meantime, Aung San Suu Kyi would gain a strong and surprising ally in the White House.

CHAPTER THIRTEEN

FRIENDS IN HIGH PLACES

"Well, I can tell you that the United States will work very hard with other members of the Security Council to get a good resolution about Burma. And the sooner the better it would be."
—Laura Bush, United Nations, September 18, 2006

While Aung San Suu Kyi was under guard at 54 University Avenue, a parade of political leaders around the world became her champions. They spoke out when she could not. Senator John McCain came to see Suu Kyi in 1995 and came away impressed that she could still treat the generals with exquisite courtesy whenever they met, serving them tea like guests of honor despite all the harm that they had caused her, her loved ones, her friends, her countrymen. He asked her how she could control her anger in their presence. She looked puzzled and asked what did he mean?

"How do you deal with them? Don't you find it difficult, considering what they have done to you and your country?"

"How do I deal with them?"

"Yes."

"Quite like I am talking to you. Civilly. I address them as 'Uncle.'"

He couldn't imagine anyone less deserving of the respectful title. But whether they merited courtesy or not, he wrote later, Suu Kyi extended it to the generals because "she knew that even though they had the guns and all the power, her cause was just, and that distinction was reinforced by her manners—and their lack of them." He imagined that they realized that, too, and it must have frustrated them immensely. "They are used to frightening people," he wrote. "She must have made them feel ridiculous."

McCain had walked out of his own meeting with the generals in anger during the same trip to Burma. General Khin Nyunt had harangued him for an hour and then insisted he watch a video of villagers being beheaded with machetes by what he described as Communists. His point may have been that the junta was more effective at rooting out Communists than Aung San Suu Kyi, but it was appalling hospitality nonetheless. The footage was so sickening, McCain's wife had to leave the room. "These are *bad* people," McCain said after he left. He became a strong supporter of sanctions against the release and a champion of the release of all political prisoners, including Aung San Suu Kyi.

British prime minister Gordon Brown also started calling for Suu Kyi's release when he was a Parliamentarian in the 1990s. He had promised her husband Michael Aris that he would do whatever he could to be helpful, and did. Throughout his tenure as prime minister, Brown was a staunch supporter of sanctions and U.N. resolutions to bring the junta to the negotiating table. One of the last official letters Brown wrote as he left office at 10 Downing Street in 2010 was to write Suu Kyi a letter of encouragement.

One of Suu Kyi's most surprising—and tenacious—advocates turned out to be American First Lady Laura Bush, who had been written off by some detractors as a "fembot," the kind of bland helpmate who baked cookies and smiled her way through morning talk shows. Yet as one astute *Washington Post* reporter observed, Laura Bush's polite and bemused Cheshire cat smile "both conceals and protects her independence."

In truth, Laura Welch Bush was no "mouse-burger," as Helen Gurley Brown would say. She took great delight when reporters underestimated her. "I read in the morning's newspaper that I was *prim*," she announced gleefully to a group of historians she had invited to the White House.

What few people knew was that while she was living at 1600 Pennsylvania Avenue, Mrs. Bush worked through back channels to do everything within her power—and then some—to help the struggle for democracy in Burma.

At a time when the rest of the world was preoccupied with the problems in the Middle East, the First Lady quietly began providing personal support for Suu Kyi. Sometime in 2002, Mrs. Bush began corresponding with the democracy leader through a network of Burma democracy activists. Even during times when Aung San Suu Kyi was supposedly "freed" from house arrest, access was difficult. Mrs. Bush provided private notes of encouragement for Suu Kyi, along with items that were hard for her to get under the circumstances. Her staff slipped out of the White House to buy cloth to make clothing and books for Suu Kyi to read, as well as seaweed tablets and aloe that she could share with friends in prison. The seaweed provided much-needed nutrients of iodine, calcium, and vitamins A and C. The aloe helped with healing wounds.

The First Lady somehow managed to keep her private mission a secret from the press corps down the hall. The unique relationship had to be kept quiet to protect those who helped along the way and to avoid a diplomatic flap.

The First Lady's confidential diplomacy was not what anyone would have expected her to do. Laura Bush had intended to follow a traditional path as First Lady, and did so in many ways, supporting reading programs and creating the National Book Festival. Profiles of her at the time tended to describe her as "bland" or "low-key"—or as a "former librarian," which was a way of saying the same thing. Then 9/11 happened.

When terrorists crashed into the World Trade Center towers in New York, Laura Bush was on her way to Capitol Hill. She was going to meet with Sen. Ted Kennedy at the Russell Senate Office Building and give a speech on early education. When the second plane crashed into a tower and then another plane crashed into the Pentagon, the First Lady was rushed out of the building by armed guards in black who shouted at the panicked employees who were fleeing their offices into the hall, "Get back!" The guards covered the First Lady with drawn guns as they ran down the hallway. Mrs. Bush was taken through an underground entrance to a secure location. She couldn't reach her husband by phone, and he couldn't reach her when he tried to call from Air Force One. Her staff members had been evacuated from the White House in such a hurry that some lost their shoes running out and were barefoot in Lafayette Park across the street. There were reports that Camp David had been attacked and then reports that their home in Crawford, Texas had been attacked (both reports later disproved).

The country was under siege. Yet Laura Bush stayed almost preternaturally calm. She immediately issued a statement offering condolences and prayers to the families of those killed in the attacks. As soon as she could leave the secure location, she went on national TV urging people to comfort their children, who had just seen the shock of their young lives on their TV screens—planes full of people crashing into flaming twin towers. "Parents need to reassure children everywhere in our country that they are safe," she said.

The next day, she went to Walter Reed Army Hospital to visit injured Pentagon workers, and then to a blood bank to thank employees for donating blood. In the emotional days ahead, while the attack sites were still smoldering, she went on *Good Morning America* and *Oprah* to assure Americans that they could and would survive this challenge. Hug your children, she reminded TV audiences again. When the country needed reassurance, she provided it. Some headlines dubbed her "First Mother" and "Comforter in Chief."

Speaking at the memorial service on September 17 for the lives lost when Flight 93 crashed into a Pennsylvania field, she kept her composure as she talked about the final calls made by the passengers to their loved ones. It was wrenching stuff, but she did not falter.

Little did people know that Mrs. Bush had gotten little rest herself during those chaotic days. She and her husband had been evacuated from the White House twice during the week after 9/11, once during a false alarm when an airplane strayed into Washington, D.C. airspace, and again when a tornado struck the capital city, a rare occurrence.

It was an extraordinary time. Many Americans still were afraid to fly, so for the next weeks the First Lady made a highly visible display of traveling while many others were canceling flights. She traveled to other parts of the country to speak in classrooms and to recruit volunteers for Teach for America. Even when an anthrax scare added new jeopardy to the nerve-racked capital, she kept an openly busy schedule. She wanted to send the message: Daily life must go on.

I was fortunate to interview Mrs. Bush in her East Wing office during that period and was struck by how focused and unruffled she appeared. Didn't she *ever* get rattled, I asked? She confessed that during the most confusing hours of 9/11, she called her mother in West Texas to let her know she was okay, "but really I called to hear her voice."

Her sense of humor had been a saving grace—she was in the middle of getting dressed both times that she was evacuated from the White House and had to tromp out to a secure area in a makeup smock and house slippers. She apologized to the Secret Service for "wearing the same outfit."

And how had she kept her composure while speaking at emotional memorial services? She said she had practiced her speeches over and over—and over yet again—so she wouldn't cry. To downplay that discipline, she said that she actually didn't cry very often, adding with a deep chuckle, "on the other hand, my husband. . . ."

Yet there were times when even her studied composure cracked during those months of grieving and grappling with reality. During the Pentagon memorial service in October, a sea of people outside the scorched walls of the defense building began spontaneously singing along with the choir to "The Battle Hymn of the Republic." When a single African-American woman stood up holding a small American flag, President and Mrs. Bush stood up to join her. Then the rest of the crowd followed, rising to their feet in a dramatic tribute to the fallen as they sang. You could see Mrs. Bush wipe away the tears streaming down her face with a tissue.

If ever there were a crucible in public life, the months after 9/11 were a test of strength for Laura Welch Bush. The searing experience prepared her to step onto a new stage. She moved onto a global platform that would include Afghanistan, Iraq, Africa—and Burma.

Her transformation was signaled when she ventured away from the domestic side of White House issues to deliver the president's weekly radio address on November 17, 2001. With her husband's strong encouragement, Mrs. Bush became the first presidential spouse to give the national broadcast. She called on the people of the world to support the women of Afghanistan who had suffered under Taliban rule. She pointed out that 70 percent of the Afghan people were malnourished . . . that one in every four children would not live past the age of five because healthcare was not available. . . . That women were denied access to doctors. Life under the Taliban was so hard and repressive, she said, that even small displays of joy were outlawed—"Children aren't allowed to fly kites; their mothers face beatings for laughing out loud. Women cannot work outside the home, or even leave their homes by themselves."

The response was overwhelmingly positive. The broadcast became a watershed moment for Mrs. Bush because she found her voice as a person of influence. Later that week when she visited a department store with one of her daughters, the sales clerks at the cosmetics counter all thanked her for speaking up for the women of Afghanistan. "I realized that people *are* watching, people *are* listening if you speak out on issues that are important to them," Mrs. Bush said later. She felt empowered enough to start the U.S. Afghan Women's Council to rally support for educational and medical programs in the ravaged country. She bought Arzu rugs handwoven by women in Afghanistan for the White House. And despite the unsettled conditions, she traveled to Afghanistan three times under heavy security to lend support with her presence.

The post-9/11 period seemed to bring out steel in the First Lady that her friends say was there all the time, just carefully guarded. She was indeed cautious—when reporters would dig in for a "gotcha" sound bite in interviews, Laura Bush would sidestep them with a gracious smile. The very observant *New York Times* columnist Maureen Dowd once complained, "You don't get any fingerprints from Laura Bush. When you look into her eyes during an interview, you feel as if she is there somewhere, deep inside herself, miles and miles down. But though she is lovely and gracious, the main vibe she gives off is an emphatic: 'I am not going to show you anything.'"

That "game face" came in handy when Laura Bush decided to secretly take on the cause of democracy in Burma. She kept it quiet that she was reaching out to a woman she had never met but would call "a sister."

—ʍ—

The First Lady's involvement started with casual conversations with Elsie Walker Kilborne, a Bush cousin who grew up playing with young George W. Bush at family gatherings at Walker Point in Maine.

Elsie Kilborne's early life had been marked with mourning. Her father, Dr. John Walker, uncle of George H. W. Bush and a prominent New York surgeon, had been crippled by polio and lost the use of his arms and legs in 1949. Her sister died of the same disease when Elsie was seven. She turned to religion for comfort and eventually was drawn to Buddhism when a friend suggested that studying Buddhism could lead to deeper understanding about the inevitability of suffering in life.

She began to meet more people with an interest in Buddhism and the exiled Dalai Lama. By then she had a husband and children, but she was increasingly drawn to help the Tibetan people in their struggle to be free of Chinese rule. She helped establish Tibet House, a cultural organization, in New York and served as president for several years before moving to Washington, D.C. She continued to work as an advocate for the oppressed people of Tibet, which led to an interest in the people in nearby Burma, who were struggling to be free of military rule.

One of Kilborne's close friends in Washington was an intense and intellectual New Yorker named Michele Bohana, who was also deeply involved in Burma issues. Bohana had co-founded the International Campaign for Tibet in 1988 and in the 1990s became the director of the Institute for Asian Democracy, a small nonprofit organization. With a distinctive raspy voice, Bohana seemed to work around the clock, navigating multiple time zones, networking with democracy activists around the world to rally support for Tibet and Burma.

When Elsie's childhood friend George W. Bush moved into the White House, the network expanded. It wasn't long before Kilborne shared her concern for Tibet and Burma with the president and his wife Laura.

"I thought Laura and Suu Kyi were a natural match," Kilborne told me. "Both are bookish, both are women who have been put in demanding roles. I thought they would hit it off."

Kilborne gave Suu Kyi's classic book of essays, *Freedom from Fear*, to Laura Bush. "Lo and behold, she really read it! The next time I saw her, we talked more about it," Kilborne remembered.

Mrs. Bush expanded her reading on Burma and began getting briefings from informed sources, including Bohana. It wasn't long before she was working very closely with her staff to keep the democracy struggle alive in policy circles. She did not want Suu Kyi or her cause to be lost while the world was focused on other issues. The U.N. was not making Burma a priority, so she decided that she would.

To be sure, there were some internal eyebrows raised about the First Lady's outreach to Burma. She wasn't the president, and yet she was involved in foreign policy. Mrs. Bush had to navigate protocols inside the White House and the State Department. Yet her aides say the First Lady was more concerned about doing something to help the Burmese than any political ramifications for herself, positive or negative. "She was already involved in women's issues and became more and more involved in human freedom. This was just her doing. She really took an interest in Aung San Suu Kyi and as time went on got more and more involved," recalled her chief of staff at the time, Andi Ball. "She spoke to me many times about how she felt oppression never works."

Kilborne added, "Her biggest contribution was just having Aung San Suu Kyi know the First Lady of the United States was making an effort for her. There were some very bleak years in there for Suu Kyi."

—~—

After Aung San Suu Kyi was attacked at Depayin in 2003 and held incommunicado, Laura Bush looked for more ways to support her. When she hired a new chief of staff, she chose Anita McBride, a seasoned Washington insider. The First Lady made it clear that she intended to be more involved in foreign affairs, not less. McBride had experience at the State Department that included working with the U.N., so she had the skills to bring issues such as Burma to the U.N. The problem was whether the U.N. had the *will* to act.

The U.N. had made a series of failed efforts to address concerns in Burma since the 1988 massacre of demonstrators and the nullified 1990 election:

The first person the U.N. Human Rights Commission (UNHRC) sent to the country to "study" possible violations was Sadako Ogata, a distinguished Japanese professor. He made one visit and submitted a report.

He was followed by Yozo Yokota, a former lawyer for the World Bank and also a distinguished professor, who made four visits between 1992 and 1995 with little progress.

His successor, Rajsoomer Lallah, a former chief justice of Mauritius, was not even allowed by the military government to visit the country during the four years that he served as the Special Human Rights Rapporteur.

The next human-rights rapporteur was Paulo Pinheiro, a Brazilian law expert whose initial reports were optimistic. His view changed when he discovered that the junta had wiretapped his supposedly confidential interviews, hiding a microphone under a desk in the prison where he interviewed prisoners. He left the country in protest in March 2003 and tried again in 2007.

Because of international pressure, Pinheiro's successor, Tómas Ojea Quintana, was able to conduct private meetings with political prisoners in Insein Prison. He also visited a prison in Karen State where he met with inmates who had been forced to serve as porters in the regime's army. When they had tried to escape from their military captors, they had been thrown in prison. Their only crime was being kidnapped by the military. Quintana called for the release of all 2,156 political prisoners in Burma before the 2010 election in order to ensure national reconciliation and a transition to democracy. The junta ignored him.

In addition to the UNHRC representatives, there also were several "special envoys," sent by the U.N. Secretary General himself. Peruvian diplomat Alvaro de Soto made six futile visits between 1995 and 1999. During that time, Suu Kyi was repeatedly accosted when she tried to travel. Following de Soto's departure, she was placed under house arrest again.

De Soto was succeeded in 2000 by a Malaysian diplomat named Tan Sri Razali Ismail, who had an impressive record of postings. He had served as ambassador to Poland and high commissioner to India before being named his country's permanent representative to the U.N. in New York. He was considered a seasoned senior diplomat and was able to help secure Suu Kyi's release in May 6, 2002. He advised the U.N. to give more time to the junta, saying "I think there is a commitment on the part of the military to make the transition." However, after twelve trips, his efforts made no more difference; Suu Kyi was attacked again and placed back under arrest.

Although Razali would continue to serve as the U.N. special envoy until late 2005, his impartiality came under serious question. Information surfaced that while Razali was negotiating with the generals, he was also doing business with them. In addition to being a Malaysian government civil servant and a U.N. envoy, he had private business interests in Burma. Those interests included being chairman and a 30-percent owner of IRIS Technologies, a company that during one of his visits managed to secure a contract with the Burmese government for high-tech passports with biometric features.

Razali protested that the IRIS interest in Burma had happened before he became the special envoy. He said it was a "general interest" and then "developed into something specific." He insisted, "I have never once spoken to the leaders in (Burma) about IRIS."

It later was reported that Razali also was head of Leader Universal, another tech firm hoping to expand into Burma, and was on the board of Wah Seong, a Malaysian engineering firm with interests in Rangoon.

A controversy ensued—and the U.N. response raised as many eyebrows as the allegations. Secretary General Kofi Annan's office said it was satisfied that there was no conflict of interest in Razali's dual role, because he was only a part-time employee, and part-time contracts did not carry any restrictions on business activities. A spokesperson said, "What he does in his spare time is his own business." Razali's contract was renewed.

In a 2003 diplomatic cable, the American chargé d'affaires in Rangoon worried about the business conflicts and whether Razali had the resolve to deal with General Than Shwe's intransigent dictatorial style. "He needs to know that he is expected to stand up to Than Shwe and not fold as he did last time," the cable said.

Their concerns were valid. Razali made no further progress. He quit his post in January 2006 after he was refused entry to Myanmar for two years.

Overall, during the time when Aung San Suu Kyi was under arrest in her home, there were more than 20 General Assembly Resolutions calling for human rights to be respected in Burma. All were ignored by the regime. The General Assembly repeatedly called on the junta to respect international law, yet violations increased rather than decreasing. There also were dozens of reports over the years confirming human-rights abuse, including the widespread use of rape as a weapon. The regime ignored the reports. The U.N. was an invaluable forum for airing grievances, but not so successful at resolving them.

—∾—

In the face of those diplomatic disappointments, Laura Bush decided to lean in and press the U.N. to do more. She reached out to Secretary General Kofi Annan. Annan, an urbane diplomat from Ghana, had risen through the ranks at the U.N. A *New Yorker* profile in 2003 described him as an aristocrat "with perfect posture and an unflappable air of amiable gravity. His impeccable tailoring, stately bearing, and elegant, expressive hands suggest a personal fastidiousness, even preciousness." With his perfectly groomed white goatee, Annan was the picture of a suave world figure. He socialized in New York with fashion designer Óscar de la Renta and NBC anchor Tom Brokaw. People liked him; he appeared on Jon Stewart's *Daily Show* and with the Muppets on *Sesame Street.* Yet Annan had a poor record of resolving conflicts and became known for his passivity at critical moments. In the mid-nineties, he served as head of the U.N.'s Peacekeeping department. During that time, he oversaw the tragic withdrawal of the U.N.'s force from Somalia and the catastrophic failures of its missions in Bosnia and Rwanda. The 1994 mass slaughter of some 800,000 Tutsi and Hutu people in Rwanda during a nightmarish 100 days took place after Annan failed to respond to repeated faxes from French troops trying to hold off the slaughter. The 1995 slaughter in Srebrenica of as many as 7,000 Bosnian Muslims by Bosnian Serbs happened after Annan refused to authorize troops to defend an area that the U.N. had designated as a "safe area" for Muslims. These failures of diplomatic communication and leadership happened on Annan's watch—and yet he was adroit enough in other ways to advance in the U.N. ranks. His U.N. career progressed, and he became Secretary General in 1997. He had gained support for making fighting AIDs a global priority and for leading efforts to reform the U.N. bureaucracy. He enhanced his moral authority by promoting the "Responsibility to Protect" measure to allow the international community to step in when countries can't protect their own people. Annan was unanimously reelected in 2001 to a second five-year term. His career peaked when he won the Nobel Peace Prize that year for his efforts to bring new life to the beleaguered U.N.

But his record on Burma was far from impressive. Annan and Razali had praised the regime's constitutional convention as progress even though the generals had packed the membership with allies and excluded the NLD for objecting to provisions that guaranteed military control. Human-rights organizations complained that as Secretary General, Annan could have brought the issue of ethnic persecution in Burma to the attention of the Security Council for action, but he did not. As Annan often said in his defense, the Secretary General does not have a vote himself in the General Assembly or Security Council, does not command troops himself, and has no authority outside of the U.N. bureaucracy. But he *does* have the power of his voice and convening authority. For example, the Secretary General could on his own initiative establish a Commission of Inquiry to investigate crimes against humanity in Burma, which could lead to prosecutions before the International Criminal Court, but Annan did not.

Laura Bush urged Annan to use more of his voice and convening power on behalf of Burma. She added her strong support to placing Burma on the Security Council's formal agenda. This was a critical step—getting on the agenda meant that any Security Council member would then be free to raise Burma as an item for discussion. It would mean that regular updates on the situation in the country could be requested from the U.N. Secretariat. In contrast, items that are not on the Security Council agenda may not be discussed, a procedural rule that protects members from being forced to discuss issues they would rather not draw attention to. It was vitally important to get Burma on the agenda and keep the democracy struggle in the spotlight.

Mrs. Bush also wanted to do something that no American First Lady had done before: hold a special hearing on Burma while the General Assembly was meeting in New York City in September 2006. There were plenty of other pressing issues for the delegates to consider that fall: Violence in the Middle East. Violence in Afghanistan. Violence in the Congo. Mrs. Bush wanted to add violence in Burma to the agenda. She was prepared to put herself on the line in a very public way.

As she wrote in her memoirs, after she began her quiet support for Suu Kyi, her office had been attending weekly meetings at the White House on Burma. She was watching closely as conditions worsened in Burma. When Aung San Suu Kyi was nearly killed in 2003 and her party's offices shut down, Mrs. Bush was determined to act.

"I could no longer remain publicly silent," she said in her memoir.

Her Burma roundtable at the U.N. became part of a concerted push by the U.S. to make something positive happen at the U.N. for the people of Burma.

- On Sept. 16, a vote was scheduled to put Burma on the formal agenda.
- On Sept. 19, Mrs. Bush would hold her unprecedented session at the U.N. on Burma.
- On Jan. 12, 2007, the U.S. would press for a vote on a Security Council resolution urging Burma to free political prisoners and take steps toward democracy.

It was an audacious agenda; a major international effort that involved many actors. It was partly successful.

First came the move to put Burma on the formal agenda on September 16. The U.S. representative asserted that Burma's refugee crisis, illicit narcotics trade, HIV-AIDS problem, and human-rights situation were "destabilizing" factors in the region.

China—a major trading partner with Burma and also its closest ally—led Russia, Qatar, and Congo in opposing the motion. The Chinese said it amounted to unwarranted interference. Referring to the human-rights problems identified by the U.S., China's U.N. envoy Wang Guangya said: "This means that all countries, any country, that faces similar issues should all be inscribed on the agenda of this council. This is preposterous." He said Burma had made strides in solving its problems.

U.N. VOTE TO ADD BURMA TO THE AGENDA

FOR: U.S., U.K., France, Argentina, Denmark, Greece, Japan, Ghana, Peru, Slovakia
AGAINST: China, Russia, Qatar, Congo
ABSTAINED: Tanzania

In the end, ten members of the Security Council supported the U.S. proposal, enough to pass a procedural measure. The majority ruled and the Security Council voted to put Burma on its formal agenda. At long last, council members would be able to keep the spotlight on the situation in the country.

—∾—

A few days later, Laura Bush held her special colloquy on Burma issues at the U.N., to take advantage of media attention at the opening of the 61st General Assembly session. As delegates milled around the building, a colorful parade of business suits and dashikis and turbans, the First Lady's roundtable was taking place not far from the wood-paneled General Assembly. What had begun as a small, personal effort to help another woman on the other side of the world had turned into a calculated, full-bore mission by the First Lady to help all the people of Burma.

It had not been easy to get U.N. officials to agree to the session. Like the royal bureaucracy at Buckingham Palace, the palace guard at the U.N. was resistant to departures from protocol. It took considerable pressure up until the last minute to get the U.N. to let the First Lady have her day. Elsie Kilborne and Michele Bohana were there for moral support.

I had been invited to attend the roundtable as an observer, since I had written often on Burma issues. It turned out to be an introduction to a side of Laura Bush that I had never seen before. As an editorial-page editor in Dallas from 1986 to 2002, I had watched Laura Welch Bush take her first tentative steps as First Lady of Texas. She was so unaccustomed to public speaking that she would speak from index cards when she talked to women's groups, barely looking up to make eye contact. When she made a speech for her husband in Muleshoe, Texas, she literally ran out of words to say. She was a non-politician, which had a charm of its own. She dressed without ostentation—no Dallas bling, no Malolo Blahnik high heels, only minimal makeup. What you saw was what you got—an attractive, unpretentious woman who happened to be married to the governor.

She grew steadily in her public persona while her husband was governor, gaining poise as a speaker thanks to professional coaching and hours of practice. By the time "Dubya" ran for president in 2000, Laura Bush was able to give one of the best-received speeches at the national convention in Philadelphia. Mrs. Bush spoke with warmth, saying that the place where she and her husband grew up was "a small town in a vast desert—a place where neighbors had to help each other because any other help was too far away." She said that their years in Midland "had formed value reserves as deep [as] and longer lasting than any of its oil wells. "

By the time she convened her session at the U.N. in 2006, she had come miles from that dry outpost in West Texas and the days of index cards. When I saw Laura Bush walk into the halls of the United Nations that fall with a look of fierce determination, I could tell the reticent librarian from Midland was a person of the past. Laura Bush looked in command. She had a set to her jaw I had not seen before. She moved through the formalities of greeting all the U.N. dignitaries in the briefing room with aplomb, nodding her head, shaking a hand, moving steadily forward around the briefing room. She was poised, confident—and totally serious.

Paula Dobriansky, the Under Secretary of State for Democracy and Global Affairs, ushered the First Lady into the room, guiding her through the crowd like a ship tender, providing a buffer of protocol and introductions to the U.N. dignitaries one by one. It was a star moment for the First Lady. Anyone who thought she was simply there to fill her dance card for the day while her husband made speeches next door needed only to look at the way she locked eyes with the diplomats sitting around the table, taking their measure. There was no coy Cheshire smile that day.

The room was filled with important portfolios: Chris Hill, the Assistant Secretary of State for East Asian and Pacific Affairs, who much of the time was huddled in the corner on his cell phone, dealing with breaking news from North Korea; Elliott Abrams, the Deputy National Security Advisor for Global Democracy Strategy; and Ibrahim Gambari, the U.N. Under Secretary for Political Affairs and new envoy to Burma. I noticed that Ellen Sauerbrey, the Assistant Secretary of State for Population, Refugees and Migration, was also prominently featured. She would later prove helpful in opening the way for more Burmese refugees to seek freedom in the U.S.

Mrs. Bush began the session by explaining that she had been interested in Burma and Aung San Suu Kyi for a while. "Of course, the story of her life is a story that I think women around the world are interested in," she said. But because of the attention that Aung San Suu Kyi receives, she went on, more people around the world now look at Burma and want to see what they can do, "to make sure she, as well as *all* the other political prisoners, are released and that her country can reconcile."

Her remarks were straightforward and controlled. She wasn't there to make a headline by flubbing up. She was there to get the U.N. Security Council to speak out more forcefully on Burma. She told the experts who had been invited to speak, "I want to hear *everything* you have to say, to find out what you think about what we can do, now that—and especially now that the subject of Burma can be on the Security Council's agenda."

The First Lady already knew much of what the experts were going to say about the atrocities in Burma before they said it, but the point was for them to say it before the media.

Zaid Ibrahim, the founder of the largest law firm in Malaysia, said he had become passionate about helping the people of Burma because "The human-rights violations are very clear and getting worse."

Hseng Noung, founding member of the Shan Women's Action Network (SWAN), said the practice of Burmese soldiers raping ethnic women and children was taking a horrific toll. Recent documentation of thousands of girls and women who were raped showed that 61 percent were gang-raped. Thirty percent were under the age of 18. Among the oldest to be raped was a woman of 80; the youngest was a girl of eight. Nearly a quarter of the victims did not survive their assault. In one of the notorious incidents, she said, 30 young schoolgirls were called to an army barracks and forced to walk a catwalk "beauty show" for leering soldiers who raped them and forced them to serve as "comfort girls" for the barracks.

Dr. Chris Beyrer, director of the Johns Hopkins Center for Public Health and Human Rights, reported that the Burmese military junta spends less than $1 a year per person on health and education. The entire budget for HIV/AIDS was $75,000 at a time when the AIDS was soaring, he said. Because the government was not spending sufficient sums on health issues,

Dr. Beyrer said, the country now had drug-resistant strains of tuberculosis and malaria that could be carried across borders.

Jim Jacobson, the president of Christian Freedom International, which was providing medicine and care for more than 100,000 displaced refugees from Burma, said the junta was using religion to target Christians, especially the Karen and Karenni villagers who were Christianized by American missionaries more than 200 years ago. "Their churches have been burned and their pastors singled out," he said, describing the persecution as "a willful tragedy."

Mrs. Bush listened intently to their grim reports, occasionally asking questions such as whether the care in hospitals for members of the junta's military forces was better than the care for everyday citizens in the public hospitals (considerably) and about trafficking in people (on the increase).

Midway through the discussion, Dr. Gambari, the professor-turned diplomat from Nigeria who recently had been named to replace Ismail Razali as the U.N. emissary to Burma, stood up to leave. Excusing himself politely, he said he had an obligation to attend another meeting, and left.

As it turned out, Professor Gambari did not fare much better than his predecessors in his mission to Burma.

Though he was well schooled—London School of Economics, Columbia University—and was a familiar face on U.N. committees, Gambari steadily lost ground in Burma. Toward the end of his tenure, he could not persuade either Senior General Than Shwe or Aung San Suu Kyi to meet with him.

Gambari made eight trips to Burma, only to discover how disingenuous the generals could be. After his first visit, he called a press conference announcing "They want to open up a new chapter of relationship with the international community." Three days later, the junta extended Suu Kyi's house arrest by a year. He had been suckered.

After his second trip, the regime closed the five Red Cross offices.

Gambari made a conspicuous show of traveling around the region to rally support for his negotiations, but it did not help. ASEAN neighbors who were doing business with the regime simply were not inclined to help.

Gambari took tea with Aung San Suu Kyi on his first visits, but over time she lost confidence in him. In meeting photos, she started leaning away and refused to smile. Democracy leaders felt the Nigerian diplomat had been too compliant with the generals, who had undercut and snubbed him. They believed he had had lost so much face, he could not be effective. They had a point:

In 2007, Gambari was kept waiting several days to deliver a letter from U.N. Secretary General Ban Ki-moon to Senior General Than Shwe. Than Shwe said he was too busy to meet with him. Despite being rebuffed, Gambari claimed the visit was successful.

For the junta, manipulating U.N. emissaries like Gambari had become a standard tactic. Stalling the envoys while sporadically giving false hopes to the international community bought time while the generals continued their hold.

Mrs. Bush was determined to add some potency to the diplomatic efforts and closed the roundtable session by promising that the United States would be working hard with other members of the Security Council to get a strong resolution passed about Burma, adding, pointedly, "the sooner the better."

She then delivered a surprisingly blunt appeal to the members of the press who were crowded at one side of the room with their cameras and notepads: "I also want to call on the members of the press who are here to get the story out. If stories were in the press, at least the leadership of Burma would know that people were watching and that they know what's happening and that Burma is not forgotten . . . that they can't get away with the terrible mistreatment of their citizens because nobody knows it's happening." It was up to them, she underscored again in closing, "to get the story out."

Overall, it was a commanding public debut of Mrs. Bush's private mission to help the people of Burma. The *Washington Post* observed: "On Monday, Laura Bush convened an international conference on literacy. Tuesday, she hosted a roundtable aimed at prodding the United Nations into action on the humanitarian crisis in Burma. Wednesday, she will address the Clinton Global Initiative. And Thursday, she is to receive a major international award. By any measure, it is a busy week. It is particularly so for a first lady praised by some admirers as the 'anti-Hillary' for her seeming preference for eschewing controversy and for embracing a more traditional role as first lady." But now she was doing anything but shying away from global issues.

Within a few months, the U.S. made its move: A strongly worded resolution on Burma was proposed in January 2007 in the Security Council. The resolution called on Burma's rulers to release Suu Kyi and more than 1,100 of her political supporters who were in prison, to cease attacks on the country's ethnic minority, and to begin a democratic transition. It also called on Burma to halt the widespread use of rape by the armed forces and to back efforts by the International Labor Organization to end forced labor in Burma. The resolution accused Burma's armed forces of causing a refugee crisis in the region, enabling narcotics traffic, and permitting international transmission of communicable diseases such as HIV/AIDS and avian flu.

Despite the strong American push, the resolution failed. The vote was 9 to 3. It wasn't a surprise that China and Russia would side with the military junta; it was a jolt that South Africa joined them in voting no. Under U.N. rules, resolutions must be approved by all five permanent members (U.S., U.K., China, Russia, France).

U.N. VOTE ON BURMA RESOLUTION

FOR: Belgium, France, Ghana, Italy, Panama, Peru, Slovakia, United Kingdom, United States
AGAINST: China, Russia, South Africa
ABSTAIN: Congo Republic, Indonesia, Qatar

After the vote, the Burmese ambassador thanked China and Russia for blocking the move. He claimed the charges against his country in the resolution were "patently false."

China and Russia—both of whom had billion-dollar dealings with Burma—contended that they shared concerns about conditions in Burma, but considered them "internal matters" that did not constitute threats to international peace and security, the criteria for a crisis to warrant Security Council action.

Russia's ambassador claimed "Not a single one of the neighboring countries regards the situation in Myanmar as a threat to them, and on the basis of that, there were no grounds for the Security Council to consider the matter."

The Chinese ambassador added: "No country is perfect. Similar problems exist in other countries as well."

R. Nicholas Burns, the Under Secretary of State for Political Affairs, disagreed strongly. He told the *New York Times*, "When a million people flee the country because of the abusive practices of the government, *that's* a threat to international peace and security. . . ."

Burns dismissed suggestions that the proper forum should have been the Human Rights Council. "We forced this onto the agenda for one reason," he said. "The Security Council is the only place that can deal with human rights. The Human Rights Council is a discredited institution. All it has done is to bash Israel; it has ignored North Korea, it has ignored Sudan, and it has ignored Burma."

The Bush administration's acting U.N. ambassador, Alejandro Wolff, said that while the United States was "deeply disappointed," he wanted to assure the Burmese people that "we won't forget you."

The *Washington Post* reported that the vote initially had faced resistance from some officials within the State Department and from European envoys, who feared it would damage U.S. and European relations with China while exposing the depth of Third World opposition to Security Council interference in Burma's affairs. But President Bush and Secretary of State Condoleezza Rice decided it was worth making the point on a matter of principle, according to U.S. officials.

Undersecretary Burns challenged suggestions that the effort had backfired or indicated a rift between the West and the developing world over human rights. "We don't consider this a defeat," Burns said. "We did the right thing. We stood up for universal human values."

—∾—

Throughout the same period, others around the world were mobilizing grassroots support to press the Burmese regime toward change. One of the distinguishing features of the Burma movement was that it inspired people of all political stripes to get involved who normally might not be found on the same side of issues.

In one of the "odd bedfellows" juxtapositions, controversial billionaire George Soros has funded a multi-million-dollar Burma Project at the same time he was a constant, vitriolic critic of the Bush administration, lampooning Mr. Bush in TV spots during the 2004 presidential election. At the same time that the Soros organization's website was calling for Aung San Suu Kyi's release, ads on the site were offering a million free "Obama for President" bumper stickers. Soros also helped finance full-page ads in the *New York Times* mocking "General Betrayus" during the war in Iraq.

However, the Hungarian-born financier and philanthropist and the Bush administration agreed on one thing—democracy should be brought to Burma. The egregious human-rights violations had to end. The Burma Project funded by Soros's Open Society Foundations was so instrumental in assisting democracy efforts that the military government called a press conference after monks took to the streets in protest to claim that the Soros Open Society was part of a foreign conspiracy to bring down the regime. As George Packer, who has led coverage of Burma with his reporting at the *New Yorker* pointed out, the generals only got that partly right. The Soros foundation had provided nearly $40 million to the Burma Project since 1994 for democracy education and advocacy efforts. Over the years, the Soros foundation had promoted independent media, encouraged reconciliation efforts, and supported programs to empower women, youth, and ethnic minorities. Leadership training had been provided to more than 2,000 Burmese to help Burma make a transition from a "closed" society to an "open" society. Those seminal efforts were directed by Maureen Aung Thwin, who had escaped from Burma after the 8-8-88 protests were crushed.

Another Burma expatriate, Aung Din, who was imprisoned after the 8-8-88 protests for four years, helped launch the U.S. Campaign for Burma. The Washington-based nonprofit has led grassroots campaigns for sanctions and U.N. action on human-rights issues. It also led the charge during the Clinton administration for a nationwide boycott, which resulted in 45 major companies cutting ties to Burma's military regime.

One of the campaign's most effective leaders was a young graduate student named Jeremy Woodrum. Woodrum made some 25 trips to refugee camps along the Thai border to give Congressional and Hollywood delegations a view of the human damage from the Burmese repression. Woodrum also brought a new-age energy to the Burma campaign by recruiting rock musicians and Hollywood stars to the democracy cause. He produced a CD of top musicians dedicating songs for Burma including R.E.M., U2,

Coldplay, Damien Rice, and Ani Difranco. And in 2008, Woodrum helped produce "Burma: It Can't Wait," 35 short videos created by Hollywood celebrities that included Will Farrell, Jennifer Anniston, Jackson Browne, Sarah Silverman, Ellen Page, Jason Seagal, Eva Longoria, Sylvester Stallone, director James Cameron, and Kim Kardashian.

The list of celebrities who started championing the democracy movement looked like the lobby of the *Vanity Fair* party at the Academy Awards. Supporting Aung San Suu Kyi had become hip.

After Cyclone Nargis devastated the Burma Delta, actors Brad Pitt, George Clooney, and Matt Damon launched an ad campaign through their "Not On Our Watch" organization to raise relief funds. Pitt also helped fund Human Rights Watch efforts in Burma and his wife Angelina Jolie later made several trips to the Thai border to spotlight refugee issues.

The biggest celebrity boost the democracy campaign received was from rock star Bono, the front man for the globally successful U2 band. Bono had become an admirer of Suu Kyi's when they both received an award in Dublin in 2009, but she could not accept in person. He was intrigued by her story and began dedicating a song to her on his concert tour: "Walk On," a tribute to her courage.

Seven million people who attended his concerts saw video messages from Suu Kyi played on giant screens. In the video, she told the concert audiences their voices were powerful and could be heard all the way to Burma—and the concert-goers roared their approval. In effect, Suu Kyi went on the road with one of the most successful rock bands of the time and a new audience heard her story.

The U2 song soon was banned in Burma by the generals. Anyone who attempted to import it risked a prison sentence of three to 20 years.

Laura Bush's efforts predated most of those celebrity efforts, but her earliest support was done in private or without fanfare. After the defeat of the U.N. resolution in 2007, Mrs. Bush doubled up on her efforts on Burma, perhaps in realization that she only had a couple more years to use her White House platform for change. The situation in Burma was still dire. The First

Lady's staff was working impossible hours coordinating her involvement in the President's Emergency Plan for AIDS Relief (PEPFAR), the anti-Malarial campaign in Africa, the Afghan Women's Council, her breast cancer campaign for women in the Middle East, and medical care for children in Iraq. It was a full load on top of her continuing interest in early childhood education and women's health. But she wasn't going to give up on Burma.

In the next few months, Mrs. Bush met with members of the Burma Ethnic Nationalities Council—whose populations were under fire from the Burmese army—at the White House. The delegation implored her to keep up her work, saying "When America speaks, it gives us hope."

In May, she helped launch the first women's caucus in the U.S. Senate on Burma to keep up pressure on the regime. The unprecedented caucus included all 16 female senators, including the new Senator from New York, former First Lady Hillary Clinton. The bipartisan group of women banded together to call for Aung San Suu Kyi's immediate release.

And in June, the First Lady penned a half-page op-ed piece in the *Wall Street Journal* in honor of Suu Kyi's 62nd birthday on June 19. The First Lady pointed out that Aung San Suu Kyi was still under house arrest and democracy advocates were still being arrested. In fact, one of the NLD party members had just been sentenced to 14 years simply for giving a fellow university student a list of the Nobel Prize winner's honors.

She credited her husband with calling for the "immediate and unconditional release" of Suu Kyi at a conference in Prague. And she noted that the week before, Senators Mitch McConnell and Dianne Feinstein had introduced the Burmese Freedom and Democracy Act to continue U.S. sanctions on the junta. "President Bush looks forward to signing this bill into law," she said with the certainty that she'd already been assured by what is known as a "high-level source."

—∾—

The U.S. first imposed an arms embargo on Burma in 1993 and then widened its sanctions four years later in the Clinton administration to include a ban on all new investment. However, existing investment—including Unocal's (later Chevron's) gas project—was exempted.

In 2003, during the Bush administration, the Burma Freedom and Democracy Act expanded the sanctions by banning imports from Burma. However, teak and gems that had been processed in a third country were allowed. The act also restricted financial transactions, froze the assets of some financial institutions, and extended visa restrictions on key Burmese officials.

Also, during the Bush administration, the Tom Lantos Block Burmese Jade (Junta's Anti-Democratic Efforts) Act of 2008 imposed a specific ban on jadite and rubies that were mined in Burma, and on jewelry containing either of these precious stones.

U.S. president Barack Obama renewed existing sanctions against Burma in May 2009. But a review was instituted to determine whether the sanctions policy was effective and how to proceed.

—∾—

Burma had become a high-profile issue, not just for the First Lady, but for the Bush administration. President Bush made Burma a key part of his speech at the 62nd General Assembly of the U.N. in 2007. He chided nations to live up to the rights and freedoms that the United Nations had pledged six decades before and announced new sanctions on Burma. He outlined a tightening of financial sanctions and an extension of the ban on visas of officials who were "responsible for the most egregious violations of human rights."

"Every civilized nation also has a responsibility to stand up for the people suffering under dictatorship," Mr. Bush emphasized.

Secretary of State Condoleezza Rice had also been drawing attention to Burma. She included Burma as an "outpost of tyranny" in her confirmation hearings as Secretary of State in 2005, along with Cuba, North Korea, Iran, Belarus, and Zimbabwe.

Rice suggested that the world should apply to those countries what Soviet dissident Natan Sharansky called the "Town Square Test": *If an individual cannot walk into the middle of the town square and express his or her views without fear of arrest, imprisonment, or physical harm, then that person is living in a fear society, not a free society.*

Burma failed that standard and then some.

When Secretary Rice traveled to the Asia-Pacific Economic Cooperation (APEC), she pushed Burma's Asian neighbors to speak out. She said, "I understand that a lot of countries that are neighbors of Burma feel the need to engage them, but I would hope that that engagement also takes the form of being serious about the really quite appalling human-rights situation," Rice told reporters.

By 2008, Rice had given up on Envoy Gambari's ability to have a constructive conversation with the regime. The genial, but hapless, envoy had earned the nickname "Gullible Gambari."

A classified cable was sent to the U.S. representative at the U.N., requesting that moves be started to remove Garbari as the Special Representative to Burma, saying the *demarche* should occur as soon as practical. As justification, the cable said there had been no progress during his missions to Burma on core steps such as the release of political prisoners and the opening of meaningful, "time-bound" dialogue with the democratic and ethnic minority leaders.

"Gambari appears unrealistically upbeat, pursuing and reporting progress on peripheral matters (e.g., a possible economic forum, the possible placement of a U.N. staff member in Rangoon) that are a distraction from what the Security Council has articulated as critical goals and identified as Gambari's mandate," the cable said.

There were complications to consider. Gambari had a concurrent role as U.N. adviser on the International Compact on Iraq. Then, too, Secretary General Ban Ki-moon would be understandably sensitive to pressure to remove his envoy.

Secretary Rice suggested talking points:

- The U.S. had become increasingly concerned that the UN good offices mission in regard to Burma was in dire jeopardy.
- Special Representative Gambari's latest trip to Burma continued a disturbing pattern of regime-managed itineraries; restricted access to key officials and activists; and complete lack of progress on critical issues.
- "While the main responsibility for this lack of progress should be attributed to regime intransigence, Mr. Gambari has not been willing to acknowledge it," the cable said. "His unwillingness to

> press the regime more forcefully for progress has caused us to conclude that his continued involvement undermines the good offices mission and should therefore be ended," the cable directed.

While there was no wish to embarrass Gambari, the facts spoke for themselves: In the first two years of Gambari's mission, the number of political prisoners in Burma had nearly doubled. More than 130,000 people were forced from their homes in an "ethnic cleansing campaign." And he was never able to start talks between the regime and the NLD.

A year later, Gambari was reassigned. He was sent to another hotspot, Darfur.

While the regime temporized and the U.N. was stalled, Mrs. Bush accelerated her own efforts. She presented a statement to the Senate Committee on Foreign Relations Subcommittee, calling for the U.N. and other governments to join the United States in condemning the junta's use of violence. She presented a special award to the women of Burma at the prestigious Vital Voices ceremony in Washington honoring women of courage from around the world. In addition to Aung San Suu Kyi, Mrs. Bush singled out women whose names were less well known in the U.S. She wanted them to know about Su Su Nway, who was imprisoned for challenging forced labor in Burma; Nilar Thein, who was forced to leave her newborn child to hide from military persecutors; and Charm Tong, who was brave enough to testify about rapes in Burma in front of representatives from the Burmese military.

Hillary Clinton had started the trend toward East Wing involvement in Burma at the Beijing Women's Conference, and Madeleine Albright had ramped up administration during the Clinton administation. Now Laura Bush brought the campaign for democracy squarely into the White House, using her podium as First Lady in a more outspoken way. Her private help for Aung San Suu Kyi had grown into sharp public criticism of the junta.

When the generals attacked the peaceful protests of monks, she was quick to respond. She told VOA, "I'm very concerned. I pray for the people of Burma. I'm awed by their courage." And she appealed to the Burmese army: "I want to say to the armed guards and to the soldiers: Don't fire on your people. Don't fire on your neighbors."

She called Secretary General Ban Ki-moon directly to discuss the situation. During the call, she reportedly expressed deep concern that the situation was deteriorating while the U.N. failed to act. She made it clear that if the U.N. stayed quiet, it was condoning the abuses. She put out her own official statement, referring to the assaults on the monks as "deplorable acts of violence."

The Secretary General got the message and made it a point to telephone Mrs. Bush to update her personally when Envoy Ibrahim Gambari returned from his most recent meeting with the junta. The results weren't encouraging. She followed up with a strongly worded op-ed piece the next day in the *Wall Street Journal*, calling point-blank for the removal of the military regime. She wrote, "This swelling outrage presents the generals with an urgent choice: Be part of Burma's peaceful transition to democracy, or get out of the way for a government of the Burmese people's choosing."

When her call to the Secretary General created a stir, she told reporters that it was something of a myth "that I was baking cookies and then they fell off the cookie sheet and I called Ban Ki-moon." Her comment was a reminder of another cookie comment from her predecessor, Hillary Clinton, who once told reporters she was not one to stay home and bake cookies. And neither was Laura Bush.

Suu Kyi's example and the courage of the Afghan women had brought Laura Bush's own moxie to the forefront. "She's always been what she is," Elsie Kilborne told a reporter when asked to comment, "but she is coloring herself in bolder colors."

Mrs. Bush had provided some clues to her independent thinking when she first met her future in-laws, President George H. W. Bush and Barbara Bush. She explained herself to them in seven words: "I read, I smoke, and I admire." Some of her favorite books included Dostoyevsky's *The Brothers Karamazov*, Truman Capotes's *Music For Chameleons,* and Willa Cather's *Death Comes to the Archbishop*. Enigmatic? Yes. A superficial goody-two-shoes? No. But in order to support Burma, Laura Bush had to step out of her carefully guarded comfort zone. She was generally so modest that she asked speechwriters to omit the personal pronoun "I" from her scripted remarks. Yet because the issues in Burma were so little known, she had to inject herself into the story to get the kind of media attention that could keep Burma from falling back into darkness. So she did.

When asked in an interview with *Time* magazine why she had taken on the issue of Burma, Mrs. Bush replied that like many people, especially women, she got interested because of Aung San Suu Kyi. "I learned about Burma and how she represents the hopes of the people of Burma, and how those hopes were being dashed by her house arrest and the fact that her party won the elections and never had the opportunity to have power at all. I did work with women senators to make sure we sent out a letter to Ban Ki-moon. I've also met with ethnic minorities and talked with them."

Observant journalists like Sheryl Stolberg at the *New York Times* took note. "She is not the traditional First Lady that a lot of people expected her to be. Anybody who has watched her closely when she visited Afghanistan or traveled internationally will tell you she has stepped out in a different way. I can't think of another instance where a First Lady has helped announce sanctions that this country has placed on another country, like Burma. She did. She really almost single-handedly brought the plight of Aung San Suu Kyi to the American public through her platform. When she started talking about it, people like me started to take notice. It was a *big* deal."

Her efforts were not without criticism. Political blogs like Wonkette mocked, "What does a lame-ass-duck administration do when basically nobody in the entire world listens to anything it says because every Senior Administration Officer is either a worn-out loser or a hapless placeholder? Get Laura Bush to freak out on the Burma military dictatorship, that's what."

David Steinberg, longtime Burma watcher at Georgetown University, said, "Laura Bush has been detrimental to the process. She doesn't have the knowledge and is talking to only one side of the deal and nobody else. She has taken a moral position that one understands, but not one carefully thought through. Nobody else has access to her except the State Department and NSC, who are under White House control."

Others in the foreign policy community, such as former Secretary of State Madeleine Albright, applauded the First Lady's campaign for Burma. Albright said she was "very impressed" by Mrs. Bush's Burma outreach.

Her interventions "absolutely" were having an impact in keeping the Burma struggle in the public eye, she said, and that could make a difference.

Historian Doris Kearns Goodwin said Mrs. Bush's direct involvement in foreign diplomacy had been more extensive than previous First Ladies—and involved more risk. Goodwin said in an interview for this book, "It is unprecedented what she has done. I suspect her increasing interest and active support of the people of Burma paralleled her increasing understanding of the role of the First Lady. Here is this woman who starts out saying she didn't sign on to give speeches, someone who was not expected to move beyond her role with subjects that seemed tailored for her like literacy and the book festival, which would have been a terrific legacy in itself. The Burma issue must have touched something deep within her because she has apparently used every resource within her power and then more. It seems that with each step she became more involved and more committed."

Laura Bush's foray in to foreign affairs as First Lady was built on an evolving tradition of American First Ladies overseas, which continues to grow.

Martha Washington sat in on informal talks about treaties with Indian nations.

Edith Wilson accompanied her husband, Woodrow, to Paris for treaty negotiations after World War I and screened all his documents while he was ailing.

Eleanor Roosevelt was the first presidential spouse to travel alone overseas to check the welfare of troops in Europe and the Pacific. (After her husband's death, she was named a delegate to the U.N. by Harry Truman and, as chair of the Human Rights Commission, was instrumental in creating the historic Universal Declaration of Human Rights.)

President Carter tapped his wife, Rosalynn, to be his envoy at a meeting with Latin American leaders.

Nancy Reagan encouraged her husband's Cold War diplomacy and helped him prepare for his first summit with Soviet leader Mikhail Gorbachev.

During her husband's two terms in the White House, Hillary Rodham Clinton visited more than 80 countries and boldly raised the issue of female infanticide in her celebrated 1995 speech on women's rights in Beijing.

Laura Bush upped the ante by speaking out directly on foreign policy issues with her radio address on Afghanistan and her U.N. conference on Burma. Her concerted campaigns for women in Afghanistan, democracy in Burma, global literacy, women's health in the Middle East, and AIDS-HIV in Africa set new precedents.

By the last year of the administration, the First Lady was being invited to speak at high-level foreign affairs events, sounding more like an ambassador from the U.S. than a First Lady. She held a videoconference with the Ladies in White human-rights activists in Cuba to cheer them on. She addressed the international conference of donors to Afghanistan in France in 2008 about increasing aid to Afghanistan—and briefed the White House press corps "gaggle" on Air Force One about the status of international aid to Afghanistan, another precedent for a First Lady. She was invited to speak to the Council on Foreign Relations in New York, the top echelon in foreign affairs, and held her own with a discerning audience. The issues she talked about most? Afghanistan and Burma.

One of the highlights of her global involvement as First Lady, she told the CFR, was her trip to the border of Burma and Thailand during the summer of 2008 to see refugee conditions for herself. While she and her husband were on their way to the Beijing Olympics, they had made a point of stopping in Thailand to support the Burmese democracy movement, something that their Chinese hosts surely noticed and their Burmese neighbors as well.

The Bushes had only six months left in office, so they put on a full-court press for progress in Burma. President Bush had lunch at the U.S. ambassador's residence in Bangkok with nine Burmese dissidents and told them that the "American people care deeply about the people of Burma, and we pray for the day in which the people will be free." He also spoke about Burma in a radio interview heard inside that country and gave a policy address in the Thai capital. "Together, we seek an end to tyranny in Burma," the president said. "The noble cause has many devoted champions, and I happen to be married to one of them."

In the meantime, his wife was making a seven-hour trip to the rugged Thai border with Burma. The next day was the 20th anniversary of the 8-8-88 protests in Burma; the timing was not coincidental. It was raining softly and the ground was soggy as the First Lady arrived with her daughter Barbara and a press contingent to tour a refugee camp and meet the legendary "Dr. Cynthia" at her Mae Sot clinic. Mrs. Bush had already hosted a video conference at the White House with Cynthia Maung. Now she wanted to meet her in person to showcase her life-saving work.

Dr. Cynthia was becoming known as "the Mother Teresa of Burma" in foreign aid circles but was not well known in the U.S. She had been born in a woven bamboo house on a dirt road on the edge of Moulmein, a languid port town near the mouth of the wide Salween River. As a young soldier, Rudyard Kipling had made the town famous by writing a poem about a young beauty on the steps of the great pagoda who left him spellbound: *"By the old Moulmein Pagoda, lookin' lazy at the sea, There's a Burma girl a-settin', and I know she thinks o' me. . . ."* The slopes around the port were dotted with Baptist church spires, as well as pagodas and palms, thanks to the Christian missionaries of the 1800s. Cynthia was the fourth of eight children in a family that was poor, ethnic Karen, and Christian—triple jeopardy under Burman military regime. Despite the fact the only light in her home was by kerosene lantern and study resources were limited, Cynthia scored near the top in the end-of-school exams and was selected to attend medical school. While she was studying to be a doctor, things began unraveling as Ne Win closed schools and the economy spiraled out of control. She was a newly qualified doctor working in a village clinic when student protests flared up in 1988. She joined in local rallies calling for "Democracy, democracy!" When the 8-8-88 crackdown came, Dr. Maung fled across the border into Thailand, walking through the jungle at night, sleeping in the fields by day. So many people were fleeing into the border area with gunshot wounds and malaria that she set up a makeshift clinic to care for them. All she had brought with her was a small bag with a medical textbook, a few medical instruments like a stethoscope, and some medicine for malaria. She had to sterilize her instruments in a rice cooker to do her first surgeries.

Dr. Maung thought she would be gone three months. Twenty years later, the military was still in control in Burma and the clinic was still operating on the Thai border. Only now it had become a compound that treated up to 130,000 patients a year—including those with cerebral malaria, HIV/AIDS, pregnant mothers, malnutrition, gunshot wounds, limbs ripped off by landmines, and anyone else in desperate need of help. Every year, the modest clinic delivered more than 3,000 babies.

When I met "Dr. Cynthia" in 2007, I was struck by how Spartan the facilities were, yet how clean and orderly and quiet, with the exception of a child with third-degree burns who whimpered in her mother's arms. I was startled as I walked through a ward to see a man lying in the shadows under his bed; he was so thin and motionless, I had to look twice to make sure there was a person there. His leg had been amputated and he was in such pain that he couldn't remain on the hard wooden bed; he had taken refuge on the earth floor underneath. "These people vanish into their pain. They shut their eyes and go somewhere else," a volunteer doctor making rounds said.

Dr. Cynthia turned out to be an unassuming woman in a white cotton blouse and plain longyi and flip-flops. She had kind eyes. Her expression remained benignly impassive, and she thought cautiously before she spoke; she had to be careful not to provoke the Thai government into shutting down her clinic. "At first, we thought the military would collapse and we could go home," she said. (long pause) "But when we arrived here, we realized there was a shortage of medical supplies and a lot of malaria. We began helping the wounded students at first, and then we had to deal with the seriously sick . . . and the injured refugees. . . ." As she spoke, she made her way around the hospital grounds, checking on babies, smiling, nodding, noticing every detail, directing someone to the girl with the burns, inquiring about the man under the bed.

There several photos of Aung San Suu Kyi on the wall, so I asked if she were a fan. "Oh, yes," she said, with another smile and an emphatic nod.

It took artful diplomacy as well as courage to keep the clinic open for two decades with a war zone not far away. By the time Mrs. Bush arrived in 2008, the original Mae Sot campus had grown to include a prosthetics building to equip the many land-mine victims, a maternity wing, and a small school.

Mrs. Bush toured the prosthetics center and presented Dr. Cynthia with gifts—not the usual diplomatic knick-knacks, but 5,000 mosquito nets from Nothing But Nets and the President's Malaria Initiative. Her staff also had brought hygienic supplies, including boxes of biodegradable soap donated by Tom's Natural Products of Maine, and boxes of school supplies for the schoolchildren.

"I want the people of Burma to know that the people of the United States want to help in whatever way they can," she said.

Then she visited the Mae La refugee camp, the largest of nine camps in that area. It had grown into a virtual city of 35,000 Burmese, most of them members of the persecuted Karen minority, living in huts that they built themselves. Mrs. Bush sat in on English and math lessons and then gathered the press to deliver a message that she knew would be heard by the generals while she was at their doorstep.

"Twenty years have gone by—everything is still the same or maybe worse in Burma," she said. "We know that Burma is a very rich country, rich in natural resources. And the junta uses those resources to prop themselves up for their own benefit, not for the benefit of the people of Burma."

The First Lady pointed out that China, in particular, had leverage over the Burmese regime, its economic partner: "We urge the Chinese to do what other countries have done—to sanction, to put a financial squeeze on the Burmese generals," she said.

But her strongest push was on behalf of the Burmese refugees trapped along the Burma/Thai border. In the last three years, more than 30,000 Burmese had been resettled in the U.S. Many of them, she said, were like the family she had just stopped to talk to. "The man in that family is about 30 years old; he has lived in this camp for 20 years," she said. "He moved here as a 10-year-old child."

"And I know that a lot of these families would rather go home, but because of the situation in Burma, they can't," she said. She pointed out that the United States had taken steps to admit more of the refugees, along with countries such as Canada, New Zealand, and the Netherlands. "I want to encourage other countries as well to take Burmese, to allow Burmese to resettle in countries where people will have an opportunity to build their life," she said.

One of the refugees who was leaving soon for the U.S. was 39-year-old Hay Lary. She was part of the ethnic Karen group being hounded by the military for their resistance to Burman domination. She was leaving the barbed-wire confines of the camp shortly to go to South Carolina with her husband and five children. "It's better to go to America," she said. "If we go back to Burma, they would torture us."

She was part of a quiet exodus that had received little attention. The number of refugees leaving Burma had surged since Congress exempted the refugees from a law barring anyone related to armed insurgents, which had blocked the ethnic groups resisting military rule.

Dennis Wilder, President Bush's adviser on Asian affairs, said removing the technicality meant "We have an open policy now. We're taking as many as we can."

When one of the refugees at Mae La asked the First Lady why the U.S. was accepting so many Burmese refugees, she replied, "The United States is a very welcoming country. We're a country made up of immigrants from all across the world. It's in our moral interest to welcome them to the United States."

What she didn't say was that she had been quietly supporting the refugee cause for some time. And she had learned the power of presence. By showing up at Dr. Cynthia's medical clinic, a signal was sent to Thai authorities, who had been threatening to shut down the clinic. They didn't dare after the First Lady showed her support.

Prime Minister Thaksin Shinawatra, who had business dealings with the Burmese junta, also had refused to allow Cynthia Maung to travel to other countries to accept major humanitarian awards, which could bring revenue to her work. After Mrs. Bush's visit, the doctor was allowed to do so. When he was in exile and his daughter Yingluck Shinawatra became prime minister, she closed down the U.N. Refugee Processing Center for Burmese refugees. That misguided closure meant that refugees who were already approved for travel to the U.S. had to be processed from Malaysia; refugee departures were slowed from then on.

At the time the First Lady visited the refugee camps, it was believed there were as many as 650,000 internally displaced people in Burma, nearly 107,000 of them in Karen State. Another 146,000 lived in the cluster of bamboo refugee camps on the Thai side of the border, trapped in limbo, unable to return to Burma, unable to leave Thailand.

An estimated 100,000 Burmese refugees have been resettled in the United States, one of the largest refugee resettlements in recent decades. (Some 200,000 Hungarians were resettled in Canada and the U.S. after the failed Hungarian Revolution of 1956. After Saigon fell in 1975, approximately 125,000 Vietnamese refugees were resettled in America between 1975 and 1982.)

The resettlement effort began during the Clinton administration and was escalated during the Bush administration.

1992–1996: 3,000 (First Clinton Administration)
1997–2000: 3,000 (Second Clinton Administration)
2001–2003: admissions interrupted due to post-9/11 security
2004: 10,442
2005: 6,968
2006: 2,681
2007: 10,436
2008: 14,406
2009: 13,033
2010: 10,013
2011: 8,137
2012: 6,333

Departures of Burmese refugees from Thailand declined after 2011, when the Thai government closed the U.N. agency in the country processing and certifying Burmese refugees.

In 2011, 2012, and 2013, approximately 15,000 Burmese refugees were resettled from Malaysia.

As the Bush administration was winding down, the post-mortems of what went wrong and what went right over the eight-year term agreed on one thing: Laura Bush had done her best and had done well. *New York Times* columnist Gail Collins, while shredding the rest of the team in a critique, was careful to add, "Nobody blames you, Laura."

The White House, *USA Today*/Gallup poll in 2008 found that 76 percent of Americans said they had a favorable opinion of the First Lady. The public had viewed her very positively during both of her husband's terms as president, with favorability ratings ranging between 63 percent and 80 percent.

Washington Post columnist Kathleen Parker gave the First Lady a positive review for her White House legacy, commending her breast cancer initiative in the Middle East, her global literacy campaign, her ongoing efforts to help women and children in Afghanistan, and her daring outreach to Burma. "Many readers may be learning these things for the first time and wonder why. In part, it may be because Mrs. Bush's demure librarian-teacher persona has minimized her appeal to the media. But Mrs. Bush's Texas manners should not be confused with passivity. Her mission has been anything but modest: to save women, educate girls, end poverty, reduce disease, expand democracy and promote freedom. Women may not save the world—at least not without the help of enlightened men—but history will judge that one Laura Bush did her part."

After her trip to the Thai border, Brian McCartin, an *Asia Times* columnist, commended her efforts, saying, "Whether Mrs. Bush's stance on Myanmar is genuine, or based on rhetoric that attempts to associate her husband's administration with a cause that nearly everyone agrees is worthy but which few are willing to do anything concrete about, her comments and actions have at least served to keep Myanmar in the news. The country's generals have become adept at riding out storms of criticism until fickle world attention moves elsewhere.

"The regime's slow grind against ethnic minority groups has resulted in decades of small military clashes, killings of civilians and the destruction of villages and livelihoods in remote places that, until Bush took up the cudgel, seldom made international headlines. This despite hard statistics indicating that Myanmar has one of the largest internally displaced populations in the world, more destroyed villages than Darfur, one of the largest land areas contaminated with landmines and the largest use of child soldiers by a government army. By keeping Myanmar in the news, more international attention, and criticism, has been placed on the regime.

"Many in Myanmar's exile community hope that Laura Bush will continue her interest and remain a close friend even after her husband's term as president expires in a few months."

British activist and author Benedict Rogers summed up in an op-ed: "Whatever else one thinks of George Bush, few could deny the contribution he, and particularly his wife Laura, made to raising the profile of the suffering in Burma. In 2005, he spent almost an hour in the Oval Office with a young Shan woman activist from Burma, Charm Tong, and heard about the military regime's use of rape as a weapon of war. In 2006, a day after former Czech President Václav Havel and former Archbishop of Cape Town Desmond Tutu published a report calling for Burma to be placed on the U.N. Security Council agenda, the U.S. declared its support for the initiative. The U.S. consistently led the way in raising Burma at the Security Council and seeking a resolution, initially with slow and grudging support from its natural allies. The U.S. has the only meaningful set of sanctions against the regime, and in the past two years it has sought to tighten and target them further."

During his last year in office, President Bush approved legislation to award the U.S. Congressional Gold Medal, the highest award the country can bestow, to Aung San Suu Kyi "in recognition of her courageous and unwavering commitment to peace, nonviolence, human rights, and democracy in Burma."

The bill was sponsored by two of the stalwart supporters of the Burmese democracy leader in the Senate, Mitch McConnell and Dianne Feinstein, and Rep. Joseph Crowley in the House of Representatives.

The award placed Aung San Suu Kyi in the diverse and distinguished company of George Washington, the Wright Brothers, Charles Lindbergh, Sir Winston Churchill, Robert Frost, Pope John Paul II, and Mother Teresa, as well as other Nobel Peace Laureates such as Elie Wiesel, the Dalai Lama, and Nelson Mandela.

In announcing to the White House press corps that her husband would sign the bill to award the Congressional Gold Medal to Suu Kyi the next day, Laura Bush was asked if Aung San Suu Kyi would be coming to accept the award. "They might let her come accept" the medal, the First Lady said. "It's unclear that they'd ever let her come back."

Aung San Suu Kyi was confined to her house at the time the Gold Medal was approved and could not leave the country or acknowledge the award. However, American diplomatic cables showed that although Suu Kyi was cut off from the world for five years, she knew that her secret "sister" had been doing everything she could to help her. When her physician was allowed to come see her, she told him she deeply appreciated the U.S. efforts to keep the issue of Burma on the world stage, "especially the First Lady."

Other cables indicated that the generals had noticed the First Lady's involvement as well. A 2008 diplomatic cable revealed that Yin Yin Oo, a Foreign Ministry official close to Number Three General Thura Shwe Mann and the sister of Deputy Foreign Minister Kyaw Thu, had been authorized by the Burmese generals to engage in discussions with the U.S. and British embassies.

As a result of the dinner discussions with Yin Yin Oo, embassy officials came away with useful insights as to the thinking of the ruling generals. The conversations confirmed: They were deeply xenophobic and feared change. They had paranoid delusions about the United States coming to get them. The discussions with Yin Yin Oo helped explain why it was so darned difficult to deal with the generals.

Yin Yin Oo acknowledged the need for Burma to change, but cited the leaders' desire to proceed cautiously. Chargé Shari Villarosa retorted that they had an excess of caution and needed to just get moving, even if slowly. Yin Yin Oo explained that the senior generals were afraid of change because they might not be able to control it. Villarosa shared with her the Vietnamese ambassador's tale of how hard change had been to start in Vietnam, but once it began, change moved faster as the leaders realized the benefits of opening up. She added that change tends to take on its own momentum, beyond any one person's control, and while there are always a few people unhappy with change, most welcome it. Since the impetus for change in Vietnam came from relatively enlightened leaders, according to the ambassador, Villarosa asked if Burma had any relatively enlightened leaders? Yin Yin Oo thought carefully and replied, "Maybe two."

Revealing the regime's paranoia toward the United States, Yin Yin Oo probed several times about the First Lady's interest in Burma. The chargé confirmed that the First Lady's interest was very deep and very sincere, and for that reason she kept very well informed about developments in Burma. "Isn't that unusual for a First Lady?" Yin Yin Oo asked. The chargé replied that a former First Lady, Hillary Clinton, was running for president. Yin Yin Oo persisted, mentioning reports that Mrs. Bush had met with U.N. Secretary General Ban Ki-moon and U.N. envoy Gambari. She said this showed that the U.S. controlled the U.N. Chargé Villarosa responded that most Americans think the U.N. does not listen to the U.S. enough.

Villarosa concluded in her report: "That Yin Yin Oo has been instructed to reach out again to the U.S. and British Embassies is an indication that some within the regime are interested in resuming some dialogue with us. She knew that much of what she asserted made little sense, regularly prefacing her remarks with 'just so you know how these people think.' We do need to know how they think, their xenophobia, their paranoia, their fear of change, their lack of awareness of how the rest of the world thinks. We also need to understand that their poor communication is not only with us, but with each other because they do not know whom they can trust, which adds to the dysfunctionality of the regime. No one speaks truth to power for fear of losing their privileged positions."

Villarosa estimated that few of her points would filter very far up in the regime hierarchy, and those that do would likely be edited to present a good news story. "For this reason, to get the attention of Than Shwe," she wrote, "we must keep raising Burma at the U.N. This irritates him to no end because it challenges his legitimacy. He can try to control the news coming into and going from Burma, but he cannot stop the outside world from criticizing his stranglehold on power in Burma. Steady criticism of Than Shwe, and how he has destroyed this country, might persuade those few generals ready to open up to risk his wrath.—VILLAROSA"

The cable was an indication that at least some of the generals were looking for an opening and were testing the waters. The pressure that Laura Bush had helped stir in the international community was being felt. But before things could get better, they got much worse.

CHAPTER FOURTEEN

THE MONKS GO ON THE MARCH

"We adhere to nonviolence, but our spine is made of steel. There is no turning back. It matters little if my life or the lives of colleagues should be sacrificed on this journey. Others will fill our sandals, and more will join and follow."

—U Gambira, leader of the Saffron Revolution

Four years after the massacre at Depayin, Aung San Suu Kyi was still being held in her home. She was not seen. She was not heard. During that time, conditions in the country steadily deteriorated. Much of the population was cooking over open wood fires while the military lived in corrupt luxury, a state within a state. By 2007, discontent began boiling over again.

To the generals' alarm, this time it was the monks throughout the country who started leading new protests, a *cri de coeur* for the suffering of the poor. Burma had become one of the 20 poorest countries in the world, according to the United Nations. Back in the fifties, before the first military takeover in 1962, it had been one of the most prosperous and highly educated in Southeast Asia. Now Than Shwe's military kleptocracy was draining the life out of the economy and the people. The cost of basic commodities such as rice, eggs, and cooking oil had recently gone up by 30 to 40 percent. Resentment was stoked when videos leaked out showing the lavish wedding of Senior General Than Shwe's daughter Thandar Shwe. Not only that, the generals also had spent some $4 billion on their new capital in Naypyidaw, where they could live like kings in splendid isolation. The memory of those excesses was still fresh when the generals callously canceled subsidies that had kept fuel prices low. In less than a week, the cost of gasoline jumped from $1.40 to $2.80 a gallon. The price of natural gas went up 500 percent.

The steep hikes meant that people couldn't get to work; it was nearly impossible to get crops to market. Food prices soared. Most people lived on less than a $1 a day and spent three fourths of that on food. Now millions of them could no longer afford to feed their families. They were a step away from starvation, while the generals were pocketing fortunes from oil and gas operations. In June 2007, the International Committee of the Red Cross (ICRC) took the unprecedented step of publicly rebuking the regime for the "immense suffering" it was causing to people.

Protests began erupting around the country, small at first, with monks joining groups of townspeople. Nearly two decades had passed since democracy protests were brutally stifled in 1988. Pent-up frustrations could no longer be held back. Members of Suu Kyi's National League for Democracy party demonstrated in central Burma, then Rangoon, then the Delta region, varying the locations to keep the military off-balance.

Su Su Nway was one of the NLD members who stepped forward to protest. The 35-year-old activist had come to the world's attention in 2005. She challenged the military government in court for forcing her and her village neighbors to repair a road without pay. Her bravery paid off when a judge sentenced the village chairman and a deputy to eight months in prison under a law that banned forced labor. The verdict was hailed as the first ever against the military regime's long-standing practice of coerced labor.

The legal victory was short-lived. A few months later, Su Su Nway was charged with allegedly defaming the village's replacement chairman. She was sentenced to 18 months in prison despite the fact that she suffered from a serious heart condition. Before her sentencing, she told reporters, "I have no responsibility, no power, and no position. They plot against a common girl, a disease sufferer, and sue her because they are afraid. If they are afraid like that, our side is winning." She endured nine months in prison before authorities finally bowed to international pressure and released her in 2006.

After the onerous fuel hikes were announced, she staged a small protest in downtown Rangoon in August 2007, calling out, "Lower fuel prices! Lower commodity prices!" Thugs from the USDA and Swan Arr Shin immediately attacked her as supporters linked arms around her to protect her. She was knocked down in the fracas, but managed to slip away in the confusion and did not stay silent long.

Authorities arrested as many protesters as they could track down, even dragging in Mya Mya San, an NLD member whose only crime was leading a regular prayer vigil at Shwedagon Pagoda for Suu Kyi's release. Veterans of the 8-8-88 demonstrations, who had only recently been released from "dog cells" in prison, went back to the streets. The military extinguished their new protests with chilling efficiency, like a giant blowing out a candle. Prominent pro-democracy leaders such as Min Ko Naing, Ko Ko Gyi, and Ko Jimmy were taken into custody once again. That might have been the end of it, another failed surge of conscience, but then the monks of the country began standing up en masse.

For centuries, monks have held the greatest moral authority in Burma. That made a principled stand by the monastic community highly threatening for a regime that lacked moral agency.

The religious community also was the only civic organization with numbers equal to the military. Before the "Saffron Revolution," there were more than 400,000 monks in the country plus some 50,000 nuns. The military ranks were estimated at 400,000 to 500,000.

More than 45,000 monasteries served as the moral backbone of the country, places of refuge, learning, and healing. Monks had dispensed teaching and guidance to past kings. On some occasions, they were even dispatched as royal peace emissaries to foreign powers to avoid wars.

In 2007, more than 80 percent of the population in Burma still adhered to Theravāda Buddhist beliefs—and held monks sacrosanct. Although the military regime had managed to subvert some of the monks in leadership positions with payoffs and perks, most of the saffron-robed monks stayed true to their principles and were deeply offended by the suffering that the military had inflicted on the populace.

First, the monks in Sittwe began demonstrating in August. Sittwe was a highly symbolic location because that is where the monk U Ottoma launched a series of heroic appeals for the British to leave Burma in the 1920s. His lectures inspired generations of followers, including young Aung San, the hero of Burma's independence. An immediate signal was sent when the monks who initiated protests in August 2007 were from U Ottama's monastery, the Shwe Zedi. The Sittwe monks were calling the nation to rise up.

The monks in Pakokku heard the call. Their show of unity in September proved a turning point. Something serious was happening. Thousands more were inspired to take to the streets in the sleepy river town. To outsiders, Pakokku might have seemed an unlikely birthplace for a revolution. It's a quiet backwater on the western banks of the Irrawaddy River. Farmers bring their peanuts and beans and corn to ship downriver. The pace is unhurried. The musky smells of tobacco and spices drift out from tea shops. Dogs sleep in the street. But Pakokku also is home to some 80 monasteries and 10,000 monks. The town is the second most important for monastic teaching after Mandalay. Monks comprise about a third of the population, which gave the generals good cause for fear. Under military rule, the monasteries had assumed an increasingly important role in educating young boys from poor families who could not afford to send them to state schools. The monasteries gave the village poor a chance to read and write. After the military closed most universities to keep students from organizing, the monasteries became the best option for learning—and ferment.

As the Pakokku monks marched down the town's potholed streets, they passed by ancient wooden monasteries, weathered gray by time, that have been centers of study since the time of the kings. The monks chanted the *metta sutra*, the Buddha's words on loving-kindness: "May all beings be happy and safe, and may their hearts be filled with joy. . . ."

They were not met with kindness. Regime soldiers—assisted by members of the thuggish Swan Arr Shin militia and the junta's civilian arm, the USDA—confronted the demonstrators with "warning" shots and tear gas. One monk was shot dead on the spot.

Another monk was tied with a rope around his neck to a tree all day, then jailed and stripped of his robes, a humiliation and a blasphemy.

Three others were tied to a light pole with ropes and beaten savagely. Their faces were smashed in with rifle butts.

The brutality sent shock waves through the monasteries. Killing, beating, or forcing a monk to disrobe are considered heinous offenses in Buddhism, dooming the offender to dire prospects in the next life.

The Pakokku monks met and decided to send their own shock wave back to the military: the monks refused to accept alms from government officials, army officers, and their families. They turned their alms bowls upside down as they filed somberly down the town streets. Refusing alms—*patta nikkujjana kamma*—is a powerful gesture. For Buddhists, giving alms is a privilege and a way to gain "merit." Gaining positive merit is essential in order to secure a better rebirth in the next life. Refusing alms from the military was tantamount to excommunication. It meant the military could not atone for their sins in this life or accrue merit for a better station in the life to come. They would be damned.

The majority of the members of the Burmese military are Buddhist, so they would have been schooled as youngsters in the five Buddhist precepts:

- not to take the life of anything living
- not to take anything not freely given
- to abstain from sexual misconduct and sensual overindulgence
- to refrain from untrue speech
- to avoid intoxication, losing mindfulness

The military government—which had directed the killing, rape, torture, and dislocation of thousands of human beings—had not lived up to those teachings. They knew that. And the monks knew that. By denying alms from anyone associated with the military, the monks were condemning them in both this life and the next.

The Pakokku monks did not stop with refusing alms from the military. They formed the All Burma Monks' Alliance to present a list of demands to the military government. They chose an auspicious date to give their ultimatum: September 9, 2007. Numerically, it lined up as 9-9-9 when the 2 and 7 from the year 2007 were added and also when all numbers 9+9+2+7=27 were added, including the sum of 27: 2+7=9. Like many Burmese, the monks placed great value in symbolic numbers. And at this moment, they needed all the good luck they could find.

The monks' alliance demanded an official apology and the immediate reversal of the price hikes. But the ABMA also added several overtly political demands: the release of all political prisoners, including Aung San Suu Kyi, and the start of a dialogue to end military rule. The demands changed the character of the protests from a humanitarian movement to an insurrection.

The generals did not meet the demands. Instead, they tried to buy the loyalty of individual monasteries with financial gifts, a familiar tactic. Many of the senior abbots were already beholden to the authorities. The State Sangha Maha Nayaka Committee was considered a puppet controlled by the military.

But the many rank-and-file monks who were supporting the ABMA stood by their demands. The wounds from the Pakokku attacks were deep. As one monk explained, "Even under the British, we were not treated like this."

Word of the Pakokku showdown spread across the country. When the deadline for an apology had passed, monasteries throughout Burma took up the cause. Soon tens of thousands of monks were mobilizing for marches that initially seemed to leave the military paralyzed.

As the marches grew, the international media took notice and started calling the protests the "Saffron Revolution." That was a misnomer since Burmese monks primarily wear robes that are the color of cinnamon or rust. But to many people, the saffron name called up the image of holy men in robes, so it stuck.

U Gawsita became one of the symbols of the protests as photos hit the front pages of him encouraging the monks with a bullhorn. Normally his pudgy cheeks were framed with a bemused smile, but now he looked desperately serious, his fingers clenched tightly around a bullhorn. At the time, Gawsita was a 27-year-old philosophy teacher. He had started learning Buddhist literature at the age of nine as a novice in his village and became a monk when he was 19. He had a quiet intelligence and a calm way of speaking sense that drew respect. After several years of advanced study, he was assigned to teach philosophy at the Maggin Monastery in Rangoon.

In addition to his teaching, Gawsita was drawn to help in the monastery's hospice program for HIV/AIDS patients. The Maggin hospice was the first in the country to be run by monks and was routinely harassed by the military government, which was doing little to address the AIDS epidemic. Because of the growing heroin industry in the "Golden Triangle" of northern Burma as well as the rise in human trafficking, Burma had one of the highest HIV rates in Asia. In recent years, the number of HIV/AIDS sufferers has been variously estimtated at 220,000 to 500,000. UNAIDS estimated one in 50 people were living with HIV infection; the National Institutes of Health estimated the figure was more like one in 29. Either way, those effected had little access to medical care and were outcasts in society. An estimated 15,000 to 18,000 were dying a year.

U Gawsita believed the dying deserved compassionate care and spiritual counseling in their last days. He worked closely with Phyu Phyu Thin, a young NLD leader who had been encouraged by Aung San Suu Kyi to open an AIDS hospice. She had found caring support for the frail patients at the monastery. She and the monks had been trying to get antiretroviral medicines so they could save patients, not just bury them. But medicines of all kinds were unavailable in the country. And donations were more difficult to come by as the economy worsened.

When the fuel hikes were imposed in 2007, U Gawsita was already talking with other monks about organizing demonstrations. He had witnessed enough suffering. "I couldn't stand the oppression and injustice anymore," he said later. "This was the time."

As the protest marches gained steam after Pakokku, laymen left their shops and market stalls to walk behind the monks in support, clapping and shouting. Farmers in bamboo hats joined in. People in the crowd offered the monks water, medicine, candy, and donations of money. Often they linked arms to form human chains of protection around the columns of crimson marchers. Even when monsoon rains poured down, laypeople stood in water up to their knees to shield the monks. To them, the treatment of the monks in Pakokku was not merely an offense against the *sangha*, the community of monks; it was an affront to all the Buddhists in the nation. It was a blasphemy.

Very few aspects of everyday life in Burma are untouched by Buddhism. Laypeople have a symbiotic relationship with the monks. They provide donations of food and material support, while the monks provide spiritual guidance, comfort, schooling for children, and social mediation, even marriage counseling.

Because the government provided a paucity of funds for social services and healthcare, monasteries and their abbots played critical roles in providing food for the hungry and traditional medicines for the sick and dying.

Most Burmese men spend some time as a monk during their lives. Boys shave their heads and don robes to join the *sangha* for a few weeks, or longer. As novices, the boys are immersed in the teachings of Buddha, the *Dharma*. They experience living as monks without the comforts of home, sleeping on the floor on simple woven mats. They learn the humility of carrying an alms bowl to seek donations. In the process, they earn considerable merit for themselves and their families. The result is a strong generational bond to the community of monks. When the monks began protesting, the people sided with them.

The monks who led the 2007 protests were smart and well organized. They had computers donated by overseas benefactors, along with cell phones, walkie-talkies, and bullhorns for communications. Communicating covertly, the monks made plans for a show of strength in Rangoon. Rangoon was the site of two high-profile protest sites—Shwedagon Pagoda, the country's holiest shrine, and the home of Aung San Suu Kyi. The monks would make pilgrimages to both.

On September 22, several thousand monks massed on the street in front of Aung San Suu Kyi's house. It was not quite the end of monsoon season, so it was raining steadily. The monks had come to ask Suu Kyi's blessing before heading to an uncertain fate in the heavily guarded city.

Suu Kyi had not been seen publicly for more than four years. A phalanx of heavily armed police with large riot shields stood defiantly around her home, forbidding the monks to come closer. In contrast, the unarmed monks stood with calm dignity in the rain and chanted softly, "May all human beings be free and happy; may all human beings be free from danger; may all human beings be free from physical suffering and mental suffering; may all human beings be free from fear and anger."

Suu Kyi, who was still under house arrest, could hear the monks chanting outside the wall around her compound. The monks asked the guards to please open the gate to her compound so she could accept the blessings of the monks and bless them in return. There were several tense moments of suspense while one of the guards called commanding officers with his walkie-talkie to find out what to do. The monks waited and prayed. Would the authorities allow the monks a moment with Suu Kyi, their star prisoner? Or would they use force to turn them away? The tension was eased when the guard put down the walkie-talkie and ordered the gate be opened. Either in a moment of rare generosity or out of fear, someone in the chain of command had okayed the request. For the first time in five years, people could see Aung San Suu Kyi.

Monks in attendance say her appearance was a powerful moment, one they will never forget and one that sustained them throughout the hardships ahead. Aung San Suu Kyi stood in front of them with the palms of her hands held reverently together. Some said they saw her smile. Others said she spoke a few sentences and said *"sandu"* to them—"well done" in Burmese. Many said she had tears streaming down her face, but it was difficult to tell in the rain. The monks' faces were wet with tears and rain as well.

"Many people were crying when they saw her face," one of the monks told me later. "I know what they were feeling—this was our leader to get democracy. We elected Aung San Suu Kyi in 1990, but she is always under house arrest. We all felt deep compassion for her."

When the security police ushered Suu Kyi back inside her compound, the monks turned back to their march with renewed purpose. As they walked down University Avenue in the rain, they were joined by students and other protesters. They carried banners that read "Untruth Will Be Overcome by Truth" and "Injustice Will Be Overcome by Justice." Some shouted "Free Aung San Suu Kyi." They were hoping that perhaps this time, their protests would be a final, and successful, push for freedom.

The next day, they were joined by thousands more monks and 150 nuns, whose pale pink robes stood out like flowers in the army of burnt orange marchers. Altogether, some 15,000 monks and laymen filed somberly through the streets of Rangoon. Momentum was building. The All Burma Monks' Alliance vowed to continue the protests until the military junta, "the enemy of the people," was deposed.

By September 24, more than 100,000 monks and ordinary citizens were marching in Rangoon, a giant river of crimson. Demonstrations were taking place in every state and division in Burma. Marches occurred simultaneously in 25 cities, with columns of monks often stretching nearly a mile. In Mandalay, the country's second city and religious heartland, a demonstration of more than 30,000 was led by around 1,000 monks. In audio recordings, people in the crowd could be heard shouting, "Doh-ah-yay, Doh-ah-yay!" That translated to "Our rights!"—a slogan used in the failed 1988 demonstrations.

Writers, social activists, and even some movie stars were now supporting the movement. The BBC reported that the popular comedian Zarganar and film star Kyaw Thu went to the golden Shwedagon Pagoda to offer food and water to the monks as they marched. Both had been helping organize the marches behind the scenes.

There was a kind of exhilaration in the air. A Swedish National Radio correspondent reported that people on the street were filled with such admiration for the brave monks that they had been spontaneously coming up to him and voicing their opinions about the government in a way they had never dared do before.

Then the military began cracking down. A dusk-to-dawn curfew was imposed. Any gathering of more than five people was banned. Thousands of military and police forces poured into Rangoon and Mandalay. Rumors swirled that Suu Kyi was moved from her home to the infamous Insein Prison, but diplomatic sources say she remained in her home, surrounded by a growing army of guards. She would not be seen again, but her image was everywhere in the streets as many of the demonstrators carried her photo.

U.N. Secretary General Ban Ki-moon warned the military government to exercise maximum restraint in responding to any demonstrations. They did not listen.

On September 25, the junta threatened protesters with military force and placed army trucks around Shwedagon Pagoda, the assembly point for monks. Thousands of monks and laypeople marched into the pagoda anyway. Reuters reported that ordinary people had formed a double chain around the monks at the giant pagoda, shielding them with their bodies. Government troops broke through with batons and tear gas and sealed off the area around the pagoda. Even that failed to stop the marchers, who regrouped and continued to protest their way through Rangoon, some wearing gas masks and hand-made cloth masks in anticipation of gas attacks.

Across town at the ancient Sule Pagoda, more protesters gathered in the large traffic circle in the center of Rangoon. The golden stupa had been a rallying point in the 1988 uprisings, so monks had designated it as another key protest site. U Gawsita was there with his bullhorn, chanting prayers and calling for calm. Phyu Phyu Thin and other NLD leaders had come to support the monks. U Gawsita had negotiated with police not to harm onlookers, but when truckloads of police roared up, a melee broke out. Gawsita was struck in the head by a police baton and knocked off his feet. He stumbled and crawled away. Phyu Phyu Thin also was battered and injured. She went into hiding. She had been arrested before: in 2000 while rallying for Aung San Suu Kyi's release and again in May 2007 for conducting a prayer vigil for Suu Kyi's release. This time, she got away.

A witness told TV reporters that a six-truck military convoy had driven straight toward the Sule Pagoda that mid-afternoon. As the trucks passed demonstrators, rounds of automatic gunfire ripped through the air. People threw their bicycles down, covered their heads with their hands, or clung to their friends on the ground. As the military moved in, a stampede of terrified human beings filled the street as people ran in all directions.

The ground was littered with grim reminders of the suddenness of the attack: A woman's small cloth bag splattered with blood. The flip-flop sandals of people who had lost them as they ran away or were dragged away. Rumors swirled that the military was equipping fire trucks to spray the crowd at the Sule Pagoda with insecticide.

"We knew they would crack down," said Gawsita later. "We just didn't realize it would be so cruel."

Many of the protesters ran pell-mell back to their monasteries. One leader, U Pyinyarthiri, retreated all the way to Monywa, 500 miles to the north. Yet even there, he was not safe. When he visited an internet café to check his e-mail, he was arrested. The café owner had tipped off police. He later told Human Rights Watch that police handcuffed his hands behind him in jail and then tortured him by stomping in his chest and face and shins with their boots. Every question was accompanied by hard slaps to his temples. When he could endure it no longer, the monk began banging his head on the table so he would lose consciousness. "Please don't do that, my reverend," he was told. "We are acting under the command of higher authority."

Truckloads of troops were now confronting monks throughout Rangoon and Mandalay. Security forces clubbed the clergymen to the ground, then dragged them away, loading them like lumber into vans and trucks. "They made some monks crawl to the trucks," survivors reported. "They were beating them from behind until they threw up blood."

The military had ordered hospitals not to treat any of the protesters. As a result, most of the injured monks received little or no care. Many of the wounded took refuge in monasteries, only to have security forces storm into the monasteries and subject them to more beating. The Democratic Voice of Burma posted a photo of a bloodied monk floating lifeless in water, his robe stained with blood.

Civilians who were protesting alongside the monks were beaten and seized as well. So many were arrested that there was not enough jail space to house them, so they were locked in classrooms in the Government Technical Institute, usually more than a hundred in a room, with no room to sleep and no sanitary facilities. Several a day died as the siege went on.

A young shopkeeper taken to a Mandalay jail later told a reporter from *The Guardian* that he was packed into a cell with 85 people, mostly young people, many with broken bones and head wounds. One boy in the cell had been arrested for wearing an American flag on his head. The young shopkeeper had been identified from surveillance photos of the protesters and pulled into jail for questioning. "Who organized the protests? Who organized the monks?" the interrogators wanted to know. He told them that the people in the crowd were following the monks; the monks were not following them. The interrogators beat him and then pressed again: *"Was this really a foreign-backed political plot to bring down the regime?"* He was questioned relentlessly for three days and nights, kicked, slapped, and punched. The shopkeeper told them: "You can ask anything, my answer will always be the same. I don't know who organized the monks."

But the interrogators didn't like his answer. As punishment, they subjected him to a torture well known in Burma prisons: the motorcycle torture. He was forced to half-crouch as if he were sitting on a motorbike, holding out his arms as if gripping handlebars, and imitating the sound of an engine. While that pose may sound like nothing more than a child's pantomime, staying in the half-crouch position for hours eventually brought intense, shooting pains in his legs and arms. When the shopkeeper fell over, he was beaten again.

The acknowledged "mastermind" of the protests, a brilliant monk named U Gambira, fared even worse. U Gambira, whose birth name was Nyi Nyi Lwin, came from a village in the central farmlands of Burma. He had started school at age five and showed considerable promise. Yet he was unable to continue his studies because the military closed the local schools after the 1988 democracy uprising. Aimless and frustrated, he ran away from home at age 12. He was spotted by the military and forcibly recruited as a child soldier. His desperate parents searched for months until they found him and brought him back home. After authorities came looking for him several times, they enrolled their son in a local monastery to protect him from arrest or re-conscription. Monastery life provided the discipline and academic challenge Gambira needed, as well as safety. He flourished in the monastery environment. When the Saffron Revolution protests began, he was 29. Daring and articulate, Gambira was a natural to become one of the leaders of the All Burma Monks' Alliance when it was formed. He had already been quietly preparing for a protest for several years; the fuel hikes and the Pakokku uprising provided sparks for action. As the 2007 protests got under way, Gambira traveled back and forth between Rangoon and Mandalay, marshalling the monks and planning larger protests.

When the military began hauling in suspects for questioning, it did not take them long to wring out the information that Gambira was one of the ringleaders. Gambira went into hiding, but not without cost: The military arrested his father and brother as hostages in order to force him to surrender. In the weeks ahead, the junta would arrest six of Gambira's family members and send them to prison, but Gambira did not surrender. He was trying to get the word out to the world about the monks' struggle.

From hiding, Gambira wrote a passionate opinion piece for the *Washington Post* and *The Guardian*, saying:

"Military rule has brought Burma to collapse. Our economy is in ruins. Once the breadbasket of Asia, Burma cannot feed itself. Once we were a light for education and literacy; now, the regime has closed schools and universities. . . . We are an enslaved people."

Even though he was wanted by the military and forced to hide, he said he was awed by the bravery of so many, including sympathetic security agents who opened their homes to him and other democracy leaders.

"We have taken their best punch," he wrote. "Now it is the generals who must fear the consequences of their actions. We adhere to nonviolence, but our spine is made of steel. There is no turning back. It matters little if my life or the lives of colleagues should be sacrificed on this journey. Others will fill our sandals, and more will join and follow."

It would be his last message for a long time. As his article was being read in Washington and London, a convoy of soldiers was headed toward his hiding place.

—~—

One of Gambira's best friends in the monastery community, Ashin Issariya, also had been crisscrossing the country to organize the monasteries. Issariya handed out pamphlets in monasteries and encouraged monks to participate in the marches. A lanky man with glasses and a firm set to his chin, he made an impressive case. Changing monasteries every day, he created an underground monk network to relay news and information around Burma. Issariya e-mailed photographs of protests from Internet cafés to the media organizations around the world. After seeing most of his comrades arrested, Ashin Issariya went underground. He adopted a bold pseudonym, "King Zero," to say the country did not need any more kings. He continued his work in hiding.

The junta had started planting informers in the monk's ranks. Large numbers of monastic robes were ordered to distribute to soldiers. The soldiers were ordered to shave their heads and infiltrate the monasteries, apparently to learn the monks' plans and betray leaders. Monks in the Old Ma Soe monastery in Mandalay put out the word that criminals were being freed from jail to pose as monks and cause trouble. In order to detect the bogus monks, senior monks began testing new arrivals for their knowledge of Buddhist literature. If the monks who showed up on their doorstep couldn't answer basic questions about The Three Gems or The Four Noble Truths, they were sent away.

On September 26, soldiers shifted emphasis from the streets to the monasteries, carrying out coordinated raids on 52 monasteries at dawn. Monks were forcibly disrobed, mauled, and taken away. During a raid in monasteries in Myitkyina, in the northern part of the country, government security forces reportedly beat four monks to death.

In some locations, local people rushed out of their homes in the middle of the night, banging pots and pans, to ward off police who were trying to break into monasteries. The distractions sometimes bought time for monks to flee.

Despite the heavy military presence around the monasteries and in the street, people found ways to defy the regime with nonviolent acts of resistance. In several townships, dogs were seen roaming with pictures of Senior General Than Shwe and other regime leaders strung around their necks. Associating anybody with a dog is a serious insult in Burma.

Trains were painted with anti-junta slogans. Leaflets calling for renewed struggle were secretly distributed.

In an example of how humor can be found in even deadly serious circumstances, a recording of military radio communications during the protests revealed that the call sign "oranges" had been designated for the monks and "potatoes" for ordinary people. According to diplomatic sources, soldiers can be heard on the recording frantically describing reports of great numbers of marching potatoes and oranges as the demonstrators made their way through Rangoon.

A struggle for the soul of the country was underway, in the barracks as well as the streets. There were scattered reports of soldiers and policemen who balked at harming the clergymen—including light infantry units in Mandalay and Rangoon. In Mandalay, warning shots were fired in the air and there were fewer casualties. One soldier reportedly turned his rifle on himself rather than obey orders to shoot a monk praying in front of him. And there were rumors that several high-ranking officers initially refused the order from Senior General Than Shwe to carry out a mass attack on the monks. It was said the Senior General took charge of the crackdown himself. According to biographer Benedict Rogers, as the protests and violence continued, Than Shwe reportedly went into a deep depression and refused to eat anything except chicken rice soup.

Not all the monks in the country's 45,000 monasteries participated in the demonstrations—some thought the marches were too political, some had been bribed by the military, some were afraid of the consequences. But most did.

In some monasteries, monks were given time by authorities to pack up and get out. In others, the monks fled before security forces could arrive, leaving neatly made beds in their austere living quarters as well as the single key that each monk is permitted to possess. Stray cats and dogs wandered the empty halls while statues of the Buddha looked on. In the largest of Pakokku's monasteries, the Bawdimandine, almost half of the 1,200 monks were gone, most never to return.

In Rangoon, police stormed into the Mingalayama monastery at midnight. Normally, more than 200 monks lived at the monastery's university where Pali script was taught. Monks came from across the country to master the ancient teachings of The Elders. On September 26, the authorities came for them while they were asleep on their mats. One young monk reported that their quarters were ransacked, vandalized, and emptied. Books and furniture were strewn on the floor. Torn robes and blood were everywhere.

U Gawsita, the monk who had helped lead the protest at Sule Pagoda with his bullhorn, had predicted that the soldiers would come next to the Maggin monastery, because it was known as a hotbed of resistance. The AIDS hospice was associated with the NLD, which was an invitation to trouble. Gawsita was hiding at another location when soldiers swept into the monastery. Hundreds of monks who had sought sanctuary inside the walls from attacks in the streets were rounded up at gunpoint, along with the resident monks. The abbot, U Indaka, was arrested along several senior monks who were over 80 years old. Soldiers pillaged the monastery with a vengeance and barricaded the doors. It would be locked up and off-limits to monks for the next five years.

By September 27, the nation's monasteries had become war zones. According to reports from the U.S. Campaign for Burma, security forces stormed the Ngwe Kyar Yan monastery in Rangoon at two in the morning. Local residents that gathered around the monastery saw soldiers lining up the monks against the brick monastery wall. One by one, the soldiers bashed the monks' heads into the wall until they were lifeless. The senior abbot was tied up in the middle of the room and forced to watch while he was being tortured himself. He died from his injuries before dawn. Everything of value was looted from the monastery, including 40 or more Buddha statues and the head of a statue that contained valuable gems. By early October, raids were still under way and casualties of bystanders reported, included at the Kyaik Ka San monastery when a young man was beaten to death when he mistakenly beeped his car horn near soldiers.

According to Wikileaks of American diplomatic cables during the Saffron crackdown, the American chargé d'affaires, Shari Villarosa, was summoned to Naypyidaw to meet with the deputy foreign minister, Maung Myint, in early October. He warned her rather ominously that he had information that democracy activists might disguise themselves as soldiers and attack the American embassy. She found the idea ludicrous but could tell the information was meant to convey the message that the embassy was vulnerable. Maung Myint also advised her that the embassy employees should not go near the demonstrations because they could not be protected from "destructive elements"—which appeared to be another veiled threat. She demurred that embassy officials would need to continue monitoring the situation to get accurate information.

Villarosa brought up the recent offer by Than Shwe to meet with Aung San Suu Kyi. Apparently in response to international pressure after the attacks, the senior general had sent out word that he would meet with the democracy leader—if she would give up her approval of economic sanctions and the "utter devastation" he claimed the sanctions had caused to the economy, as opposed to government mismanagement. This was widely interpreted as a feint to blame the lack of dialogue on Aung San Suu Kyi, who was not likely to agree to such conditions. Villarosa inquired, who would be the intermediary? When Maung Myiunt coyly suggested perhaps she should be the intermediary, it reinforced the interpretation that Than Shwe's offer was merely intended to deflect blame for lack of progress to Aung San Suu Kyi or the Americans. The meeting with Aung San Suu Kyi was never scheduled.

Villarosa then asked when Generation 88 leaders Min Ko Naing and Ko Ko Gyi would be released. Maung Myint replied that some of the activists must undergo "more interrogation." Villarosa asked if that involved torture. Maung Myint turned to her with a big smile and said, "We don't torture," then touched her on her arm and again repeated, "We don't torture." She repressed a shudder.

Subsequent reports from prison inmates confirmed that at the time, Min Ko Naing and other democracy leaders had been tortured so severely that they had been hospitalized in the prison. Screens were placed around their beds to keep others from seeing how badly they had been beaten.

Su Su Nway, who had protested against forced labor and the fuel hikes, tried to protest the human-rights violations in November. She went to the hotel where U.N. Special Rapporteur for Human Rights, Paulo Sergio Pinheiro, was staying in Rangoon. She raised a banner outside the hotel parodying the junta's propaganda billboards that said, "Oppose those relying on China, acting as thieves, holding murderous views."

She was immediately arrested and sentenced to twelve and a half years in prison.

The arrests and torture of protesters and monks continued. The monks in Pakokku tried one more brave demonstration that fall. Once again, they were hemmed in and stopped by force. It was becoming clear that the junta's massive military machine had overwhelmed the opposition. Most of the monks' leaders were dead, in prison, or in hiding. The Saffron Revolution had been decapitated and dispersed.

—≈—

Hundreds of people are believed to have died in the military crackdown, but accounts vary: the U.S. Campaign for Burma, a pro-democracy group based in Washington, D.C., said more than 100 people were killed when troops fired automatic weapons at the demonstrators at the Shwedagon and Sule pagodas. At least a hundred more were killed at a high school in Tamwe, a township in Rangoon. As some protesting students had marched toward the high school, soldiers turned from shooting in the air to shooting at the students. When parents arrived to pick up the elementary children in the school, they were hit by the spray of bullets along with some of the young students inside the building.

Getting an accurate count of casualties was difficult because security forces often carried away the dead and dying. Credible sources told U.N. Human Rights Envoy Paulo Sergio Pinheiro that numerous bodies had been cremated hurriedly at the Yae Way crematorium on the outskirts of Rangoon between September 27 and September 30. The Chinese army reportedly had carried out a similar practice after Tiananmen Square, disposing of unidentified bodies at the Babaoshan crematorium in Beijing. After the nighttime cremations in Burma, grisly stories circulated that some demonstrators rushed into the ovens had been badly injured but were still alive.

The military government put the death toll from the Saffron Revolution at only 13. The Democratic Voice of Burma reported that 138 people had been killed, based on corroborated names. The Burma Campaign in the United Kingdom said the regime had arrested more than 6,000 people during the crackdown, including approximately 1,400 monks. Many of those arrested were held in makeshift detention centers set up at universities, factories, and the Kayaikkason race track in Rangoon.

The police and government later acknowledged that 2,927 people had been interrogated, including 596 monks. Human Rights Watch said at least 240 of the monks who survived were still in prison two years later.

The great difference between the 2007 Saffron Revolution and the protests in 1988 was that this time, the world was watching. The Democratic Voice of Burma, which is based in nearby Thailand, sent out trained observers with video cameras and then supplied the images to the news media. Courageous bloggers like 27-year-old Nay Phone Latt, who owned an Internet café, transmitted photographs to news organizations. As a result, people around the world could see the rows of russet-robed monks marching through the streets. They witnessed the screams and panic as government troops attacked the unarmed protesters with tear gas, batons, bamboo sticks, and assault weapons.

One of the shocking images captured the death of a Japanese photographer, Kenji Nagai. Nagai was shot as he tried to document the killings around him at Sule Pagoda. A sequence of photos taken by others from across the street showed Nagai lying flat on his back, looking up at a soldier. Just a heartbeat later, he appears dead. In the next frame, a soldier takes Nagai's camera from his lifeless hand. The military government claimed he had been killed by protesters throwing rocks.

As the images of the protests were circulated worldwide, the Burmese junta responded by restricting media coverage. The military curtailed all unapproved travel, censored news stories, and targeted those caught carrying cameras, beating and arresting them.

The government also attempted to block all websites and Internet services that could carry information about the protests. They barred access to web-based e-mail. However, younger activists who were Internet-savvy were able to circumvent the censors, posting pictures and videos on blogs.

When Aung San Suu Kyi had stepped outside her home to greet the marching monks and supporters, the only photos of that moment were blurry cell-phone images posted on blogs. The Mizzima news organization, which is operated by exiled dissidents in India, published one of the photos of Suu Kyi facing the monks. More than 50,000 people accessed the photo in one day.

A manhunt was under way across the country for the protest leaders. The Burmese military fanned across the country, searching door to door for organizers and anyone who helped them. Buses were stopped and searched for monks. Bloggers like Nay Phone Latt were arrested for providing assistance to the media. The comedian Zarganar and actor Kyaw Thu were arrested for assisting the monks.

To make sure that no one could approach Aung San Suu Kyi's gate again, the army set up a machine-gun station outside her home. Foreign journalists were barred from openly entering Burma. Soldiers and police began going door-to-door at some Rangoon hotels, looking for foreigners. Intelligence officers matched photos taken of protesters with photos recently compiled in a "home registry" and tracked the protestors to their doorsteps.

Guards were posted around monasteries that were known to have been involved in the demonstrations. United States diplomats who visited 15 monasteries found them completely empty. The whereabouts of the monks were unknown. Bloodstains began turning brown on the floors.

—w—

> *"Every civilized nation has a responsibility to stand up for people suffering under a brutal military regime—like the one that has ruled Burma for too long."*
>
> —President George W. Bush,
> announcing new sanctions of Burma, 2007

As the coverage of the carnage was beamed around the globe, many world leaders began condemning the junta's actions, but some countries looked away. The United States took the lead on pressing the United Nations to act. As the crisis deepened, President George W. Bush spoke out at least six times, accusing the military dictatorship of imposing "a

19-year reign of fear" that denied basic freedoms of speech, assembly, and worship. First Lady Laura Bush took increasingly bold public positions on the "horrifying" violence, calling for the generals to meet with the U.N. envoy and begin a dialogue with the democratically elected Aung San Suu Kyi. The First Lady made headlines when she said in a *Wall Street Journal* op-ed that the junta generals "are a friendless regime. They should step aside to make way for a unified Burma governed by legitimate leaders. The rest of the armed forces should not fear this transition—there is room for a professional military in a democratic Burma."

In an interview with *USA Today* on October 9, 2007, she said "The crackdown has been brutal" and that tougher sanctions were needed if the junta did not take steps toward democracy. She was skeptical of the Burmese government's assertion that the nation's streets were quiet after weeks of violence. "I'm sure that's because people are afraid. . . . The arrests are happening in the middle of the night, where the military break into people's houses and . . . take them off to jail."

When the regime still failed to take any positive steps, the Bush administration moved to impose tougher financial sanctions on "the leaders of the regime and its financial backers."

Other nations responded with varying degrees of courage and cynical self-interest.

- China's initial response was that it has a policy of not interfering with its allies' domestic matters. However, Beijing reportedly urged Burma's military rulers behind the scenes to meet with U.N. Envoy Ibrahim Gambari. China wanted Burma to tone down its strife—the bloody turmoil next door was adding to tensions in the region on the eve of the 2008 Olympics.
- India, although the world's largest democracy, was likewise reluctant to criticize its neighbor publicly. While the monks' marches were in progress, India's oil ministry announced it would be investing $150 million in gas exploration in Burma, a boost for the military government. When violence broke out, the government in New Delhi expressed concern and said it was "closely monitoring the situation."

- The government in Laos did not release any statements. Unconfirmed regional news reports said Senior General Than Shwe's wife, family members, and pets had flown to Vientiane for safety.
- The Association of Southeast Asian Nations (ASEAN) issued an uncharacteristically blunt statement, expressing its "revulsion" at reports that peaceful demonstrations in Rangoon were being violently crushed by the security forces. But no actions of substance were taken.
- In Thailand, Prime Minister Surayud Chulanont took the high road, saying that as a Buddhist he was trying to persuade the Burmese government not to use harsh measures or violence against the monks, as "it will be against the way of life of the Buddhists." But again, there was little follow-up as violence worsened.

Others took more direct action:

- The European Union's foreign policy chief, Javier Solana, urged China to lean harder on Burma. The European Union already had a broad array of sanctions on Burma, which included bans on arms sales and visa restrictions on regime leaders. Those were extended after the 2007 violence and were expanded to include a ban on imports of gems, timber, and metals. However, as critics pointed out, there was no monitoring mechanism to enforce the ban.
- The government in France was quick to warn the ruling junta in Burma that it would be held accountable if it harmed the protesters. President Nicolas Sarkozy asked French businesses to freeze investments in Burma, including the oil company Total, which operates the Yadana natural gas pipeline from Burma to Thailand. Sarkozy stood out by calling on the U.N. Security Council to adopt sanctions against the regime without delay.
- In England, Prime Minister Gordon Brown, who had spoken often in support of democracy leader Aung San Suu Kyi, deplored the violent suppression of peaceful demonstrations and called for the release of all political prisoners, including Suu Kyi. Foreign Secretary David Miliband added, with verbal brio, "I for one

thought it was brilliant to see Aung San Suu Kyi alive and well outside her house last week. I think it will be a hundred times better when she takes her rightful place as the elected leader of a free and democratic Burma."

- Japan canceled funding for a human-resources center at Rangoon University and threatened to cut aid to Burma.
- In Poland, democracy leader and Nobel Prize winner Lech Wałęsa, who knew what it was like to march in the streets, joined with former Communist military leader Wojciech Jaruzelski to issue a symbolic joint statement. The two former adversaries urged the Burmese junta to sit down and talk with protestors, just as they had. "In Myanmar, as in Poland, only a bloodless transition to democracy is in the interest of all," they said.
- The Philippines urged the Burmese leaders to take steps toward democracy—and threatened to stop financial aid to Burma if opposition leader Aung San Suu Kyi was not released.
- Rolls-Royce said it would have no further business involvement in Burma, ceasing all aircraft-engine repair work and terminating the lease of an aircraft to a Burmese airline.
- The world's religious leaders also spoke out. Pope Benedict XVI stated that he was hoping for a peaceful solution to the "extremely serious" events in Burma and expressed sorrow for the poor during the "painful trial." The Dalai Lama offered his support to the monks and appealed to Buddhist members of the Burmese regime to act in accordance with the teachings of Buddha in the spirit of compassion and nonviolence. "I pray for the success of this peaceful movement and the early release of fellow Nobel Peace laureate Aung San Suu Kyi," he said. South African Nobel Prize winner Bishop Tutu also appealed for the release of political prisoners and said he wanted "our brave sisters and brothers in Burma" to know that "we support their peaceful protests to end a vicious rule of oppression and injustice."
- Canada called for the release of Aung San Suu Kyi and all other political prisoners and genuine dialogue with members of the democratic opposition.

- The Czech Republic called for the immediate release of the activists arrested during the protests and all political prisoners, including Daw Aung San Suu Kyi.
- The government in South Africa had shocked the world by voting with China and Russia against Security Council action on Burma earlier in the year, on the grounds that Burma's unrest did not represent a threat to the rest of the region. That prompted a loud uproar. After the Saffron attacks, South Africa's deputy foreign minister summoned the Burmese ambassador to condemn the violent repression of peaceful protests. Former president Nelson Mandela had only recently formed a group of international leaders called "The Elders" to protest injustice around the world. When the group was announced, Mandela left an empty chair on the stage in honor of Aung San Suu Kyi, who was still under arrest. Though he was no longer in office, the 89-year-old Mandela criticized the new violence in Burma and withdrew an invitation to golf star Gary Player to host a charity golf tournament in South Africa because of his alleged business links with Burma.

The mixed reaction was a textbook example of how difficult it is to get an effective international response to violence inside a country—even the massacre of unarmed clergymen.

The U.S. and the EU put concerted pressure on the U.N. Security Council to take serious action on the violence in Burma. The council held a series of meetings behind closed doors about the situation, once in September and twice in October. The result was a Presidential Statement saying the Security Council "strongly deplored the use of violence against peaceful demonstrations in Myanmar." The statement called for the "early release of all political prisoners and remaining detainees" and urged the Burmese junta to prepare for a "genuine dialogue" with democratically elected leader Aung San Suu Kyi.

Although the statement had a sharp edge, it had no teeth. It did not mention sanctions. It did not have the power of a resolution, although the statement required the consent of all the council members. That consensus indicated a slight concession on the part of China, which previously had blocked any action against the Burma junta. In the months ahead, however, China quietly resumed its "hands-off" position that the issue should be resolved internally in Burma. India and ASEAN continued making business deals with the junta.

Throughout the U.N. discussions, monks were still being rounded up in Burma. Monasteries were being placed under heavy guard. And more protesters were being sent to prison.

U.N. special envoy Ibrahim Gambari was allowed to meet twice with Aung San Suu Kyi and once with Senior General Than Shwe after the crackdown on the Saffron Revolution.

No substantial progress was reported.

On October 24, 2007, Aung San Suu Kyi reached a total of 12 years in detention.

—

And what happened to the monks?

A year later, I visited Pakokku to see what had become of the monks. It takes five to six hours to drive from Mandalay, including stops to raise the hood on the vintage car to let the engine cool off. The scenery is worth the while: towering temples framed by blue skies, children riding oxen in the fields. The picture was marred by dark green military trucks stationed at intervals along the road. To avoid notice, we parked our car some distance from one of the monasteries that had been involved in the protests. Motorcycles were lined up near the front gate, a telltale sign. The monks did not own motorcycles. Security forces did. At the tea shop nearby, several men sat near the front who were wearing the white shirts and green longyis associated with the government's USDA organization. They were eyeing the traffic on the street.

To avoid their attention, I ducked into a nearby temple. Inside, it was quiet and cool and dusty. On the dark altar, ancient statues of the Buddha glowed with the unmistakable patina of gold. Thick layers of gold leaf had been faithfully applied over the years by devotees as gifts for "merit." In recent years, blinking electric lights have been installed around many of the statues of the Buddha in Burma like a halo. To believers, the lights signify the Buddha's radiance and enlightenment, but as they blink on and off and sometimes change colors, they can be a garish distraction from the serenity of the spaces. I focused instead on a thin woman who was hunched down on her knees on the stone floor. She was bent over in quiet prayer with her arms stretched out ahead of her on the floor. I could see that her cotton blouse and longyi were faded and worn. She had brought a small gathering of flowers as an offering. She remained there, motionless, a small bump in front of the tall, glittering altar, for a very long time. I couldn't help but wonder what concerns were weighing on her so heavily. A death? An illness? A child to feed?

While I waited, a Burmese colleague had gone to walk by the monastery across the street. He was less likely to attract notice and might be able to sneak a peek through the padlocked gate. When he rejoined me in the temple, his face was ashen. Even after a year, there were still signs of disarray in the courtyard, upturned chairs, sandals, broken windows. The monastery was eerily quiet. No one appeared to be inside. He saw one of the men at the tea shop taking his photo as he paused at the gate, so he hurried on by. We made a donation at the temple and left. We were trying to be inconspicuous as we walked to our car, so it was unsettling when several women and clamoring children followed us noisily down the street. The children begged for pencils. The women asked for money and my mascara.

We drove back to Mandalay, home to some of the largest monasteries in Burma. Monks there are normally part of the tourist attraction, providing bright splashes of color on the streets. Yet there were noticeably fewer monks in view. When we tried to drive by one of the monasteries that had been involved in the 2007 demonstrations, we could not. The surrounding streets still were barricaded and heavily guarded. The closest we could get to the off-limits monasteries was two blocks away. My driver was too frightened to drive by more than once. Soldiers stood guard on the corners of the streets. If they noticed his license plate, it would be hard for him to get work.

And so we drove on to Rangoon. When I asked people, where are the monks? They would shrug and say, they went back to their villages. Are they safe? Some were arrested, people would say, but most have been left alone, provided they do not try to return to their monasteries.

According to the monks with the All Burma Monks' Alliance, the community of monks was drastically diminished by the end of 2007. In Bago, there had been 1,500 monks at the Kha Khat Wain Kyaung monastery; now there were 500. In Rangoon, there had been 25,000–30,000 monks; now it was said that less than a third remained. The Sin Phyu monastery in Moulmein, where nearly 600 students had been studying, was emptied. It would take years to restore the vitality of the monasteries.

As one of chief monks at the Old Ma Soe monastery in Mandalay had said, "It was all about silencing them."

—~—

I was able to meet some of the protest leaders in person when the International Burmese Monks Association (IBMO) arranged a press conference in New York City for the monks in fall 2008. The briefing was being held in an office building just down the street from the United Nations. The idea was to coincide with the U.N. General Assembly meeting across the street to remind the diplomats that repression was still occurring, monks were still being hunted and arrested a year after the demonstrations. Monks who had fled to the U.S. were bused in from around the country. It was a small-budget event, with gray folding chairs and refreshments on paper plates. A nondescript conference room had been reserved for one hour. But when the monks filed somberly in, they filled the space with their dignity.

A small audience was present, mostly composed of staffers from human-rights organizations. One asked the monks, "How many monks are left in Burma to organize?"

Through translators, the monks answered that to the best of their knowledge 61 monasteries had been raided and emptied. Eleven monks were still among the missing. But they said there were still many monks inside who supported the Saffron marches.

Will there be more demonstrations?

The monks answered carefully: It would be impossible to predict when another demonstration might take place, because no one had predicted the previous demonstration. It just happened when it seemed necessary.

Did they consider the protest a failure, since the regime was still in control?

Our aim was not to bring the fall of the government, but to bring a dialogue that would bring change, the monks said. Every movement leaves important seeds. Important seeds of democracy were planted for the future.

Would the Burmese military go to hell for torturing and killing monks?

"According to Buddhist principles, those who commit crimes against monks are definitely going to hell," said the most senior monk.

The small crowd cheered. So did the monks.

—ʌʌʌ—

The Buddhist levels of hell look much like the tiers of punishment in Dante's *Inferno*. Yet the Buddhist "Naraka" differs from the hells of Abrahamic religions in that people are not sent to Naraka as a result of divine judgment, but their own misdeeds. The length of stay is not eternal, though it is usually very long—and unpleasant.

Narakas are described as a series of cavernous layers in the earth below the ordinary human world. The most common way of describing the torments is as Eight Cold Narakas and Eight Hot Narakas.

The torments in the cold Narakas include being trapped naked and alone in blizzards that are so cold that they raise blisters on the body of the sufferer. Other layers are so cold that bodies are cracked into pieces, so that the internal organs are exposed and frozen.

The torments in the hot Narakas are more varied and include being trapped in blazing hot ground, being attacked with iron claws, having molten metal dropped on you, being cut into pieces with saws and sharp axes, being crushed by rocks into bloody jelly over and over, and being locked in a burning shelter.

In one level, animals that beings have killed in life return to torment them and eat their flesh. In yet another torment, beings are roasted in an oven and mired in endless excrement and urine. It was the kind of prospect that should have given the generals pause.

—ʌʌʌ—

One of the monks present at the New York briefing was U Gawsita, the monk whose photo with a bullhorn became an iconic image. He had escaped from the violence in Rangoon to a remote village. The military was close behind. Gawsita disguised himself as a ticket collector and mechanic to slip out of the country on a bus. Every stop at every village meant an opportunity to be arrested, but he was not detected. He escaped Burma only to be detained by the Thai police when he reached Thailand. His heart sank. Had he come so far only to be sent back to a prison in Burma? Pro-democracy organizations in Thailand came to his rescue. Gawsita was one of 38 monks given rare visas to the U.S. as political refuges. He was settled in Utica, New York, a blue-collar former textile town, where a monastery had been established by the All Burma Monks' Alliance for the refugee monks. Utica was welcoming but painfully cold for monks who had never had coats before.

Shortly after his arrival, Gawsita became a media celebrity of sorts, invited to speak at events sponsored by PEN, the Open Society Institute, *The New York Review of Books*, Columbia University, and Yale University. He was invited to the White House and interviewed on TV. He was prominently featured in *Burma VJ*, the award-winning documentary about the monks' rebellion.

When asked in an interview why he had joined the protests, Gawsita explained with the preternatural calm that so many monks project: "People were scrounging for work. . . . They were lined up to get visas to get out of the country. . . . Children as young as 10 were working in tea shops. . . . Housewives could not get food for their families."

When he went to the Sule Pagoda to lead the demonstrators, he said he was shocked to see that soldiers were not shooting into the air—they were shooting *at the crowd*. "The government was shooting people who were praying for peace," he told the U.S. Campaign for Burma. "The role of the army is no longer to protect the people. The Burmese army has become a bunch of terrorists."

U Gawsita later moved from Utica to the Metta Parami monastery in Brooklyn and then to Buffalo, N.Y., where he tried to keep up Buddhist traditions for weddings, funerals, and novice ceremonies for displaced Burmese. Raising the money for rent every month through donations was difficult. Seven years after picking up that bullhorn to lead the monks in prayer in Rangoon, U Gawsita gave up his monks' robes to become a bus driver.

—ʌʌ—

U Kovida also was at the New York briefing. He was one of the monks who had gathered in front of Aung San Suu Kyi's house on Sept. 22 to get her blessing. He caught my notice at the briefing because he had the sad face of a poet, a gravity beyond his years. Kovida was only 23 at the time of the Saffron marches. After the attacks in Pakokku, he made copies of posters announcing rallies, traveling around Rangoon by bus with the posters hidden under his robes. "September 18," the fliers read, "Three o'clock."

When the authorities cracked down, internet videos showed Kovida raising up his hand in protest as police tried to drag off a student. The government identified Kovida from photos taken of the crowds and posted "Wanted" posters of him throughout Rangoon. He was charged with hiding explosives in the monasteries, which was not true.

Kovida took refuge in a tiny bamboo hut on the outskirts of Rangoon, afraid to show his face. At night, friends brought him food and rice. When authorities raided the homes of his family members, Kovida decided to leave. He didn't want to put his family in more danger. Disguised as a Christian with a large crucifix necklace, he made his way to the Thai border.

Refugee officials in Thailand were impressed with the serious young monk. He wasn't concerned about what was going to happen to him, but about what was going to happen to Buddhism. He worried, who would keep the faith?

Within weeks, Kovida was in the U.S. testifying before Congress about the attacks on the monks and briefing the president at the White House. It was a heady introduction to the free world.

But the afterglow from the Washington meetings was fleeting. Refugee agencies resettled Kovida in Oakland, California. He did not know anyone in Oakland. He did not speak English. He found roommates on Craigslist and got work washing dishes. During his time off, he took English classes at a community college. The rest of the time, he studied and read. His bookshelf was filled with biographies of Gandhi, Churchill, Truman, MacArthur, and Lincoln—as well as Aung San Suu Kyi's *Freedom from Fear.* He had large poster of "The Lady" on his wall.

His cultural adjustment included being robbed at gunpoint his first year in Oakland. He was on his way to English class. The robber put a gun to his head and demanded his money. He didn't believe Kovida when he said he didn't have any and searched his book bag. "It was really kind of funny, you know," the monk said.

We kept in touch from time to time by e-mail. Kovida moved from Oakland to Berkeley to work for a medical-supply company. He had to switch his monk's robes for blue jeans and T-shirt. "I have long hair!" he said with a rare laugh, surprised himself by his transformation. Often he worked until 2:30 in the morning so he could get overtime pay. He was still taking college courses, he said. His goal is to get a science degree and return home someday to help young people rebuild the country. "Many people in the villages are so poor, they don't have shoes to go to the school. I would like to provide education programs for them. I want them to know, whatever happens in life, do not give up. If you try hard, it can happen. You can succeed."

Did he think the Saffron Revolution succeeded? "Before the revolution, people did not know where Burma was," he said. "When the Burmese military shot the monks, it really shocked the world. Now they know."

Of the 38 monks who fled to the U.S. after the protests, only five were still functioning as monks after six years. There was not enough density in the American Burmese community to support them; monks could not walk through the streets of Utica or Oakland with their alms bowls like they had in Rangoon. They were in exile 8,500 miles from home.

Many other monks found exile along the Thai border, which had become a second home to more than 140,000 refugees since the 8-8-88 protests. Most lived in overcrowded bamboo cities in the jungle around Mae Sot, waiting for a chance to return home, find work in Malaysia, or, if they were lucky, a ticket to America. By the time of the Saffron Generation, there was a second generation of refugees in the chain of camps that had never lived in Burma. The camps were their country. It was dangerous to go back home. And difficult to go elsewhere.

Gawsita's friend Ashin Issariya, now known as "King Zero," was able to stay a step or two ahead of the military for a year after the crackdown—until two of his helpers were arrested.

His young friends were members of the "Generation Wave" movement, which had been founded by youth in their teens and twenties to support the Saffron Revolution. Generation Wave adopted the logo of an upraised fist with a thumbs-up and used prankish guerrilla tactics such as graffiti to mock the junta. They stuck bumper stickers saying "Change New Government" to cars bearing CNG signs for compressed natural gas. They recorded a protest hip-hop album, which they left in tea shops. And they circulated bootleg copies of anti-government films, including the American action movie *Rambo*, in which actor Sylvester Stallone battled the Burmese military for persecuting Christian villagers in Karen State. The government had banned the film for depicting its soldiers in an unflattering light.

When the two young Generation Wave members were captured, they were beaten and tortured until they revealed that King Zero was in his home village. The monk got word the military was coming for him and fled to the Thai border. He began a new life in the refugee camps, teaching migrant factory workers and establishing libraries. His goal: educate a new generation of Burmese who someday might be able to restore democracy in their country.

King Zero is counting on the border libraries and literacy classes to change the minds of Burmese refugees who think there is nothing they can do about their situation. The main challenge, he said, is that many of the Burmese who are Buddhists rely on reincarnation to improve their lives. They assume the rich elite are making money because they did well in their past lives. At the same time, he said, the poor people believe they are poor because they did not do well in their past life. Rather than make changes in their present life, they simply hope they will have better circumstances in the next life. "The library can change their mind if they read more," King Zero said. "These books changed me."

—w—

Difficult and lonely as exile has been for the Burmese refugees, the hardships faced by the monks taken to prison have been infinitely worse. Some were chained, forced to break stones and dig ditches, seven days a week, dawn to dusk, no breaks. Meals were rationed. The most notorious concoction was called "Briyani." It was a mixture of small stones, un-husked rice paddy, and often mouse feces. Within two to three weeks of prison food, most prisoners lost weight and fell ill. Many developed bruises and abscesses from their leg irons. Few received medical care.

Some of the harshest treatment was reserved for the "mastermind" of the monks' movement, U Gambira.

On the same day that his impassioned opinion piece was published in the *Washington Post* and *The Guardian*, Gambira was arrested at a gas station near Mandalay. He was preparing a speech urging the people to "keep fighting the military dictatorship." Suddenly, Gambira was surrounded by more than a hundred soldiers on motorcycles and in trucks. Within hours, he was in an army camp. He was sentenced to 68 years in prison, including 12 years of hard labor.

Gambira was stripped of his monk's robes, shunted from prison to prison, and continually tortured. He protested by chanting and going on hunger strikes, which only tended to make his punishments worse. Sometimes he was strapped to a chair for weeks at a time, force-fed and beaten on the head. In the evenings, prison guards would come to his cell, put a black bag on his head, stuff a cloth in his mouth, handcuff his wrists and chain his feet to the floor, then hit him repeatedly over the head with wooden batons. He would then be interrogated all night under harsh spotlights.

As a result of his many beatings, Gambira sustained a skull fracture and a traumatic brain injury, which left him with reoccurring headaches. When he was finally released in an amnesty five years after the Saffron Revolution, he was a physical and mental wreck. His face had been battered almost beyond recognition.

Gambira had difficulty finding a doctor to treat him, because most feared government reprisals. He was unable to rejoin the monastic community, because no monastery would accept him. He was unable to seek medical care outside of the country, because he was not allowed official papers for travel. The military had freed him into a limbo with no way out.

With characteristic determination, Gambira attempted to enter the monasteries that had been closed by the military, insisting they had no right to close religious institutions. He was arrested three times the year of his release for trespassing after he repeatedly broke into the locked monasteries. No longer able to function as a monk, Gambira resumed his birth name of Nyi Nyi Lwin. He returned to his home village to live with his mother. He continued to struggle with the damage from his beatings.

For all his troubles, Gambira told reporters he had no regrets about helping launch the 2007 Revolution. "Many monks died and others were sent to prison, but we started a revolution that had a lot of impact. It was a milestone in history."

U Gambira was right: the Saffron Revolution was a milestone in Burmese history. While there had been assaults on the *sangha* before, the consensus was that the 2007 attacks on the monks' marches were the worst, in numbers and ferocity. They were worse than the suppression under the British in the 1800s. They were worse than the crackdowns on political activities in 1988, 1990, 1996, and 2003.

The military regime did not come away from the 2007 attacks unscathed. The merciless crackdown cost the military government any legitimacy it had in the eyes of its citizens and the world. By insisting on the brutal assault instead of pursuing a dialogue, Senior General Than Shwe had crossed the line of human decency. Top leaders in the military were deeply troubled by the role they played. Ordinary soldiers were fearful of the spiritual price they might pay. They knew that brutalizing the clergy was moral suicide. The damage could not be undone by building new pagodas or handing out donations to obedient monasteries.

Weeks after the protests, the military held belated press conferences to claim "foreign elements" had fomented the revolution. In a finale worthy of Gilbert and Sullivan, they insisted they had saved the nation.

Instead, they had exposed their ruthlessness to the world. And introduced a new generation—who had been too young to witness the 8-8-88 violence—to the regime's use of terror against its own population.

The Saffron Revolution proved a turning point. The military was forced to speed up the implementation of its long-promised "Roadmap to

Democracy" as a result. The generals assumed that reviving the stalled constitutional process had three benefits for them: By giving the appearance of change, the regime would stave off international pressure. By providing a framework for continued military rule, the rigged document would protect the generals from repercussions. And by specifying that future national leaders could not be married to a foreigner or have children with a foreign passport, the new constitution would keep Aung San Suu Kyi from power.

Or so the generals thought.

Within months, there would be more dramatic events that tarnished the regime's image. And Aung San Suu Kyi would demonstrate a staying power that the generals had underestimated.

CHAPTER FIFTEEN

THE KILLER STORM

> "The cyclone was one of the deadliest storms in recorded history. It blew away 700,000 homes in the delta. It killed three-fourths of the livestock, sank half the fishing fleet and salted a million acres of rice paddies with its seawater surges."
>
> —*The New York Times*

Burma was still in shock from the junta's attacks on the monks when a fresh hell stormed in.

Cyclone Nargis slammed into the southern Delta just eight months after the Saffron Revolution was beaten down and locked up. It was the worst natural disaster in the history of the country.

The powerful cyclone hit on May 2, just as monsoon season was beginning. According to government figures, more than 146,000 lives were lost in the storm. Another 56,000 were missing and presumed dead.

Aid workers believe the toll was considerably higher than the Burmese government reported. They estimate as many as 300,000 lives were lost, possibly half a million or more. That would make Nargis one of the deadliest cyclones ever recorded. The full extent of the loss may never be known, because the military regime simply stopped keeping a tally of the casualties. The generals were afraid there would be political ramifications if they acknowledged the staggering number of lives lost.

The generals had good reason to fear a negative response. Many of the deaths could have been prevented. There was some doubt about the cyclone's direction and force as it stalled in the Bay of Bengal, but the Asian Disaster Preparedness Center (ADPC) maintained that it had provided the Burmese government with model forecasts of the storm, with accurate predictions of its landfall and strength, *seven days before the cyclone hit*. Indian authorities became so concerned by the regime's lack of preparation that they made a point of directly informing the Burmese leaders that the deadly cyclone was bearing down on them *48 hours in advance*. The head of the Indian Meteorological Department, B. P. Yadav, later said, "We continuously updated authorities in Myanmar and on April 30 we even provided them [with] details of the likely route, speed and locations of landfall [of the cyclone]."

With some impressive shoe-leather journalism, writer Emma Larkin tracked down the head of Burma's Department of Meteorology, Htun Lwin, who apparently had tried on his own to get out a warning with his limited resources. He said he tried to telephone authorities on Haing Gyi Island, the first land in the cyclone's path. In its post-mortem report, Human Rights Watch confirmed that Htun Lwin had warned in a local Burmese-language newspaper interview the day the storm hit that the winds could approach 160 m.p.h. The International Federation of Red Cross and Red Crescent Societies (IFRC) also issued a storm warning on their own that day.

Yet inexplicably, the Burmese government did not issue a wider alert or warning. Human Rights Watch concluded that better warnings from the Burmese state-run television and radio media, relayed to radio stations abroad that had large Burmese audiences—such as BBC Burmese Service, Radio Free Asia, Democratic Voice of Burma, and Radio Free Asia—could have given some Delta communities several more hours to reach higher land or seek hard-walled shelters.

"Heavy rain expected'" was all that the regime's state-owned media reported as the killer storm barreled toward Burma with peak winds of 135 m.p.h. Rather than warn people in the path to evacuate or seek shelter, the generals looked after their own interests. They moved their assets—cars, planes, cash—to their luxurious redoubt in Naypyidaw and hunkered down. Some family members reportedly were flown to safety out of the country.

Most of the villagers in the Delta did not know what hit them. The majority lived in bamboo houses tied together with grass. Their homes were dotted through a watery archipelago of low-lying islands connected by channels. As in Venice, but worlds away, residents of the Delta travel almost everywhere in shallow boats.

Cyclone Nargis crashed into the Delta at midnight, when it was dark. Twenty inches of rain hammered down in a few hours. The wind was howling so loud that villagers could not hear their own screams for help. Then they were hit with a 12-foot wall of water. Workers sleeping in small huts near the rice paddies tried to dash to their villages, only to run into the tsunami of water. Some 40 percent of the dead and missing were children, swept away.

Twenty-six-year-old Than Lwin told the *New York Times* that when the water tore apart his house, his family rushed to their small boat in a desperate attempt to get away. The boat capsized in the turbulence. Than Lwin struggled for his life in the rising river of water and found himself propelled past the tops of trees, like a plastic bottle in a stream. Six harrowing hours later, when the storm had passed through, he was washed onto an island miles from his home. All his clothes had been ripped off by the raging waters. He and some other survivors found a boat that was still usable and paddled with their hands to the mainland, dodging floating bodies and the carcasses of oxen. When he finally made it back to his village, Than Lwin discovered that only 600 people had survived out of the 7,000 who had lived there. His parents and brothers and sisters were never seen again. He assumed that their bodies had flowed out to sea, along with thousands of others.

The Labutta township alone was reported to have 80,000 dead, and nearby Bogale 10,000. Coastal villages in the path of the storm, such as Hi Gyi and Maw Kyune, were blown entirely away. There was nothing left but bare ground. Nearly two million people in the region were left homeless before dawn. More than a thousand ancient temples were destroyed. Steel electric poles were bent at a 45-degree angle, like drinking straws.

By sunrise, the cyclone was roaring into the city of Rangoon with 81 m.p.h. winds. More roofs were taken than lives, including chunks of the roof on Aung San Suu Kyi's house. As rains poured through her ceiling, the Nobel laureate ran back and forth in her house, placing pots and pans under the streaming water. The military later sent work crews to repair her damaged gate—which kept her locked in—but did not repair her roof. It would continue to leak for the next two years.

Nearly every home in Rangoon was damaged, and 75 percent of the trees were blown down. Sewage erupted into the streets. "It looks like the end of the world here," one resident reported.

Burma was in a state of shock. But what followed made matters even worse.

Senior General Than Shwe did not appear for two weeks or issue a statement. There were no comforting words for the shattered nation, not even Alexander Haig–like assurances, "I am in control here." Police and soldiers were sent to the Delta region, not to assist, but to block the roads so members of the news media and international observers could not see the devastation. A CNN reporter was hounded for a week and deported. A *Time* magazine reporter was kicked out. A *New York Times* reporter had to hide in the bottom of a boat to slip by the barriers.

Despite the blockades, news seeped out about the scale of the disaster. The United Nations and aid agencies began mobilizing to help. The regime told them no, thank you. They were not welcome. No visas would be granted for international aid organizations to enter the country. U.N. Secretary General Ban Ki-moon tried repeatedly to call Than Shwe personally to persuade him to allow the assistance, but Than Shwe did not answer his calls.

When it became apparent that the government was not about to render assistance, everyday people—hotel waiters, taxi drivers, shopkeepers—took action. They packed their cars with clothing and food and headed down to the Delta on muddy back roads. Priests at St. Mary's cathedral gathered up everything they could find to help, plastic sheeting for shelter, blankets, water. Monasteries opened their doors to refugees—one small monastery took in 900 people.

AIDS hospice director Phyu Phyu Thin came out of hiding to take part in the cyclone-relief efforts, making multiple trips to the hardest-hit townships. The comedian Zarganar coordinated food drives with 88 Generation activists. The government may have lost touch with basic humanity, but the Burmese people had not.

One of those who stepped forward was the celebrated actor Kyaw Thu, who mobilized his charitable Free Funeral Society to help bury the many dead. For two decades, the actor had won accolades for playing heroes. Then he became one by helping the monks in the Saffron Revolution and the victims of Cyclone Nargis. One of the most successful leading men in Burma, Kyaw Thu had starred in over 200 films and directed six films, winning several Burmese Academy Awards.

When the government kept pressing him to make propaganda films supporting their attacks on ethnic minorities, he refused. He was shunned from future awards after that. Kyaw Thu began using his prominence for social work. He took over leadership of the Free Funeral Society, then started a health clinic, a library, a school, and vocational training.

In 2007, he was put in jail seven days for helping the monks in the Saffron Revolution. When I interviewed him in 2013, he related with a chuckle that while he in jail, he was able to hear police in the next room training snitches how to eavesdrop on the democracy leaders and report their plans to the authorities. He could also hear the sound of inmates being tortured until the police turned up a radio to muffle the noise.

Because of his help for the monks in 2007, Kyaw Thu was barred from any future work in cinema. He said he was content to continue his humanitarian work because the need was so great—there were "more and more people" coming to him for help. A longtime admirer of Aung San Suu Kyi, he proudly displayed one of the artworks she made in captivity in his office.

When the cyclone struck, Kyaw Thu used his funeral organization to raise the equivalent of $400,000 for supplies. Not only that, he also went into some of the worst-hit areas to distribute food and water. Cyclone victims often were surprised to see that the handsome man in a shaggy goatee who was handing out rice was once the Brad Pitt of Burma.

The volunteers and reporters who got past the military blockades to help the cyclone victims came back with horrific stories of death and destruction.

Dead bodies were strewn everywhere, rotting in fields and waterways. One reporter counted 66 bodies in a canal before he had to look away.

People had little or no food or clean water. They had no shelter and no medicine. Delta residents were starting to die, not from the force of the storm, but from starvation and illness.

The question of the hour was, *where was the government?*

As a trishaw driver in Rangoon complained to the BBC: "Where are all those uniformed people who are always ready to beat civilians?" Why weren't the security forces bringing in water and restoring electricity?

World leaders started calling for the military regime to allow more aid from abroad. U.N. Secretary General Ban Ki-moon expressed "deep concern" and "immense frustration" with the unacceptably slow response by the government. Than Shwe still would not return his calls or answer his letters. United Kingdom Prime Minister Gordon Brown accused the junta of turning the disaster into a "man-made catastrophe." He considered violating Burmese sovereignty by authorizing forced airdrops to deliver aid.

Three of the most influential women in America—First Lady Laura Bush, Senator Hillary Clinton, and House Speaker Nancy Pelosi—were among the first to speak up. Three days after the cyclone hit, Mrs. Bush took the unprecedented step of convening a press conference in the White House Press Room. The conference marked the first time that a First Lady had presided at the White House briefing room, which is generally used for official pronouncements by the president or senior aides. Those who did not know how involved Mrs. Bush had become in Burma issues were surprised when she chastised the Burmese government in blunt terms for its "inept" response and for not informing its people of the impending disaster. Mrs. Bush implored the regime to admit U.S. State Department disaster-response teams that had been barred from entering the country.

Her attempt to dramatize the urgent need for action seemed to backfire at first. Some in the American media criticized her remarks as unwarranted and untimely. It was not widely known at the time that the junta had not responded to the explicit 48-hour warning in any kind of meaningful way. While the generals had issued a public appeal for donations of billions in cash, they were doing everything they could to thwart access to relief teams on the ground. And would seek ways to profit personally from the donations.

Senator Hillary Clinton, who was campaigning for president, made a statement on the same day urging the regime to "put aside politics." She appealed to the government to allow the global community to bring in aid, calling the disaster "a tremendous human tragedy and humanitarian challenge." House Speaker Nancy Pelosi urged the regime to "provide for the basic survival needs of the Burmese people."

With international pressure mounting, the regime made small concessions to deflect the criticism. A few planeloads of aid were allowed in, first from neighbors such as Thailand, India, and Bangladesh. But there were soon reports that supplies were being pilfered by authorities. Two planeloads of high-energy biscuits from the World Food Program were stolen by soldiers, enough to feed 95,000 people. Tin sheeting intended for roofing was sold at inflated prices in the market instead of being delivered.

International frustration with the situation grew so intense that by May 7, France even suggested ignoring Burma's national sovereignty by invoking the U.N. "Responsibility to Protect" clause. Under that special clause, assistance could be provided to citizens *without* their government's approval. Other countries dismissed the idea, claiming the clause was only intended to apply during a time of war. Some countries were fearful of the precedent; they certainly didn't want the U.N. interfering with their own mistreatment of their citizens, rain or shine.

But the French had cut to the heart of the matter: *Didn't the Burmese government have a responsibility to protect its own people? Didn't the community of nations have a moral obligation to save lives when a country would not? How could the U.N. stand by when the Burmese leaders committed manslaughter by neglect?*

It was uncharted legal territory; for lack of unified support, the debate on applying Responsibility to Protect (R2P) to the cyclone relief faded from the agenda.

The Burmese government retaliated against the French by accusing France of deploying an amphibious assault ship on the Burmese coast. The French U.N. ambassador pointed out the ship in question was bringing 1,500 tons of badly needed relief supplies. He warned that the regime's refusal to allow aid into the country "could lead to a true crime against humanity."

~

While that debate was going on at the United Nations, a fierce internal debate was under way inside the Burmese regime about the cyclone response. According to diplomatic sources, General Maung Aye, the second most powerful general next to Than Shwe, and a hard-liner against dissent, reportedly was outraged that foreigners would dare interfere in Burma's internal matters. But some of the other army leaders felt that a humanitarian response was needed. They had readied a four-division-strong rescue team to deploy to the Delta, but were ordered to stand down by Generals Than Shwe and Maung Aye.

Prime Minister Thein Sein, who had been put in charge of the disaster response, and the eight ministers on the national rescue committee were said to be increasingly concerned and desperate. Thein Sein privately warned that the number of casualties could reach 300,000 if water, food, and medicine were not delivered immediately. Yet the aid continued to be delayed by higher-ups.

The lack of action should have been particularly frustrating for the prime minister because the cyclone destroyed an area he knew intimately. Thein Sein was born in Kyonku, a small Irrawaddy Delta village near Hainggyi Island. His parents were landless farmers; his father also made a living loading cargo onto boats at the river jetty and weaving bamboo mats. His mother was a homemaker who helped run a small tea shop owned by the family. Thein Sein knew how desperately poor most people already were. He knew most of the streets were unpaved. He knew that oxen and buffalo were the farmer's only assets, their life savings on four legs. And he now knew that people in the path of the cyclone—including his home village—had lost what little they had.

Not being able to provide more assistance—and having to take the blame as the head of the recovery effort for decisions made by others—was said to have troubled Thein Sein. But as a career military man, he knew well not to question authority. The day would come when he could do more on his own.

U.S. diplomats put the blame for the delays squarely on Senior General Than Shwe. One classified cable published by Wikileaks said, "Than Shwe's isolation and paranoia know no bounds. All fingers point to him as the obstacle to delivering the humanitarian assistance the Burmese so desperately need, much like he is the obstacle to an inclusive political dialogue.

"Our many contacts are visibly distraught as they watch Burma's humanitarian catastrophe worsen by the day because of the intransigence of Than Shwe. The question is, who is brave enough to shunt Than Shwe aside? Most Burmese tell us no one. Other senior officials may passively sit while thousands needlessly die rather than challenge Than Shwe."

While the junta's tug-of-war with other countries continued, three fourths of the cyclone survivors still had not received any assistance. Heavy monsoon rains were pouring down. Survivors of the storm huddled under plastic sheeting for shelter. Many were barefoot in water up to their ankles, their sandals long lost. Save the Children International estimated that 30,000 children in the cyclone area were already suffering severe acute malnourishment, the most serious level of hunger. When children reach that stage, the agency warned, "They can die in a matter of days."

Yet as precious days slipped by, the man-made bottleneck on aid continued. By May 11, the United Nations World Food Program said only one visa had been approved of 16 requested. The aid group World Vision said it had requested 20 visas but received two. Doctors Without Borders, the French medical aid group, said it was still awaiting approval of dozens of visa applications for technical support staff. Paul Risley, a spokesman for the World Food Program, estimated that the volume of aid being allowed into the country amounted to one tenth of what was needed.

By May 19, the U.N. Secretary General had grown so frustrated by the delays that he flew to Burma to make his case in person. Ban Ki-moon met with Senior General Than Shwe for two hours. The Secretary General came away with the understanding that the general had agreed to let more international aid workers in, regardless of nationality. The same week, Burma's neighbors in the Association of Southeast Asian Nations (ASEAN) brokered a deal with the general to coordinate aid through a Tripartite Core Group (TCG) that included ASEAN, the government of Burma, and the U.N. Once other Asian countries became part of the process, access gradually improved, though many restrictions and much red tape remained in place. Some of those lucky enough to get visas into the country discovered that they were not allowed to leave the city of Rangoon. Assistance from ships or helicopters was still barred, although cargo planes were landing under strict military controls.

The regime then made a series of clumsy attempts to apply its own PR spin to the crisis. The government dismissed aid complaints as "a storm of rumors designed to deal a devastating blow to our country." According to a commentary in the *New Light of Myanmar*, the junta's mouthpiece newspaper, "The rumors are invented and circulated by certain Western countries and internal and external ax-handlers." The paper said, "In other words, it is just a scheme conspired by a crafty tiger that is desperate to eat the flesh and the fox that is waiting for leftovers."

The New Light of Myanmar also proclaimed that the Burmese people did not need "chocolate bars from (the) international community." The newspaper maintained that people could easily catch fish in the fields and ditches and that "large edible frogs are abundant."

Leaders and editorial writers around the world were taken aback. In the midst of a humanitarian crisis, Burma's government was saying: Let them eat frogs.

At the same time, the *Los Angeles Times* was reporting that families in the devastated area were forced to sift through rice paddies littered with corpses for food. The *Times* reporter wrote that starving people were scooping up the reeking muck in their bare hands "like prospectors working claims," fingering through the contaminated goo for grains of un-milled rice left by the cyclone.

Diarrhea and dysentery and cholera began breaking out because of the lack of clean drinking water. The government's response on radio was, "Eat fresh fruit, use clean toilets, and dispose of your rubbish. Also look out for mosquitoes and snakes."

According to Associated Press news stories, the junta also was modifying donated aid from other countries to make it look as if it had come from the military regime. State-run television ran footage of Senior General Than Shwe handing out disaster relief with the names of generals written over the names of the actual donors.

Eventually, the military set up more than 400 relief camps, which appeared to be clean and well-run. Disturbing reports later surfaced that when international visitors or reporters left the sites, cyclone victims were often evicted and forced back to their devastated villages, where there was nothing for them. Some of the cyclone survivors reportedly were forced to do hard labor in exchange for food in the camps. Relief workers complained that storm victims from ethnic minority groups, such as the ethnic Christians from Karen State, who made up 60 percent of the Delta population, often were denied care by the government.

—∾—

Thousands of children were orphaned overnight by Cyclone Nargis. Some of their poignant stories were captured by Democratic Voice of Burma cameramen who slipped into the Delta:

Ten-year-old Ye Pyint lost both of his parents to the cyclone. He became the surrogate parent to his six-year-old sister and three-year-old brother. A gap-toothed little boy in a checked blue shirt too big for him, Ye Pyint was surviving by trying to catch fish or crabs. When he couldn't catch anything, he had to "buy food from the market without paying." He hoped to repay the money some day. His mother's body was never found. Someone told him they saw his father's body in the rubbish on the beach.

Thirteen-year-old Silver Moo, a member of the Christian Karen ethnic minority, was one of 140,000 children sent to the crowded refugee camps along the Thai-Burma border. There was no place for her elsewhere. Her mother, father, two sisters, and younger brother had drowned. The memory of that night still haunted her. "The water was rising more and more, and when the house leaned over my mother stood up. She said, 'Pray to God because he listens to the prayers of children.' Soon, the house couldn't stand any more and collapsed, and we all had to swim," she remembered. "I kept calling out, but nobody could hear me. I kept shouting and shouting but nobody came. I closed my eyes and floated away."

The desperate circumstances of two other young girls typified the difficulties facing the thousands of new orphans. When they were first orphaned, 16-year-old Khine and her 14-year-old sister Hlaing scavenged for food. Starving, they took a job pushing a heavy roller at a military-owned salt field. They made a three-hour trip on foot every day to push the big roller for 10 hours, earning just enough to buy rice and vegetables.

Despite the ongoing obstacles, international organizations managed to get more aid into the Delta. Heroic efforts were made in wretched conditions—90-degree heat, 100-percent humidity. Groups that braved the elements included Rotary International's Shelterbox, the British Merlin health charity, UNICEF, CARE, Doctors Without Borders, Red Cross, the World Food Program, the Adventist Development and Relief Agency (ADRA), and Save the Children, among others. Relief workers from Texas worked side by side with doctors from India. Monks who had been hiding from the military were now providing more care for the people than the military.

Aung San Suu Kyi's NLD party was in the trenches and in the rain as well. Most of the NLD offices had been shuttered since the deadly Depayin attack on Suu Kyi's convoy in 2003, but the party's network of people was still intact. Organizing relief in the Delta breathed new life into the NLD ranks—and reaffirmed the party's message that major change in the government was needed. The wheel of karma was beginning to turn for the party.

Yet because of the long delay getting workers and helicopters into the devastated area, more than half of the estimated 2.4 million people affected still had not received assistance a full month after the cyclone struck. Throughout that time, a U.S. naval task force consisting of the USS *Essex* and three other vessels had been steaming in circles off the Burma coast. For weeks, the Pacific Command task force had been ready to deliver 250,000 pounds of relief material a day, by plane, helicopter, and amphibious landing craft. On June 5, after 15 requests to deliver the life-saving assistance, the American carrier group left with its aid undelivered. France's *Mistral* and Britain's HMS *Westminster* also withdrew after being refused permission to operate. The French *Mistral* alone carried 1,500 tons of aid—the equivalent of 30 cargo planes. That shipment would have provided water purification tablets, rice, tents, and mosquito nets for 100,000 people, and shelter for 60,000 people.

Instead of allowing the ships' rescue teams into the Delta, the Burmese regime turned to people it could control: its business cronies. Leading businessmen who had benefited from sweetheart deals with the government were ordered to help distribute aid—in return for valuable concessions on land and future business contracts. Instead of trained disaster workers distributing food and medicine, airline employees were.

All donated goods had to be channeled through the military or their business minions. That sometimes that meant inferior rice ruined by the storm was substituted for cyclone victims while the donated rice was sold on the market at inflated prices. One local official in the Delta told the *New York Times* that the four bags of rice allotted to what was left of his village were rotten: "Even the pigs and dogs wouldn't eat it."

Rice, the staple of life for so many, was in short supply. The cyclone had hit the Delta region—the "rice bowl" of Burma—during prime growing season. Rice in the warehouses was flooded and ruined, along with 65 percent of the country's rice paddies. That meant there was little or no rice available just when people needed it most. But that didn't stop the generals and their cronies from profiting on rice sales. Rice traders confirmed to the U.S. embassy that a company owned by several military cronies was exporting 50,000 metric tons of quality rice to Sri Lanka as soon as loading cranes could be cleared from the debris in the harbor. The generals, who generally got a percentage of such deals, were helping expedite the shipment.

Later reports would confirm that instead of seeing the tragic human loss in the Delta, the generals saw dollar signs. The regime called for the world to provide a stunning $11.7 billion in cash donations for reconstruction—while providing little of its own.

The United Nations later reported that $10 million of aid intended for cyclone survivors was skimmed off by banks run by the military junta. The scam involved forcing the U.N. to buy the local currency, the kyat, at a government-fixed rate, rather than the market rate. At that time a dollar bought around K1,100, while the official rate was only K880. The regime banks pocketed the difference. John Holmes, the under-secretary-general for humanitarian affairs at the U.N., estimated that 15 per cent of aid transferred in this way had been lost.

What made the junta's grab for humanitarian money all the more galling was the subsequent Wikileaks release of U.S. diplomatic cables revealing that only months after the cyclone, Senior General Than Shwe was pursuing the possibility of buying the Manchester United Football team in

Britain. At the suggestion of a favored grandson, Than Shwe was prepared to offer $1 billion. That would have given the dictator a 56 per cent controlling stake in the football club. The general decided the expenditure could look bad, so he opted to create a Burmese league—and ordered business cronies to pay for the teams.

Although it was impossible to obtain accurate figures on how much the Burmese government actually spent on cyclone relief, the Burma Campaign U.K. estimated that the junta spent only $5 million of its own money. That was a meager sum considering the government had an estimated $3.5 billion in foreign reserves at the time and was receiving $150 million a month in gas-export revenues. Critics in the country complained that the junta's Delta spending was less than the amount that Than Shwe's daughter received in wedding gifts.

In contrast, Britain, the European Union, the United States, and Australia—who were generally considered enemies by the junta—were among the top donors coming to Burma's assistance, along with China, which had substantial investments at stake in Burma. According to the *New York Times*, by fall 2008, international donors had provided some $240 million, or about $100 for every person who survived Cyclone Nargis. The problem was, all the donations weren't passed along by the military.

Months after Cyclone Nargis struck, U.N. helicopters were reaching some storm survivors with aid for the first time.

When I visited the Delta region a year after the cyclone, the region was still ravaged. The wooden skeletons of fishing boats were piled in a jumble on the banks of the Irrawaddy tributaries, too shattered to be rebuilt. Toddy palm trees stood like toothpicks against the sky. Here and there, a shiny new tin roof could be seen on houses. Some new structures were under construction with fresh wooden beams instead of bamboo.

My boat driver waved with his bare arm to an area along the riverbank with nothing but short grass on it. "That was the Kansa Village," he said. "All gone." Leik Kyun village up ahead was also washed away. "People climbed coconut trees to escape," he said. "They gone, too." His family had taken refuge in a monastery but lost what little they owned. The government was offering installment loans so people could buy new boats, but they could not afford the loans. The boatman said that people were no longer starving. but they had "no hope." They were poor, but not insensible to misfortune. He had a small clutch of flowers tied to the bow of the battered old boat as a gift to the Nat spirits to ward off evil.

In village after village, the story was the same: If they had received assistance at all, it had come from non-government sources. In one village surrounded by splintered trees and large mounds of unwelcome mud, people pointed to a new road—constructed by a Japanese foundation and a group of actors. They said Senior General Than Shwe himself came to their village with TV crews several months after the storm to publicize the junta's work to restore the Delta region. This was awkward, they tittered, because the government actually had not done anything to help them. They did not dare tell the truth while the camera crews were filming. The senior general brought the minister of energy with him to send the message that the government was working to restore electricity to villages. "But we have never had electricity!" one woman said. The crowd broke into laughter, some hiding their smiles behind their hands. "They promised they would bring electricity for us. But they never did. You can see," she said, motioning to the bamboo home a few feet away. There was an open wood fire on the ground and a bamboo latrine in the back with an ingenious architecture of ladders and chutes, but no electricity.

The memory of the cyclone was still raw. One young man had become a hero by carrying his 83-year-old grandmother on his back to safety as the water rose. Most others weren't so lucky. One woman wept openly at the memory of finding her daughter dead in a tree.

Like most Burmese, the villagers smiled reflexively, but their faces showed the strain of the last year. The worst thing now was the ghosts, several said. There were still ghosts of the dead all around them. The dozen or so people who were gathered around all shook their heads yes, yes in agreement. The ghosts came every night in their dreams.

They explained that many of the people from their village had been washed away. Because their bodies were never recovered, they did not receive a proper funeral—and a proper funeral is an intrinsic part of the country's culture. To their horror, the bodies of strangers from other villages, more than they could even count, had washed up in their village and did not receive proper rites with their own families. Many bodies were still out there somewhere in the tall green rushes and mangrove forests, they said, in limbo between two worlds.

At night, they said, they hear the cries and shouts of the ghosts, who now have no place to go in death. Again, the young and old nodded their heads; they had heard the blood-curdling sounds of the dead, the wails, the sobs.

Other journalists as well as relief workers encountered similar stories about cyclone ghosts, along with widespread signs of depression. Many people were so traumatized that they could no longer eat or speak. The *Seattle Times* told of a young woman who lost five family members, including her mother, father, and a baby. "She didn't speak anymore," the writer said. "Her eyes were not moving."

The *New York Times* reported that people in a village where half the population of 200 was killed in the storm were scarred deeply by the death around them. One farmer confided that a ghost appears to him at night, every night. The ghost, he said, throws rice in his face. Another 81-year-old survivor said she still heard a girl shouting for help. When she goes to look, no one is there.

The name Nargis meant "daffodil" in Urdu, but to the people in the Delta it meant the sound of terror. Nargis was a name they would not forget.

In the aftermath, the question that remained unanswered was, why did the junta wait so callously to come to the aid of the helpless and dying? There were three likely reasons.

First, the ruling generals' paranoia about being invaded by foreigners was as real to them as the ghosts were to the villagers. The generals had never been comfortable having foreigners in their country. Why would they invite in hundreds of people who might stir up a revolt?

One of the primary reasons the generals had relocated the capital from Rangoon to Naypyidaw was that they feared an invasion, from the coast in particular. A fortuneteller had warned them an attack was coming. The seer also predicted Rangoon would be subject to street disturbances and a horrific storm. After the monks took to the streets in the Saffron Revolution and Cyclone Nargis hit, the generals feared an attack was imminent. When an American amphibious assault ship sailed into Burmese territorial waters for humanitarian purposes, the regime was convinced that the U.S. was prepared to invade. After all, the seer had told them so.

Senior General Than Shwe, who was in ill health and 75 at the time, was especially fearful of being arrested and held accountable for his crimes against the people. U.S. embassy officials reported in diplomatic cables—later published by Wikileaks—that no high-level government officials dared to frankly describe the full scope of the disaster to the ill-tempered Senior General. "Unpleasant pictures in the media reportedly make the Senior General retreat even further into isolation. According to our contacts, Than Shwe is above all concerned with saving face and holding on to power. He does not want the Burma Army to be seen as needing assistance to deliver relief and would rather let thousands of Burmese die than accept massive international assistance. . . . Our contacts emphasized that Than Shwe remained worried about a U.S. invasion and determined to hold on to power for the last few years of his life," the dispatch said.

Secondly, the military rulers—who were from the majority Burman ethnic group and were predominantly Buddhist—had a deep-seated antipathy toward the people in the Delta region, who were from the Karen ethnic group and were predominantly Christian. There was no sympathy in Naypyidaw for them.

A post-mortem on the cyclone compiled by the Johns Hopkins School of Public Health, *After the Storm: Voices from the Delta*, confirmed that "discrimination existed in the distribution of aid to cyclone victims, particularly in the Irrawaddy Delta, which had significant non-Burman and non-Buddhist populations." Relief workers told of Christian victims being pushed away from rescue boats by soldiers or being left out of aid deliveries.

Benedict Rogers, a journalist and human-rights advocate, wrote that one widely held view in the Delta was: "The junta saw the storm doing their dirty work for them, eliminating a proportion of an ethnic group they had been trying to eliminate for years." Rogers said that some Delta survivors pointed to the fact that General Than Shwe had been the regional commander in the Irrawaddy Delta in the early 1980s, and had supervised attacks against the Karen insurgency at that time. Rogers wrote, "In 1991, Than Shwe presided over a military offensive ironically called 'Operation Storm,' in which several hundred Karen were killed. In some villages, all the young men were taken away, tortured, and executed."

In that light, the junta's neglect of the Karen cyclone victims in the Delta was not much different than their destruction of ethnic villages in the ethnic Kachin, Chin, and Shan areas in other parts of the country. In the generals' eyes, it all served to weaken their perceived enemies and strengthen majority Burman control.

And third, Than Shwe was determined not to let the cyclone interfere with his plans to hold a national vote on the constitution May 10, a week after the cyclone. Ramming through the approval was his life insurance policy: the constitution guaranteed that no Burmese officials would be held liable for their actions. And as Than Shwe had confided to Indonesian president Yudhoyono during a visit, he was determined NOT to appear before an international tribunal.

"We have heard from many that Than Shwe is tired and wants to step aside, but fears for his family's financial future. We will not be able to persuade him directly, or through close advisers to step aside unless we are willing to offer him guaranteed protection. He fears democracy because he fears retribution," embassy officials wrote before the constitution vote.

The rigged constitution would allow Than Shwe to retire without retribution because it had been carefully crafted to perpetuate military control:

- It gave a National Defense and Security Council (NDSC), largely composed of generals, final oversight of the president and the head of the armed forces. The commander in chief of the military was granted more appointees than the president, which meant hard-line generals were in charge of the nation's top officials, not the other way around.
- The NDSC was given the right to suspend democratic freedoms in case of an emergency. This meant any civil unrest could be used as an excuse to declare martial law.
- It required that all top leaders in the future must have experience with military affairs—presumably ruling out most democracy activists.

Section 59 was widely regarded as Than Shwe's revenge on Aung San Suu Kyi. At last, he had found a way to deny Suu Kyi her family destiny by making her ineligible to become her country's leader.

While she was under house arrest, Aung San Suu Kyi had continued offering to meet with the generals to begin a dialogue that could lead to reconciliation.

In 2007, junta chief Senior Gen. Than Shwe said he would hold talks with Suu Kyi only if she publicly agreed to a set of conditions. Those conditions included that Suu Kyi abandon her "confrontational" positions on political issues and stop her support for international sanctions against the regime—an indication that the sanctions were hurting them.

Aung San Suu Kyi found those conditions unsupportable. And so did the United Nations and the United States.

In 2009, Suu Kyi asked to meet junta leader Senior General Than Shwe in several letters, saying she wanted to work with his government in the interests of the country. In one letter, she stated she would work with Western countries and the junta to bring about the lifting of sanctions.

The junta responded in a newspaper commentary that her letters were dishonest, designed to tarnish the image of the ruling government, and putting all the blame on the government.

Than Shwe then criticized her for allowing her letter offering to meet to be reported in the media. He refused to meet with her.

Although many in the country considered Than Shwe to be colorless and witless, "a toad in uniform," he had managed to outmaneuver all his competitors with cold-blooded skill. He had steamrollered the "Roadmap to Democracy" forward by shutting out the opposition. Critics either were barred from the constitutional convention sessions or ignored when they could attend.

As Debbie Stothard, the director of the pro-democracy Altsean group, put it, "The Burmese military has organized a game where only one team is allowed to play and there is only one goal post."

After the sham constitution had been stage-managed, the generals scheduled a sham vote. A national referendum set for May 10, only days after Cyclone Nargis hit. When democracy activists tried to protest peacefully in April by wearing T-shirts with the single word "No" on them, more than 70 people were arrested for interfering with the polling.

In the weeks before the referendum, the front page of the state press was headlined "Let's Vote Yes for National Interest." Bouncy pop songs urging people to vote "yes" were played on radio and TV.

The junta's plan to go ahead with the vote immediately after the cyclone—while simultaneously obstructing aid deliveries—drew widespread international criticism. The only concession made was delaying the vote until May 25 in the areas that had been severely affected by the storm, such as Rangoon and the Irrawaddy Delta. The rest of the country would vote on May 10.

On the day before the election, a public poll conducted by the Mizzima news agency showed that 71 percent of those surveyed did not know what the proposed constitution included.

On election day, the full weight of the government was put into getting the referendum approved. Soldiers were sent to polling places instead of helping with relief efforts. Cyclone survivors who had sought refuge in schools were forced out into the rain so the buildings could be used as polling places.

No international election observers were allowed in to monitor the process, but U.S. embassy political officers visited numerous polling stations and solicited feedback from trusted sources. There were widespread indications that the voting had been neither free nor fair:

- Police Special Branch forces with radios monitored who entered polling places at some locations and some took photos of voters' faces. In other locations, referendum officials photographed and videotaped voters.
- Ballot-counters accepted wads of "Yes" ballots clearly marked with the same hand.
- Many voters in Chin State and Shan State were given ballots that had already been marked in favor of the constitution.
- Government officials went to some homes and ordered a family member to fill out the "Yes" ballot for everyone else.
- Polls closed several hours early in numerous locations and voters were told that officials cast their ballots on their behalf.

Five days after the election, the military government reported that 99 percent of the electorate had turned out to vote in the referendum and that 92.4 percent had approved the constitution. The government declared victory even before voters in Rangoon and the Delta had their say. The generals had kept their iron grip on the country, but forfeited any remaining regard in the international community.

"The regime's announcement that the draft constitution was approved comes as no surprise," Chargé d'Affaires Shari Villarosa cabled to Washington. "The massive margin of victory they claimed, however, demonstrates how politically tone-deaf Than Shwe is. Few anticipated the referendum would be free and fair. But now it seems Than Shwe does not even care about passing the laugh test."

The government quickly turned its attention to locking up its opponents. In June, authorities arrested 22 people for providing assistance to the cyclone victims—even though the junta had previously stated that private donors could do so.

Those arrested included the comedian Zarganar, who had recruited more than 400 volunteers to help in the Delta. He was sentenced to 45 years imprisonment for providing unauthorized aid and for criticizing the government's response to the crisis in the media. Officials also searched the comedian's home and found a cache of videos, including DVDs of Than Shwe's daughter's opulent wedding; the banned Sylvestor Stallone movie *Rambo 4*, in which the action hero battles the Burmese military; and footage of the damage caused by Cyclone Nargis. As a result, Zarganar was sentenced to an additional 14 years for alleged crimes such as disrespecting the government, defaming religion, and illegal use of video communications.

In some democracy movements, it has been the poets and playwrights who have captured the public's imagination and led the war of ideas, but in Burma, it has often been comedians who have often articulated the issues, like the Moustache Brothers and Zarganar.

Zarganar, who attended the elite Methodist English High School in Rangoon, trained as a dentist but discovered that his true calling was in tweaking the military regime. He changed his name from Maung Thura to the pseudonym "Zarganar," which means "Tweezers." With his bald head and bushy dark eyebrows that looked like big Velcro strips on his brow, the comedian became instantly recognizable. He regaled the crowds that congregated at General Hospital in the early days of the democracy movement and became known as the Charlie Chaplin of Burma. One of his most popular jibes was that in order to have their teeth fixed, Burmese always have to travel abroad—not because the Burmese dentists weren't competent, but because no one dared to open their mouths at home.

The ruling generals did not share Zarganar's sense of humor and relentlessly persecuted him. He was first arrested in October 1988 and held for six months after making fun of the government. Two years later, he was detained again after impersonating General Saw Maung, who was head of the military government at the time, in front of a crowd of thousands. This time he was sentenced to five years in prison. Held in solitary confinement in a tiny cell, Zarganar began to write poetry. Forbidden to read and write in prison, he had to scratch his poems on his cell floor using a piece of pottery, then committed them to memory. Following his release in March 1994, Zarganar was banned from performing in public, but he continued to make tapes and videos, which were strictly censored by the authorities.

In 1996, after speaking out against censorship to a foreign journalist, he was banned from performing his work altogether and even denied the freedom to write and publish. Undaunted, Zarganar continued to spread his jokes and poetry by word of mouth, until his re-arrest on September 25, 2007 for his support of the monks demonstrating in Rangoon. By this time, however, he had gained international recognition for his efforts and a barrage of appeals helped to secure his release a month later. When Nargis struck, the comedian went immediately to help. He was arrested when he spoke to the international media about the paucity of the junta's relief effort and about the appalling conditions.

In an effort to block international criticism of its relief efforts in the Delta, the generals also stepped up control of cameras in the region. Equipment was seized from private homes to prevent people from filming or photographing cyclone victims. In addition, the junta closed another Rangoon monastery closely associated with the Saffron Revolution protests and democracy activists. The generals seemed determined to prevent the opposition from capitalizing on its bungled response to Cyclone Nargis.

Security also was tightened around Aung San Suu Kyi's house and the NLD headquarters. Suu Kyi's birthday was coming up on June 19. The generals did not want her supporters to draw any media attention. According to witnesses, at least 300 NLD members and supporters gathered at the NLD headquarters in downtown Rangoon to mark the birthday. Many stood outside the office to release birds and chant for Aung San Suu Kyi's freedom. Watching carefully were more than 100 uniformed police and over 200 plainclothes security, USDP members, and Swan Arr Shin security forces. The roads around the headquarters were blocked, an ominous sign. An hour after the ceremony began, a truckload of Swan Arr Shin members moved in rapidly. They arrested four NLD supporters, who were beaten and taken away.

The American chargé d'affaires, Shari Villarosa, reported after the attack that hundreds of supporters, not all of them NLD members, had risked arrest to publicly celebrate Aung San Suu Kyi's birthday. "Despite spending almost 13 of the past 19 years in detention, Aung San Suu Kyi remains an iconic figure. For that reason, Than Shwe fears her. He may send thugs to attack peaceful supporters, but Aung San Suu Kyi's popularity endures."

After the constitutional referendum, Suu Kyi remained sealed off from the world in her home. A late-night visitor soon set dramatic events in motion that would bring her back into the spotlight in an unexpected way.

CHAPTER SIXTEEN

THE INTRUDER

"Everyone is very angry with this wretched American. He is the cause of all these problems. He's a fool."

—U Kyi Win, one of Suu Kyi's lawyers

A year after the Cyclone Nargis crisis, Aung San Suu Kyi was looking forward to her release. The six long years of house arrest that the junta had heaped on her after the Depayin massacre were supposed to expire on May 27, 2009. But before she could be released, a strangely obsessed American sneaked into her home in the middle of the night. He claimed he had come to save Suu Kyi. Instead, he gave the generals an excuse to lock her up again.

Suu Kyi's longtime companions, Khin Khin Win and her daughter Win Ma Ma, arose just before dawn on May 5, like any other day. This time, they were startled to discover an American named John Yettaw, crouching in the upstairs area of the home. He had swum across Inya Lake and sneaked into Suu Kyi's compound in the dark. Yettaw claimed he had been sent by God to warn Suu Kyi that she would be assassinated. He had tried to see her the previous November, but had been turned away by her housemates. Now, improbably, he had slipped past the guards again. His return was unexpected and unnerving. This time, he had gotten all the way up the stairs in the house to the private area.

Who on earth was this eccentric interloper who wore homemade cardboard flippers on his sandals? Why was he so intent on barging into Suu Kyi's house?

John William Yettaw turned out to be a 53-year-old disabled veteran from Falcon, Missouri. He was a sometime building contractor and bus driver, who was most generally out of work. He often told people he was a Vietnam veteran and had served in various Southeast Asian countries, but his military records show he spent only a year of Army service in Germany. Yettaw said he suffered some kind of head injury during his service that left him with blackouts and headaches. He had received small disability payments for post-traumatic stress disorder.

Yettaw was living with his current wife in a mobile home in Missouri. He had been married several times and had six children. Neighbors described him as somewhat intelligent and articulate, but erratic. A Mormon, he sometimes claimed to be writing faith-based books. When he was in his early 40s, he pursued studies in psychology at Drury University and professed that he had graduated *cum laude* in multiple majors of psychology, sociology, criminal justice, and biology. According to press reports, he struggled with debt and a temper—once putting his thumb through a man's eye during a fight in a bar parking lot. After a son died in a motorcycle crash, Yettaw was so distraught that he decided to write a book about healing and forgiveness. He became obsessed with the idea of meeting Aung San Suu Kyi, a woman he believed had also suffered much, to get her thoughts on forgiveness and resilience.

Yettaw made his first attempt to see Suu Kyi in fall 2008. He traveled to Mae Sot on the border of Burma and Thailand, a town teeming with refugees, trafficking, and shady characters. Yettaw told people he wanted to bring international attention to Suu Kyi's situation. He settled into a hotel, bought a motorcycle, and struck up a friendship with a Thai woman. He spent some time talking with Burmese refugees and activists who had congregated in the border community. A heavy-set man with close-cropped gray hair, bushy black brows, and LBJ-sized ears, Yettaw looked like a middle-aged bus driver who had wandered off track, which he was. He was well-spoken and intelligent enough to seem credible at first acquaintance, but activists sensed there was something amiss in his grandiose ramblings about messages from God. With typical Burmese courtesy, they were polite to the American, but wary.

Yettaw tried unsuccessfully to get work with a Thai non-governmental organization. Then in October, he believed he had a vision. He was convinced that he was a defender of the oppressed. He left Mae Sot without paying his bills and went to Bangkok. In Bangkok, he managed to get a visa to travel to Burma. He flew to Rangoon and under the cover of darkness on November 30, he swam nearly two kilometers across Inya Lake to Suu Kyi's home. He was able to sneak onto the property by going through a big culvert near her house on University Avenue. Then Yettaw climbed over the fence surrounding the house.

At the time, Suu Kyi's residence was surrounded by security guards 24 hours a day. She was forbidden to have visits from outsiders. Police boats frequently patrolled the lake. Yet somehow, the arguably mentally unstable American slipped through the cordon of security and entered Suu Kyi's house that first visit. Her housemates were justifiably alarmed when they discovered the stranger trespassing in the lower level of the home. Concerned for Suu Kyi's safety, they prevented him from communicating with her. While Suu Kyi remained upstairs in the private quarters of the house, they explained to Yettaw that it is a serious crime for Burmese citizens to provide lodging to a foreigner and illegal to have a guest stay overnight at one's home without notifying the authorities first. But it took them two days to persuade Yettaw, who was several times larger in size than they were, to leave. He pleaded that he was in poor health and suffered from diabetes, heart trouble, and asthma. The women said they would allow him to rest for a short while, but insisted he must leave. He then spent some time resting and praying. When Yettaw headed out, he left behind a half dozen books for Suu Kyi, including *The Book of Mormon*. While he was making his way back to the lake, several police officers apprehended him. They aimed their guns at him and asked "What are you doing here?" but then let him go.

Not knowing whether the intrusion was simply the act of an unstable man or an attempt by authorities to snare her for harboring a visitor, Suu Kyi decided her best defense was to report the intrusion truthfully. Under Burmese law, all overnight visitors must be reported to the government. She informed her doctor when he came to check on her, and he alerted authorities. No action was taken. As months passed, she and her companions assumed the peculiar incident was over.

In the meantime, Yettaw had been unable to fly back to the U.S. because political protesters had seized the Suvarnabhumi International Airport in Bangkok. Yettaw found his way back to the border town of Mae Sot, where more than 100,000 refugees from Burma were living in makeshift camps. He stayed there for a month, visiting refugee schools and the famous Mae Tao clinic operated by Cynthia Maung. He talked openly to people about his failed attempt to see Suu Kyi and said he was planning to try again. By early 2009, Yettaw was back in the U.S. and trying to raise money from friends and an ex-wife to pay for the bills he left behind in Mae Sot. He was still paying off those bills when he decided he must visit Rangoon again. He was determined to try again to see Aung San Suu Kyi.

—∾—

John Yettaw was not the first foreigner to get tangled up in Burmese matters: A British citizen named Rachel Goldwyn was sentenced in September 1999 to seven years of hard labor for singing pro-democracy songs in Burma. She was released after two months. Her detention came shortly after another Briton, James Mawdsley, was arrested for handing out anti-government leaflets. He was sentenced to 17 years in prison, serving just under a year. Yettaw would become the next infiltrator to be detained.

By April 2009, Yettaw had made his way back to Thailand. While he was waiting for another visa to enter Burma, Yettaw told activists in Bangkok that he was writing a faith-based book on heroism. According to *Newsweek*, he sent a final cheerful e-mail to his family: "Pray. Study peace. Live calmness. Kindness toward everyone. Love and pray."

On May 3, he was back in Rangoon and waded into the soupy brown-gray waters of Inya Lake as it was growing dark. Some policemen saw him as he swam near the shore and threw rocks at him rather than fire warning shots. Yettaw paddled away. He was determined to reach Suu Kyi's darkened house.

Once again, Yettaw sneaked past guards by crawling through the nearby culvert and over the fence around Suu Kyi's compound. At 5 A.M., he entered the house by climbing up a drain. Once inside, he encountered Khin Khin Win and her daughter Win Ma Ma, who were terrified at the sight of the wet, hulking American in the private upstairs portion of the house. The younger woman, Win Ma Ma, was so frightened by Yettaw that she cowered in a room with a stick for protection.

Yettaw said he was hungry and sick. When Suu Kyi came to check his condition, he asked to stay a few days. He had a video camera and wanted to videotape her. She refused politely and told him he must go. He complained of leg cramps and fatigue. Out of compassion, the women allowed him to rest on the ground floor and gave him enough sustenance to regain the strength to leave. That compassion would cost them all dearly.

Yettaw swam away from the house later on the same day that he had entered, just before midnight. He left behind an puzzling assortment of items: two black abayas like the kind Muslim women wear, two black scarves, two long skirts, one red torch light, six colored pencils in a plastic bag, three pairs of sunglasses, two signal lights, a pair of swimming glasses, several pieces of wire, one recharger, two pairs of gray socks, parts of an English book, and a bag with pieces of torn paper sheets in it. The dark abayas and scarves remained a mystery. Was he planning to use the women's garments and sunglasses as a disguise? Or was he offering them to Suu Kyi as disguises for an escape? Yettaw said later the Muslim garments were a gift to Suu Kyi, although he did not explain why a Mormon would give Islamic garb to a Buddhist woman.

Around 5 A.M., Yettaw was apprehended by police less than 100 feet from the U.S. embassy, which was near the lake's west bank. He was arrested and taken to Insein Prison. A week later, he was charged with entering a restricted zone, "illegal swimming," and breaking immigration laws. He shared his cell with two Burmese prisoners, who very likely were informers. He refused to eat, claiming he was fasting to induce another vision.

John Yettaw may have suffered from delusions, but he had enough wherewithal to carefully plan his route to Suu Kyi's house by using Google Earth and to make elaborate preparations for his covert swim.

When he was arrested, he was carrying two empty five-liter plastic bottles that may have been used for flotation, two small bags, his U.S. passport, a flashlight, a camera protected by plastic wrap, a pair of pliers, a screwdriver, a pair of folding pliers with laser, six memory cards, a torch light with dry cells, 28 separate dry cells, a hat, a white shirt with long sleeves, a pair of trousers, seven paper sheets with written English words, two paper sheets with printed words, two envelopes, two $100 bills, two $10 bills, one $50 bill, ninety-three 1,000-kyat notes, and 10 visiting cards.

Pictures on his camera included photographs that he surreptitiously took inside Suu Kyi's home of her father's portrait, a fighting-peacock democracy emblem, and a bookshelf.

Police later testified that they had seized 61 items from Yettaw's room at the Beauty Land Hotel, including: a Sony Camcorder, a pair of Bushnell night binoculars, a vocal translator, a Nokia cell phone, a pair of scissors, a tourist map, and money hidden in a phone book.

A few days after the incident, Aung San Suu Kyi was arrested and charged with violating the terms of her house arrest. She was charged under the Orwellian "Law Safeguarding the State from the Dangers of Subversive Elements," which carried a three-to-five-year jail term. Her two helpers—who were actually NLD members who had volunteered to assist her during her house arrest—were charged under the same law. All three were taken to Insein Prison. Suu Kyi's doctor, Tin Myo Win (known as "Douglas"), also was held initially as a co-conspirator, but was later released.

When news got out that Suu Kyi had been placed in prison because an uninvited, possibly mentally unstable American had broken into her quarters, an international uproar ensued. U.N. chief Ban Ki-moon expressed grave concern. Hillary Clinton, who was then serving as U.S. Secretary of State, called the charges against Suu Kyi "baseless" and accused the junta of "continuing resistance to a free and open electoral process."

The farce had turned into a stunning setback for Suu Kyi. She had only been weeks away from being released. Instead, she now faced the possibility of more years of house arrest. That would keep her conveniently out of public view while the military conducted the election phase of their "Roadmap to Democracy" in fall 2010. The election was being stage-managed to ensure military rule—and the generals did not want Aung San Suu Kyi on the stage.

International observers couldn't help but wonder: Had the generals somehow facilitated Yettaw's quixotic missions as way of getting their most powerful critic out of the way during the elections? *Newsweek* quoted a Western diplomat as saying that intelligence reports showed senior Burmese officials were told to come up with some way to keep "The Lady" locked up as her release date neared. The unnamed diplomat said a week before Yettaw's second swim, two men posing as members of Suu Kyi's NLD party were believed to have approached Yettaw in Mae Sot and told him "The Lady" was ready to receive him. The government refused requests from *Newsweek* to comment on the allegation. Yettaw also would not comment on what had given him the idea to swim again across the lake, other than to say he wanted to warn Suu Kyi that terrorists were going to try to kill her.

—∾—

Yettaw, Suu Kyi, and her helpers all pleaded not guilty to the criminal charges against them. Her attorneys were preparing for the trial when another legal problem came up: Suu Kyi's estranged brother, Aung San Oo, was suing to keep her from repairing her cyclone-damaged house.

When their mother had died, her will left the house to both her children, with the proviso that if they sold the property, the proceeds must go to a charity. Since he resided in the U.S., Aung San Oo told his sister she could live in the house as long as necessary. He changed his mind in 2000 and filed suit, apparently at the urging of the generals, who would not mind seeing Aung San Suu Kyi dispossessed.

A court had ruled against the brother because he could not own property in Burma as an American citizen. But now he was trying again. A year after her house had been damaged by Cyclone Nargis, Suu Kyi had gotten permission from the regime to repair her leaking roof. Her brother filed an injunction, citing his claim on the property. That meant her house would be in disrepair through another rainy season.

Aung San Suu Kyi shrugged off the nuisance suit, although it was a needless distraction during a precarious time. The court eventually allowed the remodeling, but the legal sparring over the house would continue.

Suu Kyi's trial in the John Yettaw case was held in a courtroom inside the Insein Prison complex. Initially, the junta refused to allow observers in the courtroom, then made a rare concession to international pressure and allowed journalists and foreign diplomats to attend some of the proceedings. The generals' intent may have been to show the world that they were allowing their celebrity defendant her day in court, as opposed to several previous occasions when her sentence was extended arbitrarily without a stated reason or trial. The generals soon may have regretted the move. Suu Kyi's dignified demeanor and the flimsiness of the government's case only served to heighten criticism of the show trial.

Wearing a red-and-pink longyi, Suu Kyi smiled graciously at the diplomats in the courtroom after guards refused permission for her to speak to them individually. "Thank you very much for coming and for your support," Suu Kyi said to the group as she was being escorted from the courtroom. "I can't meet you one by one, but I hope to meet you all in better days."

She appeared healthy and focused, despite reports that she had been given an intravenous drip after suffering from dehydration and loss of appetite in the weeks before. The British ambassador, Mark Canning, said afterward, "She was composed, upright, crackling with energy, and very much in charge of her defense team." Swedish diplomat Liselott Martynenko said, "Everyone says that she has such personal charm that I had really expected to be disappointed. But when she stepped out onto the cement floor, she was 100 percent charisma." The chargé d'affaires of the Philippines, Joselito Chad Jacinto, reported, "She sat listening intently and alertly to what was going on. She exuded a type of aura which can only be described as moving, quite awe-inspiring."

Prosecutors submitted as *prima facie* evidence the video that Yettaw had created of himself inside Suu Kyi's house, presumably with the intent of uploading it onto YouTube. Yettaw stated in his voiceover commentary that he was in Suu Kyi's home and had asked her if he could film her, but she declined. "She looked nervous," he said, "and I am sorry for that."

When Suu Kyi took the stand to defend herself, she testified that she and her assistants had urged Yettaw repeatedly to leave. Out of compassion, they agreed to let him rest there during the day if he would leave that evening.

When Yettaw testified, he stated repeatedly that he was sent on his journey by God to protect Suu Kyi from a terrorist group that was trying to assassinate her. He said that he was seen by policemen as he swam across the lake, but was not intercepted or arrested. He also confirmed that during his previous visit, police had apprehended him, questioned him briefly, and let him go.

The judges would only allow Suu Kyi's defense team to present one witness, her lead attorney U Kyi Win, known as "Neville." He contended that the government's own security guards had violated the law because they had allowed intrusions into Suu Kyi's restricted residence not once but twice. He further maintained that the charges against Suu Kyi were invalid because they fell under a law that was based on the 1974 constitution, which the military government had abolished and replaced with the 2008 constitution.

As the trial went on through the summer rainy season, Suu Kyi appeared more fatigued. She continued to thank the foreign diplomats for attending as she passed by them. "It means a lot that you are here," she said. "I really appreciate your support. It's difficult to talk this way." One of her attorneys told U.S. officials that when his spirits had flagged during the sham trial, she had encouraged him, "Uncle, have a stout heart."

In the midst of the trial, something happened that many faithful Burmese interpreted as a harsh judgment on the military regime. The Danok Pagoda, a 2,300-year-old gold-domed pagoda on the outskirts of Rangoon, collapsed into a pile of timbers and dust.

The pagoda had been blessed only a few weeks before by Kyaing Kyaing, the supreme leader's wife, with an audience of what amounts to the A-list of Burmese society, generals, crony CEOs, and other sycophants. Kyaing

Kyaing had led the way in fixing a diamond orb to the top of the ancient pagoda and sprinkling holy water on the tiers of a golden umbrella.

When the pagoda collapsed, 20 workmen were killed who were completing the restoration. The golden umbrella tumbled to the ground. The diamond orb was lost in the rubble.

Many interpreted the collapse as a rebuke for the 2007 attack on the monks in the Saffron Revolution—soldiers had invaded the monasteries without removing their boots and had beaten and imprisoned the unarmed holy men. Despite their ostentatious efforts to legitimize their rule by making displays of their Buddhist fealty, the collapse was seen as a sign that Than Shwe no longer had the spiritual power to benefit from calculated acts of merit. He had lost the Mandate of Heaven.

But that did not deter his vendetta against Suu Kyi.

—w—

After first conferring with Than Shwe, the judges returned their verdict on August 11, 2009. Yettaw was sentenced to a total of seven years. He was given three years in prison for violating Suu Kyi's house arrest, three years of hard labor for breaking immigration laws, and one year of hard labor for trespassing. Suu Kyi was initially sentenced to three years of hard labor, but after a five-minute recess, it was announced that Senior General Than Shwe had magnanimously commuted the sentence to 18 months of house arrest. Khin Khin Win and Win Ma Ma were also sentenced to 18 months house arrest. (An examination of Than Shwe's directive later revealed that he had signed the sentence reduction on August 10, a day before the "independent" court presented its verdict.)

By the time the verdict was announced, Yettaw's health had deteriorated seriously. He had continued to refuse food in prison on religious grounds. Authorities had been feeding him through an intravenous tube during the trial. After he suffered a series of epileptic seizures, Yettaw was transferred to Rangoon General Hospital.

Although the negative verdict was not unexpected, the prolonged trial seemed a cruel charade, one that the hapless Yettaw might not survive. The saving grace was that highly sensitive diplomacy was under way behind the scenes while the Alice in Wonderland trial played out. There was a surprising twist no one had expected: The end of the bizarre Yettaw episode led to the beginning of serious talks between the American government and the junta.

—~—

The minute the verdict was delivered, U.S. Senator Jim Webb, a feisty Vietnam War veteran-turned-politician, flew to Rangoon August 14, 2009 to help untangle the mess that Yettaw had created. Webb was a highly decorated Marine who had shown remarkable bravery storming enemy strongholds in Vietnam. He received the Navy Cross for heroism after he captured a series of bunkers under fire and shielded one of his soldiers from a grenade blast with his own body. He went on to serve as secretary of the Navy before winning a seat in the Senate from Virginia. He was chair of the Senate Foreign Relations subcommittee on East Asia and Pacific Affairs and well versed in Southeast Asia politics. A Scotch-Irish redhead, Webb was known to be quick-tempered and independent-minded.

Webb had long harbored doubts that the tough U.S. sanctions on Burma were producing results. While the sanctions gave the U.S. the moral high ground, they were being undercut by neighboring countries that continued dealing with Burma. Webb had discussed the Burma stalemate with Hillary Clinton and Barack Obama when they were serving together in the Senate. Now they were all in positions to do something about it: Obama in the White House, Clinton as secretary of state, and Webb with a key position on the Senate Foreign Relations committee.

Webb often compared the Burma standoff to the decades-long deadlock with Vietnam, so much so that activists started wearing T-shirts to his subcommittee hearings that said "Burma is not Vietnam." Their complaint was that Vietnam may have opened trade relations with the U.S., but it was still dominated by the Communist Party and far from a democracy. Yet Webb was convinced it was time to seek an opening with Burma that might lead to a more positive relationship. He told the press, "We are in a situation where if we do not push some sort of constructive engagement, Burma is going to basically become a province of China. It does us no good to be out of there."

President Obama shared many of those concerns and had begun a "pivot to Asia" to focus more strategically on the region. He opened the door to dialogue with Burma in his inaugural address in January 2009 when he said he was willing to extend a hand to the dictators if they would "unclench their fists."

The next month, Secretary Clinton announced a major review of Burma policy at a press conference in Jakarta, pointing out that the economic sanctions imposed by the United States and other Western governments had failed to move the repressive Burmese government to meaningful change. "We are looking at possible ideas that can be presented," she said. "Clearly, the path we have taken in imposing sanctions hasn't influenced the Burmese junta," she said, adding that the route taken by Burma's neighbors of "reaching out and trying to engage them has not influenced them, either."

Back in Washington, she began quietly building Congressional support for a fresh look at Burma engagement. She had learned in the Senate to count her votes before making a move. She met with staunch Burma advocate Senator Mitch McConnelll of Kentucky. The conservative Republican had agreed with Clinton on little in the Senate, but had both championed democracy in Burma. McConnell kept a framed note from Aung San Suu Kyi on the wall. He was initially skeptical about a policy shift, but agreed outreach might be worth a try. Clinton promised to consult him regularly. She then reached out to Rep. Joe Crowley, a former Democratic colleague from New York and also a staunch supporter of human rights in Burma. He, too, agreed outreach was worth a try. She also took care to touch base with key leaders overseas, contacting the president of Indonesia, Susilo Bambang Yudhoyono. A former military man himself, he had talked recently with the Burmese generals and believed progress was possible.

It was time to take next steps. Clinton sent Stephen Blake, a senior State Department diplomat, to Burma. As a tenative show of good faith, the regime arranged a meeting with their foreign minister in Naypyidaw. It was the first time an American official had been invited to the remote capital. Blake came back convinced that the generals were interested in a dialogue, but he was still skeptical—the generals were well known for faking steps toward progress.

Then the surreal Yettaw incident happened. The diplomatic flap and a sideshow trial threatened to torpedo any progress that had been made. Yet while Suu Kyi's trial on the Yettaw intrusion dragged on that summer, Secretary Clinton kept pressing on the diplomatic front. She tested a carrot-and-stick approach at a conference of foreign ministers in Phuket, Thailand. She said that it was critical that Aung San Suu Kyi be released from "this persecution that she has been under," and hinted that if she was released, "that would open up opportunities, at least for my country, to expand our relationship with Burma, including investments in Burma."

Clinton then called on McConnell and Webb again, this time for advice on how to resolve the Yettaw dilemma. According to her memoir, Webb offered to negotiate Yettaw's release. Clinton gave him the go-ahead.

The Yettaw case provided Webb with the opportunity he was waiting for. He requested meetings with the top leadership and Aung San Suu Kyi. To his surprise, the junta agreed. That meant that Webb would be the first high-level American politician to meet with Than Shwe during his 16-year rule as senior general and the first American in six years to meet with Aung San Suu Kyi. Diplomats across Asia took note. What was going on? Just a few weeks before, the generals had refused to give U.N. Secretary General Ban Ki-moon permission to see Suu Kyi. Why were they giving a lesser-known senator the red carpet?

There had been some confidential clues in the months before the Yettaw incident that the military regime might be ready to engage with Washington. The American embassy had gotten the impression from its sources that the generals were intrigued by President Obama's stated interest in talking to those with whom the U.S. had disagreements. Secretary Clinton's announcement of a Burma policy review had further piqued their interest. The generals indirectly let the American embassy know that they would like to upgrade mutual diplomatic designations from chargé d'affaires to ambassador. They also suggested that more cooperation was possible on narcotics and POW/MIA issues left over from World War II. Symbolic gestures were important to the generals, and there were hints that it would be a positive signal if the U.S. used the military-preferred country name "Myanmar" instead of Burma.

A whirlwind series of meetings was set up for Webb with the generals and Aung San Suu Kyi in Naypyidaw, where there would be the highest security. Webb's first meeting was with the prime minister, Thein Sein. The orchestrated session was clearly a practice run for the subsequent meeting with Than Shwe. It gave the junta the opportunity to vet the senator up close and establish some boundaries for the talks.

According to Wikileaks of the embassy notes from the talks, Webb suggested to Thein Sein that there could be a "new road" forward. He asked to see Aung San Suu Kyi and requested that Yettaw be released on a humanitarian basis because of his health.

Thein Sein responded with standard regime rhetoric—Suu Kyi had been judged in court for breaking the law, but if she followed rules, the sentence might be further reduced. Likewise, Yettaw was being punished for his crimes, but the government would consider Webb's request positively.

Then the prime minister ventured into what appeared to be the regime's intended talking points. He pointed out that the two countries had enjoyed bilateral relations even before Burma's independence in 1947 and that Vice President Nixon had visited in 1958 and 1985. He said the military government was willing to appoint a new special representative to improve communications with Washington. He pointedly emphasized to Webb that the new constitution had been approved by 92.48 percent of the voters and that the regime's "Roadmap to Democracy" was a deliberate process toward elections. Burma had learned the lessons of Iraq, he said: Don't move forward toward democracy in haste.

The prime minister invited Webb to return for another visit and asked him to tell President Obama, "We wish him very well." He proposed that the two countries upgrade their diplomatic representatives to Ambassadors in both capitals. And he urged Senator Webb to "please tell the U.S. Government" that Burma wanted direct relations with the U.S.

For a regime with a history of ordering citizens to "beware of foreign elements and their stooges," this was a change of tone. The calculated charm campaign resumed the next day when Webb met with Senior General Than Shwe. Than Shwe had assembled all of his senior leaders for the meeting—including Vice Senior General Maung Aye; General Thura Shwe Mann, chief of General Staff (who would later become Speaker of the House); and General Thein Sein, prime minister (who would later become president).

The assemblage of top brass sent a clear signal: Something was afoot. Than Shwe was so eager to talk with Webb that he hurried through the traditional "camera spray" photoshoot at the beginning. He gave the senator a warm welcome, saying that Burma considered every nation a friendly nation; that while at times there might be difficulties, they are not permanent, difficult problems can be worked out.

Once again, Webb began by requesting a meeting with Aung San Suu Kyi. He stated that resolution of her status would be necessary for bilateral relations. Her release would send a positive signal to the world, he said. Than Shwe granted him the meeting with Suu Kyi, but deftly avoided the issue of her release. When Webb offered U.S. assistance with the upcoming elections in 2010, Than Shwe also sidestepped that offer. He did, however, immediately agree to Webb's request that John Yettaw be allowed to leave with him on his plane. Than Shwe said the State Peace and Development Council (SPDC), which was basically the generals in the room, had already discussed the issue and decided to grant the request as a goodwill gesture.

The 25-minute exchange was the first time embassy staff had had a chance to observe the reclusive senior general in person. I had interviewed Charge d'Affaires Larry Dinger not long after he assumed his position the year before, and he said he fully expected to finish his posting without ever meeting Than Shwe, like most of his predecessors. Now he was face to face with *all* the top leaders. Dinger and his staff were somewhat surprised to see that Than Shwe appeared to understand English well. Although he used a translator, Than Shwe seemed to follow Webb's remarks and mixed English words such as "trial" and "soldier" into his Burmese. He even seemed to understand Webb's colloquial use of humorous quotes such as President Truman's comment, "In politics if you are looking for a loyal friend, get a dog." For once, the dour senior general seemed to be at ease. He mentioned the words "friend" and "friendship" several times. He posed for final photos like a gracious host. The senior general had reason to be pleased. He had gotten rid of the ailing Yettaw, who would be a nuisance to keep in custody. He had kept Suu Kyi under his control. And he had delivered the message personally to America that sanctions ought to be withdrawn.

Webb's meeting with Aung San Suu Kyi later that afternoon was less convivial. She greeted him with folded arms and a frown. There were no bright flowers tucked into her hair as usual. "The Lady" clearly was not happy about being forced to meet with a man who had repeatedly criticized sanctions and said the U.S. should not hinge its Burma policy on one person, namely her.

Webb began by apologizing for the intrusion into her home by the American John Yettaw. Perhaps hoping to warm her up, he said he had asked the generals to release her. Suu Kyi ignored the overture, like a bouquet from an unwanted suitor. She coolly noted the limited time for the meeting and inquired, *what was the purpose of the Senator's trip?*

Not one to fade under fire, Webb was unfazed by her chilly challenge. He replied that they shared the same goal: Burma should be part of the international community again. He said he was looking for ways to help, particularly as the Obama administration reviewed its Burma policy and the effects of U.S. sanctions.

Suu Kyi kept her distance and kept her arms folded. She was understandably mistrustful—first, her home had been invaded by a delusional American, and now she had been forced to travel to Naypyidaw to meet with a cocky American who had disdained her efforts. For the next 45 minutes, the two sparred politely about the sanctions, testing each other and defending their positions. The embassy staff watched, utterly fascinated. It had been six years since they had seen Suu Kyi in person, and they were as interested in hearing her thoughts as Webb was. Suu Kyi pointed out that she had never called for the sanctions to be imposed, although she supported those working for human rights who advocated sanctions as a way to pressure the regime on human rights abuses. She noted that during her current period of arrest she had received a message from Than Shwe that the NLD should give up confrontation and oppose sanctions. She had replied that she was prepared to go on record opposing confrontation, supporting a legal solution to Burma's political problems, and pledging cooperation with the SPDC to remove sanctions "that are harmful to the country." The regime was not happy with the addition of that final phrase. The generals claimed publicly that Suu Kyi had not responded.

Suu Kyi emphasized to Webb that she and the NLD wanted a good and fair compromise; they were willing to work for the removal of sanctions and had said so many times. The problem was that to the regime, "anything short of capitulation was seen as confrontation."

Webb continued to express concern about the adverse impact of the sanctions, which he said had harmed Burma's economy and severed people-to-people ties. In particular, he noted, the separation was keeping Burma from contact with more democratic countries, which by default empowered countries like China and created a growing regional imbalance.

Suu Kyi countered that regime mismanagement, not sanctions, had damaged the economy. She pointed to a 2008 IMF report that stated the government of Burma's misguided economic policies, not sanctions, were responsible for Burma's poor economic performance. In fact, she said, a number of Asian businesses had left Burma due to the poor business climate.

She did concede some points—she acknowledged that Burma had moved closer to China and India than the West. And she agreed that there was a need for openness, exchanges, and official American visits involving talks with the regime, provided those who came got a balanced impression by talking to all sides.

Webb circled back to his anti-sanctions position, saying the American sanction policy against Burma was contradictory—China and Vietnam still had one-party systems and lacked fair elections, but they were not subject to sanctions. U.S. policy toward the region has been inconsistent, he argued. He contended that interaction and education would be more effective in changing people's consciousness than sanctions.

"I am very much for openness," Suu Kyi insisted, but she said the regime needed to talk with its *own* people before interacting with the rest of the world. As evidence, she cited her repeated attempts, even during her six years of highly restrictive house arrest, to dialogue with the regime. She noted she had reached agreement in 2004 on certain principles, including no vengeance or prosecution of individuals from the military regime. However, she had wanted an official inquiry into the Depayin incident in the interests of "justice, peace, and stability" and to prevent such events in the future. She had not asked for the release of all political prisoners, only for the release of those arrested at Depayin. At that point, she said, the regime stopped talking.

Throughout the meeting, Suu Kyi emphasized her practicality: "We have a dream list. We have a wish list. But we're practical. We want solutions." She also stressed her willingness to talk to the regime without preconditions. She reminded that after the monks' "Saffron Revolution" was suppressed in 2007, she had told SPDC representative Aung Gyi, "Let's agree we won't stop talking. Let's take things step by step." If they disagreed about something, they agreed to talk about something else. But the regime had not continued the talks. The American chargé d'affaires broke into the conversation at that point to say that he had been trying to persuade the regime to resume the dialogue with her, but the government claimed Suu Kyi had refused a meeting in September 2008 after the cyclone. Suu Kyi flatly denied the claim. She said she had been ill at the time the meeting was scheduled and simply had proposed another time to meet. The regime never responded.

Suu Kyi said she was deeply concerned about the decay in Burma's educational system. Burma had one of the best educational systems in Southeast Asia until 1962, she reminded; now only those with means could receive a decent education. She worried that the regime was using the education system to teach what they wanted people to believe and not to equip students with skills to build a better country.

As the meeting wrapped up, Aung San Suu Kyi asked Senator Webb to convey thanks to Secretary Clinton for her strong support. She added that President Obama, as a lawyer, would appreciate the great need for rule of law and an independent judiciary in Burma. Webb presented her with a copy of the president's statement on her recent conviction, which commended her "profound patriotism" and condemned her trial on "spurious charges."

The embassy staff wrote in its notes that despite the recent stress of the trial, Suu Kyi appeared physically and mentally strong. "She was extremely direct, eloquent, and detailed in her responses and despite her isolation, well informed of current economic and social conditions in Burma, as well as world events," the embassy cables concluded. "Throughout the conversation with Senator Webb, ASSK returned repeatedly to the need for direct talks with the regime and stressed the NLD's pragmatism, flexibility, and willingness to engage the SPDC without precondition. She made quite clear the breakdown in dialogue is solely the fault of the regime."

In a final note on the meeting, the cable observed that "ASSK never once raised her own release from custody, but when the Senator raised the topic, she quickly added that others must be released as well."

—w—

The day after Webb's meetings in Naypyidaw, John Yettaw was released. The Burmese authorities commuted Yettaw's sentence by half and suspended the remaining three and a half years upon his deportation.

When Yettaw arrived in the United States, he was in a wheelchair at the airport and wore a surgical mask. He said to reporters, "If I had to do it again, I would do it a hundred times, a hundred times, to save her life," also adding, "That they locked her up; it just breaks my heart." He refused a later question by saying "I wish I could talk more. I can't." He then made a zipper motion over his lips.

The quixotic Yettaw kept a low profile after his return to Missouri, but in one interview with *Newsweek*, Yettaw said he was "brokenhearted" that Suu Kyi was under house arrest again, but that he didn't consider his actions as the cause of her misfortune, saying, "I didn't put her there, I didn't imprison that woman." In fact, he contended, his visit might have saved Suu Kyi from the terrorists he believes were out to get her. He said he was going to devote his time to a "dissertation" about forgiveness, although he was not enrolled in an academic program, and a book "about a higher power, about recognizing the bitter and the sweet."

Though her attorneys were at times highly critical of Yettaw for the predicament that he had placed her in, Suu Kyi stoically accepted the prospect of longer house arrest. She stated that she bore no grudge toward Mr. Yettaw or his family. She resumed her house arrest, noting that in prison she had enjoyed wide access to magazines and books, while under house arrest she had been limited by the regime to one book a year. She asked only that repairs be allowed to her home that she had been seeking for some time and that security be improved. A new security wall around her house subsequently was constructed, reportedly paid for by one of the government's business cronies. The new wall completely blocked Suu Kyi's property from street view and was sturdier than the previous fence. It also had broken glass across the top that made it more difficult for anyone to enter. Or leave.

After a stressful summer in prison and in the courtroom, the Nobel Prize winner was under guard in her weather-beaten home once again. Yet something had changed. There was a shift in tone in the government's comments.

The government mouthpiece newspaper, *The New Light of Myanmar*, hailed Senator Webb's visit as a success in an article headlined "The first step of a long journey." The article claimed that the military government had enthusiastically cooperated with Senator Webb because of "its stance to deepen bilateral relations and relieve the disagreements between the two countries." In conclusion, the article said the Senator's visit was "the first step to promotion of the relations between the two countries . . . the first step toward marching to a 1,000-mile destination."

Before Webb had arrived, Chargé d'Affaires Dinger sent him a prescient analysis of what might be motivating the generals to reach out and how the U.S. might respond. "Burma's military machine is top-down, xenophobic, and utterly focused on preserving national unity," he summarized. "At the same time, senior generals are embarrassed by their international pariah status and crave respect. Some are concerned with Burma's ever-growing dependence on China and its geostrategic location amidst historical foes. Others having seen a glimpse of the international community's benevolence following Cyclone Nargis, no doubt wish for a lifting of sanctions and economic assistance. No matter the motivations, a dialogue with Burma's senior military leaders will be slow, frustrating, and within the U.S., politically charged. While dialogue is unlikely to yield major, near-term political outcomes such as changes to the constitution, it might sow seeds for future change by illustrating to the next line of leaders what an improved relationship with the U.S. could look like. Above all, a dialogue could lead to tangible benefits for Burma's long-suffering people, a worthwhile goal in itself."

Cyclone Nargis, while tragic, had allowed the U.S. to demonstrate vividly its commitment to the welfare of Burma's people, Dinger believed. The U.S. provided nearly $75 million in post-cyclone assistance, with more in the pipeline. The American response had been impressive and had prompted discussion of future humanitarian assistance. The regime had subtly indicated that additional assistance might be a possible avenue for future engagement.

A joint post-mortem by the U.N. and ASEAN after the cyclone, which correlated the reports of 300 relief experts, confirmed that the impact of the storm was major: at least 150,000 people were dead or missing; more than 61 percent of those were women and children; and more than one quarter of survivors reported serious psychological trauma.

True to Burma's deep-seated religious culture, 58 percent of the survivors placed more emphasis on the need to rebuild religious buildings than other structures.

According to the report, approximately 75 percent of the health centers were either destroyed or damaged; 50–60 percent of public schools were ruined; more than 600,000 hectares of rice fields were flooded; 450,000 homes destroyed and 350,000 damaged; and 50 percent of farm animals were killed.

Overall, Cyclone Nargis caused more than $4 billion in loss and damages, which was more than 27 percent of Burma's GDP. The U.N. and ASEAN estimated that Burma would need $1 billion over the next three years to rebuild the affected areas.

The Burmese government claimed to have spent $65 million on cyclone relief. Few were sure the regime could be trusted, but it was clear rebuilding would require help. And that could be a chance for a better relationship.

Dinger, who had a Harvard law degree and had studied at the National War College, sized up the junta's strengths and weaknesses in his cables:

All the major decisions were made at the very top. "Senior general Than Shwe, Vice Senior General Maung Aye and their inner circles call the shots. Than Shwe's dominant personality is keenly felt," he wrote. "Subordinates appear to share only good news, leaving the senior generals potentially ignorant of many realities." In that information vacuum, the generals were continuing to press ahead with their self-serving "Roadmap to Democracy" and their ruinous, top-down economic policies. "While self-interest clearly is a factor in their thinking, it would be a mistake to think they are motivated exclusively by self-enrichment. These are true believers who are convinced they are divinely entrusted in the tradition of the 'warrior kings,' with doing what is best for the country and the people. They feel they are simply misunderstood by the outside world."

The generals believe they are keeping the country from being torn apart and "Balkanized" by ethnic conflicts. Dinger explained that the career military leaders, most with combat experience in Burma's internal conflicts, were convinced that it was up to them to provide stability. As a result, they see a continued governance role by the military as essential in keeping the country together.

The generals see themselves as preserving the country's Buddhist heritage. Although outsiders might consider the military's attacks on ethnic groups and dissidents as betrayals of compassionate Buddhist precepts, Dinger said they see themselves as devout Buddhists. State media recently had inundated the public with scenes of senior generals and their families consecrating the newly-constructed replica of the revered Shwedagon Pagoda in Naypyidaw. "Of course, such acts of Buddhist merit-making have a public relations aspect," he noted, but they also reflect the generals' "philosophical base." The generals had forfeited much merit in the crack-down on the monks; there was atoning to do.

Families matter. Dinger underscored that the generals all spoil their children and grandchildren. When Cyclone Nargis drew near, they flew their loved ones to luxurious safety in Dubai. Although Dinger didn't mention it, many had intermarried like European royalty, with the military princelings given preferences in contracts for fueling stations, telecommunications, and construction. Than Shwe's favored grandson in particular, Nay Shwe Thway Aung, was infamous as a playboy who flaunted his influence.

Dinger did note that the Western visa bans on the generals' immediate family members were particularly unpopular. The generals' wives could not travel to fashionable cities in the U.S. or Europe. Their children could not study abroad like many of their friends.

As they aged, the generals needed a retirement plan. "It is entirely possible most senior generals are looking for an escape strategy," Dinger speculated. "Retirement has never been an option for Burmese leaders.

Historically, Burmese kings or generals, and those close to them either have died in office, been killed, or been deposed or imprisoned. The current senior generals are getting old, but they have no desire to be held to account for what the outside world perceives as their crimes against the people . . . all the top generals undoubtedly want assurances that, if they step aside, they and their families will retain their assets and not be prosecuted."

Despite its vast natural resources, the country was going bankrupt. Though the generals liked to claim the sanctions were wrecking the economy, Aung San Suu Kyi was right: their own crony capitalism and mismanagement was stifling growth. The sweetheart deals, the bureaucratic inefficiencies, corruption, and self-serving controls on agriculture, imports and exports, were crippling. Burma's GDP was half that of neighboring Laos and Cambodia, a shock to a country that was once a regional powerhouse, Dinger pointed out. The global recession also was taking a toll. Repatriated funds from Burmese overseas had declined. Migrant workers who had been laid off in other countries were returning home, but there were even fewer jobs inside Burma because textile and tourism industries were laying off workers as the global economy slowed. In sum, Burma's economy was a shaky house of cards. The government had claimed growth was 13 percent in 2007–2008, but experts estimated it was more like 1 percent. Inflation was up to 30 percent.

Dinger didn't dwell on it, but Burma also had become dangerously dependent on investment from China. China's foreign direct investment in Burma had grown to nearly 50 percent of Burma's GDP. Most Burmese also resented the fact that ethnic Chinese were dominating commerce in cities such as Mandalay as well as the lawless border areas.

More than that, China was planning a series of hydropower projects on Burma's mighty rivers that would ship needed electricity to Chinese citizens, while 75 percent of Burmese lacked power. Burma needed to somehow recalibrate its standing with its overbearing neighbor to the north.

For its part, China was leaning on the regime to step up the pace of reform. China had gotten frustrated with the regime's failure to control the ethnic conflicts on its border, because the fighting had florced flows of unwanted refugees into China.

Change was needed, but superstition was skewing decision-making. There were rational reasons for wanting a better relationship with the generals, but as Dinger warned, rationality was not always apparent in the regime decision-making. Than Shwe, in particular, relied on favored soothsayers and numerology, he said, such as the release of exactly 9,002 prisoners the previous fall, reportedly to ensure an auspicious 2009.

The senior generals are genuinely and deeply xenophobic. As Dinger put it, they didn't seem to understand foreigners and certainly didn't trust them. "This may be a reason why Than Shwe reportedly abhors Aung San Suu Kyi, who grew up overseas, married a U.K. citizen and then returned to Burma to challenge the military's authority," he wrote. Resentment of their second-class status under British rule still rankled the older officers. Their mistrust also extended to their neighbors because the Burmese had fought wars in their long history with the countries around them, including China, India, and Thailand. In many ways, the past continued to overshadow the present in Burma.

Than Shwe and his cohorts view the current period as one chapter in Burma's long history. They insist that democracy will require a guided process of "gradual maturity." They believe the West and the U.S. in general are trying to force democracy on a country that is not yet developed enough to handle it. "This is more than a cynical excuse to retain power," Dinger observed. "They think they know best."

At the same time, the generals are proud and crave the acceptance of the international community. "They hate being subject to the sanctions and aspire to be treated with the respect accorded other world leaders, including some authoritarian ones," Dinger wrote.

All those factors added up to a growing impetus for change. Even before the 2008 election that brought President Obama to office and before the Yettaw incident, Burmese officials were hinting that a visit by a high-ranking military official might be welcome. As military men, they seemed more comfortable with peers in the military than with unctuous diplomats from the U.N. As a war hero and former secretary of the Navy, Senator Webb filled the bill.

"Burma's senior generals used Senator Webb's visit to deliver an unequivocal message: The GOB (Government of Burma) wants better relations with the United States," Dinger cabled to the State Department immediately after Webb's visit.

He underscored that Than Shwe's agreement to meet with a U.S. official—for the first time—should have particular resonance. "The regime uses access to signal where countries stand in the pecking order," he explained. "China gets SPDC members [top leaders] at its national day event—we get MOFA [Ministry of Foreign Affairs] bureaucrats."

"They want direct communication with Washington and have identified an envoy—regime insider and former Ambassador to the United States U Thaung," he wrote. "It is certain Than Shwe believes he has unclenched his fist—granting a first-ever meeting with a U.S. official, arranging a session with Senator Webb and Aung San Suu Kyi, and deporting an American prisoner as a sign of 'friendship.' The generals will look for a response."

But how should the U.S. respond?

A series of steps could build confidence and provide assurances that the U.S. has no intention of invading or dominating, Dinger suggested in his cables. This could include:

- Upgrade the diplomatic posts from chargé d'affaires to ambassador as requested.
- Ease the sanctions on a quid-pro-quo basis, calibrating the American concessions as the regime takes concrete steps such as releasing political prisoners, including Aung San Suu Kyi. At the time, there were more than 2,100 political prisoners behind bars.
- Allow the regime's foreign minister to visit the renovation of the Burmese embassy in Washington, as the junta had requested.
- Schedule a meeting with the designated envoy, U Thaung, as soon as appropriate, to sketch out mutual expectations.
- Seek permission for a meeting with Aung San Suu Kyi to follow up on Webb's visit.
- Encourage the regime to allow Suu Kyi to meet with her party members before the 2010 elections.
- Ask to send international observers to the 2010 elections.
- Ask the regime to allow access to prisons again for the International Red Cross.

- Accept the generals' offer to help resolve POW/MIA issues from World War II.
- Increase cooperation on perceived win-win issues such as counter-narcotics and anti-trafficking.
- Consider recognizing Myanmar at the official country name.
- Increase military-to-military relationships.
- Offer help obtaining World Bank and International Monetary Fund technical assistance, and with progress, loan packages.
- Open a public diplomacy outreach center in Mandalay.
- Increase educational exchanges such as the Fulbright program.

Just as the U.S. had achieved mutually beneficial relationships with other former adversaries, it could be possible in Burma, Dinger wrote. He predicted that the process would be "flawed," but might be "stage one of a transition toward a next set of (mostly military) leaders." A constructive dialogue could "signal to that next generation what a positive relationship with the U.S. might offer, planting seeds for future change," he mused.

Dinger's prognosis proved more accurate that he could have imagined. The process was indeed flawed, but once the conversation started, changes were more dramatic than anyone expected, including Aung San Suu Kyi. Almost everything he suggested would happen, and yet the military managed to retain its tight control.

CHAPTER SEVENTEEN

FREE AT LAST

> "The aura surrounding her is still an extraordinary thing to witness. Her appearance—and she is always impeccably dressed—at any public event, is akin to watching the arrival of royalty, or a Hollywood superstar. Even seasoned diplomats are reduced to begging for photos with her like gushing fans. When she turns her attention to you, her charm and charisma can be overpowering."
>
> —Jonathan Head, BBC News

After Senator Jim Webb flew to Burma in 2009 to free the star-crossed John Yettaw, the American relationship with Burma zig-zagged forward. A series of secret conversations began between the U.S. and the Burmese regime, like messages slipped through cracks in the Berlin Wall.

The Obama administration had indicated that it was willing to talk about relaxing economic sanctions if—a big IF—the Burmese generals would release political prisoners and take meaningful steps toward democratic reform.

Secretary of State Clinton was intent on making something happen to end the stalemate in Burma. While the U.S. had stood by its sanctions on principle, China had moved in to fill the vacuum and was turning Burma into a vassal state. Something had to change.

The man tasked with exploring an opening and making it happen was Kurt Campbell, the Assistant Secretary of State for East Asian and Pacific Affairs. Campbell had touched all the right bases in foreign policy circles: Oxford degree. White House Fellow. Defense Department. Center for Strategic and International Studies. As one Washington insider put it, "Kurt is the Asia hand. Hillary wanted to get Burma going. Kurt designed the program." Campbell was smart and capable and personable. He would need all those traits for the battle ahead.

After an exploratory meeting in New York with Burmese diplomats, a "fact-finding" mission to Burma was arranged for Campbell in November 2009. He met with Prime Minister Thein Sein in Naypyidaw and Aung San Suu Kyi in Rangoon. No details were given, but it seemed the beginning of a beginning.

Then talks bogged down. Photos of a second meeting the next May showed Campbell conferring with a pensive Suu Kyi under an umbrella in the rain. The photo made headlines around the world. But not in Burma. Showing Suu Kyi's photo was still forbidden. Since everyone in the country knew about the meetings anyway from television coverage of Campbell coming and going, the state-controlled *New Light of Myanmar* eventually published the photo—but without Suu Kyi. The doctored photo showed Campbell and Chargé d'Affaires Larry Dinger standing several feet apart, looking inward at an empty space under the umbrella where Suu Kyi should have been.

Campbell came away from the meetings impressed by Aung San Suu Kyi and less so with the generals. The generals seemed to be stonewalling again. He told the press, "I was again moved by the perseverance and the commitment Aung San Suu Kyi has shown to the cause of a more just and benevolent Burma and to the Burmese people themselves. She has demonstrated compassion and tolerance for her captors in the face of repeated indignities. It is simply tragic that Burma's generals have rebuffed her countless appeals to work together to find a peaceable solution for a more prosperous future."

Campbell called on the military to open a dialogue with the opposition and ethnic minority groups that were seeking assurances of some measure of autonomy. He also urged the military government to allow Suu Kyi more freedom to meet with people involved in the political process, particularly her own party's senior executives. The goals of the new U.S. policy, he said, are: "Strong support for human rights, the release of Aung San Suu Kyi and all other political prisoners, and the promotion of democratic reform."

The U.S. would take steps to improve the relationship, he said, if the Burmese government would make *concrete* efforts. Pointedly, he added, those efforts should include adhering to U.N. resolutions on nuclear proliferation. Translation: No more funny business with North Korea.

The junta publicly praised the new U.S. outreach, but showed no signs of releasing Aung San Suu Kyi or changing its plans. First, the generals wanted to push through the election in October 2010, which would ensure their continued control. Then, they might talk about Aung San Suu Kyi, the troublesome woman who had spoiled their private buffet for so long.

The junta's hand-picked election commission set terms for the 2010 election that would benefit the military—and reduce NLD support:

- Those with criminal convictions could not take part—ruling out activists who had been jailed, of which there were thousands
- Members of religious orders could not take part—ruling out monks, another large subset of the population that would be inclined to vote for democracy.

The junta's lopsided election laws meant that the NLD would have to expel Aung San Suu Kyi as it leader. The party couldn't register for the November 2010 election with her at the helm, because she allegedly had a "criminal record" and could not participate. That presented the NLD with a Hobson's choice of bad alternatives:

- If the party *refused to register* without Suu Kyi at the helm, the NLD candidates would not be included on the ballot. That would give the military party an even bigger advantage.

- If the NLD *did register without their founder*, that would be tacit acceptance of the regime's rigged constitution and election laws.

The NLD decided to sit out the elections rather than endorse the regime's terms. Even though it was the first election in two decades, it was a foregone conclusion that it would not be a fair election. The NLD chose not to be an accomplice to the theft. The decision divided the party, but party leaders felt it was the only honorable choice. Some NLD members left the party to form new parties in order to run for office, but they did not have strength in numbers or organizational depth to seriously challenge the junta's well-funded Union Solidarity and Development Party (USDP). The USDP was offering low-interest loans to people who joined the party.

In the weeks before the election, the generals dangled the possibility that they might discuss Aung San Suu Kyi's status after the election. Voters could only speculate, did they really mean it? Would they release Aung San Suu Kyi after the election? Or was this yet another public relations ploy to swing more voters in the polls? With past behavior as a guide, most voters remained skeptical.

The general election in November 2010 was supposedly the fifth step of the seven-step roadmap to democracy: "free and fair election" for Parliament. The sixth step would be the convening of elected representatives in the next year. The seventh would be "the building of a modern, democratic nation," which would take much longer.

When election day came on November 7, the regime's party and other surrogates ran away with the election, with the NLD sitting on the sidelines. The military won 883 of the 1,154 parliamentary seats, or 76.5 percent. A party with close ties to the military was runner-up. The "opposition" parties won only 9 percent of the seats.

Notably, at least six of the new Parliamentarians were known drug lords. Three were business partners with junta leaders.

The junta had hijacked the election as easy as a trailer full of cigarettes, and called it democracy. Senior General Than Shwe had his way. The military was still in control, but in civilian clothes. The future looked difficult.

Then the week after the election, word began spreading that the generals—having locked in their control with the election—were going to release Aung San Suu Kyi after all.

People began gathering outside of her home in anticipation. Some waited for over 24 hours in front of her house. Then at last, on November 13, 2010, Aung San Suu Kyi walked out of the door of her house to the gate at 54 University Avenue and greeted a crowd of thousands that was cheering so loudly that she could not be heard. Thirty riot police with guns and tear gas stood nearby.

Aung San Suu Kyi waved over the gate. She laughed and waved and seemed overcome with emotion at times as the crowd cheered and chanted and held up cameras to take photos.

"We haven't seen each other for so long, I have so much to tell you! The military gave me seven years of rest. Now I am full of energy to continue my work," she tried to shout over the noise from the crowd. But telling them more than that would have to wait until another time, when she at least had a microphone and a plan.

She had been freed before—in 1995 and 2002—only to be locked up again when crowds who came to cheer her became so large that the junta couldn't abide her popularity and started attacking her supporters. After seven years of nearly total isolation, she seemed game to try again. She told the cheering supporters at her gate, "There is a time to be quiet and a time to talk. People must work in unison. Only then can we achieve our goal. We have a lot of things to do. If we are united, we can get what we want."

"Amay! Amay! (mother, mother)," some shouted. Many had on T-shirts that said "We stand with Aung San Suu Kyi." Paula Helfrich, the daughter of an OSS soldier who had fought with the Kachin Rangers in Burma during World War II, was one of those who waited for hours for Suu Kyi to come to the fence. "It was such an emotional moment," she recalled, tearing up herself at the memory. "People in the crowd spontaneously began singing the national anthem, *Kaba Ma Kyei*, all together." The people sang "Where prevail justice and independence, it's our country . . . our land. Where prevail equal rights and correct policies, for people to lead a peaceful life, It's our country . . . our land."

After someone handed up a small clutch of flowers to her, the crowd urged, "Put them in your hair!"

Suu Kyi obliged as the crowd roared its approval. It may have been the first time five thousand people have cheered a cluster of flowers.

—ꝏ—

Aung San Suu Kyi had been under house arrest for 15 out of 21 years.

That time period spanned the terms of five American presidents: Ronald Reagan, George H. W. Bush, Bill Clinton, George W. Bush, and Barack Obama:

July 20, 1989—Aung San Suu Kyi is placed under house arrest for the first time, under charges of attempting to divide the military.

July 10, 1995—Released from house arrest, but monitored, harassed, and accosted in numerous incidents.

September 23, 2000—Arrested after she attempted to travel to the city of Mandalay against travel restrictions.

May 6, 2002—Released supposedly "unconditionally," but monitored and harassed, visitors screened.

May 30, 2003—Arrested after she and her supporters are attacked by a mob backed by the government at Depayin.

September 22, 2007—Her first public appearance since 2003, to greet monks participating in the "Saffron Revolution."

May 14, 2009—Arrested for a fourth time, charged with government subversion, after American John Yettaw entered her home uninvited.

August 10, 2009—Sentenced to 18 more months of house arrest for breaching terms of her house arrest by admitting Yettaw.

March 10, 2010—Barred from upcoming election by a law which states that prisoners cannot run for elected office.

November 13, 2010—Released from house arrest.

After her release, Aung San Suu Kyi immediately reached out to her sons. Her son Kim was in Bangkok, waiting for her release and a visa. She spoke to her son Alexander by phone.

Then she met with her party leaders, the first time they had seen each other in a very long time. The party was in serious need of rebuilding. When Cyclone Nargis hit, she had instructed the party to liquidate whatever assets the party had and use the money for cyclone relief. As a result, the NLD had impoverished itself, selling buildings or property, whatever it took to help the cyclone survivors. Many precious resources were used up, but the party had demonstrated that it cared about people when the government did not. Having Suu Kyi back on the scene was a tonic; the NLD headquarters was full of people and reporters again. The Lady was back.

She went next to the HIV/AIDS hospice that Phyu Phyu Thin was managing. Suu Kyi wanted to encourage compassion for the sick and needy. She brought the flowers that people had brought to her gate to share with the patients, handing out the flowers personally to many who were too weak to stand up. She told the crowd of press and supporters who had followed her, "We need money for drugs, we need money for food, we need money for more housing. So I'd be very, very grateful if you could do something about that." One AIDS patient said he was so happy, he could cry because General Aung San's daughter had taken the time to show compassion.

The day after the highly publicized visit, local officials closed the hospice. They claimed it might spread disease to neighbors. After a loud international outcry, the officials backpedaled. The hospice was allowed to continue its work.

It was 10 days more before the regime would approve a visa for Suu Kyi's son Kim to come see her. While he was waiting in Bangkok, he acquired a puppy for her and named it "Tai Chi Toe," after a popular Bangkok drink that he had grown fond of while counting the days.

As she walked into the Rangoon airport terminal to meet him, Suu Kyi told the press with typical understatement, "I am very happy." When she first saw her son walking toward her, tears welled up in her eyes. She had not seen him since he was a young boy. He had become a tall, handsome man and the father of two children she had never seen. They hugged and she slipped her arm around his waist as the two posed briefly for photographers. To show his support for his mother's cause, Kim held up his left arm for the crowd to see: it had a tattoo of the NLD flag and the fighting-peacock democracy symbol. They walked out of the airport holding hands.

It looked like a fairy-tale ending, but it wasn't the end yet, and like all families, they had issues to deal with. Both sons had struggled to find their own role in life. Her son Alexander, who was devoted to his commune of Buddhist meditation practitioners in Oregon, did not come to Rangoon, but did speak on the phone with his mother as often as possible in the weeks to come.

In a moment of candor about her personal life, Suu Kyi conceded to the media that while her family had supported her during her long detentions, her sons had suffered considerably. "They haven't done very well after the breakup of the family, especially after their father died, because Michael was a very good father," she told the media. "Once he was no longer there, things were not as easy as they might have been." Despite those difficulties, she and her sons had not been estranged, as the media sometimes reported. She said she had always had their support. "My sons are very good to me," she said. "They've been very kind and understanding all along."

A month later, in January, the government allowed Aung San Suu Kyi to have Internet access. Like Rip van Winkle emerging from a long sleep, she also discovered the marvel of cell phones. She marveled that they seemed so "insubstantial" in the palm of her hand and yet could perform miraculous tasks.

When I returned to see her that month, her house was buzzing with activity. Flowers were being planted. The house was getting some new shutters and a coat of much-needed paint. There were new red tiles on the roof.

It had been even more difficult to get in to see Suu Kyi this visit than in 2003, when there were guards on the street. It took dozens of calls to a series of people who would not commit until the day before the meeting. The price of fame was that Aung San Suu Kyi was besieged with calls and requests for meetings and interviews, many dozens a day, hundreds a week. She now had volunteers serving as secretaries and gatekeepers, but they were not yet a precision team. It was a new experience. While I waited in the garden, her longtime adviser, former general U Tin Oo, now in his eighties but still fit and feisty, emerged from the house and was driven away. An assistant cleared away the tea cups from their meeting and brought out a fresh setting.

When Aung San Suu Kyi entered the room, I was struck again by her calm presence. Once again she was the gracious hostess, pouring tea, smiling, nodding, thinking through her answers carefully. But as opposed to my impressions from my first visit, she now looked thinner and more drawn than when I had seen her eight years before, more so than photos revealed. Still, when she was engaged and animated, when she turned on whatever it is that gives her that "aura" that so many mention—a charisma, a presence—she looked much younger than her 66 years. It was only in repose that you could see the wear of years, which she shook off to focus on my questions:

Since your release, you have gone from total seclusion to hundreds of requests for meetings. What is your life like now?
Very tiring. Sometimes I wish they would put me back under house arrest one day each week! Just one day a week, that's all. We're trying to manage the same thing by keeping people out, one day each week. I hardly have time to read, and that is the most difficult thing of being released.

You have been reaching out to young people. How is that working?
That has been a great success. Actually, I did not have to reach out too far—one of the things I noticed when I was released was how many young people there were among our supporters. And this was a great change from seven years ago. There were young people then, but they were not that active, not that

forthcoming. This time, the first thing I noticed was how young the greater part of the crowd was and how enthusiastic they were and how brave. Really, they seem braver now than they used to be.

The women in Liberia wore white to protest violence in their country and sat outside government offices, which led to the election of the first woman president there. Do you see a special role for women in Burma?
I would like the women to play a more active role. There are many, many women in the NLD, and they do a very good job. I think there are more than 400 women among the political prisoners, which shows women are involved in politics. I would like to see more women involved. I have always admired the grandmothers of Argentina who spoke up for the grandchildren who had been lost. I like that kind of movement—it is a family movement, but it is also a national movement, not just keeper of the hearth and home, but also the rights of those families, and I think this is a very good thing. The more grandmothers out on the street, the better. [As a grandmother herself, she smiles.]

You've talked about a "Second Panglong Conference" to bring together all ethnic groups. What are the prospects?
The main purpose is to strengthen the spirit of union among *all* the ethnic nationalities of Burma. . . . We don't want disputes settled under the barrel of gun. We want people to sit down and talk to each other. What we are trying to teach through a Second Panglong is the kind of unifying spirit that will stop violent solutions to political problems. We've had a very good response from many ethnic groups and parties. We've even looked at the idea of doing it electronically, a sort of Internet conference, but that may not be possible, because the access is so difficult.

Is adjusting economic sanctions a possibility?
The IMF and many others agree that the economy has been affected more by mismanagement than by sanctions. Still, we

are going to look into how sanctions affect people, and we are thinking that perhaps there may be a means of modifying the sanctions and making them smarter.

The first thing you did after your release was visit an AIDS clinic. Do you see your party doing more people-to-people activities as opposed to political activity?
No, we are not going to decrease our political activities, but we are going to expand our humanitarian activities—because we want to be closer to the people and because we *need* it. I have heard we are 191 out of 192 nations when it comes to health care. . . . There is so much that needs to be done! We want to fill the gap as much as we can, but we are going to be a *political* party.

The "Wikileaks" articles included a report that the senior general in Burma considered buying the Manchester United football team after Cyclone Nargis in 2008. Did you have any thoughts on that?
I would have thought if anybody in Burma was considering spending a lot of money at that time, they should have given it to the Nargis refugees.

You have offered repeatedly to have a dialogue with the military leadership—have you received any response?
Not yet.

What kind of leverage do you have to bring the government to a dialogue?
I don't like to think of it as *leverage*. Our greatest strength is *the people want dialogue*. They want the problems of this country to be settled across the table in a civilized manner.

On a lighter note, she said she had taken up painting during her seven-year detention and had designed some note cards on her computer that her party was selling. She ran up to her room to get one and wrote a note to be delivered to First Lady Laura Bush to thank her for some books she had sent. She noted that one of the first calls she received was from the First Lady and said she hoped to meet her some time.

Her new dog was barking louder and louder in the background; she asked that he be brought in. She scooped him up in her arms and held on to him affectionately as we posed for photos in front of the giant pop-art painting of her father in the room. She was still holding on to the puppy as she saw us off at the door, with a few of her aides standing by, ready to set up the next meeting. The tea set had to be refreshed again. The next in a stream of visitors was arriving at 54 University Avenue. There was a frisson in the air, a mixture of optimism and anxiety. Had things finally begun to change?

Just a few months later, in March 2011, former prime minister Thein Sein was named president by Parliament. He had resigned his military position to head up the USDP, the regime's party, and run for Parliament. Not surprisingly, he was elected with 91 percent of the vote and then was chosen to serve as president from a pool of three vice-presidents, who were all former generals. Thein Sein was proclaimed the first non-interim "civilian" president in 49 years. His military uniforms were probably still hanging, freshly pressed, in his closet.

His selection took Burma watchers and most of his countrymen somewhat by surprise. Shwe Mann, another loyal general, had been widely assumed to be Senior General Than Shwe's favorite for president. Instead, Shwe Mann was named Speaker of the Lower House. He would be in a prime position to run for president after Thein Sein's five-year term. Longtime observers speculated that the wily Than Shwe was making sure that loyalists were in key places for the foreseeable future, safeguarding his family and his fortune.

Although many people around the world now assumed that Burma had become a democracy with an elected president, the military was still very much in control.

Many expected Thein Sein to be a weak, one-term, status-quo president. He was 68 and had a pacemaker. Even Hillary Clinton had described him in her memoir as small and stoop-shouldered with thinning hair. With his wire-rim glasses, she wrote, he "looked more than an accountant than a general." But his soft-spoken manner may have been part of his success. Thein Sein was career army and had made his way up the ranks by following orders. He had served as commander in the lawless "Golden Triangle" region and in areas where ethnic populations were under attack—but was considered "less cruel" than other commanders. That didn't mean he was better liked, just less hated. He had a modest manner and was said to be a good listener. Some referred to him as "Senior Clerk."

True to his cautious nature, Thein Sein's first moves were carefully calibrated.

Two months after he was elected, Thein Sein freed thousands of prisoners, although few political prisoners were among them. They were still being held tight.

Six months after taking office, he invited Aung San Suu Kyi to meet with him at his home in Naypyidaw, which the government press described as a "farm cottage." It was her first visit to Naypyidaw and first meeting with Thein Sein since he became president. The occasion was well orchestrated: A portrait of Suu Kyi's father, Aung San, was prominently displayed on the wall. Suu Kyi was introduced to the president's wife and they seemed to have a warm exchange—a smart personal touch on the part of the planners to break the ice.

The state-run media reported that Aung San Suu Kyi and Thein Sein held "frank and friendly discussions" to "find ways and means of cooperation." Suu Kyi said, "It went well. I thought he was somebody who could be trusted and that he was genuine about wishing to bring reform to the country. We've said very, very openly that the military needs to be behind the reform process if it is to be irreversible."

It wasn't a "Burma Spring" yet, but it seemed like a winter thaw. More changes or, at least, promises of change followed.

Daily criticism of foreign media was removed from the newspapers.

Restrictions on the media were reduced and a process was started to rewrite restrictive press laws.

Greater access to the Internet and cell phones was promised.

Overseas Burmese citizens were invited to return home and help rebuild the economy.

And talks were called for with armed ethnic groups.

It *was* beginning to look like a spring awakening, but it seemed too good to be true, or too early to trust.

Then there were two announcements that made it look as if real reforms might be under way. Thein Sein announced that work would be stopped on the controversial Myitsone Dam project. He said the Chinese-led project would be suspended until the end of his tenure. It was a bold, unexpected step. Thein Sein was saying "No" to the powerful Chinese, or at least "Not now."

The Parliament also made amendments to the election commission law that would allow Aung San Suu Kyi to campaign in by-elections to fill vacancies in Parliament. The woman who had spent most of her life protesting against the government finally would have the chance to become part of it.

The National League for Democracy registered as a political party again. Only 48 seats would be open in the April 1 election, but the NLD aimed to get as many as possible, especially the seat Aung San Suu Kyi would seek.

—∾—

Throughout this time, Kurt Campbell's meetings with Aung San Suu Kyi and the new Burmese government had continued. More than 15 sessions had quietly taken place. As part of the review of Burma policies, the U.S. was looking for a workable carrot-and-stick approach. As Campbell put it, the administration had recognized that "conditions in Burma were deplorable and that neither isolation nor engagement, when implemented alone, had succeeded in improving those conditions." The U.S. was exploring an action-for-action approach. If the Burmese government released political prisoners, and moved toward reconciliation with the opposition and peace with the ethnic groups, then sanctions might be eased. Secretary Clinton wanted to see if the ruling generals were ready, after a harsh decade of sanctions, to re-engage.

By the end of 2011, enough tentative progress had been made for Aung San Suu Kyi to agree, it was time for Secretary of State Hillary Clinton to come survey the progress. The opening to Burma was one of Mrs. Clinton's top priorities. Richard Holbrooke was working on Afghanistan and Pakistan as a special negotiator for President Obama, and former senator George Mitchell was working on Iraq. Burma was hers. She had been thinking about Burma since 1996 in Beijing. After the Beijing Conference, she had given a speech in Chaing Mai in Thailand, calling for a "real political dialogue between Aung San Suu Kyi and the military regime." Fifteen years later, the chance seemed at hand. As the new "rebalance" was being worked out, Clinton often called her friend Kwan Kwan Wang to touch base.

Adjusting the sanctions policy would not be an easy sell in Washington. Many powerful members of Congress were committed to them, including Senators McConnell, Feinstein, and McCain. Vice President Joe Biden had been a champion of the Jade Act to limit imports from Burma; that act also had tightened financial and travel restrictions on the junta and their associates. Some human-rights groups said Clinton should be pursuing a multilateral arms embargo on Burma to stop the continuing human-rights violations instead of easing sanctions.

But others in the international community were having doubts about the sanctions policies. The Brussels-based International Crisis Group (ICG) issued a report arguing that more humanitarian aid should be directed to the country and bans on Burmese garments, agriculture, and fishery products and restrictions on tourism should be lifted.

With these political issues in play in Washington, the stage was set for Hillary Clinton to become the first American secretary of state to visit Burma since John Foster Dulles back in 1955.

When Clinton and Aung San Suu Kyi met for dinner on December 2, 2011, at the U.S. mission, after so many years of reading about each other, they quickly established a comfort level after the diplomatic formalities. They already knew each other's story well. Suu Kyi told Mrs. Clinton she had read her autobiography, *Living History*, as well as books written by former president Clinton. Mrs. Clinton had read Aung San Suu Kyi's *Freedom from Fear*. By coincidence, they showed up in similar white outfits—Mrs. Clinton in one of her trademark pants suits and Suu Kyi in a traditional longyi and white top.

They had plenty of time to compare notes over a three-hour dinner on the verandah of the mission. In an interview with the BBC, Mrs. Clinton later said that meeting Suu Kyi felt "very familiar, perhaps because I have certainly followed her over the years and have communicated with her directly and indirectly." She said it was "like seeing a friend you hadn't seen for a very long time, even though it was our first meeting."

Suu Kyi told Clinton she still had the poster of the 1995 U.N. conference on women in Beijing that Madeleine Albright brought her in 1995. Mrs. Clinton presented her with rare editions of books authored and signed by Eleanor Roosevelt—and a dog bowl and chew toy for her new puppy. For her part, Suu Kyi gifted the Secretary with a silver necklace that she had fashioned herself out of a traditional ethnic necklace.

The next morning, the two women met again at Suu Kyi's lakeside home and got down to business with their staffs in attendance. According to reports, they talked about how to keep up global pressure to keep the reforms in Burma moving. They compared impressions of President Thein Sein and seemed inclined to reserve judgment until they could weigh more of his actions. "There has to be a momentum behind reform, and we're waiting and watching for that," said Mrs. Clinton. Suu Kyi said she had been reading books about military men who became politicians, including President Eisenhower.

After the meeting, the two spoke to the media from the porch of Suu Kyi's aging home. Suu Kyi indicated she was planning to run for Parliamentary office in the spring. A few of her remarks sounded like a future stump speech as she called for equal rights for all ethnic communities in this "union of many people."

The usually reserved Suu Kyi held on to Mrs. Clinton's hand while she thanked the U.S. for its help and its "calibrated" approach to re-engagement with Burma's government.

Clinton later had the chance to meet with President Thein Sein at the presidential palace surrounded by a moat in Naypyidaw. Seated on gold thrones, the two discussed upgrading diplomatic ties—the U.S. had withdrawn its ambassador after the repression of the 1988 student protests and the nullification of the 1990 election. She indicated that the U.S. would support some modest changes in Burma's relationship with the World Bank and the International Monetary Fund. But she stopped short of supporting any easing of sanctions on Burma, linking their removal to further progress on reform.

Thein Sein hailed a "new chapter" in relations with the U.S. He and his wife stood on the steps of the giant marble palace to bid farewell and watched as Clinton's black limousine drive away over the bridge. When one of the occupants of a van in the motorcade waved good-bye to Thein Sein, he obligingly waved back.

Looking back, one BBC journalist observed that the slightly built president on the steps seemed dwarfed by the oversize building. Although Thein Sein repeatedly had said he was committed to reforms, observers remained skeptical that he had the temperament or power to push beyond the first stages of reform, especially since some hard-liners in the government were not on board. There still were important milestones to be met. The Burmese government had not released all of its political prisoners—and was still arresting critics for demonstrating without permission. Despite cease-fire talks, Tatmadaw troops were still being trucked into ethnic areas. Reports of rapes had not abated. Land confiscations were on the increase. As transitions go, it was a fast-moving but inconsistent beginning.

—w—

To check the pulse of the country for myself, I revisited Burma in that spring of 2012, just in time to see Aung San Suu Kyi on the campaign trail.

The Nobel Peace Prize winner was opening an office for her political party in a dusty suburb of Rangoon, part of her new campaign for a seat in Parliament. The guessing game of the hour was whether the April 1 election would be free and fair as promised, or another cruel disappointment for the people in Burma.

Two hours before the mid-morning campaign stop, thousands of people were already filling the streets, jostling for a place to see the balcony where Suu Kyi would appear. A man wearing a T-shirt with Suu Kyi's picture on it proudly carried his toddler daughter in his arms so she could see "The

Lady." On one side of me was a farmer in a traditional peasant straw hat, and on the other a shopgirl in a cotton sarong who waved a tiny red flag with the fighting-peacock symbol of the NLD.

Buddhist monks in burnt-orange robes walked slowly through the swelling crowd as if they were out seeking morning alms and just "happened" to be on the block where Suu Kyi was speaking. They had paid a deadly price for their protests in the "Saffron Revolution" of 2007. They seemed less visible on the streets five years later.

Just a year before, the monks and the farmer and the shopgirl might have been arrested for attending the rally. There was a lot of nervous looking-around in the crowd, as if the army trucks could roll up at any moment.

The only one who seemed totally at ease was Aung San Suu Kyi herself. When she emerged on the balcony, she spoke to the tens of thousands of people as if they were visitors in her living room. With her trademark spray of flowers tucked into the back of her dark hair, she noted that some people were dismissing the upcoming election because it was only to fill 48 vacant seats in the 656-member Parliament; but her teasing answer to them was, "Please help us to get all the seats." She added with a laugh, "People from other parties can vote for us—we don't discriminate."

She talked about the need for "rule of law" and building bridges to the ethnic minorities in the country, as she had over the years, but this time she also emphasized the need for solutions to the widespread poverty in Burma. New foreign investment would help short-term with the jobless problem, she said, but "if our people are not educated, the country can't develop."

Health also must be a priority, she said—a nod to the fact that less than 2 percent of the national budget is spent on health and education combined, while an estimated 30–50 percent is spent on the military. After the Nargis debacle, Suu Kyi consistently maintained that humanitarian aid going forward must be structured in a way to ensure that more of it actually reaches people. She called for more accountability, monitoring, and transparency.

Yet Suu Kyi said she had come that day primarily to support another NLD candidate in the district, Dr. May Win Myint. She said Dr. Myint had stayed with the democracy movement "among many struggles and troubles." Indeed—Dr. Myint was elected to Parliament in the 1990 election but, like Suu Kyi, was never allowed by the military to serve. She was arrested in 1997 for trying to arrange a meeting between Suu Kyi and NLD leaders and spent more than seven years in prison, where she suffered from serious heart difficulties. After her release, she used her medical training to treat victims of leprosy who the junta had ignored. When the new military/civilian government announced that an election would be held to fill vacancies in Parliament, Suu Kyi and Dr. Myint were among the first to step forward to run, despite knowing that if the government reneged, they would be among the first to be arrested.

People in the crowd knew their photos were probably being taken by the military plants in the audience, but they came anyway. If this was indeed a Burma Spring, they were going to do their part. There were tentative signs of change all around:

- The business lounges in four-star hotels that had been sparse after the Saffron Revolution were now crowded with foreign businessmen—butter salesmen from Australia and real-estate speculators from Hong Kong. Many of them discovered fairly quickly the people in Burma had no money to buy their goods. They were worried the Burmese laws and the banks could not protect their investments. But the government said it was working on that.
- Human-rights workers and church leaders confirmed that yes, there were fewer soldiers on the corners in Rangoon—but brutal assaults by the army were still taking place in ethnic areas. More than 70,000 Kachins in northern Burma had been displaced as a result. The stranded people were in dire need of humanitarian assistance, and yet the military wouldn't allow aid workers in.
- Cab drivers pointed out that a SIM card for a cell phone that used to cost $2,000 now only cost around $500. That was still unreachable for the many living on less than $1 a day. Burma's mobile penetration rate was less than 4 percent at the time, one of the lowest in the world, below even North Korea, Cuba, Somalia, and South Sudan. Communication like the text messaging that brought crowds to protest in Tahrir Square in Cairo was difficult.

After the rally, I talked to three democracy activists who had just been released from prison. They were students when they had first been arrested and had served 65 years in prison among them. Much of the life they had dreamed of as college students had passed them by. I asked how they could see themselves five years from now. They looked surprised by the question. One replied with a bitter laugh, "We could all be back in prison in five years!!"

So was spring really coming to Rangoon? "We'll see," they said. Come back next year.

As April 1 neared, Suu Kyi encountered the same type of harassment she had endured back in 1989, 1996, and 2003. Permission was denied to hold rallies in public spaces large enough to accommodate her crowds, such as football stadiums. NLD posters were defaced.

After so many years of isolation, the hectic campaign schedule began to wear on Suu Kyi. She threw up at one event and felt faint at another. She made light of the incidents in a press conference, telling reporters that if they asked a question that was too tough, "I will faint straight away."

Despite those difficulties and more than a few voting irregularities, when the by-election results came in, the NLD won a landslide 43 out of 44 seats it had contested. At long last, "The Lady" would be a member of the Burmese Parliament. "We won! We won!" the crowds cheered in front of the NLD headquarters. She told them, 'We hope that this will be the beginning of a new era, when there will be more emphasis on the role of the people in the everyday politics of our country." She called on all parties to support national reconciliation to create a "genuinely democratic" Burma.

~

While the overwhelming victory largely was an indicator of Aung San Suu Kyi's continuing popularity, it also was a success for the Thein Sein government's reforms: Three days later, the U.S. responded by announcing it would relax some of its sanctions on Burma to reflect the democratic transition, including a ban on companies investing in or offering financial services there.

Secretary of State Hillary Clinton hailed the "dramatic demonstration of popular will" that brought the Nobel Peace Prize laureate Aung San Suu Kyi to a seat in the Lower House of Parliament. She said the administration would continue its process of engagement, but it would move cautiously. The Southeast Asian country still had a long way to go.

The package Secretary Clinton presented was a modest first step toward lifting the complex web of U.S. sanctions that had been put in place over the years. It was announced that the U.S. would set up an office of the U.S. Agency for International Development in Burma and would support a regular U.N. Development Program operation in the country. Clinton hinted at more changes, saying in carefully couched diplomatic-speak that the administration was committed to "beginning the process of a targeted easing of our ban on the export of U.S. financial services and investment as part of a broader effort to help accelerate economic modernization and political reform." U.S. officials said some of the areas that might be ripe for an easing of the investment ban were agriculture, tourism, telecommunications, and banking but said these were simply possibilities and no decisions had been taken.

Clinton also said the United States was also ready to allow private U.S. aid groups to pursue nonprofit activities on projects such as democracy building, health, and education, and to give select Burma officials and lawmakers permission to visit the United States, relaxing longstanding visa bans. The European Union followed suit by suspending many of its economic restrictions. The game was on. Business representatives for Ford, Pepsi, GE, MasterCard, Heineken, Google, and, yes, Starbucks sent scouts to check out the possibilities in "the Golden Land."

—∾—

Oil companies took particular interest in the new opportunities. The oil industry began several centuries ago in Burma as a family business. Crude oil was extracted from shallow pits by bucket brigades in the area around Yenangyaung in southwest-central Burma. Workers with ropes tied around their waists, so they could be pulled back out, descended into the oil pits to scoop out buckets of the black gold. Those early oilfields generally were in the hands of families who passed control from one generation to another generation.

British soldier-diplomats noted the existence of oil drilling as early as 1755. The Burmah Company (later to become British Petroleum) was founded in 1886 by a Scotsman named David Sime Cargill to develop oil interests. Burmah Oil held a monopoly until 1901, when Standard Oil Company began operating. Halliburton's first foreign operation was selling equipment in Burma in 1926.

In World War II, Yenangyaung was the location of a strategically important oil refinery. When the Japanese advanced with rapid speed through Burma, the retreating Allied forces were forced to blow up the oilfields and refinery to prevent them falling into the hands of the Japanese.

All the oil interests were nationalized after 1962 when General Ne Win took over. A state oil company was created from the nationalized assets of Burmah Oil, first under the name the People's Oil, then as Myanma Oil and Gas Enterprise (MOGE). Over time, MOGE would become known as a prime resource for laundering drug profits and producing profits for the generals that are tucked away in Singapore banks.

It is estimated thay the military government earns more than $3 billion a year from sales of natural gas. The government also earns $1 billion a year from the Yadana pipeline that ships gas to Thailand and will earn $1 billion a year from a new gas pipeline to China.

Under the quasi-civilian government of Thein Sein, 20 offshore blocks have put up for tender to foreign interests, such as Royal Dutch Shell, ConocoPhillips, and Total.

Though Burma has less than 1 percent of the world's total reserves, the oil and gas are strategically placed. The fuel that was once a magnet for the British and the Japanese, is now drawing interest from China, India, and Thailand.

For Aung San Suu Kyi, there was a special bonus from the new openness: she would be able to go to Norway to give her Nobel Prize acceptance speech at long last. Two decades had gone by. Her husband—who had sought the prize for her to protect her life—had since died. Oceans and time had distanced her from her sons. This time she would go to Oslo and speak for herself, with the tacit understanding from Thein Sein that she would be able to return to Burma to continue her mission.

Suu Kyi traveled to Norway from Switzerland, her first stop on a two-week sentimental victory tour of Europe. In Geneva, she spoke before the International Labor Organization, a United Nations agency that was working to eliminate the practice of forced labor. The practice is still widespread in Burma, and she wanted to encourage their work.

The real drama was ahead in Norway. Her appearance in Oslo was described by Nobel authorities as the "most remarkable in the entire history of the Nobel prizes." A trumpet fanfare sounded as Suu Kyi entered the grand city hall, looking impossibly petite in the cavernous space. She had chosen a deep purple tunic and lavender silk scarf, which gave her an almost royal look. Before she could say a word, she received a sustained standing ovation. Suu Kyi blinked a few times, composed herself and began to speak in her measured, calm voice. She shared her feelings of isolation under house arrest, her understanding of the Buddhist concept of suffering, her hopes and fears for her country's future, and the importance of the peace prize itself. It had drawn the attention of the world to the struggle for democracy and human rights in Burma. "We were not going to be forgotten," she said.

She pointed out that the French say that to part is to die a little and added, "To be forgotten too is to die a little. It is to lose some of the links that anchor us to the rest of humanity. When I met Burmese migrant workers and refugees during my recent visit to Thailand, many cried out: 'Don't forget us!' They meant: 'Don't forget our plight, don't forget to do what you can to help us, don't forget we also belong to your world.'"

When the Nobel Committee awarded the Peace Prize to her, she said, they were recognizing that the oppressed and the isolated in Burma "were also a part of the world; they were recognizing the oneness of humanity."

Suu Kyi then recalled how her ordeal had prompted her to examine the six concepts of suffering within her Buddhist faith, and two in particular: To be separated from those one loves, and to be forced to live in propinquity with those one does not love. It made her think of "prisoners and refugees, of migrant workers and victims of human trafficking, of that great mass of the uprooted of the earth who have been torn away from their homes, parted from families and friends, forced to live out their lives among strangers who are not always welcoming."

The global aim, she said, should be to create a world where no one is displaced, homeless, or hopeless. She warned, "Wherever suffering is ignored, there will be the seeds for conflict, for suffering degrades and embitters and enrages." She appealed for help in freeing the remaining Burmese political prisoners who had not been included in recent amnesties. She lamented that in her own country, "hostilities have not yet ceased in the far north. To the west, communal violence resulting in arson and murder were taking place just several days before I started out on the journey that has brought me here today."

She spoke of the need for ethnic inclusion and national reconciliation, but noted that over the past year there had been changes in a positive direction. "If I advocate cautious optimism, it is not because I do not have faith in the future, but because I do not want to encourage blind faith." She then spoke of the lessons she had learned in isolation, a quote seemed destined for books of quotations and commencement addresses: "Of the sweets of adversity, and let me say that these are not numerous, I have found the sweetest, the most precious of all, is the lesson I learned on the value of kindness. Every kindness I received, small or big, convinced me that there could never be enough of it in our world. To be kind is to respond with sensitivity and human warmth to the hopes and needs of others. Even the briefest touch of kindness can lighten a heavy heart. Kindness can change the lives of people."

She closed with the thank-you she had not been able to give in 1990: "When I joined the democracy movement in Burma, it never occurred to me that I might ever be the recipient of any prize or honor. The prize we were working for was a free, secure, and just society where our people might be able to realize their full potential. The honor lay in our endeavor. History had given us the opportunity to give of our best for a cause in which we believed. When the Nobel Committee chose to honor me, the road I had chosen of my own free will became a less lonely path to follow. For this I thank the Committee, the people of Norway, and peoples all over the world whose support has strengthened my faith in the common quest for peace. Thank you."

When she had initially received the Nobel Prize in 1990, the chairman had said her struggle for democracy was a reminder of the "power of good." Her speech in 2012 was a reminder of the power of honor and duty.

Aung San Suu Kyi's "victory lap" took her on to Dublin to receive an Amnesty International award from Bono, the lead singer for U2, who had done so much to take her message to the younger generation. Then back to England to receive an honorary degree from her alma mater Oxford, "a city full of memories" of her young married life. She had not been back to England since the time she answered the 1988 call that her mother was ailing in Burma and she was needed. It was surely a bittersweet homecoming; she seemed thoughtful as she walked through the pomp and circumstance. Then she was on to London, where she planted a tree with the Prince of Wales and Duchess of Cornwall. She was invited to speak before both Houses of Parliament from Westminster Hall, an honor traditionally reserved for major heads of state. As London's *Daily Mail* cheekily put it, "The Steel Butterfly will now outrank such figures as Ethiopia Emperor Haile Selassie, Nikita Khrushchev, U.S. presidents Bill Clinton and Ronald Reagan, and French presidents Mitterrand, Chirac, and Sarkozy who were only received in the Royal Gallery."

In a less grandiose moment, she stopped by the BBC to thank all those whose broadcasts had provided her with a lifeline to the rest of the world for many years—including a disk jockey with the improbable name of "The Hairy Cornflake," who hosted one of her favorite programs, *Desert Island Discs*. (And what would the democracy leader choose to take with her if she were stranded on a desert island, or, in her case, her home? For pop music, she chose "Here Comes the Sun" by the Beatles; John Lennon's "Imagine"; and Welsh singer Tom Jones' "Green, Green Grass of Home." Her list also included traditional Burmese music, Mozart's Overture to *The Magic Flute,* and Pachelbel's Canon. Her chosen book was the Buddhist *Abhidhamma,* and her luxury item was a pot of roses that would change color every day.) While she chatted about her favorites, the halls were jammed with BBC journalists and news anchors. They threw professional decorum out of the way to get a glimpse of the woman they'd been writing and talking about for two decades.

Then there was a stop in France for more grand dinners and awards, and the long trip back to steamy Rangoon and the house by the lake. The international support she stoked while abroad would be important, but the real test would come when she would begin her new job as a member of Parliament in July.

Aung San Suu Kyi made her debut in the Pyithu Hluttaw, the Lower House of Parliament, on July 9, 2012. "I will try my best for the country," she told Agence France-Press.

At the time, she was surrounded on all sides by allies of the military in Parliament. There were rows and rows of members still in full military uniform. In a classic example of speaking truth to power, her first speech was a call for laws that would protect the rights of the nation's ethnic minorities.

—w—

For his part, President Thein Sein was moving to consolidate his own position. He announced a major cabinet shuffle over the summer of nine ministers and 15 deputy ministers, filling the positions previously held by hard-liners tied to Than Shwe with political allies, or so it seemed.

Thein Sein's management team was getting more savvy about public relations, and they scheduled interviews with key media organizations such as the BBC. When Thein Sein was asked whether he was afraid he would be swept away by the winds of change like Mikhail Gorbachev after the fall of the Soviet Union, he answered sharply, "I would like to say that Gorbachev and I are not alike, I tell you that."

Both he and Aung San Suu Kyi would make historic trips to the United States that fall: she to accept her Gold Medal from Congress, he to attend the United Nations General Assembly in New York, the first head of state from Burma to do so. On September 27, he told the U.N. audience that "amazing changes" were happening in Burma that were "tangible, irreversible steps in the democratic reform process." Myanmar, he said, "is now ushering in a new era."

In an example of exactly how fast the changes were occurring, he had just been taken off the American sanctions blacklist the week before so he could enter the country. Secretary of State Clinton met with him the day before his U.N. speech to announce that the U.S. would ease a ban on imports from Burma as a reward for his efforts.

It was a week of firsts. According to the Associated Press, Thein Sein's U.N. address was the first time a leader from Burma had mentioned Aung San Suu Kyi by name at a world body. He had taken care to congratulate her for the honors she had received "in recognition of her efforts for democracy." His remarks were also broadcast live in Burma, another first.

Still, as NPR noted, the international community remained wary and watchful. It was unclear how far Thein Sein would be willing, and able, to go in implementing more democratic changes. He had said he was no Gorbachev, and in time it would be clear he was not going to be a DeKlerk to Suu Kyi's Mandela and hand over power to her either.

The week before, Suu Kyi had completed the last big event on her victory tour, the presentation of the Congressional Gold Medal. She was originally awarded the medal during the last year of the Bush administration, making her the first person to receive the award while incarcerated.

Now she was coming to Washington to collect the honor and thank the Americans who had stood up for her in Congress, in the U.N., and in the press. The event was held in the Capitol rotunda—with a fresco on the ceiling of George Washington looking down from the heavens and the Marine Band thundering out Sousa marches on the side, it was a stirring occasion. Washington usually does not do pomp as well as Europeans, but this was a respectable effort. One after another, Aung San Suu Kyi's most stalwart supporters stood up to praise her, while she sat with folded hands and looked vaguely uncomfortable at being praised over and over.

I winced as a few of the speakers stumbled over her name, but she seemed unfazed with her expression unchanged, surely the result of a lifetime of hearing her name mispronounced and pretending not to notice.

Senator Mitch McConnell praised her for making sacrifices for "generations she would not know." Speaker Pelosi saluted her as a "soul pilgrim." Laura Bush, who got to meet her "secret sister" for the first time in person that day, said that the transition in Burma, like the past events in South Africa or Eastern Europe, "shows that history has a hopeful direction. It is capable of miracles. . . . As Mandela and Havel demonstrated, vast historical changes often begin in a single mind, a single heart. And the hope that now grows in Burma is a tribute to Daw Suu." She hailed Suu Kyi as "the mother of her country."

Senator John McCain verged on tears as he recalled his first meeting with Suu Kyi fifteen years before and being amazed that this "picture of gentleness and serenity" could be the same "implacable lady" who had defied the men of Burma's military-backed regime. "I might have hoped, but I would never have expected that one day I would have the honor of welcoming my personal hero Aung San Suu Kyi to the Congress of the United States." It was a genuinely emotional moment as the former POW's voice broke and he struggled to go on.

Secretary Clinton broke the tension with a light moment: During her recent visit to Burma, the Speaker of the House, Shwe Mann, had asked her to help them learn how to be a democratic congress. "He went on to tell me that they were trying to teach themselves by watching old segments of *The West Wing*," she said. "I told him, 'I think we can do better than that, Mr. Speaker.'"

When it was Aung San Suu Kyi's turn, she won the day with her concise, dignified response. "From the depths of my heart, I thank you, the people of America, and you, their representatives, for keeping us in your hearts and minds during the dark years when freedom and justice seemed beyond our reach," she said. "This is one of the most moving days of my life," she said. "A house joined together to welcome a stranger from distant land."

That evening, she met with President Obama and invited him to come see her. A few months later, he did just that, becoming the first sitting president to visit Burma.

Although President Obama's visit on November 19, 2012 was for only six hours—some wags called it the diplomatic equivalent of speed-dating—his visit was seen as a validation of the new direction in Burma. And recognition that the U.S. was sufficiently anxious about China's growing aggressiveness in the region to restore bonds with Burma. In deference to his hosts, the president even departed from U.S. policy to refer to the country as Myanmar.

The mood was welcoming, although the atmosphere was uncomfortably muggy when President Obama made the obligatory pilgrimage to Aung San Suu Kyi's home on Inya Lake. Her house now gleamed with a coat of white paint. Roses were blooming in the garden. It looked much more like the home of a national leader.

Aung San Suu Kyi welcomed the leader of the free world with warmth and candor. The United States had been "staunch" in its support of the democracy movement in Burma, she said, "and we are confident that this support will continue through the difficult years that lie ahead. I say difficult because the most difficult time in any transition is when we think that success is in sight. Then we have to be very careful that we are not lured by a mirage of success and that we are working to a genuine success for our people and for the friendship between our two countries."

President Obama observed that the day marked the next step in a new chapter between the United States and Burma and took ownership of that change. He noted that it had only been a year, "in response to early flickers of reform," since he had asked Secretary Clinton to visit Burma "and explore with Aung San Suu Kyi and the government whether the United States could empower reform efforts and begin a new relationship between our peoples.

"In the year since, we've seen some very encouraging progress, including Daw Aung San Suu Kyi's release and election to Parliament; the release of political prisoners; the lifting of restrictions on the press; and new laws to expand labor rights and eliminate the use of child soldiers. And at my direction, the United States has responded to support these reforms, including the easing of sanctions."

He said the administration's goal was to sustain the momentum for democratization. "That includes building credible government institutions, establishing rule of law, ending ethnic conflicts, and ensuring that the people of this country have access to greater education, healthcare, and economic opportunity."

He promised that if progress continued, bilateral ties would grow stronger.

Then he gave a collegial "shout-out" to Secretary of State Hillary Clinton, who had stayed deferentially in the background while he spoke. "I'm so happy, by the way, to be joined by Secretary Clinton. This is her last foreign trip that we're going to take together, and it is fitting that we have come here to a country that she has done so much to support. Where did Hillary go? Where is she? There she is. (Applause.) I could not be more grateful, not only for your service, Hillary, but also for the powerful message that you and Aung San Suu Kyi send about the importance of women and men everywhere embracing and promoting democratic values and human rights."

It was a timely valedictory for the Secretary of State, who would be leaving her post after the first of the year to return to a "normal life." She would count normalization of relations with Burma as one of her accomplishments, and so would her boss. President Obama would later be criticized for prematurely counting Burma as a foreign-policy success in a speech to graduates of the West Point military academy in May 2014. Obama said that with the courage of the Burmese people, U.S. diplomatic initiative was a driver of democratic reform in Burma. "We're now supporting reform and badly needed national reconciliation through assistance and investment, through coaxing and, at times, public criticism," he said. "Progress there could be reversed, but if Burma succeeds, we will have gained a new partner without having fired a shot."

It was a catchy sound bite, but it came back to bite him. Burmese officials shot back that that the claim was a "boast," saying reform in Burma was driven by itself without any help from the U.S.

Clinton was careful to hedge her bets more explicitly in her memoir, *Hard Choices*. She had been warned privately by Aung San Suu Kyi during her Washington visit that further reforms had been slowed. Clinton wrote, "The end of Burma's story is yet to be written and there are many challenges ahead. Ethnic strife has continued, raising alarms about new human rights abuses." She singled out the mob violence against the Rohingya Muslims, saying it threatened to undermine progress and weaken international support. "It is sometimes hard to resist getting breathless about Burma. But we have to remain clear-eyed and levelheaded about the challenges and difficulties that lie ahead. Some in Burma lack the will to complete the democratic journey. Other possess the will, but lack the tools. There is still a long way to go."

Even as she tested the waters for a presidential campaign in 2016, Mrs. Clinton kept up her telephone conversations with Aung San Suu Kyi and stayed in close touch with Deputy National Security Advisor Ben Rhodes on Burma issues. It was clear that whatever her role in public life would be going forward, her interest in Burma would continue. And there was more work to be done.

—~—

The president's historic speech in Burma was a prime example of the difficulty of separating reality from illusion in Burma, which so often is like a political house of mirrors. Just before President Obama had arrived, President Thein Sein offered additional gestures of reform. His office announced that the government would set up a process to review the fate of remaining political prisoners by the end of the year, allow international human-rights organizations more access to prisons and conflict zones, and take "decisive action" to stop violence against the country's minority Muslim population.

At the time, more than 200 political prisoners remained in custody. A process was indeed started to review those cases, but in the meantime more arrests were being made. Peace talks were indeed under way, but in the meantime the government was continuing a brutal campaign against insurgents in Kachin State. Permission for a promised U.N. Human Rights Commission office in Rangoon was on hold. Human Rights Watch said that week that satellite imagery showed violence, arson, and extensive destruction of homes in the Rohingya Muslim areas in western Burma; violence that reportedly was carried out with the support of state security forces and local government officials. The upshot was that despite President Thein Sein's assurances, violence and repression were continuing.

The "invisible hand" of the *ancien regime* was suspected in the violence, perhaps to stir up enough trouble to warrant a return to direct military control if the democratic liberalization got out of hand. Although Senior General Than Shwe was said to be retired, all the men in positions of power had been selected by him. "It's his game plan, his appointees," said a long-time human-rights activist after a visit to Burma. "This is a government that is anti-Muslim, anti-Christian, anti-anything that is not Buddhist nationalist. And if there is something good that comes from the earth, they own it. You have to be realistic."

—⁓—

Later in the day, President Obama announced the return of the United States Agency for International Development along with $170 million for projects over the next two years, reminding that in his inaugural address he had vowed to reach out to those "willing to unclench your fist."

"So today, I have come to keep my promise and extend the hand of friendship," he said in a major address at the University of Rangoon.

The president promised to help rebuild the economy and develop new institutions that can be sustained. "The flickers of progress that we have seen must not be extinguished—they *must* become a shining north star for *all* this nation's people," he said.

Although human-rights activists criticized his visit as premature because of the remaining political prisoners and violence racking parts of the country, Mr. Obama gave one of the strongest human-rights speeches of his administration at the university. He used the occasion to nudge Burma to move further. He warned that greater improvements in human rights must be made before *real* partnerships can take effect and Western economic sanctions completely removed. He took clear aim at the military's iron grip on Parliament when he said, "those in power must accept constraints," pointing to the restraints on his own presidential power.

And he told the students in the audience, "As more wealth flows into your borders, we hope and expect that it will lift up more people. It can't just help the folks at the top; it has to help everybody." He even got a smattering of applause when he encouraged national reconciliation between warring groups.

"That is how you must reach for the future you deserve," he said. "A future where a single prisoner of conscience is one too many and the law is stronger than any leader, where no child is made to be a soldier and no woman is exploited, where national security is strengthened by a military that serves under civilians and a constitution guarantees that only those who are elected by the people may govern. . . . *This* is what the 21st century should look like."

He received solid applause, the best that could be expected from a hand-picked audience that knew they were being watched carefully. On the front row was Ashin Gambira; the monk had been released earlier in the year from a six-decade sentence that he received for helping lead the 2007 "Saffron Revolution" democracy uprising. His presence was seen as one of the signs of the softening of oppression in the country that the president referred to.

A few weeks later, however, Gambira was back behind bars again, in what his family said was the latest incident of harassment by authorities. Once released, he retreated to Thailand, to get out of harm's way, and began teaching refuges.

There were more telling exaples that things weren't always what they seemed in the new Naypyidaw government. The government had ordered a quick fresh coat of white paint for the deteriorating auditorium building just before Obama's speech. The Rangoon campus had been closed on and off since the 1980's to discourage student dissent and had been left to go downhill, along with the country's education system.

But only the front façade of columns got the new paint, to present a perfect view for TV cameras. The back of the British-era building was still faded and in disrepair. And most of the classrooms were still closed to students after the president flew away.

A TIMELINE OF THE BURMA SPRING

2009

February 19: Secretary of State Hillary Clinton announces a review of Burma policy

July 23: In Phuket, Clinton calls on the Burmese junta to release democracy leader Aung San Suu Kyi and encourages ASEAN members to pressure the generals to "change their direction"

August 15: Senator Jim Webb meets with Senior General Than Shwe and Aung San Suu Kyi; secures the release of John Yettaw

2010

November 7: First general elections in Burma in 20 years

November 13: Aung San Suu Kyi freed from house arrest

March 30: Formal transfer of power to new government

May 16: 14,600 prisoners released, but only 58 political prisoners

August 19: Aung San Suu Kyi meets Burmese President Thein Sein

September 2010: President Obama announces his administration will pursue a policy of engaging the generals who rule Burma rather than rebuffing them

September 30: President Thein Sein suspends work on Myitsone Dam

October 6: Human rights commission established

October 12: Some 200 political prisoners freed

October 28: New labor laws allowing unions passed

November 17: Burma granted ASEAN chair in 2014

November 21: Aung San Suu Kyi says she will stand for election

December 2: Secretary of State Hillary Clinton visits Burma

December 3: Thein Sein signs a law allowing peaceful demonstrations, but requiring prior registration

December 8: Burmese authorities agree to a truce with rebels of the Shan ethnic group and order the military to stop operations against Kachin rebels, although fighting continues

December 23: NLD registers as political party

2012

January 12: Karen ceasefire signed

January 13: Highest-profile political prisoners freed, including Shan leader U Khun Htun Oo, 88 Generation leader Min Ko Naing, and U Gambira, the monk who led the Saffron Revolution

January 13: Secretary Clinton announces the U.S. will normalize relations with Burma and exchange ambassadors

April 1: Aung San Suu Kyi elected to Parliament

June: Suu Kyi gives Nobel Prize Lecture, visits Oxford, Dublin, London, and Paris

August: Burma removes 2,082 names from its blacklist that bars people deemed a threat to national security from entering or leaving the country—the list including former Secretary of State Madeline Albright

September: President Thein Sein addresses the U.N.; Aung San Suu Kyi receives Congressional Gold Medal

October: Violence spreads in the Rakhine area of western Burma and in Muslim areas of the country

November: President Barack Obama visits Burma

December: The government announces that privately owned newspapers are to be allowed in Burma for the first time in 50 years

Burma ushers in the New Year for the first time with a public countdown

CHAPTER 18

THE GAME OF THRONES

"Never forget what you are, for surely the world will not. Make it your strength. Then it can never be your weakness. Armor yourself in it, and it will never be used to hurt you."

—George R. R. Martin, *A Game of Thrones*

When I first came to Rangoon in 2003, there were large, threatening signs at the major intersections. The blood-red billboards warned that the mighty Tatmadaw army was watching. "BEWARE OF FOREIGN STOOGES," the signs said.

A decade later, those ominous billboards had all but vanished. Instead, there were smaller, baby blue signs that advised, "Warmly welcome and take care of tourists." The new signs got less notice because they were dwarfed by giant billboards for Samsung mini-tablets, Elizabeth Taylor-sized jewels, and face-whitening cream, evidence of an evolving society with aspirations.

There was plenty of time to ponder the signs of change while stuck in traffic. Gridlock was the new norm in Rangoon. Fleets of new cars, mostly Toyotas, had been imported by elites and foreign investors after most restrictions were dropped. The narrow byways from the colonial era were jammed like Times Square at rush hour. Rangoon had become a boomtown. It was quite a change from my first arrival in Rangoon. My first taxi from the airport in 2003 was so ancient, it died mid-way to the hotel; the engine in the second went up in smoke; and the third ran out of gas a block from the hotel.

Now Rangoon was a boom town. Hotel room prices had doubled and tripled. Tourism was expected to leap from one million to three million by 2015. You could now rent a cell phone at the airport. And there was a handy ATM in the hotel lobby that sometimes worked.

Even more surprising, photos of Aung San Suu Kyi could be bought openly in the market, a criminal offense when I had first visited. Skinny street kids who used to tap desperately on car windows to sell hand-made flower necklaces were now walking between the cars in traffic selling real-estate listings.

Every day seemed to bring a new breakthrough. Burma participated in the Miss Universe competition for the first time in 50 years. The BBC and Democratic Voice of Burma, stern watchdogs of the military regime in years past, had been given permission to open news bureaus. And women were invited to join the army.

Burma was making up for lost time. At the posh new French restaurant "Agnes," you can get a respectable *foie gras* and mushroom soup with a view of the magnificent Shwedagon Pagoda. Coca-Cola had entered the market and already needed to add another bottling site to keep up with demand.

But at the same time, there were daily signs that the *ancien regime* was not giving up power easily. The government was still arresting demonstrators, still punishing reporters who challenged their established order, still grabbing land, still rewarding cronies with sweetheart deals. There was not a happy ending to the Burma Spring story yet.

Ancient hatreds were flaring up in abhorrent ways. Disagreements in villages spiraled out of control into riots between Buddhists and Muslims. People of different faiths who used to live in peace, perhaps united by their overall fear of the junta, now turned on each other in ugly reprisals. Anti-Muslim and anti-Rohingya hate speech and violence grew. The government forced more than 140,000 of the outcast Rohingya in western Rakhine State into holding areas that were quasi-concentration camps. The Médecins Sans Frontières (Doctors Without Borders) humanitarian organization was booted out of the country for confirming to the media that its doctors had treated injuries from anti-Muslim violence. The doctors' removal left thousands of people in the squalid Rohingya holding areas without medical care. So strong was anti-Muslim sentiment in some areas of the country that Buddhist monks stepped away from their pacifist teachings to take part in slugfests themselves. Monks marched in the streets demanding the expulsion of humanitarian workers providing aid to Muslims. A radical monk named Wirathu rallied thousands with messages of hate. The worldwide admiration that the russet-robed monks had earned for standing up to the military in the Saffron Revolution was sadly diminished.

At the same time, military attacks against ethnic populations in northern Burma continued with ferocity while peace talks moved by fits and starts. Soldiers continued to rape ethnic women with impunity. Out of 100 of the cases documented in 2014, 47 cases were brutal gang rapes. Several victims were as young as eight years old. More than two dozen of the women were killed in the rape or died from their injuries.

Thousands of farmers across the country were losing land to make way for government-approved deals. When they protested the confiscations, they were arrested. Farmers were the new political prisoners. Suspicions grew that the government was delaying peace talks so more rich lands could be seized in conflict areas. In 2014, the Asian Human Rights Commission slammed what it called a "frenzy" of land grabs by the government or government-linked companies.

Were these troubling issues merely "transition wobbles"—or a sign that the hard-line generals were still calling the shots? Had the talk about a "Burma Spring" been premature? And what would happen to Aung San Suu Kyi and her dream of a more just, caring country?

As I returned to Burma in 2013 and 2014, I could see signs of a society struggling to move into the modern world. I took mental snapshots of what was happening, because it took a mosaic of pictures to piece together what was going on.

SNAP: In the elegant executive club of a five-star hotel in Rangoon, a Western executive with a British accent could be overhead pitching a deal to an impassive Burmese businessman. "Could we schedule something before I have to leave? Otherwise it will have to wait until your boss comes to Singapore. And that is *months* away. What about breakfast tomorrow? Six A.M.—would that work for you? You could get your boss to come? We bring money, yes, but we also bring *expertise*. We are in Hong Kong and the Mainland, many years of experience there. If you want to go into the U.S., we have offices in New York. And in London. What we do is bring *capital*. We work closely with your company, but we don't get involved unless you want us to. Would 6 A.M. work? You tell me and we'll be there."

SNAP: On the old Ady Road, one of the houses where General Ne Win used to hold parties was being remodeled for the new European Union ambassador's home. The EU had jettisoned its economic restrictions and was racing to get a foothold in Burma. In what surely set a record for the runaway rents in Rangoon, the EU reportedly was paying $80,000–$100,000 a month for the Ady Road house. General Ne Win, who tossed all foreigners out of the country after his 1962 coup, would no doubt be surprised to hear one of his party houses was being rented to a foreigner for a million dollars per year. The EU staff set up offices in Hledan Center—which happened to be owned by regime crony Steven Law, who was still on America's sanctions list for illicit activities. Previous landowners still were complaining that they were not compensated for vacating the site.

SNAP: Hkun Tun Oo, the senior spokesman for the Shan people, was still recovering from six years in prison when we talked. He had difficulty walking but had not slowed down his efforts to gain more autonomy for the Shan, who account for more than nine percent of the population in Burma. The conflicts with the Burman majority had been going on for nearly three generations. He sighed, "If there's no peace with the ethnic nationalities, how can Burma go forward? There are casualties every day. The president says the fighting will stop. But the Burmese army keeps attacking. There is too much *Burmanism*. The ethnic nationalities do not trust the majority Burmans. They are still in the habit of not honoring their words. Peace with them is *impossible*. It is *impossible*. But we must keep trying."

SNAP: A middle-aged Australian tourist paused to talk in the hotel's business lounge before flying home. "It's been a perfectly lovely trip and I used to be in the travel business, so I *know* what it takes. We just finished this incredible river trip down the Irrawaddy for several really *nice* days. But I couldn't help feeling a twinge of guilt, you know, about the discrepancy between the *wealth* of the people on the tour and the *poverty* of the villages along the way. There was almost a riot when this woman tried to give away pens to the children who were begging, and there weren't enough for everyone. They were all crowding up around us. We tried to give them what we could, but the poverty! They were desperate to have a pen, just a pen, can you imagine? I'm still trying to process it. It stays with you, but the cruise down the river was lovely. And the food was good."

SNAP: U.S. Ambassador Derek Mitchell posed for photos with a new Ford Ranger truck and a Ford Taurus as Ford Motor Company announced its first dealership in Rangoon. Ford executives said the auto market holds great promise. With a population of more than 50 million, Burma has the lowest car ownership per capita in the world. Ford joined PepsiCo, Coca-Cola, GE, the Gap, and Danish brewer Carlsberg in signing deals in Burma, gambling that the recent political and economic reforms will pay off. Thirty-four international banks had opened offices in the country, where more than 80 percent of the population has been "unbanked."

SNAP: An abbot active in the Buddhist national movement called for people to boycott SIM cards as well as calls from cell phones provided by the Ooredoo mobile phone operator. Why? Because Ooredoo is owned by a company in Qatar. The abbot claimed the campaign was necessary to "protect the integrity of the Burmese nation and the religion" because users would not be able to talk freely over a network from an Islamic country. The abbot alleged subscribers would be "destroyers of their own race" if they used the Ooredoo phone service. Ooredoo had to issue a denial that it had NOT been planning to train its female sales force in the Middle East after rumors spread it was going to Islamize the trainees. To reassure the public of its good intentions, the Qatari company announced it was providing several mobile medical vans to bring healthcare to thousands in remote areas.

The boycott raised fears that the goal of raising cell-phone access from six percent to 80 percent of the population would be delayed. But so great was the pent-up demand, one million customers were signed up in three weeks. The cost of SIM cards was down to a mere $1.50. And another telephone provider, the Norwegian firm Telenor, was starting to offer phone service as well. More phone service before the 2015 elections would be a plus; people could talk to each other freely, access information from around the world, and provide eyewitness accounts of government abuses.

Billboards with handsome young soccer stars could be seen all around in 2013 saluting the opening of the Southeast Asian Games, a coming-out party of sorts after two years of partially relaxed military rule under Thein Sein. The opening ceremony of the SEA Games was a lavish extravaganza with fireworks—largely paid for and stage-managed by China. The Chinese not only subsidized the opening and closing ceremonies, they also trained 200 of the Burmese athletes in China and provided 700 coaches to help make the local team look good. The $33 million in support was a very visible example of Beijing's aggressive efforts to curry favor in Burma, where resistance has grown to China's heavy-handed exploitation of Burma's resources. Now that sanctions had been lifted and other countries had the ability to invest in Burma, China had competition.

While other countries had shunned Burma after the 1988 crackdown, China had no qualms about dealing with the Burmese generals. The People's Republic of China became Burma's largest trading partner, accounting for over 20 percent of its exports and 40 percent of its imports.

From 2008 to 2011, the Chinese cumulative investment in Burma jumped from the equivalent of $1 billion to nearly $13 billion, according to the Stimson Center. That was more than a third of the foreign investment in Burma.

The infusion of Chinese capital did not make the Burmese grow fonder of their Chinese benefactors. To the contrary, they developed an even greater fear of being overrun by their colossal neighbor to the north. Privately, the Burmese express great dislike for the Chinese. When I asked a Burmese businesswoman how the Burmese generals could still consider themselves faithful Buddhists after killing and impoverishing so many of their own countrymen, she snapped, "Because they are Chinese Buddhists!" It was not a compliment.

Burma and China may share a 1,300-mile border, but they have been uneasy neighbors for centuries. There is a history of conflict, from Manchu invasions across the mountains in the 18th century to the Chinese Nationalist incursions after World War II. Most recently, China has provided military support to the Wa State, a former Communist stronghold in northern Burma that has become a narco-state with its own militia of more than 30,000. China denies directly providing arms to the Wa, but *Jane's Intelligence Review* has reported Chinese assistance in the form of surface-to-air missiles, armored vehicles, and armed helicopters. Such interference inside Burma's borders rankles Burmese leaders.

Most Burmese also resent the fact that ethnic Chinese dominate commerce in cities such as Mandalay, as well as the border areas. Many of the top bankers in Rangoon have Chinese roots. The Burmese are well aware that much of the country's jade, gems, and teak holdings are being trucked off to China. Burma produces at least $4.3 billion in high-quality jade a year, and it is estimated that at least half of that is spirited over the border into China with little or no taxation. Burma has the world's only remaining golden teak forest, but the acreage covered by timber has been dramatically reduced by illegal teak shipments to China. The environmental advocacy group Global Witness reported in 2009 that one truck carrying 15 tons of illegal logs crossed the border into China's Yunnan province every seven minutes.

Then, too, many Burmese blame the Chinese for the drug trade that seeped in from China after World War II and resulted in the rise of the notorious "Golden Triangle" poppy-growing zone in northern Burma. Chinese gangs still operate much the drug-trafficking and sex-trafficking that is taking a deep toll on Burmese families.

China has invested particularly heavily in hydropower projects on Burma's rivers, with at least 45 companies developing over 60 hydropower projects. As a result, resentment grew in Burma that the environmentally questionable dams would cost local populations their ancestral homes and farmlands. Since almost all the energy will go north to China, anger has grown that residents have no say-so in the projects and no benefit. "Our government *takes* everything from us and gives *nothing* back," a young Kachin professional complained to me.

For its part, China sees neighboring Burma as a key part of President Xi Jinping's "China Dream" of rejuvenation and regional hegemony. China needs Burma's resources to make that dream a reality. Three giant projects illustrate the billions in resources that the Chinese have at stake in Burma: the Myitsone Dam, the Letpadaung copper mine, and the trans-Burma pipeline. All have stirred a backlash in Burma.

MYITSONE DAM

To the surprise of many, new President Thein Sein suspended construction of the $3.6 billion Myitsone Dam in September 2011 in response to massive demonstrations against the project. Aung San Suu Kyi was among those strongly in opposition to the dam. Since the suspension, the Chinese have been lobbying hard for a resumption of construction, which could come after the end of Thein Sein's term in 2015. The site has been declared off limits to visitors, but local residents say shipments from China of heavy construction machinery have continued. Dredging for gold reportedly has been going on behind a cordon of armed guards.

The giant Myitsone Dam—one of a cascade of seven Chinese hydropower projects on the Irrawaddy (Ayerwaddy)—has drawn criticism since its beginnings. Farmers have protested that they were not fairly compensated for their land. Environmentalists are concerned because the dam is located on the earthquake-prone Sagaing fault line.

Residents throughout the country consider the Irrawaddy their "mother river." They are angry because the dam would submerge important spiritual and historical sites. The river's headwaters, the confluence of the Mali and N'Mai rivers in Kachin State, are an especially sacred site. The proposed dam reservoir would be the size of Singapore, and the enormous flooding area would require the relocation of thousands of local villages. The dramatic changes would affect fisheries, sediment movements, and the livelihoods of people downstream. And on top of all that, villagers would still have to use candles for light while 90 percent of the electric power is sent to China.

The controversy has been exacerbated by the widespread belief that corruption was involved in the deal between the Burmese military government, China Power Investment Company (CPI), and the local partner Asia World Company, whose principal owner, Steven Law, has family ties to drug-trafficking and is on the U.S. sanctions list.

To counter criticism of the project, the Chinese investors have invested significant resources in public relations activities such as hosting Burmese media in China, increasing media access to company executives, and leafleting local communities.

LETPADAUNG MINE

The operation of the Letpadaung copper mine was suspended in November 2012, following angry local demonstrations about land seizures and pollution, yet has resumed after a compromise worked out by Aung San Suu Kyi. The $1.065 billion mine project is a joint venture between Wanbao Mining, a subsidiary of China's state-owned China North Industries Corporation (NORINCO) and Burma's Union of Myanmar Economic Holdings Ltd. (UMEHL), a military-run conglomerate.

A brutal crackdown in 2013 on protests against the expansion of the mine provoked a public uproar because white phosphorus gas was used against demonstrators, including monks. The escalating controversy prompted the government to form an inquiry commission headed by opposition leader Aung San Suu Kyi to look into the future of the mine. When the committee recommended that the project be continued with modifications to benefit residents, the democracy icon was jeered by villagers and criticized in the media. Wanbao dispatched a public relations official to win over residents with a PowerPoint presentation describing employment opportunities in a flourishing "mine city," with better schools, libraries, healthcare, water, roads, and electricity supply. Yet the controversy is still simmering.

SINO-MYANMAR PIPELINE

Only China's giant Shwe Gas project, which brings offshore natural gas and imported oil from Burma's coast to China, has proceeded comparatively smoothly. That project includes $2.54 billion parallel pipelines that connect a Burmese deep-water port on the Bay of Bengal with China's energy-hungry provinces. The $1.5 billion gas pipeline began operations in July 2013, followed by the $1.05 billion oil pipeline that fall. China's piped gas previously was imported from areas around the Malacca Strait; now China had a land line rather than a more dangerous sea lane.

Opposition to the pipeline project largely focused on human-rights abuses during construction, environmental damage, and poor revenue-sharing with localities. Learning from the rising tide of criticism against other projects, the China National Petroleum Company (CNPC) has made efforts to ameliorate criticism by increasing the share of oil and gas for local consumption and support for local communities. According to recent reports, a CNPC public relations team has helped defuse dissent with a 42-page document outlining community outreach, which included $20 million worth of schools, clinics, and other amenities.

Notably, all three of China's major projects in Burma were finalized between December 2009 and June 2010. China rushed through the closure of the deals before Burma's leadership changed in 2011.

Another mega-project, a $20 billion Burmese railroad project that would link the Chinese province of Yunnan to the coast of Burma and the Bay of Bengal, also appeared to have been a casualty of the Burmese backlash. The three-year memorandum of understanding for the project was allowed to expire in summer 2014.

The railway to the Chinese city of Kunming was supposed to follow the gas and oil pipelines across Burma. Burmese authorities said privately they did not want Burma to become "another Crimea," ripe for takeover by China, or "another province of China."

As the result of growing resistance to its projects, China's investments in Burma during 2012–13 declined to $407 million after years of billion-dollar growth. China's current priority seems to be protecting its existing investments from further damage with a charm campaign of grassroots amenities, like the ostentatious SEA Games support.

That "pause" while resentment cools does not mean China won't be a dominant figure in Burma in the future. Beijing has been currying favor with all the political players in Burma, hosting special visits by President Thein Sein; presidential contender Shwe Mann, the Speaker of the Lower House of Parliament; leaders of the Generation 88 opposition group; and leaders from Aung San Suu Kyi's NLD party. In fact, NLD party leaders have been invited to China five times. Key Chinese Communist Party leaders have been to Burma to meet with Aung San Suu Kyi and are watching closely the maneuvering before the 2015 elections. Chinese state news outlets have portrayed Aung San Suu Kyi in favorable terms, a turnaround from the past. "Before, the Chinese viewed Ms. Suu Kyi as pro-American and pro-West," said U Yan Myo Thein, a political commentator. "Now it is the Chinese turn to need her."

Burma was becoming a test of Chinese gamesmanship, and, as Henry Kissinger has observed, they play a watchful long game. He suggests the Chinese conduct foreign affairs much like they play their ancient game of *Wei qi* (known in the West by its Japanese name of *Go*). *Wei qi* is a test of wills. Players take turns placing stone pieces on a board, building up positions of strength, while working to surround and capture the opponent's stones. The balance of power may shift back and forth, as each player reacts and plans ahead. By the end of the game, the winner may not be apparent to the untrained eye, but the winner will have the margin of dominance. As Kissinger describes it, *wei qi* is about patient, subtle encirclement. He explains that the Chinese leaders were brought up on the concept of *shi*—the art of understanding matters in flux. They understand that *wei qi* is about a long campaign. They are banking that the network of business interests they have woven into the fabric of Burma's economy will be difficult to untangle.

Because of its massive investments in Burma, China also has begun taking more of an interest in ethnic conflicts on its border. When tens of thousands of ethnic refugees fled over the border in 2012 to escape attacks from the Burmese military, China squawked. China got involved with ceasefire talks between the Burmese and Kachin forces in 2013 but balked at having the United States and United Kingdom sit in as observers. China got its way; the U.S. and U.K. were sidelined.

—~—

The China Factor has added a new dimension to the democracy struggle in Burma.

After the moves toward openness began in 2011, I started asking everyone I talked to in Burma *why* they thought the military regime had finally opened up:

Was it the fear of Chinese domination?

The pressure from economic sanctions?

Than Shwe's fear of prosecution?

Worry among other generals that they would go to Buddhist hell for their misdeeds under Than Shwe?

Or was it the decades-long campaign around the world to free Aung San Suu Kyi?

"All of the above: Legacy, pride of country, Buddhist soul, fear of Chinese and need for alternative . . . all together those issues created a critical mass," said a key Western diplomat. "Sanctions forced the real need for them to do some things—open the economy and release Aung San Suu Kyi. The country was not moving forward, the economy was stagnant. Burma had become a pariah state. That affected their pride. They saw that ASEAN countries had made changes. They couldn't help but notice the ultra-modern Thai airport as they passed through. And they were insecure because of geography, flanked by China and India. Add to that they are proud people because of self regard and their long history."

The downside of the years of sanctions, however, was that they forced the Burmese regime into the arms of China. Over time, the generals began to feel exploited by the Chinese. They began looking for alternatives, reaching out more to India and Japan. The Obama administration's "Pivot to Asia" came at an opportune moment.

Following Aung San Suu Kyi's release in late 2010, Secretary of State Clinton named Derek Mitchell as the first Special Representative and Policy Coordinator for Burma (then later as ambassador, the first person to occupy the post in two decades). He and Assistant Secretary of State Kurt Campbell worked in tandem to explore openings with the generals, but continued to press on human rights. They were not expecting dramatic change. Then President Thein Sein gave an address in March 2011 and U.S. leaders noticed a "very different tone and substance." The new president talked about addressing poverty and encouraging development, something General Than Shwe had not done.

By the time Aung San Suu Kyi met with Thein Sein in August 2011 in his home, the Americans sensed there was real potential for change. The U.S. began proposing an "action for action" plan. If Thein Sein produced tangible actions, the U.S. would respond with an action. As a result, most of the sanctions were lifted in 2012 and a gold rush ensued.

As a Western diplomat put it, "We would like to see Burma more like South Korea than North Korea as models."

In other words, the "Game of Thrones" is on, Burma/Myanmar edition.

- The U.S. wants to balance China in the strategically critical region and is racing to improve military-to-military connections in Burma as well as commercial relations.

- India wants to balance China, too, and is building roads across the Himalayas to do so.
- China wants to ram through its energy projects in Burma to feed its energy-hungry economy.
- Russia wants to keep Burma as a customer for weapons of war. So does North Korea.
- Not to be left out, Japan has forgiven $5.8 billion in loans and started giant projects, such as the 5,900-acre (2,400-hectare) Thilawa Special Economic Zone. That giant project near Rangoon will include a deep-sea port, a thermal power plant, manufacturing, and large housing projects.

The questions now at hand are: Which of the great powers contending for treasure and mastery in Burma will gain the advantage? Who will have the greatest influence on what comes *next* after the Burma Spring? And will that power bend the arc of history in a positive direction in the Pacific?

Mizzima, a pro-democracy publication published in India, voiced concerns about the power struggle in Burma this way: "When the history books on Myanmar are written a generation from now, will President Thein Sein's political and economic reform era go down as the point when the West sold out—or woke up? When the history books are written, will President Thein Sein's reform process be portrayed as a genuine attempt by the Myanmar military to come in from the cold and bring real democracy to their troubled people? Or will it be described as a silent coup in which the military was able to con the West and maintain their grip on power while holding on to their ill-gotten gains and avoiding retribution?"

At the center of the kaleidoscope of challenges facing Burma stands Aung San Suu Kyi, now a member of Parliament and a grandmother. After the death of Nelson Mandela in 2013, she was lauded in much of the global news coverage as the most prominent democracy advocate in the world.

After tracing the course of her life, I could see how she had been shaped for this moment. It started with her DNA. She had a father who was a legend, but who also was flesh and blood, playfully placing a flower in her hair as he left for work for the last time on July 19, 1947. Like him, she is charismatic, fearless, visionary. On the negative side, like him, she can be moody, temperamental, difficult.

She had a mother who insisted on high standards and personal rectitude. As a result, Suu Kyi is a demanding taskmaster of herself. What carried her through, Suu Kyi often says, was the duty and discipline her mother instilled in her.

She learned to how to navigate academic life with her husband; her intellectual world expanded. Despite the stresses they would endure, his fidelity reinforced hers.

Then, too, Suu Kyi has been influenced by her close colleagues, who walked into the face of danger with her many times. She had their example to live up to.

And she had a larger-than-life image to live up to—people around the world had spoken out for her freedom because they had absorbed some of her courage by osmosis. She could not let them down. As writer Ma Thida put it, she had become a "prisoner of her applause."

On top of all that, Aung San Suu Kyi has been marinated in solitude with the company of the best in literature and history. She has a well-stocked mind. She is human enough to love chocolate and detective books—and fallible enough to lose her cool. She is more fragile than people assume, fainting with exhaustion while campaigning, vomiting from stress on multiple occasions. She is an introvert who savors time with books and meditation, yet is most radiant when speaking to crowds of thousands. She is often described by those who know her as "steely." Some mean it as a compliment. Some don't. She has been wise enough to spend time with the religions of the world as well as her own Buddhist beliefs, which gives her a perspective that bridges East and West. She is deeply serious about her faith, yet she would be criticized for not defending the faiths of others enough.

I initially had come to Burma in 2003 to see what made Aung San Suu Kyi tick. Over the next decade, I came to believe that what made her such a unique historic figure was the sum of all those remarkable parts of her life, a synthesis of inheritance and experience. She was a much more complicated figure than the glamorous photos captured.

When she was released in November 2010 and allowed to travel outside the country in 2012, she was able to revisit the phases of her life like an episode of the old TV show *This Is Your Life*. She celebrated her 67th birthday with friends at Oxford whom she had not seen since she left in 1988. She reunited with school friends in India. She retraced her father's journey to Japan. She made her first visit back to the U.S. since her youthful days at the U.N.

Over time, the adulation and press scrunity began to wear on her. As far back as the 1990s, she had complained to friends about being asked the same questions over and over again—every reporter wanted to know how she endured her house arrest, did she miss her sons. "I've already answered those questions!" she protested. She learned to give sound bites, but was never entirely comfortable with intrusions into her personal life. In the BBC documentary *The Choice*, Suu Kyi can be seen pacing back and forth in anger as she glimpsed the crowd of reporters in the garden of her house for her first real press conference after her release in 2010. "They are zooming in through the windows!" she protested while a helpless colleague stood by. "That's too much!"

Like movie stars who have to endure having autograph seekers interrupt their dinner, Suu Kyi came to appreciate that she had become a global salesperson for her country. But the adulation that came with that celebrity still made her uncomfortable. In her first TV interview after her release in 2010, she told NBC's Ann Curry that while it was flattering that President Obama and others had called her a hero, "If I were the blushing kind, I would blush to be called a hero." As for being called "The Lady," she said with a smile, "I suppose there are worse names than The Lady, but I would like to be seen as a *worker*." She wanted to be remembered, she said, "as somebody who has performed what she should have performed, who has done her duty. There is nothing more satisfying than the knowledge that you have done your duty."

On her first trip outside of Burma, to Thailand for the World Economic Forum, she was startled when a trio of Thai women fell to their knees in front of her as she walked from her speech. As *Time*'s Hannah Beech put it, "they were like supplicants in front of a deity." As her world travels continued, she seemed increasingly ill at ease when she was showered with gushing economiums. She sat quietly with her hands folded in her lap as the top leaders in the nation praised her courage in the U.S. Capitol and as luminaries introduced her at the National Endowment for Democracy.

By the time she did an interview with CNN's Christiane Amanpour in New York, she sat stone-faced as if she were in the dentist's chair:

> AMANPOUR: I see you in these amazing public events now, accepting finally the Congressional Gold Medal, the Nobel Peace Prize. You get a hero's welcome. You looked visibly pained when people are standing up in these prolonged standing O's. Is it weird for you?
>
> SUU KYI: No, it's—I appreciate it very much. But sometimes I feel a little embarrassed.
>
> AMANPOUR: Why embarrassed?
>
> SUU KYI: It doesn't seem right for anybody to get so much attention.
>
> AMANPOUR: And yet what you've done has been so dramatic.
>
> What do you think is your greatest achievement? If you had to sum it up, what would you say has brought you this Congressional Gold Medal, the Nobel prize?
>
> SUU KYI: I don't think it's yet time to say what is my greatest achievement. I think I have received these prizes for the efforts I've made to reach the goal that all my countrymen and women would like to reach.

Suu Kyi was right: she wasn't done yet. The most complex challenge of her career was waiting for her back in Burma after her sentimental journey. She needed to rebuild her battered party. She needed to get the 2008 constitution changed so her people could choose their leaders for themselves, rather than have the military do it for them. In some ways, Suu Kyi had to earn her Nobel Prize all over again.

And so, Aung San Suu Kyi got to work. She began by immersing herself in the nitty-gritty details of being a Parliamentarian, perhaps taking a page from Hillary Clinton's playbook when she became a Senator, keeping a low profile at first so as not to outshine her colleagues and doing her committee chores dutifully. Suu Kyi worked long hours as chair of the Rule of Law Committee and tried to build bridges with other Parliamentarians, whose votes she would need to get the Constitution changed.

She almost immediately ran into trouble. President Thein Sein asked her as the Rule of Law Committee Chair to resolve the festering dispute over the Letpaduang mine, a part of the controversial Ivanhoe copper mine. Suu Kyi accepted and paid a hard price for it. Her committee's investigation determined that the contract was legally binding and had to be honored, but also found that the mining operations had taken too much of the villagers' lands. The report recommended a review to establish how much land should be restored to the residents, plus compensation for others at market rates. It also noted that the project had been launched without an environmental impact assessment, a social impact assessment, a health impact assessment, or an environmental management plan. Suu Kyi's report recommended that those requirements be fulfilled before the project continued.

The copper mine owners, Burma's military-run Union of Myanmar Economic Holdings Limited (UMEHL) and China's powerhouse Wanbao Mining, agreed to provide additional amenities such as schools and a clinic.

Yet the villagers whose land had been taken by the mining company were outraged to learn Suu Kyi could not get all their homes back for them. She was mobbed and heckled when she visited the area on March 14, 2013. In particular, villagers were furious that the 10-page report failed to call for punishment of police officers who had used white phosphorus to disperse their earlier protest, seriously injuring demonstrators. The residents were so angry that they barricaded their village with thorny bushes and only allowed Suu Kyi to enter after she had shed some of her police escort and accompanying journalists. The hostile reception was unprecedented for the famous Nobel laureate. It was a public relations disaster.

Protestors taunted that Suu Kyi was a discredit to her father. One woman sobbed, "You said you wouldn't trick the people." Another said, "We have lost respect for Daw Suu . . . although we used to love her very much. We feel that Mother Suu doesn't have sympathy for us." A farmer who confronted her complained, "All we had to eat was boiled rice when we voted for you. But you are not standing with us anymore."

Suu Kyi gave a matter-of-fact speech that only seemed to inflame the residents' ire. She told villagers the project should be allowed to continue because the company had promised to implement the report's advice to uphold environmental safeguards, create benefits for the community, and to compensate villagers for seizing their lands.

"We have asked the company to first, give jobs to our people and second, to maintain a healthy environment, according to international standards, and third, to provide education and health care for the people," Suu Kyi said.

Burma could not afford to shut down the mine and risk turning away foreign investors, she told the crowd of some 500. "If we stop this project, it will not benefit local people or the country. Our country needs a lot of development. If this company has to stop, our people will lose job opportunities.

"The other country [China] might think that our country cannot be trusted on the economy," she added. "We have to get along with the neighboring country whether we like it or not."

Suu Kyi had hoped to show she could handle a tough grassroots controversy, but failed to connect with the villagers personally. When asked about the use of phosphorus to break up their protests, Suu Kyi said there would be no arrests because the incident was caused by a lack of proper police training. She added that the local people were wrong to refer to the smoke-generating devices as "fire grenades." "The right word is smoke grenade," she said. It probably was not the best moment to correct their word usage.

The images on TV and in newspapers showed a haggard-looking Suu Kyi surrounded by irate crowds. When Suu Kyi was asked by reporters to comment on the unpleasant reception, she said, "I have never done anything just for popularity. Sometimes politicians have to do things that people dislike." She added that it was not a matter of whether the reaction from the villagers made her feel bad. "They want me to do what they want. I simply said no," she told reporters. "Anyone engaged in politics should have the courage to face animosity. It is not right to engage in politics to win popularity."

—∾—

Criticism was stirred up again a few weeks later when Suu Kyi joined the military reviewing stand on Army Day, March 27, 2013. The annual parade, now held in the sprawling Naypyitaw capital, commemorates Burma's 1945 uprising against the Japanese occupation. When Suu Kyi attended, there were more than 6,000 troops as well as speeches by generals underscoring the military's "leading role in politics."

Photos and TV coverage showed Aung San Suu Kyi sitting side by side in the front row with the generals who had kept her under house arrest. Suu Kyi had hoped to send a message with her presence: She was not an enemy of the armed forces and could work with them in the national interest. That encouraged some people and alarmed others. She received criticism that she had been "co-opted" by the military. Coming on the heels of her comments on the BBC *Desert Island Discs* show that she was "fond" of the army because of her father's association with the military, her appearance with the generals offended many of those who had been victimized by the military. At the time, the Burma army was continuing to launch offensives in ethnic Kachin areas. There had been reports of army shelling and looting of villages despite peace talks. The violence had not stopped even though President Thein Sein claimed that it had during a visit to Austria, where he urged the EU to remove sanctions. He told EU leaders, "There's no more hostilities, no more fighting all over the country; we have been able to end this kind of armed conflict."

Questions then were raised: Was Aung San Suu Kyi being used as a shill, to present a façade of reform—while the Burmese government continued business as usual?

Longtime NLD member and former political prisoner Win Htein said in Suu Kyi's defense that she had to reach out to the army because national reconciliation would need to include the army. "National reconciliation means *everybody*—ethnic people, as well as the army," he said. "So her determination is to achieve her goal, and that's why she's walking a very delicate line. She won't abandon her principles."

"You have to talk to people if you want to bring about peaceful change . . . even if you know what they have done is very, very bad," Suu Kyi told NBC's Ann Curry.

Suu Kyi had hoped her participation in the Army Day event would help build a constructive relationship with Senior General Min Aung Hlaing, the new commander in chief of the armed forces. But he seemed to have other things in mind. The Tatmadaw's main responsibility under the constitution, he said, was to prevent the disintegration of the Union, national solidarity, and sovereignty—in order words, protect the status quo.

—w—

Senior General Min Aung Hlaing rose through the ranks of the military. He was born in 1956 in Tavoy. He attended the Defense Services Academy, where he reportedly was shunned by his classmates for his reserved, buttoned-down personality. Following graduation, he was sent to Mon State and in 2002 was promoted to commander of the volatile drugs-and-war Triangle Regional Command. He became a key figure in negotiations with rebel groups.

When Shwe Mann was named Speaker of the Lower House of Parliament in 2010, Min Aung Hlaing was named to replace him as head of the Joint Chiefs of Staff of the Army, Navy, and Air Force. A year later, Min Aung Hlaing paid a visit to China, where he received the red-carpet treatment and met Chinese President Xi Jinping. They developed a bilateral defense agreement. In 2012, Min Aung Hlaing was promoted to vice senior general and in 2013 to senior general of the armed forces, the same title once held by Than Shwe. The once-reticent Min Aung Hlaing became increasingly assertive, giving speeches insisting that the military has a major role to play in national politics. He sounded a lot like his powerful mentor.

—w—

Additional controversy was stirred up when word got around that Suu Kyi's NLD party had accepted donations at a charity fundraiser from junta business cronies such as Kyaw Win and Zaw Zaw. It made the news when Suu Kyi also accepted free flights for life on Asian Wings Airways from superstar crony Tay Za. Tay Za reportedly had set up Asian Wings to skirt sanctions imposed by the U.S. on his other domestic carrier, Air Bagan. Tay Za had complained that the sanctions were hurting Air Bagan because he could not purchase American-made spare parts at market prices. According to *Forbes Asia*, he eventually stepped down as chairman of Air Bagan and transferred his shares to a third party. By setting up Asian Wings through an associate travel company, the *Irrawaddy* magazine reported, Tay Za could purchase new planes and parts through the proxy airline. Suu Kyi was named an "instant platinum frequent flyer" on Asian Wings, so she could take flights, along with two other people, for free. A public relations manager for the airline said the frequent-flier award would allow Suu Kyi to travel by plane for more of her trips around the country rather than by car. The spokeswoman said Asian Wings had offered the membership because of its "deep heartfelt respect, admiration and appreciation of everything Daw Aung San Suu Kyi has done in her lifetime."

Eyebrows also were raised when Suu Kyi visited a children's hospital that was supported by the Max Myanmar Company, headed by another regime crony, Zaw Zaw. Suu Kyi said to reporters that those who became wealthy during Burma's era of military rule should be given another chance to reform themselves. If they were involved in any illegal action, it should be investigated, she said. But the right of criminals to rehabilitate themselves should be regarded as part of the rule of law, she maintained, adding that punishment that is solely intended to inflict suffering is barbaric. "What civilized people should have is a vision that punishment is for *reform*," she said.

"I don't mind if they approach the NLD or other organizations, as long as their support is beneficial to our people, democratic reforms, and our country's health and education needs. This is something we should welcome," added the NLD chairman. "What is wrong with that? Instead of spending their money on things that have no purpose, they have supported things that they should support. It's a good thing," said Suu Kyi.

Suu Kyi had pragmatically concluded that just as she could not unite the country without military support, she could not tackle corruption issues without giving military cronies the chance to change their ways. She opened the door for them to side with the democracy movement.

The U.S. was said to be pursuing a similar course of finding "least bad" cronies who could be persuaded to mend their ways and support reform. At least one, Max Myanmar's Zaw Zaw, told local media that he wanted to be a crony who contributes to the good of Burma's democracy and economic development. He said, "I don't want to be a bad crony. I want to be a good one."

To encourage more movement in that direction, when Tom Malinowski, the Assistant Secretary of State for Democracy, Human Rights and Labor, visited Burma in June 2014, he urged all the businessmen who were on the U.S. sanctions lists for illicit activities to work harder to remove themselves from the blacklist. Those invited to meetings included Tay Za, one of the country's richest men, and Steven Law, the head of the conglomerate Asia World and heir of a notorious drug lord. The military's blacklisted business arm, Union of Myanmar Economic Holdings Limited (UMEHL), was also invited. The subtext was that if they complied with legal protocols, American businesses could bring more capital and opportunities to the quickly opening country.

The American delegation also held high-level meetings with top military leaders, including Commander-in-Chief Min Aung Laing. The U.S. was moving rapidly to establish military-to-military partnerships. Some in Congress feared the administration was moving too rapidly. They raised alarms that the U.S. was befriending the Tatmadaw while the army was still committing human-rights abuses and obstructing reforms.

Both the hurried military outreach (before peace agreements were finalized) and the outreach to business leaders (with dubious reputations) carried moral and political risks. If the cronies continued illicit dealing while partnering with the U.S., or if the military continued human-rights abuses while being trained by Americans, the U.S. would forfeit considerable moral authority. But if the new outreach helped broaden reforms, the gamble would be worthwhile.

China was doing outreach of its own. While the American delegation was in Burma, President Thein Sein was in China meeting with President Xi Jinping, who was playing host to leaders from Burma and India. Xi reassured Thein Sein that China would never seek hegemony, no matter how strong it becomes. "Neither hegemony nor militarism is in the Chinese DNA," Xi Jinping claimed in his speech. He promised greater Chinese business involvement in Burma in the future. The subtext there was that China has no intention of letting the U.S. poach in its neighborhood.

—∾—

In the meantime, Aung San Suu Kyi was struggling to rebuild her standing. The controversies over Suu Kyi's copper-mine role, her Army Day appearance, and her acceptance of crony assistance, had taken the shine off her halo for some in Burma. A BBC commentator said, "The woman who was once the world's most famous political prisoner is now wearing the less glamorous mantle of a mere politician." Throughout 2013, a steady stream of negative commentaries in the international media said the Nobel laureate was having difficulty transitioning from being an icon into being a politician. She responded with a combination of exasperation and amusement, "I've always been a politician. What do you think I've been doing all these years?"

She told CNN, "I'm always surprised when people speak as if I've just become a politician. I've been a politician all along. I started in politics not as a human-rights defender or a humanitarian worker, but as the leader of a political party. And if that's not a politician, then I don't know what is."

She told *The Age* in late 2013, "I look upon myself as a politician, not as an *icon*. I always object to [the] word icon, because it's very static, it stands there, sits there, hangs on the wall, and I happen to work very, very hard. . . . Let me assure you I am no saint of any kind . . . but I do believe there is such a thing as an honest politician and I aspire to that."

Early on in the transition, Suu Kyi said she believed Thein Sein was a man who she could do business with. They had several cordial and productive meetings the first year he became president—before his talk at the U.N. in 2012, they met in New York and photos showed him in a casual cardigan sweater chatting amiably with her.

Aung San Suu Kyi felt emboldened to announce at a special World Economic Forum held in Rangoon in 2013 that she wanted to run for president. "I want to run for president and I'm quite frank about it," she said at a debate organized by the BBC and then again at a press conference.

After that, a complicated chess game was set in play. Suu Kyi remained the equivalent of the queen on the chessboard, maneuvering for power while surrounded by generals who controlled all of the other pieces on the board.

She began playing a very calculated, hard-nosed game with the endgame of changing the military-imposed constitution, the only way to ensure true reform. Winning would take three daring moves:

- Getting the military-rigged Parliament to approve amendments to the constitution that would reduce their control
- Winning more seats in Parliament in the 2015 election for her NLD party
- Gaining the presidency for herself to ensure reforms continued

The degree of difficulty was impossibly high, and she knew that going in. Changing the constitution required the votes of 75 percent of the Parliament, and the military controlled nearly 80 percent of the seats one way or another. Yet Aung San Suu Kyi threw herself into the impossible mission. She was determined to see it through. As one longtime Western diplomat put it, "She is her father's daughter. She is intent on fulfilling her father's legacy."

The battle to change the constitution would prove one of her toughest challenges yet. The first casualty was her relationship with Thein Sein. When Suu Kyi asked for a quadripartite meeting of the key leadership—President Thein Sein, House Speaker Shwe Mann, Army Commander Min Aung Hlaing, and herself—to discuss constitutional reform, President Thein Sein refused to convene the meeting. He snubbed her.

After that, Suu Kyi increasingly aligned herself with House Speaker Shwe Mann. Even though the House Speaker had expressed a desire to run for president himself, his support would be essential to move reform measures through the Parliament.

Two measures in particular needed to be changed before the 2015 elections: Section 59f, which barred candidates for the presidency who had a member of the family with a foreign citizenship, and Section 436, which required 75 percent approval to amend the constitution.

Suu Kyi and the NLD began conducting polls and collecting petitions to demonstrate that the people wanted constitutional reform. Despite fear of reprisals, more than five million signatures were gathered in the space of a few months. It was a big plus that she had the support of

Min Ko Naing, "Conqueror of Kings," the highly regarded leader of the 1988 student movement. He became one of her most effective surrogate speakers, comparing the 2008 constitution to the military seizures of power in 1962 and 1988.

"The people of Myanmar know the history; the military seized power in 1962 and 1988 by the force of their weapons," Min Ko Naing told crowds. "Now, they do not use arms but instead they rely upon the constitution."

Suu Kyi held rallies drawing crowds up to 30,000 and told them that until the military's powers were reduced, "this will be a fake democracy." She assured audiences that the changes were essential, "not so much because I want to be president of a country, but because I want the president of the country to be elected through the will of the people."

As it became more and more apparent that the military government was thwarting reforms, her tone became even more adversarial. At one rally, she issued a challenge: "I'd like to ask the military, are you really happy that the constitution has given you privileges that other people do not have? You should think seriously about this. I hate to say it, but your guns are the source of your military strength. I understand that your guns give you the upper hand," she said. "But does this make you more dignified—or less?"

—~—

Suu Kyi kept up a daunting pace in 2014. In a typical week, she might be holding a constitutional rally, meeting with the CEO of a British grocery chain to encourage responsible investment in Burma, and conferring with the Australian foreign minister. She convened a youth conference because youth unemployment was as much as 75 percent. They needed jobs, she said, and hope. She supported the renovation of General Hospital, where her mother had worked. She called for improvements in education and a "more caring world." She continued to draw crowds in the thousands, who took photos of her with their new iPhones and iPads, like teens at a rock concert.

But her momentum was undermined by the escalating tensions with the Muslim population. Prejudice had long festered in Burma as people struggled to get by—prejudice against Indians; prejudice against Jews, who had largely disappeared from the country; prejudice against Muslims; prejudice against Christians; and prejudice against Chinese. Military repression had kept some intolerance tamped down. As some controls on expression were loosened, sectarian hate-speech violence exploded with a vengeance.

The sectarian troubles started in earnest in 2012 with a series of religious brawls that spiraled out of control. The first incident in a town near Rangoon was sparked when a Muslim woman on a bicycle bumped into a young novice monk in the market area. His alms bowl was knocked onto the ground, spilling his food for the day. The novice began crying, but the woman did not apologize. As anger spread through the market, both were taken to the police station to resolve the dispute. An irate crowd gathered and went on a rampage, damaging two mosques and torching Muslim farms nearby. It took more than 100 police in riot gear to restore calm.

Another riot erupted in Meiktila over a dispute between a Muslim shopkeeper and a Buddhist couple who had come to sell some jewelry. An argument over price turned into a melee; entire neighborhoods were burned down while security forces did little. At least 20 Muslim boys were taken, from a madrassa, and hacked to death, their bodies soaked in petrol and set alight.

The violence reawakened animosity in the western part of the country toward the Rohingya. The Rohingya, who are generally Muslim, are considered illegal "Bengalis," interlopers from neighboring Bangladesh, by many in the Buddhist majority. The Rohingya have been subjected to harsh restrictions on marriage, employment, healthcare, education, and movement. When a Buddhist woman was allegedly raped and murdered by a group of Rohingya in Rakhine State, mob brutality was unleashed. Mobs largely composed of area Buddhists burned, looted, and attacked the Rohingya communities. As the violence spread, government troops forced more than 140,000 Rohingya residents into holding areas, which prompted allegations of "ethnic cleansing."

The government has been heavily criticized for not doing enough to protect Muslims in the country, who account for about 4 percent of Burma's roughly 60 million people. And Suu Kyi, now a part of government, was widely and harshly criticized for not taking a clear stand against the communal violence.

When Suu Kyi visited Sydney, Australia in late 2013, she was repeatedly accused of not speaking out against military abuse of minority populations, Christian Kachins and Karens as well as Muslims. Local members of the

Kachin ethnic group boycotted her events, accusing her of "whitewashing" the military repression of the largely Christian Kachin people. Since Thein Sein had become president, the Burma army had broken a 17-year ceasefire with the Kachin Independence Army (KIA) and mounted a major new military offensive against the Kachin people. More than 120,000 Kachin people had been displaced, forced to flee their homes. At least 200 villages had been destroyed. Even the camps where displaced persons were gathered had been attacked. Why wasn't Suu Kyi speaking out about the assaults on the Kachin?

Others accused her of failing to speak up about the treatment of the Rohingya Muslims in western Rakhine State. Her political aspirations, they said, had compromised her views and tempered her public comments. They had expected more upon her release.

Some of the sharpest criticism came from Nicolas Kristof of the *New York Times*, who wrote, "Few people have fought as courageously for human rights as Daw Aung San Suu Kyi, the Nobel Prize-winning democracy advocate who stood up to the generals here in Myanmar. Aung San Suu Kyi should be one of the heroes of modern times. Instead, as her country imposes on the Rohingya Muslim minority an apartheid that would have made white supremacists in South Africa blush, she bites her tongue. It seems as though she aspires to become president of Myanmar, and speaking up for a reviled minority could be fatal to her prospects. The moral giant has become a calculating politician."

Elliott Prasse-Freeman wrote in the *Kyoto Review of Southeast Asia*, "Daw Aung San Suu Kyi had long implored the world to use its liberty to promote hers/her country's . . . but then at the first opportunity to use her own relative power to stand up for those worse off than she, DASSK provided only silences, equivocations, and empty mumblings about the 'rule of law.'"

Nicholas Köhler wrote in *MacLean's*, "To the surprise of many, she's stopped short of condemning the violence, instead making a series of anodyne statements extolling the virtues of 'rule of law,' and following a strict program of assigning blame equally to Buddhists and Muslims."

A *New York Times* editorial said Suu Kyi was "tragically silent" on the Rohingya issue. Aung Zaw, editor of Myanmar news magazine *The Irrawaddy*, said her failure to speak out on ethnic issues and the communal violence that had racked the country was "shocking." He said, "People expected her—as she is a Nobel Peace Prize winner—to say a few words to stop the bloodshed."

Was Suu Kyi being political—or tone-deaf—as she stuck to her principles? As chairman of the Rule of Law committee, she stressed the need for rule of law to clarify and settle the issues. She reiterated her commitment to nonviolence, while refusing to condemn either side—saying she did not want to "add fire to any side of the conflict."

She explained that she and her political party remained "totally dedicated to nonviolence. Violence has been committed against us again and again, repeatedly, not over a year, not over two, but over nearly 30 years. But we never retaliated with violence. So I'm unhappy that there should be those in my country who believe that differences can be settled only through violence. . . . What we want is a society where differences can be settled without violence."

She told an Indian television interviewer in 2012 not to "forget that violence has been committed by both sides." "This is why I prefer not to take sides and also I want to work toward reconciliation between these two communities. I'm not going to be able to do that if I'm going to take sides."

She defended herself at some length to an audience in Sydney, Australia, saying "I have always defended those whose human rights have been attacked, but what people want is not defense but condemnation. Particularly they are saying, why am I not condemning this group or why am I not condemning that group, and it also applies to the military . . . I am not condemning because I have not found that condemnation brings good results.

"What I want to do is to achieve *national reconciliation*. It's very interesting in those days back from 1988 until a year or two ago when the military regime was very, very severe and when we talked about national reconciliation, everybody agreed because they thought it was not achievable. But now when we talk about national reconciliation in very, very simple, practical terms of trying to work out our differences instead of condemning one another, then people don't like it.

"So there's an inconsistency. When they thought national reconciliation was just a pipe dream they were ready to support it, but now many who supported national reconciliation as a goal do not seem to be very keen on practicing national reconciliation, which means, as I've said, trying to sort out our differences without resorting to condemnation or violence."

She did oppose the use of violence by those involved in the sectarian riots, including the police. Unfortunately, she complicated matters by making remarks to the effect that "the fear is not just on the side of the Muslims, but on the side of the Buddhists as well," then adding that there is a perception that "global Muslim power is very great."

When a bridge-building meeting was held at the NLD headquarters with Islamic religious leaders on communal violence, she said she wanted Burma/Myanmar to be a country where all people can live with peace of mind.

"There is a phrase in the Christian Bible expressing that a stone must not be given to a person who asks for bread. In this situation, we don't want to give the stone to those who are coming to ask for help through full confidence. Anyhow, we would like people of different religions to live in the country in a peaceful coexistence upholding our emotions, expectations, and objectives," Aung San Suu Kyi said.

At Buddhist nationalism began resurfacing, she criticized the two-child limit proposed by Buddhist nationalists for Rohingya as discriminatory. When asked in interviews whether she condemned Wirathu, the Buddhist monk labeled the "Burmese Bin Laden," who had been highly critical of Muslims, she answered point-blank, "I condemn any movement that is based on hatred and extremism."

At one point, after repeatedly being asked questions about sectarian violence and the Rohingya, Aung San Suu Kyi showed her frustration by replying, "I would say instead of asking us members of the opposition what we feel about it, what we intend to do about it . . . you should ask the present government of Burma what *their* policy is."

When the communal violence first erupted, President Thein Sein said in a speech that was broadcast on radio that Myanmar is a "multi-racial and religious nation" and warned against sectarian violence. "For the reform to be successful, I would like to urge all to avoid instigation and behavior that incite hatred among our fellow citizens."

However, he then seemed to shift direction and reassured Turkish diplomats on a state visit that the violence "has nothing to do with race or religion." At one point, he proposed that the minority Rohingya ethnic group be "resettled" abroad, a proposal the United Nations quickly objected to. He also said he would not support citizenship for the Rohingya.

Thein Sein then went on to defend the controversial monk Wirathu and his "969" movement, which was calling for Buddhists to boycott Muslim businesses. After *Time* magazine had placed the controversial monk on its cover, Thein Sein accused the magazine of slandering the Buddhist religion and harming the national reconciliation process by accusing the outspoken cleric of stoking anti-Muslim violence in Burma. Describing the monk as a "son of Buddha", the president defended Wirathu as a "noble person" committed to peace.

Wirathu continued to attract international condemnation for his vitriolic anti-Muslim sermons, which warn against the "Islamization" of Burma. "Muslims are breeding so fast and they are stealing our women, raping them," Wirathu told *Time*. "Around 90 percent of Muslims in Burma are radical bad people."

The monk, who had gained thousands of supporters, began championing a national law to ban interfaith marriage to "protect" the Buddhist faith.

Aung San Suu Kyi spoke out against the proposed ban against interfaith marriage, which was primarily intended to stop Buddhist women from marrying Muslim men, describing it as a "violation of women's rights and human rights." In contrast, President Thein Sein asked Parliament to discuss the proposals banning interfaith marriage and conversion.

Several years into his five-year term, international observers began wondering whether President Thein Sein had changed—or perhaps had not really changed at all from his military days. "People thought he was a reformer, but the question became reformer for what? There were certain things he wanted reformed, but his list was not the same as what the democratic opposition wanted reformed. He mainly wanted economic reform to get the Western sanctions lifted. And would do as little as possible politically to get the political side done," said Jennifer Quigley, executive director of the U.S. Campaign for Burma.

The president's defenders continued to say he was a decent man in a difficult position, trying to move by increments while keeping control. But he remained a cipher. It was hard to tell where Thein Sein really stood—he was a cipher, as opaque as a Federal Reserve president. His remarks were often at odds with government actions. He said land reform was a priority—but the confiscations continued. He said army attacks on ethnic groups would stop—but they continued. While he had seemed to voice support for constitutional reform in his initial remarks on the subject, many of his remarks were ambiguous. He said he supported amending constitutional provisions that excluded anyone whose spouse or children were overseas citizens from becoming president, the clause keeping Aung San Suu Kyi from serving. "I would not want restrictions being imposed on the right of any citizen to become the leader of the country," Thein Sein said. He then added, "At the same time, we will need to have all necessary measures in place in order to defend our national interests and sovereignty."

Thein Sein's record was inconsistent at best. A human-rights movie festival was allowed—but the Rohingya were herded into prison-like camps. Corruption was critized—but contracts still went to friends of generals and ministers. The International Red Cross was granted access to the prisons for the first time in many years, but access for humanitarian groups to help displaced ethnic people in conflict zones was often thwarted. Thein Sein has even defended the crushing of the student uprising in 1988 in which thousands were killed, saying it "saved the nation." Yet he refused to publish his own military records for the time.

Thein Sein says he supports drug eradication—but he was in charge of the ruling Union Solidarity and Development Party (USDP) in 2011 when seven known drug lords won seats in Parliament as USDP members. They reportedly persuaded locals to vote for them by promising to allow poppy growing. The president says he wants to reduce corruption in government contracting—but on his first official trip to China, he took sanctioned businessman Steven Law with him.

When Thein Sein visited Washington, D.C. in 2013, Fred Hiatt, the editor of the *Washington Post* editorial page, repeatedly pressed the president on a series of questions, such as whether he thought the constitution should be changed so Aung San Suu Kyi could serve as president and whether he would approve the opening of a U.N. High Commissioner for Human Rights office in Rangoon, as promised. The president repeatedly dodged his questions with vague, elliptical answers.

"There's an important riddle here," Hiatt wrote. "Western officials hope that Thein Sein, who has been in power for about two years, is bravely negotiating a treacherous path from the repressive regime he was once part of to a society in which people genuinely can choose their own leaders. Along this path, they believe, he has to battle hardliners who oppose change; corrupt businessmen and generals who fear exposure; reform advocates who may push too hard, too fast; ethnic and religious conflict; and rising expectations among ordinary citizens who believe political reform should quickly lead to economic improvement.

"If so, his circumspection may be a clever tactic to keep everyone on board as reform moves forward. Alternatively, it could be an indication that the generals remain firmly in control and that Thein Sein is not free to express a view that might offend them. Or it might be that he hopes the reform path can stop somewhere short of true democracy—that Aung San Suu Kyi, for example, should never have the opportunity to run for president."

In an interview with the BBC, Thein Sein talked about the possibility of Aung San Suu Kyi becoming president. "Whether she will become a leader of the nation depends on the will of the people. If the people accept her, then I will have to accept her," he said. He maintained that there wasn't any problem between him and Aung San Suu Kyi and said, "We are working together." But he carefully added that the army, which retains most of the seats in parliament, would continue to play a central role in the country's politics.

His comments were not ringing endorsements for changing the constitution, but they left the impression that Thein Sein would try to be fair and follow the will of the people. However, he then packed the influential Union Election Commission with military officers. The UEC is one of the highest authorities in Burma, with vast power conferred by the 2008 constitution *"to monitor and decide the fate of political parties, arrange or postpone or cancel election schedules, hold elections, judge election-related cases, and investigate members of parliament if just one percent of their constituents complain and fire them if allegations are found true."*

The election commission appointed by the president then sent a notice to Aung San Suu Kyi warning the opposition leader against giving speeches in favor of amending the constitution. The commission also restricted candidates to giving speeches in their own constituencies, which meant Suu Kyi could not campaign around the country for other NLD candidates.

With those kinds of threatening signals, Suu Kyi decided to take her case for constitutional reform directly to the army members. She told a crowd in Rangoon that army soldiers, officers, and representatives in Parliament were all born as ordinary citizens, and should remember that their first duty is to serve the people. "The armed forces personnel should ask themselves how they can fulfill their duties without serving their first duty."

During a Mandalay rally, Suu Kyi said that the current constitution is not democratic because it grants the military special powers. "I want to challenge them [military officials] to amend the constitution within this year, from within the boundaries of the law and via the Parliament. If they truly love the country, respect the citizens: Think of the future of the country and be brave enough," she told the crowd.

It was the equivalent of daring the military to "man up" to their responsibilities to the people. The military brass did not appreciate the challenge. Army representatives slammed Suu Kyi's comments, saying she was being "dishonest" and merely attempting to gain the presidency for herself. Members of the military-linked Union Solidarity and Development Party (USDP) were equally defensive, saying it was not the army's job to lead constitutional reform. Min Swe, a retired colonel serving as a USDP lawmaker, said, "In my opinion, our people right now are interested in making a proper living, not in fixing the charter."

The head of the election commission soon sent Suu Kyi a letter stating that her remarks were a violation of her constitutional oath as a member of Parliament, because she had challenged the military. He said he was just warning her.

—ʬ—

The new demands of serving as a Parliamentarian while running her party and waging a national campaign placed greater stress on Suu Kyi. Whereas once Suu Kyi had had long stretches of time to fill, she now had to budget her time and energy to meet the duties of being an office-holder. She had to build alliances with people who were trying to undermine her. She had to assemble a staff with the skills to run her party, navigate Parliament procedures, and control the schedule requests of an international superstar. There was a learning curve.

As her friend Timothy Garton Ash put it, "Like Nelson Mandela emerging from prison, like the Czech dissident Václav Havel catapulted to Prague Castle, the 67-year-old Daw Suu now faces a life sentence of politics, whether as opposition leader, president, or elder stateswoman. Time, an almost unlimited resource under house arrest, is now sliced and diced relentlessly into 30-minute meetings and 30-second segments of face time."

She was overwhelmed with requests for her thoughts and for her time. In effect, Suu Kyi was operating a shadow government, but without the resources or staff. Her NLD headquarters in downtown Rangoon was a dimly lit, sparsely furnished series of meeting rooms with fading posters of Aung San Suu Kyi and her father on the walls. For all practical purposes, she still was running the opposition party out of her living room, mostly with volunteers, while trying to receive the dignitaries who wanted to pay a call—British prime minister David Cameron, former president Bill Clinton, Bishop Tutu, EU leaders, Thai leaders, the list went on and on. "Everyone that arrives in Rangoon (Yangon) expects to get a photo op," said David Mathieson of Human Rights Watch. "They all want that Suu Kyi photo on the mantelpiece."

To guard her time, Suu Kyi entrusted an NLD member, Dr. Tin Mar Aung, to screen her calls and appointments. Always unfailingly polite, but firm, Dr. Tin Mar Aung said "No" to most calls and requests. Getting in to see Aung San Suu Kyi or getting information to her became more difficult. She increasingly relied on a small circle of advisers that included her lawyers, her trusted physician, and a few others. Those who could not get on Suu Kyi's schedule began to complain. They worried that she was getting out of touch. The new wall around her house kept out the busloads of gawkers that pulled up at her gate every day, like visitors to Graceland, but it also kept out former supporters and people seeking her ear. "She's more visible in the news and yet further away," one observer said. "So many people want a piece of her."

Discontent grew into complaints of diva-like behavior. The Lady was difficult, people said. Some supporters and diplomats who dared to tell her she needed more help with her messaging and staffing, were rebuffed sharply. Loyal relationships were frayed.

In truth, the complaints showed that the revered "Lady of the Lake," the almost mythical "Madonna of University Avenue," the "Steel Orchid," was merely human after all. Aung San Suu Kyi had been placed on such a high pedestal, her image so embellished while she was locked in her home, that it was only inevitable that when she was in public view 24 hours a day, seven days a week, her blemishes would be in full view.

"She hasn't changed. People just projected onto her what they wanted her to be. She has always been honest about who she is," said a seasoned Burma scholar.

And that was true. Aung San Suu Kyi repeatedly has insisted that she is not perfect. When asked if she had ever lost hope, she answered with typical frankness, "I've never lost hope. I've lost my temper from time to time, though." When asked what were her sinful qualifies, she immediately replied, "I've got a short temper." To others, she warned, "I have a hot temper."

She told one interviewer, "I never thought of myself as a saint; it makes me uncomfortable when people say I am one." She said she was more like a "sinner who keeps on trying."

"I have my own flaws and weaknesses," she told a Burmese audience in San Francisco. And in an Australian question-and-answer session, she confessed, "I suppose I do have a stubborn streak in me."

History reminds us that towering figures are not immune to temperamental lapses. Winston Churchill may have inspired his nation in wartime, but he was so hard on his staff in the process that his wife Clementine had to write him a letter urging him to please be nicer. She knew what his temper was like: he once threw a plate of spinach at her.

Nor was history-making Nelson Mandela a "secular saint." He mixed courage, humor, generosity, and empathy into a charismatic leadership—but those who knew him well said he had a cold, haughty side. His children lamented that he was not there for them, even after he left prison. He made questionable political compromises to associate with dictators like Moammar Gadhafi simply because the Libyan strongman had opposed apartheid. He was faulted for retaining incompetent ministers in his cabinet. In sum, he, too, made mistakes.

—∾—

What others saw as stubbornness or being obdurate, Suu Kyi saw as sticking to her basic principles and being resolute. Like many other politicians, the characteristics that had propelled her to popularity later undermined her when she was in a different position. If Suu Kyi had not been stubborn, she would not have stayed the course for two and a half decades, she would have not held on to her principles of nonviolence. Yet after she was released and faced with day-to-day decisions, her critics saw her stubbornness as inflexibility and high-handedness.

In the same vein, Lech Wałęsa, the feisty electrician/labor organizer in Poland, had rallied workers at the Gdansk shipyards as a "man of the people." The resulting strikes helped trigger the breakup of the Soviet Union. But once in office as President of Poland, Wałęsa was criticized for his confrontational style, for surrounding himself with questionable people, for being too plain-spoken and undignified for the post. But he was who he was.

Another prime example of the difficulty of moving from activist to elected leader was Suu Kyi's inspiration, Czech activist Václav Havel. Havel was brilliant and eloquent, but once he moved from prison to leadership in Prague Castle, his philosopher-hero image was whittled down. There was criticism that he had married his 20-years-younger girlfriend less than a year after his wife died. Some frowned when he rode a scooter down the halls of government and signed his name with a heart doodle. Old friends complained he had lost touch with the Civic Forum, the movement that propelled him into the presidency. He dressed down his staff, not knowing a television crew was filming the tirade, and had to apologize in a memo. Like Suu Kyi, he was a complicated man of many parts, not just an eloquent activist.

The criticism that was piled onto Aung San Suu Kyi once she entered Parliament seemed disproportionate when compared to the generals who were actually running the country. She might be difficult at times, but she was not deadly. Far from it. In contrast, President Thein Sein and Speaker Shwe Mann both had overseen attacks on ethnic groups and protestors during their careers. Thein Sein held a command during the 1988 crack-down on students and was commended for his actions suppressing the protests. Shwe Mann held a command when the ethnic Karen stronghold in Manerplaw was attacked and human porters abused. He also was one of the officers in charge of Rangoon during the 2007 crackdown on the monks. In those instances, they could be said to have been following orders, but now they were the ones in charge. The commander of the army, Min Aung Hlaing, was said by his friends to be "a capable officer and an efficient administrator." But he, too, had advanced in rank by leading attacks in ethnic areas and is said to have supported the crackdown on protesting monks in 2007. In speeches in 2014, he emphasized that it was the military's duty to "protect the constitution" and told officers, "the Tatmadaw will always follow policies set by retired Senior General Than Shwe."

All three military men have been mentioned as presidential candidates. Thein Sein had demurred because he was not sure his health would allow it, but if the people wanted him to serve, he would. Although Speaker Shwe Mann was said to be on friendly terms with Suu Kyi, that didn't mean he would say "Ladies First" and let her beat him to the presidency. As head of the military-dominated Union Solidarity and Development Party (USDP) as well as Speaker, Shwe Mann has said, "Our party must win in the coming election." A Reuters news story even stirred speculation that the NLD might have to partner with Shwe Mann as the party presidential candidate if Suu Kyi was barred from running. It was a wild-card option, but 2015 was shaping up as an election year with surprises.

Suu Kyi was surrounded by leaders who had been groomed under General Than Shwe to take over Parliament and the government. That certainly made the odds more difficult of gaining major changes to the constitution or gaining the presidency. According to the 2008 document, the selection of the president is not by popular vote. The military, the Upper House, and the Lower House each appoint a vice president. The Union Parliament, which comprises both houses, then votes to determine which of those three vice presidents will become president. The NLD would have to sweep the 2015 elections to gain some bargaining power, and the Election Commission rules were making that prospect more difficult.

In a troubling sign of things to come before the 2015 election, the wife of Ye Htut, the presidential spokesman for Thein Sein, posted a Photoshopped picture of Aung San Suu Kyi in a Muslim hijab being crowned with a tiara on Facebook. Her husband later apologized, but then was quoted as saying Aung San Suu Kyi's efforts for constitutional amendment were childish. Other doctored photos being circulated in the social media showed Suu Kyi next to an unflattering picture of a Muslim man. Rumors were being circulated in the blogosphere that Aung San Suu Kyi once had a Muslim boyfriend. Suu Kyi's critics—perhaps the "invisible hand" of the military—had grabbed the closest club to attack her with, religious prejudice. Suu Kyi was being pilloried for not speaking up enough about anti-Muslim violence and smeared at the same time for favoring Muslims. It was the kind of smarmy stuff spymaster Khin Nyunt used to spread.

—~—

Even some of Suu Kyi's harshest critics began recognizing the high-wire balancing act she had to navigate. Although David Mathieson, the Human Rights Watch representative in Burma, had called her "a disappointment on human rights issues," he acknowledged "She's playing a different game now. People still see her as this great Nobel Peace Prize-winning icon for human rights and democracy—what they don't get now is she wants to be a politician taking on one of the most brutal militaries in the world."

Mathieson said Suu Kyi's political fortunes depended on negotiating several challenges, including trying to strike a balance between international expectations—"most of which are outlandishly unfair and ill-informed"—and a "very complicated domestic setting where if she suddenly did do a *volte-face* and spoke out on behalf of Muslims, it would be politically disastrous." Moreover, he said, she was operating in a complicated post-authoritarian domestic environment in which she had opted to work inside the system as a lawmaker and was compelled to keep senior military figures, who still hold a strong grip on the reins of power, onside. "I can understand why she's walking on eggshells," he said.

Georgetown University expert David Steinberg, who has differed with some of Suu Kyi's decisions in the past, interpreted Suu Kyi's politically expedient stance on the Rohingya issue as motivated out of concern for Burma's national interest, rather than being a purely self-interested act. "I think she thinks she's the person in that country who best understands what democracy is about, and what's best for the future of Burma," he said. He predicted that Suu Kyi would remain "very important" to Myanmar's future, but that her significance would diminish over time, if the government's rapid reforms continued and brought about significant change. "If the government can deliver improvement in the lives of the people, if they do things with the environment and pay attention to minorities, then her status will quietly diminish," he said. Suu Kyi would likely retain a high profile to the rest of the world regardless, he predicted, "because we like Joans of Arc."

Aung Zaw, the influential editor of the news magazine *The Irrawaddy*, said that while some of her domestic support had eroded, particularly in ethnic communities, Suu Kyi remained "one of the hopes in Burma," alongside "many other democrats and ethnic leaders who continue to push for genuine change." She retained the support of many, he said—and crucially, *she was not corrupt.*

"I still think there's time for her to change her tactics, reconnect to the roots and rebuild her base," he said. "If she can mobilize people and her allies, inside and outside, the other side will negotiate and make more meaningful concessions. She is someone Burma was expecting for many decades. She should know that the country needs her."

Igor Blazevic, of the Czech-based Centre for Democracy and Culture, gave Aung San Suu Kyi credit for being willing to sacrifice her own popularity to get the military leaders to move toward a transition. "Aung San Suu Kyi has so far rightfully and politically bravely accepted the hard historic mission of helping move transition ahead by taking a conciliatory stand. She has accepted the serious political risk of alienating and disappointing her core support base in order to give a chance to Thein Sein's government, the military, and the USDP-dominated Parliament to move the country toward democracy." He credited Aung San Suu Kyi with showing "significant political maturity" in spite of criticism from many sides.

—~—

During one visit to Rangoon, I made it a point to touch base with two of Aung San Suu Kyi's oldest advisers, the journalist U Win Tin and the scrappy general U Tin Oo.

I was especially grateful to spend time with U Win Tin, the venerated and most quotable dean of Burmese journalists, because he died not long after. He received a hero's funeral with accolades from all over the world.

When I saw him, Win Tin had just celebrated his 83rd birthday with a trip to the hospital. He needed treatment for one of the many health problems that came with 19 years in prison. He still wore a blue shirt every day, the same color as his old prison uniform, to remind that in many ways, his country is still imprisoned. As Win Tin regularly pointed out to the journalists who came to his door every day like pilgrims with notepads, Burma was still one riot away from a return to military rule. As he warned, some optimism may be warranted, "but not amnesia."

He may have been an octogenarian, but Win Tin was still feisty enough to demand an apology from the military to the country for all the harm they had done, the arrests, and the tortures. There was no response from the generals in government.

Only one of the former generals, spymaster Khin Nyunt, answered Win Tin's challenge. He scoffed at claims that former political prisoners, such as Win Tin, had been arbitrarily detained. "They are looking out for their own interests by saying they were imprisoned without reason. . . . Of course they broke the law, and they are guilty," he said. He airily challenged a reporter, "To whom should I apologize?" and refused further comment.

After his own release from prison in 2011, Khin Nyunt had entered a monastery for a while in a show of repentance. Since then, he had been operating an art gallery and coffee shop next to his home. However, one visitor noticed that he had installed video cameras and microphones in his home so he could spy on visitors in his gallery without their knowledge.

Journalist Win Tin remembered the cruelty of Khin Nyunt's henchmen all too well. On the first day he was arrested, he was beaten. "They put a hood over my head so I couldn't see who was beating me. They hit me with sticks, their fists, all kinds of things. The interrogation went on day after day. They hung me from my feet. I lost all my teeth."

He was finally released in 2012 as part of an amnesty and went immediately to rallies to support Aung San Suu Kyi in her campaign for Parliament. He remained one of Aung San Suu Kyi's staunchest advisers, but he wasn't afraid to offer gentle criticism from time to time, complaining publicly that she was being "too conciliatory" to the military as she tried to win parliamentary support. He told me he still believed Aung San Suu Kyi was the only one who could hold the party together going into the 2015 elections. He said, "She is the unifying force. She is influential. She is charismatic. She is essential."

U Tin Oo, the peppy little general who helped found the NLD in 1988 with Aung San Suu Kyi, also remained a faithful but frank supporter. When I met with him, he was impressively spry at the age of 86 despite several lengthy prison stays. His house in Rangoon is a mini-military museum, with fading photographs of him in uniform at various stages of his career. But there were almost as many photos of Aung San Suu Kyi and her father. The former general agreed that Suu Kyi's charisma was holding the party together—for now. "We are not a personality cult," he said pointedly. "Aung San Suu Kyi is a prestigious lady. She is working hard so there will be democratic traditions that can remain. She can work another 10 years and then there must be others in the mold of Aung San Suu Kyi and General Aung San."

Yet it is unlikely that there will be another figure in the immediate future with the pedigree and unique gifts of Aung San Suu Kyi. She arrived on the scene at a rare hinge moment in time when a revolution was happening—and then carried on the crusade for democracy for the next 27 years, under trying and dangerous circumstances.

Aung San Suu Kyi's place as "the woman who defied a military regime" is secure in history books. Her legacy already lives on in the new generation of democracy activists who have been inspired by her example—and in her own words, which will surely be read and quoted wherever democracy and courage are discussed for many years to come. As her friend Timothy Garton Ash wrote, her words stand with some of Václav Havel's best, many of them "penned under house arrest (on occasion smuggled out from the University Avenue house on the inside of a domestic helper's skirt)."

Her book, *Freedom from Fear*, still inspires. Her Nobel Prize speech was a synthesis of East and West, ranging from World War I poets to the Buddhist concept of *dukha* (suffering). In fact, most of her speeches and lectures after her release in 2010 were well-written and wise. It is difficult to imagine another contemporary politician who could have done as well.

In the first of her Reith Lectures, smuggled out for delivery on the BBC, she said:

"Come any weekday to the headquarters of the NLD, a modest place with a ramshackle rough-hewn air of a shelter intended for hardy folk. More than once it has been described as the NLD 'cowshed.' Since this remark is usually made with a sympathetic and often admiring smile, we do not take offense. After all, didn't one of the most influential movements in the world begin in a cowshed?"

Suu Kyi noted that when many of those in her party joined the democracy movement, they were in their twenties or even in their late teens, "fresh-faced and flashing-eyed, passionate for the cause." Now they were quieter, more mature, and more determined, she said, their passion refined by the trials they had undergone. "You do not ask them if they have ever been to prison. You ask them how many times they have been to jail," she said.

She said in the Reith speech that the debilitating sense of fear that permeated the whole Burmese society was the first adversary the democracy movement had to overcome. She came to realize that freedom from fear did not have to be complete; it only had to be "sufficient to enable us to carry on." Her colleagues, Suu Kyi explained, "pretend to be unafraid as they go about their duties and pretend not to see that their comrades are also pretending. This is not hypocrisy. This is courage that has to be renewed consciously from day to day and moment to moment."

Her off-the-cuff speeches shouted out to crowds are often less than memorable. One critic complained they had "the intellectual depth of a

Chinese fortune cookie." But when she has the time to think through her speeches and interviews, they are often worth remembering.

"The price of liberty has never been cheap, and in Burma it is particularly high," she said about the attack at Depayin.

In a shrewd observation on politics and human nature, she said, "Sometimes I think that a parody of democracy could be more dangerous than a blatant dictatorship, because that gives people an opportunity to avoid doing anything about it."

She pointed out in another exchange, "All military regimes use *security* as the reason why they should remain in power. It's nothing original."

When asked after her release what she had learned during her nearly two decades in isolation, she gave a reflective response, answering that she had learned "The greatest human quality is kindness. It costs people nothing, and I don't know why people are so miserly about being kind."

In her domestic speeches, she was frank with her fellow Burmese: "We must learn to *compromise* without regarding it as *humiliation*."

When she went abroad, she was equally frank, telling foreign leaders that Burma "is not a democracy yet" and adding bluntly, "We want democracy-friendly and human rights-friendly investors."

Surveying the populist democracy movements that had sprung up in the "Arab Spring," she observed that human beings "want to be free and however long they may agree to stay locked up, to stay oppressed, there will come a time when they say 'That's it.' Suddenly they find themselves doing something that they never would have thought they would be doing, simply because of the human instinct that makes them turn their face toward freedom."

There were similarities between the Burma Spring and the Tunisian Spring, she has pointed out in talks. Each began with the death of a young man. In Tunisia, a fruit-seller set fire to himself in frustration. In Burma, a fight broke out in a teashop.

The dissimilarities were that while the Tunisian army did not fire on their people, she said, the Burmese army did. The second, and in the long run probably the more important, difference, she said, was that the Tunisian Revolution enjoyed the benefits of the communications revolution. "Having cell phones and Internet connections helped Tunisians to coordinate their movements and kept the world focused on them," she said. "Every single casualty could be made known to the world in minutes. Burma still does not have that capacity."

However, what the people of Burma did have was Aung San Suu Kyi. And she brought the world's attention and the media to them. Though there were many people who played a role in the sequence of changes that became known as "The Burma Spring," it is difficult to imagine the opening happening without Suu Kyi's long stewardship.

As the 2015 elections neared, changes from the new opening were cascading daily. The International Monetary Fund was projecting a 7.7 percent growth rate in Burma. The World Bank estimated Burma's economic growth rate at 8.5 percent for 2014 and 2015, a figure higher than any other nation it surveyed, including China. The World Bank was investing $2 billion to bring energy and health care to the poor, as well as encouraging development. The NLD was opening free schools for parents who could not afford to send their children to state schools, as well as health clinics and mobile libraries. Health insurance was being introduced for the first time. The list of corporations moving into Burma grew to include Ball Corp., Caterpillar, Chevrolet, Cisco, Dell, DuPont, HP, Intel, Met Life, Proctor and Gamble, and Visa. Hilton was opening five new hotels, and Best Western is coming as well.

Zarganar, the comedian with the bushy eyebrows who was put in prison for cracking jokes about the regime and helping cyclone victims, was working to secure the release of the remaining political prisoners—even the Military Intelligence minions who once worked for Khin Nyunt and tortured him. "I have forgiven them," the comedian said. It was time for the country to move on. He is hoping a grassroots movement toward forgiveness and reconciliation will spread. The comedian even managed to take his plea for releasing political prisoners to President Thein Sein at his "farm cottage" in Naypyidaw. Afterward, I asked the comedian in his bustling movie studio office in Rangoon what he thought about the president. "I think he is still afraid of his old boss," he said.

Indeed, many of the people I met with in late 2014 seemed to still fear the old general Than Shwe. They wouldn't mention his name in e-mails and were reluctant to discuss "the invisible hand." His influence still seemed to hang over the country.

But Zarganar's personal diplomacy did appear to bear fruit. President Thein Sein subsequently released more prisoners—promising 3,000 would be freed for their "good manners," including eight former Military Intelligence members. But in typical mixed-message military style, only two of those freed were political prisoners. An estimated 75 political prisoners and 65 wrongly imprisoned farmers remained behind bars, while more than 100 activists and over 500 farmers were facing charges that could land them in jail for political activities.

Zarganar planned to continue his unorthodox outreach. He still performs as a comedian and uses humor to leaven civic meetings with the military. In a meeting with senior military leaders, he asked them, "Do you know how you can get 100 percent of the people's love?" They asked him, "How? How?" He answered, "Well, if you completely withdraw from Parliament you will get all of their love: every single person will applaud you and want to kiss you." They laughed. They did not support withdrawal, but they did agree to take classes on federalism.

A leading example of the Burmese who are returning to help their country rebuild is the young historian Thant Myint-U, the nephew of former U.N. Secretary General U Thant, who returned from Cambridge University to serve as an adviser to President Thein Sein. Thant Myint-U is actively involved in the peace talks with ethnic groups and founded the Yangon Heritage Trust. The Trust is leading efforts to restore the rare historic buildings of Rangoon, including the Secretariat building where Aung San Suu Kyi's father was killed. Many of the buildings are being restored by international companies who are coming to invest in Burma's future and need office space.

George Soros, the controversial billionaire who supported democracy efforts behind the scenes for many years, has opened offices for his Open Society Foundations in Rangoon to support education and health projects such as Dr. Cynthia Maung's Mae Tao clinic on the border. One of his projects is funding e-libraries for the universities in Burma, which will bring hundreds of thousands of digital books and academic journals to help students catch up after decades of isolation.

Former Representative Bill Richardson's Richardson Center is providing training for members of Parliament and partnering with the Aspen Institute to encourage investment in community-based businesses in Burma.

And the American women who reached out to Aung San Suu Kyi for so many years?

Laura Bush, Madeleine Albright, and Hillary Clinton are all still doing something to help Burma. Laura Bush and Hillary Clinton are the Honorary Co-Chairs of the Suu Foundation, which is dedicated to rebuilding Burma's health and education sectors.

Mrs. Bush and the Bush Institute also have started a leadership training program for young Burmese that deliberately began in 2014 with a group of participants that was religiously diverse (Buddhist, Christian, and Muslim) and ethnically diverse (Burman, Shan, Paulaung, Kachin, Arakan).

Madeleine Albright helped Coca-Cola launch a program to empower 25,000 Burmese women with business management skills. She also helped open a National Democracy Institute office in Burma to facilitate democracy programs.

And the Clinton Foundation is working with Proctor and Gamble to provide two billion liters of clean drinking water to Burma.

Yet—and there always seemed to be a "yet" around a cheery corner—there continued to be troubling signs of repression. Four journalists and the owner of *Unity Journal* were arrested for reporting the existence of an alleged chemical weapons factory. Another journalist from *Mizzima* was arrested for protesting the arrests of journalists. Editors at the gutsy *Irrawaddy* magazine were threatened with blacklisting; the magazine's website was repeatedly hacked and shut down.

More than 100 journalists and activists were in custody in 2014 for protesting government restrictions. They included the internationally honored labor activist Su Su Nway, who had organized a demonstration by more than 1,500 farmers to protest the confiscation of 300,000 acres of farmland by the government and private companies. Graft was still a crippling problem—six key ministries were found in a government audit to have misused millions of dollars, yet when local media wrote about the audit, they were charged with libel. The charge was later dropped, but no one from the ministries was prosecuted.

For all the encouraging change from 2010 to 2014, Burma was still a place of two parallel universes in a race for time. One is of prosperity and progress, iPhones and donut shops. And another is of grinding poverty, greed, and medieval religious misunderstanding.

The continuing hope is that the positive trends will gain so much momentum that the power of the negative forces will recede. Yet so long as the military retains tight control, the "Burma Spring" will remain more of a hard-fought, step-by-step, vote-by-vote, long-term aspiration than a fully achieved reality.

As Aung San Suu Kyi said in fall 2014, "We cannot say that we have had four years of democracy; we can only say we have had four years of striving toward democracy."

The NLD still had work to do to reform itself—to reach out more effectively to young people, to come up with smart positions on the issues, to use social media more effectively, to build relationships with ethnic parties, to win back disaffected workers who had found the NLD sclerotic or arrogant or indecisive over the years. Yet even with those vulnernabilities, the NLD still had the heft and the best chance to make headway in 2015.

As 2015 neared, Aung San Suu Kyi continued traveling the country to remind people they had the power to make change. "The elections alone will not bring democracy, but democracy will not be attained without them."

In truth, the Burma challenge is the challenge of the 21st century: Can societies that are riven with ethnic and religious differences cohere? Can a country put aside the past to embrace difficult change? Can the rule of law hem in pernicious corruption?

Making a genuine transition from military rule to civilian rule and creating a more tolerant, pluralistic society would send a powerful signal to people who are struggling in the post-colonial, post–Cold War world to overcome tribal, ethnic, and religious differences.

Aung San Suu Kyi will be 70 when elections are held in 2015. As she wryly observed, "At this age, I should be leading a quiet life." Instead, she continues spending herself and her days for the democracy movement. There is little doubt among those who know her that she will keep up her struggle for democracy until she cannot. The Lady's not for quitting. As far back as her

1995 interview with *Vogue*, she said bringing democracy to Burma "could take a long time. It could take all my life."

If the presidency is kept beyond her reach, Aung San Suu Kyi could still wield considerable power as opposition leader, much like Sonia Gandhi has wielded as head of the Congress Party in India. Other scenarios suggest a possible role as Speaker of the House or some form of power-sharing. Suu Kyi has always been an underdog, but she still has formidable assets: her father's name, her intellect, an A-list Rolodex, and her charisma. As she has said, "We do the impossible each day. Miracles take a little longer."

Back in 2003, I had been impressed that Aung San Suu Kyi was standing up to the military against impossible odds. More than a decade later, I was even more impressed that she was still at it, although often with visible fatigue and dark circles under her eyes.

Her life's journey raises the question: Was it more courageous to face soldiers who were aiming at her with guns—or to continue taking on a huge task when everyone says you are licked before you begin, to extend a hand to people who had tried their best to harm you?

Suu Kyi's uniqueness was that she remained a constant, clear voice for the values that are the glue in society: citizenship, duty, the "Golden deeds" of altruism, honor, reputation, morals, manners, and integrity. When she spoke at a youth conference in 2014, she counseled the young people not to be deterred by setbacks in the pursuit of democracy. Democracy required losing as well as winning, she said; the important thing was to not give up.

Her intellectual friend Václav Havel faced a similar mid-journey challenge as he fought corruption and apathy in the Czech Republic. He wrote, "And yet if a handful of friends and I were able to bang our heads against the wall for years by speaking the truth about Communist totalitarianism while surrounded by an ocean of apathy, there is no reason why I shouldn't go on banging my head against the wall by speaking ad nauseam, despite the condescending smiles, about responsibility and morality in the face of our present social marasmus. There is no reason to think that this struggle is a lost cause. The only lost cause is one we give up on before we enter the struggle."

"There have been many times when commentators, diplomats or even the regime have attempted to dismiss her as irrelevant, sidelined, forgotten," human rights activist and author Benedict Rogers has observed. "But the most remarkable thing about Aung San Suu Kyi is that whether you agree with her or not, whether she has got things right or not, whether she has been locked up or free, she has been impossible to sideline. Twenty-five years later, she is as relevant and central to Burma's future as she became that day on 26 August 1988."

And as a leading Western diplomat told me, "She is a uniquely unifying figure . . . a uniquely talented person. As Aung San's daughter, she could bring together the country as no one else can."

The rest is up to the more far-sighted members of the military, who have the rare opportunity to share power rather than hoard it . . . to the foreign investors who could bring socially responsible business practices as well as dollars . . . to foreign governments, who still need to insist on "action for action" from the Burmese government before giving favors . . . and to the people of Burma, who have waited for such a very long time to speak for themselves.

—~—

CLICK: Like many young people in their thirties, Zin Mar Aung loves to post things on Facebook. She often posts photos of beautiful flowers and puts flowers on the dash of her car so she can look at them as she drives from meeting to meeting. She didn't get to see much of nature for 11 years, because she was arrested for distributing poetry with democracy messages at her university. She was locked in solitary confinement. "They could imprison my body, but not my mind," she says. When she was released from prison a few years ago, she started working for Aung San Suu Kyi's NLD party. Zin Mar also created an organization with several friends called "Rainfall" to empower women. They are providing leadership training and team-building skills because women have suffered disproportionately under military rule. The all-male military and their business cronies dominate almost all leadership and business positions in the country. Then, too, there are issues like sex-trafficking that need to be addressed, Zin Mar reminds. When Buddhist nationalists promoted new restrictions on interfaith marriage in Parliament, she was among the female activists who opposed the restrictions and received death threats as a result. Undaunted, Zin Mar has started a political science school to encourage more men and women to seek elected office. "This is a fragile transition period," she says while savoring a coffee at a restaurant during a rare break. Without blinking, without emotion, she adds, "We've got to rebuild our civil society. That's my life now."

CLICK: When Buddhist monks by the thousands took to the streets in 2007 to protest the hardships the poor were suffering under the military, young Nay Phone Latt, a gutsy blogger, proved the go-to source for the Western media. He was arrested in 2008 and not released until a general amnesty freed hundreds of political prisoners in 2012. He taught himself English while in prison and today is teaching classes on citizen journalism. "Everyone wants to be a citizen journalist, but they don't know anything about journalism," he says after a long day of instructing. He has a hip look and a writer's sense of irony, which have helped make him something of an international figure. He's studied at the respected Iowa Writers' Workshop and published a book called *The City I Dropped Down*. But his main focus now is preparing the new generation of citizen bloggers in advance of the 2015 elections through the Myanmar Information Development Organization (MIDO). Nay Phone Latt has established a Rangoon office of the PEN freedom of expression organization. And when bigots began using social media to stir up hate against Muslims and others in 2014, he helped launch a campaign against the use of hate speech on social media, called *Panzagar*, "flower speech." He is a frequent speaker on the need for tolerance. "There are some things changing, but so many things to change," he says. "We have passed through a very bad situation. We have a lack of capacity. We need more capacity. We have to build a new place."

A LIFE IN DETENTION

ANCIENT KINGDOM

1057—King Anawrahta founds the first unified Burmese state at Pagan and adopts Theravāda Buddhism.
1287—Mongols under Kublai Khan conquer Pagan.
1531—Toungoo dynasty, with Portuguese help, reunites Burma.
1755—Alaungpaya founds the Konbaung dynasty.
1824–26—First Anglo-Burmese war ends with the Treaty of Yandabo, according to which Burma ceded the Arakan coastal strip, between Chittagong and Cape Negrais, to British India.
1852—Britain annexes Lower Burma, including Rangoon, following the second Anglo-Burmese war.
1885–86—Britain captures Mandalay after a brief battle; Burma becomes a province of British India.
1937—Britain separates Burma from India and makes it a crown colony.

JAPANESE OCCUPATION

1942—Japan invades and occupies Burma with some help from the Japanese-trained Burma Independence Army, which later transforms itself into the Anti-Fascist People's Freedom League (AFPFL) and resists Japanese rule.

1945—Britain liberates Burma from Japanese occupation with help from the AFPFL, led by Aung San.

1947—Aung San and six members of his interim government are assassinated by political opponents led by U Saw, a nationalist rival of Aung San's. U Nu, foreign minister in Ba Maw's government, which ruled Burma during the Japanese occupation, is asked to head the AFPFL and the government.

INDEPENDENCE

1948—Burma becomes independent with U Nu as prime minister.

Mid-1950s—U Nu, together with Indian Prime Minister Nehru, Indonesian President Sukarno, Yugoslav President Tito, and Egyptian President Nasser, co-found the Movement of Non-Aligned States.

1958–60—Caretaker government, led by army Chief of Staff General Ne Win, is formed following a split in the ruling AFPFL party.

1960—U Nu's party faction wins decisive victory in elections, but his promotion of Buddhism as the state religion and his tolerance of separatism angers the military.

ONE-PARTY, MILITARY-LED STATE

1962—U Nu's faction is ousted in military coup led by Gen Ne Win, who abolishes the federal system and inaugurates "the Burmese Way to Socialism"—nationalizing the economy, forming a single-party state with the Socialist Program Party as the sole political party, and banning independent newspapers.

1974—New constitution comes into effect, transferring power from the armed forces to a People's Assembly headed by Ne Win and other former military leaders; body of former United Nations Secretary General U Thant is returned to Burma for burial.

1975—Opposition National Democratic Front is formed by regionally based minority groups, who mounted guerrilla insurgencies.

1981—Ne Win relinquishes the presidency to San Yu, a retired general, but continues as chairman of the ruling Socialist Program Party.

1982—Law designating people of non-indigenous background as "associate citizens" in effect bars such people from public office.

RIOTS AND REPRESSION

1987—Currency devaluation wipes out many people's savings and triggers anti-government riots.

August 8, 1988—Thousands of people are killed in anti-government riots. A military regime directed by General Ne Win crushes the pro-democracy uprising, known thereafter as 8-8-88. The State Law and Order Restoration Council (SLORC) is formed.

1989—SLORC declares martial law, arrests thousands of people, including advocates of democracy and human rights, renames Burma Myanmar, with the capital, Rangoon, becoming Yangon.

July 20, 1989—Opposition leader Aung San Suu Kyi, the daughter of Aung San, is put under house arrest and disqualified from running in upcoming elections.

May 27, 1990—Suu Kyi's NLD scores an unexpectedly resounding victory in a general election even though she is being detained. The result is rejected by the ruling junta.

October 14, 1991—Nobel Prize committee awards Peace Prize to Aung San Suu Kyi. She uses the $1.3 million to establish a health and education trust for the Burmese people.

July 10, 1995—Suu Kyi is released from house arrest, but her movements are restricted.

September 21, 2000—Suu Kyi tries to defy restrictions and travel by train to Mandalay with party members. They are blocked by security forces. Suu Kyi is placed under house arrest again.

May 6, 2002—Suu Kyi is released, but her house is still under heavy guard and her movements restricted.

May 30, 2003—Suu Kyi is detained after a bloody attack on her convoy at Depayin. She is later taken to Insein Prison.

September 2003—Suu Kyi is allowed to return home from Insein Prison after surgery, but is placed under strict house arrest, unable at times to see even her doctor.

May 27, 2006—Suu Kyi's house arrest is extended despite a personal appeal from United Nations Secretary General Kofi Annan to Senior General Than Shwe.

September 22, 2007—Suu Kyi is seen in public for the first time in five years when she goes to the gate of her compound to greet a huge crowd of monks who lead peaceful demonstrations that then are brutally suppressed by the regime.

May 27, 2008—Suu Kyi's house arrest is extended again without explanation.

May 14, 2009—Suu Kyi is arrested and taken from her home to Insein Prison to face trial after an American intruder named John William Yettaw swims to her lakeside residence in a quixotic attempt to warn her of danger.

August 11, 2009—Following an 86-day sham trial, Suu Kyi is sentenced to three years of hard labor for the Yettaw incident. Her sentence is commuted to 18 months of house arrest by Senior General Than Shwe, which means that Suu Kyi will still be under arrest when elections are held under a new, rigged constitution in October 2010.

November 13, 2010—Suu Kyi is released from house arrest and resumes her efforts to establish a dialogue with the generals that will lead to reconciliation and more open democracy.

April 1, 2012—Aung San Suu Kyi is resoundingly elected to a seat in Parliament to fill a vacancy.

January 2014—President Thein Sein, Speaker of the House Shwe Mann, and the leaders of the majority Union Solidarity and Development Party (USDP) initially support changing the Burmese constitution to allow Aung San Suu Kyi to run for president in 2015.

Summer 2014—Military elements subsequently begin blocking efforts to reform the constitution to reduce military control. Aung San Suu Kyi goes back to the people to campaign for meaningful change and a more open democracy.

Credit: BBC and CNN

BIBLIOGRAPHY

BOOKS

Abhaya, Burma's Fearlessness, by James Mackay, Foreword by Aung San Suu Kyi. River Books, 2011.

Adoniram Judson, God's Man in Burma, by Sharon Hambrick. Bob Jones University Press, 2001.

A History of Modern Burma, by Michael W. Charney. Cambridge University Press, 2007.

A Land without Evil: Stopping the Genocide of Burma's Karen People, by Benedict Rogers. Monarch Books, Grand Rapids, Michigan, 2004.

Aung San of Burma, by Maung Maung. Unity Publishing House, 2011.

Aung San Suu Kyi, A Biography, by Jesper Bengtsson. Potomac Books, 2012.

Aung San Suu Kyi and Burma's Struggle for Democracy, by Bertil Lintner. Silkworm Books, 2011.

Aung San Suu Kyi, A Portrait in Words and Pictures, by Christophe Loviny. Hardie Grant, 2013.

Aung San Suu Kyi, Fearless Voice of Burma, by Whitney Stewart. Lerner Publications, Minneapolis, 1997.

Aung San Suu Kyi and the Future of Burma, by Benedict Rogers. Lecture Delivered to Trinity Forum, Rhodes House, Oxford, February 11, 2013.

Aung San Suu Kyi, Standing Up for Democracy in Burma, by Bettina Ling. Feminist Press, 1999.

Bless God and Take Courage: The Judson History and Legacy, by Rosalie Hall Hunt. Judson Press, 2005.

Burma: A Nation at the Crossroads, by Benedict Rogers. Rider, 2012.

Burma and the Karens, by San C. Po. White Lotus, 2001.

Burma Baptist Chronicle, by Maung Shwe We. Burma Baptist Convention, 1963.

Burma, The Curse of Independence, by Shelby Tucker. Pluto Press, 2001.

Burma (Myanmar), by Caroline Courtauld. Odyssey, 1999.

Burma, The State of Myanmar, by David I. Steinberg. Georgetown University Press, 2001.

Burma, Time for Change. Report of an Independent Task Force Sponsored by the Council on Foreign Relations, by Mathea Falco, Chair, Council on Foreign Relations, 2003.

Burma/Myanmar: What Everyone Needs to Know, by David I. Steinberg. Oxford University Press, 2010.

Burmese Days, by George Orwell. Harcourt, 1934.

Character is Destiny, by John McCain with Mark Salter. Random House, 2003.

Courage, by Gordon Brown. Weinstein Books, 2008.

Crackdown: Repression of the 2007 Popular Protests in Burma. Human Rights Watch, 2007.

Crimes In Burma, by the International Human Rights Clinic at Harvard Law School, May 2009.

Dancing in Cambodia, At Large in Burma, by Amitav Ghosh. Ravi Dayal, 1998.

Disaster and Despair, Report on the Humanitarian Crisis in Burma, by International Monks Association, 2008.

Drugs, Oil, and War: The United States in Afghanistan, Colombia, and Indochina, by Peter Dale Scott. Rowman and Littlefield, 2003.

Everything Is Broken: A Tale of Catastrophe in Burma, by Emma Larkin. Penguin Press, 2010.

Finding George Orwell in Burma, by Emma Larkin. Penguin Group, 2004.

Freedom from Fear and Other Writings, by Aung San Suu Kyi. Penguin Books, 1991.

Golden Parasol: A Daughter's Memoir of Burma, by Wendy Law-Yone. Chatto and Windus, 2012.

Hard Choices, by Hillary Rodham Clinton. Simon and Schuster, 2014.

History of the Shan State, From Its Origins to 1962, by Sai Aung Tun. Silkworm Books, 2009.

Incendiary Circumstances, by Amitav Ghosh. Mariner Books, Houghton Mifflin, 2005.

Inked Over, Ripped Out: Burmese Storytellers and the Censors, by Anna J. Allott. PEN American Center, 1993.

Interview, by Claudia Dreifus. Seven Stories Press, 1997.

Into Hidden Burma, by Maurice Collis. Faber and Faber, 1933.

Last and First in Burma (1941–1948), by Maurice Collis. Macmillan, 1956.

Legacy of Ashes: The History of the CIA, by Tim Weiner. Doubleday, 2007.

Letters from Burma, by Aung San Suu Kyi. Penguin, 2010.

Lives of the Three Mrs. Judsons, by Arabella W. Stuart. BiblioBazaar, 2007.

Lords of the Sunset, by Maurice Collis. Faber and Faber, 1938.

Merchants of Madness: The Methamphetamine Explosion in the Golden Triangle, by Bertil Lintner. Silkworm Books, 2009.

Myanmar Politics, 1958–1962. Volume II. Ministry of Culture, 2007.

No Bad News for the King: The True Story of Cyclone Nargis and Its Aftermath in Burma, by Emma Larkin. Peguin Group, 2010.

Nowhere to be Home: Narratives From Survivors of Burma's Military Regime, compiled by Maggie Lemere and Zoe West. McSweeney's, 2011.

On China, by Henry Kissinger. Penguin Group, 2012.

Opportunities and Pitfalls: Preparing for Burma's Economic Transition, by Yuki Akimoto. Open Society Institute, 2006.

Prisoner for Peace: Aung San Suu Kyi and Burma's Struggle for Democracy, by John Parenteau. Morgan Reynolds, Greensboro, N.C., 1994.

Politics, Morality, and Civility, by Václav Havel. Alfred A. Knopf, 2006.

Sacred Sites of Burma: Myth and Folklore in an Evolving Spiritual Realm, by Donald M. Stadtner. River Books, 2011.

Soldiers and Diplomacy in Burma: Understanding the Foreign Relations of the Burmese Praetorian State, by Renaud Egreteau and Larry Jagan. NUS Press, 2013.

Spoken from the Heart, by Laura Bush. Scribner, 2010.

Teaching Democracy: The Program and Practice of Aung San Suu Kyi's Concept of People's Education, by Franziska Blum. Die Deutsche Bibliothek, 2011.

Than Shwe's Burma, by Diane Zahler. Twenty-First Century Books, Minneapolis, 2010.

Than Shwe, Unmasking Burma's Tyrant, by Benedict Rogers. Silkworm Books, Chiang Mai, Thailand, 2010.

The Face of Resistance: Aung San Suu Kyi and Burma's Fight for Freedom, by Aung Zaw. Mekong Press, 2013.

The Gathering Storm: Infectious Diseases and Human Rights in Burma. Human Rights Center, University of California, Berkeley, 2007.

The History of Shan State, From Its Origins to 1962, by Sai Aung Tun. Silkworm Books, 2009.

The Lady and the Peacock: The Life of Aung San Suu Kyi, by Peter Popham. Rider/Random House, 2011.

The Life of Adoniram Judson to the Golden Shore, by Courtney Anderson. Little, Brown, 1987.

The Moon Princess: Memories of the Shan States, by Sao Sanda. River Books, 2008.

The Perfect Hostage: A Life of Aung San Suu Kyi, Burma's Prisoner of Conscience, by Justin Wintle. Hutchinson, 2007.

The Politics of Heroin: CIA Complicity in the Global Drug Trade, by Alfred W. McCoy. Lawrence Hill Books/Harper Collins, 1972.

The River of Lost Footsteps: Histories of Burma, by Thant Myint-U. Farrar, Straus and Giroux, 2006.

The Shore Beyond Good and Evil: A Report from Inside Burma's Opium Kingdom, by Hideyuki Takano. Kotan Publishing Co., 2002.

The Snake Charmer: A Life and Death in Pursuit of Knowledge, by Jamie James. Hyperion, 2008.

The Traveller's History of Burma, by Gerry Abbott. Orchid, 1998.

The Voice of Hope: Conversations with Alan Clements, by Aung San Suu Kyi. Rider, 2008.

Trials in Burma, by Maurice Collis. Penguin Books, 1938.

Twilight Over Burma: My Life as a Shan Princess, by Inge Sargent. University of Hawaii Press, 1994.

Where China Meets India: Burma and the New Crossroads of Asia, by Thant Myint-U. Farrar, Straus and Giroux, 2011.

White Out: The CIA, Drugs and the Press, by Alexander Cockburn and Jeffrey St. Clair. Verso, 1998.

VIDEO

Aung San Suu Kyi, Securing Freedom, BBC Reith Lectures 2011, http://www.bbc.co.uk/programmes/b012402s

Aung San Suu Kyi, Nobel Lecture, 2012, http://www.nobelprize.org/nobel_prizes/peace/laureates/1991/kyi-lecture_en.html

Aung San Suu Kyi, Speech to both Houses of Parliament in Westminster Hall, London, 2012, http://ukinfrance.fco.gov.uk/en/news/?view=Speech&id=778619482

Aung San Suu Kyi, Speech at Kennedy School, Harvard, February 5, 2013, https://www.youtube.com/watch?v=0xXuyZ4WyEM

Ann Curry interviews with Aung San Suu Kyi, September 21, 2012, https://www.youtube.com/watch?v=rJD1tvb7zxY

NBC News, September 21, 2012, http://www.nbcnews.com/video/nightly-news/49126187#49126187

NBC News, January 21, 2011, http://www.today.com/video/today/41190008#41190008

Christiane Amanpour, Interview with Aung San Suu Kyi, February 5, 2013, https://www.youtube.com/watch?v=P4JNG1CznW0

ONLINE

All You Can Do Is Pray, Human Rights Watch, http://www.hrw.org/sites/default/files/reports/burma0413webwcover_0.pdf

"Aung San Suu Kyi Interview," by Leslie Kean and Dennis Bernstein, *The Progressive*, December 2, 2006, http://www.progressive.org/mag_intv0397

"Backgrounder, Understanding Myanmar," by Jayshree Bajoria, Council on Foreign Relations, June 21, 2013, http://www.cfr.org/human-rights/understanding-myanmar/p14385

"Burma and Transnational Crime," by Liana Sun Wyler, Congressional Research Service, January 21, 2010, file:///C:/Users/User/Downloads/19971%20(3).pdf

"Burma's Champion Comes to Washington," by Fred Hiatt, *Washington Post*, September 19, 2012, http://www.washingtonpost.com/opinions/fred-hiatt-burmas-champion-comes-to-washington/2012/09/19/0beeaeb4-029e-11e2-91e7-2962c74e7738_story.html

"Burma's Dear Leader," by Joshua Kurlantzick, *Washington Post*, April 23, 2006, http://carnegieendowment.org/2006/04/23/burma-s-dear-leader/rvf

"Burma: The Next Killing Fields," by Alan Clements, December 1990, www.worlddharma.com/, http://www.worlddharma.com/wd/media/BTNKF/Burma%20The%20Next%20Killing%20Fields%20-%20Ch%201.pdf

"Burma: One Year after Cyclone, Repression Continues," Human Rights Watch, April 30, 2009, http://www.hrw.org/news/2009/04/30/burma-one-year-after-cyclone-repression-continues

"Burmese Days," by Maureen Aung Thwin, *Foreign Affairs*, September 1989, http://www.foreignaffairs.com/articles/44329/maureen-aung-thwin/burmese-days

"Burmese Tycoon," Parts 1–3, by Aung Zaw, *The Irrawaddy*, June 2000, http://www2.irrawaddy.org/article.php?art_id=1923; http://www2.irrawaddy.org/article.php?art_id=1924; http://www2.irrawaddy.org/article.php?art_id=1925

"Burma's 'Godfather Of Heroin' Dies, But Drug Trade Flourishes As Rebels, Soldiers, Government Officials All Battle For Illegal Profits," International Business Times, by Palash Ghosh, http://www.ibtimes.com/burmas-godfather-heroin-dies-drug-trade-flourishes-rebels-soldiers-government-officials-all-battle

"Burma's Unmoving Generals," by Larry Jagan, BBC, February 28, 2002, http://news.bbc.co.uk/2/hi/asia-pacific/1840987.stm

"Clock Is Ticking For Aung San Suu Kyi's Presidential Bid," NPR, http://www.npr.org/2014/06/27/325500692 clock-is-ticking-for-aung-san-suu-kyis-presidential-bid

"Courageous Burmese Leader Marks Birthday Still Under House Arrest," by Fred Hiatt, *Washington Post*, June 19, 2010, http://www.washingtonpost.com/wp-dyn/content/article/2010/06/18/AR2010061804384.html

"Drugs and Astrology, How 'Bulldog' Wields Power," by Peter Beaumont and Alex Duval Smith, *The Guardian*, October 6, 2007, http://www.theguardian.com/world/2007/oct/07/burma.peterbeaumont

"Opium Through History," Frontline, http://www.pbs.org/wgbh/pages/frontline/shows/heroin/etc/history.html

"How Junta Protects Mr. Heroin," *The Guardian*, by John Sweeney, http://www.theguardian.com/world/2001/apr/08/johnsweeney.theobserver

"I Just Want to Help my People," State Control and Civil Society in Burma after Cyclone Nargis, Human Rights Watch, 2010, http://www.hrw.org/sites/default/files/reports/burma0410webwcover.pdf

"In A Land of Fear," by John Pilger, May 4, 1996, http://johnpilger.com/articles/in-a-land-of-fear; https://www.youtube.com/watch?v=g97dxvhDrjI

"In Burma, a U.N. Promise Not Kept," by Fred Hiatt, *Washington Post*, May 12, 2008, http://www.washingtonpost.com/wp-dyn/content/article/2008/05/11/AR2008051101782.html

"Letter from Burma, A Free Woman," by Joshua Hammer, *The New Yorker*, January 24, 2011, http://www.newyorker.com/reporting/2011/01/24/110124fa_fact_hammer

"Letter from Rangoon, Drowning," by George Packer, *The New Yorker*, August 25, 2008, http://www.newyorker.com/reporting/2008/08/25/080825fa_fact_packer?currentPage=all

"Lo Hsing Han, Heroin king and business tycoon," Obituary, *The Economist*, http://www.economist.com/news/obituary/21582234-lo-hsing-han-heroin-king-and-business-tycoon-died-july-6th-aged-about-80-lo-hsing-han

Methodist English High School, Frank and Karis Manton, http://www.mehsa.org/mantons.htm

"Myanmar's Black Hole, Evolution of a Mafia State in Myanmar," by Maung Zarni, *Asia Times*, October 16, 2013, http://www.atimes.com/atimes/Southeast_Asia/SEA-03-161013.html

"Myanmar's Black Hole: Fascist Roots, Rewritten History," by Maung Zarni, *Asia Times*, October 17, 2013, http://www.atimes.com/atimes/Southeast_Asia/SEA-01-171013.html

"Myanmar's Black Hole: A Class Above, The Heaven Born," by Maung Zarni, *Asia Times*, October 21, 2013, https://www.transcend.org/tms/2013/10/yanmars-black-hole-a-class-above-the-heaven-born-part-3/

"Myanmar: The Next Failed State?" by Joshua Kurlantzick, Council on Foreign Relations, September 2011, http://www.cfr.org/burmamyanmar/myanmar-next-failed-state/p25710

New Republic articles on Burma, by Joshua Kurlantzick, http://www.newrepublic.com/authors/joshua-kurlantzick

No Peace for Kofi, in *New York* magazine, http://nymag.com/nymetro/news/people/features/11839/

"Special Report: An Image Makeover for Myanmar Inc.," by Jason Szep and Andrew R. C. Marshall, *Reuters*, April 12, 2012, http://www.reuters.com/article/2012/04/12/us-myanmar-cronies-image-idUSBRE83B0YU20120412

"The Dictators," Parts 1-10, by Aung Zaw, *The Irrawaddy*, 2013, http://www.irrawaddy.org/z_the-dictators/the-dictators-part-1-the-rise-of-ne-win.html; http://www.irrawaddy.org/z_the-dictators/the-dictators-part-2-ne-win-tightens-his-grip.html; http://www.irrawaddy.org/z_the-dictators/the-dictators-part-3-military-intelligence.html; http://www.irrawaddy.org/z_the-dictators/the-dictators-part-4-ne-wins-paranoia-grows.html; http://www.irrawaddy.org/z_the-dictators/the-dictators-part-5-ne-win-promotes-than-shwe.html; http://www.irrawaddy.org/z_the-dictators/the-dictators-part-6-popular-dissent-grows.html; http://www.irrawaddy.org/z_the-dictators/the-dictators-part-7-than-shwes-reign-begins.html; http://www.irrawaddy.org/z_the-dictators/the-dictators-part-8-khin-nyunt-overplays-his-hand.html; http://www.irrawaddy.org/z_the-dictators/

the-dictators-part-9-than-shwe-becomes-king.html; http://www.irrawaddy.org/z_the-dictators/the-dictators-part-10-than-shwe-enjoys-absolute-power.html

"The Generals in Their Labyrinth," by Patrick Symes, *Outside* magazine, August 2008, http://www.outsideonline.com/adventure-travel/asia/myanmar/The-Generals-in-Their-Labyrinth.html

"The Lady Triumphs," by Edward Klein, *Vanity Fair*, September 15, 1995, http://www.burmalibrary.org/reg.burma/archives/199509/msg00096.html

"Thein Sein: Reformer or Caretaker?" by Aung Zaw, *The Irrawaddy*, February 14, 2012, http://www2.irrawaddy.org/article.php?art_id=23034

"The Optimist," *The New Yorker*, http://www.newyorker.com/archive/2003/03/03/030303fa_fact1?currentPage=all

"Too much, Too Soon," by Joshua Kurlantzick, Foreign Policy, May 21, 2013, http://www.foreignpolicy.com/articles/2013/05/21/too_fast_too_soon_myanmar_us_visit

"Troubling signs for Burma's reforms?" by Fred Hiatt, *Washington Post*, May 20, 2013, http://www.washingtonpost.com/blogs/post-partisan/wp/2013/05/20/troubling-signs-for-burmas-reforms/

"Tycoon Ta Za, Well-Connected and Well-Heeled," by Aung Zaw, *The Irrawaddy*, June 2005, http://www2.irrawaddy.org/article.php?art_id=4761

"Tycoon Turf," by Aung Zaw, *The Irrawaddy*, September 2005, http://www2.irrawaddy.org/article.php?art_id=5010

U.S. Sanctions on Burma: Issues for 113th Congress, by Michael F. Martin, Congressional Research Service, January 11, 2013, http://www.fas.org/sgp/crs/row/R42939.pdf

"Why There's So Much Heroin Use in Myitkyina, *Business Insider*, by Patrick Winn, Global Post, http://www.businessinsider.com/why-theres-so-much-heroin-use-in-myitkyina-myanmar-2013-12#ixzz3Fevn7SD0

"Will Democracy Take Root in Myanmar?" by Joshua Kurlantzick, *The National*, July 23, 2012, http://www.thenational.ae/arts-culture/books/will-democracy-take-root-in-myanmar

RESOURCES

Altsean: http://www.altsean.org/Research.php

Daw Aung San Suu Kyi site: www.dassk.com/index/php

Burma Campaign UK: http://burmacampaign.org.uk/

Burma Partnership: http://www.burmapartnership.org/

Bush Institute—Human Freedom: http://www.bushcenter.org/bush-institute/human-freedom

Human Rights Watch: http://www.hrw.org/

Nobel Prize official biography and ASSK timeline: http://www.nobelprize.org/nobel_prizes/peace/laureates/1991/kyi-bio.html

PEN America: https://www.pen.org/

U.S. Campaign for Burma: http://uscampaignforburma.org/

Yangon Heritage Trust: http://yangonheritagetrust.org/home

WIKILEAKS

http://www.networkmyanmar.org/index.php?option=com_content&view=article&id=83&Itemid=111

http://www.theguardian.com/world/the-us-embassy-cables+burma

ACKNOWLEDGMENTS

A special thanks to my agent, Charlotte Gusay, for her steadfast encouragement and to my editor, Jessica Case, and copy chief Phil Gaskill at Pegasus for their thoughtful support.

Also much appreciation to the many people who provided assistance along the way, beginning with former First Lady Laura Bush and including:

Dr. Tin Mar Aung, Andi Ball, Patrick Barta, Bonnie Bishop, John Bishop, Michele Bohana, former Secretary of State Hillary Clinton, Benelette Dedrick, Nyan Din, Aung Din, Jim Falk, Kate Friedrich, Kathy Gest, Ambassador Jim Glassman, Michael Green, Jeanne Hallacy, Paula Helfrich, Caroline Hickey, Elizabeth Hoffman, Jim Hollifield, Zoe Houser, Ariana Huffington, U Htin Kyaw, Khin Lay, Shunn Lei, Deedie Leahy, Pete Lutken, Shibani Mahatani, Thandee Maung, Anita McBride, Senator John McCain, Tim McLaughlin, Bob Mong, Thant Myint-U, Eleanor Nagy, Jennifer Repo, Cokie Roberts, Jennifer Quigley, Amanda Schnetzer, Maureen Aung Thwin, Sharon Lyle and TEDxSMU, Pansy Tun Thein, Thelma Tun Thein, Rachel Wagley, Charity Wallace, Dr. Bruce Whitehead, Jeremy Woodrum, Richard Yukhin, and Cheery Zahou.

And thanks to all those who those who made time for interviews, beginning with Daw Aung San Suu Kyi and including:

Former Secretary of State Madeleine Albright, former Deputy Secretary of State Richard Armitage, Zin Mar Aung, former Assistant Secretary of State Kurt Campbell, Ambassador Priscilla Clapp, Laurie Dawson, Ambassador Larry Dinger, Former Under Secretary of State Paula Dobriansky, David Eubank, U Gawsita, Ko Ko Gyi, former National Security Advisor Stephen Hadley, Nang Ja, U Kovida, Joshua Kurlantzick, Byron Law-Yone, Wendy Law-Yone, Rev. Arthur Ko Lay, Dr. Cynthia Maung, Bishop Zothan Mawia, Ambassador Derek Mitchell, Min Ko Naing, Ashin Nayaka, Doris Kearns Goodwin, Elsie Walker Kilborne, Joshua Kurlantzick, Htin Kyaw, Nay Phone Latt, Rev. Arthur Ko Lay, Joseph Lelyveld, Su Su Lwin, Jenny Lim, Bertil Lintner, Peter Manikas, David Matthiesen, Bishop Zothan Mawia, Ambassador Derek Mitchell, Ashin Nayaka, U Ko Ni, Sao Hkun Htun Oo, U Tin Oo, former Gov. Bill Richardson, Benedict Rogers, Lian Saigong, Former Assistant Secretary of State Kristin Silverberg, Dr. Joseph Silverstein, Kyaw Soe, Khin Maung Soe, Dr. David Steinberg, Debbie Stothard, Phyu Phyu Thin, Kyaw Thu, Dr. Sai Aung Tin, U Win Tin, Wendy Law Yone, Edward Law Yone, Zarganar (Maung Thura), and Thiha Zaw.

And much appreciation for the help and professional courtesy over the years from State Department representatives Mary Ellen Countryman, Sarah Hutchison, Stacey May, Richard Mie, Adrienne Nutzman, Ron Post, and Jamie Ravetz. They do our country proud.

And as always, my ever-supportive sons Greg and Grant Gish and their families.